OSGi in Action

OSGi in Action

CREATING MODULAR APPLICATIONS IN JAVA

RICHARD S. HALL
KARL PAULS
STUART McCULLOCH
DAVID SAVAGE

MANNING
Greenwich
(74° w. long.)

For online information and ordering of this and other Manning books, please visit www.manning.com. The publisher offers discounts on this book when ordered in quantity. For more information, please contact

Special Sales Department
Manning Publications Co.
180 Broad Street, Suite 1323
Stamford, CT 06901
Email: orders@manning.com

Manning Publications Co.
180 Broad Street, Suite 1323
Stamford, CT 06901

Development editor: Cynthia Kane
Copyeditor: Tiffany Taylor
Typesetter: Gordan Salinovic
Illustrator: Martin Murtonen
Cover designer: Marija Tudor

ISBN 9781933988917
Printed in the United States of America
1 2 3 4 5 6 7 8 9 10 – MAL – 16 15 14 13 12 11

brief contents

contents

foreword

It was during the very hot summer of 2003 that I first heard of Richard S. Hall. During a coffee break, a colleague from Deutsche Telekom told me that the local university had a teacher who was very much into OSGi. This teacher was the author of Oscar, one of the first open source OSGi frameworks. In 2003, wholeheartedly adopting OSGi was rare, so I was intrigued. Also around that time, Eclipse was investigating moving to a new module system, and I was asked to participate as an OSGi expert. I thought Richard could be valuable for this, so I asked him to join the Equinox committee. That innocent invitation started an enormously long email thread that hasn't ended yet and, I hope, never will. Richard is often abrasive when specifications aren't clear, or worse, when we attempt to violate modular purity. Sometimes I think he physically feels pain if we have to compromise on a dirty feature. As an invited OSGi researcher, he has became one of the key people behind the specifications, making sure we don't bloat the framework and always follow our principles.

When Manning sent a flattering email proposing an *OSGi in Action* book to the key OSGi people, Richard was among them. This email triggered intense discussions about collectively writing this book; the idea to write a book had been discussed many times before. We went into negotiations with Manning, but in the end I withdrew from the group, urging the others to continue. Why did I bail out? As the editor of the OSGi specifications, I was aware of how much work it is to write a book in collaboration with other opinionated people. To extend my day job into the night and weekends for free wasn't something I was looking forward to, regardless of how much I liked and appreciated these guys. Unfortunately, my desertion deflated the effort, and it faltered.

Until the day Richard told me he had picked up the book effort again from where we had stopped, now with a better team: Karl Pauls, Stuart McCulloch, and David Savage. Each of these authors is a great contributor to the open source world as well as to the OSGi specifications: Karl for his work on Felix and his testimony to modularity by doing Felix security as a separate bundle, proving that even the framework architecture is modular; Stuart for his work on the Maven bundle plugin, the popular Ops4J work, and the Peaberry extension to Guice; and David for the excellent work he is doing with Sigil at Apache and his work at Paremus. It would be hard to come up with a team that knows more about how OSGi is used in the real world. All this experience radiates from the chapters they've written in this impressive book.

While this team undertook the Herculean effort to write this book, I was in close contact with them all along the way—not only because of our work in the OSGi Alliance, but also because authoring a book about OSGi is likely to expose weakness or deficiencies in the specifications, which then obviously results in another, often heated argument over Skype or email. Unfortunately, to my chagrin, the team was too often right.

They also asked me to provide the text about the history of OSGi, an effort that resulted in probably the highest compression rate ever achieved. Of the 4,356 words I wrote, I think the word *OSGi* remained. But this is exactly what I like: the quest for quality drove this book, not only in its details but also in its form. It isn't like many books today, full of listings outlining in minute steps how to achieve a result. No, this is a book exactly the way I like it: not only showing in detail how to use OSGi, but also going to great length to point out the rationale. It's a book that *explains.*

And such a book is needed today. I understand that OSGi isn't easy. Although it builds on an object-oriented foundation, it adds a new set of design primitives to address the shortcomings of object-oriented design that were uncovered when applications became humongous assemblies of multiple open source projects and proprietary code. Objects remain an invaluable technique for building software, but the object-oriented paradigm isn't well suited to allowing large building blocks (components) collaborate without causing too much coupling. We desperately fight objects with patterns like factories and class-loading hacks, but at a certain scale the work to prevent coupling becomes a significant part of our efforts. Dependency injection alleviated much of the coding pain but moved a lot of the code into XML, a language that has the most ill-suited syntax imaginable for human programming tasks. Annotations provide another level of support for dealing with coupling—but cause a coupling problem in themselves. Many of the painkillers we use to alleviate coupling are largely cosmetic because boundaries aren't enforced at execution time in traditional Java.

OSGi is different. It treats an application as a collaboration of peer modules: modules that can adapt themselves to the environment instead of assuming that the environment is adapted to them. Adapting to the environment requires a reification of that environment, and this is where OSGi has its biggest innovation: µServices. µServices are the oil between modules that allows modules to evolve over time without affecting other modules. During a recent OSGi community event, David Savage used the term *spiky* to describe modules, to indicate how a set of modules causes friction that makes it hard to change each module. µServices are a design primitive in OSGi that is so powerful, it's even possible to update or install modules on the fly without bringing down the application. They palliate the spikes of modules by reifying the interconnection between modules.

µServices are a new paradigm that requires a way of thinking that is different from what is prevalent in Java today. In many ways, OSGi is where object-oriented programming was 25 years ago, providing new design primitives that were ill understood by the mainstream. Objects required a generation to grow up thinking in terms of design primitives like polymorphism, inheritance, classes, and objects. OSGi is on the verge of making a new paradigm shift happen with its bundles and µServices. I believe that these design primitives will be the next software paradigm after object orientation. This book is an excellent way to become part of the generation that can really think in OSGi and reap its full benefits.

PETER KRIENS
OSGI TECHNICAL DIRECTOR

preface

When I started working with OSGi technology back in 2000, I would've never guessed I'd still be working with it a decade later. Back then, OSGi was targeting the embedded market niche, but that wasn't my area of interest. I wanted to create highly dynamic, modular applications, and OSGi gave me the possibility of doing so. At the time, there weren't any freely available OSGi framework implementations; so I started working on my own open source implementation, called *Oscar*, back in December 2000 while I was working at Free University Berlin. Oscar moved with me when I moved to Grenoble to work at Josef Fourier University, where the work really started to flourish.

As OSGi technology began to gain traction, Oscar moved to the ObjectWeb open source consortium in 2004, and later it evolved into Felix at the Apache Software Foundation in 2005. I was fortunate enough to be invited by the OSGi Alliance to work directly on the OSGi specifications for the R4 release cycle in 2004. I've been involved in the OSGi specification process ever since, initially as an academic researcher and most recently in industry, when I took a position on the GlassFish team at Sun Microsystems (now Oracle Corp.) in 2008. A lot has changed over the last 10 years.

OSGi technology has moved beyond the embedded market into a full-blown module system for Java. This transformation was significantly helped along in 2004 when the Eclipse IDE refactored its plugin system to run on top of OSGi, and it has continued with the adoption of the technology in enterprise circles by Spring and all the major application servers. Although the future of Java modularity is still evolving, OSGi technology looks to play a role for a long time to come. Which brings us back to this book.

I'd been kicking around the idea of writing an OSGi book for a couple of years, but given the enormity of the task and my life-long time deficit, I never got around to it. In the summer of 2008, I finally got serious and began writing, only to find myself quickly bogged down. It wasn't until Karl and Stuart offered to help, and later David, that we were finally able to slay the beast. Our varied OSGi experience provided just the right mix. Even then, it's taken us two years, a few career changes, and the birth of several children to see it to an end. We hope you'll find our efforts helpful.

RICHARD S. HALL

acknowledgments

We thank Peter Kriens for his in-depth feedback that improved the book and for writing the foreword. Thanks also to all the early readers of the manuscript and the book forum posters who provided valuable feedback throughout the writing process.

The following peer reviewers who read the manuscript at various stages of its development deserve special thanks for their time and effort: Cheryl Jeroza, David Kemper, Gabor Paller, Jason Lee, Massimo Perga, Joseph Ottinger, Jeroen Benckhuijsen, Ted Neward, Denis Kurilenko, Robert "Kebernet" Cooper, Ken Chien, Jason Kolter, Jeremy Flowers, Paul King, Erik van Oosten, Jeff Davis, Doug Warren, Peter Johnson, Costantino Cerbo, Dmitry Sklyut, David Dossot, Mykel Alvis, Eric Swanson, Patrick Steger, Jeff Addison, Chad Davis, Peter Pavlovich, Ramarao Kanneganti, Steve Gutz, Tijs Rademakers, John Griffin, and Sivakumar Thyagarajan. Their suggestions made this a better book. We'd also like to single out Norman Richards for his technical proofreading of the final manuscript during production.

The staff at Manning have been supportive throughout this lengthy ordeal; we'd especially like to thank our development editor Cynthia Kane for putting up with us; also Marjan Bace, Michael Stephens, and the production team of Tiffany Taylor, Katie Tennant, and Gordan Salinovic.

Last, we'd like to thank the Apache Felix community for their contributions to all the code and discussions over the years.

Individually, Richard thanks his wife and daughter and apologizes for the many distractions this book caused. Karl thanks his wife Doreen and his children Elisabeth and Holger for all the love, support, and understanding. Stuart thanks his dear wife Hayfa for the motivation to finish this book. David thanks his wonderful family, and especially his wife Imogen, for the support and encouragement to finish this book.

about this book

The OSGi specifications are well written and elaborate, so if you need to know details about OSGi technology, the specifications are the place to look. If you do, you'll discover that they were written for someone who is going to implement the specifications, not use them. This book started out as an attempt to remedy this situation by creating a user-oriented companion guide for the specifications. Our goal wasn't to create an OSGi cookbook but to thoroughly describe the important aspects of OSGi and show how to use them. Our main idea was to more simply explain the OSGi specifications by ignoring the implementation details and including additional usage information.

To that end, we've tried to limit ourselves to discussing the most common concepts, features, and mechanisms needed to work with OSGi technology throughout the book. That doesn't mean we were able to avoid all the esoteric details. As you'll find when you begin working with OSGi, it enforces a new level of strictness when it comes to modularity, which will likely break some of your old practices. In the end, you need to understand what's going on under the covers in some places to be able to effectively debug and diagnose the situations in which you find yourself.

As our writing progressed, the book chapters began to separate naturally into three parts:

1. Explaining the core OSGi specification
2. Describing how to work with the specification in practice
3. Introducing advanced OSGi-related topics

In part 1 of the book, we focus on explaining the most common aspects of the OSGi core specification from the user's perspective. We introduce OSGi according to its three-layer architecture: module, lifecycle, and services. This isn't the only approach to take in explaining OSGi; most explanations of OSGi start out with a simple bundle implementing a simple service. The downside of this type of approach, in our view, is that it cuts across all three OSGi layers at once, which would require us to *explain* all three layers at once.

The advantage of following a layered approach is that doing so creates a clear division among the concepts we need to discuss. For example, the modularity chapter focuses on modularity concepts and can largely ignore lifecycle and services. This approach also creates a natural progression, because modularity is the foundation of OSGi, lifecycle builds on it, and services are on top of lifecycle. We can also highlight how to use lower layers of the OSGi architecture without using the upper layers, which is sometimes worthwhile.

Part 2 of the book takes the knowledge about the OSGi core specification from part 1 and shows how you can use the technology from a more pragmatic viewpoint. We look into converting existing JAR files to bundles as well as testing, debugging, and managing bundles. These first two parts of the book should be of general interest to anyone wanting to learn more about using OSGi.

Part 3 covers various advanced topics, such as service-oriented component models, framework launching, security, and distributed computing technologies. This last part serves as a springboard to the world of possibilities available to you in the OSGi universe.

Roadmap

Chapter 1 presents a high-level view of OSGi technology and the issues it's intended to address. To keep the chapter from being totally abstract, we present a few "Hello, world!" examples to illustrate the different layers of the OSGi framework, but the real meat of our OSGi discussion is in the following chapters. We also look at the state of modularity support in Java as well as in some related technologies.

Chapter 2 explores the module layer of the OSGi framework. We start with a general discussion of modularity in computing and then continue by describing OSGi's module concept, called a *bundle*. We present OSGi's declarative metadata-based approach for creating modules and show how to use it to modularize a simple paint program. We also investigate one of the key OSGi tasks: bundle dependency resolution.

Chapter 3 looks at the lifecycle layer of the OSGi framework. We discuss lifecycle management in general and describe how OSGi provides dynamic lifecycle management of bundles. We present OSGi's lifecycle-related APIs by creating a simple OSGi shell and also adapt our paint program to make it lifecycle aware.

Chapter 4 examines the services layer of the OSGi framework. We describe what services are and discuss why and when you need them. We walk you through providing and using services with some toy examples and then take an iterative approach to describing how to deal with the unique aspect of service dynamism. We finish our service discussion by adapting the paint program, this time to use dynamic services.

Chapter 5 returns to the module layer and examines its more advanced or nuanced capabilities. We describe additional ways for bundles to deal with dependencies and content using bundle-level dependencies and bundle fragments. You also learn how bundles can deal with execution environments and native libraries.

Chapter 6 gives practical advice for converting JAR files into bundles, including how to define bundle metadata, package your bundle content, and add lifecycle support. We also describe how to go about dividing an application into bundles, demonstrating techniques on an existing open source project.

Chapter 7 shows how to test bundles and OSGi-based applications. We look into running your existing tests in OSGi and mocking OSGi APIs. In addition to unit and integration testing, we discuss management testing and explore some tools to help you along the way.

Chapter 8 follows testing by describing how to debug your bundles. We look into simple, command-line debugging as well as debugging with the Eclipse IDE. We show how to set up your development environment to get you up to speed quickly. We also explain some of the typical issues you encounter when working with OSGi and how to deal with them.

Chapter 9 switches gears and discusses how to manage your bundles. We explain how to meaningfully define version numbers for packages and bundles. We look into managing bundle configuration data and in the process describe a handful of related OSGi services. We also cover an option for triggering automatic bundle startup and initialization.

Chapter 10 continues investigating management topics, but moves from single-bundle issues to multi-bundle ones. We look at a couple of approaches for deploying bundles and their dependencies. We also explain how you can control bundle startup order.

Chapter 11 describes how component-oriented programming relates to OSGi. As a concrete example, we look at a standard OSGi component framework called *Declarative Services*. We show how Declarative Services allows you to work with POJOs and simplifies some aspects of dealing with service dynamism.

Chapter 12 continues investigating more advanced component frameworks for OSGi. We look at Blueprint, which is targeted toward enterprise developers familiar with Spring technology. We also examine the Apache Felix iPOJO component framework. We show that one of the benefits of OSGi-based component frameworks is they can all work together via services.

Chapter 13 turns away from developing bundles and looks at launching the OSGi framework. We describe the standard approach for configuring and creating OSGi frameworks. We also show how you can use the standard API to embed an OSGi framework into an existing application.

Chapter 14 delves into operating OSGi in a secure environment. We describe the issues involved and approaches to alleviating them. We explain how OSGi extends the standard Java security architecture to make it more flexible and easier to manage. And we show how to set up an OSGi framework with security enabled and create a secure example application.

Chapter 15 closes the book with a quick look at using web-related technologies in OSGi. We discuss using some common web applications technologies, such as servlets, JSPs, and WAR files. We also look into how to publish and consume web services.

Code

The companion code for the examples in this book is freely available from Manning's website, www.manning.com/OSGiinAction.

In the text, `Courier typeface` is used to denote code as well as JAR file manifest headers. References to methods generally don't include the signature, except when it's necessary to differentiate. The coding style adopts two-space indents and same-line braces to keep everything condensed and isn't otherwise recommended. When presenting command or shell interaction, `normal Courier typeface` is used to indicate program output, while **`bold`** is used to indicate user input.

Code annotations accompany many of the listings, highlighting important concepts. In some cases, numbered bullets link to explanations that follow the listing.

Author Online

Purchase of *OSGi in Action* includes free access to a private web forum run by Manning Publications where you can make comments about the book, ask technical questions, and receive help from the authors and from other users. To access the forum and subscribe to it, point your web browser to www.manning.com/OSGiinAction. This page provides information on how to get on the forum once you are registered, what kind of help is available, and the rules of conduct on the forum.

Manning's commitment to our readers is to provide a venue where a meaningful dialog between individual readers and between readers and the authors can take place. It is not a commitment to any specific amount of participation on the part of the authors, whose contribution to the book's forum remains voluntary (and unpaid). We suggest you try asking them some challenging questions lest their interest stray!

The Author Online forum and the archives of previous discussions will be accessible from the publisher's website as long as the book is in print.

About the title

By combining introductions, overviews, and how-to examples, the *In Action* books are designed to help learning *and* remembering. According to research in cognitive science, the things people remember are things they discover during self-motivated exploration.

Although no one at Manning is a cognitive scientist, we are convinced that for learning to become permanent it must pass through stages of exploration, play, and, interestingly, re-telling of what is being learned. People understand and remember new things, which is to say they master them, only after actively exploring them.

Humans learn in action. An essential part of an *In Action* book is that it is example-driven. It encourages the reader to try things out, to play with new code, and explore new ideas.

There is another, more mundane, reason for the title of this book: our readers are busy. They use books to do a job or solve a problem. They need books that allow them to jump in and jump out easily and learn just what they want, just when they want it. They need books that aid them in action. The books in this series are designed for such readers.

About the cover illustration

The figure on the cover of *OSGi in Action* is a "Soldier." The illustration is taken from a collection of costumes of the Ottoman Empire published on January 1, 1802, by William Miller of Old Bond Street, London. The title page is missing from the collection and we have been unable to track it down to date. The book's table of contents identifies the figures in both English and French, and each illustration bears the names of two artists who worked on it, both of whom would no doubt be surprised to find their art gracing the front cover of a computer programming book...two hundred years later.

The collection was purchased by a Manning editor at an antiquarian flea market in the "Garage" on West 26th Street in Manhattan. The seller was an American based in Ankara, Turkey, and the transaction took place just as he was packing up his stand for the day. The Manning editor did not have on his person the substantial amount of cash that was required for the purchase and a credit card and check were both politely turned down. With the seller flying back to Ankara that evening the situation was getting hopeless. What was the solution? It turned out to be nothing more than an old-fashioned verbal agreement sealed with a handshake. The seller simply proposed that the money be transferred to him by wire and the editor walked out with the bank information on a piece of paper and the portfolio of images under his arm. Needless to say, we transferred the funds the next day, and we remain grateful and impressed by this unknown person's trust in one of us. It recalls something that might have happened a long time ago.

The pictures from the Ottoman collection, like the other illustrations that appear on our covers, bring to life the richness and variety of dress customs of two centuries ago. They recall the sense of isolation and distance of that period—and of every other historic period except our own hyperkinetic present. Dress codes have changed since then and the diversity by region, so rich at the time, has faded away. It is now often hard to tell the inhabitant of one continent from another. Perhaps, trying to view it optimistically, we have traded a cultural and visual diversity for a more varied personal life. Or a more varied and interesting intellectual and technical life.

We at Manning celebrate the inventiveness, the initiative, and, yes, the fun of the computer business with book covers based on the rich diversity of regional life of two centuries ago, brought back to life by the pictures from this collection.

about the authors

RICHARD S. HALL is an active member of the Apache Felix framework development team as well as other Felix subprojects. He has been involved in open source OSGi work since 2000 and directly involved in the OSGi Alliance since 2004. Richard is a member of the Apache Software Foundation and works for Oracle on the GlassFish team, helping out out on OSGi issues or anything else, if he can.

KARL PAULS implemented the Apache Felix Framework Security Provider and is an active member of the Apache Felix framework development team as well as other Felix subprojects. He is a member of the Apache Software Foundation and is involved in various Apache and other open source projects. Karl is a fellow at Luminis.

STUART MCCULLOCH is responsible for the maven-bundle-plugin at Apache Felix and the Pax-Construct tools for rapid OSGi development from OPS4j. He is also the author of Peaberry, a Guice extension for injecting dynamic services. Stuart is a consultant at Sonatype, working on dependency injection and modularization.

DAVID SAVAGE works for Paremus and has been designing and building OSGi applications since 2005 in many different areas including build tools, component models, data persistence, desktop UIs, management, messaging, provisioning, resolvers, and RPC. He contributes to the Apache Felix project especially in the area of development tooling via the Sigil subproject. He is also directly involved in developing specifications for the OSGi Alliance.

Part 1

Introducing OSGi: modularity, lifecycle, and services

The OSGi framework defines a dynamic module system for Java. It gives you better control over the structure of your code, the ability to dynamically manage your code's lifecycle, and a loosely coupled approach for code collaboration. Even better, it's fully documented in a very elaborate specification. Unfortunately, the specification was written for people who are going to implement it rather than use it. In the first part of this book, we'll remedy this situation by effectively creating a user-oriented companion guide to the OSGi framework specification. We'll delve into its details by breaking it into three layers: module, lifecycle, and services. We'll explain what you need to understand from the specification to effectively use OSGi technology.

1 OSGi revealed

This chapter covers

- Understanding Java's built-in support for modularity
- Introducing OSGi technology and how it improves Java modularity
- Positioning OSGi with respect to other technologies

The Java platform is an unqualified success story. It's used to develop applications for everything from small mobile devices to massive enterprise endeavors. This is a testament to its well-thought-out design and continued evolution. But this success has come in spite of the fact that Java doesn't have explicit support for building modular systems beyond ordinary object-oriented data encapsulation.

What does this mean to you? If Java is a success despite its lack of advanced modularization support, then you may wonder if that absence is a problem. Most well-managed projects have to build up a repertoire of project-specific techniques to compensate for the lack of modularization in Java. These include the following:

- Programming practices to capture logical structure
- Tricks with multiple class loaders
- Serialization between in-process components

But these techniques are inherently brittle and error prone because they aren't enforceable via any compile-time or execution-time checks. The end result has detrimental impacts on multiple stages of an application's lifecycle:

- *Development*—You're unable to clearly and explicitly partition development into independent pieces.
- *Deployment*—You're unable to easily analyze, understand, and resolve requirements imposed by the independently developed pieces composing a complete system.
- *Execution*—You're unable to manage and evolve the constituent pieces of a running system, nor minimize the impact of doing so.

It's possible to manage these issues in Java, and lots of projects do so using the custom techniques mentioned earlier, but it's much more difficult than it should be. We're tying ourselves in knots to work around the lack of a fundamental feature. If Java had explicit support for modularity, then you'd be freed from such issues and could concentrate on what you really want to do, which is developing the functionality of your application.

Welcome to the OSGi Service Platform. The OSGi Service Platform is an industry standard defined by the OSGi Alliance to specifically address the lack of support for modularity in the Java platform. As a continuation of its modularity support, it introduces a service-oriented programming model, referred to by some as *SOA in a VM*, to help you clearly separate interface from implementation. This chapter will give you an overview of the OSGi Service Platform and how it helps you create modular and manageable applications using an interface-based development model.

When we've finished this chapter, you'll understand what role OSGi technology plays among the arsenal of Java technologies and why Java and/or other Java-related technologies don't address the specific features provided by OSGi technology.

1.1 The what and why of OSGi

The $64,000 question is, "What is OSGi?" The simplest answer to this question is that it's a modularity layer for the Java platform. Of course, the next question that may spring to mind is, "What do you mean by *modularity*?" Here we use *modularity* more or less in the traditional computer-science sense, where the code of your software application is divided into logical parts representing separate concerns, as shown in figure 1.1. If your software is modular, you can simplify development and

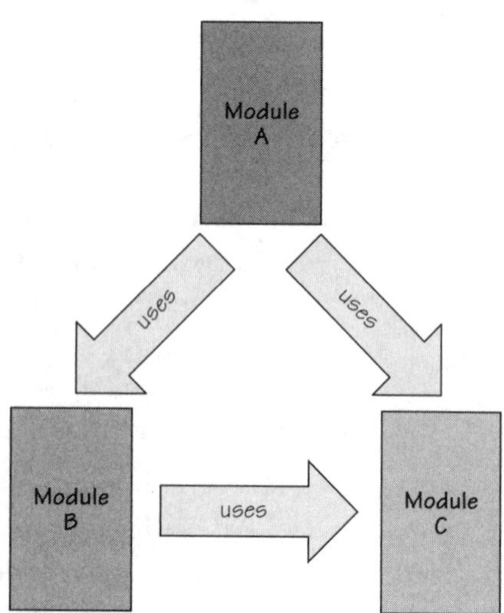

Figure 1.1 ***Modularity*** **refers to the logical decomposition of a large system into smaller collaborating pieces.**

improve maintainability by enforcing the logical module boundaries; we'll discuss more modularity details in chapter 2.

The notion of modularity isn't new. The concept became fashionable back in the 1970s. OSGi technology is cropping up all over the place—for example, as the runtime for the Eclipse IDE and the GlassFish application server. Why is it gaining popularity now? To better understand why OSGi is an increasingly important Java technology, it's worthwhile to understand some of Java's limitations with respect to creating modular applications. When you understand that, then you can see why OSGi technology is important and how it can help.

1.1.1 Java's modularity limitations

Java provides some aspects of modularity in the form of object orientation, but it was never intended to support coarse-grained modular programming. Although it's not fair to criticize Java for something it wasn't intended to address, the success of Java has resulted in difficulty for developers who ultimately have to deal with their need for better modularity support.

Java is promoted as a platform for building all sorts of applications for domains ranging from mobile phone to enterprise applications. Most of these endeavors require, or could at least benefit from, broader support for modularity. Let's look at some of Java's modularity limitations.

LOW-LEVEL CODE VISIBILITY CONTROL

Although Java provides a fair complement of access modifiers to control visibility (such as `public`, `protected`, `private`, and package private), these tend to address low-level object-oriented encapsulation and not logical system partitioning. Java has the notion of a *package*, which is typically used for partitioning code. For code to be visible from one Java package to another, the code must be declared `public` (or `protected` if using inheritance). Sometimes, the logical structure of your application calls for specific code to belong in different packages; but this means any dependencies among the packages must be exposed as `public`, which makes them accessible to everyone else, too. Often, this can expose implementation details, which makes future evolution more difficult because users may end up with dependencies on your nonpublic API.

To illustrate, let's consider a trivial "Hello, world!" application that provides a public interface in one package, a private implementation in another, and a main class in yet another.

Listing 1.1 Example of the limitations of Java's object-orientated encapsulation

Greeting.java

```
package org.foo.hello;

public interface Greeting {        ❶ Simple interface
  void sayHello();
}
```

GreetingImpl.java

```
package org.foo.hello.impl;

import org.foo.hello.Greeting;
```

```
public class GreetingImpl implements Greeting {
  final String m_name;

  public GreetingImpl(String name) {          <-- 2 Interface implementation
    m_name = name;
  }

  public void sayHello() {
    System.out.println("Hello, " + m_name + "!");
  }
}
```

Main.java

```
package org.foo.hello.main;

import org.foo.hello.Greeting;
import org.foo.hello.impl.GreetingImpl;

public class Main {
  public static void main(String[] args) {
    Greeting greet = new GreetingImpl("Hello World");     <-- 3 Main method
    greet.sayHello();
  }
}
```

Listing 1.1's author may have intended a third party to only interact with the application via the `Greeting` interface ❶. They may mention this in Javadoc, tutorials, blogs, or even email rants, but nothing stops a third party from constructing a new `GreetingImpl` using its public constructor ❷ as is done at ❸.

You may argue that the constructor shouldn't be public and that there is no need to split the application into multiple packages, which could well be true in this trivial example. But in real-world applications, class-level visibility when combined with packaging turns out to be a crude tool for ensuring API coherency. Because supposedly private implementation details can be accessed by third-party developers, you need to worry about changes to private implementation signatures as well as to public interfaces when making updates.

This problem stems from the fact that although Java packages appear to have a logical relationship via nested packages, they don't. A common misconception for people first learning Java is to assume that the parent-child package relationship bestows special visibility privileges on the involved packages. Two packages involved in a nested relationship are equivalent to two packages that aren't. Nested packages are largely useful for avoiding name clashes, but they provide only partial support for the logical code partitioning.

What this all means is that, in Java, you're regularly forced to decide between the following:

1. Impairing your application's logical structure by lumping unrelated classes into the same package to avoid exposing nonpublic APIs
2. Keeping your application's logical structure by using multiple packages at the expense of exposing nonpublic APIs so they can be accessed by classes in different packages

Neither choice is particularly palatable.

ERROR-PRONE CLASS PATH CONCEPT

The Java platform also inhibits good modularity practices. The main culprit is the Java class path. Why does the class path pose problems for modularity? Largely due to all the issues it hides, such as code versions, dependencies, and consistency. Applications are generally composed of various versions of libraries and components. The class path pays no attention to code versions—it returns the first version it finds. Even if it did pay attention, there is no way to explicitly specify dependencies. The process of setting up your class path is largely trial and error; you just keep adding libraries until the VM stops complaining about missing classes.

Figure 1.2 shows the sort of "class path hell" often found when more than one JAR file provides a given set of classes. Even though each JAR file may have been compiled to work as a unit, when they're merged at execution time, the Java class path pays no attention to the logical partitioning of the components. This tends to lead to hard-to-predict errors, such as `NoSuchMethodError`, when a class from one JAR file interacts with an incompatible class version from another.

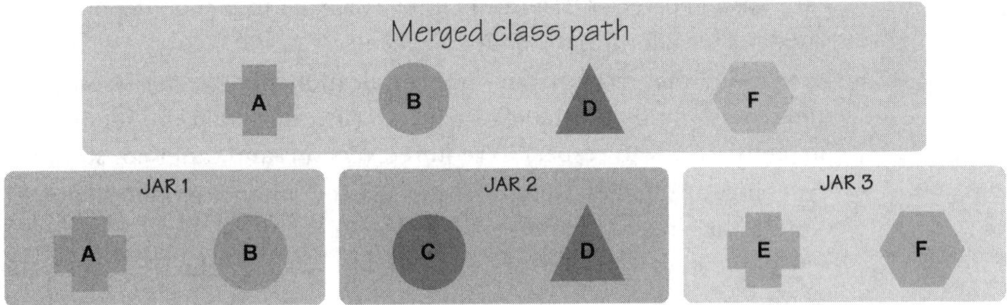

Figure 1.2 Multiple JARs containing overlapping classes and/or packages are merged based on their order of appearance in the class path, with no regard to logical coherency among archives.

In large applications created from independently developed components, it isn't uncommon to have dependencies on different versions of the same component, such as logging or XML parsing mechanisms. The class path forces you to choose one version in such situations, which may not always be possible. Worse, if you have multiple versions of the same package on the class path, either on purpose or accidentally, they're treated as split packages by Java and are implicitly merged based on order of appearance.

Overall, the class path approach lacks any form of consistency checking. You get whatever classes have been made available by the system administrator, which is likely only an approximation of what the developer expected.

LIMITED DEPLOYMENT AND MANAGEMENT SUPPORT

Java also lacks support when it comes to deploying and managing your application. There is no easy way in Java to deploy the proper transitive set of versioned code dependencies and execute your application. The same is true for evolving your application and its components after deployment.

Consider the common requirement of wanting to support a dynamic plugin mechanism. The only way to achieve such a benign request is to use class loaders, which are low level and error prone. Class loaders were never intended to be a common tool for application developers, but many of today's systems require their use. A properly defined modularity layer for Java can deal with these issues by making the module concept explicit and raising the level of abstraction for code partitioning.

With this better understanding of Java's limitations when it comes to modularity, we can ponder whether OSGi is the right solution for your projects.

1.1.2 Can OSGi help you?

Nearly all but the simplest of applications can benefit from the modularity features OSGi provides, so if you're wondering if OSGi is something you should be interested in, the answer is most likely, "Yes!" Still not convinced? Here are some common scenarios you may have encountered where OSGi can be helpful:

- `ClassNotFoundExceptions` when starting your application because the class path wasn't correct. OSGi can help by ensuring that code dependencies are satisfied before allowing the code to execute.
- Execution-time errors from your application due to the wrong version of a dependent library on the class path. OSGi verifies that the set of dependencies are consistent with respect to required versions and other constraints.
- Type inconsistencies when sharing classes among modules: put more concretely, the dreaded appearance of `foo instanceof Foo == false`. With OSGi, you don't have to worry about the constraints implied by hierarchical class-loading schemes.
- Packaging an application as logically independent JAR files and deploying only those pieces you need for a given installation. This pretty much describes the purpose of OSGi.
- Packaging an application as logically independent JAR files, declaring which code is accessible from each JAR file, and having this visibility enforced. OSGi enables a new level of code visibility for JAR files that allows you to specify what is and what isn't visible externally.
- Defining an extensibility mechanism for an application, like a plugin mechanism. OSGi modularity is particularly suited to providing a powerful extensibility mechanism, including support for execution-time dynamism.

As you can see, these scenarios cover a lot of use cases, but they're by no means exhaustive. The simple and non-intrusive nature of OSGi tends to make you discover more ways to apply it the more you use it. Having explored some of the limitations of the standard Java class path, we'll now properly introduce you to OSGi.

1.2 An architectural overview of OSGi

The OSGi Service Platform is composed of two parts: the OSGi framework and OSGi standard services (depicted in figure 1.3). The framework is the runtime that implements and provides OSGi functionality. The standard services define reusable APIs for common tasks, such as Logging and Preferences.

Figure 1.3 The OSGi Service Platform specification is divided into halves, one for the OSGi framework and one for standard services.

The OSGi specifications for the framework and standard services are managed by the OSGi Alliance (www.osgi.org/). The OSGi Alliance is an industry-backed nonprofit corporation founded in March 1999. The framework specification is now on its fourth major revision and is stable. Technology based on this specification is in use in a range of large-scale industry applications, including (but not limited to) automotive, mobile devices, desktop applications, and more recently enterprise application servers.

> **NOTE** Once upon a time, the letters *OSGi* were an acronym that stood for the Open Services Gateway Initiative. This acronym highlights the lineage of the technology but has fallen out of favor. After the third specification release, the OSGi Alliance officially dropped the acronym, and OSGi is now a trademark for the technology.

In the bulk of this book, we'll discuss the OSGi framework, its capabilities, and how to use these capabilities. Because there are so many standard services, we'll discuss only the most relevant and useful services, where appropriate. For any service we miss, you can get more information from the OSGi specifications. For now, we'll continue our overview of OSGi by introducing the broad features of the OSGi framework.

1.2.1 The OSGi framework

The OSGi framework plays a central role when you create OSGi-based applications, because it's the application's execution environment. The OSGi Alliance's framework specification defines the proper behavior of the framework, which gives you a well-defined API to program against. The specification also enables the creation of multiple implementations of the core framework to give you some freedom of choice; there are a handful of well-known open source projects, such as Apache Felix (http://felix.apache.org/), Eclipse Equinox (www.eclipse.org/equinox/), and Knopflerfish (www.knopflerfish.org/). This ultimately benefits you, because you aren't tied to a particular vendor and can program against the behavior defined in the specification. It's sort of like the reassuring feeling you get by knowing you can go into any McDonald's anywhere in the world and get the same meal!

OSGi technology is starting to pop up everywhere. You may not know it, but if you use an IDE to do your Java development, it's possible you already have experience with OSGi. The Equinox OSGi framework implementation is the underlying runtime for the Eclipse IDE. Likewise, if you use the GlassFish v3 application server, you're also using OSGi, because the Apache Felix OSGi framework implementation is its runtime. The diversity of use cases attests to the value and flexibility provided by the OSGi framework through three conceptual layers defined in the OSGi specification (see figure 1.4):

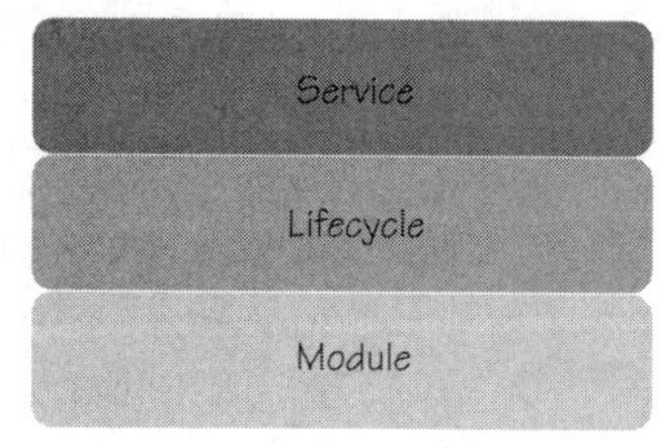

Figure 1.4 OSGi layered architecture

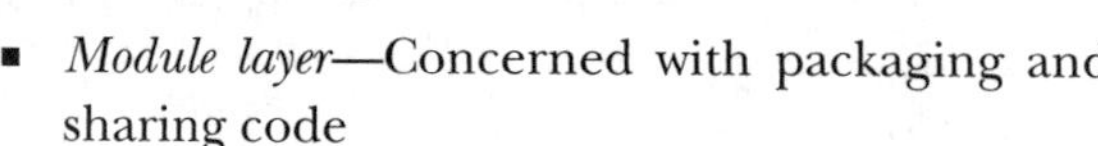

- *Module layer*—Concerned with packaging and sharing code
- *Lifecycle layer*—Concerned with providing execution-time module management and access to the underlying OSGi framework
- *Service layer*—Concerned with interaction and communication among modules, specifically the components contained in them

Like typical layered architectures, each layer is dependent on the layers beneath it. Therefore, it's possible for you to use lower OSGi layers without using upper ones, but not vice versa. The next three chapters discuss these layers in detail, but we'll give an overview of each here.

MODULE LAYER

The module layer defines the OSGi module concept, called a *bundle*, which is a JAR file with extra *metadata* (data about data). A bundle contains your class files and their related resources, as depicted in figure 1.5. Bundles typically aren't an entire application packaged into a single JAR file; rather, they're the logical modules that combine to form a given application. Bundles are more powerful than standard JAR files, because you can explicitly declare which contained packages are externally visible (that is, *exported packages*). In this sense, bundles extend the normal access modifiers (`public`, `private`, and `protected`) associated with the Java language.

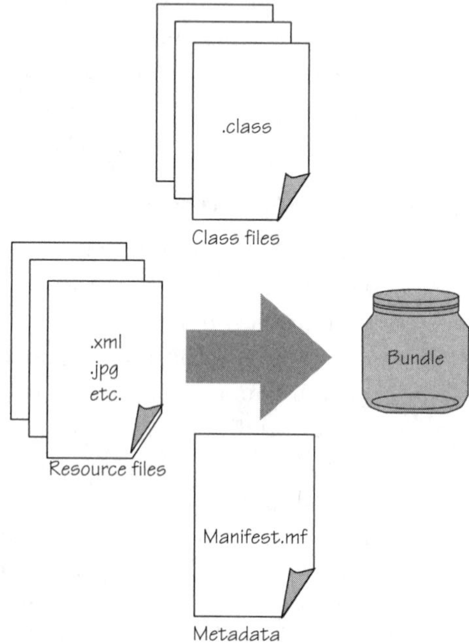

Figure 1.5 A bundle contains code, resources, and metadata.

Another important advantage of bundles over standard JAR files is the fact that you can explicitly declare on which external packages the bundles depend (that is, *imported packages*). The main benefit of explicitly declaring your bundles' exported and imported packages is that the OSGi framework can manage and verify their consistency automatically; this process is called *bundle resolution* and involves matching exported packages to imported packages. Bundle resolution ensures consistency among bundles with respect to versions and other constraints, which we'll discuss in detail in chapter 2.

LIFECYCLE LAYER

The lifecycle layer defines how bundles are dynamically installed and managed in the OSGi framework. If you were building a house, the module layer would provide the foundation and structure, and the lifecycle layer would be the electrical wiring. It makes everything run.

The lifecycle layer serves two different purposes. External to your application, the lifecycle layer precisely defines the bundle lifecycle operations (install, update, start, stop, and uninstall). These lifecycle operations allow you to dynamically administer, manage, and evolve your application in a well-defined way. This means bundles can be safely added to and removed from the framework without restarting the application process.

Internal to your application, the lifecycle layer defines how your bundles gain access to their execution context, which provides them with a way to interact with the OSGi framework and the facilities it provides during execution. This overall approach to the lifecycle layer is powerful because it lets you create externally (and remotely) managed applications or completely self-managed applications (or any combination).

SERVICE LAYER

Finally, the service layer supports and promotes a flexible application programming model incorporating concepts popularized by service-oriented computing (although these concepts were part of the OSGi framework before service-oriented computing became popular). The main concepts revolve around the service-oriented publish, find, and bind interaction pattern: service providers publish their services into a service registry, while service clients search the registry to find available services to use (see figure 1.6). Nowadays, this service-oriented architecture (SOA) is largely associated with web services; but OSGi services are local to a single VM, which is why some people refer to it as *SOA in a VM*.

The OSGi service layer is intuitive, because it promotes an interface-based development approach, which is generally considered good practice. Specifically, it promotes the separation of interface and implementation. OSGi *services* are Java interfaces representing a conceptual contract between service providers and service clients. This makes the service layer lightweight, because service providers are just Java objects accessed via direct method invocation. Additionally, the service layer expands

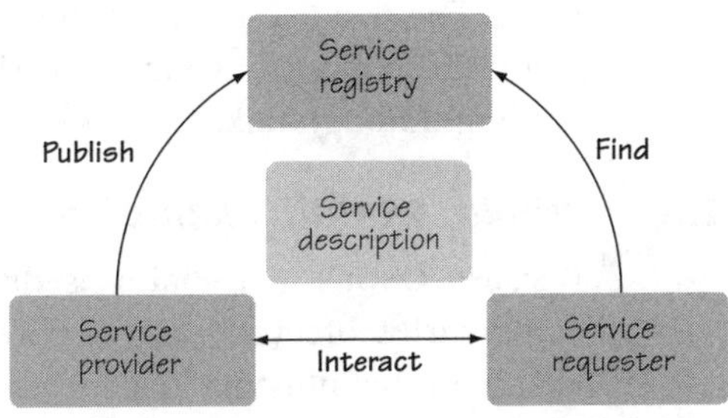

Figure 1.6 The service-oriented interaction pattern. Providers publish services into a registry where requesters can discover which services are available for use.

the bundle-based dynamism of the lifecycle layer with service-based dynamism—services can appear or disappear at any time. The result is a programming model eschewing the monolithic and brittle approaches of the past, in favor of being modular and flexible.

This sounds well and good, but you may still be wondering how these three layers fit together and how you go about using them to create an application on top of them. In the next couple of sections, we'll explore how these layers fit together using some small example programs.

1.2.2 Putting it all together

The OSGi framework is made up of layers, but how do you use these layers in application development? We'll make it clearer by outlining the general approach you'll use when creating an OSGi-based application:

1. Design your application by breaking it down into service interfaces (normal interface-based programming) and clients of those interfaces.
2. Implement your service provider and client components using your preferred tools and practices.
3. Package your service provider and client components into (usually) separate JAR files, augmenting each JAR file with the appropriate OSGi metadata.
4. Start the OSGi framework.
5. Install and start all your component JAR files from step 3.

If you're already following an interface-based approach, the OSGi approach will feel familiar. The main difference will be how you locate your interface implementations (that is, your services). Normally, you might instantiate implementations and pass around references to initialize clients. In the OSGi world, your services will publish themselves in the service registry, and your clients will look up available services in the registry. After your bundles are installed and started, your application will start and execute as normal, but with several advantages. Underneath, the OSGi framework provides more rigid modularity and consistency checking, and its dynamic nature opens up a world of possibilities.

Don't fret if you don't or can't use an interfaced-based approach for your development. The first two layers of the OSGi framework still provide a lot of functionality; in truth, the bulk of OSGi framework functionality lies in these first two layers, so keep reading. Enough talk: let's look at some code.

1.3 "Hello, world!" examples

Because OSGi functionality is divided over the three layers mentioned previously (modularity, lifecycle, and service), we'll show you three different "Hello, world!" examples that illustrate each of these layers.

1.3.1 Module layer example

The module layer isn't related to code creation as such; rather, it's related to the packaging of your code into bundles. You need to be aware of certain code-related issues when developing, but by and large you prepare code for the module layer by adding packaging metadata to your project's generated JAR files. For example, suppose you want to share the following class.

Listing 1.2 Basic greeting implementation

```
package org.foo.hello;

public class Greeting {
  final String m_name;

  public Greeting(String name) {
    m_name = name;
  }

  public void sayHello() {
    System.out.println("Hello, " + m_name + "!");
  }
}
```

During the build process, you compile the source code and put the generated class file into a JAR file. To use the OSGi module layer, you must add some metadata into your JAR file's META-INF/MANIFEST.MF file, such as the following:

```
Bundle-ManifestVersion: 2
Bundle-Name: Greeting API
Bundle-SymbolicName: org.foo.hello
Bundle-Version: 1.0
Export-Package: org.foo.hello;version="1.0"
```

The first line indicates the OSGi metadata syntax version. Next is the human-readable name, which isn't strictly necessary. This is followed by the symbolic name and version bundle identifier. The last line shares packages with other bundles.

In this example, the bulk of the metadata is related to bundle identification. The important part is the `Export-Package` statement, because it extends the functionality of a typical JAR file with the ability for you to explicitly declare which packages contained in the JAR are visible to its users. In this example, only the contents of the `org.foo.hello` package are externally visible; if the example included other packages, they wouldn't be externally visible. This means that when you run your application, other modules won't be able to accidentally (or intentionally) depend on packages your module doesn't explicitly expose.

To use this shared code in another module, you again add metadata. This time, you use the `Import-Package` statement to explicitly declare which external packages are required by the code contained in the client JAR. The following snippet illustrates:

```
Bundle-ManifestVersion: 2
Bundle-Name: Greeting Client
Bundle-SymbolicName: org.foo.hello.client
Bundle-Version: 1.0
Import-Package: org.foo.hello;version="[1.0,2.0)"
```

In this case, the last line specifies a dependency on an external package.

To see this example in action, go in the chapter01/greeting-example/modularity/ directory in the book's companion code, and type `ant` to build it and `java -jar main.jar` to run it. Although the example is simple, it illustrates that creating OSGi bundles out of existing JAR files is a reasonably non-intrusive process. In addition, there are tools that can help you create your bundle metadata, which we'll discuss in appendix A; but in reality, no special tools are required to create a bundle other than what you normally use to create a JAR file. Chapter 2 will go into all the juicy details of OSGi modularity.

1.3.2 *Lifecycle layer example*

In the last subsection, you saw that it's possible to take advantage of OSGi functionality in a non-invasive way by adding metadata to your existing JAR files. Such a simple approach is sufficient for most reusable libraries, but sometimes you need or want to go further to meet specific requirements or to use additional OSGi features. The lifecycle layer moves you deeper into the OSGi world.

Perhaps you want to create a module that performs some initialization task, such as starting a background thread or initializing a driver; the lifecycle layer makes this possible. Bundles may declare a given class as an *activator*, which is the bundle's hook into its own lifecycle management. We'll discuss the full lifecycle of a bundle in chapter 3, but first let's look at a simple example to give you an idea of what we're talking about. The following listing extends the previous `Greeting` class to provide a singleton instance.

Listing 1.3 Extended greeting implementation

```
package org.foo.hello;

public class Greeting {
  static Greeting instance;                          <- Singleton instance
  final String m_name;

  Greeting(String name) {                            <- Constructor now package private
    m_name = name;
  }

  public static Greeting get() {                     <- Clients must use singleton
    return instance;
  }

  public void sayHello() {
    System.out.println("Hello, " + m_name + "!");
  }
}
```

Listing 1.4 implements a bundle activator to initialize the `Greeting` class singleton when the bundle is started and clear it when it's stopped. The client can now use the preconfigured singleton instead of creating its own instance.

Listing 1.4 OSGi bundle activator for our greeting implementation

```
package org.foo.hello;

import org.osgi.framework.BundleActivator;
import org.osgi.framework.BundleContext;

public class Activator implements BundleActivator {

  public void start(BundleContext ctx) {
    Greeting.instance = new Greeting("lifecycle");
  }

  public void stop(BundleContext ctx) {
    Greeting.instance = null;
  }
}
```

A bundle activator must implement a simple OSGi interface, which in this case is composed of the two methods `start()` and `stop()`. At execution time, the framework constructs an instance of this class and invokes the `start()` method when the bundle is started and the `stop()` method when the bundle is stopped. (What we mean by *starting* and *stopping* a bundle will become clearer in chapter 3.) Because the framework uses the same activator instance while the bundle is active, you can share member variables between the `start()` and `stop()` methods.

You may wonder what the single parameter of type `BundleContext` in the `start()` and `stop()` methods is all about. This is how the bundle gets access to the OSGi framework in which it's executing. From this context object, the module has access to all the OSGi functionality for modularity, lifecycle, and services. In short, it's a fairly important object for most bundles, but we'll defer a detailed introduction of it until later when we discuss the lifecycle layer. The important point to take away from this example is that bundles have a simple way to hook into their lifecycle and gain access to the underlying OSGi framework.

Of course, it isn't sufficient to just create this bundle activator implementation; you have to tell the framework about it. Luckily, this is simple. If you have an existing JAR file you're converting to be a module, you must add the activator implementation to the existing project so the class is included in the resulting JAR file. If you're creating a bundle from scratch, you need to compile the class and put the result in a JAR file. You must also tell the OSGi framework about the bundle activator by adding another piece of metadata to the JAR file manifest. For this section's example, you add the following metadata to the JAR manifest:

```
Bundle-Activator: org.foo.hello.Activator
Import-Package: org.osgi.framework
```

Notice that you also need to import the `org.osgi.framework` package, because the bundle activator has a dependency on it. To see this example in action, go to the chapter01/greeting-example/lifecycle/ directory in the companion code and type ant to build the example and `java -jar main.jar` to run it.

We've now introduced how to create OSGi bundles out of existing JAR files using the module layer and how to make your bundles lifecycle aware so they can use framework functionality. The last example in this section demonstrates the service-oriented programming approach promoted by OSGi.

1.3.3 Service layer example

If you follow an interfaced-based approach in your development, the OSGi service approach will feel natural to you. To illustrate, consider the following `Greeting` interface:

```
package org.foo.hello;
public interface Greeting {
  void sayHello();
}
```

For any given implementation of the `Greeting` interface, when the `sayHello()` method is invoked, a greeting will be displayed. In general, a service represents a contract between a provider and prospective clients; the semantics of the contract are typically described in a separate, human-readable document, like a specification. The previous service interface represents the syntactic contract of all `Greeting` implementations. The notion of a contract is necessary so that clients can be assured of getting the functionality they expect when using a `Greeting` service.

The precise details of how any given `Greeting` implementation performs its task aren't known to the client. For example, one implementation may print its greeting textually, whereas another may display its greeting in a GUI dialog box. The following code depicts a simple text-based implementation.

Listing 1.5 Implementation of the `Greeting` interface

```
package org.foo.hello.impl;

import org.foo.hello.Greeting;

public class GreetingImpl implements Greeting {
  final String m_name;

  GreetingImpl(String name) {
    m_name = name;
  }

  public void sayHello() {
    System.out.println("Hello, " + m_name + "!");
  }
}
```

Your may be thinking that nothing in the service interface or listing 1.5 indicates that you're defining an OSGi service. You're correct. That's what makes the OSGi's service approach so natural if you're already following an interface-based approach; your code will largely stay the same. Your development will be a little different in two places: how you make a service instance available to the rest of your application, and how the rest of your application discovers the available service.

All service implementations are ultimately packaged into a bundle, and that bundle must be lifecycle aware in order to register the service. This means you need to create a bundle activator for the example service, as shown next.

Listing 1.6 OSGi bundle activator with service registration

```
package org.foo.hello.impl;

import org.foo.hello.Greeting;
import org.osgi.framework.BundleActivator;
import org.osgi.framework.BundleContext;

public class Activator implements BundleActivator {

  public void start(BundleContext ctx) {
    ctx.registerService(Greeting.class.getName(),
        new GreetingImpl("service"), null);
  }

  public void stop(BundleContext ctx) {}
}
```

This time, in the `start()` method, instead of storing the `Greeting` implementation as a singleton, you use the provided bundle context to register it as a service in the service registry. The first parameter you need to provide is the interface name(s) that the service implements, followed by the actual service instance, and finally the service properties. In the `stop()` method, you could unregister the service implementation before stopping the bundle; but in practice, you don't need to do this. The OSGi framework automatically unregisters any registered services when a bundle stops.

You've seen how to register a service, but what about discovering a service? The following listing shows a simplistic client that doesn't handle missing services and that suffers from potential race conditions. We'll discuss a more robust way to access services in chapter 4.

Listing 1.7 OSGi bundle activator with service discovery

```
package org.foo.hello.client;

import org.foo.hello.Greeting;
import org.osgi.framework.*;

public class Client implements BundleActivator {

  public void start(BundleContext ctx) {
    ServiceReference ref =
        ctx.getServiceReference(Greeting.class.getName());   <- (1) Looks up service reference

    ((Greeting) ctx.getService(ref)).sayHello();   <- (2) Retrieves and uses service
  }

  public void stop(BundleContext ctx) {}
}
```

Notice that accessing a service in OSGi is a two-step process. First, an indirect reference is retrieved from the service registry (1). Second, this indirect reference is used to access the service object instance ❷. The service reference can be safely stored in a member variable; but in general it isn't a good idea to hold on to references to service object instances, because services may be unregistered dynamically, resulting in stale references that prevent garbage collection of uninstalled bundles.

Both the service implementation and the client should be packaged into separate bundle JAR files. The metadata for each bundle declares its corresponding activator, but the service implementation exports the `org.foo.hello` package, whereas the client imports it. Note that the client bundle's metadata only needs to declare an import for the `Greeting` interface package—it has no direct dependency on the service implementation. This makes it easy to swap service implementations dynamically without restarting the client bundle. To see this example in action, go to the chapter01/greeting-example/service/ directory in the companion code and type `ant` to build the example and `java -jar main.jar` to run it.

Now that you've seen some examples, you can better understand how each layer of the OSGi framework builds on the previous one. Each layer gives you additional capabilities when building your application, but OSGi technology is flexible enough for you to adopt it according to your specific needs. If you only want better modularity in your project, use the module layer. If you want a way to initialize modules and interact with the module layer, use both the module and lifecycle layers. If you want a dynamic, interface-based development approach, use all three layers. The choice is yours.

1.3.4 Setting the stage

To help introduce the concepts of each layer in the OSGi framework in the next three chapters, we'll use a simple paint program; its user interface is shown in figure 1.7.

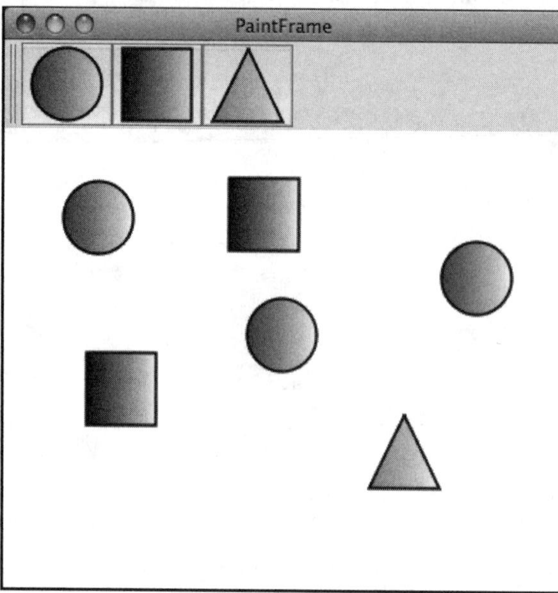

Figure 1.7 Simple paint program user interface

The paint program isn't intended to be independently useful; rather, it's used to demonstrate common issues and best practices.

From a functionality perspective, the paint program only allows the user to paint various shapes, such as circles, squares, and triangles. The shapes are painted in predefined colors. Available shapes are displayed as buttons in the main window's toolbar. To draw a shape, the user selects it in the toolbar and then clicks anywhere in the canvas to draw it. The same shape can be drawn repeatedly by clicking in the canvas numerous times. The user can drag drawn shapes to reposition them. This sounds simple enough. The real value of using a visual program for demonstrating these concepts will become evident when we start introducing execution-time dynamism.

We've finished our overview of the OSGi framework and are ready to delve into the details; but before we do, we'll put OSGi in context by discussing similar or related technologies. Although no Java technology fills the exact same niche as OSGi, several tread similar ground, and it's worth understanding their relevance before moving forward.

1.4 Putting OSGi in context

OSGi is often mentioned in the same breath with many other technologies, but it's in a fairly unique position in the Java world. Over the years, no single technology has addressed OSGi's exact problem space, but there have been overlaps, complements, and offshoots. Although it isn't possible to cover how OSGi relates to every conceivable technology, we'll address some of the most relevant in roughly chronological order. After reading this section, you should have a good idea whether OSGi replaces your familiar technologies or is complementary to them.

1.4.1 Java Enterprise Edition

Java Enterprise Edition (Java EE, formerly J2EE) has roots dating back to 1997. Java EE and OSGi began targeting opposite ends of the computing spectrum (the enterprise vs. embedded markets, respectively). Only within the last couple of years has OSGi technology begun to take root in the enterprise space.

In total, the Java EE API stack isn't related to OSGi. The Enterprise JavaBeans (EJB) specification is probably the closest comparable technology from the Java EE space, because it defines a component model and packaging format. But its component model focuses on providing a standard way to implement enterprise applications that must regularly handle issues of persistence, transactions, and security. The EJB deployment descriptors and packaging formats are relatively simplistic and don't address the full component lifecycle, nor do they support clean modularity concepts.

OSGi is also used in the Java EE domain to provide a more sophisticated module layer beneath these existing technologies. Because the two ignored each other for so long, there are some challenges in moving existing Java EE concepts to OSGi, largely due to different assumptions about how class loading is performed. Still, progress is being made, and today OSGi plays a role in all major application servers, such as IBM's WebSphere, Red Hat's JBoss, Oracle's GlassFish, ObjectWeb's JOnAS, and Apache's Geronimo.

1.4.2 Jini

An often-overlooked Java technology is Jini, which is definitely a conceptual sibling of OSGi. Jini targets OSGi's original problem space of networked environments with a variety of connected devices.

Sun began developing Jini in 1998. The goal of Jini is to make it possible to administer a networked environment as a flexible, dynamic group of services. Jini introduces the concepts of service providers, service consumers, and a service lookup registry. All of this sounds completely isomorphic to OSGi; where Jini differs is its focus on distributed systems. Consumers access clients through some form of proxy using a remote procedure call mechanism, such as Remote Method Invocation (RMI). The service-lookup registry is also a remotely accessible, federated service. The Jini model assumes remote access across multiple VM processes, whereas OSGi assumes everything occurs in a single VM process. But in stark contrast to OSGi, Jini doesn't define any modularity mechanisms and relies on the execution-time code-loading features of RMI. The open source project Newton is an example of combining OSGi and Jini technologies in a single framework.

1.4.3 NetBeans

NetBeans, an IDE and application platform for Java, has a long history of having a modular design. Sun purchased NetBeans in 1999 and has continued to evolve it.

The NetBeans platform has a lot in common with OSGi. It defines a fairly sophisticated module layer and also promotes interface-based programming using a lookup pattern that is similar to the OSGi service registry. Whereas OSGi focused on embedded devices and dynamism, the NetBeans platform was originally an implementation layer for the IDE. Eventually, the platform was promoted as a separate tool in its own right, but it focused on being a complete GUI application platform with abstractions for file systems, windowing systems, and much more. NetBeans has never been seen as comparable to OSGi, even though it is; perhaps OSGi's more narrow focus is an asset in this case.

1.4.4 Java Management Extensions

Java Management Extensions (JMX), released in 2000 through the Java Community Process (JCP) as JSR 3, was compared to OSGi in the early days. JMX is a technology for remotely managing and monitoring applications, system objects, and devices; it defines a server and a component model for this purpose.

JMX isn't comparable to OSGi; it's complementary, because it can be used to manage and monitor an OSGi framework and its bundles and services. Why did the comparisons arise in the first place? There are probably three reasons: the JMX component model was sufficiently generic that it was possible to use it for building applications; the specification defined a mechanism for dynamically loading code into its server; and certain early adopters pushed JMX in this direction. One major perpetrator was JBoss, which adopted and extended JMX for use as a module layer in its application server (since eliminated in JBoss 5). Nowadays, JMX isn't (and shouldn't be) confused with a module system.

1.4.5 Lightweight containers

Around 2003, lightweight or inversion of control (IoC) containers started to appear, such as PicoContainer, Spring, and Apache Avalon. The main idea behind this crop of IoC containers was to simplify component configuration and assembly by eliminating the use of concrete types in favor of interfaces. This was combined with dependency injection techniques, where components depend on interface types and implementations of the interfaces are injected into the component instance. OSGi services promote a similar interface-based approach but employ a service-locator pattern to break a component's dependency on component implementations, similar to Apache Avalon.

At the same time, the Service Binder project was creating a dependency injection framework for OSGi components. It's fairly easy to see why the comparisons arose. Regardless, OSGi's use of interface-based services and the service-locator pattern long predated this trend, and none of these technologies offer a sophisticated dynamic module layer like OSGi. There is now significant movement from IoC vendors to port their infrastructures to the OSGi framework, such as the work by VMware (formerly SpringSource) on the OSGi Blueprint specification (discussed in chapter 12).

1.4.6 Java Business Integration

Java Business Integration (JBI) was developed in the JCP and released in 2005. Its goal was to create a standard SOA platform for creating enterprise application integration (EAI) and business-to-business (B2B) integration solutions.

In JBI, plugin components provide and consume services after they're plugged in to the JBI framework. Components don't directly interact with services, as in OSGi; instead, they communicate indirectly using normalized Web Services Description Language (WSDL)-based messages.

JBI uses a JMX-based approach to manage component installation and lifecycle and defines a packaging format for its components. Due to the inherent similarities to OSGi's architecture, it was easy to think JBI was competing for a similar role. On the contrary, its fairly simplistic modularity mechanisms mainly addressed basic component integration into the framework. It made more sense for JBI to use OSGi's more sophisticated modularity, which is ultimately what happened in Project Fuji from Sun and ServiceMix from Apache.

1.4.7 JSR 277

In 2005, Sun announced JSR 277 ("Java Module System") to define a module system for Java. JSR 277 was intended to define a module framework, packaging format, and repository system for the Java platform. From the perspective of the OSGi Alliance, this was a major case of reinventing the wheel, because the effort was starting from scratch rather than building on the experience gained from OSGi.

In 2006, many OSGi supporters pushed for the introduction of JSR 291 (titled "Dynamic Component Support for Java"), which was an effort to bring OSGi technology properly into JCP standardization. The goal was twofold: to create a bridge between the two communities and to ensure OSGi technology integration was considered by JSR 277. The completion of JSR 291 was fairly quick because it started from the OSGi R4 specification and resulted in the R4.1 specification release. During this period, OSGi technology continued to gain momentum. JSR 277 continued to make slow progress through 2008 until it was put on hold indefinitely.

1.4.8 JSR 294

During this time in 2006, JSR 294 (titled "Improved Modularity Support in the Java Programming Language") was introduced as an offshoot of JSR 277. Its goal was to focus on necessary language changes for modularity. The original idea was to introduce the notion of a *superpackage* into the Java language—a package of packages.

The specification of superpackages got bogged down in details until it was scrapped in favor of adding a module-access modifier keyword to the language. This simplification ultimately led to JSR 294 being dropped and merged back into JSR 277 in 2007. But when it became apparent in 2008 that JSR 277 would be put on hold, JSR 294 was pulled back out to address a module-level access modifier.

With JSR 277 on hold, Sun introduced an internal project, called *Project Jigsaw*, to modularize the JDK. The details of Jigsaw are still evolving after the acquisition of Sun by Oracle.

1.4.9 Service Component Architecture

Service Component Architecture (SCA) began as an industry collaboration in 2004 and ultimately resulted in final specifications in 2007. SCA defines a service-oriented component model similar to OSGi's, where components provide and require services. Its component model is more advanced because it defines *composite components* (components made of other components) for a fully recursive component model.

SCA is intended to be a component model for declaratively composing components implemented using various technologies (such as Java, Business Process Execution Language [BPEL], EJB, and C++) and integrated using various bindings (such as SOAP/HTTP, Java Message Service [JMS], Java EE Connector Architecture [JCA], and Internet Inter-Orb Protocol [IIOP]). SCA does define a standard packaging format, but it doesn't define a sophisticated module layer like OSGi provides. The SCA specification leaves open the possibility of other packaging formats, which makes it possible to use OSGi as a packaging and module layer for Java-based SCA implementations; Apache Tuscany and Newton are examples of an SCA implementation that use OSGi. In addition, bundles could be used to implement SCA component types, and SCA could be used as a mechanism to provide remote access to OSGi services.

1.4.10 .NET

Although Microsoft's .NET (released in 2002) isn't a Java technology, it deserves mention because it was largely inspired by Java and did improve on it in ways that are similar to how OSGi improves Java. Microsoft not only learned from Java's example but also learned from the company's own history of dealing with DLL hell. As a result, .NET includes the notion of an *assembly*, which has modularity aspects similar to an OSGi bundle. All .NET code is packaged into an assembly, which takes the form of a DLL or EXE file. Assemblies provide an encapsulation mechanism for the code contained inside of them; an access modifier, called `internal`, is used to indicate visibility within an assembly but not external to it. Assemblies also contain metadata describing dependencies on other assemblies, but the overall model isn't as flexible as OSGi's. Because dependencies are on specific assembly versions, the OSGi notion of provider substitutability isn't attainable.

At execution time, assemblies are loaded into application domains and can only be unloaded by unloading the entire application domain. This makes the highly dynamic and lightweight nature of OSGi hard to achieve, because multiple assemblies loaded into the same application domain must be unloaded at the same time. It's possible to load assemblies into separate domains; but then communication across domains must use interprocess communication to collaborate, and type sharing is greatly complicated. There have been research efforts to create OSGi-like environments for the .NET platform, but the innate differences between the .NET and Java platforms results in the two not having much in common. Regardless, .NET deserves credit for improving on standard Java in this area.

1.5 Summary

In this chapter, we've laid the foundation for everything we'll cover in the rest of the book. What you've learned includes the following:

- The Java platform is great for developing applications, but its support for modularity is largely limited to fine-grained object-oriented mechanisms, rather than more coarse-grained modularity features needed for project management.
- The OSGi Service Platform, through the OSGi framework, addresses the modularity shortcomings of Java to create a powerful and flexible solution.
- The declarative, metadata-based approach employed by OSGi provides a non-invasive way to take advantage of its sophisticated modularity capabilities by modifying how projects are packaged with few, if any, changes to the code.
- The OSGi framework defines a controlled, dynamic module lifecycle to simplify management.
- Following good design principles, OSGi promotes an interface-based programming approach to separate interfaces from implementations.

With this high-level understanding of Java's limitations and OSGi's capabilities, we can start our adventure by diving into the details of the module layer in chapter 2. This is the foundation of everything else in the OSGi world.

2 Mastering modularity

This chapter covers

- Understanding modularity and why it's desirable
- Using metadata to describe OSGi bundles (aka modules)
- Explaining how bundle metadata is used to manage code visibility
- Illustrating how bundles are used to create an application

In the previous chapter, we took a whistle-stop tour of the OSGi landscape. We made a number of observations about how standard Java is broken with respect to modularity and gave you examples where OSGi can help. We also introduced you to some OSGi concepts, including the core layers of the OSGi framework: module, lifecycle, and service.

In this chapter, we'll deal specifically with the module layer, because its features are the initial attraction for most Java developers to OSGi. The module layer is the foundation on which everything else rests in the OSGi world. We'll provide you with a full understanding of what OSGi modularity is, why modularity is important in a general sense, and how it can help you in designing, building, and maintaining Java applications in the future.

The goal of this chapter is to get you thinking in terms of modules rather than JAR files. We'll teach you about OSGi module metadata, and you'll learn how to describe your application's modularity characteristics with it. To illustrate these concepts, we'll continue the simple paint program example that we introduced in chapter 1; you'll convert it from a monolithic application into a modular one. Let's get started with modularity.

2.1 What is modularity?

Modularity encompasses so many aspects of programming that we often take it for granted. The more experience you have with system design, the more you know good designs tend to be modular—but what precisely does that mean? In short, it means designing a complete system from a set of logically independent pieces; these logically independent pieces are called *modules*. You may be thinking, "Is that it?" In the abstract, yes, that is it; but of course there are a lot of details underneath these simple concepts.

A module defines an enforceable logical boundary: code either is part of a module (it's on the inside) or it isn't part of a module (it's on the outside). The internal (implementation) details of a module are visible only to code that is part of a module. For all other code, the only visible details of a module are those that it explicitly exposes (the public API), as depicted in figure 2.1. This aspect of modules makes them an integral part of designing the logical structure of an application.

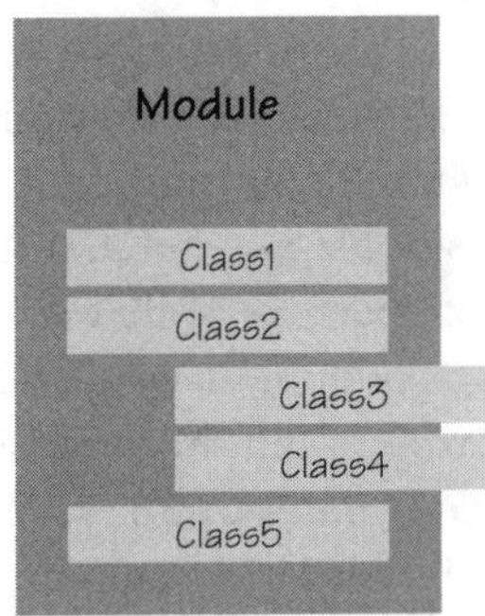

Figure 2.1 A module defines a logical boundary. The module itself is explicitly in control of which classes are completely encapsulated and which are exposed for external use.

2.1.1 Modularity vs. object orientation

You may wonder, "Hey, doesn't object orientation give you these things?" That's correct: object orientation is intended to address these issues too. You'll find that modularity provides many of the same benefits as object orientation. One reason these two programming concepts are similar is because both are forms of *separation of concerns*. The idea behind separation of concerns is you should break down a system into minimally overlapping functionality or *concerns*, so that each concern can be independently reasoned about, designed, implemented, and used. Modularity is one of the earliest forms of separation of concerns. It gained popularity in the early 1970s, whereas object orientation gained popularity in the early 1980s.

With that said, you may now be wondering, "If I already have object orientation in Java, why do I need modularity too?" Another good question. The need for both arises due to *granularity*.

Assume you need some functionality for your application. You sit down and start writing Java classes to implement the desired functionality. Do you typically implement all your functionality in a single class? No. If the functionality is even remotely complicated, you implement it as a set of classes. You may also use existing classes from other parts of your project or from the JRE. When you're done, a logical relationship exists among the classes you created—but where is this relationship captured? Certainly it's captured in the low-level details of the code, because there are compilation dependencies that won't be satisfied if all classes aren't available at compilation time. Likewise, at execution time, these dependencies will fail if all classes aren't present on the class path when you try to execute your application.

Unfortunately, these relationships among classes can only be known through low-level source code inspection or trial and error. Classes allow you to encapsulate the state and behavior of a single, logical concept. But numerous classes are generally necessary to create a well-designed application. Modules encapsulate classes, allowing you to express the logical relationship among the classes—or concepts—in your application. Figure 2.2 illustrates how modules encapsulate classes, and the resulting inter-module relationships. You may think that Java packages allow you to capture such logical code relationships. Well, you're right. Packages are a form of built-in modularity provided by Java, but they have some limitations, as discussed in section 1.1.1. So packages are a good starting point in understanding how modularity helps you encapsulate code, but you need a mechanism that goes further. In the end, object orientation and modularity serve different but complementary purposes (see figure 2.3).

When you're developing in Java, you can view object orientation as the implementation approach for modules. As such, when you're developing classes, you're *programming in the small*, which means you aren't thinking about the overall structure of your application, but instead are thinking in terms of specific functionality. After you begin to logically organize related classes into modules, then you start to concern yourself with *programming in the large*, which means you're focusing on the larger logical pieces of your system and the relationships among those pieces.

In addition to capturing relationships among classes via module membership, modules also capture logical system structure by explicitly declaring dependencies on external code. With

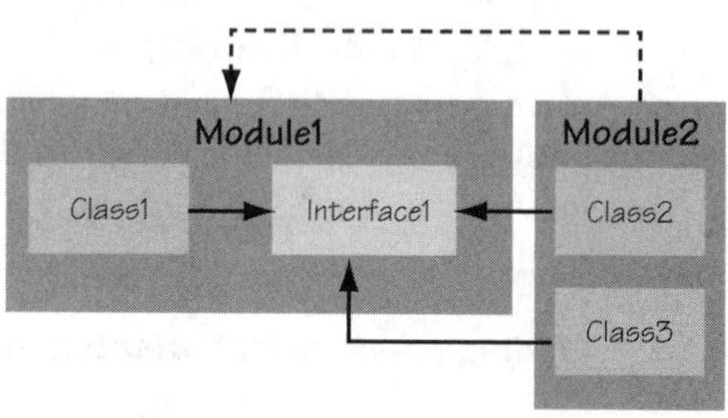

Figure 2.2 Classes have explicit dependencies due to the references contained in the code. Modules have implicit dependencies due to the code they contain.

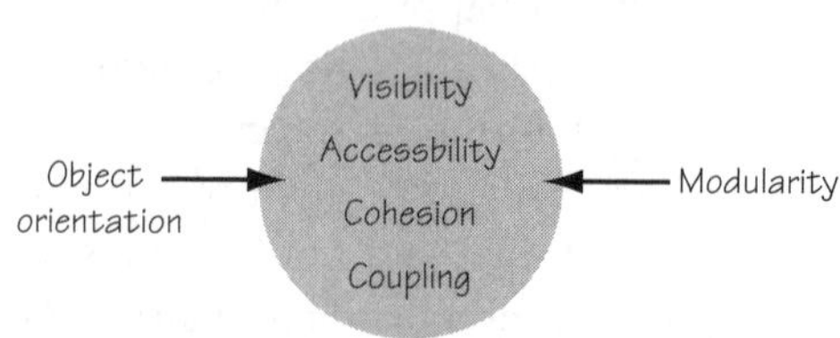

Figure 2.3 Even though object orientation and modularity provide similar capabilities, they address them at different levels of granularity.

this in mind, we now have all the pieces in place to more concretely define what we mean by the term *module* in the context of this book.

> **MODULE** A set of logically encapsulated implementation classes, an optional public API based on a subset of the implementation classes, and a set of dependencies on external code.

Although this definition implies that modules contain classes, at this point this sense of containment is purely logical. Another aspect of modularity worth understanding is *physical modularity*, which refers to the container of module code.

> **Logical vs. physical modularity**
>
> A module defines a logical boundary in your application, which impacts code visibility in a fashion similar to access modifiers in object-oriented programming. *Logical modularity* refers to this form of code visibility. *Physical modularity* refers to how code is packaged and/or made available for deployment.
>
> In OSGi, these two concepts are largely conflated; a logical module is referred to as a *bundle*, and so is the physical module (that is, the JAR file). Even though these two concepts are nearly synonymous in OSGi, for modularity in general they aren't, because it's possible to have logical modularity without physical modularity or to package multiple logical modules into a single physical module. Physical modules are sometimes also referred to as *deployment modules* or *deployment units*.

The OSGi module layer allows you to properly express the modularity characteristics of applications, but it's not free. Let's look in more depth at why you should modularize your applications, so you can make up your own mind.

2.2 Why modularize?

We've talked about what modularity is, but we haven't gone into great depth about why you might want to modularize your own applications. In fact, you may be thinking, "If modularity has been around for almost 40 years and it's so important, why isn't everyone already doing it?" That's a great question, and one that probably doesn't have any single answer. The computer industry is driven by the next best thing, so we tend to throw out the old when the new comes along. And in fairness, as we discussed in the last section, the new technologies and approaches (such as object orientation and component orientation) do provide some of the same benefits that modularity was intended to address.

Java also provides another important reason why modularity is once again an important concern. Traditionally, programming languages were the domain of logical modularity mechanisms, and operating systems and/or deployment packaging systems were the domain of physical modularity. Java blurs this distinction because it's both a language and a platform. To compare to a similar situation, look at the .NET platform. Microsoft, given its history of operating system development and the pain of

DLL hell, recognized this connection early in .NET, which is why it has a module concept called an *assembly*. Finally, the size of applications continues to grow, which makes modularity an important part of managing their complexity—divide and conquer!

This discussion provides some potential explanations for why modularity is coming back in vogue, but it doesn't answer this section's original question: Why should you modularize your applications? Modularity allows you to reason about the logical structure of applications. Two key concepts arose from modularity decades ago:

- *Cohesion* measures how closely aligned a module's classes are with each other and with achieving the module's intended functionality. You should strive for high cohesion in your modules. For example, a module shouldn't address many different concerns (network communication, persistence, XML parsing, and so on): it should focus on a single concern.
- *Coupling*, on the other hand, refers to how tightly bound or dependent different modules are on each other. You should strive for low coupling among your modules. For example, you don't want every module to depend on all other modules.

As you start to use OSGi to modularize your applications, you can't avoid these issues. Modularizing your application will help you see your application in a way that you couldn't before.

By keeping these principles of cohesion and coupling in mind, you'll create more reusable code, because it's easier to reuse a module that performs a single function and doesn't have a lot of dependencies on other code.

More specifically, by using OSGi to modularize your applications, you'll be able to address the Java limitations discussed in section 1.1.1. Additionally, because the modules you'll create will explicitly declare their external code dependencies, reuse is further simplified because you'll no longer have to scrounge documentation or resort to trial and error to figure out what to put on the class path. This results in code that more readily fits into collaborative, independent development approaches, such as in multiteam, multilocation projects or in large-scale open source projects.

Now you know what modularity is and why you want it, so let's begin to focus on how OSGi provides it and what you need to do to use it in your own applications. The example paint program will help you understand the concepts.

2.3 Modularizing a simple paint program

The functionality provided by OSGi's module layer is sophisticated and can seem overwhelming when taken in total. You'll use a simple paint program, as discussed in chapter 1, to learn how to use OSGi's module layer. You'll start from an existing paint program, rather than creating one from scratch. The existing implementation follows an interfaced-based approach with logical package structuring, so it's amenable to modularization, but it's currently packaged as a single JAR file. The following listing shows the contents of the paint program's JAR file.

Listing 2.1 Contents of existing paint program's JAR file

```
META-INF/
META-INF/MANIFEST.MF
org/
org/foo/
org/foo/paint/
org/foo/paint/PaintFrame$1$1.class
org/foo/paint/PaintFrame$1.class
org/foo/paint/PaintFrame$ShapeActionListener.class
org/foo/paint/PaintFrame.class
org/foo/paint/SimpleShape.class
org/foo/paint/ShapeComponent.class
org/foo/shape/
org/foo/shape/Circle.class
org/foo/shape/circle.png
org/foo/shape/Square.class
org/foo/shape/square.png
org/foo/shape/Triangle.class
org/foo/shape/triangle.png
```

The listing begins with a standard manifest file. Then come the application classes, followed by various shape implementations.

The main classes composing the paint program are described in table 2.1.

Table 2.1 Overview of the classes in the paint program

Class	Description
`org.foo.paint.PaintFrame`	The main window of the paint program, which contains the toolbar and drawing canvas. It also has a static `main()` method to launch the program.
`org.foo.paint.SimpleShape`	An interface representing an abstract shape for painting.
`org.foo.paint.ShapeComponent`	A GUI component responsible for drawing shapes onto the drawing canvas.
`org.foo.shape.Circle`	An implementation of `SimpleShape` for drawing circles.
`org.foo.shape.Square`	An implementation of `SimpleShape` for drawing squares.
`org.foo.shape.Triangle`	An implementation of `SimpleShape` for drawing triangles.

For those familiar with Swing, `PaintFrame` extends `JFrame` and contains a `JToolBar` and a `JPanel` canvas. `PaintFrame` maintains a list of available `SimpleShape` implementations, which it displays in the toolbar. When the user selects a shape in the toolbar and clicks in the canvas to draw the shape, a `ShapeComponent` (which extends `JComponent`) is added to the canvas at the location where the user clicked. A `ShapeComponent` is associated with a specific `SimpleShape` implementation by name, which it retrieves from a reference to its `PaintFrame`. Figure 2.4 highlights some of the UI elements in the paint program GUI.

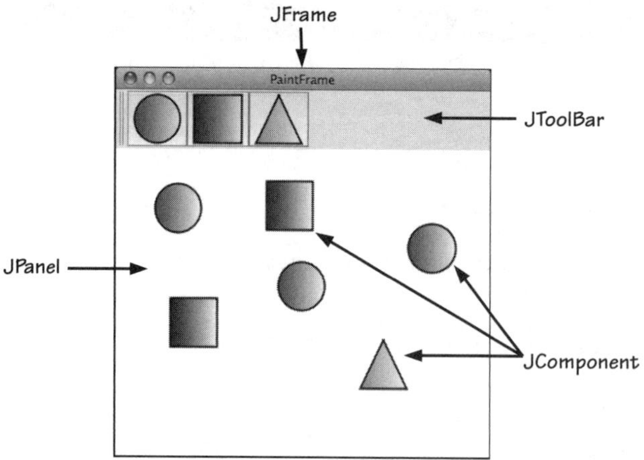

Figure 2.4 The paint program is a simple Swing application.

A static `main()` method on `PaintFrame` launches the paint program, which creates an instance of the `PaintFrame` and each shape implementation, adding each shape instance to the created `PaintFrame` instance. For further explanation, figure 2.5 captures the paint program classes and their interrelationships.

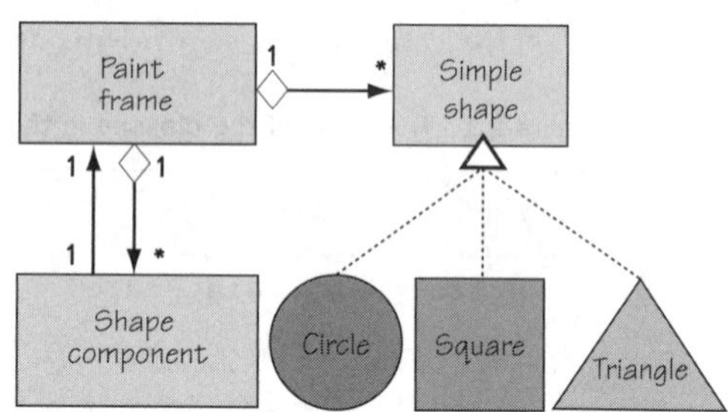

Figure 2.5 Paint program class relationships

To run this nonmodular version of the paint program, go into the chapter02/ paint-nonmodular/ directory of the companion code. Type `ant` to build the program, and then type `java -jar main.jar` to run it. Feel free to click around and see how it works; we won't go into any more details of the program's implementation, because GUI programming is beyond the scope of this book. The important point is to understand the structure of the program. Using this understanding, you'll divide the program into bundles so you can enhance and enforce its modularity.

Currently, the paint program is packaged as a single JAR file, which we'll call version 1.0.0 of the program. Because everything is in a single JAR file, this implies that the program isn't already modularized. Of course, single-JAR-file applications can still be implemented in a modular way—just because an application is composed of multiple JAR files, that doesn't mean it's modular. The paint program example could have both its logical and physical modularity improved. First, we'll examine the program's logical structure and define modules to enhance this structure. Where do you start?

One low-hanging fruit you can look for is public APIs. It's good practice in OSGi (you'll see why later) to separate your public APIs into packages so they can be easily shared without worrying about exposing implementation details. The paint program has a good example of a public API: its `SimpleShape` interface. This interface makes it easy to implement new, possibly third-party shapes for use with the program. Unfortunately, `SimpleShape` is in the same package as the program's implementation classes. To remedy this situation, you'll shuffle the package structure slightly. You'll move `SimpleShape` into the `org.foo.shape` package and move all shape implementations into a new package called `org.foo.shape.impl`. These changes divide the paint program into three logical pieces according to the package structure:

- `org.foo.shape`—The public API for creating shapes
- `org.foo.shape.impl`—Various shape implementations
- `org.foo.paint`—The application implementation

Given this structure (logical modularity), you could package each of these packages as separate JAR files (physical modularity). To have OSGi verify and enforce the modularity, it isn't sufficient to package the code as JAR files: you must package them as bundles. To do this, you need to understand OSGi's bundle concept, which is its logical and physical unit of modularity. Let's introduce bundles.

2.4 Introducing bundles

If you're going to use OSGi technology, you may as well start getting familiar with the term *bundle*, because you'll hear and say it a lot. *Bundle* is how OSGi refers to its specific realization of the module concept. Throughout the remainder of this book, the terms *module* and *bundle* will be used interchangeably; but in most cases we're specifically referring to bundles and not modularity in general, unless otherwise noted. Enough fuss about how we'll use the term *bundle*—let's define it.

BUNDLE A physical unit of modularity in the form of a JAR file containing code, resources, and metadata, where the boundary of the JAR file also serves as the encapsulation boundary for logical modularity at execution time.

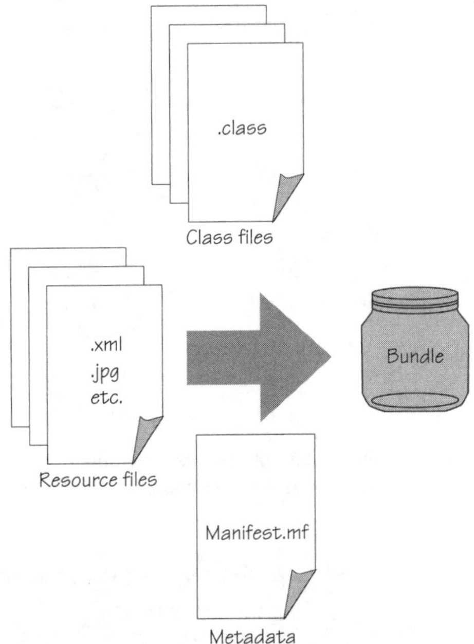

Figure 2.6 A bundle can contain all the usual artifacts you expect in a standard JAR file. The only major difference is that the manifest file contains information describing the bundle's modular characteristics.

The contents of a bundle are graphically depicted in figure 2.6. The main thing that makes a bundle JAR file different than a normal JAR file is its module metadata, which is used by the OSGi framework to manage its modularity characteristics. All JAR files, even if they aren't bundles, have a place for metadata, which is in their manifest file or, more specifically, in the

`META-INF/MANIFEST.MF` entry of the JAR file. This is where OSGi places its module metadata. Whenever we refer to a bundle's *manifest file*, we're specifically referring to the module-related metadata in this standard JAR manifest file.

Note that this definition of a bundle is similar to the definition of a module, except that it combines both the physical and logical aspects of modularity into one concept. So before we get into the meat of this chapter, which is defining bundle metadata, let's discuss the bundle's role in physical and logical modularity in more detail.

2.4.1 The bundle's role in physical modularity

The main function of a bundle with respect to physical modularity is to determine module membership. No metadata is associated with making a class a member of a bundle. A given class is a member of a bundle if it's contained in the bundle JAR file. The benefit for you is that you don't need to do anything special to make a class a member of a bundle: just put it in the bundle JAR file.

This physical containment of classes leads to another important function of bundle JAR files as a deployment unit. The bundle JAR file is tangible, and it's the artifact you share, deploy, and use when working with OSGi. The final important role of the bundle JAR file is as the container of bundle metadata, because, as we mentioned, the JAR manifest file is used to store it. These aspects of the bundle are shown in figure 2.7. The issue of metadata placement is part of an ongoing debate, which we address in the sidebar for those interested in the issue.

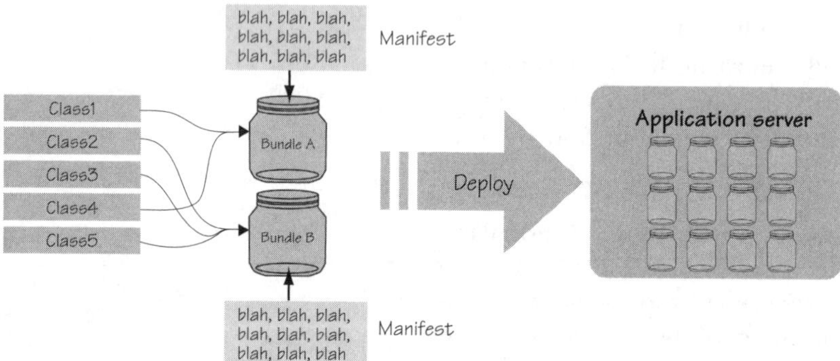

Figure 2.7 A class is a member of a bundle if it's packaged in it, the bundle carries its module metadata inside it as part of its manifest data, and the bundle can be deployed as a unit into a runtime environment.

Where should metadata go?

Is it a good thing to store the module metadata in the physical module and not in the classes themselves? There are two schools of thought on this subject. One says it's better to include the metadata alongside the code it's describing (in the source file itself), rather than in a separate file where it's more difficult to see the connection to the code. This approach is possible with various techniques, such as doclets or the annotations mechanism introduced in Java 5.

(continued)

Annotations are the choice du jour today. Unfortunately, when OSGi work started back in 1999, annotations weren't an option because they didn't exist yet. Besides, there are some good reasons to keep the metadata in a separate file, which brings us to the second school of thought.

This school of thought argues that it's better to not bake metadata into the source code, because it becomes harder to change. Having metadata in a separate file offers you greater flexibility. Consider the following benefits of having separate module metadata:

- You don't need to recompile your bundle to make changes to its metadata.
- You don't need access to the source code to add or modify metadata, which is sometimes necessary when dealing with legacy or third-party libraries.
- You don't need to load classes into the JVM to access the associated metadata.
- Your code doesn't get a compile-time dependency on OSGi API.
- You can use the same code in multiple modules, which is convenient or even necessary in some situations when packaging your modules.
- You can easily use your code on older or smaller JVMs that don't support annotations.

Regardless of whether your preferred approach is annotations, you can see that you gain a good deal of flexibility by maintaining the module metadata in the manifest file.

2.4.2 The bundle's role in logical modularity

Similar to how the bundle JAR file physically encapsulates the member classes, the bundle's role in logical modularity is to logically encapsulate member classes. What precisely does this mean? It specifically relates to code visibility. Imagine that you have a utility class in a `util` package that isn't part of your project's public API. To use this utility class from different packages in your project, it must be `public`. Unfortunately, this means anyone can use the utility class, even though it's not part of your public API.

The logical boundary created by a bundle changes this, giving classes inside the bundle different visibility rules to external code, as shown in figure 2.8. This means `public` classes inside your bundle JAR file aren't necessarily externally visible. You may be thinking, "What?" This isn't a misstatement: it's a major differentiator between bundles and standard JAR files. Only code explicitly exposed via bundle metadata is visible externally. This logical boundary effectively extends standard Java access modifiers

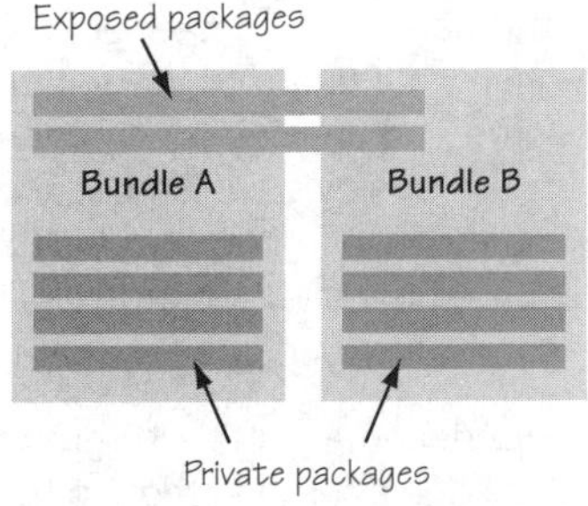

Figure 2.8 Packages (and therefore the classes in them) contained in a bundle are private to that bundle unless explicitly exposed, allowing them to be shared with other bundles.

(`public`, `private`, `protected`, and package private) with module private visibility (only visible in the module). If you're familiar with .NET, this is similar to the `internal` access modifier, which marks something as being visible in an assembly but private from other assemblies.

As you can see, the bundle concept plays important roles in both physical and logical modularity. Now we can start to examine how you use metadata to describe bundles.

2.5 Defining bundles with metadata

In this section, we'll discuss OSGi bundle metadata in detail, and you'll use the paint program as a use case to understand the theory. The main purpose of bundle metadata is to precisely describe the modularity-related characteristics of a bundle so the OSGi framework can handle it appropriately, such as resolving dependencies and enforcing encapsulation. The module-related metadata captures the following pieces of information about the bundle:

- *Human-readable information*—Optional information intended purely as an aid to humans who are using the bundle
- *Bundle identification*—Required information to identify a bundle
- *Code visibility*—Required information for defining which code is internally visible and which internal code is externally visible

We'll look at each of these areas in the following subsections. But because OSGi relies on the manifest file, we've included a sidebar to explain its persnickety syntax details and OSGi's extended manifest value syntax. Luckily, there are tools for editing and generating bundle metadata, so you don't have to create it manually, but it's still worthwhile to understand the syntax details.

JAR file manifest syntax

The JAR file manifest is composed of groups of name-value pairs (attributes). The general format for an attribute declaration is

```
name: value
```

The name isn't case sensitive and can contain alphanumeric, underscore, and hyphen characters. Values can contain any character information except carriage returns and line feeds. The name and the value must be separated by a colon and a space. A single line can't exceed 72 characters. If a line must exceed this length, you must continue it on the next line, which you do by starting the next line with a single space character followed by the continuation of the value. Manifest lines in OSGi can grow quite long, so it's useful to know this.

You define an attribute group by placing attribute declarations on successive lines (one line after the other) in the manifest file. An empty or blank line between attribute declarations signifies different attribute groups. OSGi uses the first group of attributes, called the *main attributes*, for module metadata. The order of attributes in a group isn't important. If you look in a manifest file, you may see something like this:

(continued)

```
Manifest-Version: 1.0
Created-By: 1.4 (Sun Microsystems Inc.)
Bundle-ManifestVersion: 2
Bundle-SymbolicName: org.foo.api
Bundle-Version: 1.0.0.SNAPSHOT
Bundle-Name: Simple Paint API
Export-Package: org.foo.api
Import-Package: javax.swing,org.foo.api
Bundle-License: http://www.opensource.org/licenses/apache2.0.php
```

We'll get into the exact meaning of most of these attributes throughout the remainder of this section. But for now, we'll focus on the syntax. Whereas the standard Java manifest syntax is a name-value pair, OSGi defines a common structure for OSGi-specified attribute values. Most OSGi manifest attribute values are a list of clauses separated by commas, such as

```
Property-Name: clause, clause, clause
```

Each clause is further broken down into a target and a list of name-value pair parameters separated by semicolons:

```
Property-Name: target1; parameter1=value1; parameter2=value2,
 target2; parameter1=value1; parameter2=value2,
 target3; parameter1=value1; parameter2=value2
```

Parameters are divided into two types, called *attributes* and *directives*. Directives alter framework handling of the associated information and are explicitly defined by the OSGi specification. Attributes are arbitrary name-value pairs. You'll see how to use directives and attributes later. Slightly different syntax is used to differentiate directives (:=) from attributes (=), which looks something like this:

```
Property-Name: target1; dir1:=value1; attr1=value2,
   target2; dir1:=value1; attr1=value2,
   target3; dir1:=value1; attr1=value2
```

Keep in mind that you can have any number of directives and attributes assigned to each target, all with different values. Values containing whitespace or separator characters should be quoted to avoid parsing errors. Sometimes you'll have lots of targets with the same set of directives and attributes. In such a situation, OSGi provides a shorthand way to avoid repeating all the duplicated directives and attributes, as follows:

```
Property-Name: target1; target2; dir1:=value1; attr1=value2
```

This is equivalent to listing the targets separately with their own directives and attributes. This is pretty much everything you need to understand the structure of OSGi manifest attributes. Not all OSGi manifest values conform to this common structure, but the majority do, so it makes sense for you to become familiar with it.

2.5.1 Human-readable information

Most bundle metadata is intended to be read and interpreted by the OSGi framework in its effort to provide a general module layer for Java. But some bundle metadata serves no purpose other than helping humans understand what a bundle does and from where it comes. The OSGi specification defines several pieces of metadata for this purpose, but none of it is required, nor does it have any impact on modularity. The OSGi framework completely ignores it.

The following code snippet shows human-readable bundle metadata for the paint program's `org.foo.shape` bundle (the other program bundles are described similarly):

```
Bundle-Name: Simple Paint API
Bundle-Description: Public API for a simple paint program.
Bundle-DocURL: http://www.manning.com/osgi-in-action/
Bundle-Category: example, library
Bundle-Vendor: OSGi in Action
Bundle-ContactAddress: 1234 Main Street, USA
Bundle-Copyright: OSGi in Action
```

The `Bundle-Name` attribute is intended to be a short name for the bundle. You're free to name your bundle anything you want. Even though it's supposed to be a short name, there's no enforcement of this; just use your best judgment. The `Bundle-Description` attribute lets you be a little more long-winded in describing the purpose of your bundle. To provide even more documentation about your bundle, `Bundle-DocURL` allows you to specify a URL to refer to documentation. `Bundle-Category` defines a comma-separated list of category names. OSGi doesn't define any standard category names, so you're free to choose your own. The remaining attributes, `Bundle-Vendor`, `Bundle-ContactAddress`, and `Bundle-Copyright`, provide information about the bundle vendor.

Human-readable metadata is reasonably straightforward. The fact that the OSGi framework ignores it means you can pretty much do what you want to with it. But don't fall into a laissez-faire approach just yet—the remaining metadata requires more precision. Next, we'll look at how you use metadata to uniquely identify bundles.

2.5.2 Bundle identification

The human-readable metadata from the previous subsection helps you understand what a bundle does and where it comes from. Some of this human-readable metadata also appears to play a role in identifying a bundle. For example, `Bundle-Name` seems like it could be a form of bundle identification. It isn't. The reason is somewhat historical. Earlier versions of the OSGi specification didn't provide any means to uniquely identify a given bundle. `Bundle-Name` was purely informational, and therefore no constraints were placed on its value. As part of the OSGi R4 specification process, the idea of a unique bundle identifier was proposed. For backward-compatibility reasons, `Bundle-Name` couldn't be commandeered for this purpose because it wouldn't be possible to place new constraints on it and maintain backward compatibility. Instead, a new manifest entry was introduced: `Bundle-SymbolicName`.

In contrast to `Bundle-Name`, which is only intended for users, `Bundle-SymbolicName` is only intended for the OSGi framework to help uniquely identify a bundle. The value of the symbolic name follows rules similar to Java package naming: it's a series of dot-separated strings, where reverse domain naming is recommended to avoid name clashes. Although the dot-separated construction is enforced by the framework, there's no way to enforce the reverse-domain-name recommendation. You're free to choose a different scheme; but if you do, keep in mind that the main purpose is to provide unique identification, so try to choose a scheme that won't lead to name clashes.

IDENTIFYING THE PAINT PROGRAM (PART 1)

The paint program is divided into bundles based on packages, so you can use each package as the symbolic name, because they already follow a reverse-domain-name scheme. For the public API bundle, you declare the symbolic name in manifest file as

```
Bundle-SymbolicName: org.foo.shape
```

Although it would be possible to solely use `Bundle-SymbolicName` to uniquely identify a bundle, it would be awkward to do so over time. Consider what would happen when you released a second version of your bundle: you'd need to change the symbolic name to keep it unique, such as `org.foo.shapeV2`. This is possible, but it's cumbersome; and worse, this versioning information would be opaque to the OSGi framework, which means the modularity layer couldn't take advantage of it. To remedy this situation, a bundle is uniquely identified not only by its `Bundle-SymbolicName` but also by its `Bundle-Version`, whose value conforms to the OSGi version number format (see the sidebar "OSGi version number format"). This pair of attributes not only forms an identifier, it also allows the framework to capture the time-ordered relationship among versions of the same bundle.

IDENTIFYING THE PAINT PROGRAM (PART 2)

For example, the following metadata uniquely identifies the paint program's public API bundle:

```
Bundle-SymbolicName: org.foo.shape
Bundle-Version: 2.0.0
```

Although technically only `Bundle-SymbolicName` and `Bundle-Version` are related to bundle identification, the `Bundle-ManifestVersion` attribute also plays a role. Starting with the R4 specification, it became mandatory for bundles to specify `Bundle-SymbolicName`. This was a substantial change in philosophy. To maintain backward compatibility with legacy bundles created before the R4 specification, OSGi introduced the `Bundle-ManifestVersion` attribute. Currently, the only valid value for this attribute is `2`, which is the value for bundles created for the R4 specification or later. Any bundles without `Bundle-ManifestVersion` aren't required to be uniquely identified, but bundles with it must be.

IDENTIFYING THE PAINT PROGRAM (PART 3)

The following example shows the complete OSGi R4 metadata to identify the shape bundle:

```
Bundle-ManifestVersion: 2
Bundle-SymbolicName: org.foo.shape
Bundle-Version: 2.0.0
```

This is the complete identification metadata for the public API bundle. The identification metadata for the other paint program bundles are defined in a similar fashion. Now that bundle identification is out of the way, we're ready to look at code visibility, which is perhaps the most important area of metadata.

OSGi version number format

One important concept you'll visit over and over again in OSGi is a *version number*, which appears here in the bundle-identification metadata. The OSGi specification defines a common version number format that's used in a number of places throughout the specification. For this reason, it's worth spending a few paragraphs exploring exactly what a version number is in the OSGi world.

A version number is composed of three separate numerical component values separated by dots; for example, 1.0.0 is a valid OSGi version number. The first value is referred to as the *major number*, the second value as the *minor number*, and the third value as the *micro number*. These names reflect the relative precedence of each component value and are similar to other version-numbering schemes, where version-number ordering is based on numerical comparison of version-number components in decreasing order of precedence: in other words, 2.0.0 is newer than 1.2.0, and 1.10.0 is newer than 1.9.9.

A fourth version component is possible, which is called a *qualifier*. The qualifier can contain alphanumeric characters; for example, 1.0.0.alpha is a valid OSGi version number with a qualifier. When comparing version numbers, the qualifier is compared using string comparison. As the following figure shows, this doesn't always lead to intuitive results; for example, although 1.0.0.beta is newer than 1.0.0.alpha, 1.0.0 is older than both.

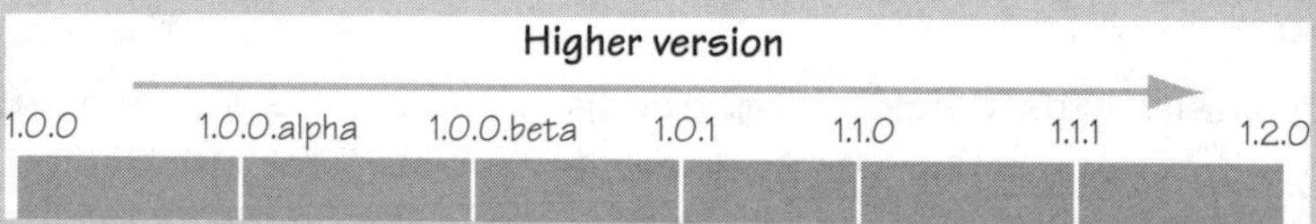

OSGi versioning semantics can sometimes lead to non-intuitive results.

In places in the metadata where a version is expected, if it's omitted, it defaults to 0.0.0. If a numeric component of the version number is omitted, it defaults to 0, and the qualifier defaults to an empty string. For example, 1.2 is equivalent to 1.2.0. One tricky aspect is that it isn't possible to have a qualifier without specifying all the numeric components of the version. So you can't specify 1.2.build-59; you must specify 1.2.0.build-59.

OSGi uses this common version-number format for versioning both bundles and Java packages. In chapter 9, we'll discuss high-level approaches for managing version numbers for your packages, bundles, and applications.

2.5.3 Code visibility

Human-readable and bundle-identification metadata are valuable, but they don't go far in allowing you to describe your bundle's modularity characteristics. The OSGi specification defines metadata for comprehensively describing which code is visible internally in a bundle and which internal code is visible externally. OSGi metadata for code visibility captures the following information:

- *Internal bundle class path*—The code forming the bundle
- *Exported internal code*—Explicitly exposed code from the bundle class path for sharing with other bundles
- *Imported external code*—External code on which the bundle class path code depends

Each of these areas captures separate but related information about which Java classes are reachable in your bundle and by your bundle. We'll cover each in detail; but before we do that, let's step back and dissect how you use JAR files and the Java class path in traditional Java programming. This will give you a basis for comparison to OSGi's approach to code visibility.

> **IMPORTANT!** Standard JAR files typically fail as bundles since they were written under the assumption of global type visibility (i.e., if it's on the class path, you can use it). If you're going to create effective bundles, you have to free yourself from this old assumption and fully understand and accept that type visibility for bundles is based purely on the primitives we describe in this section. To make this point very clear, we'll go into intricate details about type visibility rules for standard JAR files versus bundle JAR files. Although this may appear to be a lesson in the arcane, it's critical to understand these differences.

CODE VISIBILITY IN STANDARD JAR FILES AND THE CLASS PATH

Generally speaking, you compile Java source files into classes and then use the `jar` tool to create a JAR file from the generated classes. If the JAR file has a `Main-Class` attribute in the manifest file, you can run the application like this:

```
java -jar app.jar
```

If not, you add it to the class path and start the application something like this:

```
java -cp app.jar org.foo.Main
```

Figure 2.9 shows the stages the JVM goes through. First it searches for the class specified in the `Main-Class` attribute or the one specified on the command line. If it finds the class, it searches it for a `static public void main(String[])` method. If such a method is found, it invokes it to start the application. As the application executes, any additional classes needed by the application are found by searching the class path, which is composed of the application classes in the JAR file and the standard JRE classes (and anything you may have added to the class path). Classes are loaded as they're needed.

This represents a high-level understanding of how Java executes an application from a JAR file. But this high-level view conceals a few implicit decisions made by standard JAR file handling, such as these:

- Where to search inside the JAR file for a requested class
- Which internal classes should be externally exposed

With respect to the first decision, a JAR file has an implicit policy of searching all directories relative to the root of the JAR file as if they were package names corresponding to the requested class (for example, the class `org.foo.Bar` is in `org/foo/Bar.class` inside the JAR file). With respect to the second decision, JAR files have an implicit policy of exposing all classes in root-relative packages to all requesters. This is a highly deconstructed view of the behavior of JAR files, but it helps to illustrate the implicit modularity decisions of standard JAR files. These implicit code-visibility decisions are put into effect when you place a JAR file on the class path for execution.

While executing, the JVM finds all needed classes by searching the class path, as shown in figure 2.10. But what is the exact purpose of the class path with respect to modularity? The class path defines which external classes are visible to the JAR file's internal classes. Every class reachable on the class path is visible to the application classes, even if they aren't needed.

With this view of how standard JAR files and the class path mechanism work, let's look into the details of how OSGi handles these same code-visibility concepts, which is quite a bit different. We'll

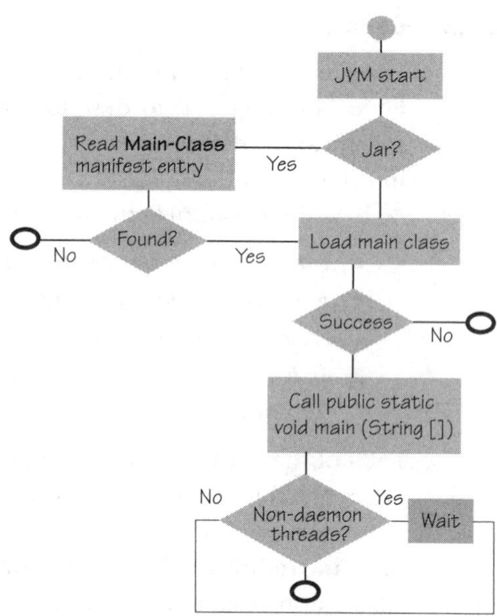

Figure 2.9 Flow diagram showing the steps the JVM goes through to execute a Java program from the class path

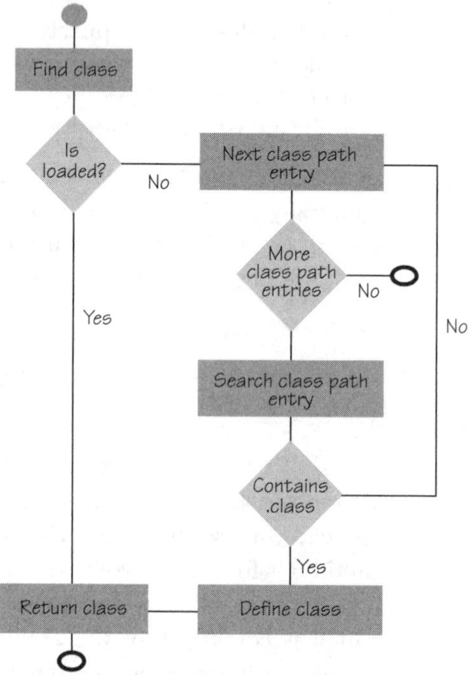

Figure 2.10 Flow diagram showing the steps the JVM goes through to load a class from the class path

start with how OSGi searches bundles internally for code, followed by how OSGi externally exposes internal code, and finally how external code is made visible to internal bundle code. Let's get started.

INTERNAL BUNDLE CLASS PATH

Whereas standard JAR files are implicitly searched for internal classes in all directories from the root of the JAR file as if they were package names, OSGi uses a more explicit approach called the *bundle class path*. Like the standard Java class path concept, the bundle class path is a list of locations to search for classes. The difference is the bundle class path refers to locations *inside* the bundle JAR file.

> **BUNDLE-CLASSPATH** An ordered, comma-separated list of relative bundle JAR file locations to be searched for class and resource requests.

When a given bundle class needs another class in the same bundle, the entire bundle class path of the containing bundle is searched to find the class. Classes in the same bundle have access to all code reachable on their bundle class path. Let's examine the syntax for declaring it.

Bundles declare their internal class path using the `Bundle-ClassPath` manifest header. The bundle class path behaves in the same way as the global class path in terms of the search algorithm, so you can refer to figure 2.10 to see how this behaves; but in this case, the scope is limited to classes contained in the bundle. With `Bundle-ClassPath`, you can specify a list of paths in the bundle where the class loader should look for classes or resources. For example:

```
Bundle-ClassPath: .,other-classes/,embedded.jar
```

This tells the OSGi framework where to search inside the bundle for classes. The period (`.`) signifies the bundle JAR file. For this example, the bundle is searched first for root-relative packages, then in the folder called other-classes, and finally in the embedded JAR in the bundle. The ordering is important, because the bundle class path entries are searched in the declared order.

`Bundle-ClassPath` is somewhat unique, because OSGi manifest headers don't normally have default values. If you don't specify a value, the framework supplies a default value of period (`.`). Why does `Bundle-ClassPath` have a default value? The answer is related to how standard JAR files are searched for classes. The bundle class path value of `.` corresponds to the internal search policy of standard JAR files. Putting `.` on your bundle class path likewise treats all root-relative directories as if they were packages when searching for classes. Making `.` the default gives both standard and bundle JAR files the same default internal search policy.

> **NOTE** It's important to understand that the default value of `Bundle-ClassPath` is `.` if and only if there is no specified value, which isn't the same as saying the value `.` is included on the bundle class path by default. In other words, if you specify a value for `Bundle-ClassPath`, then `.` is included only if you explicitly specify it in your comma-separated list of locations. If you specify a value and don't include `.`, then root-relative directories aren't searched when looking for classes in the bundle JAR file.

As you can see, the internal bundle class path concept is powerful and flexible when it comes to defining the contents and internal search order of bundles; refer to the sidebar "Bundle class path flexibility" for some examples of when this flexibility is useful. Next, you'll learn how to expose internal code for sharing with other bundles.

> **Bundle class path flexibility**
>
> You may wonder why you'd want to package classes in different directories or embed JAR files in the bundle JAR file. First, the bundle class path mechanism doesn't apply only to classes, but also to resources. A common use case is to place images in an image/ directory to make it explicit in the JAR file where certain content can be found. Also, in web applications, nested JAR files are embedded in the JAR file under the WEB-INF/lib/ directory and classes can be placed in the WEB-INF/classes/ directory.
>
> In other situations, you may have a legacy or proprietary JAR file that you can't change. By embedding the JAR file into your bundle and adding bundle metadata, you can use it without changing the original JAR. It may also be convenient to embed a JAR file when you want your bundle to have a private copy of some library; this is especially useful when you want to avoid sharing static library members with other bundles.
>
> Embedding JAR files isn't strictly necessary, because you can also unpack a standard JAR file into your bundle to achieve the same effect. As an aside, you can also see a performance improvement by not embedding JAR files, because OSGi framework implementations must extract the embedded JAR files to access them.

EXPORTING INTERNAL CODE

`Bundle-ClassPath` affects the visibility of classes in a bundle, but how do you share classes among bundles? The first stage is to export the packages you wish to share with others.

Externally useful classes are those composing the public API of the code contained in the JAR file, whereas *non-useful* classes form the implementation details. Standard JAR files don't provide any mechanism to differentiate externally useful classes from non-useful ones, but OSGi does. A standard JAR file exposes everything relative to the root by default, but an OSGi bundle exposes nothing by default. A bundle must use the `Export-Package` manifest header to explicitly expose internal classes it wishes to share with other bundles.

EXPORT-PACKAGE A comma-separated list of internal bundle packages to expose for sharing with other bundles.

Instead of exposing individual classes, OSGi defines sharing among bundles at the package level. Although this makes the task of exporting code a little simpler, it can still be a major undertaking for large projects; we'll discuss some tools to simplify this in appendix A. When you include a package in an `Export-Package` declaration, every public class contained in the package is exposed to other bundles. A simple example for the paint program shape API bundle is as follows (figure 2.11 shows how we'll graphically represent exported module packages):

```
Export-Package: org.foo.shape
```

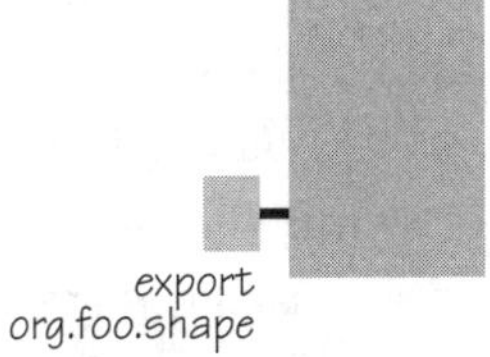

Figure 2.11 Graphical depiction of an exported package

Here, you're exporting every class in the `org.foo.shape` package. You'll likely want to export more than one package at a time from your bundles. You can export multiple packages by separating them with commas:

```
Export-Package: org.foo.shape,org.foo.other
```

You can also attach attributes to exported packages. Because it's possible for different bundles to export the same packages, a given bundle can use attributes to differentiate its exports from other bundles. For example:

```
Export-Package: org.foo.shape; vendor="Manning", org.foo.other;
 vendor="Manning"
```

This attaches the `vendor` attribute with the value `"Manning"` to the exported packages. In this particular example, `vendor` is an arbitrary attribute because it has no special meaning to the framework—it's something we made up. When we talk about importing code, you'll get a better idea of how arbitrary attributes are used in package sharing to differentiate among exported packages. As we mentioned previously in the sidebar "JAR file manifest syntax," OSGi also supports a shorthand format when you want to attach the same attributes to a set of target packages, like this:

```
Export-Package: org.foo.shape; org.foo.other; vendor="Manning"
```

This is equivalent to the previous example. This shorthand comes in handy, but it can be applied only if all attached attributes are the same for all packages. Using arbitrary attributes allows a bundle to differentiate its exported packages, but there's a more meaningful reason to use an attribute for differentiation: version management.

Code is constantly evolving. Packages contain classes that change over time. It's important to document such changes using version numbers. Version management isn't a part of standard Java development, but it's inherent in OSGi-based Java development. In particular, OSGi supports not only bundle versioning, as discussed previously, but also *package versioning*, which means every shared package has a version number. Attributes are used to associate a version number with a package:

```
Export-Package: org.foo.shape; org.foo.other; version="2.0.0"
```

Here, you attach the `version` attribute with the value `"2.0.0"` to the exported packages, using OSGi's common version-number format. In this case, the attribute isn't arbitrary, because this attribute name and value format is defined by the OSGi specification. You may have noticed that some of the earlier `Export-Package` examples don't specify a version. In that case, the version defaults to `"0.0.0"`, but it isn't a good idea to use this version number. We'll discuss versioning in more detail in chapter 9.

With `Bundle-ClassPath` and `Export-Package`, you have a pretty good idea how to define and control the visibility of the bundle's internal classes; but not all the code you need will be contained in the bundle JAR file. Next, you'll learn how to specify the bundle's dependencies on external code.

IMPORTING EXTERNAL CODE

Both `Bundle-ClassPath` and `Export-Package` deal with the visibility of internal bundle code. Normally, a bundle is also dependent on external code. You need some way to declare which external classes are needed by the bundle so the OSGi framework can make them visible to it. Typically, the standard Java class path is used to specify which external code is visible to classes in your JAR files, but OSGi doesn't use this mechanism. OSGi requires all bundles to include metadata explicitly declaring their dependencies on external code, referred to as *importing*.

Importing external code is straightforward, if not tedious. You must declare imports for all packages required by your bundle but not contained in your bundle. The only exception to this rule is for classes in the `java.*` packages, which are automatically made visible to all bundles by the OSGi framework. The manifest header you use for importing external code is appropriately named `Import-Package`.

> **IMPORT-PACKAGE** A comma-separated list of packages needed by internal bundle code from other bundles.

> **`Import-Package` vs. `import` keyword**
>
> You may be thinking that you already do imports in your source code with the `import` keyword. Conceptually, the `import` keyword and declaring OSGi imports are similar, but they serve different purposes. The `import` keyword in Java is for namespace management; it allows you to use the short name of the imported classes instead of using its fully qualified class name (for example, you can refer to `SimpleShape` rather than `org.foo.shape.SimpleShape`). You can `import` classes from any other package to use their short name, but it doesn't grant any visibility. In fact, you never need to use `import`, because you can use the fully qualified class name instead. For OSGi, the metadata for importing external code is important, because it's how the framework knows what your bundle needs.

The value of the `Import-Package` header follows the common OSGi manifest header syntax. First, let's start with the simplest form. Consider the main paint program bundle, which has a dependency on the `org.foo.shape` package. It needs to declare an import for this package as follows (figure 2.12 shows how we'll graphically represent imported module packages):

```
Import-Package: org.foo.shape
```

Figure 2.12 Graphical depiction of an imported package

This specifically tells the OSGi framework that the bundle requires access to `org.foo.shape` in addition to the internal code visible to it from its bundle class path. Be aware that importing a package doesn't import its subpackages; remember, there's no relationship among nested packages. If your bundle needs access to `org.foo.shape` and `org.foo.shape.other`, it must import both packages as comma-separated targets, like this:

```
Import-Package: org.foo.shape,org.foo.shape.other
```

Your bundles can import any number of packages by listing them on `Import-Package` and separating them using commas. It's not uncommon in larger projects for the `Import-Package` declaration to grow large (although you should strive to minimize this).

Sometimes, you'll want to narrow your bundle's package dependencies. Recall how `Export-Package` declarations can include attributes to differentiate a bundle's exported packages. You can use these export attributes as matching attributes when importing packages. For example, we previously discussed the following export and associated attribute:

```
Export-Package: org.foo.shape; org.foo.other; vendor="Manning"
```

A bundle with this metadata exports the two packages with the associated `vendor` attribute and value. It's possible to narrow your bundle's imported packages using the same matching attribute:

```
Import-Package: org.foo.shape; vendor="Manning"
```

The bundle with this metadata is declaring a dependency on the package `org.foo.shape` with a `vendor` attribute matching the `"Manning"` value. The attributes attached to `Export-Package` declarations define the attribute's value, whereas attributes attached to `Import-Package` declarations define the value to match; essentially, they act like a filter. The details of how imports and exports are matched and filtered is something we'll defer until section 2.7. For now, it's sufficient to understand that attributes attached to imported packages are matched against the attributes attached to exported packages.

For arbitrary attributes, OSGi only supports equality matching. In other words, it either matches the specified value or it doesn't. You learned about one non-arbitrary attribute when we discussed `Export-Package` and the `version` attribute. Because this attribute is defined by the OSGi specification, more flexible matching is supported. This is an area where OSGi excels. In the simple case, it treats a value as an infinite range starting from the specified version number. For example:

```
Import-Package: org.osgi.framework; version="1.3.0"
```

This statement declares an import for package `org.osgi.framework` for the version range of 1.3.0 to infinity, inclusive. This simple form of specifying an imported package version range implies an expectation that future versions of `org.osgi.framework` will always be backward compatible with the lower version. In some cases, such as specification packages, it's reasonable to expect backward compatibility. In situations where you wish to limit your assumptions about backward compatibility, OSGi allows you to specify an explicit version range using interval notation, where the characters `[` and `]` indicate inclusive values and the characters `(` and `)` indicate exclusive values. Consider the following example:

```
Import-Package: org.osgi.framework; version="[1.3.0,2.0.0)"
```

This statement declares an import for package `org.osgi.framework` for the version range including 1.3.0 and up to but excluding 2.0.0 and beyond. Table 2.2 illustrates the meaning of the various combinations of the version range syntax.

Syntax	Meaning
`"[min,max)"`	min ≤ x < max
`"[min,max]"`	min ≤ x ≤ max
`"(min,max)"`	min < x < max
`"(min,max]"`	min < x ≤ max
`"min"`	min ≤ x

Table 2.2 Version range syntax and meaning

If you want to specify a precise version range, you must use a version range like `"[1.0.1,1.0.1]"`. You may wonder why a single value like `"1.0.1"` is an infinite range rather than a precise version. The reason is partly historical. In the OSGi specifications prior to R4, all packages were assumed to be specification packages where backward compatibility was guaranteed. Because backward compatibility was assumed, it was only necessary to specify a minimum version. When the R4 specification added support for sharing implementation packages, it also needed to add support for arbitrary version ranges. It would have been possible at this time to redefine a single version to be a precise version, but that would have been unintuitive for existing OSGi programmers. Also, the specification would have had to define syntax to represent infinity. In the end, the OSGi Alliance decided it made the most sense to define versions ranges as presented here.

You may have noticed that some of the earlier `Import-Package` examples didn't specify a version range. When no version range is specified, it defaults to the value `"0.0.0"`, which you may expect from past examples. Of course, the difference here is that the value `"0.0.0"` is interpreted as a version range from 0.0.0 to infinity.

Now you understand how to use `Import-Package` to express dependencies on external packages and `Export-Package` to expose internal packages for sharing. The decision to use packages as the basis for interbundle sharing isn't an obvious choice to everyone, so we discuss some arguments for doing so in the sidebar "Depending on packages, not bundles."

We've now covered the major constituents of the OSGi module layer: `Bundle-ClassPath`, `Export-Package`, and `Import-Package`. We've discussed these in the context of the paint program you'll see running in the next section, but the final piece of the puzzle we need to look at is how these various code-visibility mechanisms fit together in a running application.

Depending on packages, not bundles

Importing packages seems fairly normal for most Java programmers, because you import the classes and packages you use in the source files. But the `import` statements in the source files are for managing namespaces, not dependencies. OSGi's choice of using package-level granularity for expressing dependencies among bundles is novel, if not controversial, for Java-based module-oriented technologies. Other approaches typically adopt module-level dependencies, meaning dependencies are expressed in terms of one module depending on another. The OSGi choice of package-level dependencies has created some debate about which approach is better.

The main criticisms leveled against package-level dependencies is that they're too complicated or fine-grained. Some people believe it's easier for developers to think in terms of requiring a whole JAR file rather than individual packages. This argument doesn't hold water, because a Java developer using any given technology must know something about its package naming. For example, if you know enough to realize you want to use the `Servlet` class in the first place, you probably have some idea about which package it's in, too.

Package-level dependencies are more fine-grained, which does result in more metadata. For example, if a bundle exports 10 packages, only 1 module-level dependency is needed to express a dependency on all of them, whereas package-level dependencies require 10. But bundles rarely depend on all exported packages of a given bundle, and this is more of a condemnation of tooling support. Remember how much of a nuisance it was to maintain import declarations before IDEs started doing it for you? This is starting to change for bundles, too; in appendix A, we describe tools for generating bundle metadata. Let's look at some of the benefits of package-level dependencies.

The difference between module- and package-level dependencies is one of *who* versus *what*. Module-level dependencies express which specific module you depend on (who), whereas package-level dependencies express which specific packages you depend on (what). Module-level dependencies are brittle, because they can only be satisfied by a specific bundle even if another bundle offers the same packages. Some people argue that this isn't an issue, because they want the specific bundle they've tested against, or because the packages are implementation packages and won't be provided by another bundle. Although these arguments are reasonable, they usually break down over time.

For example, if your bundle grows too large over time, you may wish to refactor it by splitting its various exported packages into multiple bundles. If you use module-level dependencies, such a refactoring will break existing clients, which tends to be a real bummer when the clients are from third parties and you can't easily change them. This issue goes away when you use package-level dependencies. Also, a bundle doesn't usually depend on *everything* in another bundle, only a *subset*. As a result, module-level dependencies are too broad and cause transitive fanout. You end up needing to deploy a lot of extra bundles you don't use, just to satisfy all the dependencies.

(continued)

Package-level dependencies represent a higher-level view of the code's real class dependencies. It's possible to analyze a bundle's code and generate its set of imported packages, similar to how IDEs maintain import declarations in source files. Module-level dependencies can't be discovered in such a fashion, because they don't exist in the code. Package-level dependencies sound great, right? You may now wonder if they have any issues.

The main issue is that OSGi must treat a package as an atomic unit. If this assumption weren't made, then the OSGi framework wouldn't be free to substitute a package from one bundle for the same package from another bundle. This means you can't split a package across bundles; a single package must be contained in a single bundle. If packages were split across bundles, there would be no easy way for the OSGi framework to know when a package was complete. Typically, this isn't a major limitation. Other than this, you can do anything with package-level dependencies that you can with module-level dependencies. And truth be told, the OSGi specification *does* support module-level dependencies and some forms of split packages, but we won't discuss those until chapter 5.

2.5.4 Class-search order

We've talked a lot about code visibility, but in the end all the metadata we've discussed allows the OSGi framework to perform sophisticated searching on behalf of bundles for their contained and needed classes. Under the covers, when an importing bundle needs a class from an exported package, it asks the exporting bundle for it. The framework uses class loaders to do this, but the exact details of how it asks are unimportant. Still, it's important to understand the ordering of this class-search process.

When a bundle needs a class at execution time, the framework searches for the class in the following order:

1. If the class is from a package starting with `java.`, the parent class loader is asked for the class. If the class is found, it's used. If there is no such class, the search ends with an exception.
2. If the class is from a package imported by the bundle, the framework asks the exporting bundle for the class. If the class is found, it's used. If there is no such class, the search ends with an exception.
3. The bundle class path is searched for the class. If it's found, it's used. If there is no such class, the search ends with an exception.

These steps are important because they also help the framework ensure consistency. Specifically, step 1 ensures that all bundles use the same core Java classes, and step 2 ensures that imported packages aren't split across the exporting and importing bundles.

That's it! We've finished the introduction to bundle metadata. We haven't covered everything you can possibly do, but we've discussed the most important bundle metadata for getting started creating bundles; we'll cover additional modularity issues in chapter 5. Next, you'll put all the metadata in place for the paint program and then step back to review the current design. Before moving on, if you're wondering if it's possible to have a JAR file that is both a bundle and an ordinary JAR file, see the sidebar "Is a bundle a JAR file or a JAR file a bundle?"

Is a bundle a JAR file or a JAR file a bundle?

Maybe you're interested in adding OSGi metadata to your existing JAR files or you want to create bundles from scratch, but you'd still like to use them in non-OSGi situations too. We've said before that a bundle is just a JAR file with additional module-related metadata in its manifest file, but how accurate is this statement? Does it mean you can use any OSGi bundle as a standard JAR file? What about using a standard JAR file as a bundle? Let's answer the second question first, because it's easier.

A standard JAR file can be installed into an OSGi framework unchanged. Unfortunately, it doesn't do anything useful. Why? The main reason is that a standard JAR file doesn't expose any of its content; in OSGi terms, it doesn't export any packages. The default `Bundle-ClassPath` for a JAR file is `.`, but the default for `Export-Package` is nothing. So even though a standard JAR file is a bundle, it isn't a useful bundle. At a minimum, you need to add an `Export-Package` declaration to its manifest file to explicitly expose some (or all) of its internal content.

What about bundle JAR files? Can they be used as a standard JAR file outside of an OSGi environment? The answer is, it depends. It's possible to create bundles that function equally well in or out of an OSGi environment, but not all bundles can be used as standard JAR files. It comes down to which features of OSGi your bundle uses. Of the metadata features you've learned about so far, only one can cause issues: `Bundle-ClassPath`. Recall that the internal bundle class path is a comma-separated list of locations inside the bundle JAR file and may contain

- A `.` representing the root of the bundle JAR file
- A relative path to an embedded JAR file
- A relative path to an embedded directory

Only bundles with a class path entry of `.` can be used as standard JAR files. Why? The OSGi notion of `.` on the bundle class path is equivalent to standard JAR file class searching, which is to search from the root of the JAR file as if all relative directories are package names. If a bundle specifies an embedded JAR file or directory, it requires special handling that's available only in an OSGi environment. Luckily, it isn't too difficult to avoid using embedded JAR files and directories.

It's a good idea to try to keep your bundle JAR files compatible with standard JAR files if you can, but it's still best to use them in an OSGi environment. Without OSGi, you lose dependency checking, consistency checking, and boundary enforcement, not to mention all the cool lifecycle and service stuff we'll discuss in the coming chapters.

2.6 Finalizing the paint program design

So far, you've defined three bundles for the paint program: a shape API bundle, a shape implementation bundle, and a main paint program bundle. Let's look at the complete metadata for each. The shape API bundle is described by the following manifest metadata:

```
Bundle-ManifestVersion: 2
Bundle-SymbolicName: org.foo.shape
Bundle-Version: 2.0.0
Bundle-Name: Paint API
Import-Package: javax.swing
Export-Package: org.foo.shape; version="2.0.0"
```

The bundle containing the shape implementations is described by the following manifest metadata:

```
Bundle-ManifestVersion: 2
Bundle-SymbolicName: org.foo.shape.impl
Bundle-Version: 2.0.0
Bundle-Name: Simple Shape Implementations
Import-Package: javax.swing, org.foo.shape; version="2.0.0"
Export-Package: org.foo.shape.impl; version="2.0.0"
```

And the main paint program bundle is described by the following manifest metadata:

```
Bundle-ManifestVersion: 2
Bundle-SymbolicName: org.foo.paint
Bundle-Version: 2.0.0
Bundle-Name: Simple Paint Program
Import-Package: javax.swing, org.foo.shape; org.foo.shape.impl;
 version="2.0.0"
```

As you can see in figure 2.13, these three bundles directly mirror the logical package structure of the paint program.

This approach is reasonable, but can it be improved? To some degree, you can answer this question only if you know more about the intended uses of the paint program; but let's look more closely at it anyway.

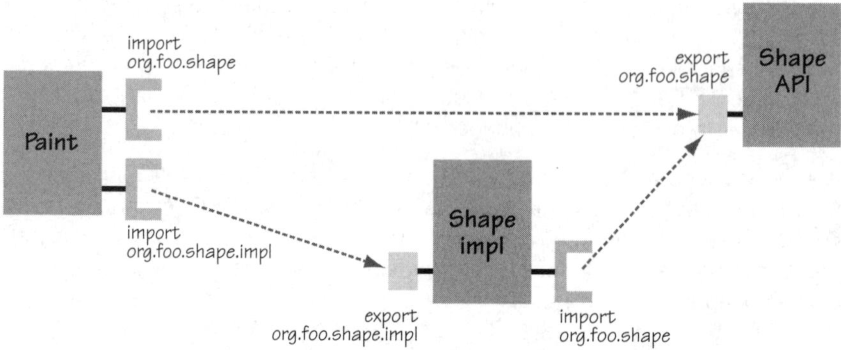

Figure 2.13 Structure of the paint program's bundles

2.6.1 Improving the paint program's modularization

In the current design, one aspect that sticks out is the shape-implementation bundle. Is there a downside to keeping all shape implementations in a single package and a single bundle? Perhaps it's better to reverse the question. Is there any advantage to separating the shape implementations into separate bundles? Imagine use cases where not all shapes are necessary; for example, small devices may not have enough resources to support all shape implementations. If you separate the shape implementations into separate packages and separate bundles, you have more flexibility when it comes to creating different configurations of the application.

This is a good issue to keep in mind when you're modularizing applications. Optional components or components with the potential to have multiple alternative implementations are good candidates to be in separate bundles. Breaking your application into multiple bundles gives you more flexibility, because you're limited to deploying configurations of your application based on the granularity of your defined bundles. Sounds good, right? You may then wonder why you don't divide your applications into as many bundles as you can.

You pay a price for the flexibility afforded by dividing an application into multiple bundles. Lots of bundles mean you have lots of artifacts that are versioning independently, creating lots of dependencies and configurations to manage. So it's probably not a good idea to create a bundle out of each of your project's packages, for example. You need to analyze and understand your needs for flexibility when deciding how best to divide an application. There is no single rule for every situation.

Returning to the paint program, let's assume the ultimate goal is to enable the possibility for creating different configurations of the application with different sets of shapes. To accomplish this, you move each shape implementation into its own package (`org.foo.shape.circle`, `org.foo.shape.square`, and `org.foo.shape.triangle`). You can now bundle each of these shapes separately. The following metadata captures the circle bundle:

```
Bundle-ManifestVersion: 2
Bundle-SymbolicName: org.foo.shape.circle
Bundle-Version: 2.0.0
Bundle-Name: Circle Implementation
Import-Package: javax.swing, org.foo.shape; version="2.0.0"
Export-Package: org.foo.shape.circle; version="2.0.0"
```

The metadata for the square and triangle bundles is nearly identical, except with the correct shape name substituted where appropriate. The shape-implementation bundles have dependencies on Swing and the public API and export their implementation-specific shape package. These changes also require changes to the program's metadata implementation bundle; you modify its metadata as follows:

```
Bundle-ManifestVersion: 2
Bundle-SymbolicName: org.foo.paint
Bundle-Version: 2.0.0
Bundle-Name: Simple Paint Program
Import-Package: javax.swing, org.foo.shape; org.foo.shape.circle;
 org.foo.shape.square; org.foo.shape.triangle; version="2.0.0"
```

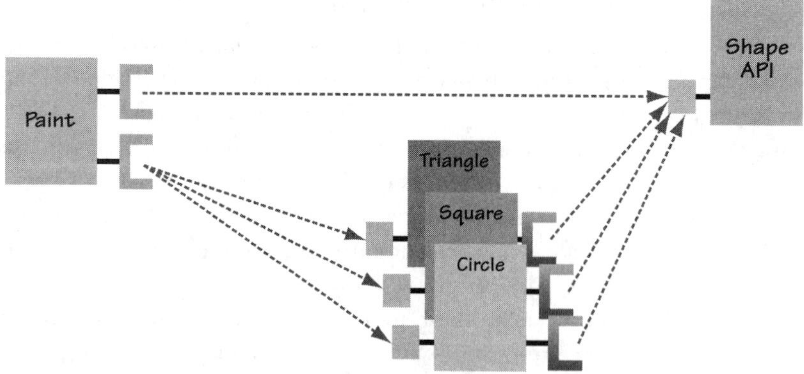

Figure 2.14 Logical structure of the paint program with separate modules for each shape implementation

The paint program implementation bundle depends on Swing, the public API bundle, and all three shape bundles. Figure 2.14 depicts the new structure of the paint program.

Now you have five bundles (shape API, circle, square, triangle, and paint). Great. But what do you do with these bundles? The initial version of the paint program had a static `main()` method on `PaintFrame` to launch it; do you still use it to launch the program? You could use it by putting all the bundle JAR files on the class path, because all the example bundles can function as standard JAR files, but this would defeat the purpose of modularizing the application. There'd be no enforcement of modular boundaries or consistency checking. To get these benefits, you must launch the paint program using the OSGi framework. Let's look at what you need to do.

2.6.2 Launching the new paint program

The focus of this chapter is on using the module layer, but you can't launch the application without a little help from the lifecycle layer. Instead of putting the cart before the horse and talking about the lifecycle layer now, we created a generic OSGi bundle launcher to launch the paint program for you. This launcher is simple: you execute it from the command line and specify a path to a directory containing bundles; it creates an OSGi framework and deploys all bundles in the specified directory. The cool part is that this generic launcher hides all the details and OSGi-specific API from you. We'll discuss the launcher in detail in chapter 13.

Just deploying the paint bundles into an OSGi framework isn't sufficient to start the paint program; you still need some way to kick-start it. You can reuse the paint program's original static `main()` method to launch the new modular version. To get this to work with the bundle launcher, you need to add the following metadata from the original paint program to the paint program bundle manifest:

```
Main-Class: org.foo.paint.PaintFrame
```

As in the original paint program, this is standard JAR file metadata for specifying the class containing the application's static `main()` method. Note that this feature isn't defined by the OSGi specification but is a feature of the bundle launcher. To build and launch the newly modularized paint program, go into the chapter02/paint-modular/ directory in the companion code and type `ant`. Doing so compiles all the code and packages the modules. Typing `java -jar launcher.jar bundles/` starts the paint program.

The program starts up as it apparently always has; but underneath, the OSGi framework is resolving the bundles' dependencies, verifying their consistency, and enforcing their logical boundaries. That's all there is to it. You've now used the OSGi module layer to create a nicely modular application. OSGi's metadata-based approach didn't require any code changes to the application, although you did move some classes around to different packages to improve logical and physical modularity.

The goal of the OSGi framework is to shield you from a lot of the complexities; but sometimes it's beneficial to peek behind the curtain, such as to help you debug the OSGi-based applications when things go wrong. In the next section, we'll look at some of the work the OSGi framework does for you, to give you a deeper understanding of how everything fits together. Afterward, we'll close out the chapter by summarizing the benefits of modularizing the paint program.

2.7 OSGi dependency resolution

You've learned how to describe the internal code composing the bundles with `Bundle-ClassPath`, expose internal code for sharing with `Export-Package`, and declare dependencies on external code with `Import-Package`. Although we hinted at how the OSGi framework uses the exports from one bundle to satisfy the imports of another, we didn't go into detail. The `Export-Package` and `Import-Package` metadata declarations included in bundle manifests form the backbone of the OSGi bundle dependency model, which is predicated on package sharing among bundles.

In this section, we'll explain how OSGi resolves bundle package dependencies and ensures package consistency among bundles. After this section, you'll have a clear understanding of how bundle modularity metadata is used by the OSGi framework. You may wonder why this is necessary, because bundle resolution seems like an OSGi framework implementation detail. Admittedly, this section covers some of the more complex details of the OSGi specification; but it's helpful when defining bundle metadata if you understand a little of what's going on behind the scenes. Further, this information can come in handy when you're debugging OSGi-based applications. Let's get started.

2.7.1 Resolving dependencies automatically

Adding OSGi metadata to your JAR files represents extra work for you as a developer, so why do it? The main reason is so you can use the OSGi framework to support and enforce the bundles' inherent modularity. One of the most important tasks performed by the OSGi framework is automating dependency management, which is called *bundle dependency resolution*.

A bundle's dependencies must be resolved by the framework before the bundle can be used, as shown in figure 2.15. The framework's dependency resolution algorithm is sophisticated; we'll get into its gory details, but let's start with a simple definition.

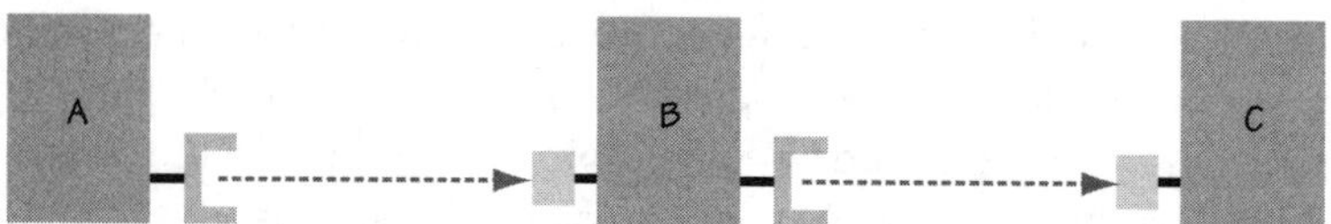

Figure 2.15 Transitive dependencies occur when bundle A depends on packages from bundle B and bundle B in turn depends on packages from bundle C. To use bundle A, you need to resolve the dependencies of both bundle B and bundle C.

> **RESOLVING** The process of matching a given bundle's imported packages to exported packages from other bundles and doing so in a consistent way so any given bundle only has access to a single version of any type.

Resolving a bundle may cause the framework to resolve other bundles transitively, if exporting bundles themselves haven't yet been resolved. The resulting set of resolved bundles are conceptually *wired* together in such a fashion that any given imported package from a bundle is wired to a matching exported package from another bundle, where a *wire* implies having access to the exported package. The final result is a graph of all bundles wired together, where all imported package dependencies are satisfied. If any dependency can't be satisfied, then the resolve fails, and the instigating bundle can't be used until its dependencies are satisfied.

This description likely makes you want to ask three questions:

1. When does the framework resolve a bundle's dependencies?
2. How does the framework gain access to bundles to resolve them in the first place?
3. What does it mean to wire an importing bundle to an exporting bundle?

The first two questions are related, because they both involve the lifecycle layer, which we'll discuss in the next chapter. For the first question, it's sufficient to say that the framework resolves a bundle automatically when another bundle attempts to use it. To answer the second question, we'll say that all bundles must be *installed* into the framework in order to be resolved (we'll discuss bundle installation in more depth in chapter 3). For the discussion in this section, we'll always be talking about installed bundles. As for the third question, we won't answer it fully because the technical details of wiring bundles together isn't important; but for the curious, we'll explain it briefly before looking into the resolution process in more detail.

At execution time, each OSGi bundle has a class loader associated with it, which is how the bundle gains access to all the classes to which it should have access (the ones determined by the resolution process). When an importing bundle is wired to an exporting bundle, the importing class loader is given a reference to the exporting class loader so it can delegate requests for classes in the exported package to it. You don't need to worry about how this happens—relax and let OSGi worry about it for you. Now, let's look at the resolution process in more detail.

SIMPLE CASES

At first blush, resolving dependencies is fairly straightforward; the framework just needs to match exports to imports. Let's consider a snippet from the paint program example:

```
Bundle-Name: Simple Paint Program
Import-Package: org.foo.shape
```

From this, you know that the paint program has a single dependency on the `org.foo.shape` package. If only this bundle were installed in the framework, it wouldn't be usable, because its dependency wouldn't be satisfiable. To use the paint program bundle, you must install the shape API bundle, which contains the following metadata:

```
Bundle-Name: Paint API
Export-Package: org.foo.shape
```

When the framework tries to resolve the paint program bundle, it knows it must find a matching export for `org.foo.shape`. In this case, it finds a candidate in the shape API bundle. When the framework finds a matching candidate, it must determine whether the candidate is resolved. If the candidate is already resolved, the candidate can be chosen to satisfy the dependency. If the candidate isn't yet resolved, the framework must resolve it first before it can select it; this is the transitive nature of resolving dependencies. If the shape API bundle has no dependencies, it can always be successfully resolved. But you know from the example that it does have some dependencies, namely `javax.swing`:

```
Bundle-Name: Paint API
Import-Package: javax.swing
Export-Package: org.foo.shape
```

What happens when the framework tries to resolve the paint program? By default, in OSGi it wouldn't succeed, which means the paint program can't be used. Why? Because even though the `org.foo.shape` package from the API bundle satisfies the main program's import, there's no bundle to satisfy the shape API's import of `javax.swing`. In general, to resolve this situation, you can conceptually install another bundle exporting the required package:

```
Bundle-Name: Swing
Export-Package: javax.swing
```

Now, when the framework tries to resolve the paint program, it succeeds. The main paint program bundle's dependency is satisfied by the shape API bundle, and its dependency is satisfied by the Swing bundle, which has no dependencies. After resolving the main paint program bundle, all three bundles are marked as resolved, and the framework won't try to resolve them again (until certain conditions require it, as we'll describe in the next chapter). The framework ends up wiring the bundles together, as shown in figure 2.16.

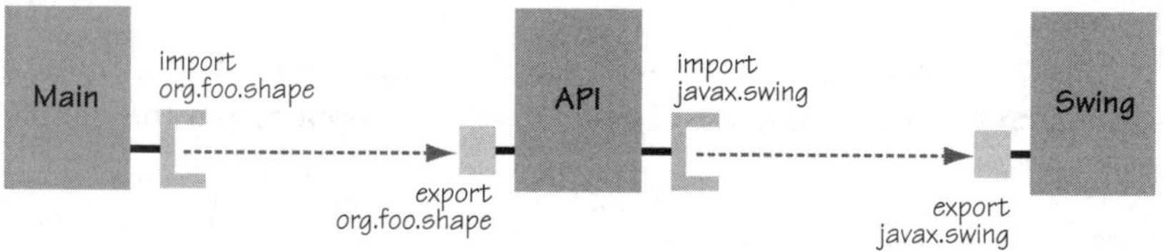

Figure 2.16 Transitive bundle-resolution wiring

What does the wiring in figure 2.16 tell you? It says that when the main bundle needs a class in package `org.foo.shape`, it gets it from the shape API bundle. It also says when the shape API bundle needs a class in package `javax.swing`, it gets it from the Swing bundle. Even though this example is simple, it's largely what the framework tries to do when it resolves bundle dependencies.

> **System class path delegation**
>
> In actuality, the `javax.swing` case in the previous example is a little misleading if you're running your OSGi framework with a JRE that includes `javax.swing`. In such a case, you may want bundles to use Swing from the JRE. The framework can provide access using system class path delegation. We'll look at this area a little in chapter 13, but this highlights a deficiency with the heavyweight JRE approach. If it's possible to install a bundle to satisfy the Swing dependencies, why are they packaged in the JVM by default? Adoption of OSGi patterns could massively trim the footprint of future JVM implementations.

You've learned that you can have attributes attached to exported and imported packages. At the time, we said it was sufficient to understand that attributes attached to imported packages are matched against attributes attached to exported packages. Now you can more fully understand what this means. Let's modify the bundle metadata snippets to get a deeper understanding of how attributes factor into the resolution process. Assume you modify the Swing bundle to look like this:

```
Bundle-Name: Swing
Export-Package: javax.swing; vendor="Sun"
```

Here, you modify the Swing bundle to export `javax.swing` with an attribute `vendor` with value `"Sun"`. If the other bundles' metadata aren't modified and you perform the resolve process from scratch, what impact does this change have? This minor change has no impact at all. Everything resolves as it did before, and the `vendor` attribute never comes into play. Depending on your perspective, this may or may not seem confusing. As we previously described attributes, imported attributes are matched against exported attributes. In this case, no import declarations mention the `vendor` attribute, so it's ignored. Let's revert the change to the Swing bundle and instead change the API bundle to look like this:

```
Bundle-Name: Paint API
Export-Package: org.foo.shape
Import-Package: javax.swing; vendor="Sun"
```

Attempting to resolve the paint program bundle now fails because no bundle is exporting the package with a matching `vendor` attribute for the API bundle. Putting the `vendor` attribute back on the Swing bundle export allows the main paint program bundle to successfully resolve again with the same wiring, as shown earlier in figure 2.16. Attributes on exported packages have an impact only if imported packages specify them, in which case the values must match or the resolve fails.

Recall that we also talked about the `version` attribute. Other than the more expressive interval notation for specifying ranges, it works the same way as arbitrary attributes. For example, you can modify the shape API bundle as follows:

```
Bundle-Name: Paint API
Export-Package: org.foo.shape; vendor="Manning"; version="2.0.0"
Import-Package: javax.swing; vendor="Sun"
```

And you can modify the paint program bundle as follows:

```
Bundle-Name: Simple Paint Program
Import-Package: org.foo.shape; vendor="Manning"; version="[2.0.0,3.0.0)"
```

In this case, the framework can still resolve everything because the shape API bundle's export matches the paint program bundle's import; the vendor attributes match, and 2.0.0 is in the range of 2.0.0 inclusive to 3.0.0 exclusive. This particular example has multiple matching attributes on the `import` declaration, which is treated like a logical AND by the framework. Therefore, if any of the matching attributes on an import declaration don't match a given export, the export doesn't match at all.

Overall, attributes don't add much complexity to the resolution process, because they add additional constraints to the matching of imported and exported package names already taking place. Next, we'll look into slightly more complicated bundle-resolution scenarios.

MULTIPLE MATCHING PACKAGE PROVIDERS

In the previous section, dependency resolution is fairly straightforward because there's only one candidate to resolve each dependency. The OSGi framework doesn't restrict bundles from exporting the same package. Actually, one of the benefits of the OSGi framework is its support for side-by-side versions, meaning it's possible to use different versions of the same package in the same running JVM. In highly collaborative environments of independently developed bundles, it's difficult to limit which versions of packages are used. Likewise, in large systems, it's possible for different teams to use different versions of libraries in their subsystems; the use of different XML parser versions is a prime example.

Let's consider what happens when multiple candidates are available to resolve the same dependency. Consider a case in which a web application needs to import the `javax.servlet` package and both a servlet API bundle and a Tomcat bundle provide the package (see figure 2.17).

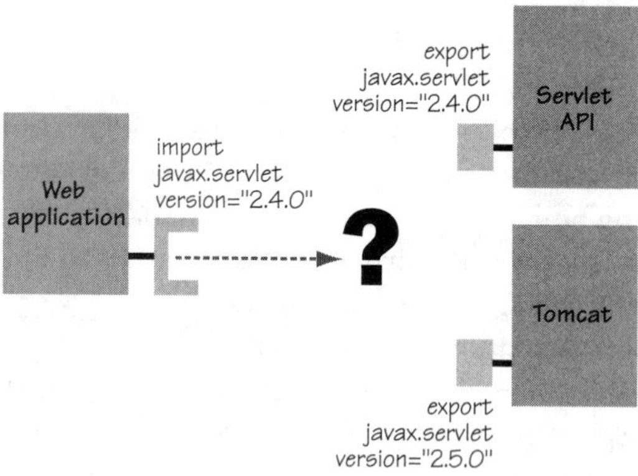

Figure 2.17 How does the framework choose between multiple exporters of a package?

When the framework tries to resolve the dependencies of the web application, it sees that the web application requires `javax.servlet` with a minimum version of 2.4.0 and both the servlet API and Tomcat bundles meet this requirement. Because the web application can be wired to only one version of the package, how does the framework choose between the candidates? As you may intuitively expect, the framework favors the highest matching version, so in this case it selects Tomcat to resolve the web application's dependency. Sounds simple enough. What happens if both bundles export the same version, say 2.4.0?

In this case, the framework chooses between candidates based on the order in which they're installed in the framework. Bundles installed earlier are given priority over bundles installed later; as we mentioned, the next chapter will show you what it means to install a bundle in the framework. If you assume the servlet API was installed before Tomcat, the servlet API will be selected to resolve the web application's dependency. The framework makes one more consideration when prioritizing matching candidates: maximizing collaboration.

So far, you've been working under the assumption that you start the resolve process on a cleanly installed set of bundles. But the OSGi framework allows bundles to be dynamically installed at any time during execution. In other words, the framework doesn't always start from a clean slate. It's possible for some bundles to be installed, resolved, and already in use when new bundles are installed. This creates another means to differentiate among exporters: already-resolved exporters and not-yet-resolved exporters. The framework gives priority to already-resolved exporters, so if it must choose between two matching candidates where one is resolved and one isn't, it chooses the resolved candidate. Consider again the example with the servlet API exporting version 2.4.0 of the `javax.servlet` package and Tomcat exporting version 2.5.0. If the servlet API is already resolved, the framework will choose it to resolve the web application's dependency, even though it isn't exporting the highest version, as shown in figure 2.18. Why?

It has to do with maximizing the potential for collaboration. Bundles can only collaborate if they're using the same version of a shared package. When resolving, the

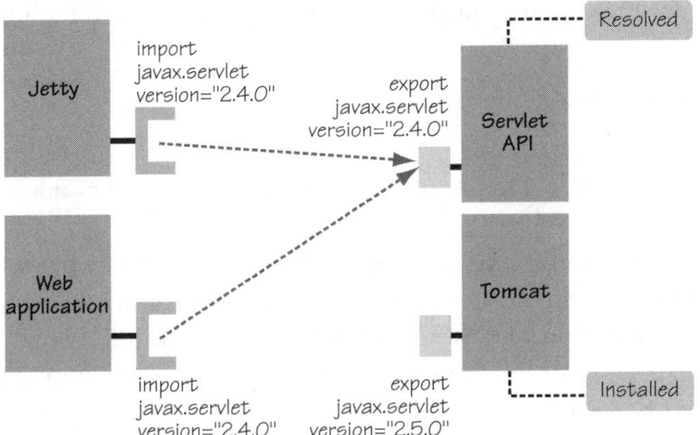

Figure 2.18 If a bundle is already resolved because it's in use by another bundle, this bundle is preferred to bundles that are only installed.

framework favors already-resolved packages as a means to minimize the number of different versions of the same package being used. Let's summarize the priority of dependency resolution candidate selection:

- Highest priority is given to already-resolved candidates, where multiple matches of resolved candidates are sorted according to version and then installation order.
- Next priority is given to unresolved candidates, where multiple matches of unresolved candidates are sorted according to version and then installation order.

It looks like we have all the bases covered, right? Not quite. Next, we'll look at how an additional level of constraint checking is necessary to ensure that bundle dependency resolution is consistent.

2.7.2 Ensuring consistency with uses constraints

From the perspective of any given bundle, a set of packages is visible to it, which we'll call its *class space*. Given your current understanding, you can define a bundle's class space as its imported packages combined with the packages accessible from its bundle class path, as shown in figure 2.19.

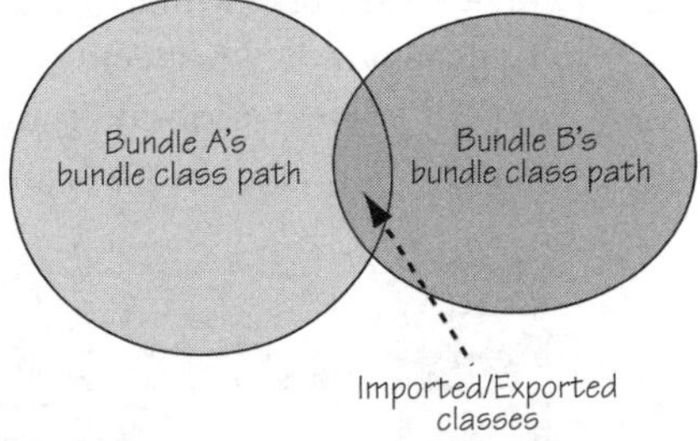

Figure 2.19 Bundle A's class space is defined as the union of its bundle class path with its imported packages, which are provided by bundle B's exports.

A bundle's class space must be consistent, which means only a single instance of a given package must be visible to the bundle. Here, we define *instances* of a package as those with the same name, but from different providers. For example, consider the previous example, where both the servlet API and Tomcat bundles exported the `javax.servlet` package. The OSGi framework strives to ensure that the class spaces of all bundles remain consistent. Prioritizing how exported packages are selected for imported packages, as described in the last section, isn't sufficient. Why not? Let's consider the simple API in the following code snippet:

```
package org.osgi.service.http;
import javax.servlet.Servlet;
public interface HttpService {
  void registerServlet(Sting alias, Servlet servlet, HttpContext ctx);
}
```

This is a snippet from an API you'll meet in chapter 15. The details of what it does are unimportant at the moment; for now, you just need to know its method signature. Let's assume the implementation of this API is packaged as a bundle containing the `org.osgi.service.http` package but not `javax.servlet`. This means it has some metadata in its manifest like this:

```
Export-Package: org.osgi.service.http; version="1.0.0"
Import-Package: javax.servlet; version="2.3.0"
```

Let's assume the framework has the HTTP service bundle and a servlet library bundle installed, as shown in figure 2.20. Given these two bundles, the framework makes the only choice available, which is to select the version of `javax.servlet` provided by the Servlet API bundle.

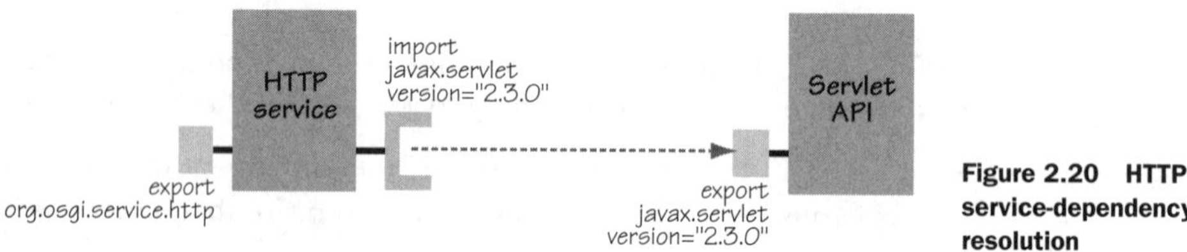

Figure 2.20 HTTP service-dependency resolution

Now, assume you install two more bundles into the framework: the Tomcat bundle exporting version 2.4.0 of `javax.servlet` and a bundle containing a client for the HTTP service importing version 2.4.0 of `javax.servlet`. When the framework resolves these two new bundles, it does so as shown in figure 2.21.

The HTTP client bundle imports `org.osgi.service.http` and version 2.4.0 of `javax.servlet`, which the framework resolves to the HTTP service bundle and the Tomcat bundle, respectively. It seems that everything is fine: all bundles have their dependencies resolved, right? Not quite. There's an issue with these choices for dependency resolution—can you see what it is?

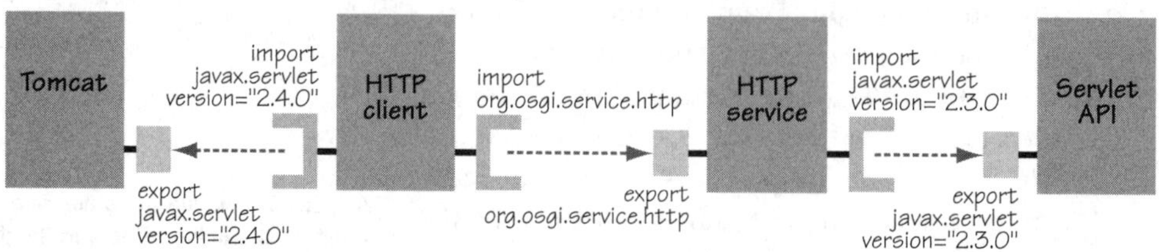

Figure 2.21 Subsequent HTTP client-dependency resolution

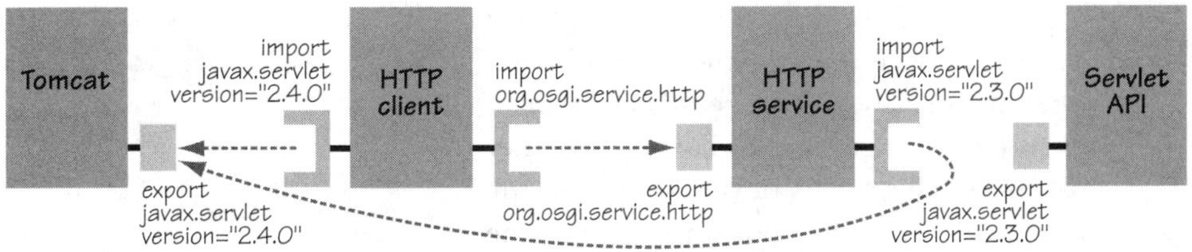

Figure 2.22 Consistent dependency resolution of HTTP service and client bundles

Consider the servlet parameter in the `HTTPService.registerServlet()` method. Which version of `javax.servlet` is it? Because the HTTP service bundle is wired to the Servlet API bundle, its parameter type is version `2.3.0` of `javax.servlet.Servlet`. When the HTTP client bundle tries to invoke `HTTPService.registerServlet()`, which version of `javax.servlet.Servlet` is the instance it passes? Because it's wired to the Tomcat bundle, it creates a 2.4.0 instance of `javax.servlet.Servlet`. The class spaces of the HTTP service and client bundles aren't consistent; two different versions of `javax.servlet` are reachable from both. At execution time, this results in class cast exceptions when the HTTP service and client bundles interact. What went wrong?

The framework made the best choices at the time it resolved the bundle dependencies; but due to the incremental nature of the resolve process, it couldn't make the best overall choice. If you install all four bundles together, the framework resolves the dependencies in a consistent way using its existing rules. Figure 2.22 shows the dependency resolution when all four bundles are resolved together.

Because only one version of `javax.servlet` is in use, you know the class spaces of the HTTP service and client bundles are consistent, allowing them to interact without issue. But is this a general remedy to class-space inconsistencies? Unfortunately, it isn't, as you'll see in chapter 3, because OSGi allows you to dynamically install and uninstall bundles at any time. Moreover, inconsistent class spaces don't only result from incremental resolving of dependencies. It's also possible to resolve a static set of bundles into inconsistent class spaces due to inconsistent constraints. For example, imagine that the HTTP service bundle requires precisely version 2.3.0 of `javax.servlet`, whereas the client bundle requires precisely version 2.4.0. These constraints are clearly inconsistent, but the framework will happily resolve the example bundles given the current set of dependency resolution rules. Why doesn't it detect this inconsistency?

INTER- VS. INTRA-BUNDLE DEPENDENCIES

The difficulty is that `Export-Package` and `Import-Package` only capture inter-bundle dependencies, but class-space consistency conflicts result from intra-bundle dependencies. Recall the `org.osgi.service.http.HttpService` interface; its `registerServlet()` method takes a parameter of type `javax.servlet.Servlet`, which means `org.osgi.service.http` uses `javax.servlet`. Figure 2.23 shows this intra-bundle `uses` relationship between the HTTP service bundle's exported and imported packages.

How do these uses relationships arise? The example shows the typical way, which is when the method signatures of classes in an exported package expose classes from other packages. This seems obvious, because the used types are visible, but it isn't always the case. You can also expose a type via a base class that's downcast by the consumer. Because these types of uses relationships are important, how do you capture them in the bundle metadata?

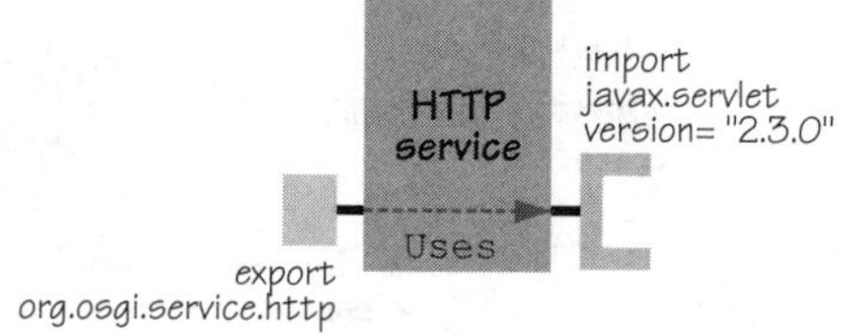

Figure 2.23 Bundle export uses import

USES DIRECTIVE A directive attached to exported packages whose value is a comma-delimited list of packages exposed by the associated exported package.

The sidebar "JAR file manifest syntax" in section 2.5 introduced the concept of a directive, but this is the first example of using one. *Directives* are additional metadata to alter how the framework interprets the metadata to which the directives are attached. The syntax for capturing directives is similar to arbitrary attributes. For example, the following modified metadata for the HTTP service example shows how to use the uses directive:

```
Export-Package: org.osgi.service.http;
 uses:="javax.servlet"; version="1.0.0"
Import-Package: javax.servlet; version="2.3.0"
```

Notice that directives use the := assignment syntax, but the ordering of the directives and the attributes isn't important. This particular example indicates that `org.osgi.service.http` uses `javax.servlet`. How exactly does the framework use this information? uses relationships among packages act like grouping constraints for the packages. In this example, the framework ensures that importers of `org.osgi.service.http` also use the same `javax.servlet` used by the HTTP service implementation.

This captures the previously missing intra-bundle package dependency. In this specific case, the exported package expresses a uses relationship with an imported package, but it could use other exported packages. These sorts of uses relationships constrain which choices the framework can make when resolving dependencies, which is why they're also referred to as *constraints*. Abstractly, if package `foo` uses package `bar`, importers of `foo` are constrained to the same `bar` if they use `bar` at all. Figure 2.24 depicts how this would impact the original incremental dependency resolutions.

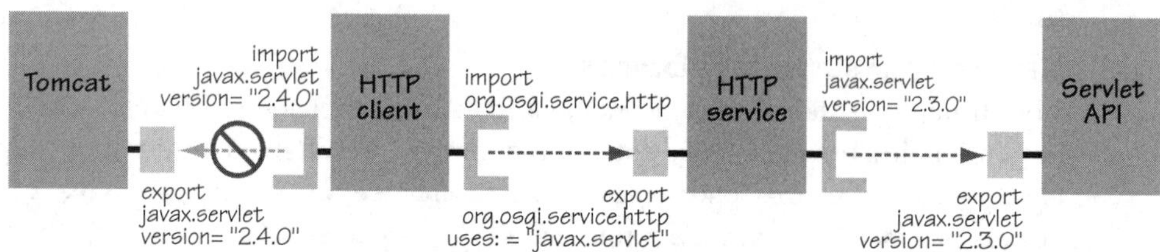

Figure 2.24 Uses constraints detect class-space inconsistencies, so the framework can determine that it isn't possible to resolve the HTTP client bundle.

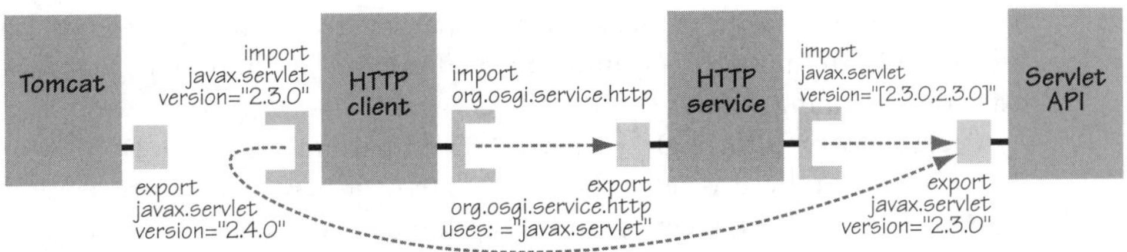

Figure 2.25 `Uses` **constraints guide dependency resolution.**

For the incremental case, the framework can now detect inconsistencies in the class spaces, and resolution fails when you try to use the client bundle. Early detection is better than errors at execution time, because it alerts you to inconsistencies in the deployed set of bundles. In the next chapter, you'll learn how to cause the framework to re-resolve the bundle dependencies to remedy this situation.

You can further modify the example, to illustrate how `uses` constraints help find proper dependency resolutions. Assume the HTTP service bundle imports precisely version 2.3.0 of `javax.servlet`, but the client imports version 2.3.0 or greater. Typically, the framework tries to select the highest version of a package to resolve a dependency; but due to the `uses` constraint, the framework ends up selecting a lower version instead, as shown in figure 2.25.

If you look at the class space of the HTTP client, you can see how the framework ends up with this solution. The HTTP client's class space contains both `javax.servlet` and `org.osgi.service.http`, because it imports these packages. From the perspective of the HTTP client bundle, it can use either version 2.4.0 or 2.3.0 of `javax.servlet`, but the framework has only one choice for `org.osgi.service.http`. Because `org.osgi.service.http` from the HTTP service bundle uses `javax.servlet`, the framework must choose the same `javax.servlet` package for any clients. Because the HTTP service bundle can only use version 2.3.0 of `javax.servlet`, this eliminates the Tomcat bundle as a possibility for the client bundle. The end result is a consistent class space where a lower version of a needed package is correctly selected even though a higher version is available.

ODDS AND ENDS OF USES CONSTRAINTS

Let's finish the discussion of `uses` constraints by touching on some final points. First, `uses` constraints are *transitive*, which means that if a given bundle exports package `foo` that uses imported package `bar`, and the selected exporter of `bar` uses package `baz`, then the associated class space for a bundle importing `foo` is constrained to have the same providers for both `bar` and `baz`, if they're used at all.

Also, even though `uses` constraints are important to capture, you don't want to create blanket `uses` constraints, because doing so overly constrains dependency resolution. The framework has more leeway when resolving dependency on packages not listed in `uses` constraints, which is necessary to support side-by-side versions. For example, in larger applications, it isn't uncommon for independently developed subsystems to use different versions of the same XML parser. If you specify `uses` constraints too broadly, this isn't possible. Accurate `uses` constraints are important, but luckily tools exist for generating them for exported packages.

OK! You made it through the most difficult part and survived. Don't worry if you didn't understand every detail, because some of it may make more sense after you have more experience creating and using bundles. Let's turn our attention back to the paint program to review why you did all this in the first place.

2.8 Reviewing the benefits of the modular paint program

Even though the amount of work required to create the modular version of the paint program wasn't great, it was still more effort than if you left the paint program as it was. Why did you create this modular version? Table 2.3 lists some of the benefits.

Table 2.2 Benefits of modularization in the paint program

Benefit	Description
Logical boundary enforcement	You can keep the implementation details private, because you're only exposing what you want to expose in the `org.foo.shape` public API package.
Reuse improvement	The code is more reusable because you explicitly declare what each bundle depends on via `Import-Package` statements. This means you know what you need when using the code in different projects.
Configuration verification	You no longer have to guess if you've deployed the application properly, because OSGi verifies whether all needed pieces are present when launching the application.
Version verification	Similar to configuration verification, OSGi also verifies whether you have the correct versions of all the application pieces when launching the application.
Configuration flexibility	You can more easily tailor the application to different scenarios by creating new configurations. Think of this as paint program a la carte.

Some of these benefits are more obvious than others. Some you can demonstrate easily. For example, assume you forgot to deploy the shape API bundle in the launcher, which you can simulate by deleting bundles/shape-2.0.jar before launching the paint program. If you do this, you'll see an exception like this:

```
org.osgi.framework.BundleException: Unresolved constraint in bundle 1:
    package; (&(package=org.foo.shape)(version>=2.0.0)(!(version>=3.0.0)))
```

The exact syntax of this message will become familiar to you when you read chapter 4; but ignoring the syntax, it tells you the application is missing the `org.foo.shape` package, which is provided by the API bundle. Due to the on-demand nature of Java class loading, such errors are typically only discovered during application execution when the missing classes are used. With OSGi, you can immediately discover such issues with missing bundles or incorrect versions. In addition to detecting errors, let's look at how OSGi modularity helps you create different configurations of the application.

Creating a different configuration of the paint program is as simple as creating a new static `main()` method for the launcher to invoke. Currently, you're using the original static `main()` method provided by `PaintFrame`. In truth, it isn't modular to have the static `main()` on the implementation class; it's better to create a separate class so you don't need to recompile the implementation classes when you want to change the application's configuration. The following listing shows the existing static `main()` method from the `PaintFrame` class.

Listing 2.2 Existing `PaintFrame.main()` method implementation

```
pcublic class PaintFrame extends JFrame
    implements MouseListener, MouseMotionListener {
  ...
  public static void main(String[] args) throws Exception {
    SwingUtilities.invokeAndWait(new Runnable() {
      public void run() {
        PaintFrame frame = new PaintFrame();                    // 1 Creates PaintFrame instance
        frame.setDefaultCloseOperation(JFrame.DO_NOTHING_ON_CLOSE);
        frame.addWindowListener(new WindowAdapter() {           // 2 Adds listener
          public void windowClosing(WindowEvent evt) {
            System.exit(0);
          }
        });
        frame.addShape(new Circle());                           // 3 Injects shape implementations
        frame.addShape(new Square());
        frame.addShape(new Triangle());
        frame.setVisible(true);
      }
    });
  }
```

The existing static `main()` is simple. You create a `PaintFrame` instance ❶ and add a listener ❷ to cause the VM to exit when the `PaintFrame` window is closed. You inject the various shape implementations into the paint frame ❸ and make the application window visible. The important aspect from the point of view of modularity is at ❸. Because the configuration decision of which shapes to inject is hardcoded into the method, if you want to create a different configuration, you must recompile the implementation bundle.

For example, assume you want to run the paint program on a small device only capable of supporting a single shape. To do so, you could modify `PaintFrame.main()` to only inject a single shape, but this wouldn't be sufficient. You'd also need to modify the metadata for the bundle so it would no longer depend on the other shapes. Of course, after making these changes, you'd lose the first configuration. These types of issues are arguments why the static `main()` method should be in a separate bundle.

Let's correct this situation in the current implementation. First, delete the `PaintFrame.main()` method and modify its bundle metadata as follows:

```
Bundle-ManifestVersion: 2
Bundle-SymbolicName: org.foo.paint
Bundle-Version: 2.0.0
Bundle-Name: Simple Paint Program
Import-Package: javax.swing, org.foo.shape; version="2.0.0"
Export-Package: org.foo.paint; version="2.0.0"
```

The main paint program bundle no longer has any dependencies on the various shape implementations, but it now needs to export the package containing the paint frame. You can take the existing static `main()` method body and put it inside a new class called `org.foo.fullpaint.FullPaint`, with the following bundle metadata:

```
Bundle-ManifestVersion: 2
Bundle-SymbolicName: org.foo.fullpaint
Bundle-Version: 1.0.0
Bundle-Name: Full Paint Program Configuration
Import-Package: javax.swing, org.foo.shape; org.foo.paint;
 org.foo.shape.circle; org.foo.shape.square; org.foo.shape.triangle;
 version="2.0.0"
Main-Class: org.foo.fullpaint.FullPaint
```

To launch this full version of the paint program, use the bundle launcher to deploy all the associated bundles, including this `FullPaint` bundle. Likewise, you can create a different bundle containing the `org.foo.smallpaint.SmallPaint` class in this listing to launch a small configuration of the paint program containing only the circle shape.

Listing 2.3 New launcher for smaller paint program configuration

```
package org.foo.smallpaint;

public class SmallPaint {
  public static void main(String[] args) throws Exception {
    SwingUtilities.invokeAndWait(new Runnable() {
      public void run() {
        PaintFrame frame = new PaintFrame();
        frame.setDefaultCloseOperation(JFrame.DO_NOTHING_ON_CLOSE);
        frame.addWindowListener(new WindowAdapter() {
          public void windowClosing(WindowEvent evt) {
            System.exit(0);
          }
        });
        frame.addShape(new Circle());          <-- Injects only circle shape implementation
        frame.setVisible(true);
      }
    });
  }
```

The metadata for the bundle containing the small paint program configuration is as follows:

```
Bundle-ManifestVersion: 2
Bundle-SymbolicName: org.foo.smallpaint
Bundle-Version: 1.0.0
Bundle-Name: Reduced Paint Program Configuration
Import-Package: javax.swing, org.foo.shape; org.foo.paint;
 org.foo.shape.circle; version="2.0.0"
Main-Class: org.foo.smallpaint.SmallPaint
```

This small configuration only depends on Swing, the public API, the paint program implementation, and the circle implementation. When you launch the full configuration, all shape implementations are required; but for the small configuration, only the circle implementation is required. Now you can deploy the appropriate configuration of the application based on the target device and have OSGi verify the correctness of it all. Pretty sweet. For completeness, figure 2.26 shows the before and after views of the paint program.

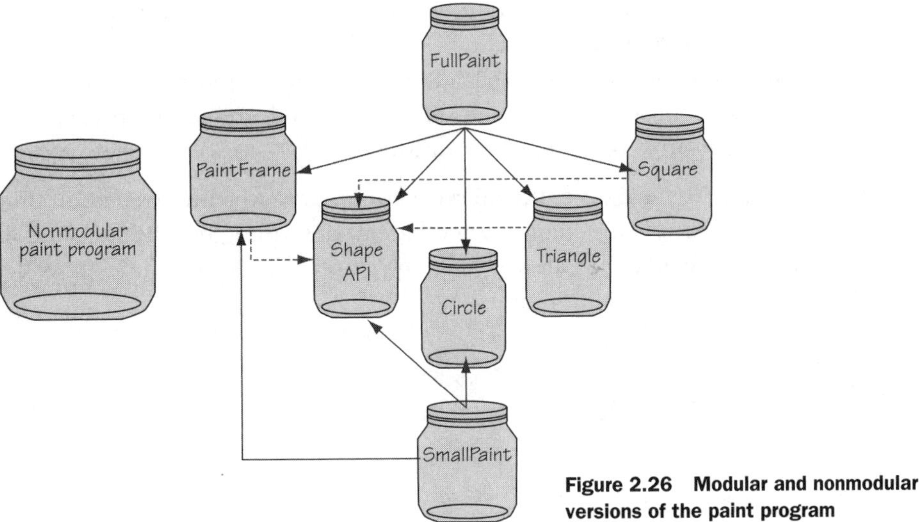

Figure 2.26 Modular and nonmodular versions of the paint program

2.9 Summary

We've covered a lot of ground in this chapter. Some of the highlights include the following:

- Modularity is a form of separation of concerns that provides both logical and physical encapsulation of classes.
- Modularity is desirable because it allows you to break applications into logically independent pieces that can be independently changed and reasoned about.
- *Bundle* is the name for a module in OSGi. It's a JAR file containing code, resources, and modularity metadata.
- Modularity metadata details human-readable information, bundle identification, and code visibility.
- Bundle code visibility is composed of an internal class path, exported packages, and imported packages, which differs significantly from the global type assumption of standard JAR files.
- The OSGi framework uses the metadata about imported and exported packages to automatically resolve bundle dependencies and ensure type consistency before a bundle can be used.
- Imported and exported packages capture inter-bundle package dependencies, but `uses` constraints are necessary to capture intra-bundle package dependencies to ensure complete type consistency.

From here, we'll move on to the lifecycle layer, where we enter execution time aspects of OSGi modularity. This chapter was all about describing bundles to the OSGi framework; the lifecycle layer is all about using bundles and the facilities provided by the OSGi framework at execution time.

3 Learning lifecycle

This chapter covers

- Understanding software lifecycle management
- Introducing the lifecycle of a bundle
- Exploring the lifecycle layer API
- Extending an application to make it lifecycle aware
- Explaining the relationship between the module and lifecycle layers

In the last chapter, we looked at the OSGi module layer and introduced you to bundles: a *bundle* is OSGi terminology for a module, which is a JAR file with the extra modularity metadata. You use bundles to define both the logical (code encapsulation and dependencies) and physical (deployable units) modularity of an application.

The OSGi module layer goes to great lengths to ensure that class loading happens in a consistent and predictable way. But to avoid putting the cart before the horse, in chapter 2 we glossed over the details of how you install bundles into an OSGi framework. No longer: in this chapter, we'll look at the next layer of the OSGi stack—the lifecycle layer.

As we mentioned in chapter 2, to use a bundle you install it into a running instance of the OSGi framework. So creating a bundle is the first half of leveraging OSGi's modularity features; the second half is using the OSGi framework as a runtime to manage and execute bundles. The lifecycle layer is unique in allowing you to create externally (and remotely) managed applications or completely self-managed applications (or any combination of the two). It also introduces dynamism that isn't normally part of an application.

This chapter will familiarize you with the features of the lifecycle layer and explain how to effectively use them. In the next section, we'll take a closer look at what lifecycle management is and why you should care about it, followed by the definition of the OSGi bundle lifecycle. In subsequent sections, you'll learn about the API for managing the lifecycle of bundles. Throughout this chapter, we'll bring all the points home via examples of a simple OSGi shell and a lifecycle-aware version of the paint program.

3.1 Introducing lifecycle management

The OSGi lifecycle layer provides a management API and a well-defined lifecycle for bundles at execution time in the OSGi framework. The lifecycle layer serves two different purposes:

- External to your application, the lifecycle layer precisely *defines the bundle lifecycle operations.* These lifecycle operations allow you to manage and evolve your application by dynamically changing the composition of bundles inside a running framework.
- Internal to your application, the lifecycle layer *defines how your bundles gain access to their execution context,* which provides them with a way to interact with the OSGi framework and the facilities it provides at execution time.

But let's take a step back. It's fine to state what the OSGi lifecycle layer does, but this won't necessarily convince you of its worth. Instead, let's look at a quick example of how it can improve your applications with a real-world scenario.

3.1.1 What is lifecycle management?

Imagine you have a business application that can report management events via JMX. Do you always want to enable or even install the JMX layer? Imagine running in a lightweight configuration and only enabling the JMX notifications on demand. The lifecycle layer allows you to install, start, update, stop, and uninstall different bundles externally, to customize your application's configuration at execution time.

Further, imagine that a critical failure event in your application must trigger the JMX layer to send out a notification regardless of whether the administrator previously enabled or installed the layer. The lifecycle layer also provides programmatic access to bundles so they can internally modify their application's configuration at execution time.

Generally speaking, programs (or parts of a program) are subject to some sort of lifecycle, which may or may not be explicit. The lifecycle of software typically has four distinct phases, as shown in figure 3.1.

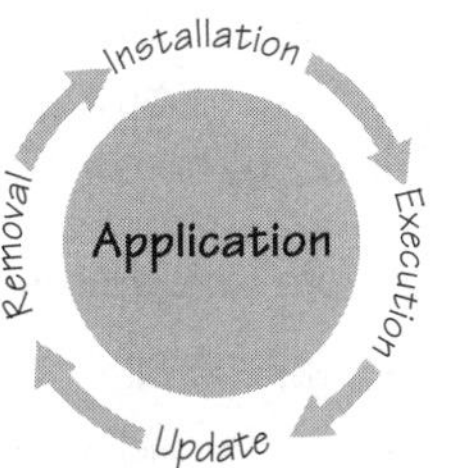

Figure 3.1 The four phases of the software lifecycle. An application is installed so you can execute it. Later, you can update it to a newer version or, ultimately, remove it if you no longer need it.

If you're creating an application, think about the typical lifecycle of the application as a whole. First you need to install it. Assuming all its dependencies are satisfied, you can execute it, which allows it to begin acquiring resources. When the application is no longer needed, you stop it, which allows it to release any resources and perhaps persist any important state. Over time, you may want to update the application to a newer version. Ultimately, you may remove the application because you no longer need it. For nonmodular applications, the lifecycle operates on the application as a whole; but as you'll see, for modular applications, fine-grained lifecycle management is possible for individual pieces of the application.

The following are two of the more popular models for creating applications in Java and how they manage software lifecycle:

- *Standard Java*—For the purposes of this discussion, we'll equate an application in standard Java to a JAR file containing the `Main-Class` header in its manifest, which allows it to be easily executed. In standard Java development, the lifecycle of an application is simple. Such a JAR-based Java application is *installed* when downloaded. It's *executed* when the user launches a JVM process, typically by double-clicking it. The application is stopped when the program terminates. *Updating* is usually done by replacing the JAR with a newer version. *Removal* is achieved by deleting the JAR from the file system.
- *Servlet*—In servlet development, the lifecycle of the web application is managed by the servlet container. The application is *installed* via a container-specific process; sometimes this involves dropping a WAR file containing the application in a certain directory in the file system or uploading a WAR file via a web-management interface. The servlet container calls various lifecycle API methods such as `Servlet.init()` and `Servlet.destroy()` on the WAR file's subcomponents during the *execution* phase of the application's lifecycle. To *update* the application, a completely new WAR file is generated. The existing WAR must be stopped and the new WAR file started in its place. The application is *removed* by a container-specific process, again sometimes removing the WAR from the file system or interacting with a management interface.

As you know, many different lifecycle-management approaches are used in Java today. In traditional Java applications, the lifecycle is largely managed by the platform-specific mechanism of the underlying operating system via installers and double-clicking desktop icons. For modular development approaches, such as servlets, Java EE, and NetBeans, each has its own specific mechanism of handling the lifecycle of its components. This leads us to the question of why you need lifecycle management at all.

3.1.2 Why lifecycle management?

Cast your mind back to the earlier discussion about why you should modularize your application code into separate bundles. We talked about the benefits of separating different concerns into bundles and avoiding tight coupling among them. The OSGi module layer provides the necessary means to do this at the class level, but it doesn't address *when* a particular set of classes or objects is needed in an application.

An explicit lifecycle API lets the providing application take care of how to configure, initialize, and maintain a piece of code that's installed so it can decide how it should operate at execution time. For example, if a database driver is in use, should it start any threads or initialize any cache tables to improve performance? If it does any of these things, when are these resources released? Do they exist for the lifetime of the application as a whole? And if not, how are they removed? Because the OSGi specification provides an explicit lifecycle API, you can take any bundle providing the functionality you need and let it worry about how to manage its internal functions. In essence, it's a matter of *compose* versus *control*.

Because you can architect your application such that parts of it may come and go at any point in time, the application's flexibility is greatly increased. You can easily manage installation, update, and removal of an application and its required modules. You can configure or tailor applications to suit specific needs, breaking the monolithic approach of standard development approaches. Instead of "you get what you get," wouldn't it be great if you could offer "you get what you need"?

Another great benefit of the standard lifecycle API is that it allows for a diverse set of management applications that can manage your application. There's no magic going on; lifecycle management can be done completely using the provided API.

We hope this discussion has piqued your interest. Now, let's focus specifically on defining the OSGi bundle lifecycle and the management API associated with it.

3.2 OSGi bundle lifecycle

The OSGi lifecycle layer is how you use the bundles; it's where the rubber meets the road. The module metadata from chapter 2 is all well and good, but creating bundles in and of itself is useful only if you use them. You need to interact with the OSGi lifecycle layer in order to use the bundles. Unlike the module layer, which relies on metadata, the lifecycle layer relies on APIs. Because introducing APIs can be a boring endeavor (Javadoc, anyone?), we'll move in a top-down fashion and use an example to show what the lifecycle layer API allows you to do.

It's important to note that the OSGi core framework doesn't mandate any particular mechanism of interacting with the lifecycle API (such as the command line, a GUI, or an XML configuration file); the core is purely a Java API. This turns out to be extremely powerful, because it makes it possible to design as many different ways of managing the OSGi framework as you can think of; in the end, you're limited only by your imagination as a developer.

Because there's no standard way for users to interact with the lifecycle API, you *could* use a framework-specific mechanism. But using this approach here would be a disservice to you, because it's a great opportunity for learning. Instead of reusing someone else's work in this chapter, we'll lead you through some basic steps for developing your own command line interface for interacting with the OSGi framework. This gives you the perfect tool, alongside the paint program, to explore the rich capabilities provided by the OSGi lifecycle API.

> **Shells, shells, everywhere**
>
> If you have some familiarity with using OSGi frameworks, you're likely aware that most OSGi framework implementations (such as Apache Felix, Eclipse Equinox, and Knopflerfish) have their own shells for interacting with a running framework. The OSGi specification doesn't define a standard shell (although there has been some work toward this goal recently; see http://felix.apache.org/site/apache-felix-gogo.html), but shells need not be tied to a specific framework and can be implemented as bundles, just as you'll do here.

3.2.1 *Introducing lifecycle to the paint program*

Enough with the talk—let's see the lifecycle API in action by kicking off the shell application and using it to install the paint program. To do this, type the following into your operating system console (Windows users, substitute \ for /):

```
$ cd chapter03/shell-example/
$ ant
$ java -jar launcher.jar bundles
Bundle: org.foo.shell started with bundle id 1 - listening on port 7070
```

The shell is created as a bundle that, on starting, begins listening for user input on a telnet socket. This allows clients to connect and perform install, start, stop, update, and uninstall actions on bundles. It also provides some basic diagnostic facilities. Here's a session that connects to the newly launched framework and uses the shell to install the paint example:

```
$ telnet localhost 7070
-> install file:../paint-example/bundles/paint-3.0.jar
Bundle: 2
-> install file:../paint-example/bundles/shape-3.0.jar
Bundle: 3
-> start 2
-> install file:../paint-example/bundles/circle-3.0.jar
Bundle: 4
-> install file:../paint-example/bundles/square-3.0.jar
```

```
Bundle: 5
-> start 4
-> start 5
-> install file:../paint-example/bundles/triangle-3.0.jar
Bundle: 6
-> start 6
-> stop 4
```

In figure 3.2, you can see that in step 1, you first install the shape API bundle, and then you install and start the paint program bundle. This causes an empty paint frame to appear with no available shapes, which makes sense because you haven't installed any other bundles yet. In step 2, you install and start the circle and square bundles. As if by magic, the two shapes dynamically appear in the paint frame's toolbar and are available for drawing. In step 3, you install and start the triangle bundle; then, you draw some shapes on the paint canvas. What happens if you stop a bundle? In step 4, you stop the circle bundle, which you see is replaced on the canvas with the placeholder icon (a construction worker) from `DefaultShape`.

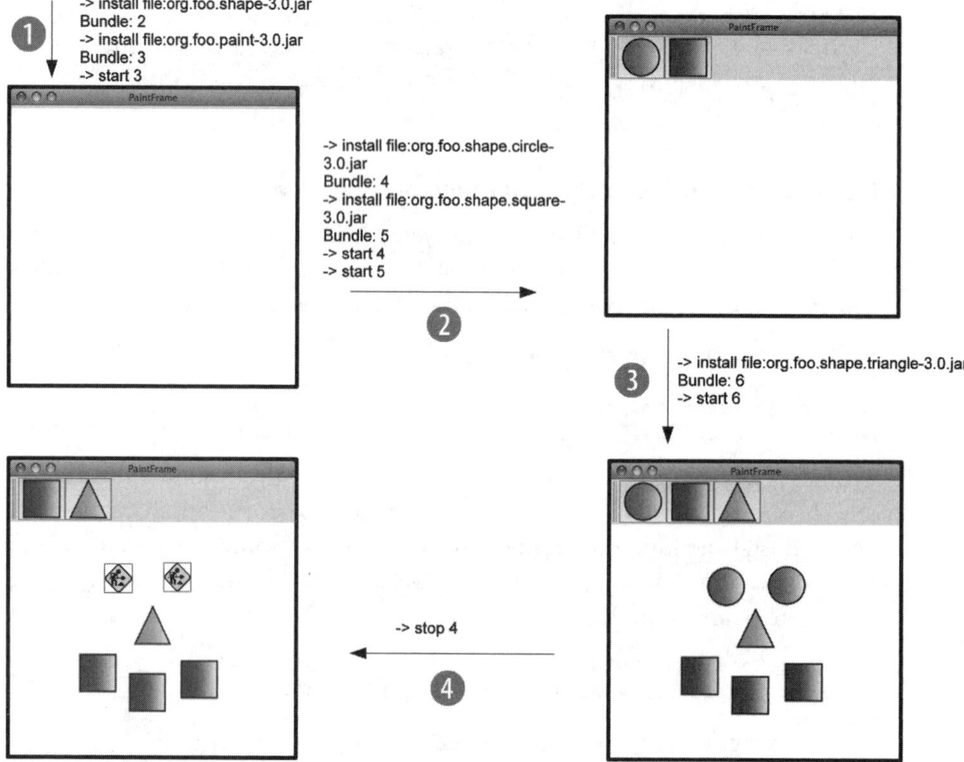

Figure 3.2 Execution-time evolution: dynamically adding shapes to and removing shapes from the paint program as if by magic

This shows you in practice that you can use the lifecycle API to build a highly dynamic application, but what's going on in this example? To understand, we'll take a top-down approach, using the shell and paint example for context:

- In section 3.2.2, we'll explain the framework's role in the application's lifecycle.
- In section 3.2.3, we'll look at the changes you need to make to the bundle manifest to hook the bundles into the OSGi framework.
- In section 3.2.4, we'll investigate the key API interfaces used by the OSGi lifecycle: `BundleActivator`, `BundleContext`, and `Bundle`.
- In section 3.2.5, we'll wrap up with a review of the OSGi lifecycle state diagram.

Let's get started.

3.2.2 The OSGi framework's role in the lifecycle

In standard Java programming, you use JAR files by placing them on the class path. This isn't the approach for using bundles. A bundle can only be used when it's installed into a running instance of the OSGi framework. Conceptually, you can think of installing a bundle into the framework as being similar to putting a JAR file on the class path in standard Java programming.

This simplified view hides some important differences from the standard class path, as you can see in figure 3.3. One big difference is the fact that the OSGi framework supports full lifecycle management of bundle JAR files, including install, resolve, start, stop, update, and uninstall. At this point, we've only touched on installing bundles and resolving their dependencies. The remainder of this chapter will fully explain the lifecycle activities and how they're related to each other. For example, we've already mentioned that the framework doesn't allow an installed bundle to be used until its dependencies (`Import-Package` declarations) are satisfied.

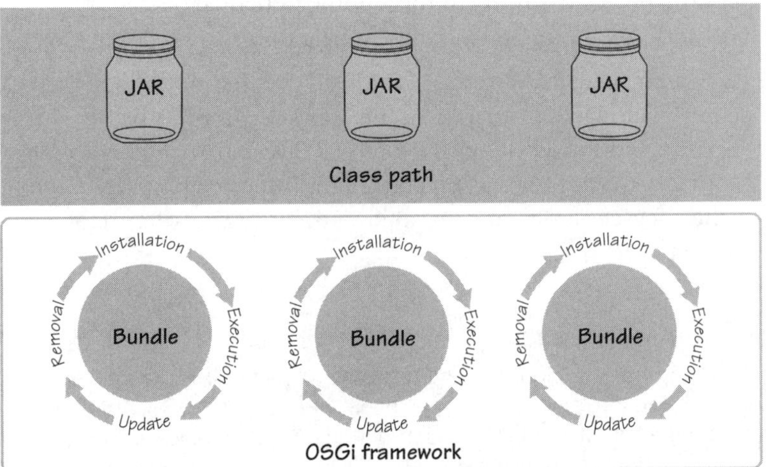

Figure 3.3 Class path versus OSGi framework with full lifecycle management

Another huge difference from the standard class path is inherent dynamism. The OSGi framework supports the full bundle lifecycle at execution time. This is similar to modifying what's on the class path dynamically.

As part of lifecycle management, the framework maintains a persistent cache of installed bundles. This means the next time you start the framework, any previously installed bundles are automatically reloaded from the bundle cache, and the original JAR files are no longer necessary. Perhaps we can characterize the framework as a fully manageable, dynamic, and persistent class path. Sounds cool, huh? Let's move on to how you have to modify the metadata to allow bundles to hook into the lifecycle layer API.

3.2.3 The bundle activator manifest entry

How do you tell the framework to kick-start the bundles at execution time? The answer, as with the rest of the modularity information, is via the bundle metadata. Here's the JAR file manifest describing the shell bundle you'll create:

```
Manifest-Version: 1.0
Bundle-ManifestVersion: 2
Bundle-SymbolicName: org.foo.shell
Bundle-Version: 1.0
Bundle-Activator: org.foo.shell.Activator
Import-Package: org.osgi.framework;version="[1.3,2.0)",
 org.osgi.service.packageadmin;version="[1.2,2.0)",
 org.osgi.service.startlevel;version="[1.1,2.0)"
Bundle-Name: remote_shell
Bundle-DocURL: http://code.google.com/p/osgi-in-action/
```

You should already be familiar with most of these headers from chapter 2. But to recap, most of the entries are related to the class-level modularity of the bundle. This metadata does the following:

- Defines the bundle's identity
- Specifies the packages on which this bundle depends
- Declares additional human-readable information

The only new header is `Bundle-Activator`. This is the first sighting of the OSGi lifecycle API in action! The `Bundle-Activator` header specifies the name of a reachable class (that is, either imported or on the bundle class path) implementing the `org.osgi.framework.BundleActivator` interface. This interface provides the bundle with a hook into the lifecycle layer and the ability to customize what happens when it's started or stopped.

Is an activator necessary?

Keep in mind that not all bundles need an activator. An activator is necessary only if you're creating a bundle and wish to specifically interact with OSGi API or need to perform custom initialization/de-initialization actions. If you're creating a simple library bundle, it isn't necessary to give it an activator because it's possible to share classes without one.

> ***(continued)***
> This doesn't mean your bundles won't be able to do anything. Bundles don't necessarily need to be started in order to do useful things. Remember the paint program you created in chapter 2: none of the bundles had activators, nor did any of them need to be started, but you still created a fully functioning application.

To understand what's going on in the shell example, we'll now introduce you to three interfaces (`BundleActivator`, `BundleContext`, and `Bundle`) that are the heart and soul of the lifecycle layer API.

3.2.4 *Introducing the lifecycle API*

The last section described how the shell bundle declares a `BundleActivator` to hook into the framework at execution time. We can now look into the details of this interface and the other lifecycle APIs made available from it to the bundle. This is the bundle's hook into the world of OSGi.

BUNDLE ACTIVATOR

As you've seen, adding an activator to the bundle is straightforward, because you only need to create a class implementing the `BundleActivator` interface, which looks like this:

```
public interface BundleActivator {
  public void start(BundleContext context) throws Exception;
  public void stop(BundleContext context) throws Exception;
}
```

For the shell example, the activator allows it to become lifecycle aware and gain access to framework facilities. The following listing shows the activator for the shell bundle.

Listing 3.1 Simple shell bundle activator

```
package org.foo.shell;

import org.osgi.framework.BundleActivator;
import org.osgi.framework.BundleContext;

public class Activator implements BundleActivator {
  private volatile Binding m_binding;

  public void start(BundleContext context) {
    int port = getPort(context);
    int max = getMaxConnections(context);
    m_binding = getTelnetBinding(context, port, max);
    m_binding.start();
    System.out.println("Bundle " +
      context.getBundle().getSymbolicName() +
      " started with bundle id" +
      context.getBundle().getBundleId() +
      " listening on port " + port);
  }
```

❶ Declares volatile member field
❷ Gets configuration property values
❸ Passes context into telnet binding
❹ Starts binding

```
  public void stop(BundleContext context) {
    m_binding.stop();
  }

    ...
}
...

public interface Binding {
  public void start();
  public void stop() throws InterruptedException;
}
```

This class implements the OSGi `BundleActivator` interface. When the bundle is installed and started, the framework constructs an instance of this activator class and invokes the `start()` method. When the bundle is stopped, the framework invokes the `stop()` method. The `start()` method is the starting point for your bundle, sort of like the static `main()` method in standard Java. After it returns, your bundle is expected to function until the `stop()` method is invoked at some later point. The `stop()` method should undo anything done by the `start()` method.

We need to mention a few technical but potentially important details about the handling of the `BundleActivator` instance:

- The activator instance on which `start()` is called is the same instance on which `stop()` is called.
- After `stop()` is called, the activator instance is discarded and isn't used again.
- If the bundle is subsequently restarted after being stopped, a new activator instance is created, and the `start()` and `stop()` methods are invoked on it as appropriate.

As you can see, the rest of the activator isn't complicated. In the `start()` method, you get the port on which the bundle listens for connection requests and the number of allowed concurrent connections. You also create a `TelnetBinding`, which does the work of listening on a socket for user input and processes it; the details of creating the telnet binding are omitted here for reasons of simplicity and brevity. The next step is to start the binding, which creates a new `Thread` to run the shell. How this happens is left to the binding, which you start next ❹.

The point about the binding starting its own thread is important because the activator methods shouldn't do much work. This is best practice as with most callback patterns, which are supposed to return quickly, allowing the framework to carry on managing other bundles. But it's also important to point out that the OSGi specification doesn't mandate you start a new thread if your application's startup doesn't warrant it—the ball is in your court.

For the activator `stop()` method, all you do is tell the binding to stop listening to user input and cease to execute. You should make sure it does stop by waiting until its thread is finished; the binding method waits for its thread to stop. Sometimes, you may have special cases for certain situations because, as you'll see later, the shell thread itself may call

> **Threading**
>
> OSGi is designed around the normal Java thread abstraction. Unlike other, more heavyweight frameworks, it assumes that you do your own thread management. You gain a lot of freedom by doing this, but at the same time you have to make sure your programs are correctly synchronized and thread safe. In this simple example, nothing special is needed; but in general, it's likely that `stop()` will be called on a different thread than `start()` (for this reason, you make the member at ❶ `volatile`).
>
> The OSGi libraries are thread safe, and callbacks are normally done in a way to give you some guarantees. For example, in the case of the bundle activator, `start()` and `stop()` are guaranteed to be called in order and not concurrently. So, technically, in this particular case the `volatile` might not be necessary, but in general your code must take thread visibility into account.

the `stop()` method, which will cause the bundle to freeze. We'll cover these and other advanced use cases later. In general, if you use threads in your bundles, do so in such a way that all threads are stopped when the `stop()` method returns.

Now you've seen how you can handle starting and stopping a bundle, but what if you want to interact with the OSGi framework? We'll now switch the focus to the `BundleContext` object passed into the `start()` and `stop()` methods of the activator; this allows a bundle to interact with the framework and manage other bundles.

BUNDLE CONTEXT

As you learned in the previous section, the framework calls the `start()` method of a bundle's activator when it's started and the `stop()` method when it's stopped. Both methods receive an instance of the `BundleContext` interface. The methods of the `BundleContext` interface can be roughly divided into two categories:

- The first category is related to deployment and lifecycle management.
- The second category is related to bundle interaction via services.

We're interested in the first category of methods, because they give you the ability to install and manage the lifecycle of other bundles, access information about the framework, and retrieve basic configuration properties. This listing captures these methods from `BundleContext`.

Listing 3.2 `BundleContext` methods related to lifecycle management

```
public interface BundleContext {
  ...
  String getProperty(String key);
  Bundle getBundle();
  Bundle installBundle(String location, InputStream input)
    throws BundleException;
  Bundle installBundle(String location) throws BundleException;
  Bundle getBundle(long id);
  Bundle[] getBundles();
```

```
  void addBundleListener(BundleListener listener);
  void removeBundleListener(BundleListener listener);
  void addFrameworkListener(FrameworkListener listener);
  void removeFrameworkListener(FrameworkListener listener);
  ...
}
```

We'll cover most of these methods in this chapter. The second category of `BundleContext` methods related to services will be covered in the next chapter.

> **Unique context**
>
> One important aspect of the bundle context object is its role as the unique execution context of its associated bundle. Because it represents the execution context, it's only valid while the associated bundle is active, which is explicitly from the moment the activator `start()` method is invoked until the activator `stop()` method completes and the entire time in between. Most bundle context methods throw an exception if used when the associated bundle isn't active. It's a unique execution context because each activated bundle receives its own context object. The framework uses this context for security and resource allocation purposes for each individual bundle. Given this capability of `BundleContext` objects, they should be treated as sensitive or private objects and not passed freely among bundles.

The shell activator in listing 3.1 uses the bundle context to get its configuration property values ❷. It also passes the context into the telnet binding ❸, which client connections will use to interact with the running framework. Finally, it uses the context to obtain the bundle's `Bundle` object to access the identification information. We'll look at these details shortly, but for now we'll continue the top-down description by looking at the final lifecycle layer interface: `org.osgi.framework.Bundle`.

BUNDLE

For each installed bundle, the framework creates a `Bundle` object to logically represent it. The `Bundle` interface defines the API to manage an installed bundle's lifecycle; a portion of the interface is presented in the following listing. As we discuss the `Bundle` interface, you'll see that most lifecycle operations have a corresponding method in it.

Listing 3.3 `Bundle` interface methods related to lifecycle management

```
public interface Bundle {
  ...
  BundleContext getBundleContext();
  long getBundleId();
  Dictionary getHeaders();
  Dictionary getHeaders(String locale);
  String getLocation();
  int getState();
  String getSymbolicName();
```

```
    Version getVersion();
    void start(int options) throws BundleException;
    void start() throws BundleException;
    void stop(int options) throws BundleException;
    void stop() throws BundleException;
    void update(InputStream input) throws BundleException;
    void update() throws BundleException;
    void uninstall() throws BundleException;
    ...
}
```

Each installed bundle is uniquely identified in the framework by its `Bundle` object. From the `Bundle` object, you can also access two additional forms of bundle identification: the bundle identifier and the bundle location. You might be thinking, "Didn't we talk about bundle identification metadata back in chapter 2?" Yes, we did, but don't get confused. The identification metadata in chapter 2 was for static identification of the bundle JAR file. The bundle identifier and bundle location are for execution-time identification, meaning they're associated with the `Bundle` object. You may wonder why you need two different execution-time identifiers.

The main difference between the two is who defines the identifier; see figure 3.4. The bundle identifier is a Java language `long` value assigned by the framework in ascending order as bundles are installed. The bundle location is a `String` value assigned by the installer of the bundle.

Both the bundle identifier and location values uniquely identify the `Bundle` object and persist across framework executions when the installed bundles are reloaded from the framework's cache.

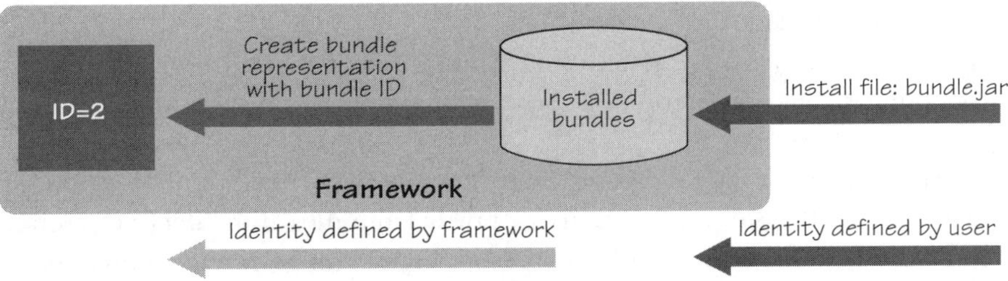

Figure 3.4 Difference between the bundle identifiers

> **Bundle location interpretation**
>
> The bundle location has a unique characteristic because most OSGi framework implementations interpret it as a URL pointing to the bundle JAR file. The framework then uses this URL to download the contents of the bundle JAR file during bundle installation. The specification doesn't define the location string as an URL, nor is it required, because you can install bundles from an input stream as well.

You may still be thinking, "I'm not convinced that all these identification mechanisms are necessary. Couldn't you find the `Bundle` object using the bundle's symbolic name and version from chapter 2?" Yes, you could, because the framework allows only one bundle with a given symbolic name and version to be installed at a time. This means the bundle symbolic name and version pair also act as an execution-time identifier.

> **Why so many forms of identification?**
>
> History plays a role here. As mentioned in chapter 2, the notion of using a bundle's symbolic name and version to uniquely identify it didn't exist in versions of the specification prior to R4. Therefore, prior to R4, it made sense to have internally and externally assigned identifiers. Now it makes less sense, because the bundle's symbolic name and version pair are externally defined and explicitly recognized internally by the framework.
>
> There's still a role for the bundle identifier because in some cases the framework treats a lower identifier value as being better than a higher one when deciding between two otherwise equal alternatives, such as when two bundles export the same version of a given package. The real loser here is the bundle location, which doesn't serve a useful purpose other than potentially giving the initial URL of the bundle JAR file.

Although one instance of `Bundle` exists for each bundle installed into the framework, at execution time there's also a special instance of `Bundle` to represent the framework itself. This special bundle is called the *system bundle*; and although the API is the same, it merits its own discussion.

THE SYSTEM BUNDLE

At execution time, the framework is represented as a bundle with an identifier of 0, called the *system bundle*. You don't install the system bundle—it always exists while the framework is running.

The system bundle follows the same lifecycle as normal bundles, so you can manipulate it with the same operations as normal bundles. But lifecycle operations performed on the system bundle have special meanings when compared to normal bundles. One example of the special meaning is evident when you stop the system bundle. Intuitively, stopping the system bundle shuts down the framework in a well-behaved manner. It stops all other bundles first and then shuts itself down completely.

With that, we conclude our high-level look at the major API players in the lifecycle layer (`BundleActivator`, `BundleContext`, and `Bundle`). You now know the following:

- `BundleActivator` is the entry point for the bundles, much like static `main()` in a standard Java application.
- `BundleContext` provides applications with the methods to manipulate the OSGi framework at execution time.
- `Bundle` represents an installed bundle in the framework, allowing state manipulations to be performed on it.

With this knowledge in hand, we'll complete the top-down approach by defining the overall bundle lifecycle state diagram and see how these interfaces relate to it.

3.2.5 Lifecycle state diagram

Until now, we've been holding off on explicitly describing the complete bundle lifecycle in favor of getting a high-level view of the API forming the lifecycle layer. This allowed you to quickly get your hands a little dirty. Now you can better understand how these APIs relate to the complete bundle lifecycle state diagram, shown in figure 3.5.

The entry point of the bundle lifecycle is the `BundleContext.installBundle()` operation, which creates a bundle in the `INSTALLED` state. From figure 3.5, you can see that there's no direct path from `INSTALLED` to `STARTING`. This is because the framework ensures all dependencies of a bundle are satisfied before it can be used (that is, no classes can be loaded from it). The transition from the `INSTALLED` to the `RESOLVED` state represents this guarantee. The framework won't allow a bundle to transition to `RESOLVED` unless all its dependencies are satisfied. If it can't transition to `RESOLVED`, by definition it can't transition to `STARTING`. Often, the transition to `RESOLVED` happens implicitly when the bundle is started or another bundle tries to load a class from it, but you'll see later in this chapter that it's also possible to explicitly resolve a bundle.

The transition from the `STARTING` to the `ACTIVE` state is always implicit. A bundle is in the `STARTING` state while its activator's `start()` method executes. Upon successful completion of the `start()` method, the bundle's state transitions to `ACTIVE`; but if the activator throws an exception, it transitions back to `RESOLVED`.

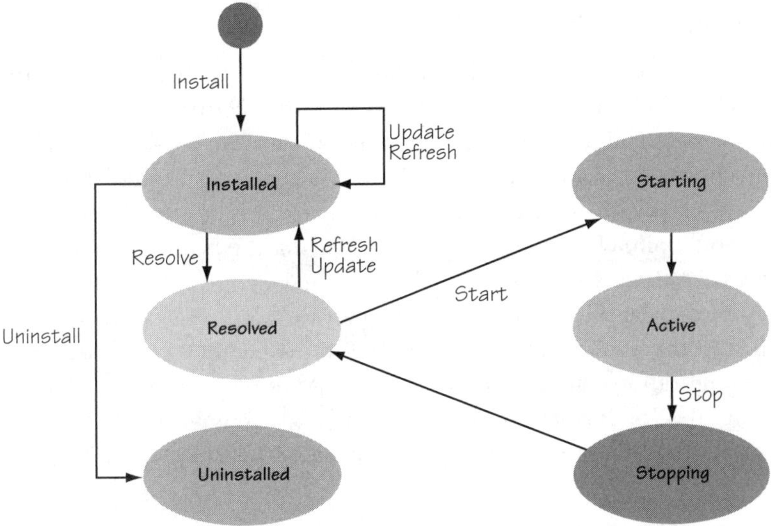

Figure 3.5 OSGi bundle lifecycle

An ACTIVE bundle can be stopped, which also results in a transition back to the RESOLVED state via the STOPPING state. The STOPPING state is an implicit state like STARTING, and the bundle is in this state while its activator's stop() method executes. A stopped bundle transitions back to RESOLVED instead of INSTALLED because its dependencies are still satisfied and don't need to be resolved again. It's possible to force the framework to resolve a bundle again by refreshing it or updating it, which we'll discuss later. Refreshing or updating a bundle transitions it back to the INSTALLED state.

A bundle in the INSTALLED state can be uninstalled, which transitions it to the UNINSTALLED state. If you uninstall an active bundle, the framework automatically stops the bundle first, which results in the appropriate state transitions to the RESOLVED state and then transitions it to the INSTALLED state before uninstalling it.[1] A bundle in the UNINSTALLED state remains there as long as it's still needed (we'll explain later what this means), but it can no longer transition to another state. Now that you understand the complete bundle lifecycle, let's discuss how these operations impact the framework's bundle cache and subsequent restarts of the framework.

3.2.6 Bundle cache and framework restarts

To use bundles, you have to install them into the OSGi framework. Check. But what does this mean? Technically, you know you must invoke BundleContext.installBundle() to install a bundle. In doing so, you must specify a location typically interpreted as a URL to the bundle JAR file or an input stream from which the bundle JAR file is read. In either case, the framework reads the bundle JAR file and saves a copy in a private area known as the *bundle cache*. This means two things:

- Installing a bundle into the framework is a persistent operation.
- After the bundle is installed, the framework no longer needs the original copy of the bundle JAR file.

The exact details of the bundle cache are dependent on the framework implementation; the specification doesn't dictate the format nor structure other than that it must be persistent across framework executions. If you start an OSGi framework, install a bundle, shut down the framework, and then restart it, the bundle you installed will still be there, as shown in figure 3.6. If you compare this approach to using the class path, where you manually manage everything, having the framework cache and manage the artifacts relieves you of a lot of effort.

In terms of your application, you can think of the bundle cache as the deployed configuration of the application. This is similar to the chapter 2 discussion of creating different configurations of the paint program. Your application's configuration is whichever bundles you install into the framework. You maintain and manage the configuration using the APIs and techniques discussed in this chapter.

---

[1] This is a change in the R4.2 version of the OSGi specification. You can't go to UNINSTALLED from RESOLVED; you have to go to INSTALLED first, and only INSTALLED goes to UNINSTALLED. This detail is listed in the R4.2 specification errata.

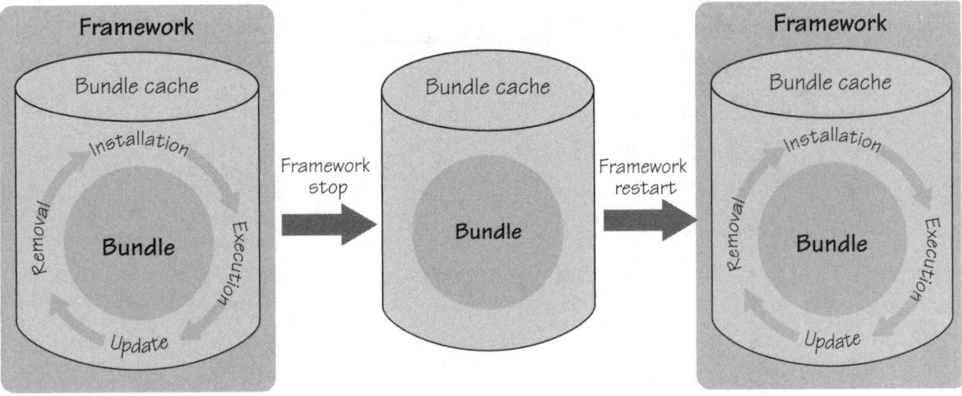

Figure 3.6 Bundle cache during framework restarts

Bundle installation isn't the only lifecycle operation to impact the bundle cache. When a bundle is started using `Bundle.start()`, the framework persistently marks the bundle as started, even if `Bundle.start()` throws an exception, such as when the bundle can't be resolved or the bundle's `BundleActivator.start()` method throws an exception. When a bundle is persistently marked as started, subsequent executions of the framework not only reinstall the bundle but also attempt to start it. From a management perspective, you deploy a configuration of your application by installing a set of bundles and activating them. Subsequent framework executions automatically restart your application. If you stop a bundle using `Bundle.stop()`, this removes the persistently started status of the bundle; subsequent framework executions no longer restart the bundle, although it's still reinstalled. This is another means of modifying your application's configuration.

You may want to ask, "What about updating and uninstalling a bundle? These must impact the bundle cache, right?" The short answer is, yes, but this isn't the whole answer. `Bundle.update()` and `Bundle.uninstall()` impact the bundle cache by saving a new bundle JAR file or removing an existing bundle JAR file, respectively. But these operations may not affect the cache immediately. We'll explain these oddities when we discuss the relationship between the modularity and lifecycle layers in section 3.5. Next, we'll delve into the details of the shell bundle as we more fully explore how to use the lifecycle layer API.

3.3 Using the lifecycle API in your bundles

So far, you haven't implemented much functionality for the shell—you just created the activator to start it up and shut it down. In this section, we'll show you how to implement the bulk of its functionality. You'll use a simple command pattern to provide the executable actions to let you interactively install, start, stop, update, and uninstall bundles. You'll even add a persistent history to keep track of previously executed commands.

A high-level understanding of the approach will be useful before you start. The main piece is the telnet binding, which listens to the configured port for

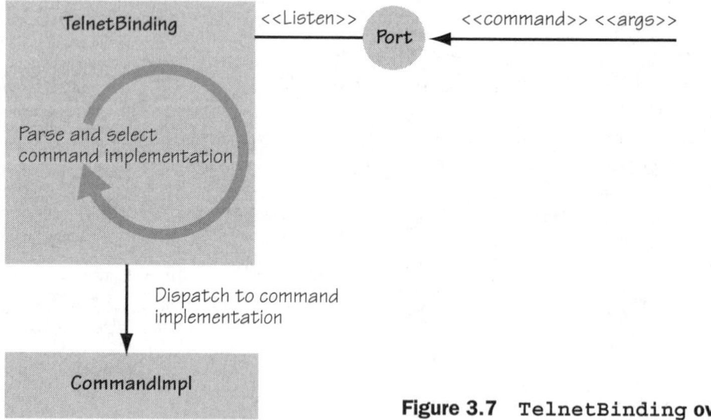

Figure 3.7 `TelnetBinding` overview

connection requests. It spawns a new thread for each connecting client. The client sends command lines to its thread, where a command line consists of a command name and the arguments for the command. The thread parses the command line, selects the appropriate command, and invokes it with any specified arguments, as shown in figure 3.7.

Commands process the arguments passed in to them. We won't discuss the implementation of the telnet binding and the connection thread, but full source code is available in the companion code. We'll dissect the command implementations to illustrate how to use `Bundle` and `BundleContext`. Let's get the ball rolling by showing how you configure the bundle.

3.3.1 Configuring bundles

The shell needs two configuration properties: one for the port and one for the maximum number of concurrent connections. In traditional Java programming, you'd use the `System.getProperty()` method to retrieve them. When creating a bundle, you can use the `BundleContext` object to retrieve configuration properties instead. The main benefit of this approach is that it avoids the global aspect of `System.getProperty()` and allows properties per framework instance.

The OSGi specification doesn't specify a user-oriented way to set bundle configuration properties, so different frameworks handle this differently; typically, they provide a configuration file where the properties are set. But the specification does require bundle-configuration properties to be backed by system properties, so you can still use system properties in a pinch. Retrieving bundle-configuration property values is standardized via the `BundleContext.getProperty()` method, as shown next.

Listing 3.4 Bundle configuration by example

```
package org.foo.shell;

import org.osgi.framework.Bundle;
import org.osgi.framework.BundleContext;
```

```
public class Activator implements BundleContext {
...
  private int getPort(BundleContext context) {
    String port = context.getProperty("org.foo.shell.port");        <-
    if (port != null) {
      return Integer.parseInt(port);
    }
    return 7070;                                          Retrieves properties (1)
  }

  private int getMaxConnections(BundleContext context) {
    String max = context.getProperty("org.foo.shell.connection.max");   <-
    if (max != null) {
      return Integer.parseInt(max);
    }
    return 1;
  }
}
```

This listing continues the activator implementation from listing 3.1; in the activator, you use these two methods to get configuration properties. Here, the methods use the `BundleContext.getProperty()` method to retrieve the properties ❶. This method looks in the framework properties to find the value of the specified property. If it can't find the property, it searches the system properties, returning `null` if the property isn't found. For the shell, you return default values if no configured value is found. The OSGi specification also defines some standard framework properties, shown in table 3.1. If you need to use these standard properties, you can use the constants for them defined in the `org.osgi.framework.Constants` class.

Table 3.1 Standard OSGi framework properties

Property name	Description
org.osgi.framework.version	OSGi framework version
org.osgi.framework.vendor	Framework implementation vendor
org.osgi.framework.language	Language being used; see ISO 639 for possible values
org.osgi.framework.os.name	Host computer operating system
org.osgi.framework.os.version	Host computer operating system version number
org.osgi.framework.processor	Host computer processor name

There you have it: your first real interaction with the OSGi framework. This is only a small part of the API that you can use in your bundles, but we'll cover a lot of ground in the next section, so don't worry. And those of you thinking, "Hey, this configuration mechanism seems overly simplistic!" are correct. There are other, more sophisticated ways to configure your bundle, but we won't discuss them until chapter 9. Bundle properties are the simplest mechanism available and should only be used for properties that don't change much. In this regard, they may not be the best choice for the shell, but it depends on what you want to achieve; for example, it makes it difficult to change the shell's port dynamically. For now, we'll keep things simple, so this is sufficient.

3.3.2 Deploying bundles

Each bundle installed into the framework is represented by a `Bundle` object and can be identified by its bundle identifier, location, or symbolic name. For most of the shell commands you'll implement, you'll use the bundle identifier to retrieve a `Bundle` object, because the bundle identifier is nice and concise. Most of the commands accept a bundle identifier as a parameter, so let's look at how you can use it and the bundle context to access `Bundle` objects associated with other bundles. As part of the design, you create an abstract `BasicCommand` class to define a shared method, `getBundle()`, to retrieve bundles by their identifier, as shown here:

```
protected volatile BundleContext m_context;
...
public Bundle getBundle(String id) {
  Bundle bundle = m_context.getBundle(Long.parseLong(id.trim()));
  if (bundle == null) {
    throw new IllegalArgumentException("No such bundle.");
  }
  return bundle;
}
```

All you do is call `BundleContext.getBundle()` on the context object with the parsed bundle identifier, which is passed in as a `String`. The only special case you need to worry about is when no bundle with the given identifier exists. In such a case, you throw an exception.

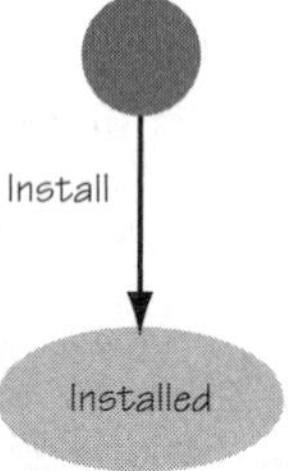

Figure 3.8 The install-related portion of the bundle lifecycle state diagram

INSTALL COMMAND

With this basic functionality in place, you can start the first command. The next listing shows the implementation of an `install` command, and figure 3.8 reminds you which portion of the bundle lifecycle is involved.

Listing 3.5 Bundle `install` command

```
package org.foo.shell;

import org.osgi.framework.Bundle;
import org.osgi.framework.BundleContext;

public class InstallCommand extends BasicCommand {
  public void exec(String args, PrintStream out, PrintStream err)
    throws Exception {
    Bundle bundle = m_context.installBundle(args);
    out.println("Bundle: " + bundle.getBundleId());
  }
}
```

You use `BundleContext.installBundle()` to install a bundle. In most framework implementations, the argument to `installBundle()` is conveniently interpreted as a URL in `String` form from which the bundle JAR file can be retrieved. Because the user enters the URL argument as a `String`, you can use it directly to install the bundle. If the install succeeds, then a new `Bundle` object corresponding to the newly installed bundle is returned. The bundle is uniquely identified by this URL, which is used as its location. This location value will also be used in the future to determine if the bundle is already installed. If a bundle is already associated with this location value, the `Bundle` object associated with the previously installed bundle is returned instead of installing it again. If the install operation is successful, the command outputs the installed bundle's identifier.

The bundle context also provides an overloaded `installBundle()` method for installing a bundle from an input stream. We won't show this method here, but the other form of `installBundle()` accepts a location and an open input stream. When you use this other form of the method, the location is used purely for identification, and the bundle JAR file is read from the passed-in input stream. The framework is responsible for closing the input stream.

START COMMAND

Now you have a command to install bundles, so the next operation you'll want to do is start bundles. The `start` command shown in listing 3.6 does just that (see figure 3.9).

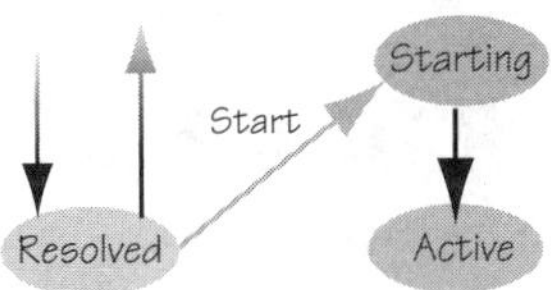

Figure 3.9 The start-related portion of the bundle lifecycle state diagram

Listing 3.6 Bundle `start` command

```
package org.foo.shell;

import org.osgi.framework.Bundle;
import org.osgi.framework.BundleContext;

  public class StartCommand extends BasicCommand {
    public void exec(String id) throws Exception {
    Bundle bundle = getBundle(id);
    bundle.start();
  }
}
```

Again, the implementation is pretty easy. You use the method from the base command class to get the `Bundle` object associated with the user-supplied identifier, and then you invoke `Bundle.start()` to start the bundle associated with the identifier.

The result of `Bundle.start()` depends on the current state of the associated bundle. If the bundle is `INSTALLED`, it transitions to `ACTIVE` via the `RESOLVED` and `STARTING` states. If the bundle is `UNINSTALLED`, the method throws an `IllegalStateException`. If the bundle is either `STARTING` or `STOPPING`, `start()` blocks until the bundle enters either `ACTIVE` or `RESOLVED`. If the bundle is already `ACTIVE`, calling `start()` again has no effect. A bundle must be resolved before it can be started. You don't need to explicitly resolve the bundle, because the specification requires the framework to implicitly resolve the bundle if it's not already resolved. If the bundle's dependencies can't be resolved, `start()` throws a `BundleException` and the bundle can't be used until its dependencies are satisfied. If this happens, you'll typically install additional bundles to satisfy the missing dependencies and try to start the bundle again.

If the bundle has an activator, the framework invokes the `BundleActivator.start()` method when starting the bundle. Any exceptions thrown from the activator result in a failed attempt to start the bundle and an exception being thrown from `Bundle.start()`. One last case where an exception may result is if a bundle tries to start itself; the specification says attempts to do so should result in an `IllegalStateException`.

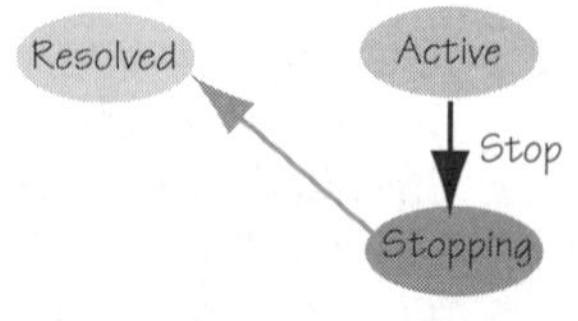

Figure 3.10 The stop-related portion of the bundle lifecycle state diagram

STOP COMMAND

That's it for starting bundles. Now we can look at stopping bundles, which is similar to starting them; see the next listing and figure 3.10.

Listing 3.7 Bundle `stop` command

```
package org.foo.shell;

import org.osgi.framework.Bundle;
import org.osgi.framework.BundleContext;

   public class StopCommand extends BasicCommand {
  public void exec(String id) throws Exception {
    Bundle bundle = getBundle(id);
    bundle.stop();
  }
}
```

Like starting a bundle, stopping a bundle takes a simple call to `Bundle.stop()` on the `Bundle` object retrieved from the specified identifier. As before, you must be mindful of the bundle's state. If it's `UNINSTALLED`, an `Illegal-StateException` results. Either `STARTING` or `STOPPING` blocks until `ACTIVE` or `RESOLVED` is reached, respectively. In the `ACTIVE` state, the bundle transitions to `RESOLVED` via the `STOPPING` state. If the bundle has an activator and the activator's `stop()` method throws an exception, a `BundleException` is thrown. Finally, a bundle isn't supposed to change its own state; trying to do so may result in an `IllegalStateException`.

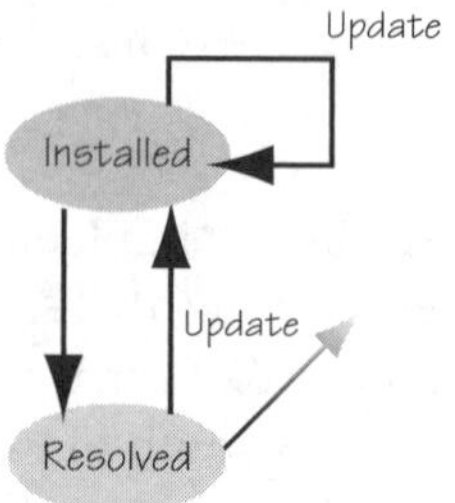

Figure 3.11 The update-related portion of the bundle lifecycle state diagram

UPDATE COMMAND

Let's continue with the `update` command in the following listing (see figure 3.11).

Listing 3.8 Bundle `update` command

```
package org.foo.shell;

import org.osgi.framework.Bundle;
import org.osgi.framework.BundleContext;

  public class UpdateCommand extends BasicCommand {
    public void exec(String id) throws Exception {
    Bundle bundle = getBundle(id);
    bundle.update();
  }
}
```

By now, you may have noticed the pattern we mentioned in the beginning. Most lifecycle operations are methods on the `Bundle` and `BundleContext` objects. The `Bundle.update()` method is no exception, as you can see. The `update()` method is available in two forms: one with no parameters (shown) and one taking an input stream (not shown). The `update` command uses the form without parameters here, which reads the updated bundle JAR file using the original location value as a source URL. If the bundle being updated is in the `ACTIVE` state, it needs to be stopped first, as required by the bundle lifecycle. You don't need to do this explicitly, because the framework does it for you, but it's still good to understand that this occurs because it impacts the application's behavior. The update happens in either the `RESOLVED` or `INSTALLED` state and results in a new revision of the bundle in the `INSTALLED` state. If the bundle is in the `UNINSTALLED` state, an `IllegalStateException` is thrown. As in the `stop` command, a bundle shouldn't try to update itself.

The `Bundle-UpdateLocation` anti-pattern

We should point out an anti-practice for updating a bundle. The OSGi specification provides a third option for updating bundles based on bundle metadata. A bundle may declare a piece of metadata in its bundle manifest called `Bundle-UpdateLocation`. If it's present, `Bundle.update()` with no parameters uses the update location value specified in the metadata as the URL for retrieving the updated bundle JAR file. Using this approach is discouraged because it's confusing if you forget it's set, and it doesn't make sense to bake this sort of information into the bundle.

UNINSTALL COMMAND

You can now wrap up the lifecycle operations by implementing the `uninstall` command, as shown next (see figure 3.12).

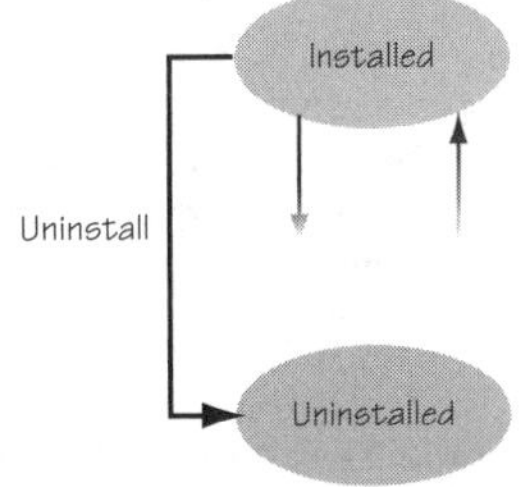

Figure 3.12 The uninstall-related portion of the bundle lifecycle state diagram

To uninstall a bundle, you call the `Bundle.uninstall()` method after retrieving the `Bundle` object associated with the user-supplied bundle identifier. The framework stops the bundle, if necessary. If the bundle is already

UNINSTALLED, an IllegalStateException is thrown. As with the other lifecycle operations, a bundle shouldn't attempt to uninstall itself.

Listing 3.9 Bundle uninstall command

```
package org.foo.shell;

import org.osgi.framework.Bundle;
import org.osgi.framework.BundleContext;

public class UninstallCommand extends BasicCommand {
  public void exec(String id) throws Exception {
    Bundle bundle = getBundle(id);
    bundle.uninstall();
  }
}
```

That's it. You've created a telnet-based shell bundle that you can use in any OSGi framework. But there is one fly in the ointment. Most of the shell commands require the bundle identifier to perform their action, but how does the shell user know which identifier to use? You need some way to inspect the state of the framework's installed bundle set. You'll create a command for that next.

3.3.3 Inspecting framework state

You need one more command to display information about the bundles currently installed in the framework. The next listing shows a simple implementation of a bundles command.

Listing 3.10 Bundle information example

```
package org.foo.shell;

import org.osgi.framework.Bundle;
import org.osgi.framework.BundleContext;
import org.osgi.framework.Constants;

public class BundlesCommand extends BasicCommand {
  public void exec(String args, PrintStream out, PrintStream err)
    throws Exception {
    Bundle[] bundles = m_context.getBundles();

    out.println("  ID      State       Name");

    for (Bundle bundle : bundles) {
      printBundle(
        bundle.getBundleId(), getStateString(bundle.getState()),
        (String) bundle.getHeaders().get(Constants.BUNDLE_NAME),
        bundle.getLocation(), bundle.getSymbolicName(), out);
    }
  }

  private String getStateString(int state) {
    switch (state) {
```

```
        case Bundle.INSTALLED:
          return "INSTALLED";
        case Bundle.RESOLVED:
          return "RESOLVED";
        case Bundle.STARTING:
          return "STARTING";
        case Bundle.ACTIVE:
          return "ACTIVE";
        case Bundle.STOPPING:
          return "STOPPING";
        default:
          return "UNKNOWN";
      }
    }

    private void printBundle(long id, String state, String name,
      String location, String symbolicName) {...}
}
```

The implementation of this command is pretty easy too, because you only need to use `BundleContext.getBundles()` to get an array of all bundles currently installed in the framework. The rest of the implementation loops through the returned array and prints out information from each `Bundle` object. Here you print the bundle identifier, lifecycle state, name, location, and symbolic name for each bundle.

With this command in place, you have everything you need for the simple shell. You can install, start, stop, update, and uninstall bundles and list the currently installed bundles. That was fairly simple, wasn't it? Think about the flexibility at your fingertips versus the amount of effort needed to create the shell. Now you can create applications as easily deployable configurations of bundles that you can manage and evolve as necessary over time.

Before you move back to the paint program, two final lifecycle concepts are worth exploring in order to fully appreciate the approach you'll take to make the paint program dynamically extensible: persistence and events. We'll describe them in the context of the shell example; but as you'll see in the paint example in a couple of pages, they're generally useful tools to have in mind when building OSGi applications.

3.3.4 Persisting bundle state

As we mentioned when discussing bundle activators, the framework creates an instance of a bundle's activator class and uses the same instance for starting and subsequently stopping the bundle. An activator instance is used only once by the framework to start and stop a bundle, after which it's discarded. If the bundle is subsequently restarted, a new activator instance is created. Given this situation, how does a bundle persist state across stops and restarts? Stepping back even further, we mentioned how the framework saves installed bundles into a cache so they can be reloaded the next time the framework starts. How does a bundle persist state across framework sessions? There are several possibilities.

One possibility is to store the information outside the framework, such as in a database or a file, as shown in figure 3.13. The disadvantage of this approach is that the state isn't managed by the framework and may not be cleaned up when the bundle is uninstalled.

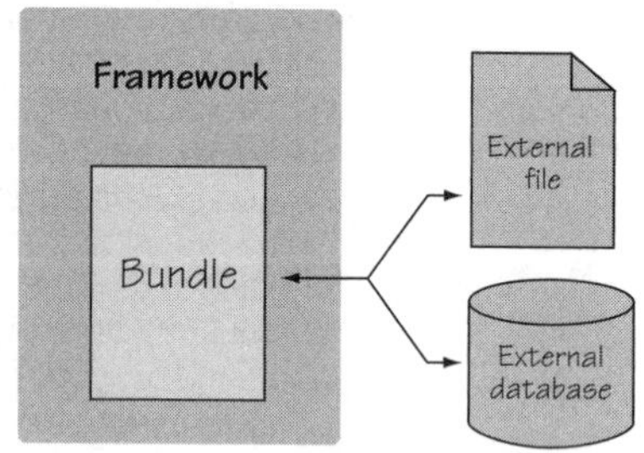

Figure 3.13 Storing state externally

Another possibility is for a bundle to give its state to another bundle that isn't being stopped; then, it can get the state back after it restarts, as shown in figure 3.14. This is a workable approach, and in some cases it makes the most sense.

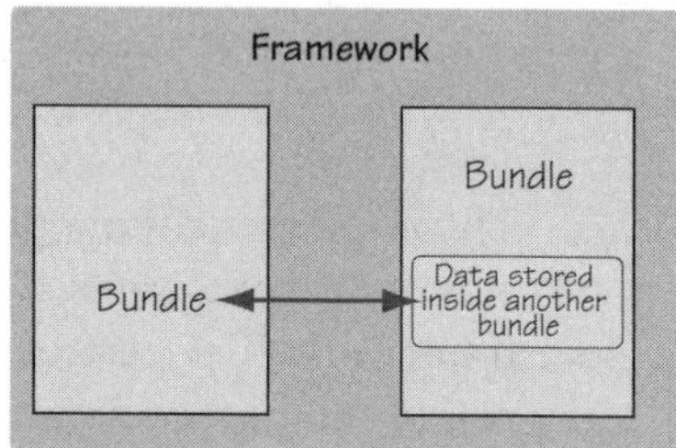

Figure 3.14 Storing state with other bundles

For simplicity, it would be nice to be able to use files, but have them managed by the framework. Such a possibility exists. The framework maintains a private data area in the file system for each installed bundle.

The `BundleContext.getDataFile()` method provides access to your bundle's private data area. When using the private data area, you don't need to worry about where it is on the file system because the framework takes care of that for you, as well as cleaning up in the event of your bundle being uninstalled (see figure 3.15). It may seem odd to not directly use files to store your data; but if you did, it would be impossible for your bundle to clean up during an uninstall. This is because a bundle isn't notified when it's uninstalled. Further, this method simplifies running with security enabled, because bundles can be granted permission to access their private area by the framework.

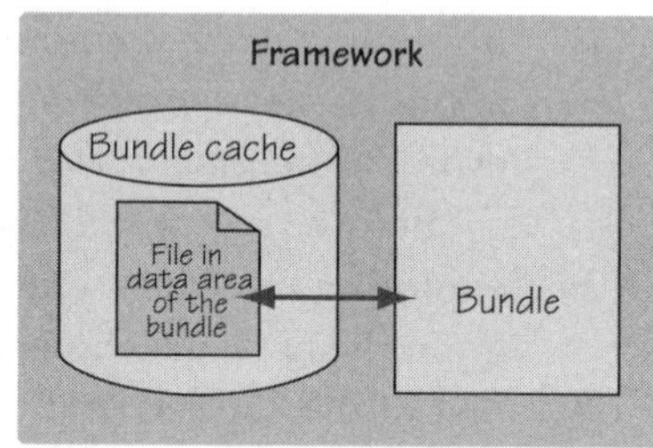

Figure 3.15 Storing state internally

For the shell example, you want to use the private area to persistently save the command history. Here's how the `history` command should work; it prints the commands issued via the shell in reverse order:

```
-> history
bundles
uninstall 2
bundles
update 2
bundles
stop 2
bundles
start 2
bundles
install file:foo.jar
bundles
```

Listing 3.11 shows how you use the bundle's private storage area to save the command history. The bundle activator's `start()` and `stop()` methods also need to be modified to invoke these methods, but these changes aren't shown here, so please refer to the companion code for complete implementation details.

Listing 3.11 Bundle persistent storage example

```
package org.foo.shell;

import java.util.List;

public interface History {
  public List<String> get();
}

public class Activator implements BundleActivator {
  ...
  private void writeHistory(History history, BundleContext context) {
    List<String> list = history.get();
    File log = context.getDataFile("log.txt");
    if (log == null) {
      System.out.println(
        "Unable to persist history - no storage area");
    }
    if (log.exists() && !log.delete()) {
      throw new IOException("Unable to delete previous log file!");
    }
    write(list, log);
  }

  private List<String> readHistory(BundleContext context) {
    List<String> result = new ArrayList<String>();
    File log = context.getDataFile("log.txt");
    if ((log != null) && log.isFile()) {
      read(log, result);
    }
    return result;
  }
}
```

❶ Gets File object

❷ Handles null result when bundle requests file

You use `BundleContext.getDataFile()` to get a `File` object in the bundle's private storage area ❶. The method takes a relative path as a `String` and returns a valid `File` object in the storage area. After you get the `File` object, you can use it normally to create the file, make a subdirectory, or do whatever you want. It's possible for a framework to return `null` when a bundle requests a file; so as you can see ❷, you need to handle this possibility. This can happen because the OSGi framework was designed to run on a variety of devices, some of which may not support a file system. For the shell, you ignore it if there's no file system support, because the `history` command is non-critical functionality.

If you want to retrieve a `File` object for the root directory of your bundle's storage area, you can call `getDataFile()` with an empty string. Your bundle is responsible for managing the content of its data area, but you don't need to worry about cleaning up when it's uninstalled, because the framework takes care of this.

Plan ahead

Keep in mind that your bundle may be updated. Due to this possibility, you should design your bundles so they properly deal with previously saved state, because they may start with a private area from an older version of the bundle. The best approach is for your bundles to seamlessly migrate old state formats to new state formats if possible. One tricky issue, though, is that the update lifecycle operation may also be used to downgrade a bundle. In this case, your bundle may have difficulty dealing with the newer state formats, so it's probably best if you implement your bundles to delete any existing state if they can't understand it. Otherwise, you can always uninstall the newer bundle first and then install the older version instead of downgrading.

You could finish the `history` command, but let's try to make it a little more interesting by keeping track of what's going on inside the framework. You can record not only the issued commands, but also the impact they have on the framework. The next section shows how you can achieve this using the framework's event-notification mechanism.

3.3.5 Listening for events

The OSGi framework is a dynamic execution environment. To create bundles and, ultimately, applications that are flexible enough to not only cope with but also take advantage of this dynamism, you need to pay attention to execution-time changes. The lifecycle layer API provides access to a lot of information, but it isn't easy to poll for changes; it's much more convenient if you can be notified when changes occur. To make this possible, the OSGi framework supports two types of events: `BundleEvents` and `FrameworkEvents`. The former event type reports changes in the lifecycle of bundles, whereas the latter reports framework-related issues.

You can use the normal Java listener pattern in your bundles to receive these events. The `BundleContext` object has methods to register `BundleListener` and `FrameworkListener` objects for receiving `BundleEvent` and `FrameworkEvent` notifications, respectively. The following listing shows how you implement the `history` command. You record all executed commands as well as the events they cause during execution.

Listing 3.12 Bundle and framework event listener example

```
package org.foo.shell;

import java.io.PrintStream;
import java.util.ArrayList;
import java.util.Collections;
import java.util.List;

import org.osgi.framework.BundleEvent;
import org.osgi.framework.BundleListener;
```

```
import org.osgi.framework.FrameworkEvent;
import org.osgi.framework.FrameworkListener;

public class HistoryDecorator implements Command,
  History, FrameworkListener, BundleListener {
  private final List<String> m_history =
    Collections.synchronizedList(new ArrayList<String>());     <-- 1 Defines m_history member
  private final Command m_next;

  public HistoryDecorator(Command next, List<String> history) {
    m_next = next;
    m_history.addAll(history);
  }

  public void exec(String args, PrintStream out, PrintStream err)
    throws Exception {
    try {
      m_next.exec(args, out, err);        <-- 2 Forwards command execution
    } finally {
      m_history.add(args);
    }
  }

  public List<String> get() {
    return new ArrayList<String>(m_history);
  }

  public void frameworkEvent(FrameworkEvent event) {
    m_history.add("\tFrameworkEvent(type=" + event.getType() +
      ",bundle=" + event.getBundle() +
      ",source=" + event.getSource() +
      ",throwable=" + event.getThrowable() + ")");
  }

  public void bundleChanged(BundleEvent event) {
    m_history.add("\tBundleEvent(type=" + event.getType() +
      ",bundle=" + event.getBundle() +
      ",source=" + event.getSource() + ")");
  }
}
```

You use an interceptor pattern to wrap the commands so you can record the issued commands. The wrapper also records any events in the history by implementing the `BundleListener` and `FrameworkListener` interfaces. You maintain a list of all issued commands and received events in the `m_history` member defined at ❶. The history wrapper command forwards the command execution to the command ❷ and stores it in the history list.

The wrapper implements the single `FrameworkListener.frameworkEvent()`. Here, you record the event information in the history list. The most important part of the event is its type. Framework events are of one of the following types:

- `FrameworkEvent.STARTED`—Indicates the framework has performed all initialization and has finished starting up.
- `FrameworkEvent.INFO`—Indicates some information of general interest in various situations.

- FrameworkEvent.WARNING—Indicates a warning. Not crucial, but may indicate a potential error.
- FrameworkEvent.ERROR—Indicates an error. Requires immediate attention.
- FrameworkEvent.PACKAGES_REFRESHED—Indicates the framework has refreshed some shared packages. We'll discuss what this means in section 3.5.
- FrameworkEvent.STARTLEVEL_CHANGED—Indicates the framework has changed its start level. We'll discuss what this means in chapter 10.

The wrapper also implements the single BundleListener.bundleChanged() method. Here, you also record the event information in the history list. Bundle events have one of the following types:

- BundleEvent.INSTALLED—Indicates a bundle was installed
- BundleEvent.RESOLVED—Indicates a bundled was resolved
- BundleEvent.STARTED—Indicates a bundle was started
- BundleEvent.STOPPED—Indicates a bundle was stopped
- BundleEvent.UPDATED—Indicates a bundle was updated
- BundleEvent.UNINSTALLED—Indicates a bundle was uninstalled
- BundleEvent.UNRESOLVED—Indicates a bundle was unresolved

You register the listeners using the bundle context as follows:

```
private void addListener(BundleContext context,
    BundleListener bundleListener, FrameworkListener frameworkListener) {
    context.addBundleListener(bundleListener);
    context.addFrameworkListener(frameworkListener);
}
```

The example doesn't show how to remove the listeners, which requires calls to the removeBundleListener() and removeFrameworkListener() methods on the bundle context. It's not necessary to remove the listeners, because the framework will do so automatically when the bundle is stopped; this makes sense because the bundle context is no longer valid after the bundle is stopped. You only need to explicitly remove your listeners if you want to stop listening to events while your bundle is active.

For the most part, the framework delivers events asynchronously. It's possible for framework implementations to deliver them synchronously, but typically they don't because it complicates concurrency handling. Sometimes you need synchronous delivery because you need to perform an action as the event is happening, so to speak. This is possible for BundleEvents by registering a listener implementing the SynchronousBundleListener interface instead of BundleListener. The two interfaces look the same, but the framework delivers events synchronously to SynchronousBundleListeners, meaning the listener is notified during the processing of the event. Synchronous bundle listeners are processed before normal bundle listeners. This allows you to take action when a certain operation is triggered; for example, you can give permissions to a bundle at the moment it's installed. The following event types are only sent to SynchronousBundleListeners:

- `BundleEvent.STARTING`—Indicates a bundle is about to be started
- `BundleEvent.STOPPING`—Indicates a bundle is about to be stopped

Synchronous bundle listeners are sometimes necessary (as you'll see in the paint example in the next section), but should be used with caution. They can lead to concurrency issues if you try to do too much in the callback; as always, keep your callbacks as short and simple as possible and don't call foreign code while holding a lock. In all other cases, the thread invoking the listener callback method is undefined. Events become much more important when you start to write more sophisticated bundles that take full advantage of the bundle lifecycle.

3.3.6 *Bundle suicide*

We've mentioned it numerous times: a bundle isn't supposed to change its own state. But what if a bundle wants to change its own state? Good question. This is one of the more complicated aspects of the lifecycle layer, and there are potentially negative issues involved.

The central issue is that if a bundle stops itself, it finds itself in a state it shouldn't be in. Its `BundleActivator.stop()` method has been invoked, which means its bundle context is no longer valid. Additionally, the framework has cleaned up its bookkeeping for the bundle and has released any framework facilities it was using, such as unregistering all of its event listeners. The situation is even worse if a bundle tries to uninstall itself, because the framework will likely release its class loader. In short, the bundle is in a hostile environment, and it may not be able to function properly.

Because its bundle context is no longer valid, a stopped bundle can no longer use the functionality provided by the framework. Most method calls on an invalid bundle context will throw `IllegalStateExceptions`. Even if the bundle's class loader is released, this may not pose a serious issue if the bundle doesn't need any new classes, because the class loader won't be garbage collected until the bundle stops using it. But you're not guaranteed to be able to load new classes if the bundle was uninstalled. In this case, the framework may have closed the JAR file associated with the bundle. Already-loaded classes continue to load, but all bets are off when attempting to load new classes.

Depending on your bundle, you may run into other issues too. If your bundle creates and uses threads, it's typically a good idea for it to wait for all of its threads to complete when its `BundleActivator.stop()` method is called. If the bundle tries to stop itself on its own thread, that same thread can end up in a cycle waiting for other sibling threads to complete. In the end, the thread waits forever. For example, the simple shell uses a thread to listen for telnet connections and then uses secondary threads to execute the commands issued on those connections. If one of the secondary threads attempts to stop the shell bundle itself, it ends up waiting in the shell bundle's `BundleActivator.stop()` method for the connection thread to stop all of the secondary threads. Because the calling thread is one of the secondary threads, it'll end up waiting forever for the connection thread to complete. You have to be careful of these types of situations, and they're not always obvious.

Under normal circumstances, you shouldn't try to stop, uninstall, or update your own bundle. OK—that should be enough disclaimers. Let's look at a case where you may need to do it anyway. We'll use the shell as an example, because it provides a means to update bundles, and it may need to update itself. What do you have to do to allow a user to update the shell bundle via the shell command line? You must do two things to be safe:

1. Use a new thread when you stop, update, or uninstall your own bundle.
2. Do nothing in the new thread after calling stop, update, or uninstall.

You need to do this to prevent yourself from waiting forever for the shell thread to return when you get stopped and to avoid the potential ugliness of the hostile environment in which the thread will find itself. The following listing shows the changes to the implementation of the `stop` command to accommodate this scenario.

Listing 3.13 Example of how a bundle can stop itself

```
package org.foo.shell;

import java.io.PrintStream;
import org.osgi.framework.Bundle;
import org.osgi.framework.BundleException;

class StopCommand extends BasicCommand {
  public void exec(String args, PrintStream out, PrintStream err)
    throws Exception {
    Bundle bundle = getBundle(args);

    if (bundle.equals(m_context.getBundle())){        ❶ Gets reference to
      new SelfStopThread(bundle).start();                bundle representation
    } else {
      bundle.stop();
    }
  }

  private static final class SelfStopThread extends Thread {
    private final Bundle m_self;

    public SelfStopThread(Bundle self) {
      m_self = self;
    }

    public void run() {
      try {                                  ❷ Executes
        m_self.stop();                          Bundle.stop()
      } catch (BundleException e) {
        // Ignore
      }
    }
  }
}
```

You use the `BundleContext.getBundle()` method to get a reference to the bundle representation and compare it to the target bundle ❶. When the target is the shell bundle, you need to stop it using a different thread. For this reason, you create and start a new thread of type `SelfStopThread`, which executes the `Bundle.stop()` method ❷. There's one final point to note in this example: you change the behavior of stopping a bundle in this case from synchronous to asynchronous. Ultimately, this shouldn't matter much, because the bundle will be stopped anyway.

You should also modify the implementation of the `update` and `uninstall` commands the same way. Using the shell to stop the framework (the system bundle) also requires special consideration. Why? Because stopping the system bundle causes the framework to stop, which stops every other bundle. This means you'll stop your bundle indirectly, so you should make sure you're using a new thread.

We hope you now have a good understanding of what is possible with OSGi's lifecycle layer. Next, you'll apply this knowledge to the paint program.

3.4 Dynamically extending the paint program

Let's look at how you can use the individual parts of the lifecycle layer to dynamically extend the paint program. As you'll recall from the last chapter, you first converted a nonmodular version of the paint program into a modular one using an interface-based programming approach for the architecture. This is great because you can reuse the resulting bundles with minimal extra work. The bundles containing the shape implementations don't need to change, except for some additional metadata in their manifest. You just need to modify the paint program to make it possible for shapes to be added and removed at execution time.

The approach you'll take is a well-known pattern in the OSGi world, called the *extender pattern*. The main idea behind the extender pattern is to model dynamic extensibility on the lifecycle events (installing, resolving, starting, stopping, and so on) of other bundles. Typically, some bundle in the application acts as the *extender*: it listens for bundles being started and/or stopped. When a bundle is started, the extender probes it to see if it's an *extension* bundle. The extender looks in the bundle's manifest (using `Bundle.getHeaders()`) or the bundle's content (using `Bundle.getEntry()`) for specific metadata it recognizes. If the bundle does contain an extension, the extension is described by the metadata. The extender reads the metadata and performs the necessary tasks on behalf of the extension bundle to integrate it into the application. The extender also listens for extension bundles to be stopped, in which case it removes the associated extensions from the application.

That's the general description of the extender pattern, which is shown in figure 3.16. Let's look at how you'll use it in the paint program.

You'll treat the shape implementations as extensions. The extension metadata will be contained in the bundle manifest and will describe which class implements the shape contained in the shape bundle. The extender will use this information to load the shape class from the bundle, instantiate it, and inject it into the application when an extension bundle is activated. If a shape bundle is stopped, the extender will remove it from the application. Figure 3.17 illustrates this usage scenario.

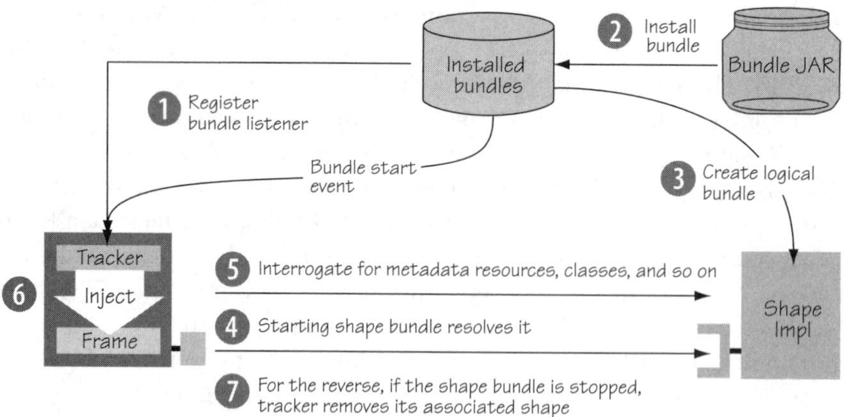

Figure 3.16 Extender pattern overview

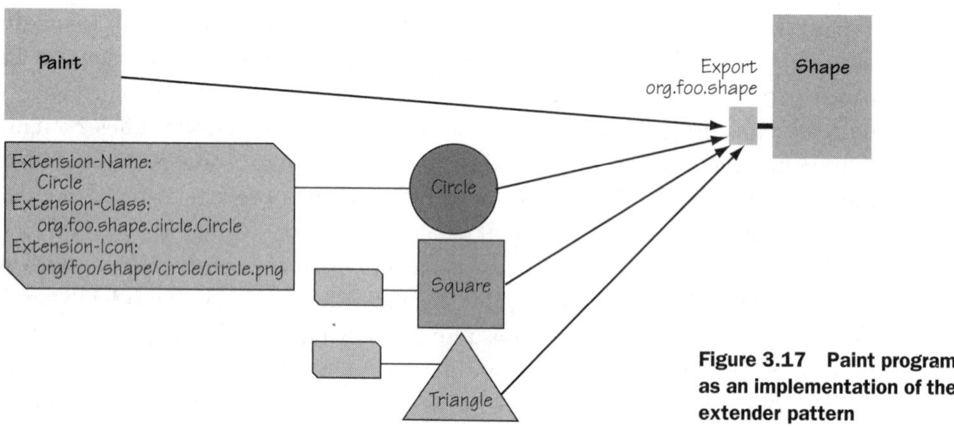

Figure 3.17 Paint program as an implementation of the extender pattern

Let's dive in and start converting the application. The first thing you need to do is define the extension metadata for shape bundles to describe their shape implementation. In the following snippet, you add a couple of constants to the `SimpleShape` interface for extension metadata property names; it's not strictly necessary to add these, but it's good programming practice to use constants:

```
package org.foo.shape;

import java.awt.Graphics2D;
import java.awt.Point;

public interface SimpleShape {
  public static final String NAME_PROPERTY = "Extension-Name";
  public static final String ICON_PROPERTY = "Extension-Icon";
  public static final String CLASS_PROPERTY = "Extension-Class";

  public void draw(Graphics2D g2, Point p);
}
```

The constants indicate the name of the shape, the bundle resource file for the shape's icon, and the bundle class name for the shape's class. The `draw()` method draws the shape on the canvas,

From the constants, it's fairly straightforward to see how you'll describe a specific shape implementation. You only need to know the name, an icon, and the class implementing the shape. As an example, for the circle implementation you add the following entries to its bundle manifest:

```
Extension-Name: Circle
Extension-Icon: org/foo/shape/circle/circle.png
Extension-Class: org.foo.shape.circle.Circle
```

The name is just a string, and the icon and class refer to a resource file and a class inside the bundle JAR file, respectively. You add similar metadata to the manifests of all shape implementation bundles, which converts them all to extensions. Next, you need to tweak the architecture of the paint program to make it cope with dynamic addition and removal of shapes. Figure 3.18 captures the updated design.

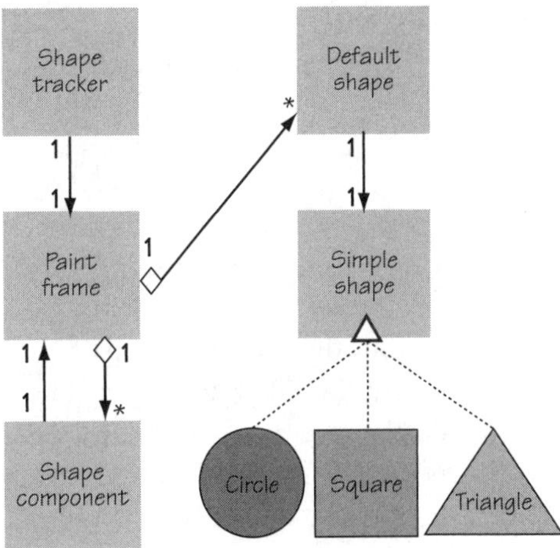

Figure 3.18 Dynamic paint program class relationships

Comparing the new design to the original, you add two new classes: `ShapeTracker` and `DefaultShape`. They help you dynamically adapt the paint frame to deal with `SimpleShape` implementations dynamically appearing and disappearing. In a nutshell, the `ShapeTracker` is used to track when extension bundles start or stop, in which case it adds or removes `DefaultShapes` to/from the `PaintFrame`, respectively.

The concrete implementation of the `ShapeTracker` is a subclass of another class, called `BundleTracker`. The latter class is a generic class for tracking when bundles are started or stopped. Because `BundleTracker` is somewhat long, we'll divide it across multiple listings; the first part is shown next.

Listing 3.14 `BundleTracker` class declaration and constructor

```
package org.foo.paint;

import java.util.*;
import org.osgi.framework.*;

public abstract class BundleTracker {
  final Set m_bundleSet = new HashSet();
  final BundleContext m_context;
  final SynchronousBundleListener m_listener;
  boolean m_open;
```

```
public BundleTracker(BundleContext context) {
  m_context = context;
  m_listener = new SynchronousBundleListener() {
    public void bundleChanged(BundleEvent evt) {        ❶ Implements bundler listener's method
      synchronized (BundleTracker.this) {
        if (!m_open) {                                   ❷ Checks if tracking bundles
          return;
        }
        if (evt.getType() == BundleEvent.STARTED) {
          if (!m_bundleSet.contains(evt.getBundle())) {
            m_bundleSet.add(evt.getBundle());            ❸ Adds bundle to list
            addedBundle(evt.getBundle());
          }
        } else if (evt.getType() == BundleEvent.STOPPING) {
          if (m_bundleSet.contains(evt.getBundle())) {
            m_bundleSet.remove(evt.getBundle());
            removedBundle(evt.getBundle());
          }
        }
      }
    }
  };
}
```

The bundle tracker is constructed with a `BundleContext` object, which is used to listen for bundle lifecycle events. The tracker uses a `SynchronousBundleListener` to listen to events because a regular `BundleListener` doesn't get notified when a bundle enters the `STOPPING` state, only `STOPPED`. You need to react on the `STOPPING` event instead of the `STOPPED` event because it's still possible to use the stopping bundle, which hasn't been stopped yet; a potential subclass might need to do this if it needed to access the stopping bundle's `BundleContext` object. The bundle listener's single method ❶ makes sure the tracker is tracking bundles ❷. If so, for started events, it adds the associated bundle to its bundle list ❸ and invokes the abstract `addedBundle()` method. Likewise, for stopping events, it removes the bundle from its bundle list and invokes the abstract `removedBundle()` method.

The following listing shows the next portion of the `BundleTracker`.

Listing 3.15 Opening and using a `BundleTracker`

```
public synchronized void open() {
  if (!m_open) {
    m_open = true;
    m_context.addBundleListener(m_listener);
    Bundle[] bundles = m_context.getBundles();
    for (int i = 0; i < bundles.length; i++) {
      if (bundles[i].getState() == ACTIVE) {
        m_bundleSet.add(bundles[i]);
        addedBundles(bundles[i]);
      }
    }
  }
}
```

```
  }

  public synchronized Bundle[] getBundles() {
    return (Bundle[]) m_bundleSet.toArray(
      new Bundle[m_bundleSet.size()]);
  }

  protected abstract void addedBundle(Bundle bundle);

  protected abstract void removedBundle(Bundle bundle);
```

To start a BundleTracker instance tracking bundles, you must invoke its open() method. This methods registers a bundle event listener and processes any existing ACTIVE bundles by adding them to its bundle list and invoking the abstract addedBundle() method. The getBundles() method provides access to the current list of active bundles being tracked. Because BundleTracker is abstract, subclasses must provide implementations of addedBundle() and removedBundle() to perform custom processing of added and removed bundles, respectively.

The last portion of the BundleTracker is as follows.

Listing 3.16 Disposing of a BundleTracker

```
  public synchronized void close() {
    if (m_open) {
      m_open = false;
      m_context.removeBundleListener(m_listener);
      Bundle[] bundles = (Bundle[])
        m_bundleSet.toArray(new Bundle[m_bundleSet.size()]);
      for (int i = 0; i < bundles.length; i++) {
        if (m_bundleSet.remove(bundles[i])) {
          removedBundle(bundles[i]);
        }
      }
    }
  }
}
```

Calling BundleTracker.close() stops it from tracking bundles. This removes its bundle listener, removes each currently tracked bundle from its bundle list, and invokes the abstract removedBundle() method.

Standardizing bundle trackers

Tracking bundles is a useful building block. It's so useful that the OSGi Alliance decided to create a standard BundleTracker for the R4.2 specification. The R4.2 BundleTracker is more complicated than the one presented here, but it follows the same basic principles; we'll discuss it in chapter 15.

Now that you know how the BundleTracker works, let's return to its subclass, ShapeTracker. The heart of this subclass is the processBundle() method shown next, which processes added and removed bundles.

Listing 3.17 Processing shapes in `ShapeTracker`

```
private void processBundle(int action, Bundle bundle) {
  Dictionary dict = bundle.getHeaders();
  String name = (String) dict.get(SimpleShape.NAME_PROPERTY);      <-- ❶ Checks if bundle is an extension
  if (name == null) {
    return;
  }

  switch (action) {
    case ADDED:                                                      <-- ❷ Adds shape to paint frame
      String iconPath = (String) dict.get(SimpleShape.ICON_PROPERTY);
      Icon icon = new ImageIcon(bundle.getResource(iconPath));
      String className = (String) dict.get(SimpleShape.CLASS_PROPERTY);
      m_frame.addShape(name, icon,
        new DefaultShape(m_context, bundle.getBundleId(), className));
      break;
    case REMOVED:                                                    <-- ❸ Removes shape
      m_frame.removeShape(name);
      break;
  }
}
```

`ShapeTracker` overrides `BundleTracker`'s `addedBundle()` and `removedBundle()` abstract methods to invoke `processBundle()` in either case. You determine whether the bundle is an extension by probing its manifest for the `Extension-Name` property ❶. Any bundle without this property in its manifest is ignored. If the bundle being added contains a shape, the code grabs the metadata from the bundle's manifest headers and adds the shape to the paint frame wrapped as a `DefaultShape` ❷. For the icon metadata, you use `Bundle.getResource()` to load it. If the bundle being removed contains a shape, you remove the shape from the paint frame ❸.

`DefaultShape`, shown in listing 3.18, serves two purposes. It implements the `SimpleShape` interface and is responsible for lazily creating the shape implementation using the `Extension-Class` metadata. It also serves as a placeholder for the shape if and when the shape is removed from the application. You didn't have to deal with this situation in the original paint program, but now shape implementations can appear or disappear at any time when bundles are installed, started, stopped, and uninstalled. In such situations, the `DefaultShape` draws a placeholder icon on the paint canvas for any departed shape implementations.

Listing 3.18 `DefaultShape` example

```
class DefaultShape implements SimpleShape {
  private SimpleShape m_shape;
  private ImageIcon m_icon;
  private BundleContext m_context;
  private long m_bundleId;
  private String m_className;

  public DefaultShape() {}                                  <-- Default constructor
```

```
  public DefaultShape(BundleContext context, long bundleId,
    String className) {
    m_context = context;
    m_bundleId = bundleId;
    m_className = className;
  }

  public void draw(Graphics2D g2, Point p) {
    if (m_context != null) {
      try {
        if (m_shape == null) {
          Bundle bundle = m_context.getBundle(m_bundleId);
          Class clazz = bundle.loadClass(m_className);
          m_shape = (SimpleShape) clazz.newInstance();
        }
        m_shape.draw(g2, p);
        return;
      } catch (Exception ex) {}
    }

    if (m_icon == null) {
      try {
        m_icon = new ImageIcon(this.getClass().getResource(
          "underc.png"));
      } catch (Exception ex) {
        ex.printStackTrace();
        g2.setColor(Color.red);
        g2.fillRect(0, 0, 60, 60);
        return;
      }
    }
    g2.drawImage(m_icon.getImage(), 0, 0, null);
  }
}
```

Constructor with extension data

Creates extension and delegates to it if available

Draws default image if no extension

In summary, when the paint application is started, its activator creates and opens a `ShapeTracker`. This tracks `STARTED` and `STOPPED` bundle events, interrogating the associated bundle for extension metadata. For every started extension bundle, it adds a new `DefaultShape` for the bundle to the paint frame, which creates the shape implementation, if needed, using the extension metadata. When the bundle stops, the `ShapeTracker` removes the shape from the paint frame. When a drawn shape is no longer available, the `DefaultShape` is used to draw a placeholder shape on the canvas instead. If the departed shape reappears, the placeholder is removed and the real shape is drawn on the canvas again.

Now you have a dynamically extensible paint program, as demonstrated in section 3.2.1. Although we didn't show the activator for the paint program, it's reasonably simple and only creates the framework and shape tracker on start and disposes of them on stop. Overall, this is a good example of how easy it is to make a modularized application take advantage of the lifecycle layer to make it dynamically extensible. As a bonus, you no longer need to export the implementation packages of the shape implementations. What you're still missing at this point is a discussion about how the lifecycle and module layers interact with each other, which we'll get into next.

3.5 Lifecycle and modularity

A two-way relationship exists between OSGi's lifecycle and module layers. The lifecycle layer manages which bundles are installed into the framework, which obviously impacts how the module layer resolves dependencies among bundles. The module layer uses the metadata in bundles to make sure all their dependencies are satisfied before they can be used. This symbiotic relationship creates a chicken-and-egg situation when you want to use your bundles; to use a bundle you have to install it, but to install a bundle you must have a bundle context, which are only given to bundles. This close relationship is also obvious in how the framework resolves bundle dependencies, especially when bundles are dynamically installed and/or removed. Let's explore this relationship by first looking into bundle dependency resolution.

3.5.1 Resolving bundles

The act of resolving a bundle happens at the discretion of the framework, as long as it happens before any classes are loaded from the bundle. Often, when resolving a given bundle, the framework ends up resolving another bundle to satisfy a dependency of the original bundle. This can lead to cascading dependency resolution, because in order for the framework to use a bundle to satisfy the requirements of another bundle, the satisfying bundle too must be resolved, and so on. Because the framework resolves dependencies when needed, it's possible to mostly ignore transitioning bundles to the `RESOLVED` state; you can start a bundle and know the framework will resolve it before starting it, if possible. This is great compared to the standard Java way, where you can run into missing dependencies at any point during the lifetime of your application.

But what if you want to make sure a given bundle resolves correctly? For example, maybe you want to know in advance whether an installed bundle can be started. In this case, there's a way to ask the framework to resolve the bundle directly, but it's not a method on `Bundle` like most other lifecycle operations. Instead, you use the Package Admin Service. The Package Admin Service is represented as an interface and is shown here:

```
public interface PackageAdmin {
  static final int BUNDLE_TYPE_FRAGMENT = 0x00000001;
  Bundle getBundle(Class clazz);
  Bundle[] getBundles(String symbolicName, String versionRange);
  int getBundleType(Bundle bundle);
  ExportedPackage getExportedPackage(String name);
  ExportedPackage[] getExportedPackages(Bundle bundle);
  ExportedPackage[] getExportedPackages(String name);
  Bundle[] getFragments(Bundle bundle);
  RequiredBundle[] getRequiredBundles(String symbolicName);
  Bundle[] getHosts(Bundle bundle);
  void refreshPackages(Bundle[] bundles);
  boolean resolveBundles(Bundle[] bundles);
}
```

You can explicitly resolve a bundle with the `resolveBundles()` method, which takes an array of bundles and returns a Boolean flag indicating whether the bundles could be resolved. The Package Admin Service can do a bit more than resolving bundles, and it's a fairly important part of the framework; it also supports the following operations, among others:

- *Determines which bundle owns a particular class*—In rare circumstances, you may need to know which bundle owns a particular class. You can accomplish this with the `getBundle()` method, which takes a `Class` and returns the `Bundle` to which it belongs.
- *Introspects how the framework resolves bundle dependencies*—You can use the `getExportedPackage()` family of methods to find out which bundles are importing a given package, whereas other methods inspect other types of dependencies we won't talk about until chapter 5, such as `getRequiredBundles()` and `getFragments()`.
- *Refreshes the dependency resolution for bundles*—Because the installed set of bundles can evolve over time, sometimes you need to have the framework recalculate bundle dependencies. You can do this with the `refreshBundles()` method.

The most important feature of the Package Admin Service isn't the ability to resolve bundles or introspect dependencies; it's the ability to refresh bundle dependencies, which is another tool needed for managing bundles. But before we get into the details of refreshing bundles, let's finish the discussion of explicitly resolving bundles.

To demonstrate how to use the Package Admin Service to explicitly resolve a bundle, you'll create a new `resolve` command for the shell to instigate bundle resolution, as shown next.

Listing 3.19 Bundle `resolve` command

```
package org.foo.shell;

import java.io.PrintStream;
import java.util.*;
import org.osgi.framework.Bundle;
import org.osgi.service.packageadmin.PackageAdmin;

public class ResolveCommand extends BasicCommand {

  public void exec(String args, PrintStream out, PrintStream err)
    throws Exception {
    boolean success;
    if (args == null) {
      success =
        getPackageAdminService().resolveBundles(null);
    } else {
      List<Bundle> bundles = new ArrayList<Bundle>();
      StringTokenizer tok = new StringTokenizer(args);
      while (tok.hasMoreTokens()) {
        bundles.add(getBundle(tok.nextToken()));
      }
      success = getPackageAdminService().resolveBundles(
        bundles.toArray(newBundle[bundles.size()]));
```

```
    }
    out.println(success ? "Success" : "Failure");
  }

  private PackageAdmin getPackageAdminService() {...}
}
```

We won't discuss the details of how you obtain the Package Admin Service until the next chapter; for now, you use the `getPackageAdminService()` method. If the `resolve` command is executed with no arguments, you invoke `resolveBundles()` with `null`, which causes the framework to attempt to resolve all unresolved bundles. Otherwise, you parse the argument as a list of whitespace-separated bundle identifiers. For each identifier, you get its associated `Bundle` object and add it to a list. After you've retrieved the complete list of bundles, you pass them in as an array to `resolveBundles()`. The framework attempts to resolve any unresolved bundles of those specified.

It's worthwhile to understand that the framework may resolve bundles in addition to those that were specified. The specified bundles are the root of the framework's resolve process; the framework will resolve any additional unresolved bundles necessary to resolve the specified roots.

Resolving a bundle is a fairly easy process, because the framework does all the hard work for you. You'd think that'd be it. As long as your bundle's dependencies are resolved, you have nothing to worry about, right? It turns out the dynamic nature of the bundle lifecycle makes this an invalid assumption. Sometimes you need to have the framework recalculate a bundle's dependencies. You're probably wondering, "Why?" We'll tell you all about it in the next section.

3.5.2 Refreshing bundles

The lifecycle layer allows you to deploy and manage your application's bundles. Up until now we've focused on installing, resolving, and starting bundles, but there are other interesting bundle lifecycle operations. How about updating or uninstalling a bundle? In and of themselves, these operations are as conceptually simple as the other lifecycle operations. We certainly understand what it means to update or uninstall a bundle. The details are a little more complicated. When you update or uninstall a resolved bundle, you stand a good chance of disrupting your system. This is the place where you can start to see the impact of the framework's dynamic lifecycle management.

The simple case is updating or uninstalling a self-contained bundle. In this case, the disruption is limited to the specific bundle. Even if the bundle imports packages from other bundles, the disruption is limited to the specific bundle being updated or uninstalled. In either case, the framework stops the bundle if it's active. In the case of updating, the framework updates the bundle's content and restarts it if it was previously active. Complications arise if other bundles depend on the bundle being updated or uninstalled. Such dependencies can cause a cascading disruption to your application, if the dependent bundles also have bundles depending on them.

Why do dependencies complicate the issue? Consider updating a given bundle. Other dependent bundles have potentially loaded classes from the old version of the bundle. They can't just start loading classes from the new version of the bundle, because they would see old versions of the classes they already loaded mixed with new versions of classes loaded after the update. This would be inconsistent. In the case of an uninstalled bundle, the situation is more dire, because you can't pull the rug out from under the dependent bundles.

It's worthwhile to limit the disruptions caused by bundle updates or uninstalls. The framework provides such control by making updating and uninstalling bundles a two-step process. Conceptually, the first step prepares the operation; and the second step, called *refreshing*, enacts its. Refreshing recalculates the dependencies of the impacted bundles. How does this help? It allows you to control when the changeover to the new bundle version or removal of a bundle occurs for updates and uninstalls, respectively, as shown in figure 3.19.

We say this is a two-step process, but what happens in the first step? For updates, the new bundle version is put in place, but the old version is still kept around so bundles depending on it can continue loading classes from it. You may be thinking, "Does this mean two versions of the bundle are installed at the same time?" Effectively, the answer is, yes. And each time you perform an update without a refresh, you introduce yet another version. For uninstalls, the bundle is removed from the installed list of bundles, but it isn't removed from memory. Again, the framework keeps it around so dependent bundles can continue to load classes from it.

For example, imagine you want to update a set of bundles. It would be fairly inconvenient if the framework refreshed all dependent bundles after each individual update. With this two-step approach, you can update all bundles in the set and then trigger one refresh of the framework at the end. You can experience a similar situation if you install a bundle providing a newer version of a package. Existing resolved bundles importing an older version of the package won't be automatically rewired to the new bundle unless they're refreshed. Again, it's nice to be able to control the point in time when this happens. It's a fairly common scenario when updating your application that some of your bundles are updated, some are uninstalled, and some are installed; so a way to control when these changes are enacted is helpful.

You trigger a refresh by using the Package Admin Service again. To illustrate how to use it, let's add a `refresh` command to the shell, as shown next.

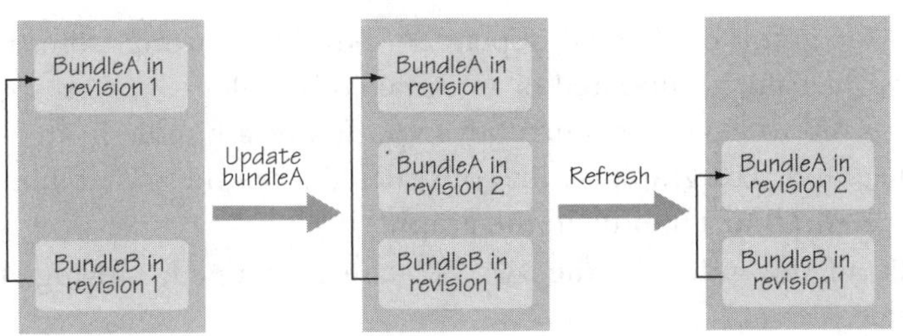

Figure 3.19 Updating and refreshing bundles is a two-step process. Most of the work normally takes place in the second step during the framework refresh operation.

Listing 3.20 Bundle `refresh` command

```
package org.foo.shell;

import java.io.PrintStream;
import java.util.*;
import org.osgi.framework.Bundle;
import org.osgi.service.packageadmin.PackageAdmin;

public class RefreshCommand extends BasicCommand {

  public void exec(String args, PrintStream out, PrintStream err)
    throws Exception {
    if (args == null) {
      getPackageAdminService().refreshPackages(null);
    } else {
      List<Bundle> bundles = new ArrayList<Bundle>();
      StringTokenizer tok = new StringTokenizer(args);
      while (tok.hasMoreTokens()) {
        bundles.add(getBundle(tok.nextToken()));       // ❶ Lists bundles to be refreshed
      }
      getPackageAdminService().refreshPackages(        // ❷ Passes array of bundles to Package Admin Service
        bundles.toArray(new Bundle[bundles.size()]));
    }
  }

  private PackageAdmin getPackageAdminService() {...}
}
```

Just as in the `resolve` command, you rely on the magic method to get the Package Admin Service. You use the `PackageAdmin.refreshPackages()` method to refresh bundles. If no arguments are given to the command, you pass in `null` to the Package Admin Service. This results in the framework refreshing all previously updated and uninstalled bundles since the last refresh. This captures the update and uninstall cases presented earlier, but it doesn't help with the rewiring case. You achieve that by passing in the specific bundles you want refreshed. For this case, the `refresh` command accepts an argument of whitespace-separated bundle identifiers. You parse their identifiers out of the supplied argument, retrieve their associated `Bundle` object, and add them to a list to be refreshed ❶. You then pass in the array of bundles to refresh to the Package Admin Service ❷.

The `PackageAdmin.refreshPackages()` method updates or removes packages exported by the bundles being refreshed. The method returns to the caller immediately and performs the following steps on a separate thread:

1. It computes the graph of affected dependent bundles, starting from the specified bundles (or from all updated or uninstalled bundles if `null` is specified). Any bundle wired to a package currently exported by a bundle in the graph is added to the graph. The graph is fully constructed when there is no bundle outside the graph wired to a bundle in the graph.
2. Each bundle in the graph in the `ACTIVE` state is stopped, moving it to the `RESOLVED` state.

3. Each bundle in the graph in the RESOLVED state, including those that were stopped, is unresolved and moved to the INSTALLED state. This means the bundles' dependencies are no longer resolved.
4. Each bundle in the graph in the UNINSTALLED state is removed from the graph and completely removed from the framework (is free to be garbage collected). You're back to a fresh starting state for the affected bundles.
5. For the remaining bundles in the graph, the framework restarts any previously ACTIVE bundles, which resolves them and any bundles on which they depend.
6. When everything is done, the framework fires an event of type FrameworkEvent.PACKAGES_REFRESHED.

As a result of these steps, it's possible that some of the previously ACTIVE bundles can no longer be resolved; maybe a bundle providing a required package was uninstalled. In such cases, or for any other errors, the framework fires an event of type FrameworkEvent.ERROR.

The following shell session shows how you can use the resolve and refresh commands in combination to manage a system:

```
-> install file:foo.jar
Bundle: 2
-> bundles
  ID      State       Name
[   0] [   ACTIVE] System Bundle
                   Location: System Bundle
                   Symbolic-Name: system.bundle
[   1] [   ACTIVE] Simple Shell
                   Location: file:org.foo.shell-1.0.jar
                   Symbolic-Name: org.foo.shell
[   2] [INSTALLED] Foo Bundle
                   Location: file:foo.jar
                   Symbolic-Name: org.foo.foo
-> resolve 2                                          ❶ Resolves bundle
-> bundles
  ID      State       Name
[   0] [   ACTIVE] System Bundle
                   Location: System Bundle
                   Symbolic-Name: system.bundle
[   1] [   ACTIVE] Simple Shell
                   Location: file:org.foo.shell-1.0.jar
                   Symbolic-Name: org.foo.shell
[   2] [ RESOLVED] Foo Bundle
                   Location: file:foo.jar
                   Symbolic-Name: org.foo.foo
-> refresh 2                                          ❷ Transitions bundle to INSTALLED state
-> bundles
  ID      State       Name
[   0] [   ACTIVE] System Bundle
                   Location: System Bundle
                   Symbolic-Name: system.bundle
[   1] [   ACTIVE] Simple Shell
                   Location: file:org.foo.shell-1.0.jar
```

```
                    Symbolic-Name: org.foo.shell
[   2] [INSTALLED]  Foo Bundle
                    Location: file:foo.jar
                    Symbolic-Name: org.foo.foo
```

You install a bundle and resolve it using the `resolve` command ❶, which transitions it to the `RESOLVED` state. Using the `refresh` command ❷, you transition it back to the `INSTALLED` state.

At this point, you've achieved a lot in understanding the lifecycle layer; but before you can finish, we need to explain some nuances about updating bundles. Let's get to it.

3.5.3 When updating isn't updated

One of the gotchas many people run into when updating a bundle is the fact that it may or may not use its new classes after the update operation. We said previously that updating a bundle is a two-step process, where the first step prepares the operation and the second step enacts it, but this isn't entirely accurate when you update a bundle. The specification says the framework should enact the update immediately, so after the update the bundle should theoretically be using its new classes; but it doesn't necessarily start using them immediately. In some situations, after a bundle is updated, new classes are used; in other situations, old classes are used. Sounds confusing, doesn't it? It is. Why not just wait until a refresh to enact the new revision completely?

The answer, as you might guess, is historical. The original R1 specification defined the update operation to update a bundle. End of story. There was no Package Admin Service. With experience, it became clear that the specified definition of *update* was insufficient. Too many details were left for framework implementations to decide, such as when to dispose of old classes and start using new classes. This led to inconsistencies, which made it difficult to manage bundle lifecycles across different framework implementations. This situation resulted in the introduction of the Package Admin Service in the R2 specification, to resolve the inconsistencies around update once and for all. Unfortunately, the original behavior of update was left intact, due to backward-compatibility concerns. These concerns leave you with the less-than-clean approach to bundle update that we have today, but at least it's fairly consistent across framework implementations.

Back to the issue of an updated bundle sometimes using old or new classes. As arcane as it may be, there is a way to understand what's going on. Whether your bundle's new classes or the old classes are used after an update depends on two factors:

- Whether the classes are from a private package or an exported package
- If the classes are from an exported package, whether they're being used by another bundle

Regarding the first factor:

- If the classes come from a private bundle package (one that isn't exported), the new classes become available immediately no matter what.

- If they're from an exported package, their visibility depends on whether other bundles are using them:
  - If no other bundles are using the exported packages, the new classes become available immediately. The old versions of the classes are no longer needed.
  - If any other bundles are using the exported packages, the new classes don't become available immediately, because the old version is still required. In this case, the new classes aren't made available until the `PackageAdmin.refreshPackages()` method is called.

There is yet another nuance. In chapter 5, you'll learn that bundles can also import the same packages they export. If a bundle imports a package it exports, and the imported package from the updated bundle matches the exported package from the old version, the updated bundle's import is wired to the old exported packages. This may work out well in some cases—when you're fixing a bug in a private package, for example. But it can potentially lead to odd situations, because the updated bundle is using new versions of private classes alongside old versions of exported classes. If you need to avoid this situation, you should specify version ranges when your bundle imports its own packages.

If the updated bundle imports its own package, but the import doesn't match the old version of the exported package, you have a different situation. It's similar to the case where the bundle only exports the package. In this case, the new classes from the exported packages become available immediately to the updated exporting bundle and for future resolves of other bundles, but not to existing importer bundles, which continue to see the old version. This situation generally requires `PackageAdmin.refreshPackages()` to bring the bundles back to a useful state.

You can avoid some of these issues through interface-based programming and bundle partitioning. For example, if you can separate shared APIs (the APIs through which bundles interact) into interfaces, and you place those interfaces into a separate set of packages contained in a separate bundle, you can sometimes simplify this situation. In such a setup, both the client bundles and the bundles implementing the interfaces have dependencies on the shared API bundle, but not on each other. In other words, you limit the coupling between clients and the providers of the functionality.

3.6 Summary

In this chapter, you've seen that whether your desire is to deploy the bundles needed to execute your application or to create a sophisticated auto-adaptive system, the lifecycle layer provides everything you need. Let's review what you've learned:

- A bundle can only be used by installing it into a running instance of the OSGi framework.
- The lifecycle layer API is composed of three main interfaces: `BundleActivator`, `BundleContext`, and `Bundle`.

- A `BundleActivator` is how a bundle hooks into the lifecycle layer to become lifecycle aware, which allows it to gain access to all framework facilities for inspecting and modifying the framework state at execution time.
- The framework associates a lifecycle state with each installed bundle, and the `BundleContext` and `Bundle` lifecycle interfaces make it possible to transition bundles though these states at execution time.
- Monitoring bundle lifecycle events is a form of dynamic extensibility available in the OSGi framework based on the dynamically changing installed set of bundles (also known as the extender pattern).
- The lifecycle and module layers have a close relationship, which is witnessed when bundles are updated and uninstalled. You use the Package Admin Service to manage this interaction.

Now we'll move on to the next layer of the OSGi framework: the service layer. Services promote interface-based programming among bundles and provide another form of dynamic extensibility.

4 Studying services

This chapter covers

- Understanding what services are and why they're useful
- Publishing and using services
- Dealing with service dynamism
- Modifying an application to use services
- Relating services to the module and lifecycle layers

So far, you've seen two layers of the OSGi framework. The module layer helps you separate an application into well-defined, reusable bundles, and the lifecycle layer builds on the module layer to help you manage and evolve bundles over time. Now we'll make things even more dynamic with the third and final layer of OSGi: services.

We'll start this chapter with a general discussion about services to make sure we're all thinking about the same thing. We'll then look at when you should (and shouldn't) use services and walk through an example to demonstrate the OSGi service model. At this point, you should understand the basics, so we'll take a closer look at how best to handle the dynamics of OSGi services, including common pitfalls and how to avoid them.

With these techniques in mind, you'll update the ongoing paint program to use services and see how the service layer relates to the module and lifecycle layers. We'll conclude with a review of standard OSGi framework services and tell you more about the *compendium*. As you can see, we have many useful and interesting topics to cover, so let's get started and talk about services.

4.1 The what, why, and when of services

Before looking at OSGi services, we should first explain what we mean by a *service*, because the term can mean different things to different people depending on their background. When you know the "what," you also need to know why and when to use services, so we'll get to that, too.

4.1.1 What is a service?

You may think a service is something you access across the network, like retrieving stock quotes or searching Google. But the classical view of a service is something much simpler: "work done for another." This definition can easily apply to a simple method call between two objects, because the callee is doing work for the caller.

How does a service differ from a method call? A service implies a contract between the provider of the service and its consumers. Consumers typically aren't worried about the exact implementation behind a service (or even who provides it) as long as it follows the agreed contract, suggesting that services are to some extent substitutable. Using a service also involves a form of discovery or negotiation, implying that each service has a set of identifying features (see figure 4.1).

If you think about it, Java interfaces provide part of a contract, and Java class linking is a type of service lookup because it "discovers" methods based on signatures and class hierarchy. Different method implementations can also be substituted by changing the JAR files on the class path. So a local method call could easily be seen as a service, although it would be even better if you could use a high-level abstraction to find services or if there was a more dynamic way to switch between implementations at execution time. Thankfully, OSGi helps with both by recording details of the service contract, such as interface names and metadata, and by providing a registry API to publish

Figure 4.1 Services follow a contract and involve some form of discovery.

and discover services. You'll hear more about this later, in section 4.2; for now, let's continue to look at services in general.

You may be thinking that a Java method call in the same process can't possibly be a service, because it doesn't involve a remote connection or a distributed system. In reality, as you'll see throughout this chapter, services do *not* have to be remote, and there are many benefits to using a service-oriented approach in a purely local application.

Components vs. services

When people discuss services, they often talk about components in the same context, so it's useful to consider how services and components compare and overlap. Service-oriented design and component-oriented design are extremely complementary. The key semantic difference between these two approaches is as follows:

- In a component-oriented approach, the architect focuses on the provider's view.
- In a service-oriented approach, the architect focuses on the consumer's view.

Typically, in a component-oriented approach, the architect is focused on ensuring that the component they provide is packaged in such a way that it makes their life easier. You know that when it comes to packaging and deploying Java code, the code will often be used in a range of different scenarios. For example, a stock-quote program can be deployed as a console, GUI, or web application by combining different components. A component design approach tries to make it as easy as possible for the architect to select what functionality they want to deploy without hardcoding this into their application.

This contrasts with a service-oriented approach, where the architect is focused on supplying a function or set of functions to consumers who typically have little interest in how the internals of the individual component are constructed, but have specific requirements for how they want the function to behave. Examples include acid transactions, low latency, and encrypted data.

You'll see in chapters 11 and 12 that component-oriented approaches can easily be built on top of the OSGi services model. With this in mind, let's continue our introduction to services by considering the benefits of services.

4.1.2 Why use services?

The main drive behind using services is to get others to do work on your behalf, rather than attempting to do everything yourself. This idea of delegation fits in well with many object-oriented design techniques, such as Class-Responsibility-Collaboration (CRC) cards.[1] CRC cards are a role-playing device used by development teams to think about what classes they need, as well as which class will be responsible for which piece of work and how the various classes should collaborate to get work done.[2] Techniques like CRC

---

1 Kent Beck and Ward Cunningham, "A Laboratory for Teaching Object-Oriented Thinking," http://c2.com/doc/oopsla89/paper.html.

2 Don Wells, "Design a Simulator for the Coffee Maker," www.extremeprogramming.org/example/crcsim.html.

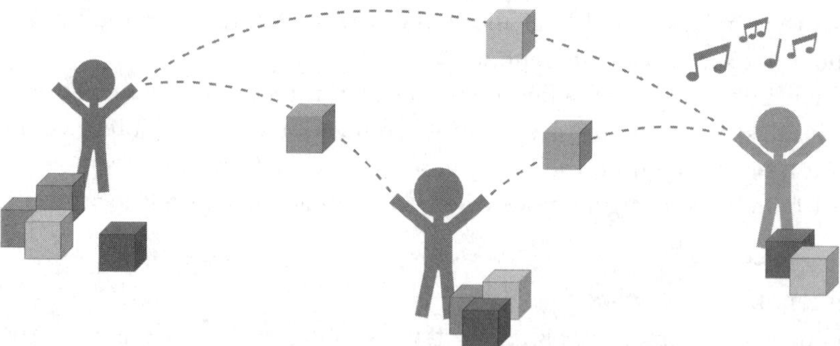

Figure 4.2 Using CRC to place responsibilities can be like playing pass-the-parcel.

cards try to push work out to other components wherever possible, which leads to lean, well-defined, maintainable components. Think of this like a game of pass-the-parcel (see figure 4.2), where each developer is trying to pass parcels of work to other developers—except in this game, when the music stops, you want the smallest pile of parcels!

A service-oriented approach also promotes

- Less coupling between providers and consumers, so it's easier to reuse components
- More emphasis on interfaces (the abstract) rather than superclasses (the concrete)
- Clear descriptions of dependencies, so you know how it all fits together
- Support for multiple competing implementations, so you can swap parts in and out

In other words, it encourages a plug-and-play approach to software development, which means much more flexibility during development, testing, deployment, and maintenance. You don't mind where a service comes from, as long as it does what you want. Still not convinced? Let's see how each of these points helps you build a better application.

LESS COUPLING

One of the most important aspects of a service is the *contract*. Every service needs some form of contract—otherwise, how could a consumer find it and use it (see figure 4.3)? The contract should include everything a consumer needs to know about the service, but no more. Putting too much detail in a contract tightens the coupling between provider and consumer and limits the possibility of swapping in other implementations

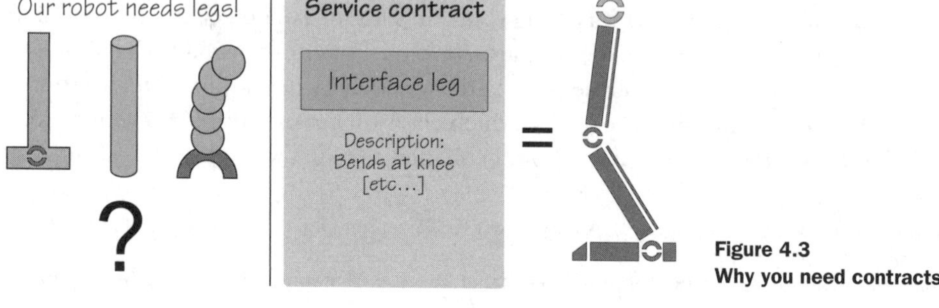

Figure 4.3 Why you need contracts

later. To put it in clothing terms, you want it nice and stretchy to give your application room to breathe.

A good service contract clearly and cleanly defines the boundary between major components and helps with development and maintenance. After the contract is defined, you can work on implementing service providers and consumers in parallel to reduce development time, and you can use scripted or *mock* services to perform early testing of key requirements. Contracts are good news for everyone—but how do you define one in Java?

MORE EMPHASIS ON INTERFACES

Java interfaces can form part of a service contract. They list the various methods that make up a service along with expected parameters and return types. After they're defined, you can begin programming against the agreed-on set of interfaces without having to wait for others to finish their implementations (see figure 4.4). Interfaces also have several advantages over concrete classes. A Java class can implement several interfaces, whereas it can only extend one concrete class. This is essential if you want flexibility over how you implement related services. Interfaces also provide a higher level of encapsulation because you're forced to put logic and state in the implementing class, not the interface.

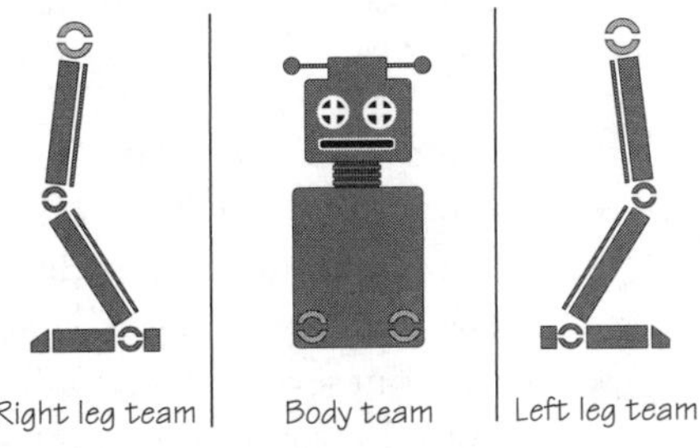

Figure 4.4 Programming to interfaces means teams can work in parallel.

You could stop at this point, assemble your final application by creating the various components with `new`, and wire their dependencies manually. Or you could use a dependency injection framework to do the construction and wiring for you. If you did, you'd have a pluggable application and all the benefits it entails, but you'd also miss out on two other benefits of a service-oriented approach: rich metadata and the ability to switch between implementations at execution time in response to events.

CLEAR DESCRIPTIONS OF DEPENDENCIES

Interfaces alone can't easily capture certain characteristics of a service, such as the quality of a particular implementation or configuration settings like supported locales. Such details are often best recorded as metadata alongside the service interface, and to do this you need some kind of framework. *Semantics*, which describe what a service does, are also hard to capture. Simple semantics like pre- and post-conditions can be recorded using metadata or may even be enforced by the service framework. Other semantics can only be properly described in documentation, but even here metadata can help provide a link to the relevant information.

Think about your current application: what characteristics may you want to record outside of classes and interfaces? To get you started, table 4.1 describes some characteristics from real-world services that could be recorded as metadata.

Table 4.1 Example characteristics of real-world services

Characteristic	Why may you be interested?
Supported locales	A price-checking service may only be available for certain currencies.
Transaction cost	You may want to use the cheapest service, even if it takes longer.
Throughput	You may want to use the fastest service, regardless of cost.
Security	You may only want to use services that are digitally signed by certain providers.
Persistence characteristics	You may only want to use a service that guarantees to store your data in such a way that it won't be lost if the JVM restarts.

As you can see, metadata can capture fine-grained information about your application in a structured way. This is helpful when you're assembling, supporting, and maintaining an application. Recording metadata alongside a service interface also means you can be more exact about what you need. The service framework can use this metadata to filter out services you don't want, without having to load and access the service itself.

But why would you want to do this? Why not just call a method on the service to ask if it does what you need?

SUPPORT FOR MULTIPLE COMPETING IMPLEMENTATIONS

A single Java interface can have many implementations; one may be fast but use a lot of memory, another may be slow but conserve memory. How do you know which one to use when they both implement the same interface? You could add a query method to the interface that tells you more about the underlying implementation, but that would lead to bloat and reduce maintainability. What would happen when you added another implementation that couldn't be characterized using the existing method? Using a query method also means you have to find and call each service implementation before you know whether you want to use it, which isn't efficient—especially when you may have hundreds of potential implementations that could be loaded at execution time.

Because service frameworks help you record metadata alongside services, they can also help you query and filter on this metadata when discovering services. This is different from classic dependency injection frameworks, which look up implementations based solely on the interfaces used at a given dependency point. Figure 4.5 shows how services can help you get exactly what you want.

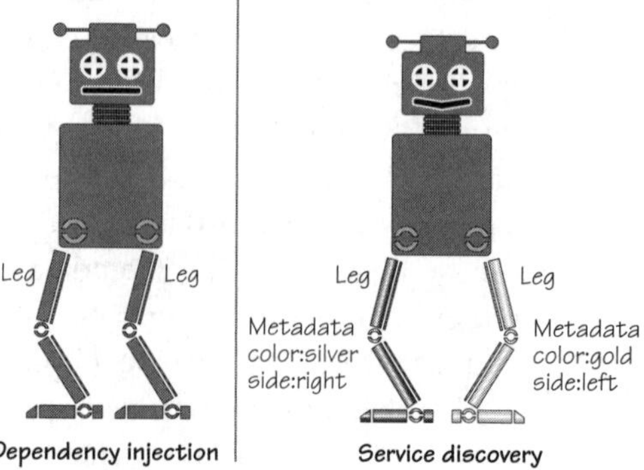

Figure 4.5 Simple dependency injection vs. service discovery

We hope that, by now, you agree that services are a good thing—but as the saying goes, you can have too much of a good thing! How can you know when you should use a service or when it would be better to use another approach, such as a static factory method or simple dependency injection?

4.1.3 When to use services

The best way to decide when to use a service is to consider the benefits: less coupling, programming to interfaces, additional metadata, and multiple implementations. If you have a situation where any of these make sense or your current design provides similar benefits, you should use a service.

The most obvious place to use a service is between major components, especially if you want to replace or upgrade those components over time without having to rewrite other parts of the application. Similarly, anywhere you look up and choose between implementations is another candidate for a service, because it means you can replace your custom logic with a standard, recognized approach.

Services can also be used as a substitute for the classic *listener pattern*.[3] With this pattern, one object offers to send events to other objects, known as *listeners*. The event source provides methods to subscribe and unsubscribe listeners and is responsible for maintaining the list of listeners. Each listener implements a known interface to receive events and is responsible for subscribing to and unsubscribing from the event source (see figure 4.6).

Implementing the listener pattern involves writing a lot of code to manage and register listeners, but how can services help? You can see a service as a more general form of listener, because it can receive all kinds of requests, not just events. Why not save time and get the service framework to manage listeners for you by registering them as services?

To find the current list of listeners, the sender queries the service framework for matching services (see figure 4.7). You can use service metadata to further define and filter the interesting events for a listener. In OSGi, this is known as the *whiteboard pattern*; you'll use this pattern when you update the paint example to use services in section 4.4.

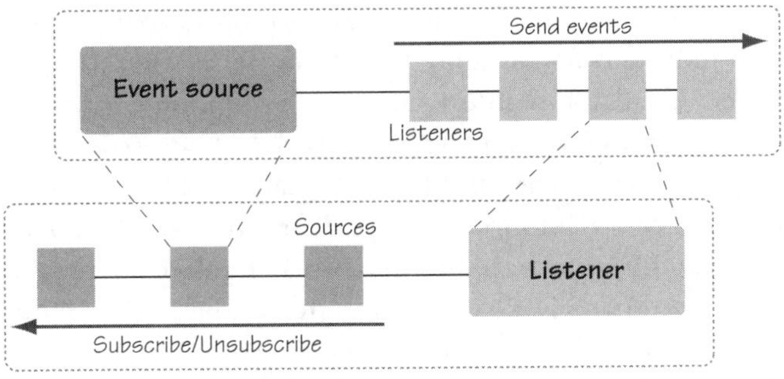

Figure 4.6 Listener pattern

3 Brian Goetz, "Java theory and practice: Be a good (event) listener," www.ibm.com/developerworks/java/library/j-jtp07265/index.html.

Figure 4.7 Whiteboard pattern

One downside of the whiteboard pattern is that it may not be clear that listeners should register a particular interface with the registry, but you can solve this by highlighting the interface in the event source's documentation. It also introduces a dependency to the service framework, which you may not want for components that you want to reuse elsewhere. Finally, the service registry must be able to scale to large numbers of services, for situations where you have lots of sources and listeners.

4.1.4 When not to use services

Another way to decide if you should use services is to consider when you *wouldn't* want to use them. Depending on the service framework, overhead may be involved when calling services, so you probably don't want to use them in performance-critical code. That said, the overhead when calling a service in OSGi can be next to zero. You may have a one-time start-up cost, but calling a service is then just a direct method call. You should also consider the work required to define and maintain the service contract. There's no point in using a service between two tightly coupled pieces of code that are always developed and updated in tandem (unless of course you need to keep choosing between multiple implementations).

4.1.5 Still not sure?

What if you're still not sure whether to use a service? Fortunately, you can use an approach that makes development easier and helps you migrate to services later: *programming to interfaces.* If you use interfaces, you're already more than halfway to using services, especially if you also take advantage of dependency injection. Of course, interfaces can be taken to extremes; there's no point in creating an interface for a class if there will only ever be one implementation. But for outward-facing interaction between components, it definitely makes sense to use interfaces wherever possible.

What have you learned? You saw how interfaces reduce coupling and promote faster development, regardless of whether you end up using services. You also saw how services help capture and describe dependencies and how they can be used to switch between different implementations. More importantly, you learned how a service-oriented approach makes developers think more about where work should be done, rather than lump code all in one place. And finally, we went through a whole section about services without once mentioning remote or distributed systems.

Is OSGi just another service model? Should we end the chapter here with an overview of the API and move on to other topics? No, because one aspect is unique to the OSGi service model: services are completely dynamic.

4.2 OSGi services in action

What do we mean by *dynamic*? After a bundle has discovered and started using a service in OSGi, it can disappear at any time. Perhaps the bundle providing it has been stopped or even uninstalled, or perhaps a piece of hardware has failed; whatever the reason, you should be prepared to cope with services coming and going over time. This is different from many other service frameworks, where after you bind to a service it's fixed and never changes—although it may throw a runtime exception to indicate a problem.

OSGi doesn't try to hide this dynamism: if a bundle wants to stop providing a service, there's little point in trying to hold it back or pretend the service still exists. This is similar to many of the failure models used in distributed computing. Hardware problems in particular should be acknowledged and dealt with promptly rather than ignored. Fortunately, OSGi provides a number of techniques and utility classes to build robust yet responsive applications on top of such fluidity; we'll look more closely at these in chapters 11 and 12. But before we can discuss the best way to handle dynamic services, you first need to understand how OSGi services work at the basic level, and to do that we need to introduce the registry.

The OSGi framework has a centralized service registry that follows a *publish-find-bind* model (see figure 4.8). To put this in the perspective of service providers and consumers,

- A providing bundle can publish Plain Old Java Objects (POJOs) as services.
- A consuming bundle can find and then bind to services.

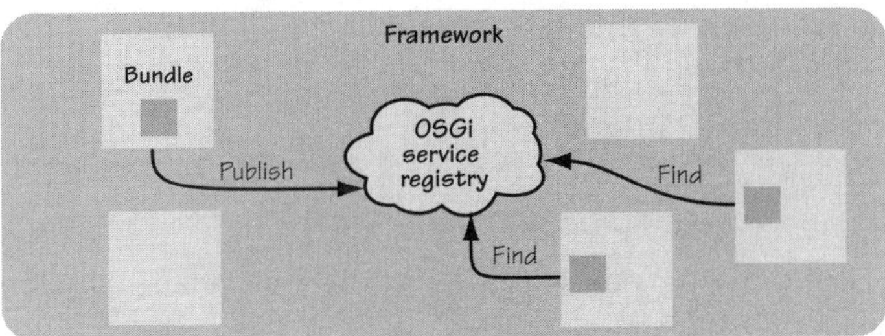

Figure 4.8 OSGi service registry

You access the OSGi service registry through the `BundleContext` interface, which you saw in section 3.2.4. Back then, we looked at its lifecycle-related methods; now we'll look into its service-related methods, as shown in the following listing.

Listing 4.1 `BundleContext` methods related to services

```
public interface BundleContext {
  ...

  void addServiceListener(ServiceListener listener, String filter)
    throws InvalidSyntaxException;
  void addServiceListener(ServiceListener listener);
  void removeServiceListener(ServiceListener listener);
```

```
  ServiceRegistration registerService(
    String[] clazzes, Object service, Dictionary properties);
  ServiceRegistration registerService(
    String clazz, Object service, Dictionary properties);
  ServiceReference[] getServiceReferences(String clazz, String filter)
    throws InvalidSyntaxException;
  ServiceReference[] getAllServiceReferences(String clazz, String filter)
    throws InvalidSyntaxException;
  ServiceReference getServiceReference(String clazz);
  Object getService(ServiceReference reference);
  boolean ungetService(ServiceReference reference);

  ...
}
```

As long as your bundle has a valid context (that is, when it's active), it can use services. Let's see how easy it is to use a bundle's `BundleContext` to publish a service.

4.2.1 Publishing a service

Before you can publish a service, you need to describe it so others can find it. In other words, you need to take details from the implemented contract and record them in the registry. What details does OSGi need from the contract?

DEFINING A SERVICE

To publish a service in OSGi, you need to provide a single interface name (or an array of them), the service implementation, and an optional dictionary of metadata (see figure 4.9). Here's what you can use for a service that provides both stock listings and stock charts for the London Stock Exchange (LSE):

```
String[] interfaces = new String[] {
    StockListing.class.getName(), StockChart.class.getName()};

Dictionary metadata = new Properties();
metadata.setProperty("name", "LSE");
metadata.setProperty("currency", Currency.getInstance("GBP"));
metadata.setProperty("country", "GB");
```

`Class.getName()` helps during refactoring. Note that metadata must be in the `Dictionary` type and can contain any Java type.

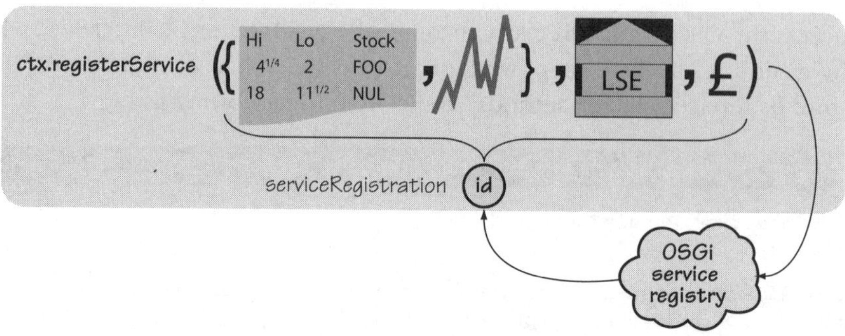

Figure 4.9 Publishing a service that provides both stock listings and stock charts

When everything's ready, you can publish your service by using the bundle context:

```
ServiceRegistration registration =
    bundleContext.registerService(interfaces, new LSE(), metadata);
```

The registry returns a service registration object for the published service, which you can use to update the service metadata or to remove the service from the registry.

> **NOTE** Service registrations are private. They shouldn't be shared with other bundles, because they're tied to the lifecycle of the publishing bundle.

The LSE implementation is a POJO. It doesn't need to extend or implement any specific OSGi types or use any annotations; it just has to match the provided service details. There's no leakage of OSGi types into service implementations. You don't even have to use interfaces if you don't want to—OSGi will accept services registered under concrete class names, but this isn't recommended.

UPDATING SERVICE METADATA

After you've published a service, you can change its metadata at any time by using its service registration:

```
registration.setProperties(newMetadata);
```

This makes it easy for your service to adapt to circumstances and inform consumers about any such changes by updating its metadata. The only pieces of metadata that you can't change are `service.id` and `objectClass`, which are maintained by the framework. Other properties that have special meaning to the OSGi framework are shown in table 4.2.

Table 4.2 Standard OSGi service properties

Key	Type	Description
`objectClass`	`String[]`	Class name the service was registered under. You can't change it after registration.
`service.id`	`Long`	Unique registration sequence number, assigned by the framework when registering the service. You can't choose or change it.
`service.pid`	`String`	Persistent (unique) service identifier, chosen by you.
`service.ranking`	`Integer`	Ranking used when discovering services. Defaults to 0. Services are sorted by their ranking (highest first) and then by their ID (lowest first). Chosen by you.
`service.description`	`String`	Description of the service, chosen by you.
`service.vendor`	`String`	Name of the vendor providing the service, chosen by you.

REMOVING A SERVICE

The publishing bundle can also remove a published service at any time:

```
registration.unregister();
```

What happens if your bundle stops before you've removed all your published services? The framework keeps track of what you've registered, and any services that haven't yet been removed when a bundle stops are automatically removed by the framework. You don't have to explicitly unregister a service when your bundle is stopped, although it's prudent to unregister before cleaning up required resources. Otherwise, someone could attempt to use the service while you're trying to clean it up.

You've successfully published the service in only a few lines of code and without any use of OSGi types in the service implementation. Now let's see if it's just as easy to discover and use the service.

4.2.2 Finding and binding services

As with publishing, you need to take details from the service contract to discover the right services in the registry. The simplest query takes a single interface name, which is the main interface you expect to use as a consumer of the service:

```
ServiceReference reference =
    bundleContext.getServiceReference(StockListing.class.getName());
```

This time the registry returns a service reference, which is an indirect reference to the discovered service (see figure 4.10). This service reference can safely be shared with other bundles, because it isn't tied to the lifecycle of the discovering bundle. But why does the registry return an indirect reference and not the actual service implementation?

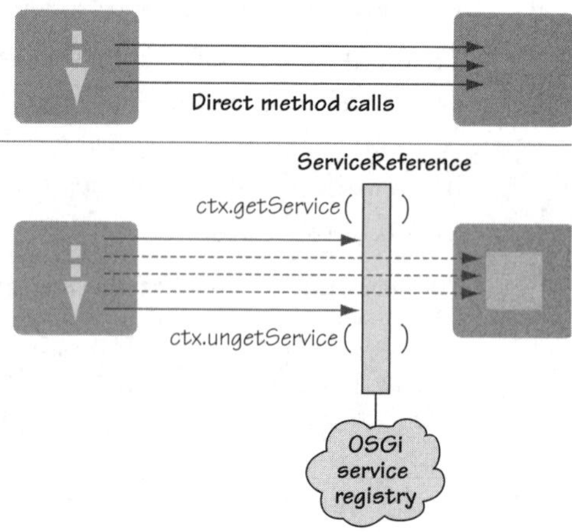

Figure 4.10 Using an OSGi service

To make services fully dynamic, the registry must decouple the use of a service from its implementation. By using an indirect reference, it can track and control access to the service, support laziness, and tell consumers when the service is removed.

CHOOSING THE BEST SERVICE

If multiple services match the given query, the framework chooses what it considers to be the "best" services. It determines the best service using the ranking property mentioned in table 4.2, where a larger numeric value denotes a higher-ranked service. If multiple services have the same ranking, the framework chooses the service with the lowest service identifier, also covered in table 4.2. Because the service identifier is an increasing number assigned by the framework, lower identifiers are associated with older services. So if multiple services have equal ranks, the framework effectively chooses the oldest service, which guarantees some stability and provides an affinity to existing services (see figure 4.11). Note that this only applies when you use `getServiceReference`—if you ask

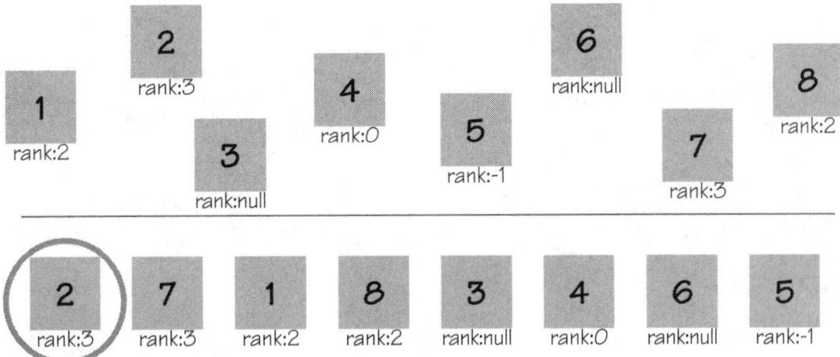

Figure 4.11 OSGi service ordering (by highest `service.ranking` and then lowest `service.id`)

for multiple services using `getServiceReferences`, the ordering of the returned array is undefined.

You've seen how to find services based on the interfaces they provide, but what if you want to discover services with certain properties? For example, in figure 4.12, if you ask for any stock listing service, you get back the first one (NYSE); but what if you want a UK-based listing? The bundle context provides another query method that accepts a standard LDAP filter string, described in RFC 1960,[4] and returns all services matching the filter.

A quick guide to using LDAP queries

Perform attribute matching:

```
(name=John Smith)
(age>=20)
(age<=65)
```

Perform fuzzy matching:

```
(name~=johnsmith)
```

Perform wildcard matching:

```
(name=Jo*n*Smith*)
```

Determine if an attribute exists:

```
(name=*)
```

Match *all* the contained clauses:

```
(&(name=John Smith)(occupation=doctor))
```

Match *at least one* of the contained clauses:

```
(|(name~=John Smith)(name~=Smith John))
```

Negate the contained clause:

```
(!(name=John Smith))
```

4 T. Howes, "A String Representation of LDAP Search Filters," www.ietf.org/rfc/rfc1960.txt.

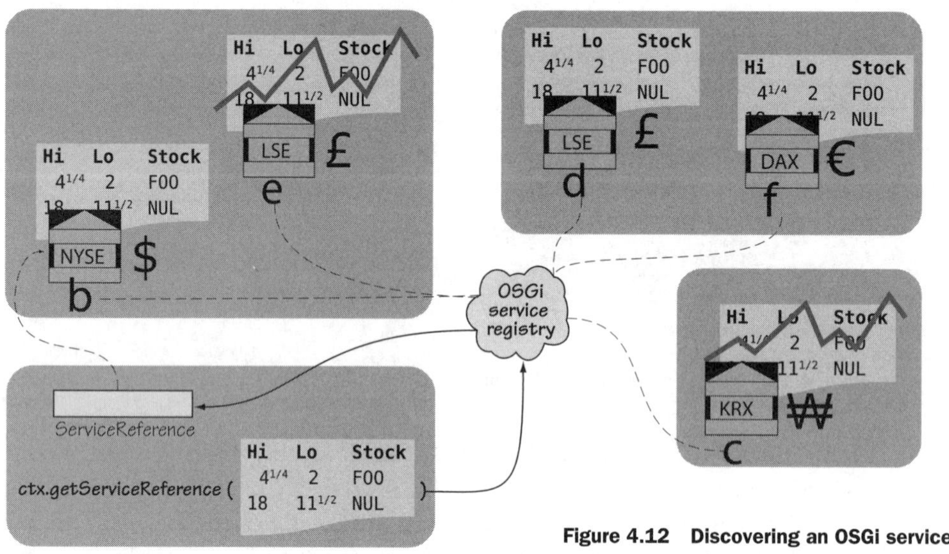

Figure 4.12 Discovering an OSGi service

Here's how you can find all stock listing services using the GBP currency:

```
ServiceReference[] references =
    bundleContext.getServiceReferences(StockListing.class.getName(),
        "(currency=GBP)");
```

This returns references to the two LSE services (`service.ids` 3 and 4 in figure 4.12).

You can also use the `objectClass` property, mentioned in table 4.2, to query for services that provide specific additional interfaces. Here, you narrow the search to those stock listing services that use a currency of GBP and also provide a chart service:

```
ServiceReference[] references =
    bundleContext.getServiceReferences(StockListing.class.getName(),
        "(&(currency=GBP)(objectClass=org.example.StockChart))");
```

This returns only one LSE service reference (`service.id` 4 from figure 4.12) because the other LSE service provides listings, but not charts.

You can look up all sorts of service references based on your needs, but how do you use them? You need to dereference each service reference to get the actual service object.

USING A SERVICE

Before you can use a service, you must bind to the actual implementation from the registry, like this:

```
StockListing listing =
    (StockListing) bundleContext.getService(reference);
```

The implementation returned is typically exactly the same POJO instance previously registered with the registry, although the OSGi specification doesn't prohibit the use of proxies or wrappers.

Revisiting the magic method

Recall that in chapter 3, when you implemented the `refresh` command for the shell, you had to use the magic `getPackageAdminService()` method to acquire the Package Admin Service. Now you have enough knowledge to see what was happening behind the scenes:

```
private PackageAdmin getPackageAdminService() {
  return (PackageAdmin) m_context.getService(
    m_context.getServiceReference(
      PackageAdmin.class.getName()));
}
```

This method is simple—probably too simple, as you'll find out later in section 4.3.1. You use the `BundleContext` to find a service implementing the Package Admin Service interface. This returns a service reference, which you use to get the service implementation. No more magic!

Each time you call `getService()`, the registry increments a usage count so it can keep track of who is using a particular service. To be a good OSGi citizen, you should tell the registry when you've finished with a service:

```
bundleContext.ungetService(reference);
listing = null;
```

Services aren't proxies

In general in OSGi, when you're making method calls on a service, you're holding a reference to the Java object supplied by the providing bundle. For this reason, you should also remember to null variables referring to the service instance when you're done using it, so it can be safely garbage collected. The actual service implementation should generally never be stored in a long-lived variable such as a field; instead, you should try to access it temporarily via the service reference and expect that the service may go away at any time.

You've now seen how to publish simple Java POJOs as OSGi services, how they can be discovered, and how the registry tracks their use. But if you remember one thing from this section, it should be that services can disappear at any time. If you want to write a robust OSGi-based application, you shouldn't rely on services always being around or even appearing in a particular order when starting your application. Of course, we don't want to scare you with all this talk of dynamism. It's important to realize that dynamism isn't created or generated by OSGi—it just enables it. A service is never arbitrarily removed; either a bundle has decided to remove it or an agent has stopped a bundle. You have control over how much dynamism you need to deal with, but it's always good to code defensively in case things change in the future or your bundles are used in different scenarios.

What's the best way to cope with potential dynamism? How can you get the most from dynamic services without continual checking and rechecking? The next section discusses potential pitfalls and recommended approaches when you're programming with dynamic services.

4.3 Dealing with dynamics

In the last section, we covered the basics of OSGi services, and you saw how easy it is to publish and discover services. In this section, we'll look more closely at the dynamics of services and techniques to help you write robust OSGi applications. To demonstrate, you'll use the OSGi Log Service.

The Log Service is a standard OSGi service, one of the so-called *compendium* or noncore services. Compendium services will be covered more in section 4.6.2. For now, all you need to know is that the Log Service provides a simple logging facade, with various flavors of methods accepting a logging level and a message, as shown in the following listing.

Listing 4.2 OSGi Log Service

```
package org.osgi.service.log;

import org.osgi.framework.ServiceReference;

public interface LogService {

  public static final int LOG_ERROR   = 1;
  public static final int LOG_WARNING = 2;
  public static final int LOG_INFO    = 3;
  public static final int LOG_DEBUG   = 4;

  public void log(int level, String message);
  public void log(int level, String message,
      Throwable exception);

  public void log(ServiceReference sr, int level, String message);
  public void log(ServiceReference sr, int level, String message,
      Throwable exception);
}
```

With OSGi, you can use any number of possible Log Service implementations in the example, such as those written by OSGi framework vendors or others written by third-party bundle vendors. To keep things simple and to help you trace what's happening inside the framework, you'll use your own dummy Log Service that implements only one method and outputs a variety of debug information about the bundles using it.

> **NOTE** The examples in the next section are intended purely to demonstrate the proper usage of dynamic OSGi services. To keep these explanatory code snippets focused and to the point, they occasionally avoid using proper programming techniques such as encapsulation. You should be able to join the dots between the patterns we show you in these examples and real-world OO design. If you aren't interested in the gory details of the OSGi service API and just want a simple, safe way to get services, skip ahead to the tracker example (section 4.3.3) or look at the component models in chapters 11 and 12.

You picked up the basics of discovering services in section 4.2.2. In the following section, you'll take that knowledge and use it to look up and call the Log Service; we'll point out and help you solve potential problems as we go along.

4.3.1 Avoiding common pitfalls

When people start using OSGi, they often write code that looks similar to the following listing.

Listing 4.3 Broken lookup example—service instance stored in a field

```
public class Activator implements BundleActivator {

  LogService m_logService;

  public void start(BundleContext context) {
    ServiceReference logServiceRef =
        context.getServiceReference(LogService.class.getName());   <-- Finds single best Log Service

    m_logService = (LogService) context.getService(logServiceRef);   <-- Stores instance in field (bad!)

    startTestThread();   <-- Starts Log Service test thread
  }

  public void stop(BundleContext context) {
    stopTestThread();
  }
}
```

Because you store the Log Service instance in a field, the test code can be simple:

```
while (Thread.currentThread() == m_logTestThread) {
  m_logService.log(LogService.LOG_INFO, "ping");
  pauseTestThread();
}
```

But there's a major problem with the bundle activator. The Log Service implementation is stored directly in a field, which means the consumer won't know when the service is retracted by its providing bundle. It only finds out when the implementation starts throwing exceptions after removal, when the implementation becomes unstable. This hard reference to the implementation also keeps it from being garbage collected while the bundle is active, even if the providing bundle is uninstalled. To fix this, let's replace the Log Service field with the indirect service reference, as shown in the following listing.

Listing 4.4 Broken lookup example—service is only discovered on startup

```
public class Activator implements BundleActivator {

  ServiceReference m_logServiceRef;
  BundleContext m_context;

  public void start(BundleContext context) {
    m_logServiceRef =
        context.getServiceReference(LogService.class.getName());   <-- Stores indirect service reference
```

```
    m_context = context;                          <-- Remembers context for later

    startTestThread();
  }

  public void stop(BundleContext context) {
    stopTestThread();
  }
}
```

You also need to change the test method to always dereference the service, as in the following listing.

Listing 4.5 Broken lookup example—testing the discovered Log Service

```
while (Thread.currentThread() == m_logTestThread) {
  LogService logService =
      (LogService) m_context.getService(m_logServiceRef);     <-- Needs saved bundle context

  if (logService != null) {                       <-- If null, service was removed
    logService.log(LogService.LOG_INFO, "ping");
  } else {
    alternativeLog("LogService has gone");
  }

  pauseTestThread();
}
```

This is slightly better, but there's still a problem with the bundle activator. You discover the Log Service only once in the `start()` method, so if there is no Log Service when the bundle starts, the reference is always `null`. Similarly, if there *is* a Log Service at startup, but it subsequently disappears, the reference always returns `null` from that point onward. Perhaps you want this one-off check, so you can revert to another (non-OSGi) logging approach based on what's available at startup. But this isn't flexible. It would be much better if you could react to changes in the Log Service and always use the active one.

A simple way of reacting to potential service changes is to always look up the service just before you want to use it, as in the following listing.

Listing 4.6 Broken lookup example—potential race condition

```
while (Thread.currentThread() == m_logTestThread) {
  ServiceReference logServiceRef =
      m_context.getServiceReference(LogService.class.getName());

  if (logServiceRef != null) {
    ((LogService) m_context.getService(logServiceRef)).log(
        LogService.LOG_INFO, "ping");              <-- Safe to dereference—or is it?
  } else {
    alternativeLog("LogService has gone");
  }

  pauseTestThread();
}
```

With this change, the bundle activator becomes trivial and just records the context:

```
public class Activator implements BundleActivator {
  BundleContext m_context;
  public void start(BundleContext context) {
    m_context = context;
    startTestThread();
  }
  public void stop(BundleContext context) {
    stopTestThread();
  }
}
```

Unfortunately, you're still not done, because there's a problem in the test method—can you see what it is? Here's a clue: remember that services can disappear at any time, and with a multithreaded application this can even happen between single statements.

The problem is that between the calls to `getServiceReference()` and `getService()`, the Log Service could disappear. The current code assumes that when you have a reference, you can safely dereference it immediately afterward. This is a common mistake made when starting with OSGi and an example of what's more generally known as a *race condition* in computing. Let's make the lookup more robust by adding a few more checks and a `try-catch` block, as in the following listing.

Listing 4.7 Correct lookup example

```
while (Thread.currentThread() == m_logTestThread) {
  ServiceReference logServiceRef =
      m_context.getServiceReference(LogService.class.getName());

  if (logServiceRef != null) {                                  <-- If null, no service available
    try {
      LogService logService =
          (LogService) m_context.getService(logServiceRef);

      if (logService != null) {                                 <-- If null, service was removed
        logService.log(LogService.LOG_INFO, "ping");
      } else {
        alternativeLog("LogService has gone");
      }

    } catch (RuntimeException re) {
      alternativeLog("error in LogService " + re);
    } finally {
      m_context.ungetService(logServiceRef);                    <-- Ungets service when not used
    }
  } else {
    alternativeLog("LogService has gone");
  }

  pauseTestThread();
}
```

The test method is now robust but not perfect. You react to changes in the Log Service and fall back to other logging methods when there are problems finding or using a service, but you can still miss Log Service implementations. For example, imagine that a Log Service is available when you first call `getServiceReference()`, but it's removed, and a different Log Service appears before you can use the original service reference. The `getService()` call returns `null`, and you end up not using any Log Service, even though a valid replacement is available. This particular race condition can't be solved by adding checks or loops because it's an inherent problem with the two-stage "find-then-get" discovery process. Instead, you must use another facility provided by the service layer to avoid this problem: service listeners.

4.3.2 Listening for services

The OSGi framework supports a simple but flexible listener API for service events. We briefly discussed the listener pattern back in section 4.1.3: one object (in this case, the framework) offers to send events to other objects, known as listeners. For services, there are currently three different types of event, shown in figure 4.13:

- `REGISTERED`—A service has been registered and can now be used.
- `MODIFIED`—Some service metadata has been modified.
- `UNREGISTERING`—A service is in the process of being unregistered.

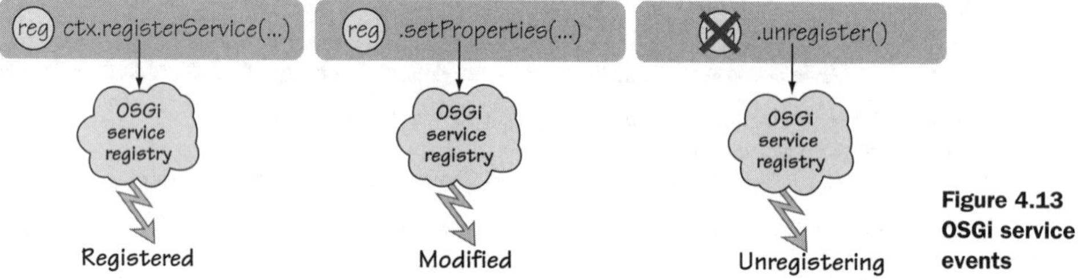

Figure 4.13 OSGi service events

Every service listener must implement this interface in order to receive service events:

```
public interface ServiceListener extends EventListener {
  public void serviceChanged(ServiceEvent event);
}
```

How can you use such an interface in the current example? You can use it to cache service instances on `REGISTERED` events and avoid the cost of repeatedly looking up the Log Service, as you did in section 4.3.1. A simple caching implementation may go something like the following listing.

Listing 4.8 Broken listener example—caching the latest service instance

```
class LogListener implements ServiceListener {
  public void serviceChanged(ServiceEvent event) {
    switch (event.getType()) {

      case ServiceEvent.REGISTERED:
        m_logService = (LogService)
            m_context.getService(event.getServiceReference());
        break;
```

```
      case ServiceEvent.MODIFIED:                 <-- Nothing to do
        break;

      case ServiceEvent.UNREGISTERING:
        m_logService = null;                      <-- Stops using service
        break;                                        (see a problem?)

      default:
        break;
    }
  }
}
```

It's safe to call the `getService()` method during the `REGISTERED` event, because the framework delivers service events synchronously using the same thread. This means you know the service won't disappear, at least from the perspective of the framework, until the listener method returns. Of course, the service could still throw a runtime exception at any time, but using `getService()` with a `REGISTERED` event always returns a valid service instance. For the same reason, you should make sure the listener method is relatively short and won't block or deadlock; otherwise, you block other service events from being processed.

REGISTERING A SERVICE LISTENER

You have the service listener, but how do you tell the framework about it? The answer is, as usual, via the bundle context, which defines methods to add and remove service listeners. You must also choose an LDAP filter to restrict events to services implementing the Log Service; otherwise, you can end up receiving events for hundreds of different services. The final code looks like the following listing.

Listing 4.9 Broken listener example—existing services aren't seen

```
public class Activator implements BundleActivator {

  BundleContext m_context;                        Threads
  volatile LogService m_logService;           <-- access field

  public void start(BundleContext context) throws Exception {
    m_context = context;

    String filter = "(" + Constants.OBJECTCLASS + "=" +
        LogService.class.getName() + ")";

    context.addServiceListener(new LogListener(), filter);

    startTestThread();
  }

  public void stop(BundleContext context) {
    stopTestThread();
  }
}
```

The LDAP filter matches `LogService` instances, and you add a listener for future Log Service events. Notice that you don't explicitly remove the service listener when you stop the bundle. This is because the framework keeps track of what listeners you've added and automatically cleans up any remaining listeners when the bundle stops. You saw something similar in section 4.2.1 when the framework removed any leftover service registrations.

The test method is now simple, because you're caching the service instance:

```
while (Thread.currentThread() == m_logTestThread) {
  if (m_logService != null) {
    m_logService.log(LogService.LOG_INFO, "ping");
  } else {
    alternativeLog("LogService has gone");
  }
  pauseTestThread();
}
```

This looks much better, doesn't it? You don't have to do as much checking or polling of the service registry. Instead, you wait for the registry to tell you whenever a Log Service appears or disappears. Unfortunately, this code sample has a number of problems. First, there are some minor issues with the test method; you don't catch runtime exceptions when using the service; and because of the caching, you don't unget the service when you're not using it. The cached Log Service could also change between the non-null test and when you use it.

More importantly, there's a significant error in the listener code, because it doesn't check that the `UNREGISTERING` service is the same as the Log Service currently being used. Imagine that two Log Services (A and B) are available at the same time, where the test method uses Log Service A. If Log Service B is unregistered, the listener will clear the cached instance even though Log Service A is still available. Similarly, as new Log Services are registered, the listener will always choose the newest service regardless of whether it has a better service ranking. To make sure you use the highest-ranked service and to be able to switch to alternative implementations whenever a service is removed, you must keep track of the current set of active service references—not just a single instance.

The bundle activator in listing 4.9 has another subtle error, which you may not have noticed at first. This error may never show up in practice, depending on how you start your application. Think back to how listeners work: the event source sends events to the listener as they occur. What about events that happened in the past? What about already-published services? In this case, the service listener doesn't receive events that happened in the dim and distant past and remains oblivious to existing Log Service implementations.

FIXING THE SERVICE LISTENER

You have two problems to fix: you must keep track of the active set of Log Services and take into account already-registered Log Services. The first problem requires the use of a sorted set and relies on the natural ordering of service references, as defined in the specification of the `compareTo()` method. You'll also add a helper method to decide which Log Service to pass to the client, based on the cached set of active service references; see the following listing.

Listing 4.10 Correct listener example—keeping track of active Log Services

```
class LogListener implements ServiceListener {

  SortedSet<ServiceReference> m_logServiceRefs =
      new TreeSet<ServiceReference>();

  public synchronized void serviceChanged(ServiceEvent event) {
    switch (event.getType()) {
      case ServiceEvent.REGISTERED:
        m_logServiceRefs.add(event.getServiceReference());
        break;
      case ServiceEvent.MODIFIED:
        break;
      case ServiceEvent.UNREGISTERING:
        m_logServiceRefs.remove(event.getServiceReference());
        break;
      default:
        break;
    }
  }

  public synchronized LogService getLogService() {
    if (m_logServiceRefs.size() > 0) {
      return (LogService) m_context.getService(
          m_logServiceRefs.last());
    }
    return null;
  }
}
```

Orders service refs by ranking

Locks listener before changing state

Locks listener before querying state

Now the last service reference has the highest ranking.

You can fix the second problem in the bundle activator by issuing pseudo-registration events for each existing service, to make it look like the service has only just appeared, as shown in the following listing.

Listing 4.11 Correct listener example—sending pseudo-registration events

```
public class Activator implements BundleActivator {

  BundleContext m_context;
  LogListener m_logListener;

  public void start(BundleContext context) throws Exception {
    m_context = context;

    m_logListener = new LogListener();

    synchronized (m_logListener) {

      String filter = "(" + Constants.OBJECTCLASS + "=" +
          LogService.class.getName() + ")";

      context.addServiceListener(m_logListener, filter);

      ServiceReference[] refs =
          context.getServiceReferences(null, filter);

      if (refs != null) {
```

Locks listener before adding it

Checks for existing services

```
        for (ServiceReference r : refs) {
          m_logListener.serviceChanged(
              new ServiceEvent(ServiceEvent.REGISTERED, r));      <-- Sends pseudo-events
        }
      }
    }

    startTestThread();
  }

  public void stop(BundleContext context) {
    m_context.removeServiceListener(m_logListener);

    stopTestThread();
  }
}
```

You deliberately lock the listener before passing it to the framework, so the pseudo-registration events are processed first. Otherwise, it would be possible to receive an `UNREGISTERING` event for a service before its pseudo-registration. Only when the listener has been added do you check for existing services, to make sure you don't miss any intervening registrations. You could potentially end up with duplicate registrations by doing the checks in this order, but that's better than missing services. The test method now only needs to call the helper method to get the best Log Service, as shown in the following listing.

Listing 4.12 Correct listener example—using the listener to get the best Log Service

```
while (Thread.currentThread() == m_logTestThread) {
  LogService logService = m_logListener.getLogService();

  if (logService != null) {
    try {
      logService.log(LogService.LOG_INFO, "ping");
    } catch (RuntimeException re) {
      alternativeLog("error in LogService " + re);
    }
  } else {
    alternativeLog("LogService has gone");
  }

  pauseTestThread();
}
```

You may have noticed that the finished listener example still doesn't unget the service after using it; this is left as an exercise for you. Here's a hint to get you started: think about moving responsibility for logging into the listener. This will also help you reduce the time between binding the service and using it.

Service listeners reduce the need to continually poll the service registry. They let you react to changes in services as soon as they occur and get around the inherent race condition of the find-then-get approach. The downside of listeners is the amount of code you need to write. Imagine having to do this for every service you want to use and having to repeatedly test for synchronization issues. Why doesn't OSGi provide a utility class to do all this for you—a class that has been battle hardened and tested in many applications, that you can configure and customize as you require? It does, and the class's name is ServiceTracker.

4.3.3 Tracking services

The OSGi ServiceTracker class provides a safe way for you to get the benefits of service listeners without the pain. To show how easy it can be, let's take the bundle activator from the last example and adapt it in the following listing to use the service tracker.

Listing 4.13 Standard tracker example

```
public class Activator implements BundleActivator {

  BundleContext m_context;
  ServiceTracker m_logTracker;

  public void start(BundleContext context) {
    m_context = context;

    m_logTracker = new ServiceTracker(context,
        LogService.class.getName(), null);

    m_logTracker.open();                          <-- Must open tracker before using it

    startTestThread();
  }

  public void stop(BundleContext context) {       <-- Closes tracker

    m_logTracker.close();

    stopTestThread();
  }
}
```

In this example, you use the basic ServiceTracker constructor that takes a bundle context, the service type you want to track, and a *customizer* object. We'll look at customizers in a moment; for now, you don't need any customization, so you pass null. If you need more control over what services are tracked, there's another constructor that accepts a filter.

> **NOTE** Before you can use a tracker, you must open it using the open() method to register the underlying service listener and initialize the tracked list of services. This is often the thing people forget to do when they first use a service tracker, and then they wonder why they don't see any services. Similarly, when you're finished with the tracker, you must close it. Although the framework automatically removes the service listener when the bundle stops, it's best to explicitly call close() so that all the tracked resources can be properly cleared.

And that's all you need to do to track instances of the Log Service—you don't need to write your own listener or worry about managing long lists of references. When you need to use the Log Service, you ask the tracker for the current instance:

```
LogService logService = (LogService) m_logTracker.getService();
```

Other tracker methods get all active instances and access the underlying service references; there's even a method that helps you wait until a service appears. Often, a raw service tracker is all you need, but sometimes you'll want to extend it. Perhaps you want to decorate a service with additional behavior, or you need to acquire or release resources as services appear and disappear. You could extend the `ServiceTracker` class, but you'd have to be careful not to break the behavior of any methods you override. Thankfully, there's a way to extend a service tracker without subclassing it: with a customizer object. The `ServiceTrackerCustomizer` interface shown here provides a safe way to enhance a tracker by intercepting tracked service instances:

```
public interface ServiceTrackerCustomizer {
  public Object addingService(ServiceReference reference);
  public void modifiedService(ServiceReference reference,
      Object service);
  public void removedService(ServiceReference reference,
      Object service);
}
```

Like a service listener, a customizer is based on the three major events in the life of a service: adding, modifying, and removing. The `addingService()` method is where most of the customization normally occurs. The associated tracker calls this whenever a matching service is added to the OSGi service registry. You're free to do whatever you want with the incoming service; you can initialize some resources or wrap it in another object, for example. The object you return is tied to the service by the tracker and returned wherever the tracker would normally return the service instance. If you decide you don't want to track a particular service instance, return `null`. The other two methods in the customizer are typically used for housekeeping tasks like updating or releasing resources.

Suppose you want to decorate the Log Service, such as adding some text around the log messages. The service tracker customizer may look something like the following listing.

Listing 4.14 Customized tracker example—decorated Log Service

```
class LogServiceDecorator implements ServiceTrackerCustomizer {
  private final BundleContext m_context;

  public LogServiceDecorator(BundleContext context) {
    m_context = context;
  }

  public Object addingService(final ServiceReference ref) {
    return new LogService() {

      public void log(int level, String message) {
        ((LogService) m_context.getService(ref)).log(level,
            "<<" + message + ">>");
      }

      public void log(int level, String message,
          Throwable exception) {}
```

Wraps code around original Log Service

```
        public void log(ServiceReference sr, int level, String message) {}
        public void log(ServiceReference sr, int level, String message,
            Throwable exception) {}
      };
    }

    public void modifiedService(ServiceReference ref, Object service) {}

    public void removedService(ServiceReference ref, Object service) {}
}
```

All you have to do to decorate the Log Service is pass the customizer to the tracker:

```
m_logTracker = new ServiceTracker(context, LogService.class.getName(),
    new LogServiceDecorator());
```

Now any Log Service returned by this tracker will add angle brackets to the logged message. This is a trivial example, but we hope you can see how powerful customizers can be. Service tracker customizers are especially useful in separating code from OSGi-specific interfaces, because they act as a bridge connecting your application code to the service registry.

You've seen three different ways to access OSGi services: directly through the bundle context, reactively with service listeners, and indirectly using a service tracker. Which way should you choose? If you only need to use a service intermittently and don't mind using the raw OSGi API, using the bundle context is probably the best option. At the other end of the spectrum, if you need full control over service dynamics and don't mind the potential complexity, a service listener is best. In all other situations, you should use a service tracker, because it helps you handle the dynamics of OSGi services with the least amount of effort.

What? No abstractions?

If none of these options suit you, and you prefer to use a higher-level abstraction, such as components, this is fine too. As we mentioned at the start of this chapter, it's possible to build component models on top of these core APIs. This is exactly what many people have been doing for the past few years, and several service-oriented component frameworks are based on OSGi; we'll discuss them in chapters 11 and 12. But remember, all these component frameworks make subtle but important semantic choices when mapping components to the OSGi service model. If you need to cut through these abstractions and get to the real deal, now you know how.

Now that you know all about OSGi services and their dynamics, let's look again at the paint program and see where it may make sense to use services.

4.4 Using services in the paint example

You last saw the paint example back in section 3.4, where you used an extender pattern to collect shapes. Why don't you try using a service instead? A shape service makes a lot of sense, because you can clearly define what responsibilities belong to a shape and use metadata to describe various nonfunctional attributes like its name and icon. Remember that the first thing to define when creating a new service is the contract. What should a shape service look like?

4.4.1 Defining a shape service

Let's use the previous interface as the basis of the new service contract—but this time, instead of extension names, you'll declare service property names. These names will tell the client where to find additional metadata about the shape:

```
public interface SimpleShape {

  public static final String NAME_PROPERTY = "simple.shape.name";
  public static final String ICON_PROPERTY = "simple.shape.icon";

  public void draw(Graphics2D g2, Point p);
}
```

This isn't much different from the interface defined in section 3.4. You can see how easy it is to switch over to services when you're programming with interfaces. With this contract in hand, you now need to update each shape bundle to publish its implementation as a service, and update the paint frame bundle to track and consume these shape services.

4.4.2 Publishing a shape service

Before you can publish a shape implementation as a service, you need a bundle context. To get the bundle context, you need to add a bundle activator to each shape bundle, as shown in the following listing.

Listing 4.15 Publishing a shape service

```
public class Activator implements BundleActivator {
  private BundleContext m_context = null;

  public void start(BundleContext context) {
    m_context = context;
    Hashtable dict = new Hashtable();

    dict.put(SimpleShape.NAME_PROPERTY, "Circle");
    dict.put(SimpleShape.ICON_PROPERTY,
        new ImageIcon(this.getClass().getResource("circle.png")));

    m_context.registerService(SimpleShape.class.getName(),
        new Circle(), dict);                          <-- Publishes new shape service
  }

  public void stop(BundleContext context) {}
}
```

You record the name and icon under their correct service properties. The shape bundles will now publish their shape services when they start and remove them when they stop. To use these shapes when painting, you need to update the paint frame bundle so it uses services instead of bundles, as shown in figure 4.14.

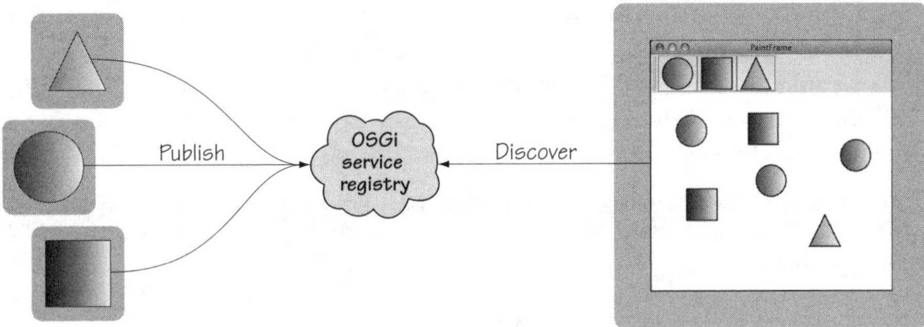

Figure 4.14 Painting with services

4.4.3 Tracking shape services

Remember the `DefaultShape` class that acted as a simple proxy to an underlying shape bundle in section 3.4? When the referenced shape bundle was active, the `DefaultShape` used its classes and resources to paint the shape. When the shape bundle wasn't active, the `DefaultShape` drew a placeholder image instead. You can use the same approach with services, except that instead of a bundle identifier, you use a service reference as shown here:

```
if (m_context != null) {
  try {
    if (m_shape == null) {
      m_shape = (SimpleShape) m_context.getService(m_ref);
    }
    m_shape.draw(g2, p);
    return;
  } catch (Exception ex) {}
}
```

This code gets the referenced shape service and draws a shape with a simple method call. A placeholder image is drawn instead if there's a problem.

You can also add a `dispose()` method to tell the framework when you're finished with the service:

```
public void dispose() {
  if (m_shape != null) {
    m_context.ungetService(m_ref);
    m_context = null;
    m_ref = null;
    m_shape = null;
  }
}
```

The new `DefaultShape` is now based on an underlying service reference, but how do you find such a reference? Remember the advice from section 4.3.3: you want to use several instances of the same service and react as they appear and disappear, but you don't want detailed control—you need a `ServiceTracker`.

In the previous chapter, you used a BundleTracker to react as shape bundles came and went. This proved to be a good design choice, because it meant the ShapeTracker class could process shape events and trigger the necessary Swing actions. All you need to change is the source of shape events, as shown in the following listing; they now come from the ServiceTracker methods.

Listing 4.16 Sending shape events from ServiceTracker methods

```
public Object addingService(ServiceReference ref) {
  SimpleShape shape = new DefaultShape(m_context, ref);
  processShapeOnEventThread(ADDED, ref, shape);
  return shape;
}

public void modifiedService(ServiceReference ref, Object svc) {
  processShapeOnEventThread(MODIFIED, ref, (SimpleShape) svc);
}

public void removedService(ServiceReference ref, Object svc) {
  processShapeOnEventThread(REMOVED, ref, (SimpleShape) svc);
  ((DefaultShape) svc).dispose();                    <-- Ungets service and clears fields
}
```

The processing code also needs to use service properties rather than extension metadata:

```
String name = (String) ref.getProperty(SimpleShape.NAME_PROPERTY);
Icon icon = (Icon) ref.getProperty(SimpleShape.ICON_PROPERTY);
```

And that's all there is to it. You now have a service-based paint example. To see it in action, go into the chapter04/paint-example/ directory of the companion code, type ant to build it, and type java -jar launcher.jar bundles to run it. The fact that you needed to change only a few files is a testament to the non-intrusiveness of OSGi services if you already use an interface-based approach.

We hope you can also see how easy it would be to do this in reverse and adapt a service-based example to use extensions. Imagine being able to decide when and where to use services in your application, without having to factor them into the initial design. The OSGi service layer gives you that ability, and the previous layers help you manage and control it. But how can the module and lifecycle layers help; how do they relate to the service layer?

4.5 Relating services to modularity and lifecycle

The service layer builds on top of the module and lifecycle layers. You've already seen one example, where the framework automatically unregisters services when their registering bundle stops. But the layers interact in other ways, such as providing bundle-specific (also known as *factory*) services and specifying when you should unget and unregister services, and how you should bundle up services. But let's start with how modularity affects what services you can see.

4.5.1 Why can't I see my service?

Sometimes you may ask yourself this question and wonder why, even though the OSGi framework shows a particular service as registered, you can't access it from your bundle. The answer comes back to modularity. Because multiple versions of service interface packages may be installed at any given time, the OSGi framework only shows your bundle services using the same version. The reasoning behind this is that you should be able to cast service instances to any of their registered interfaces without causing a `ClassCastException`.

But what if you want to query all services, regardless of what interfaces you can see? Although this approach isn't common, it's useful in management scenarios where you want to track third-party services even if they aren't compatible with your bundle. To support this, the OSGi framework provides a so-called `All*` variant of the `getServiceReferences()` method to return all matching services, regardless of whether their interfaces are visible to the calling bundle. For example:

```
ServiceReference[] references =
    bundleContext.getAllServiceReferences(null, null);
```

This returns references to all services currently registered in the OSGi service registry. Similarly, for service listeners there's an `All*` extension of the `ServiceListener` interface, which lets you receive all matching service events. The `ServiceTracker` is the odd one out, with no `All*` variant—to ignore visibility, you start the tracker with `open(true)`.

You've seen that although one bundle can see a service, another bundle with different imports may not. How about two bundles with the same imports? They see the same service instances. What if you want them to see different instances—is it possible to customize services for each consumer?

4.5.2 Can I provide a bundle-specific service?

You may have noticed that throughout this chapter, you've assumed that service instances are created first and then published, discovered, and finally used. Or, to put it another way, creation of service instances isn't related to their use. But sometimes you want to create services lazily or customize a service specifically for each bundle using it. An example is the simple Log Service implementation from section 4.3. None of the Log Service methods accept a bundle or bundle context, but you may want to record details of the bundle logging the message. How is this possible in OSGi? Doesn't the `registerService()` method expect a fully constructed service instance?

The OSGi framework defines a special interface to use when registering a service. The `ServiceFactory` interface acts as a marker telling the OSGi framework to treat the provided instance not as a service, but as a factory that can create service instances on demand. The OSGi service registry uses this factory to create instances just before they're needed, when the consumer first attempts to use the service. A factory can potentially create a number of instances at the same time, so it must be thread safe:

```
public interface ServiceFactory {
  public Object getService(Bundle bundle,
      ServiceRegistration registration);
  public void ungetService(Bundle bundle,
      ServiceRegistration registration, Object service);
}
```

The framework caches factory-created service instances, so a bundle requesting the same service twice receives the same instance. This cached instance is removed only when the bundle has completely finished with a service (that is, the number of calls to get it match the calls to unget it), when the bundle has stopped, or when the service factory is unregistered. Should you always unget a service after you use it, like closing an I/O stream?

4.5.3 When should I unget a service?

You just saw that instances created from service factories are cached until the consuming bundle has finished with the service. This is determined by counting the calls to `getService()` compared to `ungetService()`. Forgetting to call unget can lead to instances being kept around until the bundle is stopped. Similarly, agents interrogating the framework will assume the bundle is using the service when it isn't. Should you always unget after using a service, perhaps something like the following?

```
try {
  Service svc = (Service) m_context.getService(svcRef);
  if (svc != null) {
    svc.dispatch(something);
  } else {
    fallback(somethingElse);
  }
} finally {
  m_context.ungetService(svcRef);
}
```

This code records exactly when you use the service, but what happens if you want to use it again and again in a short space of time? Services backed by factories will end up creating and destroying a new instance on every call, which can be costly. You may also want to keep the instance alive between calls if it contains session-related data. In these circumstances, it makes more sense to get at the start of the session and unget at the end of the session. For long-lived sessions, you still need to track the service in case it's removed, probably using a service tracker customizer to close the session. In all other situations, you should unget the service when you're finished with it.

But what about the other side of the equation? Should bundles let the framework unregister their services when they stop, or should they be more proactive and unregister services as soon as they don't want to or can't support them?

4.5.4 When should I unregister my service?

The OSGi framework does a lot of tidying up when a bundle stops—it removes listeners, releases used services, and unregisters published services. It can often feel like you don't need to do anything yourself; indeed, many bundle activators have empty `stop()` methods. But sometimes it's prudent to unregister a service yourself. Perhaps you've received a hardware notification and need to tell bundles not to use your service. Perhaps you need to perform some processing before shutting down and don't want bundles using your service while this is going on. At times like this, remember that you're in control, and it's often better to be explicit than to rely on the framework to clean up after you.

After that salutary message, let's finish this section with a modularity topic that has caused a lot of heated discussion on OSGi mailing lists: where to package service interfaces.

4.5.5 Should I bundle interfaces separately?

Service interfaces are by definition decoupled from their implementations. Should they be packaged separately in their own bundle or duplicated inside each implementation bundle? OSGi supports both options, because as long as the metadata is correct, it can wire the various bundles together to share the same interface. But why would you want to copy the interface inside each implementation bundle? Surely that would lead to duplicated content.

Think about deploying a set of services into a framework. If each service has both an API and an implementation bundle, that doubles the number of bundles to manage. Putting the interface inside the implementation bundle means you need to provide only one JAR file. Similarly, users don't have to remember to install the API—if they have the implementation, they automatically get the API for free. This sounds good, so why doesn't everyone do it?

It comes down to managing updates. Putting interfaces inside an implementation bundle means the OSGi framework may decide to use that bundle as the provider of the API package. If you then want to upgrade and refresh the implementation bundle, all the consuming bundles will end up being refreshed, causing a wave of restarting bundles. Similarly, if you decide to uninstall the implementation, the implementation classes will be unloaded by the garbage collector only when the interface classes are no longer being used (because they share the same class loader).

In the end, there's no single right answer. Each choice has consequences you should be aware of. Just as with other topics we've discussed—service visibility, service factories, and using unget and unregister—you need to know the possibilities to make an informed choice. We'll come back to this topic in the next chapter, because packaging service interfaces with the implementation bundle also requires you to define the bundle metadata a little differently. Whatever you decide, we can all agree that services are an important feature of OSGi.

4.6 Standard services

Services are such an important feature that they're used throughout the OSGi specification. By using services to extend the framework, the core API can be kept lean and clean. Almost all extensions to OSGi have been specified as optional add-on services without requiring any changes to the core specification. These standard OSGi services are divided into two categories: core and compendium. We'll take a quick look at some of the core and compendium services in the next two subsections (see table 4.3).

Table 4.3 Standard OSGi services covered in this section

Service	Type	Description
Package Admin	Core	Manages bundle updates and discovers who exports what
Start Level	Core	Queries and controls framework and bundle start levels
URL Handlers	Core	Handles dynamic URL streams
Permission Admin	Core	Manages bundle and service permissions
HTTP	Compendium	Puts simple servlets and resources onto the web
Event Admin	Compendium	Provides a topic-based publish-subscribe event model
Configuration Admin	Compendium	Manages and persists configuration data
User Admin	Compendium	Performs role-based authentication and authorization

4.6.1 *Core services*

The following core services are generally implemented by the OSGi framework itself, because they're intimately tied to framework internals.

PACKAGE ADMIN SERVICE

The OSGi Package Admin Service, which we discussed in chapter 3, provides a selection of methods to discover details about exported packages and the bundles that export and/or import them. You can use this service to trace dependencies between bundles at execution time, which can help when upgrading because you can see what bundles may be affected by the update. The Package Admin Service also provides methods to refresh exported packages, which may have been removed or updated since the last refresh, and to explicitly resolve specific bundles.

START LEVEL SERVICE

The OSGi Start Level Service lets you programmatically query and set the start level for individual bundles as well as the framework itself, which allows you to control the relative order of bundle activation. You can use start levels to deploy an application or roll out a significant update in controlled stages. We'll discuss this more in chapter 10.

URL HANDLERS SERVICE

The OSGi URL Handlers Service adds a level of dynamism to the standard Java URL process. The Java specification unfortunately only allows one `URLStreamHandlerFactory` to be set during the lifetime of a JVM, so the framework attempts to set its own implementation at startup. If this is successful, this factory dynamically provides

URL stream handlers and content handlers, based on implementations registered with the OSGi service registry.

(CONDITIONAL) PERMISSION ADMIN SERVICE

Two OSGi services deal with permissions: the Permission Admin Service, which deals with permissions granted to specific bundles, and the Conditional Permission Admin Service, which provides a more general-purpose and fine-grained permission model based on conditions. Both of these services build on the standard Java 2 security architecture. We'll discuss security more in chapter 14.

You now know which core services you can expect to see in an OSGi framework, but what about the non-core compendium services? What sort of capabilities do they cover?

4.6.2 Compendium services

In addition to the core services, the OSGi Alliance defines a set of non-core standard services called the *compendium* services. Whereas the core services are typically available by default in a running OSGi framework, the compendium services aren't. Keeping with the desire for modularity, you wouldn't want them to be included by default because this would lead to bloated systems. Instead, these services are provided as separate bundles by framework implementers or other third parties and typically work on all frameworks.

You've already seen one example of a compendium service: the Log Service from section 4.3, which provides a simple logging API. This is one of the better-known compendium services. Let's take a brief look at other popular examples.

HTTP SERVICE

The OSGi HTTP Service supports registration of servlets and resources under named aliases. These aliases are matched against incoming URI requests, and the relevant servlet or resource is used to construct the reply. You can authenticate incoming requests using standard HTTP/HTTPS, the OSGi User Admin Service, or your own custom approach. The current HTTP Service is based on version 2.1 of the servlet specification,[5] which means it doesn't cover servlet filters, event listeners, or JSPs. Later versions of the HTTP Service specification should address this, and some implementations already support these additional features.[6] We'll talk more about the HTTP Service and OSGi web applications in chapter 15.

EVENT ADMIN SERVICE

The OSGi Event Admin Service provides a basic publish-subscribe event model. Each event consists of a topic, which is basically a semistructured string, and a set of properties. Event handlers are registered as services and can use metadata to describe which topics and properties they're interested in. Events can be sent synchronously or asynchronously and are delivered to matching event handlers by using the whiteboard

---

[5] http://java.sun.com/products/servlet/2.1/servlet-2.1.pdf.

[6] For example, Pax Web: http://wiki.ops4j.org/display/paxweb.

pattern, which we discussed in section 4.1.3. Other types of OSGi events (like framework, bundle, service, and log events) are mapped and republished by the Event Admin Service implementation.

CONFIGURATION ADMIN SERVICE

The OSGi Configuration Admin Service delivers configuration data to those services with persistent identifiers (`service.pid`) that implement the `ManagedService` interface—or `ManagedServiceFactory`, if they want to create a new service instance per configuration. These so-called *configuration targets* accept configuration data in the form of a dictionary of properties. Management bundles, which have been granted permission to configure services, can use the Configuration Admin Service to initialize and update configurations for other bundles. Nonmanagement bundles can only update their own configurations. The Configuration Admin Service is pluggable and can be extended by registering implementations of the `ConfigurationPlugin` interface with the OSGi service registry. Chapter 9 provides detailed examples of how to supply and consume configuration data.

USER ADMIN SERVICE

The OSGi User Admin Service provides a role-based model for authentication (checking credentials) and authorization (checking access rights). An authenticating bundle uses the User Admin Service to prepopulate the required roles, groups, and users along with identifying properties and credentials. This bundle can query the User Admin Service at a later date to find users, check their credentials, and confirm their authorized roles. It can then decide how to proceed based on the results of these checks.

This is a short sample of the compendium services; you can find a complete table in appendix B. You can also read detailed specifications of each service in *OSGi Service Platform Service Compendium*.[7]

4.7 Summary

That was a lot of information to digest, so don't worry if you got a bit woozy. Let's summarize this chapter:

- A service is "work done for another."
- Service contracts define responsibilities and match consumers with providers.
- Services encourage a relaxed, pluggable, interface-based approach to programming.
- You don't need to care where a service comes from as long as it meets the contract.
- The best place to use services is between replaceable components.
- Think carefully before using services in tightly coupled or high-performance code.
- Services can replace the listener pattern with a much simpler whiteboard pattern.

---

[7] OSGi Alliance, *OSGi Service Platform Service Compendium* (2009), www.osgi.org/download/r4v42/r4.cmpn.pdf

- OSGi services use a publish-find-bind model.
- OSGi services are truly dynamic and can appear or disappear at any time.
- The easiest and safest approach is to use the OSGi `ServiceTracker` utility class.
- For higher-level service abstractions, consider the component models in chapters 11 and 12.
- OSGi services build on and interact with the previous module and lifecycle layers.
- OSGi defines core framework services and additional compendium services.

Services aren't limited to distributed or remote applications. There's a huge benefit to applying a service-oriented design to a purely local, single-JVM application, and we hope you get the opportunity to experience this in your next project.

5 Delving deeper into modularity

This chapter covers

- Exploring advanced aspects of exporting packages
- Importing optional or unknown packages
- Requiring bundles instead of packages
- Splitting bundles into fragments
- Dealing with platform dependencies and native code

In the preceding chapters, we covered a myriad of details about the three layers of the OSGi framework. Believe it or not, we didn't cover everything. Instead, we focused on explaining the common specification features, best practices, and framework behavior necessary to get you started with OSGi technology. Depending on the project, the aforementioned features and best practices may not be sufficient. This can be especially true when it comes to legacy situations, where you're not able to make sweeping changes to your existing code base. Sometimes the clean theory of modularity conflicts with the messiness of reality, so occasionally compromises are needed to get things moving or to meet objectives.

In this chapter, we'll investigate more aspects of OSGi's module layer. We'll look into simple features, such as making imported packages a little more flexible, and into more complicated ones, such as splitting Java packages across multiple bundles or breaking a single bundle into pieces. You probably won't need to use most of the features described in this chapter as often as the preceding ones; if you do, you should review your design, because it may not be sufficiently modular. With that said, it's worthwhile to be aware of these advanced features of the OSGi module layer and the circumstances under which they're useful. To assist in this endeavor, we'll introduce use cases and examples to help you understand when and how to apply them.

This chapter isn't strictly necessary for understanding subsequent chapters, so feel free to postpone reading it until later. Otherwise, let's dig in.

5.1 Managing your exports

From what you've learned so far, exporting a package from a bundle is fairly simple: include it in the `Export-Package` header, and potentially include some attributes. This doesn't cover all the details of exporting packages. In the following subsections, we'll discuss other aspects, like importing exported packages, implicit attributes, mandatory attributes, class filtering, and duplicate exports.

5.1.1 Importing your exports

In chapter 2, you learned how `Export-Package` exposes internal bundle classes and how `Import-Package` makes external classes visible to internal bundle classes. This seems to be a nice division of labor between the two. You may even assume the two are mutually exclusive. In other words, you may assume a bundle exporting a given package can't import it also and vice versa. In many module systems, this would be a reasonable assumption, but for OSGi it's incorrect. A bundle importing a package it exports is a special case in OSGi, but what exactly does it mean? The answer to this question is both philosophical and technical.

The original vision of the OSGi service platform was to create a lightweight execution environment where dynamically downloaded bundles collaborate. In an effort to meet the "lightweight" aspect of this vision, these bundles collaborated by sharing direct references to service objects. Using direct references means that bundles collaborate via normal method calls, which is lightweight. As a byproduct of using direct references, bundles must share the Java class associated with shared service objects. As you've learned, OSGi has code sharing covered in spades with `Export-Package` and `Import-Package`. Still, there's an issue lurking here, so let's examine a collaboration scenario more closely.

Imagine that bundle A wants to use an instance of class `javax.servlet.Servlet` from bundle B. As you now understand, in their respective metadata, bundle A will import package `javax.servlet`, and bundle B will export it. Makes sense. Now imagine that bundle C also wants to share an instance of class `javax.servlet.Servlet` with bundle A. It has two choices at this point:

- Don't include a copy of package `javax.servlet` in its bundle JAR file, and import it instead.
- Include a copy of package `javax.servlet` in its bundle JAR file, and also export it.

If the approach in option 1 is taken (see figure 5.1), bundle C can't be used unless bundle B is present, because it has a dependency on package `javax.servlet` and only bundle B provides the package (that is, bundle C isn't self-contained).

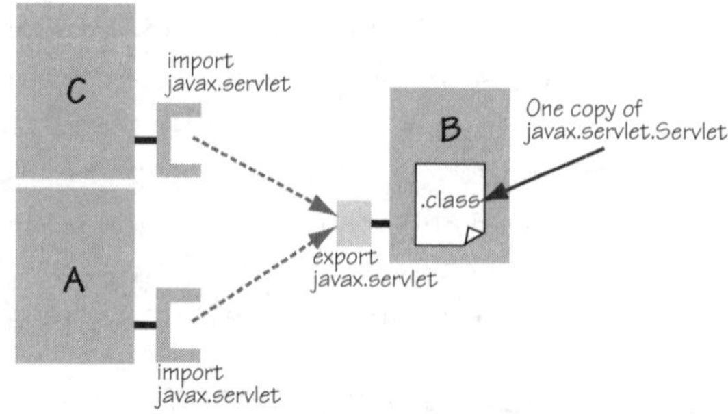

Figure 5.1 If bundle C imports from B, both can share servlet instances with A because there's only one copy of the `Servlet` class; but this creates a dependency for C on B.

On the other hand, if the approach in option 2 is taken (see figure 5.2), bundle C is self-contained, and both B and C can be used independently. But what happens if you want bundle A to interact with the `javax.servlet.Servlet` objects from bundles B and C at the same time? It can't do so. Why?

The answer is technical, so we'll only briefly explain it. To use a class, Java must load it into the JVM using a class loader. The identity of a class at execution time is not only associated with its fully qualified class name, it's also scoped by the class loader that loaded it. The exact same class loaded by two different class loaders is loaded twice by the Java VM and is treated as two different and incompatible types. This means if you try to cast an instance of one to the other, you receive a `ClassCast-Exception`. Combine this knowledge with the fact that the OSGi specification requires each bundle to have its own class loader for loading its classes, and you begin to understand the issue with the second option we described.

If bundles B and C both include and export a copy of the `javax.servlet` package, then there are two copies of the `javax.servlet.Servlet` class. Bundle A can't use both instances, because they come from different class loaders and are incompatible. Due to this incompatibility, the OSGi framework only allows bundle A to see one copy, which means A can't collaborate with both B and C at the same time.

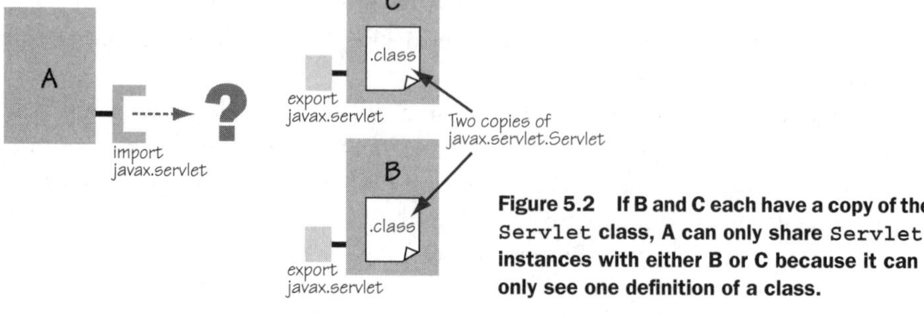

Figure 5.2 If B and C each have a copy of the `Servlet` class, A can only share `Servlet` instances with either B or C because it can only see one definition of a class.

It's not important for you to completely understand these arcane details of Java class loaders, especially because OSGi technology tries to relieve you from having to worry about them in the first place. The important point is to understand the issues surrounding the two options: option 1 results in bundle C requiring B to be present, whereas option 2 results in bundle A not being able to see the shared object instances from bundles B and C at the same time. This gets us to the crux of OSGi's special case for allowing a bundle to import a package it exports.

Neither of the previous two options is satisfactory. The solution devised by the OSGi specification is to allow a bundle to both import and export the same package (see figure 5.3). In this case, the bundle contains the given package and its associated classes, but it may not end up using its copy. A bundle importing and exporting the same package is offering the OSGi framework a choice; it allows the framework to treat it as either an importer or an exporter of the package, whichever seems appropriate at the time the framework makes the decision. Here's another way to think about this: it defines a *substitutable* export, where the framework is free to substitute the bundle's export with an imported package from another bundle. Returning to the example, both bundles B and C can include a copy of package `javax.servlet`, with both importing and exporting it, knowing they'll work independently or together.

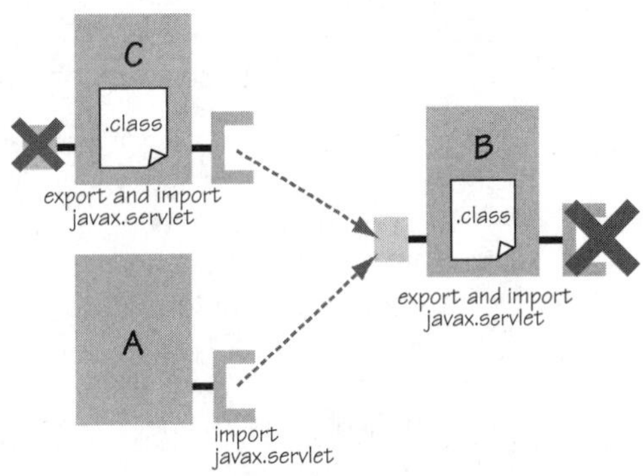

Figure 5.3 B and C can both export and import the `Servlet` package, which makes it possible for the framework to choose to substitute packages so all bundles use a single class definition.

Admittedly, this may seem odd; but as the discussion here illustrates, to simplify the OSGi vision of a collaborative environment, it's necessary to make sure bundles use the same class definitions. Up until the OSGi R4 specification, `Export-Package` implicitly meant `Import-Package`, too. The R4 specification removed this implicitness, making it a requirement to have a separate `Import-Package` to get a substitutable export; but this didn't lessen the importance of doing so in cases where collaboration is desired. An interesting side effect of this is the possibility of metadata like this:

```
Export-Package: javax.servlet; version="2.4.0"
Import-Package: javax.servlet; version="2.3.0"
```

This isn't a mistake. A bundle may include a copy of a given package at a specific version but may work with a lower range. This can make the bundle useful in a wider range of scenarios, because it can still work in an environment where an older version of the package must be used.

When to import your exports

The question on your mind probably is, "With all these benefits, shouldn't I make all my exports substitutable?" Not necessarily. If the packages in question are somehow coupled to private (non-exported) packages, or all packages are exported, you should only export them. Conversely, if other bundles can reasonably expect to get the packages from a different provider, you may want to import and export them. For example, if you're embedding and exporting common open source packages, you may want to import them too, because other bundles may reasonably expect to get them from other providers; this is especially necessary if your other exported packages have `uses` constraints on the common packages.

Importing and exporting a package is also useful when you're using an interface-based development approach. In interface-based programming, which is the foundation of the OSGi service approach, you assume there are potentially multiple implementations of well-known interfaces. You may want to package the interfaces into their implementations to keep them self-contained. In this case, to ensure interoperability, the bundles should import and export the interface packages. Because the whole point of OSGi services is to foster collaboration among bundles, the choice between importing only or exporting and importing interface packages is fairly common.

You do have an alternative approach: to always package your collaborative interface packages into a separate bundle. By never packaging your interfaces in a bundle that provides implementations, you can be sure all implementations can be used together, because all implementations will import the shared packages. If you follow this approach, none of your implementations will be self-contained, because they'll all have external dependencies on the shared packages. The trade-off is deciding whether you want more bundles with dependencies among them or fewer self-contained bundles with some content overlap. It's all about balancing coupling and cohesion.

Next, we'll look at implicit export attributes. Unlike importing exported packages, which gives the framework resolver more flexibility when resolving imports, implicit export attributes can be used to limit the framework's options for resolving an import.

5.1.2 *Implicit export attributes*

Generally speaking, OSGi regards the same package exported by multiple bundles as being completely equivalent if the package versions are the same. This is beneficial when it comes to dependency resolution, because it's possible for the framework to satisfy an import for a given package from any available matching exporter. In certain situations, you may not wish to have your bundle's imports satisfied by an arbitrary bundle; instead, you may want to import from a specific bundle. For example, perhaps you patched a bug in a common open source library, and you don't want to risk using a nonpatched version. OSGi supports this through implicit export attributes.

Consider the following bundle manifest snippet:

```
Bundle-ManifestVersion: 2
Bundle-SymbolicName: my.javax.servlet
Bundle-Version: 1.2.0
Export-Package: javax.servlet; javax.servlet.http; version="2.4.0"
```

This metadata exports the packages `javax.servlet` and `javax.servlet.http` with a `version` attribute of the specified value. Additionally, the framework implicitly attaches the bundle's symbolic name and version to all packages exported by a bundle. Therefore, the previous metadata conceptually looks like this (also shown in figure 5.4):

```
Bundle-ManifestVersion: 2
Bundle-SymbolicName: my.javax.servlet
Bundle-Version: 1.2.0
Export-Package: javax.servlet; javax.servlet.http; version="2.4.0";
 bundle-symbolic-name="my.javax.servlet"; bundle-version="1.2.0"
```

Although this is conceptually what is happening, don't try to explicitly specify the `bundle-symbolic-name` and `bundle-version` attributes on your exports. These attributes can only be specified by the framework; explicitly specifying them results in an installation exception. With these implicit attributes, it's possible for you limit the framework's resolution of an imported package to specific bundles. For example, an importing bundle may contain the following snippet of metadata:

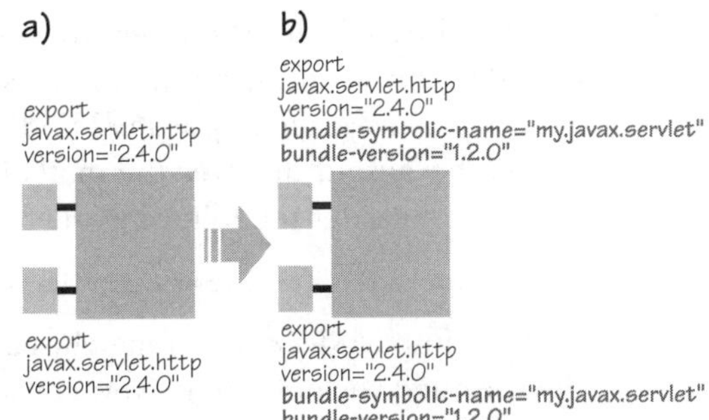

Figure 5.4 a) Your metadata declares explicit attributes that are attached to your bundle's exported packages, but b) the framework also implicitly attaches attributes explicitly identifying from which bundle the exports come.

```
Import-Package: javax.servlet; bundle-symbolic-name="my.javax.servlet";
 bundle-version="[1.2.0,1.2.0]"
```

In this case, the importer limits its dependency resolution to a specific bundle by specifying its symbolic name with a precise version range. As you can imagine, this makes the dependency a lot more brittle, but under certain circumstances this may be desired.

You may be thinking that implicit export attributes aren't completely necessary to control how import dependencies are resolved. You're correct. You can also use good old arbitrary attributes to achieve the same effect—just make sure your attribute name and/or value are sufficiently unique. For example, you can modify your exporting manifest like this:

```
Bundle-ManifestVersion: 2
Bundle-SymbolicName: javax.servlet
Bundle-Version: 1.2.0
Export-Package: javax.servlet; javax.servlet.http; version="2.4.0";
 my-provider-attribute="my.value.scheme"
```

In this case, the importer needs to specify the corresponding attribute name and value on its `Import-Package` declaration. There's an advantage to using this approach if you're in a situation where you must have brittle dependencies: it's not as brittle as implicit attributes. You're able to refactor your exporting bundle without impacting importing bundles, because these attribute values aren't tied to the containing bundle. On the downside, arbitrary attributes are easier for other bundles to imitate, even though there are no guarantees either way.

In short, it's best to avoid brittle dependencies, but at least now you understand how both implicit and arbitrary export attributes allow importing bundles to have a say in how their dependencies are resolved. Thinking about the flip side, it may also occasionally be necessary for exporting bundles to have some control over how importing bundles are resolved. Mandatory attributes can help you here.

5.1.3 Mandatory export attributes

The OSGi framework promotes arbitrary package sharing among bundles. As we discussed in the last subsection, in some situations this isn't desired.

Up until now, the importing bundle appears to be completely in control of this situation, because it declares the matching constraints for dependency resolution. For example, consider the following metadata snippet for importing a package:

```
Import-Package: javax.servlet; version="[2.4.0,2.5.0)"
```

Such an import declaration matches any provider of `javax.servlet` as long as it's in the specified version range. Now consider the following metadata snippet for exporting a package in another bundle:

```
Export-Package: javax.servlet; version="2.4.1"; private="true"
```

Will the imported package match this exported package? Yes, it will, as shown in figure 5.5. The name of the attribute, `private`, may have tricked you into thinking otherwise, but it's just an arbitrary attribute and has no meaning (if it did have meaning to the framework, it would likely be a directive, not an attribute). When it comes to matching an import to an export, only the attributes mentioned on the import declaration are compared against the attributes on the export declaration. In this case, the import mentions the package name and version range, which match the exported package's name and version. The `private` attribute isn't even considered.

In some situations, you may wish to have a little more control in your exporting bundle. For example, maybe you're exposing a package containing a nonpublic API, or you've modified a common open source library in an incompatible way, and you don't want unaware bundles to inadvertently match your exported packages. The OSGi specification provides this capability using

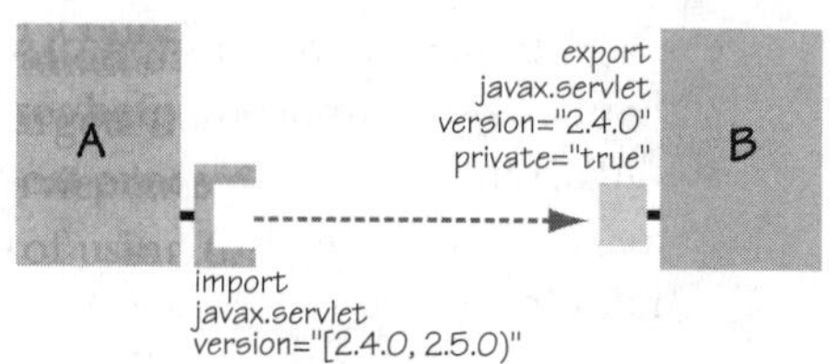

Figure 5.5 Only attributes mentioned in the imported package declaration impact dependency resolution matching. Any attributes mentioned only in the exported package declaration are ignored.

mandatory export attributes, which you declare using the `mandatory` export package directive of the `Export-Package` manifest header.

> **MANDATORY DIRECTIVE** The `mandatory` export package directive specifies a comma-delimited list of attribute names that any importer must match in order to be wired to the exported package.

To see how mandatory attributes work, let's modify the previous snippet to export its package, like this:

```
Export-Package: javax.servlet; version="2.4.1"; private="true";
 mandatory:="private"
```

You add the `mandatory` directive to the exported package to declare the `private` attribute as mandatory. Any export attribute declared as mandatory places a constraint on importers. If the importers don't specify a matching value for the attribute, then they don't match. The export attribute can't be ignored, as shown in figure 5.6. The need for mandatory attributes doesn't arise often; you'll see some other use cases in the coming sections. Until then, let's look into another more fine-grained mechanism that bundles can use to control what is exposed from their exported packages.

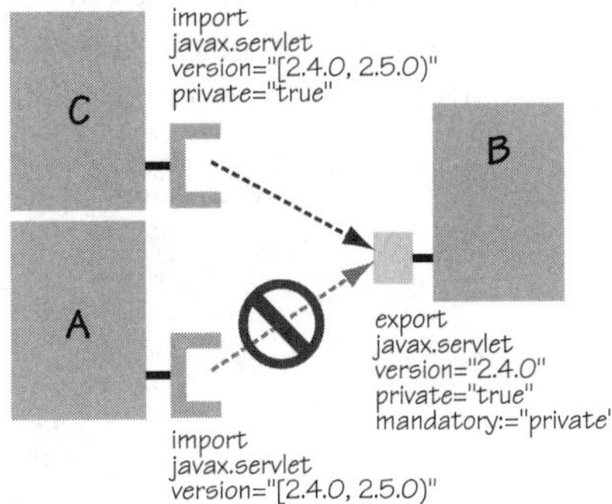

Figure 5.6 If an export attribute is declared as mandatory, importing bundles must declare the attribute and matching value; otherwise, it won't match when the framework resolves dependencies.

5.1.4 Export filtering

In chapter 1, we discussed the limitations of Java's rules for code visibility. There's no way to declare module visibility, so you must use `public` visibility for classes accessed across packages. This isn't necessarily problematic if you can keep your public and private APIs in separate packages, because bundles have the ability to hide packages by not exporting them. Unfortunately, this isn't always possible, and in some cases you end up with a `public` implementation class inside a package exported by the bundle. To cope with this situation, OSGi provides `include` and `exclude` export filtering directives for the `Export-Package` manifest header to enable fine-grained control over the classes exposed from your bundle's exported packages.

> **EXCLUDE/INCLUDE DIRECTIVES** The `exclude` and `include` export package directives specify a comma-delimited list of class names to exclude or include from the exported package, respectively.

To see how you can use these directives, consider a hypothetical bundle containing a package (`org.foo.service`) with a service interface (`public class Service`), an implementation of the service (package private `class ServiceImpl`), and a utility class (`public class Util`). In this hypothetical example, the utility class is part of the private API. It's included in this package due to dependencies on the service implementation and is `public` because it's used by other packages in the bundle. You need to export the `org.foo.service` package, but you don't want to expose the `Util` class. In general, you should avoid such scenarios, but the following metadata snippet illustrates how you can do this with export filtering:

```
Export-Package: org.foo.service; version="1.0.0"; exclude:="Util"
```

This exported package behaves like any normal exported package as far as dependency resolution is concerned; but at execution time, the framework filters the `Util` class from the package so importers can't access it, as shown in figure 5.7. A bundle attempting to load the `Util` class receives a "class not found" exception. The value of the directive specifies only class names; the package name must not be specified, nor should the .class portion of the class file name. The `*` character is also supported as a wildcard, so it's possible to exclude all classes with names matching `*Impl`, for example.

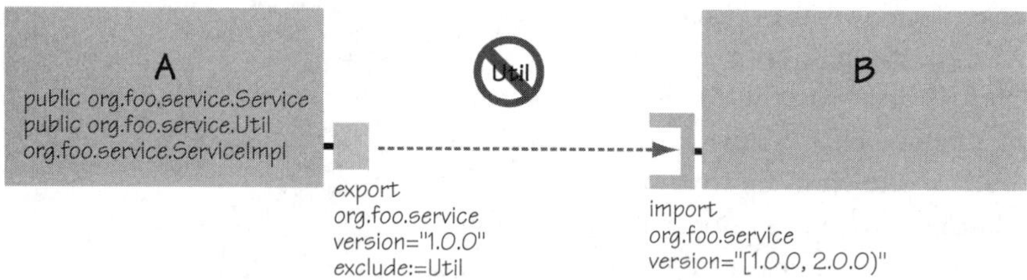

Figure 5.7 Bundle A exports the `org.foo.service` package but excludes the `Util` class. When bundle B imports the `org.foo.service` package from bundle A, it can only access the public `Service` class.

In some cases, it may be easier to specify which classes are allowed instead of which ones are disallowed. For those situations, the `include` directive is available. It specifies which classes the exported package should expose. The default value for the `include` directive is `*`, and the default value for the `exclude` directive is an empty string. You can also specify both the `include` and `exclude` directive for a given exported package. A class is visible only if it's matched by an entry in the `include` directive and not matched by any entry in the `exclude` directive.

You should definitely strive to separate your public and private APIs into different packages so these mechanisms aren't needed, but they're here to get you out of a tough spot when you need them. Next, we'll move on to another mechanism to help you manage your APIs.

5.1.5 Duplicate exports

A given bundle can see only one version of a given class while it executes. In view of this, it's not surprising to learn that bundles aren't allowed to import the same package more than once. What you may find surprising is that OSGi allows a bundle to *export* the same package more than once. For example, the following snippet of metadata is perfectly valid:

```
Export-Package: javax.servlet; version="2.3.0",
 javax.servlet; version="2.4.0"
```

How is it possible, you ask? The trick is that the bundle doesn't contain two separate sets of classes for the two exported packages. The bundle is masquerading the same set of classes as different packages. Why would it do this? Expounding on the previous snippet, perhaps you have unmodifiable third-party bundles with explicit dependencies on `javax.servlet` version `2.3.0` in your application. Because version `2.4.0` is backward compatible with version `2.3.0`, you can use duplicate exports to allow your bundle to stake a backward compatibility claim. In the end, all bundles requiring either version of `javax.servlet` can resolve, but they'll all use the same set of classes at execution time, as shown in figure 5.8.

As with export filtering, this is another mechanism to manage your APIs. You can take this further and combine it with some of the other mechanisms you've learned about in this section for additional API management techniques. For example, you generally don't want to expose your bundle's implementation details to everyone, but sometimes you want to expose implementation details to select bundles; this is similar to the friend concept in C++. A friend is allowed to see implementation details, but nonfriends aren't. To achieve something like this in OSGi, you need to combine mandatory export attributes, export filtering, and duplicate exports.

To illustrate, let's return to the example from export filtering:

```
Export-Package: org.foo.service; version="1.0.0"; exclude:="Util"
```

In this example, you excluded the `Util` class, because it was an implementation detail. This is the exported package your nonfriends should use. For friends, you need to export the package without filtering:

```
Export-Package: org.foo.service; version="1.0.0"; exclude:="Util",
 org.foo.service; version="1.0.0"
```

Now you have one export hiding the `Util` class and one exposing it. How do you control who gets access to what? That's right: mandatory export attributes. The following complete export metadata gives you what you need:

```
Export-Package: org.foo.service; version="1.0.0"; exclude:="Util",
 org.foo.service; version="1.0.0"; friend="true"; mandatory:="friend"
```

Only bundles that explicitly import your package with the `friend` attribute and matching value see the `Util` class. Clearly, this isn't a strong sense of friendship, because any bundle can specify the `friend` attribute; but at least it requires an opt-in

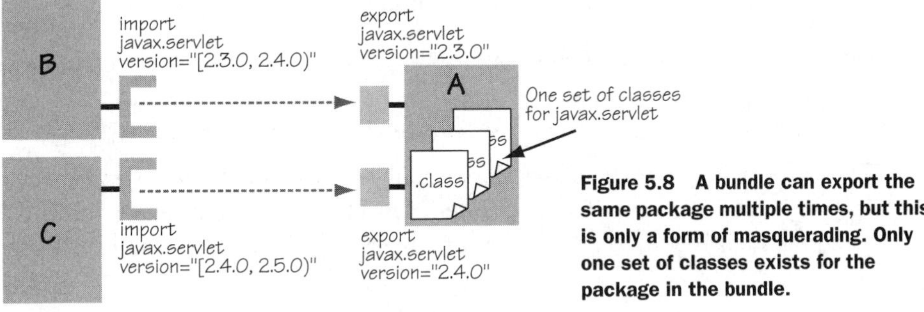

Figure 5.8 A bundle can export the same package multiple times, but this is only a form of masquerading. Only one set of classes exists for the package in the bundle.

strategy for using implementation details, signaling that the importer is willing to live with the consequences of potential breaking changes in the future.

Best practice dictates avoiding the friendship concept, because it weakens modularity. If an API is valuable enough to export, you should consider making it a public API.

In this section, we've covered additional capabilities that OSGi provides for exporting packages to help you deal with various uncommon use cases. Likewise, OSGi provides some additional capabilities for importing packages. In the next section, you'll learn how to make importing packages a little more flexible, which again can provide some wiggle room when you're trying to get legacy Java applications to work in an OSGi environment.

5.2 Loosening your imports

Explicitly declared imports are great, because explicit requirements allow you to more easily reuse code and automate dependency resolution. This gives you the benefit of being able to detect misconfigurations early rather than receiving various class-loading and class-cast exceptions at execution time. On the other hand, explicitly declared imports are somewhat constraining, because the framework uses them to strictly control whether your code can be used; if an imported package can't be satisfied, the framework doesn't allow the associated bundle to transition into the `RESOLVED` state. Additionally, to import a package, you must know the name of a package in advance, but this isn't always possible.

What can you do in these situations? The OSGi framework provides two different mechanisms for dealing with such situations: optional and dynamic imports. Let's look into how each of these can help, as well as compare and contrast them.

5.2.1 Optional imports

Sometimes a given package imported by a bundle isn't strictly necessary for it to function properly. Consider an imported package for a nonfunctional purpose, like logging. The code in a given bundle may have been programmed to function properly regardless of whether a logging facility is available. To express this, OSGi provides the `resolution` directive for the `Import-Package` manifest header to mark imported packages as optional.

> **RESOLUTION DIRECTIVE** The `resolution` import package directive can have a value of `mandatory` or `optional` to indicate whether the imported package is required to successfully resolve the bundle.

Consider the following metadata snippet:

```
Import-Package: javax.servlet; version="2.4.0",
 org.osgi.service.log; version="1.3.0"; resolution:="optional"
```

This import statement declares dependencies on two packages, `javax.servlet` and `org.osgi.service.log`. The dependency on the logging package is optional, as indicated by the use of the `resolution` directive with the `optional` value. This means the bundle can be successfully resolved even if there isn't an `org.osgi.service.log` package available. Attempts by the bundle to use classes from this package at execution time result in `ClassNotFoundExceptions`. All imported packages have a resolution associated with them, but the default value is `mandatory`. We'll look at how this is used in practice in section 5.2.4, but for now let's consider the other tool in the box: dynamic imports.

5.2.2 Dynamic imports

Certain Java programming practices make it difficult to know all the packages that a bundle may need at execution time. A prime example is locating a JDBC driver. Often the name of the class implementing the JDBC driver is a configuration property or is supplied by the user at execution time. Because your bundle can only see classes in packages it imports, how can it import an unknown package? This sort of situation arises when you deal with service provider interface (SPI) approaches, where a common interface is known in advance, but not the name of the class implementing it. To capture this, OSGi has a separate `DynamicImport-Package` manifest header.

> **DYNAMICIMPORT-PACKAGE** This header is a comma-separated list of packages needed at execution time by internal bundle code from other bundles, but not needed at resolve time. Because the package name may be unknown, you can use a `*` wildcard (matching all packages) or a trailing `.*` (matching subpackages recursively).

You may have expected from the previous examples that dynamic imports would be handled using an import directive rather than their own manifest header, but they're sufficiently different to warrant a separate header. In the most general sense, a dynamic import is expressed in the bundle metadata like this:

```
DynamicImport-Package: *
```

This snippet dynamically imports any package needed by the bundle. When you use the wildcard at the end of a package name (for example, `org.foo.*`), it matches all subpackages recursively but doesn't match the specified root package.

Given the open-ended nature of dynamic imports, it's important to understand precisely when in the class search order of a bundle they're employed. They appear in the class search order as follows:

1. Requests for classes in `java.` packages are delegated to the parent class loader; searching stops with either a success or failure (section 2.5.4).
2. Requests for classes in an imported package are delegated to the exporting bundle; searching stops with either a success or failure (section 2.5.4).
3. The bundle class path is searched for the class; searching stops if found but continues to the next step with a failure (section 2.5.4).
4. If the package in question isn't exported by the bundle, requests matching any dynamically imported package are delegated to an exporting bundle if one is found; searching stops with either a success or failure.

As you can see, dynamic imports are attempted only as a last resort. But when a dynamically imported package is resolved and associated with the importing bundle, it behaves just like a statically imported package. Future requests for classes in the same package are serviced in step 2.

Avoid the Siren's song

Dynamic imports are alluring to new OSGi programmers because they provide behavior similar to that in standard Java programming, where everything available on the class path is visible to the bundle. Unfortunately, this approach isn't modular and doesn't allow the OSGi framework to verify whether dependencies are satisfied in advance of using a bundle. As a result, dynamically importing packages should be seen as bad practice, except for explicitly dealing with legacy SPI approaches.

You can also use dynamically imported packages in a fashion more similar to optionally imported packages by specifying additional attributes like normal imported packages

```
DynamicImport-Package: javax.servlet.*; version="2.4.0"
```

or even

```
DynamicImport-Package: javax.servlet; javax.servlet.http; version="2.4.0"
```

In the first case, all subpackages of `javax.servlet` of version `2.4.0` are dynamically imported, whereas in the second only the explicitly mentioned packages are dynamically imported. More precise declarations such as these often make less sense when you're using dynamic imports, because the general use case is for unknown package names.

We apparently have two different ways to loosen bundle imports. Let's compare and contrast them a little more closely.

5.2.3 Optional vs. dynamic imports

There are intended use cases for both optional and dynamic imports, but the functionality they provide overlaps. To better understand each, we'll look into their similarities and differences. Let's start with the similarities.

SIMILARITIES

Both are used to express dependencies on packages that may or may not be available at execution time. Although this is the specific use case for optional imports, it's a byproduct of dynamic imports. Either way, this has the following impact:

- Optional/dynamic imports never cause a bundle to be unable to resolve.
- Your bundle code must be prepared to catch `ClassNotFoundExceptions` for the optionally/dynamically imported packages.

Only normally imported packages (that is, mandatory imported packages) impact bundle dependency resolution. If a mandatory imported package can't be satisfied, the bundle can't be resolved or used. Neither optionally nor dynamically imported packages are required to be present when resolving dependencies. For optional imports, this is the whole point: they're optional. For dynamic imports, they aren't necessarily optional; but because they aren't known in advance, it's not possible for the framework to enforce that they exist.

Because the packages may not exist in either case, the logical consequence is that the code in any bundle employing either mechanism must be prepared to catch `ClassNotFoundExceptions` when attempting to access classes in the optionally or dynamically imported packages. This is typically the sort of issue the OSGi framework tries to help you avoid with explicit dependencies; we shouldn't be dealing with class-loading issues as developers.

DIFFERENCES

By now, you must be wondering what the difference is between optional and dynamic imports. It has to do with when the framework tries to resolve the dependencies.

The framework attempts to resolve an optionally imported package once when the associated bundle is resolved. If the import is satisfied, the bundle has access to the package. If not, the bundle doesn't and will never have access to the package unless it's re-resolved. For a dynamically imported package, the framework attempts to resolve it at execution time when the bundle's executing code tries to use a class from the package.

Further, the framework keeps trying to resolve the dynamically imported package each time the bundle's executing code tries to use classes from it until it's successfully resolved. If a bundle providing the dynamically imported package is ever deployed into the executing framework, the framework eventually will be able to resolve it. After the resolve is successful, the bundle is wired to the provider of the package; it behaves like a normal import from that point forward.

Let's look at how you can use these mechanisms in a logging example, which is often an optional activity for bundles.

5.2.4 Logging example

The OSGi specification defines a simple logging service that you may want to use in your bundles, but you can't be certain it will always be available. One way to deal with this uncertainty is to create a simple *proxy* logger that uses the logging service if available or prints to standard output if not.

Our first example uses an optional import for the `org.osgi.service.log` package. The simple proxy logger code is shown here.

Listing 5.1 Simple proxy logger using optional import

```
public class Logger {
  private final BundleContext m_context;
  private final ServiceTracker m_tracker;
  public Logger(BundleContext context) {
    m_context = context;
    m_tracker = init(m_context);
```

```
  }
  private ServiceTracker init(BundleContext context) {
    ServiceTracker tracker = null;
    try {
      tracker = new ServiceTracker(                         ❶ Creates ServiceTracker
        context, org.osgi.service.log.LogService.class.getName(), null);
      tracker.open();
    } catch (NoClassDefFoundError error) { }
    return tracker;
  }
  public void close() {
    if (m_tracker != null) {
      m_tracker.close();
    }
  }
  public void log(int level, String msg) {
    boolean logged = false;                                  ❷ Checks for valid tracker
    if (m_tracker != null) {
      LogService logger = (LogService) m_tracker.getService();
      if (logger != null) {                                  ❸ Checks for log service
        logger.log(level, msg);
        logged = true;
      }
    }
    if (!logged) {
      System.out.println("[" + level + "] " + msg);
    }
  }
}
```

The proxy logger has a constructor that takes the `BundleContext` object to track log services, an `init()` method to create a `ServiceTracker` for log services, a `close()` method to stop tracking log services, and a `log()` method for logging messages. Looking more closely at the `init()` method, you try to use the logging package to create a `ServiceTracker` ❶. Because you're optionally importing the logging package, you surround it in a `try-catch` block. If an exception is thrown, you set your tracker to `null`; otherwise, you end up with a valid tracker.

When a message is logged, you check if you have a valid tracker ❷. If so, you try to log to a log service. Even if you have a valid tracker, that doesn't mean you have a log service, which is why you verify it ❸. If you have a log service, you use it; otherwise, you log to standard output. The important point is that you attempt to probe for the log package only once, with a single call to `init()` from the constructor, because an optional import will never be satisfied later if it's not satisfied already.

The bundle activator is shown in the following listing.

Listing 5.2 Bundle activator creating the proxy logger

```
public class Activator implements BundleActivator {
  private volatile Logger m_logger = null;
  public void start(BundleContext context) throws Exception {
    m_logger = new Logger(context);
```

```
    m_logger.log(4, "Started");
    ...
  }
  public void stop(BundleContext context) {
    m_logger.close();
  }
}
```

When the bundle is started, you create an instance of your proxy logger that's used throughout the bundle for logging. Although not shown here, the bundle passes a reference or somehow provides access to the logger instance to any internal code needing a logger at execution time. When the bundle is stopped, you invoke `close()` on the proxy logger, which stops its internal service tracker, if necessary. The manifest for your logging bundle is

```
Bundle-ManifestVersion: 2
Bundle-SymbolicName: example.logger
Bundle-Activator: example.logger.Activator
Import-Package: org.osgi.framework, org.osgi.util.tracker,
 org.osgi.service.log; resolution:=optional
```

How would this example change if you wanted to treat the logging package as a dynamic import? The impact to the `Logger` class is as follows.

Listing 5.3 Simple proxy logger using dynamic import

```
public class Logger {
  private final BundleContext m_context;
  private ServiceTracker m_tracker;
  public LoggerImpl(BundleContext context) {
    m_context = context;
  }
  private ServiceTracker init(BundleContext context) {
    ServiceTracker tracker = null;
    try {
      tracker = new ServiceTracker(
        context, org.osgi.service.log.LogService.class.getName(), null);
      tracker.open();
    } catch (NoClassDefFoundError error) { }
    return tracker;
  }
  public synchronized void close() {                          ◁─┐
    if (m_tracker != null) {                                     │
      m_tracker.close();                                         │ ❶ Synchronizes
    }                                                            │   entry
  }                                                              │   methods
  public synchronized void log(int level, String msg) {       ◁─┘
    boolean logged = false;
    if (m_tracker == null) {
      m_tracker = init(m_context);                     ◁─┐ Tries to create
    }                                                     ❷ ServiceTracker
    if (m_tracker != null) {
      LogService logger = (LogService) m_tracker.getService();
      if (logger != null) {
```

```
        logger.log(level, msg);
        logged = true;
      }
    }
    if (!logged) {
      System.out.println("[" + level + "] " + msg);
    }
  }
}
```

You can no longer make your `ServiceTracker` member variable `final`, because you don't know when it will be created. To make your proxy logger thread safe and avoid creating more than one `ServiceTracker` instance, you need to synchronize your entry methods ❶. Because the logging package can appear at any time during execution, you try to create the `ServiceTracker` instance each time you log a message ❷ until successful. As before, if all else fails, you log to standard output. The manifest metadata is pretty much the same as before, except you use `DynamicImport-Package` to import the logging package:

```
Bundle-ManifestVersion: 2
Bundle-SymbolicName: example.logger
Bundle-Activator: example.logger.Activator
Import-Package: org.osgi.framework, org.osgi.util.tracker
DynamicImport-Package: org.osgi.service.log
```

These two examples illustrate the differences between these two mechanisms. As you can see, if you plan to take advantage of the full, dynamic nature of dynamically imported packages, there's added complexity with respect to threading and concurrency. There's also potential overhead associated with dynamic imports, not only because of the synchronization, but also because it can be costly for the framework to try to find a matching package at execution time. For logging, which happens frequently, this cost can be great.

Optional imports are optional

We should point out that you can use dynamic imports in a fashion similar to optional imports. In this sense, the use of the optional import package mechanism is itself optional. For example, you can modify the metadata of the optional logger example to be a dynamic import instead, but keep the code exactly the same. If you did this, the two solutions would behave equivalently.

If this is the case, then why choose one over the other? There's no real reason or recommendation for doing so. These two concepts overlap for historical reasons. Dynamic imports have existed since the R2 release of the OSGi specification, whereas optional imports have only existed since the R4 release. Even though optional imports overlapped dynamic imports, they were added for consistency with bundle dependencies, which were also added in R4 and can also be declared as optional.

We've finished covering the advanced capabilities for importing packages, but there's still a related concept provided by OSGi for declaring dependencies. In some situations, such as legacy situations where modules are tightly coupled or contain a given package split across modules, importing a specific package isn't sufficient. For these situations, OSGi allows you to declare dependencies on specific bundles. We'll look at how this works next.

5.3 Requiring bundles

In section 5.1.2, we discussed how implicit export attributes allow bundles to import packages from a specific bundle. The OSGi specification also supports a module-level dependency concept called a *required bundle* that provides a similar capability. In chapter 2, we discussed a host of reasons why package-level dependencies are preferred over module-level dependencies, such as them being more flexible and fine-grained. We won't rehash those general issues. But there is one particular use case where requiring bundles may be necessary in OSGi: if you must deal with split packages.

> **SPLIT PACKAGE** A split package is a Java package whose classes aren't contained in a single JAR but are split across multiple JAR files. In OSGi terms, it's a package split across multiple bundles.

In standard Java programming, packages are generally treated as split; the Java class path approach merges all packages from different JAR files on the class path into one big soup. This is anathema to OSGi's modularization model, where packages are treated as atomic (that is, they can't be split).

When migrating to OSGi from a world where split packages are common, we're often forced to confront ugly situations. But even in the OSGi world, over time a package may grow too large and reach a point where you can logically divide it into disjoint functionality for different clients. Unfortunately, if you break up the existing package and assign new disjoint package names, you break all existing clients. Splitting the package allows its disjoint functionality to be used independently; but for existing clients, you still need an aggregated view of the package.

This gives you an idea of what a split package is, but how does this relate to requiring bundles? This will become clearer after we discuss what it means to require a bundle and introduce a use case for doing so.

5.3.1 Declaring bundle dependencies

The big difference between importing a package and requiring a bundle is the scope of the dependency. Whereas an imported package defines a dependency from a bundle to a specific package, a required bundle defines a dependency from a bundle to every package exported by a specific bundle. To require a bundle, you use the `Require-Bundle` manifest header in the requiring bundle's manifest file.

> **REQUIRE-BUNDLE** This header consists of a comma-separated list of target bundle symbolic names on which a bundle depends, indicating the need to access all packages exported by the specifically mentioned target bundles.

You use the Require-Bundle header to specify a bundle dependency in a manifest, like this:

```
Require-Bundle: A; bundle-version="[1.0.0,2.0.0)"
```

Resolving required bundles is similar to imported packages. The framework tries to satisfy each required bundle; if it's unable to do so, the bundle can't be used. The framework resolves the dependency by searching the installed bundles for ones matching the specified symbolic name and version range. Figure 5.9 shows a resolved bundle dependency.

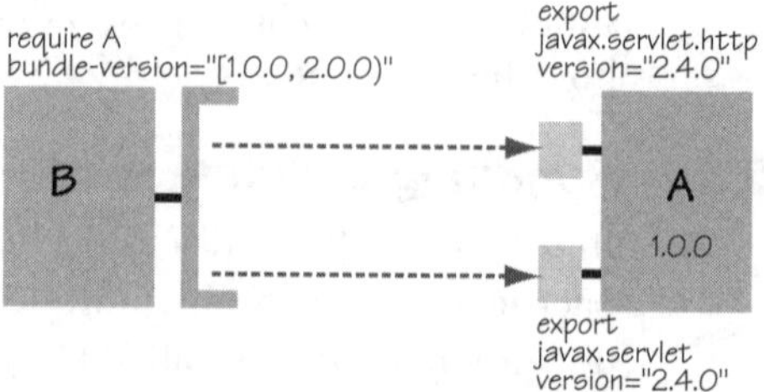

Figure 5.9 Requiring a bundle is similar to explicitly importing every package exported by the target bundle.

To a large degree, requiring bundles is just a brittle way to import packages, because it specifies *who* instead of *what*. The significant difference is how it fits into the overall class search order for the bundle, which is as follows:

1. Requests for classes in `java.` packages are delegated to the parent class loader; searching stops with either a success or failure (section 2.5.4).
2. Requests for classes in an imported package are delegated to the exporting bundle; searching stops with either a success or failure (section 2.5.4).
3. Requests for classes in a package from a required bundle are delegated to the exporting bundle; searching stops if found but continues with the next required bundle or the next step with a failure.
4. The bundle class path is searched for the class; searching stops if found but continues to the next step with a failure (section 2.5.4).
5. If the package in question isn't exported or required, requests matching any dynamically import package are delegated to an exporting bundle if one is found; searching stops with either a success or failure (section 5.2.2).

Packages from required bundles are searched only if the class wasn't found in an imported package, which means imported packages override packages from required bundles. Did you notice another important difference between imported packages and packages from required bundles in the search order? If a class in a package from a required bundle can't be found, the search continues to the next required bundle in declared order or the bundle's local class path. This is how Require-Bundle supports split packages, which we'll discuss in more detail in the next subsection. First, let's look at the remaining details of requiring bundles.

As we briefly mentioned in section 5.2.4, it's also possible to optionally require a bundle using the `resolution` directive:

```
Require-Bundle: A; bundle-version="[1.0.0,2.0.0)"; resolution:="optional"
```

The meaning is the same as when you optionally import packages, such as not impacting dependency resolution and the need to catch ClassNotFoundExceptions when

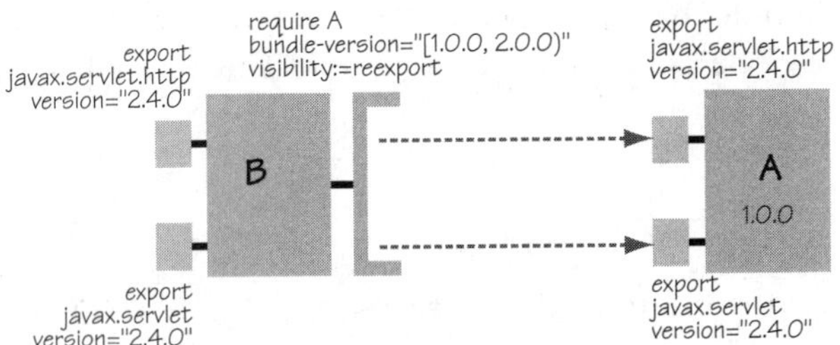

Figure 5.10 When bundle B requires bundle A with `reexport` visibility, any packages exported from A become visible to any bundles requiring B.

your bundle attempts to use potentially missing classes. It's also possible to control downstream visibility of packages from a required bundle using the `visibility` directive, which can be specified as `private` by default or as `reexport`. For example:

```
Require-Bundle: A; bundle-version="[1.0.0,2.0.0)"; visibility:="reexport"
```

This makes the required bundle dependency transitive. If a bundle contains this, any bundle requiring it also sees the packages from bundle A (they're re-exported). Figure 5.10 provide a pictorial example.

> **WARNING** There are few, if any, good reasons to use `Require-Bundle` with `reexport` visibility. This mechanism isn't very modular, and using it results in brittle systems with high coupling.

Now let's return our attention to how `Require-Bundle` supports aggregating split packages.

5.3.2 Aggregating split packages

Avoiding split packages is the recommended approach in OSGi, but occasionally you may run into a situation where you need to split a package across bundles. `Require-Bundle` makes such situations possible. Because class searching doesn't stop when a class isn't found for required bundles, you can use `Require-Bundle` to search for a class across a split package by requiring multiple bundles containing its different parts.

For example, assume you have a package `org.foo.bar` that's split across bundles A and B. Here's a manifest snippet from bundle A:

```
Bundle-ManifestVersion: 2
Bundle-SymbolicName: A
Bundle-Version: 2.0.0
Export-Package: org.foo.bar; version="2.0.0"
```

Here is a manifest snippet from bundle B:

```
Bundle-ManifestVersion: 2
Bundle-SymbolicName: B
Bundle-Version: 2.0.0
Export-Package: org.foo.bar; version="2.0.0"
```

Both bundles claim to export `org.foo.bar`, even though they each offer only half of it. (Yes, this is problematic, but we'll ignore that for now and come back to it shortly.)

Now, if you have another bundle that wants to use the entire `org.foo.bar` package, it has to require both bundles. The bundle metadata may look something like this:

```
Bundle-ManifestVersion: 2
Bundle-SymbolicName: C
Bundle-Version: 1.0.0
Require-Bundle: A; version="[2.0.0,2.1.0)", B; version="[2.0.0,2.1.0)"
```

When code from bundle C attempts to load a class from the `org.foo.bar` package, it follows these steps:

1. It delegates to bundle A. If the request succeeds, the class is returned; but if it fails, the code goes to the next step.
2. It delegates to bundle B. If the request succeeds, the class is returned; but if it fails, the code goes to the next step.
3. It tries to load the class from bundle C's local class path.

The last step allows `org.foo.bar` to be split across the required bundles as well as the requiring bundle. Because searching continues across all required bundles, bundle C is able to use the whole package.

What about a bundle wanting to use only one half of the package? Instead of requiring both bundles, it can require just the bundle containing the portion it needs. Sounds reasonable; but does this mean that after you split a package, you're stuck with using bundle-level dependencies and can no longer use package-level dependencies? No, it doesn't, but it does require some best practice recommendations.

HANDLING SPLIT PACKAGES WITH IMPORT-PACKAGE

If another bundle wants to use `Import-Package` to access the portion of the package contained in bundle B, it can do something like this:

```
Import-Package: org.foo.bar; version="2.0.0"; bundle-symbolic-name="B"
```

This is similar to using `Require-Bundle` for the specific bundle. If you add an arbitrary attribute to each exported split package—called `split`, for example—you can use it to indicate a part name instead. Assume you set `split` equal to `part1` for bundle A and `part2` for bundle B. You can import the portion from B as follows:

```
Import-Package: org.foo.bar; version="2.0.0"; split="part2"
```

This has the benefit of being a little more flexible, because if you later change which bundle contains which portion of the split package, it won't break existing clients. What about existing clients that were using `Import-Package` to access the entire `org.foo.bar` package? Is it still possible? It's likely that existing client bundles are doing the following:

```
Import-Package: org.foo.bar; version="2.0.0"
```

Will they see the entire package if it's now split across multiple bundles? No. How can the framework resolve this dependency? The framework has no understanding of split packages as far as dependency resolution is concerned. If bundles A and B are installed and another bundle comes along with the above import declaration, the framework treats A and B as both being candidates to resolve dependency. It chooses one following the normal rules of priority for multiple matching candidates. Clearly, no matter which candidate it chooses, the resulting solution will be incorrect.

To avoid such situations, you need to ensure that your split package portions aren't accidentally used by the framework to resolve an import for the entire package. But how? Mandatory attributes can help. You can rewrite bundle A's metadata like so:

```
Bundle-ManifestVersion: 2
Bundle-SymbolicName: A
Bundle-Version: 2.0.0
Export-Package: org.foo.bar; version="2.0.0"; split="part1";
 mandatory:="split"
```

Likewise for bundle B, but with `split` equal to `part2`. Now for a bundle to import either part of the split package, they must explicitly mention the part they wish to use. But what about an existing client bundle wanting to import the whole package? Because its import doesn't specify the mandatory attribute, it can't be resolved. You need some way to reconstruct the whole package and make it available for importing; OSGi allows you to create a *facade bundle* for such a purpose. To make bundle C a facade bundle, you change its metadata to be

```
Bundle-ManifestVersion: 2
Bundle-SymbolicName: C
Bundle-Version: 1.0.0
Require-Bundle: A; version="[2.0.0,2.1.0)", B; version="[2.0.0,2.1.0)"
Export-Package: org.foo.bar; version="2.0.0"
```

The only change is the last line where bundle C exports `org.foo.bar`, which is another form of re-exporting a package. In this case, it aggregates the split package by requiring the bundles containing the different parts, and it re-exports the package without the mandatory attribute. Now any client importing `org.foo.bar` will be able to resolve to bundle C and have access to the whole package.

Summarizing split package best practices

In short, if you must use a split package, make sure you follow these steps:

- Always export split packages with a mandatory attribute to avoid unsuspecting bundles from using them.
- Use either `Require-Bundle` or `Import-Package` plus the mandatory attribute to access parts of the split packages.
- To provide access to the whole package, create a facade bundle that requires the bundles containing the package parts and exports the package in question.

Admittedly, this isn't the most intuitive or straightforward way to deal with split packages. This approach wasn't intended to make them easy to use, because they're best avoided; but it *does* make it possible in those situations where you have no choice.

Despite these dire-sounding warnings, OSGi provides another way of dealing with split packages, called *bundle fragments*. We'll talk about those shortly, but first we'll discuss some of the issues surrounding bundle dependencies and split packages.

5.3.3 Issues with bundle dependencies

Using `Import-Package` and `Export-Package` is the preferred way to share code because they couple the importer and exporter to a lesser degree. Using `Require-Bundle` entails much higher coupling and lower cohesion between the importer and the exporter and suffers from other issues, such as the following:

- *Mutable exports*—Requiring bundles are impacted by changes to the exports of the required bundle, which introduce another form of breaking change to consider. Such changes aren't always easily apparent because the use of `reexport` visibility can result in chains of required bundles where removal of an export in upstream required bundles breaks all downstream requiring bundles.
- *Shadowing*—Because class searching continues across all required bundles and the requiring bundle's class path, it's possible for content in some required bundles to shadow other required bundle content and the content of the requiring bundle itself. The implications of this aren't always obvious, especially if some bundles are optionally required.
- *Ordering*—If a package is split across multiple bundles, but they contain overlapping classes, the declared order of the `Require-Bundle` header is significant. All bundles requiring the bundles with overlapping content must declare them in the same order, or their view of the package will be different. This is similar to traditional class path ordering issues.
- *Completeness*—Even though it's possible to aggregate split packages using a facade bundle, the framework has no way to verify whether an aggregated package is complete. This becomes the responsibility of the bundle developer.
- *Restricted access*—An aggregated split package isn't completely equivalent to the unsplit package. Each portion of the split package is loaded by its containing bundle's class loader. In Java, classes loaded by different class loaders can't access package-private members and types, even if they're in the same package.

This is by no means an exhaustive list of issues, but it gives you some ideas of what to look out for when using `Require-Bundle` and (we hope) dissuades you from using it too much.

Enough of the scare tactics. So far, we've introduced you to some of the more advanced features of managing OSGi dependencies, including importing exports, implicit export attributes, mandatory export attributes, export filtering, duplicate exports, optional and dynamic imports, and requiring bundles. These tools allow you to solve some of the more complex edge cases found when migrating a classic Java application to an OSGi environment. That must be it—we must have covered every possible mechanism of specifying dependencies, right? Not quite. There's one more curve ball to be thrown into the mix: bundle fragments. Fragments are another way to deal with split packages by allowing the content of a bundle to be split across multiple, subordinate bundle JAR files.

5.4 Dividing bundles into fragments

Although splitting packages isn't a good idea, occasionally it does make sense, such as with Java localization. Java handles localization by using `java.util.ResourceBundles` (which have nothing to do with OSGi bundles) as a container to help you turn locale-neutral keys into locale-specific objects. When a program wants to convert information into the user's preferred locale, it uses a resource bundle to do so. A `ResourceBundle` is created by loading a class or resource from a class loader using a base name, which ultimately defines the package containing the class or resource for the `ResourceBundle`. This approach means you typically package many localizations for different locales into the same Java package.

If you have lots of localizations or lots of information to localize, packaging all your localizations into the same OSGi bundle can result in a large deployment unit. Additionally, you can't introduce new localizations or fix mistakes in existing ones without releasing a new version of the bundle. It would be nice to keep localizations separate; but unlike the split package support of `Require-Bundle`, these split packages generally aren't useful without the bundle to which they belong. OSGi provides another approach to managing these sorts of dependencies through bundle fragments. We'll come back to localization shortly when we present a more in-depth example, but first we'll discuss what fragments are and what you can do with them.

5.4.1 Understanding fragments

If you recall the modularity discussion in chapter 2, you know there's a difference between logical modularity and physical modularity. Normally, in OSGi, a logical module and a physical module are treated as the same thing; a bundle is a physical module as a JAR file, but it's also the logical module at execution time forming an explicit visibility encapsulation boundary. Through fragments, OSGi allows you to break a single logical module across multiple physical modules. This means you can split a single logical bundle across multiple bundle JAR files.

Breaking a bundle into pieces doesn't result in a handful of peer bundles; instead, you define one *host* bundle and one or more subordinate *fragment* bundles. A host bundle is technically usable without fragments, but the fragments aren't usable without a host. Fragments are treated as optional host-bundle dependencies by the OSGi framework. But the host bundle isn't aware of its fragments, because it's the fragments that declare a dependency on the host using the `Fragment-Host` manifest header.

> **FRAGMENT-HOST** This header specifies the single symbolic name of the host bundle on which the fragment depends, along with an optional bundle version range.

A fragment bundle uses the `Fragment-Host` manifest header like this:

```
Fragment-Host: org.foo.hostbundle; bundle-version="[1.0.0,1.1.0)"
```

The `Fragment-Host` header is somewhat confusingly named, because it seems to be declaring the bundle as a host; it should be read as "require fragment host." Although this header value follows the common OSGi syntax, you can't specify multiple symbolic names. A fragment is limited to belonging to one host bundle, although it may be applicable to a range of host versions. Note that you don't need to do anything special to define a bundle as a host; any bundle without a `Fragment-Host` header is a potential host bundle. Likewise, any bundle with a `Fragment-Host` header is a fragment.

You now understand the relationship between a host and its fragments, but how do they work together? When the framework resolves a bundle, it searches the installed bundles to see if there are any fragments for the bundle being resolved. If so, it merges the fragments into the host bundle. This merging happens in two different ways:

- *Physically*—The content and metadata from the fragments are conceptually merged with the host's content and metadata.
- *Logically*—Rather than giving each fragment its own class loader, the framework attaches the fragment content to the host's class loader.

The first form of merging recombines the split physical pieces of the logical bundle, and the second form creates a single logical bundle because OSGi uses a single class loader per logical bundle to achieve encapsulation.

Fragments and package-private access

As a technical side note, Java only allows package-private access to classes loaded by the same class loader. Two classes in the same package, but loaded by two different class loaders, can't access each others' package-private members. By loading fragment classes with the host's class loader, the fragment classes are properly recombined to avoid this issue. This isn't true for split packages accessed through `Require-Bundle`. This isn't always important, but the distinction between these two forms of support for split packages is worth understanding.

Returning to the discussion about resolving a bundle, if the bundle being resolved has fragments, the framework merges their metadata with the host's and resolves the bundle as normal. Figure 5.11 illustrates the before- and after effects of the merging process.

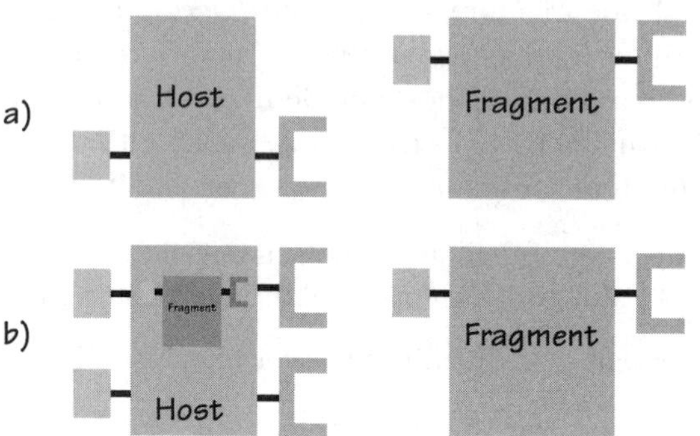

Figure 5.11 a) The host and fragment bundles are deployed as independent bundles in the framework. b) When the framework resolves the host, it effectively merges the fragment's content and metadata into the host bundle.

In addition to merging the exported and imported packages and required bundles, the bundle class paths are also merged. This impacts the overall class search order for the bundle, like this:

1. Requests for classes in `java.` packages are delegated to the parent class loader; searching stops (section 2.5.4).
2. Requests for classes in an imported package are delegated to the exporting bundle; searching stops (section 2.5.4).
3. Requests for classes in a package from a required bundle are delegated to the exporting bundle; searching continues with a failure (section 5.3.1).
4. The host bundle class path is searched for the class; searching continues with a failure (section 2.5.4).
5. Fragment bundle class paths are searched for the class in the order in which the fragments were installed. Searching stops if found but continues through all fragment class paths and then to the next step with a failure.
6. If the package in question isn't exported or required, requests matching any dynamically import package are delegated to an exporting bundle if one is found. Searching stops with either a success or a failure (section 5.2.2).

This is the complete bundle class search order, so you may want to mark this page for future reference! This search order makes it clear how fragments support split packages, because the host and all fragment class paths are searched until the class is found.

Fragments and the `Bundle-ClassPath`

The bundle class path search order seems fairly linear, but fragments do introduce one exception. When specifying a bundle class path, you can specify embedded JAR files, such as

```
Bundle-ClassPath: .,specialized.jar,default.jar
```

Typically, you'd expect both of these JAR files to be contained in the JAR file of the bundle declaring them, but this need not be the case. If fragments aren't involved, the framework ignores a non-existent JAR file on the bundle class path. But if the bundle has fragments attached to it, the framework searches the fragments for the specified JAR files if they don't exist in the host bundle.

In the example, imagine that the host contains default.jar but doesn't contain specialized.jar, which is contained in an attached fragment. The effect this has on the class search order is that the specified fragment content is searched before some of the host bundle content.

Sometimes this is useful if you want to provide default functionality in the host bundle but be able to override it on platforms where you have specialized classes (for example, using native code). You can also use this approach to provide a means for issuing patches to bundles after the fact, but in general it's better to update the whole bundle.

Some final issues regarding fragments: Fragments are allowed to have any metadata a normal bundle can have except `Bundle-Activator`. This makes sense because fragments can't be started or stopped and can only be used when combined with the host bundle. Attaching a fragment to a host creates a dependency between the two, which is similar to the dependencies created between two bundles via `Import-Package` or `Require-Bundle`. This means if either bundle is updated or uninstalled, the other bundle is impacted, and any refreshing of the one will likely lead to refreshing of the other.

We started this foray into fragments discussing localization, because it's the main use case for them. Next, we'll look at an example of how to use fragments for this purpose.

5.4.2 Using fragments for localization

To see how you can use fragments to localize an application, let's return to the service-based paint program from chapter 4. The main application window is implemented by the `PaintFrame` class. Recall its design: `PaintFrame` doesn't have any direct dependencies on the OSGi API. Instead, it uses a `ShapeTracker` class to track `SimpleShape` services in the OSGi service registry and inject them into the `PaintFrame` instance. `ShapeTracker` injects services into the `PaintFrame` using its `addShape()` method, as shown in the following listing.

Listing 5.4 Method used to inject shapes into `PaintFrame` object

```
public void addShape(String name, Icon icon, SimpleShape shape) {
  m_shapes.put(name, new ShapeInfo(name, icon, shape));
  JButton button = new JButton(icon);
  button.setActionCommand(name);
  button.setToolTipText(name);
  button.addActionListener(m_reusableActionListener);

  if (m_selected == null) {
    button.doClick();
  }

  m_toolbar.add(button);
  m_toolbar.validate();
  repaint();
}
```

The `addShape()` method is invoked with the name, icon, and service object of the `SimpleShape` implementation. The exact details aren't important, but the shape is recorded in a data structure, a button is created for it, its name is set as the button's tool tip, and, after a few other steps, the associated button is added to the toolbar. The tool tip is textual information displayed to users when they hover the mouse over the shape's toolbar icon. It would be nice if this information could be localized.

You can take different approaches to localize the shape name. One approach is to define a new service property that defines the `ResourceBundle` base name. This way, shape implementations can define their localization base name, much as they use service properties to indicate the name and icon. In such an approach, the

`PaintFrame.addShape()` must be injected with the base name property so it can perform the localization lookup. This probably isn't ideal, because it exposes implementation details.

Another approach is to focus on where the shape's name is set in the first place: in the shape implementation's bundle activator. The following listing shows the activator of the circle implementation.

Listing 5.5 Original circle bundle activator with hardcoded name

```
public class Activator implements BundleActivator {
  public void start(BundleContext context) {
    Hashtable dict = new Hashtable();
    dict.put(SimpleShape.NAME_PROPERTY, "Circle");
    dict.put(SimpleShape.ICON_PROPERTY,
      new ImageIcon(this.getClass().getResource("circle.png")));
    context.registerService(
      SimpleShape.class.getName(), new Circle(), dict);
  }

  public void stop(BundleContext context) {}
}
```

The hardcoded shape name is assigned to the service property dictionary, and the shape service is registered. The first thing you need to do is change the hardcoded name into a lookup from a `ResourceBundle`. This code shows the necessary changes.

Listing 5.6 Modified circle bundle activator with `ResourceBundle` name lookup

```
public class Activator implements BundleActivator {
  public static final String CIRCLE_NAME = "CIRCLE_NAME";        ❶ Defines constant

  public void start(BundleContext context) {
    ResourceBundle rb = ResourceBundle.getBundle(
      "org.foo.shape.circle.resource.Localize");
    Hashtable dict = new Hashtable();
    dict.put(SimpleShape.NAME_PROPERTY, rb.getString(CIRCLE_NAME));
    dict.put(SimpleShape.ICON_PROPERTY,
      new ImageIcon(this.getClass().getResource("circle.png")));
    context.registerService(
      SimpleShape.class.getName(), new Circle(), dict);          Creates ResourceBundle ❷
  }

  public void stop(BundleContext context) {}
}
```

You modify the activator to look up the shape name using the key constant defined at ❶ from a `ResourceBundle` you create ❷, whose resulting value is assigned to the service properties. Even though we won't go into the complete details of using `ResourceBundle` objects, the important part in this example is when you define it. You specify the base name of `org.foo.shape.circle.resource.Localize`. By default, this refers to a Localize.properties file in the `org.foo.shape.circle.resource` package, which contains a default mapping for your name key. You need to modify the circle implementation to have this additional package, and you add the Localize.properties file to it with the following content:

```
CIRCLE_NAME=Circle
```

This is the default mapping for the shape name. If the example was more complicated, you'd have many more default mappings for other terms. To provide other mappings to other languages, you need to include them in this same package, but in separate property files named after the locales' country codes. For example, the country code for Germany is `DE`, so for its localization you create a file called Localize_de.properties with the following content:

```
CIRCLE_NAME=Kreis
```

You do this for each locale you want to support. Then, at execution time, when you create your `ResourceBundle`, the correct property file is automatically selected based on the locale of the user's computer.

This all sounds nice; but if you have a lot of information to localize, you need to include all this information in your bundle, which can greatly increase its size. Further, you have no way of adding support for new locales without releasing a new version of your bundle. This is where fragments can help, because you can split the resource package into different fragments. You keep the default localization in your circle implementation, but all other localizations are put into separate fragments. You don't need to change the metadata of your circle bundle, because it's unaware of fragments, but the content of your circle bundle becomes

```
META-INF/MANIFEST.MF
META-INF/
org/
org/foo/
org/foo/shape/
org/foo/shape/circle/
org/foo/shape/circle/Activator.class
org/foo/shape/circle/Circle.class
org/foo/shape/circle/circle.png
org/foo/shape/circle/resource/
org/foo/shape/circle/resource/Localize.properties
```

For this example, you'll create a German localization fragment bundle for the circle using the property file shown earlier. The metadata for this fragment bundle is

```
Bundle-ManifestVersion: 2
Bundle-Name: circle.resource-de
Bundle-SymbolicName: org.foo.shape.circle.resource-de
Bundle-Version: 5.0
Fragment-Host: org.foo.shape.circle; bundle-version="[5.0,6.0)"
```

The important part of this metadata is the last line, which declares it as a fragment of the circle bundle. The content of the fragment bundle is simple:

```
META-INF/MANIFEST.MF
META-INF/
org/
```

```
org/foo/
org/foo/shape/
org/foo/shape/circle/
org/foo/shape/circle/resource/
org/foo/shape/circle/resource/Localize_de.properties
```

It only contains a resource file for the German translation, which you can see is a split package with the host bundle. You can create any number of localization fragments following this same pattern for your other shapes (square and triangle). Figure 5.12 shows the paint program with the German localization fragments installed.

Figure 5.12 Paint program with installed German localization fragments

To run this example, go into the chapter05/paint-example/ directory of the companion code and type `ant` to build and `java -Duser.language=de -jar launcher.jar bundles/` to run it using a German locale. With this approach, you only need to deploy the required localization fragments along with your shape implementations, and you can create new localizations or update existing ones without releasing new versions of the shape bundles.

We've now covered all major aspects of the OSGi module layer! As you can see, tools are available to help you deal with virtually any scenario the Java language can throw at you. But we have one more trick up our sleeves: the OSGi specification does a pretty good job of dealing with native code that runs outside of the Java environment. We'll look at this and how to deal with general factors relating to the JVM environment in the next and final section of this chapter.

5.5 Dealing with your environment

Although Java has been fairly successful at attaining its original vision of "write once, run everywhere," there are still situations where it's not entirely able to achieve this goal. One such situation is the myriad of Java platforms, such as Java ME and the different versions of Java SE. If you develop a bundle with requirements for a specific Java platform—for example, if you use classes from the `java.util.concurrent` package—you need a Java 5.0 JVM or above. Another situation is if you need to natively integrate with the underlying operating system, as may be necessary if you must communicate directly with underlying hardware.

As you may expect, in both these situations the OSGi specification provides mechanisms to explicitly declare these scenarios in your bundles to allow an OSGi framework to do whatever is necessary at execution time. In this section, we'll cover both of these topics, starting with the former.

5.5.1 *Requiring execution environments*

If you develop a bundle with a dependency on specific Java execution environments, what happens if this bundle executes in an unintended environment? Most likely, you'll get various exceptions for missing classes or methods and/or faulty results. If you have a bundle with specific execution environment requirements, you must explicitly declare these requirements to avoid people unknowingly trying to use your bundle in invalid environments. The OSGi specification defines an execution environment concept for just this purpose. Like all bundle metadata, you use a manifest header to define it. In this case, it's a manifest header with a long name: `Bundle-RequiredExecutionEnvironment`.

> **BUNDLE-REQUIREDEXECUTIONENVIRONMENT** This header specifies a comma-delimited list of supported execution environments.

The OSGi specification defines standard values for the common execution environments; table 5.1 lists them.

Table 5.1 OSGi defined standard execution environment names

Name	Description
`CDC-1.1/Foundation-1.1`	Equivalent to J2ME Foundation Profile
`CDC-1.1/PersonalBasis-1.1`	J2ME Personal Basis Profile
`CDC-1.1/PersonalJava-1.1`	J2ME Personal Java Profile
`J2SE-1.2`	Java 2 SE 1.2.x
`J2SE-1.3`	Java 2 SE 1.3.x
`J2SE-1.4`	Java 2 SE 1.4.x
`J2SE-1.5`	Java 2 SE 1.5.x
`JavaSE-1.6`	Java SE 1.6.x
`OSGi/Minimum-1.2`	Minimal required set of Java API that allows an OSGi framework implementation

Bundles should list all known execution environments on which they can run, which may look something like this:

```
Bundle-RequiredExecutionEnvironment: J2SE-1.4,J2SE-1.5,JavaSE-1.6
```

This specific example indicates that the bundle runs only on modern Java platforms. If a bundle lists a limited execution environment, such as `CDC-1.1/Foundation-1.1`, it shouldn't use classes or methods that don't exist in the declared execution environment. The framework doesn't verify this claim; it only ensures that the bundle isn't resolvable on incompatible execution environments.

Resolve-time, not install-time enforcement

Pay special attention to the previous sentence. It's possible to install a bundle on a given execution environment even if it's not compatible with it, but you won't be able to resolve it unless its required execution environment matches the current one. This is tied to the bundle's resolved state because it's possible for the execution environment to change over time. For example, you may switch between different versions of Java on subsequent executions of the framework. This way, any cached bundles not matching the current execution environment will essentially be ignored.

A given framework implementation can claim to provide more than one execution environment, because in most cases the Java platform versions are backward compatible. It's possible to determine the framework's supported execution environments by retrieving the `org.osgi.framework.executionenvironment` property from `BundleContext.getProperty()`.

Now that you understand how to declare your bundles' required execution environments, let's look at how to handle bundles with native code.

5.5.2 Bundling native libraries

Java provides a nice platform and language combination, but it's not always possible to stay purely in Java. In some situations, you need to create native code for the platform on which Java is running. Java defined Java Native Interface (JNI) precisely for this purpose; JNI is how Java code calls code written in other programming languages (such as C or C++) for specific operating systems (such as Windows or Linux). A complete discussion of how JNI works is outside the scope of this book, but the following list provides the highlights:

- Native code is integrated into Java as a special type of method implementation. A Java class can declare a method as having a native implementation using the `native` method modifier.
- Classes with native code are compiled normally. But after compilation, the `javah` command is used to generate C header and stub files, which are used to create the native method implementations.
- The native code is compiled into a library in a platform-specific way for its target operating system.
- The original Java class with the native method includes code to invoke `System.loadLibrary()`, typically in a static initializer, to load the native library when the class is loaded in the Java VM.
- Other classes can invoke the native method as if it were a normal method, and the Java platform takes care of the native invocation details.

Although it's fairly straightforward to use native code in Java, it's best to avoid it if possible. Native code doesn't benefit from the garbage collector and suffers from the typical pointer issues associated with all native code. Additionally, it hinders Java's "write once, run everywhere" goal, because it ties the class to a specific platform. Still, in those cases where it's absolutely necessary, it's nice to know that OSGi supports it. OSGi even simplifies it a little.

One of the downsides of native code is the fact that you end up with an additional artifact to deploy along with your classes. To make matters worse, what you need to do with the native library differs among operating systems; for example, you typically need to put native libraries in specific locations in the file system so they can be found at execution time (for example, somewhere on the binary search path). OSGi native code support simplifies these issues by

- Allowing you to embed your native library directly into your bundle JAR file
- Allowing you to embed multiple native libraries for different target platforms
- Automatically handling execution-time discovery of native code libraries

When you embed a native library into your bundle, you must tell the OSGi framework about it. As with all other modularity aspects, you do so in the bundle metadata using the `Bundle-NativeCode` manifest header. With this header, you can specify the set of contained native libraries for each platform your bundle supports. The grammar is as follows:

```
Bundle-NativeCode ::= nativecode (',' nativecode)* (',' optional)?
nativecode        ::= path (';' path)* (';' parameter)+
optional          ::= '*'
```

The parameter is one of the following:

- `osname`—Name of the operating system
- `osversion`—Operating system version range
- `processor`—Processor architecture
- `language`—ISO code for a language
- `selection-filter`—LDAP selection filter

For example, if you have a bundle with native libraries for Windows XP, you may have a native code declaration like this one:

```
Bundle-NativeCode: lib/math.dll; lib/md5.dll; osname=WindowsXP;
 processor=x86
```

This is a semicolon-delimited list, where the leading entries not containing an `=` character are interpreted as file entries in the bundle JAR file and the remaining entries with an `=` character are used to determine if the native library clause matches the current platform. In this case, you state the bundle has two native libraries for Windows XP on the x86 architecture.

If `Bundle-NativeCode` is specified, there must be a matching header for the platform on which the bundle is executing; otherwise, the framework won't allow the bundle to resolve. In other words, if a bundle with the previous native code header was installed on a Linux box, the framework won't allow the bundle to be used.

If these same libraries also work on Vista, you can specify this as follows:

```
Bundle-NativeCode: lib/math.dll; lib/md5.dll; osname=WindowsXP;
 osname=WindowsVista; processor=x86
```

In cases where the parameter is repeated, the framework treats this like a logical OR when matching, so these native libraries match Windows XP or Windows Vista.

If your bundle also has native libraries for Linux, you can specify that as follows:

```
Bundle-NativeCode: lib/math.dll; lib/md5.dll; osname=WindowsXP;
 osname=WindowsVista; processor=x86, lib/libmath.so; osname=Linux;
 osprocessor=x86
```

You separate different platforms using a comma instead of a semicolon. Notice also that the native libraries don't need to be parallel. In this example, you have two native libraries for the Windows platform but only one for Linux. This bundle is now usable on Windows XP, Windows Vista, and Linux on the x86 architecture, but on any other platform the framework won't resolve it.

In some cases, you may have either optional native libraries or a non-optimized Java implementation for unsupported platforms. You can denote this using the optional clause, like this:

```
Bundle-NativeCode: lib/math.dll; lib/md5.dll; osname=WindowsXP;
 osname=WindowsVista; processor=x86, lib/libmath.so; osname=Linux;
 osprocessor=x86, *
```

The `*` at the end acts as a separate platform clause that can match any platform, so this bundle is usable on any platform.

The process of how native libraries are made available when the classes containing native methods perform `System.loadLibrary()` is handled automatically by the framework, so you don't need to worry about it. Even though it isn't often necessary, it's fairly easy to use this mechanism to create bundles with native code.

That's it! You've now been introduced to many of the specialized features of the OSGi module layer. Let's review what you've learned in this chapter.

5.6 Summary

You learned that the OSGi module layer provides many additional mechanisms to deal with collaborative, dynamic, and legacy situations, such as the following:

- A bundle may import a package it exports to make its export substitutable for purposes of broadening collaboration among bundles.
- Exported packages have bundle symbolic name and version attributes implicitly attached to them, which can be useful if you need to import a package from a specific bundle.
- Exported packages may have mandatory attributes associated with them, which must be specified by an importer for it to be wired to the exported package.

- It's possible to export the same package more than once with different attributes, which is sometimes helpful if a bundle wishes to masquerade as more than one version of a package.
- The framework ignores optionally imported packages if no exporters are present when the importing bundle is resolved.
- The framework only attempts to resolve dynamically imported packages when the importing bundle tries to use a class in the dynamically imported package. Repeated attempts to use a class in the dynamically imported package will result in repeated attempts to resolve the package until successful.
- It's possible to require a bundle, rather than importing specific packages, which wires you to everything the target bundle exports. This is typically useful when aggregating split packages.
- Bundle fragments support splitting a bundle into multiple optional JAR files, which is helpful in such situations as localization.
- Bundles with dependencies on specific Java platforms can declare these dependencies with required execution environments.
- Bundles can include native libraries to integrate platform-specific functionality.

Most of these mechanisms are intended for specific use cases and shouldn't be overused to avoid less modular solutions.

We've now covered all the major functionality of OSGi specification, which closes out this part of the book. In the next section, we'll look into more practical matters that crop up while trying to use and build applications on top of OSGi technology.

Part 2

OSGi in practice

In the first part of the book, we focused on the details and theory behind the OSGi specifications, which can be a little daunting when you're first getting started. In this second part, you'll put your newfound OSGi knowledge into practice. We'll look at approaches for converting JAR files into bundles. After that, we'll explore how to test and debug bundles using tried-and-true techniques. We'll finish by explaining how to manage different aspects of bundles and OSGi-based applications, such as versioning, configuring, and deploying them. Upon completing this part of the book, you should have all the knowledge you need to successfully use OSGi technology in your own projects.

6 Moving toward bundles

This chapter covers

- Choosing a bundle identity for a JAR file
- Determining which packages a bundle should export and/or import
- Migrating an application to OSGi
- Dividing an application into a set of bundles

The first part of this book introduced the three layers of OSGi: module, lifecycle, and service. We'll now take a more practical look at how you can migrate existing code to OSGi by using one or more of these layers, beginning with examples of turning real-world JAR files into bundles. After that, we'll examine different ways of migrating a complete application to OSGi and finish up with a short discussion of situations where you might decide not to bundle.

By the end of this chapter, you'll know how to take your current application and all of its third-party libraries and turn them into bundles, step by step. You'll be able to move existing projects to OSGi, plan new projects with OSGi in mind, and understand when it may not be the right solution for you. In other words, you should be able to explain in detail to your manager and co-workers how OSGi will affect your project. But before we reach that stage, we first need to consider a simple question that often comes up on the OSGi mailing lists: how can you turn your JAR file into a bundle?

6.1 Turning JARs into bundles

As you saw in chapter 2, a *bundle* is a JAR file with additional metadata. So to turn a JAR file into a bundle, you need to add metadata giving it a unique identity and describing what it imports and exports. Simple, right? For most business-domain JAR files, it is; but for others (such as third-party GUI or database libraries), you'll need to think carefully about their design. Where is the line between what's public and what's private, which imports are required and which are optional, and which versions are compatible with one another?

In this section, we'll help you come up with this metadata by taking a series of common library JAR files and turning them into working bundles. We'll also consider some advanced bundling techniques, such as embedding dependencies inside the bundle, as well as how to manage external resources and background threads.

Before you can even load a bundle into an OSGi framework, it must have an identity. This identity should be unique, at least among the set of bundles loaded into the framework. But how should you choose such an identity? If you pick names at random, you may clash with other projects or other developers, as shown in figure 6.1.

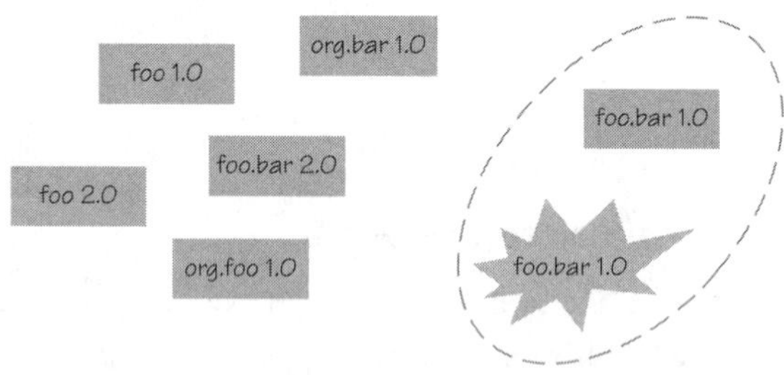

Figure 6.1 A bundle must have a unique identity.

6.1.1 Choosing an identity

Each bundle installed into an OSGi framework must have a unique identity, made up of the `Bundle-SymbolicName` and `Bundle-Version`. We'll look into approaches for defining both of these now.

CHOOSING A SYMBOLIC NAME

One of the first steps in turning a JAR file into a bundle is to decide what symbolic name to give it. The OSGi specification doesn't mandate a naming policy but recommends a reverse-domain naming convention. This is the same as Java package naming: if the bundle is the primary source of a particular package, it makes sense to use it as the `Bundle-SymbolicName`.

Let's look at a real-world example, the kXML parser (http://kxml.sourceforge.net/). This small JAR file provides two distinct top-level packages: the XmlPull API org.xmlpull.v1 and the kXML implementation org.kxml2. If this JAR was the only one expected to provide the org.xmlpull.v1 API, or if it only contained this package, it would be reasonable to use this as the symbolic name. But this JAR file also provides a particular implementation of the XmlPull API, so it makes more sense to use the name of the implementation as the symbolic name because it captures the essence of what the bundle provides:

```
Bundle-SymbolicName: org.kxml2
```

Alternatively, you can use the domain of the project that distributes the JAR file. Here, the domain is http://kxml.sourceforge.net/kxml2/:

```
Bundle-SymbolicName: net.sourceforge.kxml.kxml2
```

Or if Maven (http://maven.apache.org/) project metadata is available, you can use the Maven `groupId` + `artifactId` to identify the JAR file:

```
Bundle-SymbolicName: net.sf.kxml.kxml2
```

Sometimes, you may decide on a name that doesn't correspond to a particular package or distribution. For example, consider two implementations of the same service API provided by two different bundles. OSGi lets you hide non-exported packages, so these bundles can have an identical package layout but at the same time provide different implementations. You can still base the symbolic name on the main top-level package or the distribution domain, but you must add a suffix to ensure that each implementation has a unique identity. This is the approach that the Simple Logging Facade for Java (SLF4J; www.slf4j.org/) project used when naming its various logging implementation bundles:

```
Bundle-SymbolicName: slf4j.juli
Bundle-SymbolicName: slf4j.log4j
Bundle-SymbolicName: slf4j.jcl
```

All of these bundles export org.slf4j.impl

If you're wrapping a third-party library, you may want to prefix your own domain in front of the symbolic name. This makes it clear that you're responsible for the bundle metadata rather than the original third party. For example, the symbolic name for the SLF4J API bundle in the SpringSource Enterprise Bundle Repository (www.springsource.com/repository/app/) clearly shows that it was modified by SpringSource and isn't an official SLF4J JAR:

```
Bundle-SymbolicName: com.springsource.slf4j.api
```

Don't worry too much about naming bundles—in the end, you need to give each bundle a unique enough name for your target deployment. You're free to rename your bundle later if you wish, because by default the framework wires import packages to export packages regardless of bundle symbolic names. It's only when someone uses `Require-Bundle` (see section 5.3) that consistent names become important. That's another reason why package dependencies are preferred over module dependencies: they don't tie you to a particular symbolic name forever.

CHOOSING A VERSION

After you've decided on a symbolic name, the next step is to version your bundle. Determining the `Bundle-Version` is more straightforward than choosing the symbolic name, because pretty much every JAR file distribution is already identified by some sort of build version or release tag. On the other hand, version-numbering schemes that don't match the recognized OSGi format of *major.minor.micro.qualifier* must be converted before you can use them. Table 6.1 shows some actual project versions and attempts to map them to OSGi.

Project version	Suggested OSGi equivalent
2.1-alpha-1	2.1.0.alpha-1
1.4-m3	1.4.0.m3
1.0_01-ea	1.0.1.ea
1.0-2	1.0.2
1.0.b2	1.0.0.b2
1.0a1	1.0.0.a1
2.1.7c	2.1.7.c
1.12-SNAPSHOT	1.12.0.SNAPSHOT
0.9.0-incubator-SNAPSHOT	0.9.0.incubator-SNAPSHOT
3.3.0-v20070604	3.3.0.v20070604
4aug2000r7-dev	0.0.0.4aug2000r7-dev

Table 6.1 Mapping real-world project versions to OSGi

Not every version is easily converted to the OSGi format. Look at the last example in the table; it starts with a number, but this is part of the date rather than the major version. This is the problem with free-form version strings—there's no standard way of comparing them or breaking them into component parts. OSGi versions, on the other hand, have standardized structure and well-defined ordering. (Later, you'll use a tool called *bnd* that makes a good attempt at automated mapping based on common-sense rules, but even bnd has its limits.)

After you've uniquely identified your bundle by name and version, you can add more information: a human-friendly `Bundle-Name`, a more detailed `Bundle-Description`, license details, vendor details, a link to online documentation, and so on. Most if not all of these details can be taken from existing project information, such as the following example from the second release of Google Guice (http://code.google.com/p/google-guice/):

```
Bundle-SymbolicName: com.google.inject
Bundle-Version: 2.0
Bundle-Name: guice
Bundle-Copyright: Copyright (C) 2006 Google Inc.
Bundle-Vendor: Google Inc.
Bundle-License: http://www.apache.org/licenses/LICENSE-2.0
Bundle-DocURL: http://code.google.com/p/google-guice/
Bundle-Description: Guice is a lightweight dependency injection
 framework for Java 5 and above
```

Remember that new OSGi bundles should also have this header:

```
Bundle-ManifestVersion: 2
```

This tells the OSGi framework to process your bundle according to the latest specification. Although this isn't mandatory, it's strongly recommended because it enables additional checks and support for advanced modularity features offered by OSGi R4 specifications and beyond.

After you've captured enough bundle details to satisfactorily describe your JAR file, the next thing to decide is which packages it should export to other bundles in the framework.

6.1.2 Exporting packages

Most bundles export at least one package, but a bundle doesn't have to export any. Bundles providing service implementations via the service registry don't have to export any packages if they import their service API from another bundle. This is because their implementation is shared indirectly via the service registry and accessed using the shared API, as illustrated in figure 6.2. But what about the package containing the `Bundle-Activator` class? Doesn't that need to be exported? No, you don't need to export the package containing the bundle activator unless you want to share it with other bundles. Best practice is to keep it private. As long as the activator class has a `public` modifier, the framework can load it, even if it belongs to an internal, non-exported package. The question remains: when is it necessary for you to export packages, and which packages in your JAR file do you need to export?

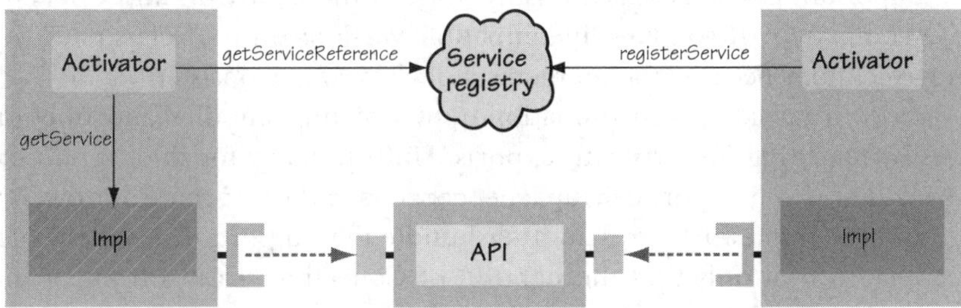

Figure 6.2 Sharing implementations without exporting their packages

SELECTING EXPORTED PACKAGES

The classic, non-OSGi approach is to export everything and make the entire contents of the JAR file visible. For API-only JAR files, this is fine; but for implementation JAR files, you don't want to expose internal details. Clients might then use and rely on these internal classes by mistake. As you'll see in a moment, exporting everything also increases the chance of conflicts among bundles containing the same package, particularly when they provide a different set of classes in those packages. When you're new to OSGi, exporting everything can look like a reasonable choice to begin with, especially if you don't know precisely where the public API begins or ends. On the contrary: you should try to trim down the list of exported packages as soon as you have a working bundle.

Let's use a real-world example to demonstrate how to select your exports. Here are some of the packages containing classes and resources inside the core BeanUtils 1.8.0 library from Apache Commons (http://commons.apache.org/beanutils/):

```
org.apache.commons.beanutils
org.apache.commons.beanutils.converters
org.apache.commons.beanutils.locale
org.apache.commons.beanutils.locale.converters
org.apache.commons.collections
```

None of these packages seem private; there isn't an `impl` or `internal` package in the list, but the `org.apache.commons.collections` package is in fact an implementation detail. If you look closely at the BeanUtils Javadoc (http://commons.apache.org/beanutils/v1.8.2/apidocs/index.html), you'll see that this package contains a subset of the original Apache Commons Collections API (http://commons.apache.org/collections/). BeanUtils uses only a few of the Collections classes; and rather than have an execution-time dependency on the entire JAR file, the project embeds a copy of what it needs. What happens when your application requires both the BeanUtils and Collections JAR files?

This typically isn't a problem in a non-OSGi environment because the application class loader exhaustively searches the entire class path to find a class. If both BeanUtils and Collections were on the same class path, they would be merged together, with classes in BeanUtils overriding those from Collections or vice versa depending on their ordering on the class path. Figure 6.3 (based on the class path diagram from chapter 2) shows an example.

One important caveat is that this only works if the BeanUtils and Collections versions are compatible. If you have incompatible versions on your class path, you'll get runtime exceptions because the merged set of classes is inconsistent.

OSGi tries to avoid this incompatibility by isolating bundles and only exposing packages by matching imports with exports. Unfortunately for the current example, this means that if you export `org.apache.commons.collections` from the BeanUtils bundle, and the framework wires another bundle that imports `org.apache.commons.collections` to it, it only sees the handful of Collections classes from BeanUtils. It doesn't see the complete set of classes sitting in the Commons Collections bundle. To make sure this doesn't happen, you must exclude the partial `org.apache.commons.collections` package from the BeanUtils exports:

```
Export-Package: org.apache.commons.beanutils,
 org.apache.commons.beanutils.converters,
 org.apache.commons.beanutils.locale,
 org.apache.commons.beanutils.locale.converters
```

You can do this because the Collections package doesn't belong to the main BeanUtils API. Now, if it was purely an implementation detail that was never exposed to

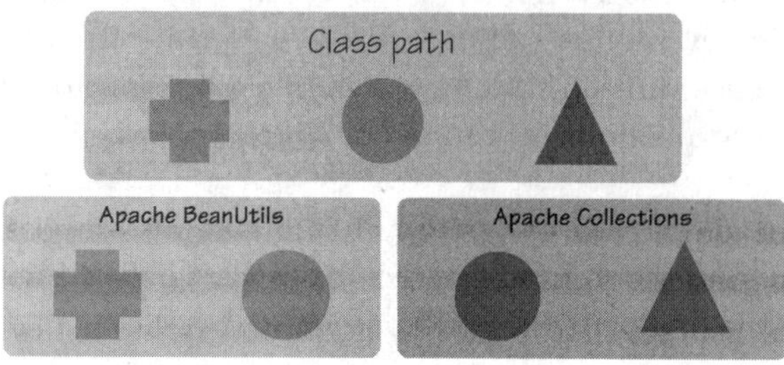

Figure 6.3 The classic application class loader merges JAR files into a single class space.

clients, your job would be complete. But there's a hitch: a class from the Collections package is indirectly exposed to BeanUtils clients via a return type on some deprecated methods. What can you do? You need to find a way to guarantee that the BeanUtils bundle uses the same Commons Collections provider as its clients. The simplest solution would be to make this dependency explicit by importing `org.apache.commons.collections` into the BeanUtils bundle, but then your bundle wouldn't resolve unless the Commons Collections bundle was also installed. Perhaps you could you use an *optional* import instead:

```
Import-Package: org.apache.commons.collections;resolution:=optional
```

Now, if the full package is available, you'll import it; but if it's not available, you can still use your internal private copy. Will this work? It's better, but it still isn't entirely accurate.

Unfortunately, the only correct way to resolve this situation is to refactor the BeanUtils bundle to not contain the partial private copy of `org.apache.commons.collections`. See the sidebar "Revisiting uses constraints" if you want more details as to why an optional import won't work.

Revisiting `uses` constraints

We hypothesized about modifying the example BeanUtils bundle to optionally import `org.apache.commons.collections`. The idea was that your bundle would import it if an exporter was available, but would use its private copy if not. This doesn't work, but why not? It's all about `uses` constraints, as discussed in section 2.7.2.

As we mentioned, BeanUtils exposes a type from the Collections package in a return type of a method in its exported types; this is a `uses` constraint by definition. To deal with this situation, you must express it somehow. Let's assume you follow the optional import case and try to model the `uses` constraint correctly, like this:

```
Export-Package:
 org.apache.commons.beanutils;
  uses:="org.apache.commons.collections",
 org.apache.commons.beanutils.converters,
 org.apache.commons.beanutils.locale;
  uses:="org.apache.commons.collections",
 org.apache.commons.beanutils.locale.converters
Import-Package: org.apache.commons.collections;resolution:=optional
```

This may work in some situations; for example, it would work if you deployed your BeanUtils bundle, another bundle importing BeanUtils and Collections, and a bundle exporting the Collections package. In this case, all the bundles would be wired up to each other, and everyone would be using the correct version of the Collections packages. Great!

But what would happen if the BeanUtils bundle was installed and resolved by itself first? In that case, it wouldn't import the Collections package (because there isn't one) and would use its private partial copy instead. Now, if the other bundles were installed and resolved, you'd end up with the wiring depicted here:

(continued)

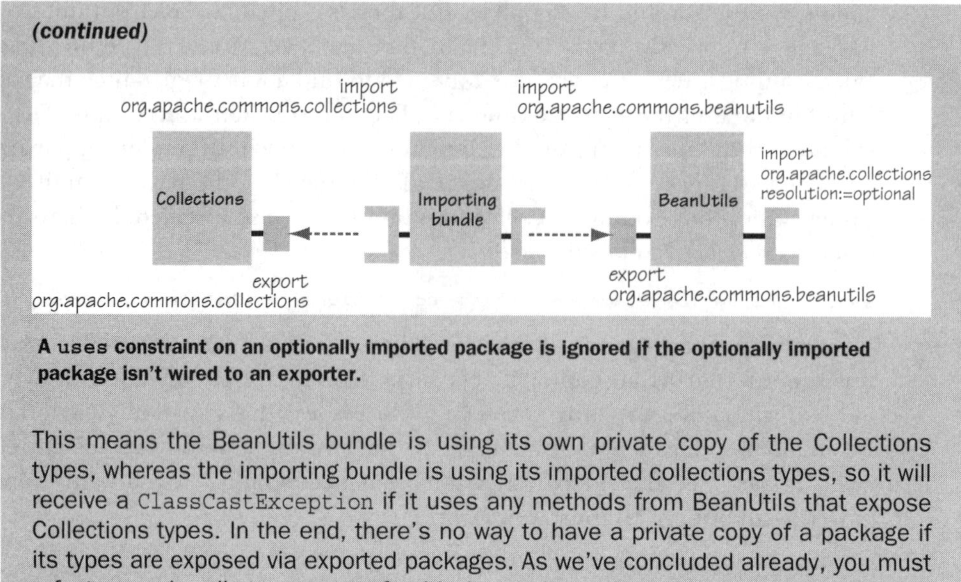

A `uses` constraint on an optionally imported package is ignored if the optionally imported package isn't wired to an exporter.

This means the BeanUtils bundle is using its own private copy of the Collections types, whereas the importing bundle is using its imported collections types, so it will receive a `ClassCastException` if it uses any methods from BeanUtils that expose Collections types. In the end, there's no way to have a private copy of a package if its types are exposed via exported packages. As we've concluded already, you must refactor your bundle to export preferably the whole package or to import the package.

A surprising number of third-party libraries include partial packages. Some want to reuse code from another large library but don't want to bloat their own JAR file. Some prefer to ship a single self-contained JAR file that clients can add to their class path without worrying about conflicting dependencies. Some libraries even use tools such as Jar Jar Links (http://code.google.com/p/jarjar/) to repackage internal dependencies under different namespaces to avoid potential conflicts. This leads to multiple copies of the same class all over the place, because Java doesn't provide modularity out of the box! Renamed packages also make debugging harder and confuse developers. OSGi removes the need for renaming and helps you safely share packages while still allowing you to hide and embed implementation details.

At this point, you may decide it's a good time to refactor the API to make it more modular. Separating interfaces from their implementations can avoid the need for partial (or so-called *split*) packages. This helps you reduce the set of packages you need to export and make your bundle more manageable. Although this may not be an option for third-party libraries, it's often worth taking time to contact the original developers to explain the situation. This happened a few years ago with the SLF4J project, which refactored its API to great effect (www.slf4j.org/pipermail/dev/2007-February/000750.html). You should also be careful to avoid accidentally leaking implementation types via method signatures. As you saw with the BeanUtils example, the more internal details are exposed through your API, the harder it is to modularize your code.

VERSIONING EXPORTED PACKAGES

After you have your list of exported packages, you should consider versioning them. Which version should you use? The common choice is to use the bundle version, which implies that the packages change at the same rate as the bundle, but some packages inevitably change faster than others. You may also want to increment the bundle version because of an implementation fix while the exported API remains at the same level. Although everything starts out aligned, you'll probably find that you need a separate version for each package (or at least each group of tightly coupled packages).

We'll take an in-depth look at managing versions in chapter 9, but a classic example is the OSGi framework itself, which provides service APIs that have changed at different rates over time:

```
Export-Package: org.osgi.framework;version="1.4",
 org.osgi.service.packageadmin;version="1.2",
 org.osgi.service.startlevel;version="1.1",
 org.osgi.service.url;version="1.0",
 org.osgi.util.tracker;version="1.3.3"
```

Knowing which packages to export is only half of the puzzle of turning a JAR into a bundle—you also need to find out what should be imported. This is often the hardest piece of metadata to define and causes the most problems when people migrate to OSGi.

6.1.3 Discovering what to import

Do you know what packages a given JAR file needs at execution time? Many developers have tacit or hidden knowledge of what JAR files to put on the class path. Such knowledge is often gained from years of experience getting applications to run, where you reflexively add JAR files to the class path until any `ClassNotFoundExceptions` disappear. This leads to situations where an abundance of JAR files is loaded at execution time, not because they're all required, but because a developer feels they may be necessary based on past experience.

The following lines show an example class path for a Java EE client. Can you tell how these JAR files relate to one another, what packages they provide and use, and their individual versions?

```
concurrent.jar:getopt.jar:gnu-regexp.jar:jacorb.jar:\
jbossall-client.jar:jboss-client.jar:jboss-common-client.jar:\
jbosscx-client.jar:jbossha-client.jar:jboss-iiop-client.jar:\
jboss-j2ee.jar:jboss-jaas.jar:jbossjmx-ant.jar:jboss-jsr77-client.jar:\
jbossmq-client.jar:jboss-net-client.jar:jbosssx-client.jar:\
jboss-system-client.jar:jboss-transaction-client.jar:jcert.jar:\
jmx-connector-client-factory.jar:jmx-ejb-connector-client.jar:\
jmx-invoker-adaptor-client.jar:jmx-rmi-connector-client.jar:jnet.jar:\
jnp-client.jar:jsse.jar:log4j.jar:xdoclet-module-jboss-net.jar
```

With OSGi, you explicitly define which packages your bundle needs, and this knowledge is then available to any developer who wants it. They no longer have to guess how to compose their class path—the information is readily available in the metadata! It can also be used by tools such as the OSGi Bundle Repository (OBR; http://felix.apache.org/site/apache-felix-osgi-bundle-repository.html) to automatically select and validate collections of bundles for deployment.

This means any developer turning a JAR file into a bundle has a great responsibility in defining the correct set of imported packages. If this list is incomplete or too excessive, it affects all users of the bundle. Unfortunately, standard Java tools don't provide an easy way to determine which packages a JAR file may use at execution time. Manually skimming the source for package names is time consuming and unreliable. Byte-code analysis is more reliable and repeatable, which is especially important for distributed teams, but it can miss classes that are dynamically loaded by name. For instance, this could load a class from any package:

```
String name = someDynamicNameConstruction(someSortOfContext);
Class<?> clazz = someClassLoader.loadClass(name);
```

The ideal solution is to use a byte-code analysis tool like bnd (http://aqute.biz/Code/Bnd) followed by a manual review of the generated metadata by project developers. You can then decide whether to keep generating the list of imported packages for every build or generate the list once and save it to a version-controlled file somewhere so it can be pulled into later builds. Most tools for generating OSGi manifests also let you supplement or override the generated list, in case the manual review finds missing or incorrect packages.

After you're happy with the metadata, you should run integration tests on an OSGi framework to verify that the bundle has the necessary imported packages. You don't want to get a `ClassNotFoundException` in production when an obscure but important piece of code runs for the first time and attempts to access a package that hasn't been imported!

USING TOOLS TO GENERATE IMPORTS

Let's continue with the BeanUtils example and use bnd to discover what imports you need. The bnd tool was developed by the OSGi director of technology, Peter Kriens, and provides a number of Ant tasks and command-line commands specifically designed for OSGi. Bnd uses a pull approach to divide a single class path into separate bundles based on a set of instructions. This means you have to tell bnd what packages you want to pull in and export, as well as those you want to pull in and keep private.

Bnd instructions use the same format as OSGi directives, which means you can mix normal manifest entries along with bnd instructions. In addition to accepting OSGi manifest headers as instructions, bnd adds some of its own, such as `Include-Resource` and `Private-Package`, to give you more control over exactly what goes into the bundle. These instructions aren't used by the OSGi framework at execution time.

The following instructions select the exported and non-exported (or so-called *private*) packages that should be contained in your final BeanUtils bundle. You start by exporting all of the BeanUtils API, as discussed in section 6.1.2. Remember that you also want to remove the partial Collections package from the internals and import it instead. Finally, you let bnd decide what this bundle needs to import. Let's put these instructions in a file named beanutils.bnd, which you can find under chapter06/BeanUtils-example/ in this book's examples:

```
Export-Package: org.apache.commons.beanutils.*
Private-Package: !org.apache.commons.collections.*, *
Import-Package: *
```

Notice that unlike the standard OSGi headers, bnd package instructions can contain wildcards and negative patterns. Bnd expands these patterns at build time according to what it finds in the project byte code on the class path, saving you the hassle of typing everything in minute detail.

After you've chosen your exported and internal packages, you invoke the bnd `build` task by passing it the original BeanUtils JAR file along with your custom bnd instructions:

```
$ cd chapter06/BeanUtils-example

$ java -jar ../../lib/bnd-0.0.384.jar \
    build -classpath commons-beanutils-1.8.0.jar beanutils.bnd
```

Bnd processes the given class path using your instructions and generates a new JAR alongside the instructions file, called beanutils.jar. You can extract the OSGi-enhanced manifest from the newly created BeanUtils bundle like so:

```
$ java -jar ../../lib/bnd-0.0.384.jar \
    print -manifest beanutils.jar
```

As you can see, it contains the following generated list of imported packages:

```
Import-Package:
 org.apache.commons.beanutils;version="1.8",
 org.apache.commons.beanutils.converters;version="1.8",
 org.apache.commons.beanutils.expression;version="1.8",
 org.apache.commons.beanutils.locale;version="1.8",
 org.apache.commons.beanutils.locale.converters;version="1.8",
 org.apache.commons.collections,
 org.apache.commons.collections.comparators,
 org.apache.commons.collections.keyvalue,
 org.apache.commons.collections.list,
 org.apache.commons.collections.set,
 org.apache.commons.logging
```

There are a couple of interesting points about this list. First, bnd has added imports for all the BeanUtils packages that you want to export. As we discussed in section 5.1.1, this is usually good practice when exporting an API that has multiple implementations, because it means that if (for whatever reason) an existing bundle already exports these packages, you'll share the same class space for the API. Without these imports, your bundle would sit on its own little island, isolated from any bundles already wired to the previous package exporter. But if you don't expect alternative implementations of Commons Collections, you can always turn off this feature with a special bnd directive:

```
Export-Package: org.apache.commons.beanutils.*;-noimport:=true
```

Bnd has also found byte code references to the Apache Collections and Logging packages, which aren't contained in the BeanUtils bundle and must therefore be imported. Just think: you can now tell what packages a JAR file needs at execution time by checking the imported package list in the manifest. This is extremely useful for automated deployment of applications. Such a system knows that when deploying

BeanUtils, it should also deploy Commons Collections and Commons Logging (or another bundle that provides the same logging package, like SLF4J). But which particular version of Logging should it deploy?

IMPORTING THE CORRECT VERSION

Just as with exported packages, you should consider versioning your imports. Chapter 2 explained how versioning helps ensure binary compatibility with other bundles. You should try to use ranges rather than leave versions open-ended, because doing so protects you against potentially breaking API changes in the future. For example, consider the following:

```
Import-Package: org.slf4j;version="1.5.3"
```

This matches any version of the SLF4J API from 1.5.3 onward, even unforeseen future releases that could be incompatible with your code.

One recommended practice is to use a range starting from the minimum acceptable version up to, but not including, the next major version. (This assumes a change in major version is used to indicated that the API isn't binary compatible.) For example, if you tested against the 1.5.3 SLF4J API, you might use the following range:

```
Import-Package: org.slf4j;version="[1.5.3,2)"
```

This ensures that only versions from the tested level to just before the next major release are used.

Not all projects follow this particular versioning scheme—you may need to tweak the range to narrow or widen the set of compatible versions. The width of the import range also depends on how you're using the package. Consider a simple change like adding a method to an interface, which typically occurs during a point release (such as 1.1 to 1.2). If you're just calling the interface, this change doesn't affect you. If, on the other hand, you're implementing the interface, this will definitely break, because you now need to implement a new method.

Adding the correct version ranges to imported packages takes time and patience, but this is often a one-time investment that pays off many times over during the life of a project. Tools such as bnd can help by detecting existing version metadata from dependencies on the class path and by automatically applying version ranges according to a given policy.

Unfortunately, tools aren't perfect. While you're reviewing the generated list of imported packages, you may notice a few that aren't used at execution time. Some code may only be executed in certain scenarios, such as an Ant build task that's shipped with a library JAR file for convenience. Other JAR files may dynamically test for available packages and adapt their behavior at execution time to match what's installed. In such cases, it's useful to mark these imports as optional to tell the OSGi framework that the bundle can still work even when these packages aren't available. Table 6.2 shows some real-world packages that are often consid-ered optional.

As you saw back in section 5.2, OSGi provides two ways to mark a package as optional. You can either mark packages with the `resolution:=optional` directive or

Table 6.2 Common optional imported packages found in third-party libraries

Package	Used for
`javax.swing.*`	GUI classes (could be interactive tests)
`org.apache.tools.ant.*`	ANT taskdefs (build time)
`antlr.*`	Parsing (maybe build/test related)
`sun.misc.*`	Sun implementation classes (like `BASE64`)
`com.sun.tools.*`	Sun tool support (javac, debugging, and so on)

list them as dynamically imported packages. For packages you never expect to be used at execution time, like the Ant packages, we suggest that you either use the `optional` attribute or remove them from the list of imported packages. Use `resolution:=optional` when you know the bundle will always be used the same way after it's installed. If you want a more adaptive bundle that reacts to the latest set of available packages, you should list them as dynamic imports.

If you're new to OSGi and unsure exactly what packages your JAR file uses, consider using

```
DynamicImport-Package: *
```

This makes things similar to the classic model, where requests to load a new class always result in a query to the complete class path. It also allows your bundle to successfully resolve regardless of what packages are available. The downside is that you're pushing the responsibility of finding the right set of bundles onto users, because you don't provide any metadata defining what you need! This approach should only be considered as a stopgap measure to get you started.

You've now chosen the exports and imports for your new bundle. Every nonoptional, nondynamic package you import (but don't export) must be provided by another bundle. Does this mean that for every JAR file you convert into a bundle, you also need to convert each of its dependencies into bundles? Not necessarily, because unlike standard JAR files, OSGi supports embedding JAR files inside bundles.

6.1.4 *Embedding vs. importing*

Sometimes a JAR file has a close dependency on another JAR file. Maybe they only work together, or the dependency is an implementation detail you want to keep private, or you don't want to share the static member fields in the JAR file with other bundles. In these situations, it makes more sense to embed the dependencies inside the primary JAR file when you turn it into a bundle. Embedding the JAR file is easier than converting both JAR files to bundles because you can ignore packages that would otherwise need to be exported and imported between them. The downside of embedding is that it adds unnecessary weight for non-OSGi users, who can't use the embedded JAR file unless the bundle is first unpacked. Figure 6.4a shows how a CGLIB bundle might embed ASM, a small utility for processing byte code.

a) 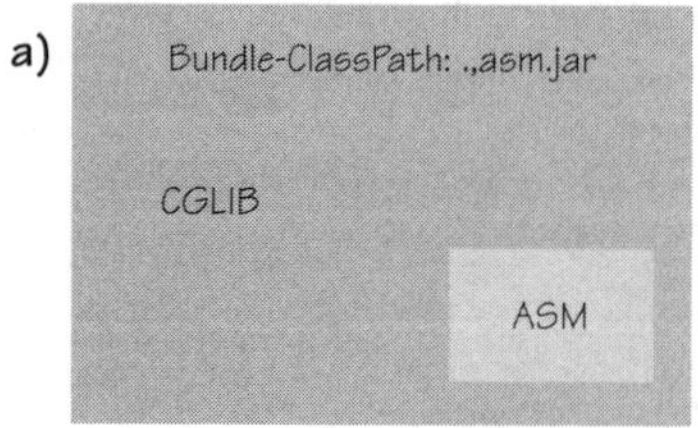

b) 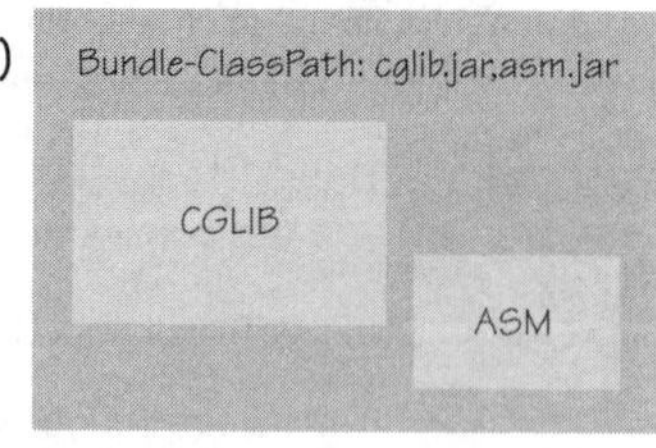

Figure 6.4 Embedding tightly coupled dependencies in a bundle

Alternatively, you can consider creating a new bundle artifact that embeds all the related JAR files together instead of turning the primary JAR file into a bundle. This aggregate bundle can then be provided separately to OSGi users without affecting users of the original JAR files. Figure 6.4b shows how you can use this approach for the CGLIB library. Although this means you have an extra deliverable to support, it also gives you an opportunity to override or add classes for better interoperability with OSGi. You'll see an example in a moment and also later on in section 6.2.1. This often happens when libraries use external connections or background threads, which ideally should be managed by the OSGi lifecycle layer. Such libraries are said to have *state*.

6.1.5 Adding lifecycle support

You may not realize it when you use a third-party library, but a number of them have a form of state. This state can take the form of a background thread, a file system cache, or a pool of database connections. Libraries usually provide methods to manage this state, such as cleaning up resources and shutting down threads. Often, you don't bother calling these methods because the life of the library is the same as the life of your application. In OSGi, this isn't necessarily the case; your application could still be running after the library has been stopped, updated, and restarted many times. On the other hand, the library could still be available in the framework long after your application has come and gone. You need to tie the library state to its bundle lifecycle; and to do that, you need to add a bundle activator (see section 3.4.1).

The original HttpClient library from Apache Commons (http://hc.apache.org/httpclient-3.x/apidocs/index.html) manages a pool of threads for multithreaded connections. These threads are started lazily so there's no need to explicitly initialize the pool, but the library provides a method to shut down and clean everything up:

```
MultiThreadedHttpConnectionManager.shutdownAll();
```

To wrap the HttpClient library JAR file up as a bundle, you can add an activator that shuts down the thread pool whenever the HttpClient bundle is stopped. This approach is as follows:

```
package org.apache.commons.httpclient.internal;

import org.apache.commons.httpclient.MultiThreadedHttpConnectionManager;
import org.osgi.framework.*;

public class Activator implements BundleActivator {
  public void start(BundleContext ctx) {}
```

```
  public void stop(BundleContext ctx) {
    MultiThreadedHttpConnectionManager.shutdownAll();
  }
}
```

You have to tell OSGi about this activator by adding metadata to the manifest:

```
Bundle-Activator: org.apache.commons.httpclient.internal.Activator
```

You can see this in action by building and running the following example:

```
$ cd chapter06/HttpClient-example

$ ant dist

$ java -jar launcher.jar bundles
```

You should see it start and attempt to connect to the internet (ignore log4j warnings):

```
GET http://www.google.com/
GOT 5500 bytes
->
```

If you use `jstack` to see what threads are running in the JVM, one of them should be

```
"MultiThreadedHttpConnectionManager cleanup" daemon
```

Stop the HttpClient bundle, which should clean up the thread pool, and check again:

```
-> stop 5
```

The `MultiThreadedHttpConnectionManager` thread should now be gone. Unfortunately, this isn't a complete solution, because if you stop and restart the test bundle, the thread pool manager reappears—even though the HttpClient bundle is still stopped! Restricting use of the HttpClient library to the bundle active state would require all calls to go through some sort of delegating proxy or, ideally, the OSGi service registry. Thankfully, the 4.0 release of the HttpClient library makes it much easier to manage connection threads inside a container such as OSGi and removes the need for this single static shutdown method.

Bundle activators are mostly harmless because they don't interfere with non-OSGi users of the JAR file. They're only referenced via the bundle metadata and aren't considered part of the public API. They sit there unnoticed and unused in classic Java applications until the bundle is loaded into an OSGi framework and started. Whenever you have a JAR file with implicit state or background resources, consider adding an activator to help OSGi users.

We've now covered most aspects of turning a JAR file into a bundle: identity, exports, imports, embedding, and lifecycle management. How many best practices can you remember? Wouldn't it be great to have them summarized as a one-page cheat sheet?

Look no further than the following section.

6.1.6 JAR file to bundle cheat sheet

Figure 6.5 presents a cheat sheet that gives you a handy summary of converting JAR files into bundles.

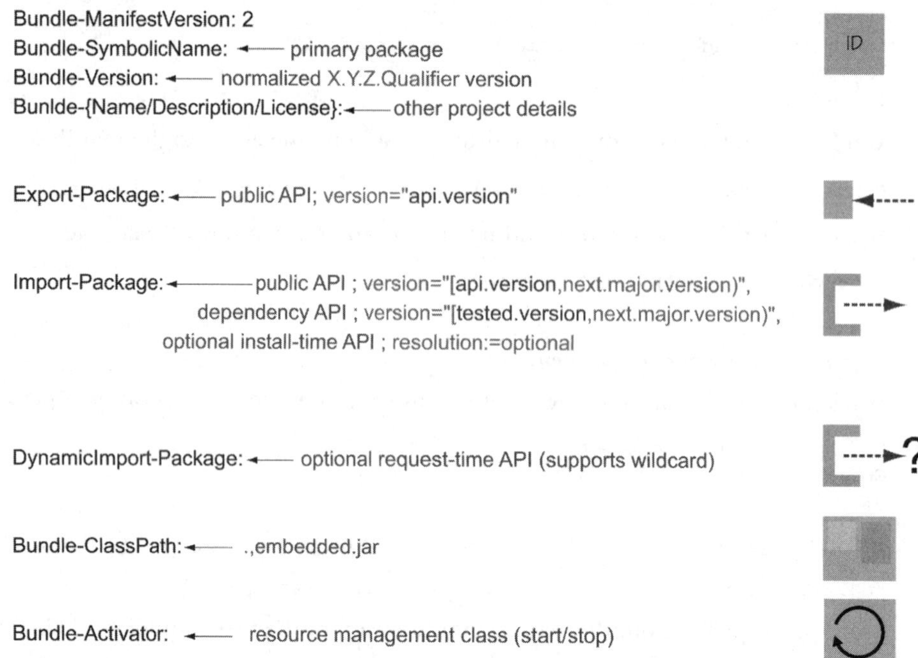
Bundle-ManifestVersion: 2
Bundle-SymbolicName: ← primary package
Bundle-Version: ← normalized X.Y.Z.Qualifier version
Bunlde-{Name/Description/License}: ← other project details
ID
Export-Package: ← public API; version="api.version"
Import-Package: ← public API ; version="[api.version,next.major.version)",
dependency API ; version="[tested.version,next.major.version)",
optional install-time API ; resolution:=optional
DynamicImport-Package: ← optional request-time API (supports wildcard)
?
Bundle-ClassPath: ← .,embedded.jar
Bundle-Activator: ← resource management class (start/stop)

Figure 6.5 JAR-to-bundle cheat sheet

OK, you know how to take a single JAR file and turn it into a bundle, but what about a complete application? You could take your existing JAR, EAR, and WAR files and turn them all into bundles; or you could choose to wrap everything up as a single application bundle. Surely you can do better than that. What techniques can you use to bundle up an application, and what are the pros and cons? For the answers to this and more, read on.

6.2 Splitting an application into bundles

Most applications are made up of one or more JAR files. One way to migrate an application to OSGi is to take these individual JAR files and convert each of them into a bundle using the techniques discussed in the previous section. Converting lots of JAR files is time consuming (especially for beginners), so a simpler approach is to take your complete application and wrap it up as a single bundle. In this section, we'll show you how to start from such a single application bundle and suggest ways of dividing it further into multiple bundles. Along the way, we'll look at how you can introduce other OSGi features, such as services, to make your application more flexible. Finally, we'll suggest places where it doesn't make sense to introduce a bundle.

Let's start with the single application bundle or so-called *mega bundle.*

6.2.1 Making a mega bundle

A mega bundle comprises a complete application along with its dependencies. Anything the application needs on top of the standard JDK is embedded inside this bundle

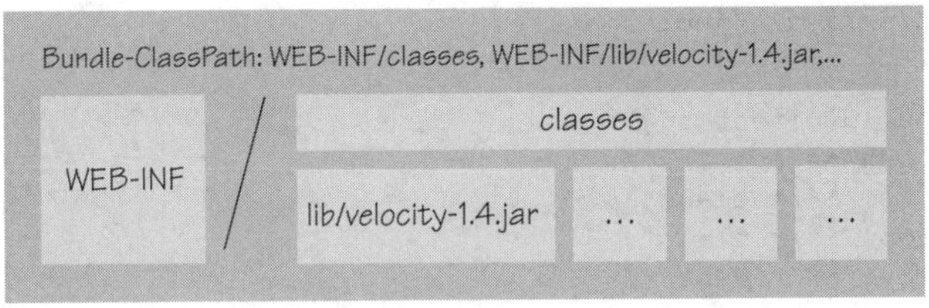

Figure 6.6 Turning a WAR file into a bundle

and made available to the application by extending the `Bundle-ClassPath` (2.5.3). This is similar to how Java Enterprise applications are constructed. In fact, you can take an existing web application archive (WAR file) and easily turn it into a bundle by adding an identity along with `Bundle-ClassPath` entries for the various classes and libraries contained within it, as shown in figure 6.6.

The key benefit of a mega bundle is that it drastically reduces the number of packages you need to import, sometimes down to no packages at all. The only packages you may need to import are non-`java.*` packages from the JDK (such as `javax.*` packages) or any packages provided by the container itself. Even then, you can choose to access them via OSGi boot delegation by setting the `org.osgi.framework.bootdelegation` framework property to the list of packages you want to inherit from the container class path. Boot delegation can also avoid certain legacy problems (see section 8.2 for the gory details). The downside is that it reduces modularity, because you can't override boot-delegated packages in OSGi. A mega bundle with boot delegation enabled is close to the classic Java application model; the only difference is that each application has its own class loader instead of sharing the single JDK application class loader.

JEDIT MEGA-BUNDLE EXAMPLE

Let's shelve the theoretical discussion for the moment and create a mega bundle based on jEdit (www.jedit.org/), a pluggable Java text editor. The sample code for this book comes with a copy of the jEdit 4.2 source, which you can unpack like so:

```
$ cd chapter06/jEdit-example
$ ant jEdit.unpack
$ cd jEdit
```

The jEdit build uses Apache Ant (http://ant.apache.org/), which is good news because it means you can use bnd's Ant tasks to generate OSGi manifests. Maven users shouldn't feel left out, though: you can use maven-bundle-plugin (http://felix.apache.org/site/apache-felix-maven-bundle-plugin-bnd.html), which also uses bnd under the covers.

How exactly do you add bnd to the build? The following listing shows the main target from the original (non-OSGi) jEdit build.xml.

Listing 6.1 Default jEdit build target

```
<target name="dist" depends="compile,compile14"
  description="Compile and package jEdit.">

  <jar jarfile="jedit.jar"
```

```
      manifest="org/gjt/sp/jedit/jedit.manifest"
      compress="false">

      <fileset dir="${build.directory}">
        <include name="bsh/**/*.class"/>
        <include name="com/**/*.class"/>
        <include name="gnu/**/*.class"/>
        <include name="org/**/*.class"/>
      </fileset>

      <fileset dir=".">
        <include name="bsh/commands/*.bsh"/>
        <include name="gnu/regexp/MessagesBundle.properties"/>
        <include name="org/gjt/sp/jedit/**/*.dtd"/>
        <include name="org/gjt/sp/jedit/icons/*.gif"/>
        <include name="org/gjt/sp/jedit/icons/*.jpg"/>
        <include name="org/gjt/sp/jedit/icons/*.png"/>
        <include name="org/gjt/sp/jedit/*.props"/>
        <include name="org/gjt/sp/jedit/actions.xml"/>
        <include name="org/gjt/sp/jedit/browser.actions.xml"/>
        <include name="org/gjt/sp/jedit/dockables.xml"/>
        <include name="org/gjt/sp/jedit/services.xml"/>
        <include name="org/gjt/sp/jedit/default.abbrevs"/>
      </fileset>
    </jar>
  </target>
```

The `jar` task is configured to take a static manifest file: org/gjt/sp/jedit/jedit.manifest. If you don't want to change the build process but still want an OSGi-enabled manifest, you can take the jEdit binary, run it through an analyzer like bnd, and add the generated OSGi headers to this static manifest. As we mentioned back in section 6.1.3, this approach is fine for existing releases or projects that don't change much. On the other hand, integrating a tool such as bnd with your build means you get feedback about the modularity of your application immediately rather than when you try to deploy it.

REPLACING THE JAR TASK WITH BND

Let's make things more dynamic and generate OSGi metadata during the build. This is the recommended approach because you don't have to remember to check and regenerate the metadata after significant changes to the project source. This is especially useful in the early stages of a project, when responsibilities are still being allocated.

There are several ways to integrate bnd with a build:

- Use bnd to generate metadata from classes before creating the JAR file.
- Create the JAR file as normal and then post-process it with bnd.
- Use bnd to generate the JAR file instead of using the Ant `jar` task.

If you need certain features of the `jar` task, such as indexing, you should use the first or second option. If you're post-processing classes or need to filter resources, choose either the second or third option. Let's go with the third option to demonstrate how easy it is to switch your build over to bnd. It will also help you later, in section 6.2.2, when you start partitioning the application into separate bundles.

First, comment out the `jar` task:

```
<!-- jar jarfile="jedit.jar"
  manifest="org/gjt/sp/jedit/jedit.manifest"
  compress="false">
...
</jar -->
```

The first line above shows where to put the JAR file, and the second lists fixed manifest entries.

Next, add the `bnd` definition and target task:

```
<taskdef resource="aQute/bnd/ant/taskdef.properties"
  classpath="../../../lib/bnd-0.0.384.jar" />

<bnd classpath="${build.directory}"
  files="jedit-mega.bnd" />
```

Here, you first give the location of the bnd JAR file to tell Ant where it can find the bnd task definition. Then you specify a `bnd` task to create your bundle JAR file, giving it the project class path and the file containing your bnd instructions.

There's one key difference between the `jar` and `bnd` tasks that you must remember:

- The `jar` task takes a list of files and directories and copies them all into a single JAR file.
- The `bnd` task takes a class path and a list of instruction files (one file per bundle) that tell it which classes and/or resources to copy from the class path into each bundle.

If you don't tell bnd to pull a certain package into the bundle, don't be surprised if the package isn't there. You're building a single mega bundle, so you need only one instruction file: call it jedit-mega.bnd. The first thing you must add is an instruction to tell bnd where to put the generated bundle:

```
-output: jedit.jar
```

The `bnd` task can also copy additional manifest headers into the final manifest, so let's ask bnd to include the original jEdit manifest rather than duplicate its content in your new file:

```
-include: org/gjt/sp/jedit/jedit.manifest
```

You could have left the manifest file where it was, added your instructions to it, and passed that into bnd, but this would make it harder for people to separate out the new build process from the original. It's also better to have the bnd instructions at the project root where they're more visible. You can now try to build the project from inside the jEdit directory:

```
$ ant dist
...
[bnd] Warnings
[bnd] None of Export-Package, Private-Package, -testpackages, or -
     exportcontents is set, therefore no packages will be included
```

```
[bnd] Did not find matching referal for *
[bnd] Errors
[bnd] The JAR is empty
```

ADDING BND INSTRUCTIONS

What went wrong? You forgot to tell bnd what packages to pull into your new bundle! Using the JAR-to-bundle cheat sheet from section 6.1.6, add the following bundle headers to jedit-mega.bnd along with a bnd-specific instruction to pull in all classes and resources from the build class path and keep them private:

```
Bundle-Name: jEdit
Bundle-SymbolicName: org.gjt.sp.jedit
Bundle-Version: 4.2

Private-Package: *
```

> **Take care with wildcards**
>
> Remember that bnd supports wildcard package names, so you can use * to represent the entire project. Although this is useful when creating mega bundles, you should be careful about using wildcards when separating a class path into multiple, separate bundles, or when already bundled dependencies appear on the class path. Always check the content of your bundles to make sure you aren't pulling in additional packages by mistake!

Getting back to the task at hand, when you rebuild the jEdit project you now see this:

```
$ ant dist
...
[bnd] # org.gjt.sp.jedit (jedit.jar) 849
```

Success! Try to run your new JAR file:

```
$ java -jar jedit.jar
```

Whoops, something else went wrong:

```
Uncaught error fetching image:
java.lang.NullPointerException
 at sun.awt.image.URLImageSource.getConnection(Unknown Source)
 at sun.awt.image.URLImageSource.getDecoder(Unknown Source)
 at sun.awt.image.InputStreamImageSource.doFetch(Unknown Source)
 at sun.awt.image.ImageFetcher.fetchloop(Unknown Source)
 at sun.awt.image.ImageFetcher.run(Unknown Source)
```

ADDING RESOURCE FILES

It seems your JAR file is missing some resources. Can you see why? Look closely at the `jar` task in listing 6.1; notice how classes come from `${build.directory}`, but the resource files come from `.` (the project root). You could write a bnd-specific `Include-Resource` instruction to tell bnd to pull in these resources, but there's an easier solution that lets you reuse instructions from the jEdit build file. Take the existing resource file set from the old `jar` task, and put it inside a `copy` task to copy matching resources to the build directory before the `bnd` task runs:

```
<copy todir="${build.directory}">
  <fileset dir=".">
    <include name="bsh/commands/*.bsh"/>
    <!-- and so on... -->
  </fileset>
</copy>
```

The resource files can now be found on the build class path. Rebuild, and run jEdit again:

```
$ ant dist
...
[bnd] # org.gjt.sp.jedit (jedit.jar) 1003

$ java -jar jedit.jar
```

Bingo! You should see the main jEdit window appear, as shown in figure 6.7.

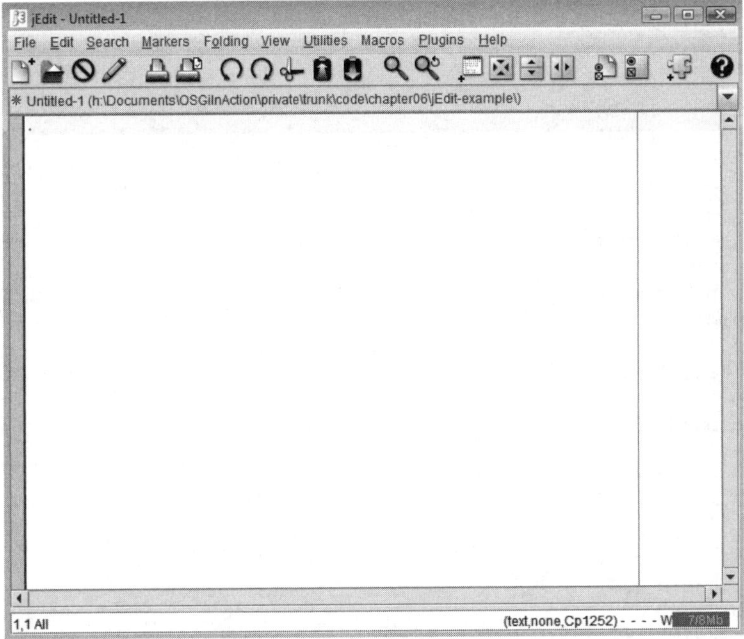

Figure 6.7 Main jEdit window

Your bundle works as a classic JAR file, but will it work as a bundle? Let's review the manifest.

Listing 6.2 jEdit mega bundle manifest

```
Manifest-Version: 1.0
Created-By: 1.6.0_13 (Sun Microsystems Inc.)
Bnd-LastModified: 1250524748304
Tool: Bnd-0.0.384
Main-Class: org.gjt.sp.jedit.jEdit
Bundle-ManifestVersion: 2
```

```
Bundle-Name: jEdit
Bundle-SymbolicName: org.gjt.sp.jedit
Bundle-Version: 4.2
Private-Package:
 bsh,
 bsh.collection,
 bsh.commands,
 bsh.reflect,
 com.microstar.xml,
 gnu.regexp,
 installer,
 org.gjt.sp.jedit,
 org.gjt.sp.jedit.browser,
 org.gjt.sp.jedit.buffer,
 org.gjt.sp.jedit.gui,
 org.gjt.sp.jedit.help,
 org.gjt.sp.jedit.icons,
 org.gjt.sp.jedit.io,
 org.gjt.sp.jedit.menu,
 org.gjt.sp.jedit.msg,
 org.gjt.sp.jedit.options,
 org.gjt.sp.jedit.pluginmgr,
 org.gjt.sp.jedit.print,
 org.gjt.sp.jedit.proto.jeditresource,
 org.gjt.sp.jedit.search,
 org.gjt.sp.jedit.syntax,
 org.gjt.sp.jedit.textarea,
 org.gjt.sp.util,
 org.objectweb.asm
Import-Package:
 javax.print.attribute,
 javax.print.attribute.standard,
 javax.swing,
 javax.swing.border,
 javax.swing.event,
 javax.swing.filechooser,
 javax.swing.plaf,
 javax.swing.plaf.basic,
 javax.swing.plaf.metal,
 javax.swing.table,
 javax.swing.text,
 javax.swing.text.html,
 javax.swing.tree
```

Your jEdit bundle doesn't export any packages, but it does use packages from Swing. These should come from the system bundle, which is typically set up to export JDK packages (although this can be overridden). You may wonder if you should add version ranges to the packages imported from the JDK. This isn't required, because most system bundles don't version their JDK packages. You only need to version these imports if you want to use another implementation that's different from the stock JDK version.

We should also mention that the final manifest contains some bnd-specific headers that aren't used by the OSGi framework (such as `Private-Package`, `Tool`, and `Bnd-LastModified`). They're left as a useful record of how bnd built the bundle, but if you don't want them, you can remove them by adding this bnd instruction to jedit-mega.bnd:

```
-removeheaders: Private-Package,Tool,Bnd-LastModified
```

The new manifest looks correct, but the real test is yet to come. You must now try to deploy and run your bundle on an actual OSGi framework. Will it work the first time or fail with an obscure exception?

RUNNING JEDIT WITH OSGI

You can deploy your jEdit bundle by using the same simple launcher used to launch the earlier paint examples. Remember, this launcher first installs any bundles found in the directory and then uses the first `Main-Class` header it finds to bootstrap the application. Your manifest already has a `Main-Class`, so you need to point the launcher at the jEdit directory, like so:

```
$ cd ..
$ cp ../../launcher/dist/launcher.jar .
$ java -jar launcher.jar jEdit
```

Unfortunately, something's not quite right. The bundle installs and the application starts, but it hangs at the splash screen shown in figure 6.8, and the main jEdit window never appears.

If you look closely at the top of the stack trace, you see the following warning message:

```
java.net.MalformedURLException: Unknown protocol: jeditresource
```

Why did this work when the bundle was run as a classic application, but not when the bundle was installed in an OSGi framework? The answer lies in the URL Handlers Service we discussed briefly back in section 4.6.1. To implement this service, the OSGi framework installs its own `URLStreamHandlerFactory`, which delegates requests to handlers installed via the service registry. Unlike the default `URLStreamHandlerFactory`, this implementation doesn't automatically scan the class path for URL handlers. Instead, all

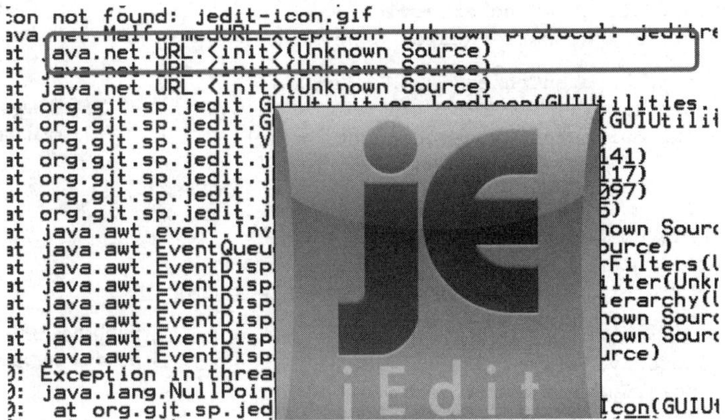

Figure 6.8 jEdit when first run as OSGi bundle

URL handlers must be registered as OSGi services, which also means the handlers are tied to their bundle lifecycle.

FIXING THE URL HANDLER ISSUE

Your first thought may be to try to disable the URL Handlers Service so it doesn't install this factory. Unfortunately, there's no standard switch for this; but to disable it in Felix, you set the `felix.service.urlhandlers` framework property to `false`. Turning off the global URL Handlers Service also has serious implications. It means no bundle can contribute dynamic protocol handlers, which would break applications that rely on the URL Handlers Service. It also won't fix this particular problem because the `jeditresource` handler isn't visible to the default `URLStreamHandlerFactory` when you run jEdit as a bundle. The JDK's URL Handler factory uses `Class.forName()` to search the application class path for valid handlers, but your `jeditresource` handler is hidden from view inside the jEdit bundle class loader.

The solution is to register the `jeditresource` handler as a `URLStreamHandlerService` when the jEdit bundle is started and remove it when the bundle is stopped. But how can you add OSGi-specific code without affecting classic jEdit users? Cast your mind back to section 6.1.5, where we talked about using lifecycles to manage external resources. This is exactly the sort of situation that requires a bundle activator, such as the one shown next.

Listing 6.3 Bundle activator to manage the `jeditresource` handler

```
package org.gjt.sp.jedit;

import java.io.IOException;
import java.net.*;
import java.util.Properties;

import org.osgi.framework.*;
import org.osgi.service.url.*;

import org.gjt.sp.jedit.proto.jeditresource.Handler;

public class Activator implements BundleActivator {
  private static class JEditResourceHandlerService
    extends AbstractURLStreamHandlerService {
    private Handler jEditResourceHandler = new Handler();        <- Real handler instance

    public URLConnection openConnection(URL url)
      throws IOException {
      return jEditResourceHandler.openConnection(url);           <- Delegates to real handler
    }
  }

  public void start(BundleContext context) {
    Properties properties = new Properties();
    properties.setProperty(URLConstants.URL_HANDLER_PROTOCOL,
        "jeditresource");

    context.registerService(                                     <- Publishes URL handler service
      URLStreamHandlerService.class.getName(),
      new JEditResourceHandlerService(),
```

```
        properties);
  }

  public void stop(BundleContext context) {}
}
```

After you've added this activator class to the build, you must remember to declare it in the OSGi metadata—otherwise, it will never be called. This is a common cause of head-scratching for people new to OSGi, because the framework can't tell when you accidentally forget a `Bundle-Activator` header. When you've added an activator, but it's having no effect, always check your manifest to make sure it's been declared—it saves a lot of hair!

```
Bundle-Activator: org.gjt.sp.jedit.Activator
```

Your activator code uses OSGi constants and interfaces, so you must add the core OSGi API to the compilation class path in the jEdit build.xml. Otherwise, your new code won't compile:

```
<javac ... >
        <classpath path="../../../lib/osgi.core.jar"/>
        <!-- the rest of the classpath -->
```

This API is only required when compiling the source; it isn't necessary at execution time unless the activator class is explicitly loaded. One more build, and you now have a JAR file that can run as a classic Java application or an OSGi bundle! The following snippet shows the final set of bnd instructions for the jEdit mega bundle:

```
-output: jedit.jar

-include: org/gjt/sp/jedit/jedit.manifest

Bundle-Name: jEdit
Bundle-SymbolicName: org.gjt.sp.jedit
Bundle-Version: 4.2

Private-Package: *

Bundle-Activator: org.gjt.sp.jedit.Activator
```

One last wrinkle: you have to tell jEdit where its installation directory is by using the `jedit.home` property. Normally, jEdit can detect the installation directory containing its JAR file by peeking at the application class path, but this won't work when running it as a bundle on OSGi because the JAR file is loaded via a different mechanism:

```
$ ant dist

$ cd ..

$ java -Djedit.home=jEdit -jar launcher.jar jEdit
```

With this last piece of configuration in place, you should see jEdit start and the main window appear, as you saw earlier in figure 6.8. It should also still work as a classic Java application.

REVISITING MEGA BUNDLES

You've successfully created a mega bundle for jEdit with a small amount of effort. What are the downsides of a mega bundle? Well, your application is still one single unit. You can't replace or upgrade sections of it without shutting down the complete application, and doing so may shut down the entire JVM process if the application calls `System.exit()`. Because nothing is being shared, you can end up with duplicate content between applications.

Effectively, you're in the same situation as before moving to OSGi, but with a few additional improvements in isolation and management. This doesn't mean the mega bundle approach is useless—as a first step, it can be reassuring to be able to run your application on an OSGi framework with the minimum of fuss. It also provides a solid foundation for further separating (or slicing) your application into bundles, which is the focus of the next section.

6.2.2 *Slicing code into bundles*

You now have a single mega bundle containing your entire application. The next step toward a full-fledged flexible OSGi application is to start breaking it into bundles that can be upgraded independently of one another. How and where should you draw the lines between bundles?

Bundles import and export packages in order to share them, so it makes sense to draw lines that minimize the number of imports and exports. If you have a high-level design document showing the major components and their boundaries, you can take each major component and turn it into a bundle. If you don't have such a document, you should look for major areas of responsibility such as business logic, data access, and graphical components. Each major area can be represented by a bundle, as depicted in figure 6.9.

Another way to approach this is to review the benefits of modularity (described in section 2.2) and think about where they make the most sense in your application. For example, do any areas need to be upgraded or fixed independently? Does the application have any optional parts? Are common utilities shared throughout the application?

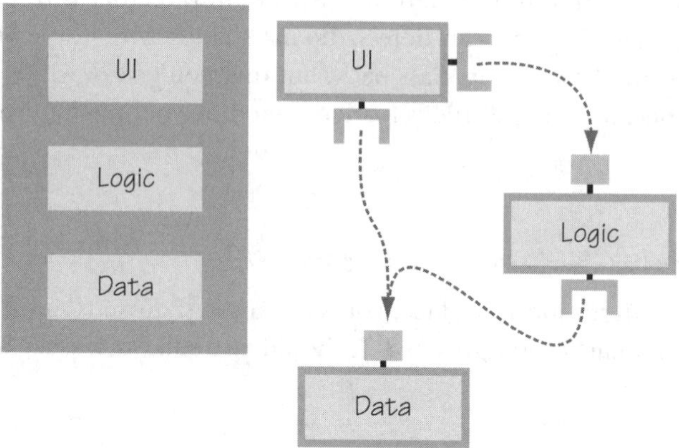

Figure 6.9 Slicing code into bundles

CUTTING ALONG THE DOTTED LINES

Returning to the jEdit example, what areas suggest themselves as potential bundles? The obvious choice to begin with is to separate the jEdit code from third-party libraries and then try to extract the main top-level package. But how do you go about dividing the project class path into different bundles?

Recall what we said about bnd back in section 6.1.3, that it uses a pull approach to assemble bundles from a project class path based on a list of instruction files. All you need to do is provide your bnd task with different instruction files for each bundle. The following example divides the class path into three bundles:

```
<bnd classpath="${build.directory}"
  files="jedit-thirdparty.bnd,jedit-main.bnd,jedit-engine.bnd" />
```

The first bundle contains all third-party classes—basically, any package from the build directory that doesn't start with `org.gjt.sp`. Bnd makes this easy by allowing negated packages. For example:

```
Private-Package: !org.gjt.sp.*, *
```

This copies all other packages into the bundle and keeps them private.

Using the earlier jedit-mega.bnd file as a template, you can flesh out the rest to get the following jedit-thirdparty.bnd file:

```
-output: jedit-thirdparty.jar

Bundle-Name: jEdit Third-party Libraries
Bundle-SymbolicName: org.gjt.sp.jedit.libs
Bundle-Version: 4.2

Private-Package: !org.gjt.sp.*, !installer.*, *
```

You also exclude the `installer` package because it isn't required at execution time and doesn't belong in the third-party library bundle.

The second bundle contains the top-level package containing the main jEdit class. You should also add the `org.gjt.sp.jedit.proto` package containing the URL handler code because it's only used by the bundle activator in the top-level package. Here's an initial attempt at jedit-main.bnd:

```
-output: jedit.jar

-include: org/gjt/sp/jedit/jedit.manifest

Bundle-Name: jEdit
Bundle-SymbolicName: org.gjt.sp.jedit
Bundle-Version: 4.2

Private-Package: org.gjt.sp.jedit, org.gjt.sp.jedit.proto.*

Bundle-Activator: org.gjt.sp.jedit.Activator
```

Notice that the only difference between this file and the mega bundle instructions shown earlier is the selection of private packages; everything else is exactly the same. The main bundle also replaces the mega bundle as the executable JAR file.

The third and final bundle contains the rest of the jEdit packages, which we'll call the *engine* for now. It should contain all packages beneath the `org.gjt.sp` namespace, except the top-level jEdit package and packages under `org.gjt.sp.jedit.proto`. The resulting jedit-engine.bnd file is as follows:

```
-output: jedit-engine.jar

Bundle-Name: jEdit Engine
Bundle-SymbolicName: org.gjt.sp.jedit.engine
Bundle-Version: 4.2

Private-Package:\
 !org.gjt.sp.jedit, !org.gjt.sp.jedit.proto.*,\      <-- Excludes main packages
 org.gjt.sp.*
```

Notice how the same packages listed in the main instructions are negated in the engine instructions. Refactoring packages between bundles is as simple as moving entries from one instruction file to another.

STITCHING THE PIECES TOGETHER

You now have three bundles that together form the original class path, but none of them share any packages. If you tried to launch the OSGi application at this point, it would fail because of unsatisfied imports between the three bundles. Should you go ahead and export everything by switching all `Private-Package` instructions to `Export-Package`? You could, but what would you learn by doing that? Let's try to export only what you absolutely need to share, keeping as much as possible private.

There are three ways you can find out which packages a bundle must export:

- Gain an understanding of the code base and how the packages relate to one other. This can involve the use of structural analysis tools such as Structure101 (www.headwaysoftware.com/products/structure101/index.php).
- Read the `Import-Package` headers from generated manifests to compile a list of packages that "someone" needs to export. Ignore JDK packages like `javax.swing`. You can use the bnd `print` command to avoid having to unpack the manifest.
- Repeatedly deploy the bundles into a live framework, and use any resulting error messages and/or diagnostic commands (such as the `diag` command on Equinox) to fine-tune the exported packages until all bundles resolve.

The first option requires patience, but the reward is a thorough understanding of the package structure. It also helps you determine other potential areas that can be turned into bundles. The third option can be quick if the framework gives you the complete list of missing packages on the first attempt, but sometimes it feels like an endless loop of "deploy, test, update." The second option is a good compromise between the other two. The bnd tool has already analyzed the code base to come up with the list of imports, and you already know that the framework will follow the import constraints listed in the manifest. The structured manifest also means you can write a script to do the hard work for you.

For example, consider this rather obscure command on Linux:

```
$ java -jar ../../lib/bnd-0.0.384.jar print jEdit/*.jar \
   | awk '/^Import-Package$/ {getline;ok=1} /^[^ ]/ {ok=0} \
         {if (ok) print $1}' | sort -u
```

It uses bnd to print a summary of each jEdit bundle, extracts the package names from the `Import-Package` part of the summary, and sorts them into a unique list. (You could also use the bnd `print -uses` command to get a tabular view of what packages use other packages.) After you remove the JDK and OSGi framework packages, you get the following:

```
bsh
com.microstar.xml
gnu.regexp

org.gjt.sp.jedit

org.gjt.sp.jedit.browser
org.gjt.sp.jedit.buffer
org.gjt.sp.jedit.gui
org.gjt.sp.jedit.help
org.gjt.sp.jedit.io
org.gjt.sp.jedit.menu
org.gjt.sp.jedit.msg
org.gjt.sp.jedit.options
org.gjt.sp.jedit.pluginmgr
org.gjt.sp.jedit.search
org.gjt.sp.jedit.syntax
org.gjt.sp.jedit.textarea
org.gjt.sp.util
```

The first group includes third-party packages, next is the main jEdit package, and the long group contains other jEdit packages.

It's clear that the third-party library bundle needs to export only three packages and the main jEdit bundle just the top-level package. Unfortunately, the jEdit engine bundle needs to export almost all of its packages, indicating a tight coupling between the engine and the top-level jEdit package. This suggests that it would be better to merge these two bundles back together, unless you were going to refactor the code to reduce this coupling. Let's ignore this for now and press on, because this separation will eventually lead to an interesting class-loading issue that's worth knowing about. Anyone who's curious can skip ahead to section 6.2.4.

What's next on the JAR-to-bundle checklist? Ah, yes: versioning. You should version all the exported jEdit packages with the current bundle version (4.2); but you won't version the individual third-party packages at the moment, because it's not obvious what releases are being used. You can always add the appropriate versions in the future, when you divide the combined third-party bundle into separate library bundles.

You should also add version ranges to your imports, as suggested back in section 6.1.3. Rather than endure the hassle of explicitly writing out all the ranges, you can take advantage of another bnd feature and compute them:

```
-versionpolicy: [${version;==;${@}},${version;+;${@}})
```

This instruction (http://aqute.biz/Code/Bnd#versionpolicy) tells bnd to take the detected version `${@}` and turn it into a range containing the current major.minor version `${version;==;...}` up to but not including the next major version `${version;+;...}`. (See appendix A for more information about the various bnd instructions.) So if the bnd tool knows that a package has a version of 4.1.8, it applies a version range of `[4.1,5)` to any import of that package. You add this to each of your bnd files (you can also put it in a shared common file) along with the changes to export the necessary packages.

Following are the final bnd instructions for the jEdit third-party library bundle:

```
-output: jedit-thirdparty.jar

Bundle-Name: jEdit Third-party Libraries
Bundle-SymbolicName: org.gjt.sp.jedit.libs
Bundle-Version: 4.2

Export-Package: bsh, com.microstar.xml, gnu.regexp
Private-Package: !org.gjt.sp.*, !installer.*, *

-versionpolicy: [${version;==;${@}},${version;+;${@}})
```

And here are the final bnd instructions for the jEdit engine bundle:

```
-output: jedit-engine.jar

Bundle-Name: jEdit Engine
Bundle-SymbolicName: org.gjt.sp.jedit.engine
Bundle-Version: 4.2

Export-Package:\
 !org.gjt.sp.jedit,\
 !org.gjt.sp.jedit.proto.*,\
 org.gjt.sp.*;version="4.2"

-versionpolicy: [${version;==;${@}},${version;+;${@}})
```

You still have one more (non-OSGi) tweak to make to the main jEdit bundle instructions. Remember that you now create three JAR files in place of the original single JAR file. Although you can rely on the OSGi framework to piece these together into a single application at execution time, this isn't true of the standard Java launcher. You need some way to tell it to include the two additional JAR files on the class path whenever someone executes:

```
$ java -jar jedit.jar
```

Thankfully, there is a way: you need to add the standard `Class-Path` header to the main JAR file manifest. The `Class-Path` header takes a space-separated list of JAR files, whose locations are relative to the main JAR file. These final main-bundle instructions allow jEdit to work both as a bundle and an executable JAR:

```
-output: jedit.jar

-include: org/gjt/sp/jedit/jedit.manifest
Class-Path: jedit-thirdparty.jar jedit-engine.jar
```

```
Bundle-Name: jEdit
Bundle-SymbolicName: org.gjt.sp.jedit
Bundle-Version: 4.2

Export-Package:\
 org.gjt.sp.jedit;version="4.2"

Private-Package:\
 org.gjt.sp.jedit.proto.*

-versionpolicy: [${version;==;${@}},${version;+;${@}})

Bundle-Activator: org.gjt.sp.jedit.Activator
```

Update your three bnd files as shown, and rebuild. Or if you want a shortcut, use this:

```
$ cd ..
$ ant jEdit.patch dist
```

Congratulations—you've successfully separated jEdit into three JAR files that work with or without OSGi! The following lines launch jEdit OSGi and jEdit classic, respectively:

```
$ java -Djedit.home=jEdit -jar launcher.jar jEdit
$ java -jar jEdit/jedit.jar
```

As we hope this example demonstrates, after you have an application working in OSGi, it doesn't take much effort to start slicing it up into smaller, more modularized bundles. But is this all you can do with jEdit on OSGi—keep slicing it into smaller and smaller pieces?

6.2.3 Loosening things up

So far, we've focused on using the first two layers of OSGi: module and lifecycle. There's another layer you haven't yet used in this chapter: service. The service layer is different from the first two layers in that it can be hard to tell when or where you should use it, especially when migrating an existing application to OSGi. Often, people decide not to use services at all in new bundles, instead relying on sharing packages to find implementations. But as you saw in chapter 4, services make your application more flexible and help reduce the coupling between bundles. The good news is, you can decide to use services at any time; but how will you know when the time is right?

There are many ways to share different implementations inside a Java application. You can construct instances directly, call a factory method, or perhaps apply some form of dependency injection. When you first move an application to OSGi, you'll probably decide to use the same tried-and-tested approach you did before, except that now some of the packages come from other bundles. As you saw in chapter 4, these approaches have certain limitations compared to OSGi services. Services in OSGi are extremely dynamic, support rich metadata, and promote loose coupling between the consumer and provider.

If you expect to continue to use your application outside of OSGi—for example, as a classic Java application—you may be worried about using the service layer in case it ties you to the OSGi runtime. No problem! You can get the benefits of services without being tied to OSGi by using component-based dependency injection. Chapters 11 and 12 introduce a number of component models that transparently support services without forcing you to depend on the OSGi API. If you already use dependency injection, moving to these component models is straightforward; sometimes it's only a matter of reconfiguring the dependency bindings in your original application. If you're itching to try out these component models, feel free to skip ahead to chapter 11. But make sure you come back and read the intervening chapters; they'll be an invaluable guide when it comes to managing, testing, and debugging your new OSGi application.

Let's get back to discussing services. Where might you use services in jEdit? Well, jEdit has its own home-grown plugin framework for developers to contribute all sorts of gadgets, tools, and widgets to the GUI. In addition, jEdit uses its own custom class loader `org.gjt.sp.jedit.JARClassLoader` to allow hot deployment and removal of jEdit plugins. Plugins hook back into jEdit by accessing implementation classes and calling static methods, such as `jEdit.getSettingsDirectory()`. These static method calls are convenient, but they make it hard to mock out (or replace) dependencies for testing purposes.

Instead of relying on static methods, you can change jEdit to use dependency injection. Plugins then have their dependencies injected, rather than call jEdit directly. After you replace the static methods calls with dependency injection, it's just another step to replace the static bindings with dynamic OSGi services (see chapters 11 and 12). This also simplifies unit testing, because you can swap out the real bindings and put in stubbed or scripted test implementations. Unfortunately, refactoring jEdit to use dependency injection throughout is outside the scope of this book, but you can use chapters 11 and 12 as a general guide. With this in mind, is there a smaller task that can help bridge the gap between OSGi bundles and jEdit plugins and make it easier to use services?

You can consider replacing the jEdit plugin framework with OSGi, much as Eclipse replaced its original plugin framework. To do this, you have to take the `JARClassLoader` and `PluginJAR` classes and extract a common API that you can then reimplement using OSGi, as shown in figure 6.10. You use the original jEdit plugin code when running in classic Java mode and the smaller OSGi mapping layer when running on an OSGi framework.

Extracting the common plugin API is left as an interesting exercise for you; one wrinkle is the fact that jEdit assumes plugins are located in the file system, whereas OSGi supports bundles installed from opaque input streams. The new plugin API can have methods to iterate over and query JAR file entries to avoid having to know where the plugin is located. These methods will map nicely to the resource-entry methods on the OSGi `Bundle` interface.

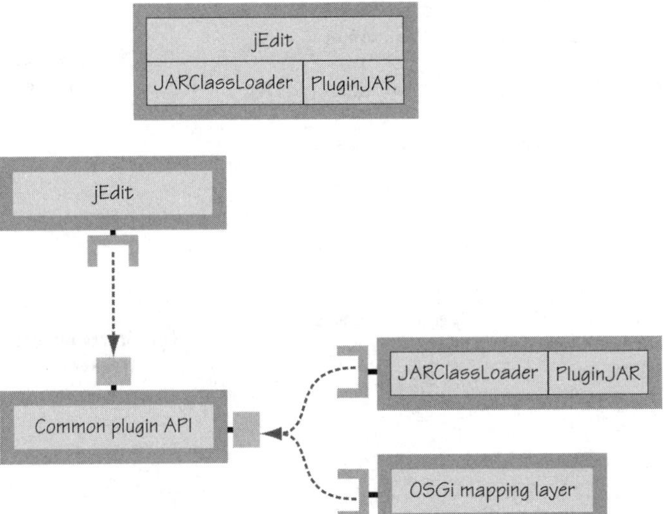

Figure 6.10 Extracting a common jEdit plugin API

How about being able to register OSGi bundles as jEdit plugins? This is a stepping stone to using services, because you need a bundle context to access OSGi services. The main jEdit class provides two static methods to add and remove plugin JAR files:

```
public static void addPluginJAR(String path);

public static void removePluginJAR(PluginJAR jar, boolean exit);
```

Following the extender pattern introduced in section 3.4, let's use a bundle tracker to look for potential jEdit plugins. The code in the following listing uses a tracker to add and remove jEdit plugin bundles as they come and go.

Listing 6.4 Using the extender pattern to install jEdit plugins

```
package org.foo.jedit.extender;

import java.io.File;
import org.gjt.sp.jedit.*;
import org.osgi.framework.*;

public class Activator implements BundleActivator {

  BundleTracker pluginTracker;

  public void start(final BundleContext ctx) {
    pluginTracker = new BundleTracker(ctx) {

      public void addedBundle(Bundle bundle) {
        String path = getBundlePath(bundle);
        if (path != null && bundle.getResource("actions.xml") != null) {   ← 1 Looks for actions.xml
          jEdit.addPluginJAR(path);
        }
      }
```

```
      public void removedBundle(Bundle bundle) {
        String path = getBundlePath(bundle);
        if (path != null) {
          PluginJAR jar = jEdit.getPluginJAR(path);
          if (jar != null) {
            jEdit.removePluginJAR(jar, false);
          }
        }
      }
    };

    EditBus.addToBus(new EBComponent() {
      public void handleMessage(EBMessage message) {
        EditBus.removeFromBus(this);
        pluginTracker.open();
      }
    });
  }

  public void stop(BundleContext ctx) {
    pluginTracker.close();
    pluginTracker = null;
  }

  static String getBundlePath(Bundle bundle) {
    String location = bundle.getLocation().trim();

    File jar;
    if (location.startsWith("file:")) {
      jar = new File(location.substring(5));
    } else {
      jar = new File(location);
    }

    if (jar.isFile()) {
      return jar.getAbsolutePath();
    }

    return null;
  }
}
```

❷ Maps to PluginJAR instance

❸ Starts bundle tracker

❹ Ignores bundles that don't map to file

The code identifies jEdit plugins by looking for a file called actions.xml in the bundle root ❶. Because the jEdit API only accepts path-based plugins, it ignores bundles whose locations don't map to a file ❹. To remove a plugin bundle, it uses another jEdit method to map the location back to the installed `PluginJAR` instance ❷. The last piece of the puzzle is to start the bundle tracker only when jEdit is ready to accept new plugins. If you look at the jEdit startup code, you may notice that one of the last things it does in `finishStartup()` is send out the initial `EditorStarted` message on the EditBus (jEdit's event-notification mechanism). The code registers a one-shot component that listens for any message event, deregisters itself, and starts the bundle tracker ❸.

Let's see this extender in action:

```
$ cd chapter06/jEdit-example
$ ant jEdit.patch dist
$ java -Djedit.home=jEdit -jar launcher.jar jEdit
-> install file:test/Calculator.jar
```

Look in the Plugins menu; no plugins should be available. Now start the calculator bundle that you just installed:

```
-> start 9
```

You should see the calculator in the Plugins menu. Selecting this item opens the window shown in figure 6.11. If you stop the calculator bundle, this window immediately disappears, and the Plugins menu once again shows no available plugins:

```
-> stop 9
```

Cool—the extender successfully bridges the gap between OSGi bundles and jEdit plugins! You can now use existing OSGi management agents, such as the Apache Felix Web Console (http://felix.apache.org/site/apache-felix-web-console.html), to manage jEdit plugins. This small example shows how standards like OSGi can make it much easier to reuse and assemble existing pieces into new applications.

Are you eager to start moving your application to OSGi? Wait, not so fast! We have one last topic to discuss before we close out this chapter, and it's something you should keep asking yourself when you're modularizing applications: is this bundle adding any value?

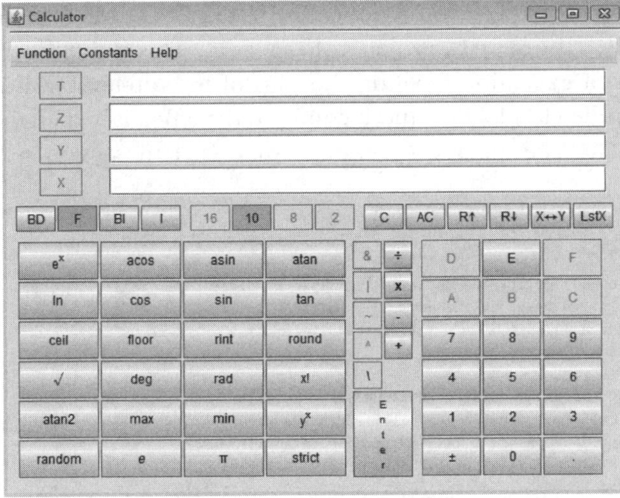

Figure 6.11
jEdit calculator plugin

6.2.4 *To bundle or not to bundle?*

Sometimes, you should take a step back and think, do I need another bundle? The more bundles you create, the more work is required during build, test, and management in general. Creating a bundle for every individual package is obviously overkill, whereas putting your entire application inside a single bundle means you're missing out on modularity. Some number of bundles in between is best, but where's the sweet spot?

One way to tell is to measure the benefit introduced by each bundle. If you find you're always upgrading a set of bundles at the same time and you never install them individually, keeping them as separate bundles isn't bringing much benefit.

You can also look at how your current choice affects developers. If a bundle layout helps developers work in parallel or enforces separation between components, it's worth keeping. But if a bundle is getting in the way of development, perhaps for legacy class-loader reasons, you should consider removing it, either by merging it with an existing bundle or by making it available via boot delegation (we briefly discussed this option at the start of section 6.2.1). Consider the jEdit example: have you reached the right balance of bundles?

A BUNDLE TOO FAR

Let's refresh your memory. Recall the `Import-Package` discussion back in the section "Stitching the pieces together." We mentioned an interesting issue caused by placing the top-level package in its own bundle, separate from the rest of the jEdit engine. You can see the problem for yourself by starting the OSGi version of jEdit and selecting File > Print. A message box pops up (see figure 6.12), describing a failure in a BeanShell script.

Why did the script fail? The error message suggests a class-loading problem. If you scroll down through the stack trace, you'll notice the last jEdit class before the call to `bsh.BshMethod.invoke()` is `org.gjt.sp.jedit.BeanShell`. This is a utility class that manages BeanShell script execution for jEdit. It's part of the top-level jEdit package loaded by the main bundle class loader, and it configures the BeanShell engine to use a special instance of `JARClassLoader` (previously discussed in section 6.2.3) that

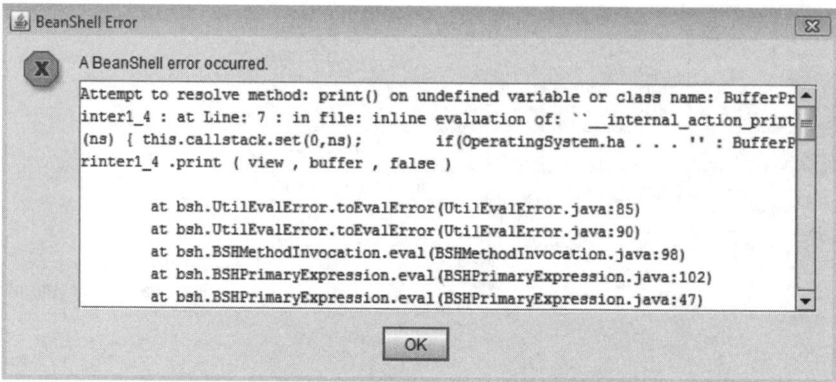

Figure 6.12 Error attempting to print from jEdit

delegates to each plugin class loader in turn. This is so BeanShell scripts can access any class in the entire jEdit application. If none of the plugin class loaders can see the class, this special class loader delegates to its parent class loader. For a classic Java application, this is the application class loader, which can see all the jEdit classes on the class path. For your OSGi application, the parent is the class loader for the main bundle, which can only see the `org.gjt.sp.jedit` and `proto` packages it contains as well as any packages it explicitly imports. One thing you know it can't see is the `BufferPrinter1_4` class.

Who owns the `BufferPrinter1_4` class? It's part of the `org.gjt.sp.jedit.print` package, belonging to the jEdit engine bundle. You could check the manifest to make sure this package is being exported as expected; but if you're using the instructions from the section "Stitching the pieces together," then it is. It's being exported from the engine bundle, but is it being imported by the main bundle? Without an import, this package isn't visible. Let's avoid cracking open the JAR file and instead use bnd to see the list of imports.

Listing 6.5 Using bnd to print imported and exported packages

```
$ java -jar ../../lib/bnd-0.0.384.jar print -impexp jEdit/jedit.jar    <- Prints imported and exported packages

[IMPEXP]
Import-Package
  bsh
  com.microstar.xml
  gnu.regexp
  javax.swing
  javax.swing.border
  javax.swing.event
  javax.swing.plaf
  javax.swing.text
  org.gjt.sp.jedit.browser
  org.gjt.sp.jedit.buffer
  org.gjt.sp.jedit.gui
  org.gjt.sp.jedit.help
  org.gjt.sp.jedit.io
  org.gjt.sp.jedit.menu
  org.gjt.sp.jedit.msg
  org.gjt.sp.jedit.options
  org.gjt.sp.jedit.pluginmgr
  org.gjt.sp.jedit.search
  org.gjt.sp.jedit.syntax
  org.gjt.sp.jedit.textarea
  org.gjt.sp.util
  org.osgi.framework
  org.osgi.service.url
Export-Package
  org.gjt.sp.jedit                          {version=4.2}
```

Aha! The main bundle manifest contains no mention of the `org.gjt.sp.jedit.print` package, which explains why the `BufferPrinter1_4` class wasn't found and the script failed. A last question before you try to fix this issue: why didn't bnd pick up the reference to the `org.gjt.sp.jedit.print` package? Remember that bnd works primarily on byte code, not source code; it won't pick up packages referenced in scripts, arbitrary strings, or runtime configuration files. The only reference to this package was in a BeanShell script, which wasn't analyzed by the bnd tool.

You now have all the answers as to why the script failed, but how should you solve the problem? Bnd supports adding custom analyzers to process additional content, so you could write your own BeanShell analyzer for bnd. But what if writing such an analyzer is outside your expertise? Can you instead fix the class-loading problem at execution time? There are two approaches to solving this type of class-loading issue:

- Attempt to use a different class loader to load the class.
- Add the necessary imports to the bundle doing the loading.

The first approach is only possible when the library provides some way of passing in the class loader or when it uses the Thread Context Class Loader (TCCL) to load classes. (You can read more about the TCCL in chapter 8.) The BeanShell library does provide a method to set the class loader, but jEdit is already using it to pass in the special class loader that provides access to all currently installed jEdit plugins. Rather than mess around with jEdit's internal `JARClassLoader` code and potentially break the jEdit plugin framework, you'll take the second approach and add the missing imports to the main bundle. This has the least impact on existing jEdit code—all you're doing is updating the OSGi part of the manifest.

You know that you need to import the `org.gjt.sp.jedit.print` package, but what else might you need? To make absolutely sure, you'd have to run through a range of tests exercising the whole of the jEdit GUI. Although this testing could be automated to save time, let's instead try the suggestion from the end of section 6.1.3 and allow the main jEdit bundle to import any package on demand:

```
DynamicImport-Package: *
```

Add this to the jedit-main.bnd instruction file, and rebuild one more time. You can now open the print dialog box without getting the error message. The application will also continue to work even if you use a more restrictive dynamic import, such as

```
DynamicImport-Package: org.gjt.sp.*
```

Why does this work? Well, rather than say up front what you import, you leave it open to whatever load requests come through the main bundle class loader. As long as another bundle exports the package, and it matches the given wildcard, you'll be able to see it. But is this the right solution? Merging the main and engine bundles back together would solve the BeanShell problem without the need for dynamic imports. You already know these bundles are tightly coupled; keeping them apart is causing you further trouble. This is a good example of when introducing more bundles doesn't make sense. OSGi isn't a golden hammer, and it won't magically make code more modular.

In short, if you're getting class-loading errors or are sharing lots of packages between bundles, that could be a sign that you should start merging them back together. You may decide to fall back to classic Java class loading by putting troublesome JAR files back on the application class path and exposing a selection of their packages via the system bundle with the `org.osgi.framework.system.packages.extra` property. You can go even further by adding their packages to the `org.osgi.framework.bootdelegation` property, which makes them automatically available to all bundles without needing to explicitly import them.

This sounds useful, but there's a catch: if you use boot delegation, you won't be able to use multiple versions or dynamically deploy them. But if it avoids tangled classloading problems and helps keep your developers sane, you may decide this is a fair trade. You can often achieve more by concentrating on modularizing your own code. Leave complex third-party library JAR files on the application class path until you know how to turn them into bundles or until an OSGi-compatible release is available. Not everything has to be a bundle. As we often say in this book, you can decide how much OSGi you want to use: it's definitely *not* an all-or-nothing approach!

6.3 Summary

In this chapter, we did the following:

- Showed how to turn an existing JAR into a bundle (abracadabra!)
- Turned Apache BeanUtils and HttpClient into example bundles
- Discussed slicing complete applications into one or more bundles
- Converted jEdit into an OSGi application that still works outside of OSGi
- Explained why you should watch for the sweet spot where you get the most value per bundle
- Looked at why too few bundles make your application less modular and less flexible
- Looked at why too many bundles can lead to exponential test and management costs

But what is involved in testing bundles? After you've split your application into many independent parts, how do you keep everything consistent, and how do you upgrade your application without bringing everything down? The next chapter will discuss this and more, as we look at testing OSGi applications.

7 Testing applications

This chapter covers

- Migrating tests to OSGi for in-container testing
- Mocking OSGi APIs for bundle testing
- Performing unit, integration, and management testing

You're now just about halfway through this book: congratulations! At this point, you should have confidence in applying OSGi to new and existing projects. Migrating applications to OSGi should be especially fresh in your mind from the last chapter. But what can you do to make sure you're on the right track to modularity and not turning your applications into tangled spaghetti? As is true for any piece of software, the best way to track quality is with regular testing. Testing can confirm that your modularized code meets the same requirements as your original application. Testing can verify that your code will continue to work when deployed inside the target container. It can even help you practice different deployment scenarios in the safety of your friendly neighborhood test server. Even a simple nonfunctional test, such as checking the number of shared packages between bundles, can avoid tangles forming early on in development.

Why wait until the end of a project to discover if your code works in the strict environment of an OSGi framework or how well your chosen bundles fit together? Migrate and modularize your tests along with your code! This chapter will help put this advice into practice by taking you through three different approaches:

- Running existing tests on OSGi
- Mocking out calls to OSGi APIs
- Advanced OSGi testing

The last section in particular takes a closer look at how unit and integration test concepts relate to modular applications and introduces the idea of management testing. If you're eager to learn more about testing modularity and you're already familiar with in-container tests and object mocking, feel free to skip ahead to section 7.3.

By the end of this chapter, you should be comfortable with testing OSGi applications, which will lead to better quality bundles for everyone. Let's start by continuing the theme from chapter 6 and get some existing tests running on an OSGi framework.

7.1 Migrating tests to OSGi

Imagine you have an application that you want to modularize and move to OSGi. You almost certainly have existing tests that check requirements and expected behavior. You can use these tests to verify and validate the modularization process, either by manually running them at key stages or by using an automated build system that runs tests on a regular schedule—say, whenever people check in code. These tests give you confidence that your modularized application is to some extent equivalent to the original, at least when run with the test framework. But what they don't tell you is whether your code behaves the same inside an OSGi container.

To find out, you need to run your tests *twice*: inside the target container as well as outside. Running these tests outside the container is a matter of using your favorite test framework, like JUnit (http://junit.sourceforge.net/) or TestNG (http://testng.org/). There are many good books on testing standard Java applications, so we assume you already know how to write unit tests and run them using Ant, Maven, or your IDE. But what about testing inside an OSGi container; how does it work in practice, and is it worth the effort?

7.1.1 In-container testing

Would you develop and deploy a web application without ever testing it inside an application server? Would you ship a product without testing its installer? Of course not! It's important to test code in the right environment. If you expect to use a class with OSGi, you should test it inside an OSGi framework—how else will you discover potential class-loading or visibility issues? But before you can run your existing JUnit or TestNG tests inside the container, you first need to deploy them.

As you saw in chapter 6, whenever you want to deploy something into an OSGi framework, you must consider packaging and placement. If the test classes are (accidentally) exposed from the external class path, the tests will effectively be running outside of the container. Does this mean you should bundle tests along with the application code? It depends on how you expect the code to be used in OSGi. Internal classes can only be tested from inside the same bundle, but public-facing code can and should be tested from another bundle to mimic real-world conditions. Testing code inside the same bundle typically means the caller and callee share the same class loader, but many OSGi-related issues only appear when different class loaders are involved. So, wherever possible, test from another bundle.

Figure 7.1 summarizes the four possible test-deployment options:

- Boot class path
- System bundle export
- Intra-bundle
- Inter-bundle

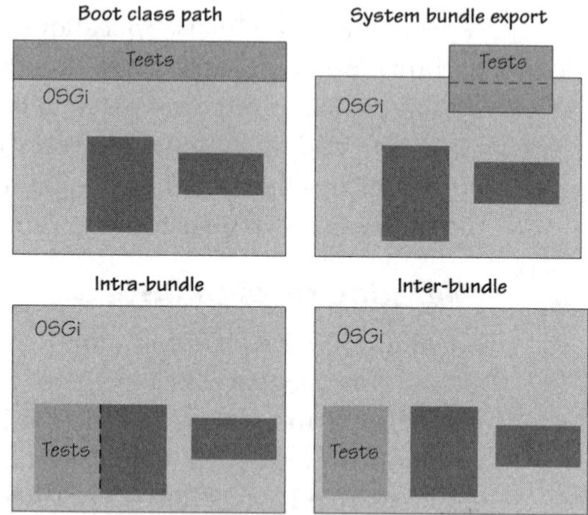

Figure 7.1 Test deployment options

We'll concentrate on the last two options (intra-bundle and inter-bundle tests) because it's much more realistic to have the test code running inside the container along with the code being tested. Bundle testing means deploying tests in bundles just like any other piece of code, but how much effort is involved in getting tests up and running in an OSGi framework? Let's find out right now by converting an existing open source library and its test suite into separate bundles.

7.1.2 Bundling tests

The Apache Commons Pool project (http://commons.apache.org/pool/) provides a small library for managing object pools. You'll use the source distribution for Commons Pool 1.5.3, which contains the code for both the library and its test suite:

```
chapter07/migration-example/commons-pool-1.5.3-src.zip
```

Begin the example by splitting the Commons Pool library and tests into two bundles. The `main` subproject extracts the library source, compiles it, and creates a simple bundle that exports the main package, but hides the implementation (.impl) package. The `test` subproject does exactly the same thing for the test source, but it appends `-test` to the bundle symbolic name to make sure the bundles are unique.

The Commons Pool tests are JUnit tests, so you also need access to the JUnit library. Should it be deployed as a bundle or placed on the external class path? Exposing the packages from the external class path means you don't have to turn JUnit into a bundle, but it also means JUnit can't see test classes unless they're on the same class path or explicitly passed in via a method call. You'd have to write your own code to scan bundles for tests and feed the class instances to JUnit, instead of relying on the standard test runner. We'll look at a tool that does this in section 7.3. Let's try the other approach here: bundling JUnit.

You can use the `bndwrap` Ant task from the bnd tool (http://aqute.biz/Code/Bnd) to quickly wrap the JAR file. The `bndwrap` task analyzes the JAR and creates a bundle that exports all packages contained inside it. It also adds *optional* imports for any packages that are needed but not contained in the JAR file. Unfortunately, this import list doesn't contain your test packages, because JUnit doesn't know about them yet. To avoid having to explicitly list your test packages at build time, you can instead use `DynamicImport-Package: *` (discussed in section 5.2.2). This dynamic import means JUnit will be able to see any future test class, as long as some bundle exports them.

Also add the following `Main-Class` header:

```
Main-Class: junit.textui.TestRunner
```

This tells your example launcher to start the JUnit test runner after deploying all the bundles. The `TestRunner` class expects to receive the name of the primary test class, so add `org.apache.commons.pool.TestAll` to the OSGi launcher command line in build.xml. (Your launcher will automatically pass any arguments after the initial bundle directory setting on to the `Main-Class`.)

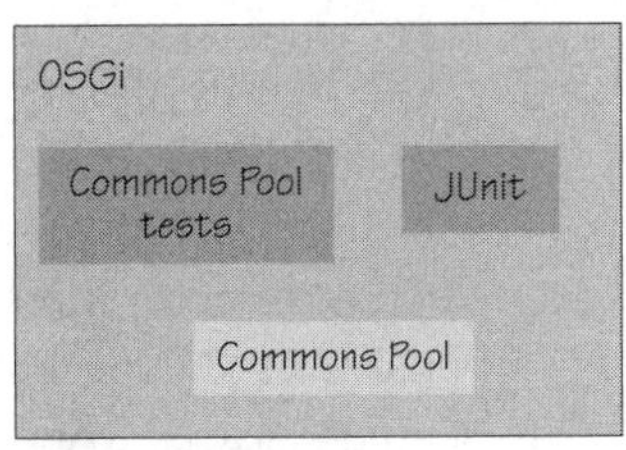

Figure 7.2 Testing Commons Pool inside an OSGi framework

Figure 7.2 shows the test deployment, which is the inter-bundle option from figure 7.1.

Let's try it for real:

```
$ cd chapter07/migration-example
$ ant clean test.osgi
...
[junit.osgi] Class not found "org.apache.commons.pool.TestAll"
[junit.osgi] Java Result: 1
```

Hmm...the JUnit bundle couldn't see the `TestAll` class even though the test bundle clearly exports it. If you look closely at the package involved and cast your mind back to the visibility discussion from section 2.5.3, you should understand why. This is the same package that's exported by the main Commons Pool bundle! Remember that packages can't be split across bundles unless you use bundle dependencies (section 5.3), and you're using package dependencies. You could use `Require-Bundle` to merge the packages together and re-export them (see section 5.3.1 for more about re-exporting packages), but you'd then need to use mandatory attributes to make sure JUnit and other related test bundles were correctly wired to the merged package. This would lead to a fragile test structure and cause problems with package-private members (to find out why, see the discussion near the start of section 5.4.1).

A better solution is to use fragments (section 5.4) to augment the original bundle with the extra test classes. To do this, you need to add one line to test/build.properties:

```
Fragment-Host: ${module}
```

The module property refers to the org.apache.commons.pool package, which you also use as the symbolic name of the main bundle. This is all you need to declare your test bundle as a fragment of the main library bundle. With this change in place, you can rebuild and repeat the test. You should see JUnit run through the complete Commons Pool test suite, which takes around two minutes:

```
$ ant clean test.osgi
...
[junit.osgi] .....................................
[junit.osgi] .....................................
[junit.osgi] .....................................
[junit.osgi] .....................................
[junit.osgi] .....................................
[junit.osgi] .................................
[junit.osgi] Time: 118.127
[junit.osgi]
[junit.osgi] OK (242 tests)
```

You're now running all your tests inside the combined library bundle (the intra-bundle option from figure 7.1) because your test fragment contains both internal and public-facing tests. You could go one step further and use a plain bundle for public tests and a fragment for internal tests, but you'd need some way to give JUnit access to your internal tests. At the moment the public org.apache.commons.pool.TestAll class loads internal tests from inside the same fragment, but this won't work when you separate them. You don't want to export any internal packages from the fragment because that would also expose internals from the main bundle, potentially affecting the test results.

The least disruptive solution is to keep a single public test class in the fragment that can be used to load the internal tests. You can move the remaining public-facing tests to a new package that doesn't conflict with the library API (such as .test) and deploy them in a separate bundle. The result is a combination of both inter-bundle and intra-bundle testing. Figure 7.3 shows an example of such a structure for testing Commons Pool.

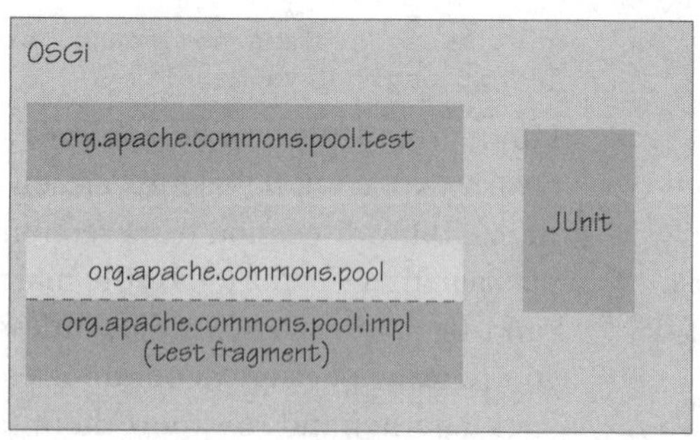

Figure 7.3 Recommended test structure for OSGi bundle tests

You can also run the test example outside of the container by invoking JUnit with the various bundles on the standard Java class path. In this case, you don't need to start the OSGi framework. To try this, use the test build target instead of test.osgi. You should see the same results as before:

```
$ ant clean test
...
[junit] .....................................
[junit] .....................................
```

```
[junit] ........................................
[junit] ........................................
[junit] ........................................
[junit] ....................................
[junit] Time: 117.77
[junit]
[junit] OK (242 tests)
```

You've seen how easy it is to run tests both inside and outside of a container, but how do you know if you're testing all possible scenarios and edge cases? Most projects use coverage to measure test effectiveness, although this doesn't guarantee you have well-written tests! Given the importance of test coverage, let's continue with the example and find out how you can record coverage statistics inside an OSGi container.

7.1.3 Covering all the bases

It's always good to know how much of your code is being tested. Like test results, coverage can vary depending on whether you're testing inside or outside a container. This makes in-container tests just as important as out-of-container tests when determining overall test coverage.

We can break the coverage-gathering process into three stages:

1. Instrument the classes
2. Execute the tests
3. Analyze the results

The first and third stages can be done outside of the OSGi container. This leaves you with the second stage: testing the instrumented classes inside the chosen container. You already know you can run the original tests in OSGi, so what difference does instrumentation make? It obviously introduces some sort of package dependency to the coverage library, but it also introduces a configuration dependency. The instrumented code needs to know where to find the coverage database so it can record results. You can deal with the package dependency in three ways: wrap the coverage JAR file up as a bundle, export its packages from the system bundle using `org.osgi.framework.system.packages.extra`, or expose them from the boot class path with `org.osgi.framework.bootdelegation`. When using boot delegation, you must make sure coverage packages are excluded from the generated `Import-Package` in the library bundle or at least made optional. (Not doing this would lead to a missing constraint during resolution, because no bundle exports these packages.)

The simplest approach is to add the coverage JAR file and its dependencies to the launcher's class path and update the system packages. Next simplest is boot delegation: here you have the extra step of removing coverage packages from the `Import-Package` of your instrumented bundle. Let's take the interesting route and turn the coverage JAR file into a bundle. Our chosen coverage tool for this example is Cobertura 1.9.3 (http://cobertura.sourceforge.net/), but all the techniques mentioned should work for other tools as well.

The first step is to create a new JAR file which contains the original Cobertura JAR file and all of its execution-time dependencies. You embed these dependencies because you want this to be a standalone bundle. Remember, this bundle will only be used during testing, so you have more leeway than if you were creating a production-quality bundle. You then use the bnd tool to wrap the JAR file in the same way you wrapped JUnit, making sure you set `Bundle-ClassPath` so the bundle can see its embedded dependencies. You can find the complete bundling process in cobertura.osgi/build.xml.

All you need to do now is instrument the classes and run the tests:

```
$ ant clean test.osgi -Dinstrument=true
```

You use the `instrument` property to enable the various instrumentation targets. Before launching the tests, the build also sets the `net.sourceforge.cobertura.datafile` system property so that instrumented tests know where to find the coverage database. As soon as the tests complete, the build runs the Cobertura `report` task to process the results. Point your browser at reports/index.html to see the results, which should look like figure 7.4.

Coverage Report - All Packages

Package	# Classes	Line Coverage		Branch Coverage		Complexity
All packages	22	79%	2274/2870	64%	657/1022	2.276
org.apache.commons.pool	27	86%	564/649	89%	111/124	1.596
org.apache.commons.pool.impl	25	76%	1710/2221	60%	546/898	2.744

Report generated by Cobertura 1.9.3 on 2/21/10 7:47 PM

Figure 7.4 Cobertura coverage report for Commons Pool

In this section, you saw how to take existing tests (and test tools) and run them inside an OSGi container. You may have noticed that this process is similar to the JAR-to-bundle process described in the first half of chapter 6. Deciding how to bundle tests is no different than deciding how to bundle an application. Visibility and modularity are just as important when it comes to testing. But what about going the other way? Can you take OSGi-related code and test it outside the container?

When you first begin to modularize and migrate an application over to OSGi, you probably won't have a direct dependency on the OSGi API. This means your code can still be tested both inside and outside the container. But at some point you'll want to use the OSGi API. It may start with one or two bundle activators, and then maybe use the bundle context to look up a service. Dependency injection, component models (discussed in chapters 11 and 12), and other similar abstractions can all help reduce the need to deal directly with the container. But what if you have code that uses the OSGi API? Such code can't be tested outside the container—or can it?

Imagine if you could mimic the container without having to implement a complete OSGi framework. There's a technique for doing this, and it goes by the name of *mocking*.

7.2 Mocking OSGi

OSGi is just a load of fancy class loaders! Oh, wait, we didn't mean that sort of mocking. (Besides, we all know by now that there's a lot more to OSGi than enhanced class loading.) We're talking about using *mock* objects to test portions of code without requiring a complete system. A mock object is basically a simulation, not a real implementation. It provides the same API, but its methods are scripted and usually return expected values or additional mocked objects. Object mocking is a powerful technique because it lets you test code right from the start of a project, even before your application is complete. You can also use it to test situations that are hard to recreate with the real object, such as external hardware failures.

Figure 7.5 represents the dynamic log client from chapter 4. Let's take this example and test it outside OSGi by mocking the API: verifying calls made to the API and scripting the desired responses. We'll show you how easy it is to script scenarios that may be hard to reproduce in a real container, look at mocking in a multithreaded environment, and wrap things up by reliably demonstrating the race condition mentioned in section 4.3.1.

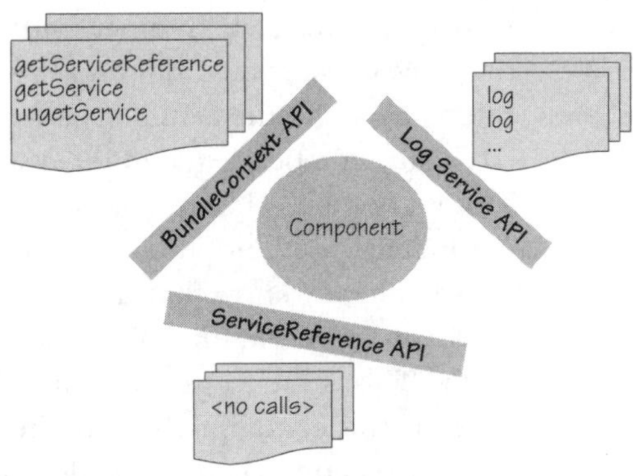

Figure 7.5 Mocking in action

7.2.1 Testing expected behavior

How might you use mocking to test an OSGi application? Let's look at code from earlier in this book: the `LogService` lookup example from chapter 4 that contained a potential race condition. Here's a quick reminder of the problematic code.

Listing 7.1 Broken service lookup containing a race condition

```
public class Activator implements BundleActivator {
  BundleContext m_context;

  public void start(BundleContext context) {
    m_context = context;
    startTestThread();
  }

  public void stop(BundleContext context) {
    stopTestThread();
  }

  class LogServiceTest implements Runnable {
    public void run() {
      while (Thread.currentThread() == m_logTestThread) {
        ServiceReference logServiceRef =
            m_context.getServiceReference(LogService.class.getName());
```

Gets service reference ❶

```
        if (logServiceRef != null) {
          ((LogService)m_context.getService(logServiceRef)).log(      <-- Gets
              LogService.LOG_INFO, "ping");                             ❷ instance
        } else {
          alternativeLog("LogService has gone");
        }

        pauseTestThread();
      }
    }
  }

  // The rest of this class is just support code...
}
```

Notice how this code interacts with the OSGi container. It receives a `context` object in the activator start method, uses this context to get a service reference ❶, and uses this reference to get the actual instance ❷. Each of these objects has a well-defined interface you can mock out, and the example code uses only a few methods from each API. This is good news because when mocking objects you only need to simulate the methods that are used, not the complete API.

You already know that this code compiles against the OSGi API, and back in chapter 4 you even tried it on an actual framework. But does it use the service API correctly? This is the sort of test that's hard to write without mocking. Sure, you can run tests on the container by invoking your code and checking the results as you did back in section 7.1, but this doesn't tell you if the code is using the container the right way. For example, the container won't complain if you forget to unget a service after you're done with it, but forgetting to do this skews service accounting and makes it look like your bundle is still using the service when it isn't. The container also doesn't know if you use the result of `getService()` without checking for `null`. In this example, you may get a `NullPointerException` if the service disappears in the short time between checking the reference and using it. Writing a test that's guaranteed to expose this race condition on a live framework is hard, but trivial with mock objects.

How exactly does mocking help? Because mock objects are scripted, you can verify that the right methods are called in the appropriate order. You can throw exceptions or return `null` values at any point in the sequence to see how the client handles it. Enough talk, let's try mocking ourselves.

7.2.2 Mocking in action

Typically, five steps are involved in mocking out an API:

1 *Mock*—Create prototype mock objects
2 *Expect*—Script the expected behavior
3 *Replay*—Prepare the mock objects
4 *Test*—Run the code using the mock objects
5 *Verify*—Check that the behavior matches

You'll use EasyMock (http://easymock.org/) in this example, but any mocking library will do. You can find the initial setup under chapter07/mocking-example in the book's companion code. It contains the log client code from listing 7.1 and a skeleton test class that you'll expand on in this section: mock_test/src/org/foo/mock/LogClientTests.java. You can also find a completed version of the unit test in the solution directory if you don't feel like typing all this code. Let's go through each of the five steps in detail and mock out the OSGi API:

1 Create prototype objects for parts of the API that you want to mock out: `BundleContext`, `ServiceReference`, and `LogService`. You can do this by adding the following lines to the empty test case:

```
BundleContext context = createStrictMock(BundleContext.class);
ServiceReference serviceRef = createMock(ServiceReference.class);
LogService logService = createMock(LogService.class);
```

You use a strict mock for the context, because you want to check the call sequence.

2 Script the expected behavior of the log client as it finds and calls the `LogService`:

```
expect(context.getServiceReference(LogService.class.getName()))
    .andReturn(serviceRef);

expect(context.getService(serviceRef))
    .andReturn(logService);

logService.log(
    and(geq(LogService.LOG_ERROR), leq(LogService.LOG_DEBUG)),
    isA(String.class));
```

Using your knowledge of the service API from chapter 4, you expect that the client will call your mock context to find a reference to the `LogService`, to which you respond by returning a mock service reference. You expect the client to pass this reference back your mock context in order to get your mock `LogService`. Finally, you expect the client to call your mock `LogService` with a valid log level and some sort of message string.

3 Replay the expected behavior to initialize your mock objects:

```
replay(context, serviceRef, logService);
```

4 Use your mock objects, and pretend to be the OSGi container:

```
BundleActivator logClientActivator = new Activator();

logClientActivator.start(context);
try {
  Thread.sleep(1000);
} catch (InterruptedException e) {}
logClientActivator.stop(context);
```

Consider the active lifecycle of an OSGi bundle: first it's started, and some time later it's stopped. You don't worry about mimicking the resolution stage in this test because you want to test service usage, not class loading. You know the client will spawn some sort of thread to use the `LogService`, so you wait one second to give that thread time to make the call and pause. (Using `sleep` here isn't ideal; later, you'll see how you can replace it with proper handshaking.) Then, when the one second is up, you stop the client bundle.

5 The last step is to make sure you saw the expected behavior during the test:

```
verify(context, serviceRef, logService);
```

This method throws an exception if the observed behavior doesn't match.

At this point, you should have a complete test that compiles and runs successfully:

```
$ cd chapter07/mocking-example
$ ant test
...
test:
[junit] Running org.foo.mock.LogClientTests
[junit] Tests run: 1, Failures: 0, Errors: 0, Time elapsed: 1.157 sec
```

Excellent: you've confirmed that your client uses the OSGi API correctly when a `LogService` is available. But what happens when a `LogService` isn't available; does it handle that too?

7.2.3 Mocking unexpected situations

As we mentioned back at the start of this section, mocking is a powerful testing technique because it lets you script situations that are hard to re-create inside a test environment. Although it's easy to arrange a test in an OSGi container without a `LogService`, it would be difficult to arrange for this service to appear and disappear at exactly the right time to trigger the race condition you know exists in your client code. With mocking, it's easy.

First, let's test what happens when no `LogService` is available by adding the following expectation between your last `expect` and the call to `replay`:

```
expect(context.getServiceReference(LogService.class.getName()))
    .andReturn(null);
```

This states that you expect the client to begin another call to look up the `LogService`, but this time you return a `null` reference to indicate no available service. If you try to run the test now, it will fail because you don't give the client enough time to make a second call before stopping the bundle. Your log client pauses five seconds between each call, so you need to add five seconds to the existing `sleep`:

```
try {
  Thread.sleep(6000);
} catch (InterruptedException e) {}
```

The client now gets enough time to begin a second log call, but the test still fails:

```
$ ant test
...
[junit] Running org.foo.mock.LogClientTests
[junit] Exception in thread "LogService Tester" java.lang.AssertionError:
[junit]   Unexpected method call getBundle():
```

It appears that your client is using another method (`getBundle()`) on the `BundleContext` to find the owning bundle when no `LogService` is available. If you look at the rest of the client code under chapter07, you'll see that it uses this to get the bundle identifier when logging directly to the console. You don't mind how many times your client calls `getBundle()`, if at all, so let's use a wildcard expectation:

```
Bundle bundle = createNiceMock(Bundle.class);

expect(context.getServiceReference(LogService.class.getName()))
    .andReturn(null);

expect(context.getBundle())
    .andReturn(bundle).anyTimes();
```

You need to provide a new mock to represent your `Bundle` object. This time, instead of simulating each method the client uses, you take a shortcut and use a *nice mock* on the first line. Nice mocks automatically provide empty implementations and default return values. You expect your log client to request this mock bundle from your mock bundle context after you return the `null` service reference, but it may ask for it zero or more times. One last thing you must remember to do is add your mock bundle to the replay list. (If you happen to forget to replay a mock before it's used, you'll get an `IllegalStateException` from EasyMock about missing behavior definitions.)

```
replay(context, serviceRef, logService, bundle);
```

With the new expectation in place and everything replayed, the test passes once more:

```
$ ant test
...
[junit] Running org.foo.mock.LogClientTests
[junit] <--> thread="LogService Tester", bundle=0 : LogService has gone
[junit] Tests run: 1, Failures: 0, Errors: 0, Time elapsed: 6.125 sec
```

Having `sleep` in your unit test is annoying, though. Every time you want to test additional log calls, you need to extend the `sleep`, which makes your tests run longer and longer. You should try to replace it with some form of handshaking. But even with handshaking, your log client will still pause for five seconds between each call. If only you could replace the pause method while keeping the rest of the code intact.

7.2.4 Coping with multithreaded tests

You're currently testing a simple log client that spawns a separate thread to make log calls. Knowing how to test multithreaded bundles is useful, because people often use threads to limit the amount of work done in the activator's start method. As we mentioned at the end of the last section, the main difficulty is synchronizing the test thread with the threads being tested. Up to now you relied on `sleep`, but this is a fragile solution. Some form

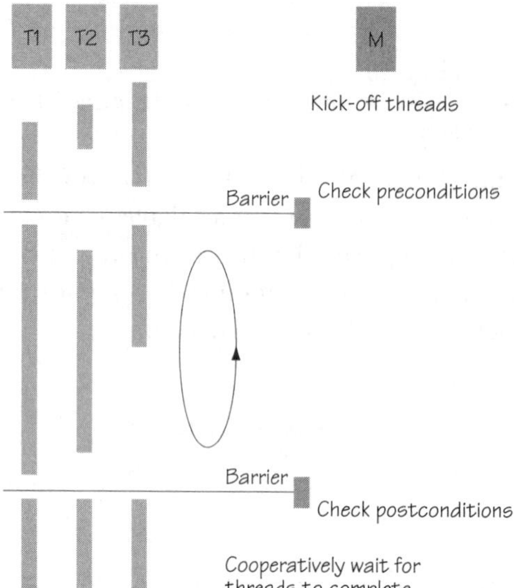

Figure 7.6 Synchronizing tests with multithreaded code

of barrier or handshake procedure (see figure 7.6) is needed to hold client threads back until the test is ready to proceed and vice versa.

Thankfully, the log client has an obvious place where you can add such a barrier: the protected pauseTestThread method, which currently puts the client thread to sleep for five seconds. You could consider using aspect-orientated programming (AOP) to add a barrier to this method, but let's avoid pulling in extra test dependencies and use an anonymous class to override it instead:

```
final CountDownLatch latch = new CountDownLatch(2);

BundleActivator logClientActivator = new Activator() {
  @Override protected void pauseTestThread() {
    latch.countDown();

    if (latch.getCount() == 0) {
      LockSupport.park();
    }
  }
};
```

The anonymous class replaces the original pauseTestThread method with one that uses a countdown latch, initialized with the number of expected log calls. Each time the client makes a log call, it calls pauseTestThread and counts down the latch. When no more log calls are expected, the client thread suspends itself and waits for the rest of the test to shut down. The test code only needs to wait for the latch to reach zero before it stops the client bundle:

```
logClientActivator.start(context);
if (!latch.await(5, TimeUnit.SECONDS)) {
  fail("Still expecting" + latch.getCount() + " calls");
}
logClientActivator.stop(context);
```

The test includes a timeout in case the client thread aborts and can't complete the countdown; but if everything goes as expected, the updated test finishes in under a second:

```
$ ant test
...
[junit] Running org.foo.mock.LogClientTests
[junit] <--> thread="LogService Tester", bundle=0 : LogService has gone
[junit] Tests run: 1, Failures: 0, Errors: 0, Time elapsed: 0.14 sec
```

So far so good: all you have to do to test additional log calls is increment the latch count. But what should you do if your client thread doesn't contain a pause method or this method can't be replaced or extended? Another solution is to add barriers to the mocked-out objects themselves by using so-called *answer objects*. Answers let you perform basic AOP by intercepting method calls, which you can use to add synchronization points. Here's an example:

```
expect(context.getServiceReference(isA(String.class)).andAnswer(
    new IAnswer<ServiceReference>() {
      public ServiceReference answer() {
        LockSupport.park();
        return null;
      }
    });
```

In this (incomplete) example, you script an answer that always returns a `null` service reference and use it to suspend the client thread whenever it makes this call. This works as long as the client thread initiates the expected call at the right time and there are no problems with suspending the client in the middle of this call. But it also leaves the client code untouched, which in this case means a five-second pause between log calls. You'll test another log call in the next section, so let's stick with the original latch solution.

7.2.5 Exposing race conditions

OSGi is dynamic: bundles and services may come and go at any time. The key to developing a robust application is being able to cope with and react to these events. This same dynamism makes testing robustness difficult. You could deploy your bundles into a real framework and attempt to script events to cover all possibilities (we'll look at this in more detail in section 7.3), but some scenarios require microsecond timing. Remember the race condition we mentioned at the start of this section? This will be exposed only if you can arrange for the `LogService` to disappear between two method invocations—a narrow window. Many factors can cause you to miss this window, such as unexpected garbage collection and differences in thread scheduling. With mocking, you can easily script the exact sequence of events you want:

```
expect(context.getServiceReference(LogService.class.getName()))
    .andReturn(serviceRef);

expect(context.getService(serviceRef))
    .andReturn(null);

expect(context.getBundle())
    .andReturn(bundle).anyTimes();
```

You begin by expecting another log call, so remember to bump the latch count up to three calls. The `LogService` is still available at this point, so you return the mock reference. The client is expected to dereference this by calling `getService()`, and at this point you pretend the `LogService` has vanished and return `null`. You follow this by expecting another wildcard call to get the bundle, just as you did in section 7.2.3, because the log client may need it to do some alternative logging to the console.

Your test is now complete. You may want to compare it with the class in the `solution` subdirectory. It covers normal and missing service conditions and the edge case where the service is there to begin with but quickly disappears. Running it should expose the problem that you know is there but couldn't re-create reliably on a real framework:

```
$ ant test
...
[junit] Running org.foo.mock.LogClientTests
[junit] <--> thread="LogService Tester", bundle=0 : LogService has gone
[junit] Exception in thread "LogService Tester"
            java.lang.NullPointerException
[junit]       at org.foo.log.Activator$LogServiceTest.run(Activator.java:66)
[junit]       at java.lang.Thread.run(Thread.java:619)
[junit] Tests run: 1, Failures: 0, Errors: 0, Time elapsed: 5.205 sec
```

At this point, adventurous readers may want to copy the working service-lookup example from chapter 4 (chapter04/dynamics/correct_lookup) and try testing it. One tip: you'll need to extend the test to expect calls to `ungetService()`, because the working example attempts to release the service reference after each successful call to `getService()`. Whether you mandate calls to `ungetService()` or make them optional by appending `times(0, 1)` to the expectation is completely up to you.

In this section, you learned how to mock out the OSGi API and script different scenarios when testing bundle-specific code that uses OSGi. Mocking helps you test situations that are next to impossible to recreate in a real container. It also provides a counterpoint to the first section where you were running existing tests inside a real container on code that often had no dependency on OSGi at all. The last section will attempt to harmonize both approaches, by explaining how to script modular tests and run them on a variety of frameworks.

7.3 Advanced OSGi testing

In the previous section, you successfully mocked out the OSGi API and ran your tests without requiring a framework. Of course, the less you depend directly on an API, the easier it is to mock. It's even easier if you use one of the component models from chapters 11 and 12, because your dependencies will be indirectly injected by the component framework. Such components rarely need to use the OSGi API themselves, so testing becomes a matter of reconfiguring bindings to inject mocked-out dependencies in place of the original instances. But as we discussed in section 7.1.1, eventually you'll want to run tests on a real OSGi framework. These container tests typically don't increase your code coverage—any unit and mocked-out tests should have already tested the critical paths. Instead, these tests verify that your code conforms to the container:

is it packaged correctly, does it follow the container programming model, does it use standard APIs?

You should run your tests on as many containers as possible to guard against container-specific behavior. But keeping all these containers up to date and managing their different settings and configurations soon becomes tiresome. The newly standardized OSGi embedding and launching API (discussed in chapter 13) helps, but it lacks features that would make testing on OSGi much easier: automatic test wrapping, dynamic bundle creation, and common deployment profiles. Luckily, several recently released OSGi test tools provide all these features and more.

OSGi-enabled test tools bring other benefits because they embrace OSGi, such as improved test modularity and management. You can use them to run a complete range of tests from basic unit tests, through various combinations of integration tests, all the way up to advanced management tests. You'll see a real-world example of this later that uses one of the more popular OSGi test tools called Pax Exam to test a service bundle in isolation, combined with client bundles, and finally with older versions of the same service to try out a proposed upgrade scenario.

Let's begin with a brief review of the various OSGi test tools available today.

7.3.1 OSGi test tools

At the time of writing this book, three major test tools are available for OSGi:

- Open Participation Software for Java's (OPS4J) Pax Exam (http://wiki.ops4j.org/display/paxexam)
- Spring DM's test support (http://static.springsource.org/osgi/docs/1.2.1/reference/html/testing.html)
- Dynamic Java's DA-Testing (www.dynamicjava.org/posts/da-testing-introduction)

All follow the same basic approach to building and deploying tests:

1. Prepare the OSGi container.
2. Deploy the selected bundles.
3. Create a test bundle on the fly.
4. Deploy and execute the tests.
5. Shut down the container.

Each tool has its own advantages and disadvantages. The Spring DM test support obviously works best with Spring-based applications. Although you can also use it to test non-Spring applications, doing so requires several Spring dependencies that make it appear rather heavy. Spring DM testing also only supports JUnit 3, which means no annotated tests. DA-Testing, on the other hand, provides its own test API, optimized for testing service dynamics such as the race condition you saw in section 7.2.5. This makes it hard to move existing JUnit or TestNG tests over to DA-Testing, because developers have to learn another test API, but it does make dynamic testing much easier. Pax Exam goes to the other extreme and supports both JUnit 3 and 4, with TestNG support in the works. Table 7.1 summarizes the differences between the tools.

Table 7.1 OSGi test tool features

Test tool	JUnit 3	JUnit 4	TestNG	OSGi mocks	OSGi frameworks	OSGi profiles
Pax Exam	✔	✔	Future		Felix / Equinox / Knopflerfish (multiple versions)	over 50
Spring DM	✔	Future		✔	Felix / Equinox / Knopflerfish (single version only)	
DA-Testing					Equinox (others planned)	

In this chapter, you'll use Pax Exam from the OPS4J community, because we believe it's a good general-purpose solution; but many of the techniques covered in this section can be adapted for use with the other tools. One of Pax Exam's strengths is its support for a wide range of different OSGi frameworks, which is important if you want to produce robust portable bundles. But why is this?

7.3.2 Running tests on multiple frameworks

OSGi is a standard, with a detailed specification and a set of framework-compliance tests. Even with all this, there can be subtle differences between implementations. Perhaps part of the specification is unclear or is open to interpretation. On the other hand, maybe your code relies on behavior that isn't part of the specification and is left open to framework implementers, such as the default Thread Context Class Loader (TCCL) setting. The only way to make sure your code is truly portable is to run the same tests on different frameworks. This is like the practice of running tests on different operating systems—even though the JDK is supposed to be portable and standardized, differences can exist, and it's better to catch them during development than to fix problems in the field.

Unfortunately, many OSGi developers only test against a single framework. This may be because they only expect to deploy their bundles on that particular implementation, but it's more likely that they believe the cost of setting up and managing multiple frameworks far outweighs the perceived benefits. This is where Pax Exam helps—testing on an extra OSGi framework is as simple as adding a single line of Java code.

Let's see how easy it to use Pax Exam. You'll continue to use Ant to run these tests, although Pax Exam is primarily Maven-based. This means you need to explicitly list execution-time dependencies in build.xml, instead of letting Maven manage this for you. You can find your initial setup under chapter07/testing-example.

Look at the `fw` subproject; it contains a simple test class that prints out various framework properties. The contents of this test class are shown next.

Listing 7.2 Simple container test

```
@RunWith(JUnit4TestRunner.class)
public class ContainerTest {

  @Configuration
```

```
  public static Option[] configure() {
    return options(
      mavenBundle("org.osgi", "org.osgi.compendium", "4.2.0")
    );
  }

  @Test
  public void testContainer(BundleContext ctx) {
    System.out.println(
      format(ctx, FRAMEWORK_VENDOR) +
      format(ctx, FRAMEWORK_VERSION) +
      format(ctx, FRAMEWORK_LANGUAGE) +
      format(ctx, FRAMEWORK_OS_NAME) +
      format(ctx, FRAMEWORK_OS_VERSION) +
      format(ctx, FRAMEWORK_PROCESSOR) +
      "\nTest Bundle is " +
      ctx.getBundle().getSymbolicName());
  }

  private static String format(
      BundleContext ctx, String key) {

    return String.format("%-32s = %s\n",
        key, ctx.getProperty(key));
  }
}
```

Deploys compendium bundle ❶

❷ **Prints symbolic name**

You begin by annotating your test class with `@RunWith`. This tells JUnit to use the named test runner instead of the standard JUnit one. The Pax Exam `JUnit4TestRunner` class is responsible for starting the relevant framework, deploying bundles, and running the tests. The `@Configuration` annotation identifies the method that provides the Pax Exam configuration. Right now, you ask it to deploy the standard OSGi compendium bundle ❶ from Maven central in to the default framework. The actual test method is annotated with the usual JUnit 4 annotation, `@Test`. It accepts a `BundleContext` argument that's supplied by Pax Exam at execution time. You use this bundle context to print out various properties, including the symbolic name of the test bundle ❷.

To run this test, type the following:

```
$ cd chapter07/testing-example
$ ant test.container
```

You should see something like the following, but with properties that match your system.

Listing 7.3 Using Pax Exam to run tests on an OSGi framework

```
[junit] Running org.foo.test.ContainerTest
[junit] __________                 ___________
[junit] \______   \_____  ___  ___ \_   _____/__  ________    _____
[junit]  |     ___/\__  \ \  \/  /  |    __)_\  \/  /\__  \  /     \
[junit]  |    |     / __ \_>    <   |        \>    <  / __ \|  Y Y  \
[junit]  |____|    (____  /__/\_ \ /_______  /__/\_ \(____  /__|_|  /
[junit]                 \/      \/         \/      \/     \/      \/
[junit]
```

```
[junit] Pax Exam 1.1.0 from OPS4J - http://www.ops4j.org
[junit] ---------------------------------------------
[junit]
[junit]
[junit]
[junit] Welcome to Felix
[junit]
[junit] ================
[junit]
[junit] org.osgi.framework.vendor        = Apache Software Foundation
[junit] org.osgi.framework.version       = 1.5
[junit] org.osgi.framework.language      = en
[junit] org.osgi.framework.os.name       = windowsvista
[junit] org.osgi.framework.os.version    = 6.0
[junit] org.osgi.framework.processor     = x86
[junit]
[junit] Test Bundle is pax-exam-probe
[junit]
[junit]
[junit] Tests run: 1, Failures: 0, Errors: 0, Time elapsed: 3.424 sec
```

You may have noticed that the symbolic name of the test bundle is `pax-exam-probe`. This bundle is generated at execution time by Pax Exam and contains your test classes. The default container is Apache Felix, but you can easily ask Pax Exam to run the same test on other frameworks as well. All you need to do is add a few lines to the configuration method in your test class fw/container/src/org/foo/test/ContainerTest.java:

```
@Configuration
public static Option[] configure() {
  return options(
    frameworks(
      felix(), equinox(), knopflerfish()
    ),
    mavenBundle("org.osgi", "org.osgi.compendium", "4.2.0")
  );
}
```

Pax Exam does the hard work of downloading the necessary JAR files and setting up any framework-specific configuration files. You just need to sit back and rerun your test:

```
$ ant test.container
```

This time you should see three distinct sets of output, as shown here.

Listing 7.4 Using Pax Exam to run tests on multiple frameworks

```
[junit] Running org.foo.test.ContainerTest
[junit] __________                 ___________
[junit] \______   \_____  ___  ___ \_   _____/__  ________    _____
[junit]  |     ___/\__  \ \  \/  /  |    __)_\  \/  /\__  \  /     \
[junit]  |    |     / __ \_>    <   |        \>    <  / __ \|  Y Y  \
[junit]  |____|    (____  /__/\_ \ /_______  /__/\_ \(____  /__|_|  /
[junit]                 \/      \/         \/      \/     \/      \/
[junit]
[junit] Pax Exam 1.1.0 from OPS4J - http://www.ops4j.org
```

```
[junit] ------------------------------------------------
[junit]
[junit]
[junit]
[junit] Welcome to Felix
[junit] ================
[junit]
[junit] org.osgi.framework.vendor          = Apache Software Foundation
[junit] org.osgi.framework.version         = 1.5
[junit] org.osgi.framework.language        = en
[junit] org.osgi.framework.os.name         = windowsvista
[junit] org.osgi.framework.os.version      = 6.0
[junit] org.osgi.framework.processor       = x86
[junit]
[junit] Test Bundle is pax-exam-probe
[junit]
[junit]
[junit] __________                 ___________
[junit] \______   \_____  ___  ___ \_   _____/__  ________    _____
[junit]  |     ___/\__  \ \  \/  /  |    __)_\  \/  /\__  \  /     \
[junit]  |    |     / __ \_>    <   |        \>    <  / __ \|  Y Y  \
[junit]  |____|    (____  /__/\_ \ /_______  /__/\_ \(____  /__|_|  /
[junit]                 \/      \/         \/      \/     \/      \/
[junit]
[junit] Pax Exam 1.1.0 from OPS4J - http://www.ops4j.org
[junit] ------------------------------------------------
[junit]
[junit]
[junit] org.osgi.framework.vendor          = Eclipse
[junit] org.osgi.framework.version         = 1.5.0
[junit] org.osgi.framework.language        = en
[junit] org.osgi.framework.os.name         = WindowsVista
[junit] org.osgi.framework.os.version      = 6.0.0
[junit] org.osgi.framework.processor       = x86
[junit]
[junit] Test Bundle is pax-exam-probe
[junit]
[junit]
[junit] __________                 ___________
[junit] \______   \_____  ___  ___ \_   _____/__  ________    _____
[junit]  |     ___/\__  \ \  \/  /  |    __)_\  \/  /\__  \  /     \
[junit]  |    |     / __ \_>    <   |        \>    <  / __ \|  Y Y  \
[junit]  |____|    (____  /__/\_ \ /_______  /__/\_ \(____  /__|_|  /
[junit]                 \/      \/         \/      \/     \/      \/
[junit]
[junit] Pax Exam 1.1.0 from OPS4J - http://www.ops4j.org
[junit] ------------------------------------------------
[junit]
[junit]
[junit] Knopflerfish OSGi framework, version 4.1.10
[junit] Copyright 2003-2009 Knopflerfish. All Rights Reserved.
[junit]
[junit] See http://www.knopflerfish.org for more information.
[junit]
[junit] Loading xargs url file:knopflerfish/config.ini
```

```
[junit] Installed and started:
    file:bundles/org.ops4j.pax.exam_1.1.0.jar (id#1)
[junit] Installed and started:
    file:bundles/org.ops4j.pax.exam.junit.extender_1.1.0.jar (id#2)
[junit] Installed and started:
    file:bundles/org.ops4j.pax.exam.junit.extender.impl_1.1.0.jar (id#3)
[junit] Installed and started:
    file:bundles/org.ops4j.pax.url.dir_1.0.0.jar (id#4)
[junit] Installed and started:
    file:bundles/com.springsource.org.junit_4.4.0.jar (id#5)
[junit]
[junit] Installed and started:
    file:bundles/org.ops4j.pax.exam.rbc_1.1.0.jar (id#6)
[junit] Installed and started:
    file:bundles/osgi.cmpn_4.2.0.200908310645.jar (id#7)
[junit] Framework launched
[junit] org.osgi.framework.vendor         = Knopflerfish
[junit] org.osgi.framework.version        = 1.3
[junit] org.osgi.framework.language       = en
[junit] org.osgi.framework.os.name        = Windows Vista
[junit] org.osgi.framework.os.version     = 6.0
[junit] org.osgi.framework.processor      = x86
[junit]
[junit] Test Bundle is pax-exam-probe
[junit]
[junit]
[junit] Tests run: 3, Failures: 0, Errors: 0, Time elapsed: 12.513 sec
```

Notice how some of the properties vary slightly between frameworks, in particular the OS name. This is a reminder of why it's a good idea to test on a variety of frameworks: to make sure you aren't depending on unspecified or undocumented behavior.

You just saw how easy it is to run a test on many different frameworks using Pax Exam. But how well does it work with existing unit tests and existing test tools?

7.3.3 Unit testing

At the start of this section, we mentioned how OSGi test tools can help you modularize and manage tests. Because Pax Exam integrates with JUnit as a custom runner, you can use it in any system that can run JUnit tests. This means you can mix non-OSGi unit and integration tests with Pax Exam–based tests and have the results collected in one place. A good example of this mixture can be found in the Configuration Admin Service implementation from the Apache Felix project (http://felix.apache.org/site/apache-felix-config-admin.html). The Configuration Admin Service is a compendium service that provides and persists configuration data for bundles.

The Felix Configuration Admin Service build uses Maven and has a single test directory. This test directory contains mocked-out unit tests to test internal details along with Pax Exam integration tests to test the expected Configuration Admin Service behavior. We've taken these tests and separated them into unit and integration tests so you can see the difference. The unit tests are in the `ut` subproject, and you can run them with this command from the chapter07/testing-example/ directory:

```
$ ant test.unit
...
[junit] Running
    org.apache.felix.cm.file.FilePersistenceManagerConstructorTest
[junit] Tests run: 2, Failures: 0, Errors: 0, Time elapsed: 0.027 sec
[junit] Running org.apache.felix.cm.file.FilePersistenceManagerTest
[junit] Tests run: 8, Failures: 0, Errors: 0, Time elapsed: 0.255 sec
[junit] Running org.apache.felix.cm.impl.CaseInsensitiveDictionaryTest
[junit] Tests run: 10, Failures: 0, Errors: 0, Time elapsed: 0.012 sec
[junit] Running org.apache.felix.cm.impl.ConfigurationAdapterTest
[junit] Tests run: 3, Failures: 0, Errors: 0, Time elapsed: 0.013 sec
[junit] Running org.apache.felix.cm.impl.ConfigurationManagerTest
[junit] Tests run: 3, Failures: 0, Errors: 0, Time elapsed: 0.037 sec
[junit] Running org.apache.felix.cm.impl.DynamicBindingsTest
[junit] Tests run: 4, Failures: 0, Errors: 0, Time elapsed: 0.055 sec
```

These are still considered unit tests because they don't run inside an OSGi container. You could bundle them into a fragment as you did in section 7.1 and deploy them using Pax Exam, in which case they would be called *bundle tests*. Bundle tests are somewhere between unit and full-blown integration tests. They test more than a single class or feature but don't involve more than one bundle. Figure 7.7 shows the difference.

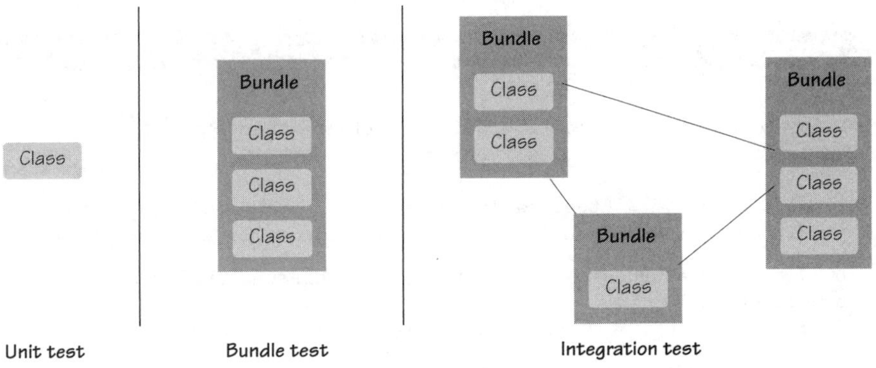

Figure 7.7 Unit, bundle, and integration testing

After you've tested your core functionality both inside and outside the OSGi container, you can move on to integration testing. Integration testing is where Pax Exam shines.

7.3.4 Integration testing

Integration tests are where you start to piece together your application and test interactions between individual components. To test combinations of components, you need some way to compose them. For standard Java applications, it can be tricky deciding which JAR files you need to load; but with OSGi applications, all the dependency information is available in the metadata. Deployment becomes a simple matter of picking a set of bundles.

Let's look at a concrete example. You can find the Apache Felix Configuration Admin Service integration tests under the `it` subproject. To run all these tests in sequence, type the following in the chapter07/testing-example/ directory:

```
$ ant test.integration
...
[junit] Tests run: 2, Failures: 0, Errors: 0, Time elapsed: 26.523 sec
...
[junit] Tests run: 7, Failures: 0, Errors: 0, Time elapsed: 24.664 sec
...
[junit] Tests run: 15, Failures: 0, Errors: 0, Time elapsed: 55.839 sec
...
[junit] Tests run: 4, Failures: 0, Errors: 0, Time elapsed: 14.45 sec
...
[junit] Tests run: 4, Failures: 0, Errors: 0, Time elapsed: 13.809 sec
...
[junit] Tests run: 2, Failures: 0, Errors: 0, Time elapsed: 5.723 sec
```

You may wonder why there isn't much output during the tests. This is because you've set the local logging threshold to `WARN`. To see more details about what Pax Exam is running, edit the local log4j.properties file, and change the threshold from `WARN` to `INFO`.

Let's take a closer look at one of the integration tests from `ConfigurationBaseTest`.

Listing 7.5 Basic configure-then-start integration test

```
@Test
public void test_basic_configuration_configure_then_start()
  throws BundleException, IOException
{
  final String pid = "test_basic_configuration_configure_then_start";
  final Configuration config = configure( pid, null, true );            ❶ Sets configuration data

  bundle = installBundle( pid, ManagedServiceTestActivator.class );
  bundle.start();
  delay();

  final ManagedServiceTestActivator tester =
      ManagedServiceTestActivator.INSTANCE;

  TestCase.assertNotNull( tester.props );                               ❷ Checks for correct configuration
  TestCase.assertEquals( pid, tester.props.get(
      Constants.SERVICE_PID ) );
  TestCase.assertNull( tester.props.get(
      ConfigurationAdmin.SERVICE_FACTORYPID ) );
  TestCase.assertNull( tester.props.get(
      ConfigurationAdmin.SERVICE_BUNDLELOCATION ) );
  TestCase.assertEquals( PROP_NAME, tester.props.get( PROP_NAME ) );
  TestCase.assertEquals( 1, tester.numManagedServiceUpdatedCalls );

  config.delete();
  delay();
  TestCase.assertNull( tester.props );
  TestCase.assertEquals( 2, tester.numManagedServiceUpdatedCalls );    ❸ Verifies notification
}
```

This integration test checks that the Configuration Admin Service implementation successfully records configuration data that is registered before the managed bundle starts. The managed bundle is the bundle being configured. The test method has the standard JUnit 4 annotation and extends a base class called `ConfigurationTestBase` that provides general helper methods. One such method is used to set configuration data using the current Configuration Admin Service ❶. The test creates and installs a managed bundle on the fly and waits for the configuration to be delivered to this managed bundle. It makes sure the delivered configuration is correct ❷ before removing the configuration. The test waits for the managed bundle to be notified about this removal and verifies it was correctly notified ❸.

This is a clear test. It almost looks like a unit test, except calls are being made between components instead of inside a single component or class. The other tests under the `it` subproject follow the same basic pattern, which may be repeated several times:

1. Check the initial system state.
2. Disrupt the state (by calling services, or adding or removing bundles).
3. Check the resulting system state.

As you just saw, the Configuration Admin Service integration tests all extend a single base class called `ConfigurationTestBase` that defines helper methods to deal with configurations, synchronize tests, and create additional bundles at execution time. These additional bundles consume and validate the configuration data. Right now, the tests are only configured to run on Apache Felix, but let's see if they also pass on other frameworks.

Add the following lines to the Pax Exam options inside the `configuration()` method in `ConfigurationTestBase`, just as you did with the container test back in section 7.3.2, like this:

```
@Configuration
public static Option[] configuration() {
  return options(
    frameworks(felix(), equinox(), knopflerfish()),
    provision(
      bundle(new File("bundles/configadmin.jar").toURI().toString()),
      mavenBundle(
        "org.ops4j.pax.swissbox", "pax-swissbox-tinybundles", "1.0.0"))
  );
}
```

Pax Exam now runs each test three times—once per framework. You can see this by typing the following command in the chapter07/testing-example/ directory:

```
$ ant test.integration
...
[junit] Tests run: 6, Failures: 0, Errors: 0, Time elapsed: 84.585 sec
...
[junit] Tests run: 21, Failures: 0, Errors: 0, Time elapsed: 99.05 sec
...
[junit] Tests run: 45, Failures: 0, Errors: 0, Time elapsed: 220.184 sec
```

```
...
[junit] Tests run: 12, Failures: 0, Errors: 0, Time elapsed: 55.269 sec
...
[junit] Tests run: 12, Failures: 0, Errors: 0, Time elapsed: 54.686 sec
...
[junit] Tests run: 6, Failures: 0, Errors: 0, Time elapsed: 26.417 sec
```

No failures or errors! The Apache Felix Configuration Admin Service implementation works the same on all three frameworks. This shouldn't be unexpected, because one of the goals driving OSGi is reusable modules. Many framework bundles can be reused on other frameworks. When you find you need a particular compendium service, and your current framework doesn't provide it, look around in case you can reuse a bundle from another site. You can even use Pax Exam to try different combinations of compendium bundles.

Pax Exam makes integration testing as simple as unit testing, but like any good tool you have to be careful not to overuse it. Each integration test has the overhead of starting and stopping an OSGi container, so the overall test time can build up as you add more and more tests. People are looking into reusing containers during testing, but for some tests you need complete isolation. Although work is being done to reduce the cost of each test, this cost will never be zero. In practice, this means you should look carefully at your tests and try to get the most from each one.

Integration testing is normally considered the last phase of testing before starting system or acceptance tests. You've tested each piece of functionality separately and tested that the pieces work together. There's nothing else to test before verifying that your application meets the customers' requirements—or is there?

7.3.5 Management testing

This book contains an entire chapter (chapter 10) about how to manage OSGi applications, so it's clear that management is an important aspect. You should reflect that by testing applications to make sure they can be successfully managed, upgraded, and restarted before releasing them into production. Too often, we see bundles that work perfectly until they're restarted or bundles that can't be upgraded without causing ripples that affect the whole application.

What might management testing cover? Table 7.2 has some suggestions.

Table 7.2 Management testing ideas

Task	Involves
Install	Installing new bundles (or features) alongside existing used implementations
Uninstall	Uninstalling old bundles (or features) that may or may not have replacements
Upgrade	Upgrading one or more bundles with new functionality or bug fixes
Downgrade	Downgrading one or more bundles because of an unexpected regression
Graceful degradation	Seeing how long the application functions as elements are stopped or uninstalled

We'll show you how OSGi and Pax Exam can help with management testing. The current test example exercises the latest Configuration Admin Service implementation from Apache Felix. But what if you have an application that uses an earlier version? Can you upgrade to the latest version without losing any configuration data? Why not write a quick test to find out?

You can find the example upgrade test under mt/upgrade_configadmin_bundle. It's based on the `listConfiguration` test from the existing Apache Felix integration test suite. Listing 7.6 shows the custom configuration for the upgrade test. You want to reuse the helper classes from the earlier tests, so you explicitly deploy the integration test bundle alongside your management test. You also deploy the old Configuration Admin Service bundle and store the location of the new bundle in a system property so you can use it later to upgrade Configuration Admin Service during the management test. You use a system property because the configuration and test methods are executed by different processes, and system properties are a cheap way to communicate between processes.

Listing 7.6 Configuring the upgrade management test

```
private static String toFileURI(String path) {
  return new File(path).toURI().toString();
}

@org.ops4j.pax.exam.junit.Configuration
public static Option[] configuration() {
  return options(
    provision(
      bundle(toFileURI("bundles/integration_tests-1.0.jar")),
      bundle(toFileURI("bundles/old.configadmin.jar")),
      mavenBundle("org.osgi", "org.osgi.compendium", "4.2.0"),
      mavenBundle("org.ops4j.pax.swissbox", "pax-swissbox-tinybundles",
                  "1.0.0")
    ),
    systemProperty("new.configadmin.uri").
      value(toFileURI("bundles/configadmin.jar"))
  );
}
```

The rest of the test follows the same script as the original `listConfiguration` test with three key differences. First, you make sure the installed Configuration Admin Service bundle is indeed the older 1.0.0 release, by checking the OSGi metadata:

```
Dictionary headers = getCmBundle().getHeaders();
TestCase.assertEquals("org.apache.felix.configadmin",
    headers.get(Constants.BUNDLE_SYMBOLICNAME));
TestCase.assertEquals("1.0.0",
    headers.get(Constants.BUNDLE_VERSION));
```

Second, you do an in-place update of the Configuration Admin Service bundle to the new edition:

```
cmBundle.update(new URL(
    System.getProperty("new.configadmin.uri")).openStream());
```

You perform an in-place update to preserve the existing configuration data in the bundle's persistent data area (see section 3.3.4). This works only when you're upgrading bundles to a new version. If you wanted to switch to a Configuration Admin Service implementation from another vendor, you'd need both bundles installed while you copied the configuration data between them.

Third, you make sure the Configuration Admin Service bundle was successfully updated to the new version before finally checking that the configuration data still exists:

```
headers = cmBundle.getHeaders();
TestCase.assertEquals("org.apache.felix.configadmin",
    headers.get(Constants.BUNDLE_SYMBOLICNAME));
TestCase.assertEquals("1.2.7.SNAPSHOT",
    headers.get(Constants.BUNDLE_VERSION));
```

You can run this management test with a single command from the chapter07/ testing- example/ directory:

```
$ ant test.management

[junit] Running org.apache.felix.cm.integration.mgmt.ConfigAdminUpgradeTest
...
[junit] Tests run: 1, Failures: 0, Errors: 0, Time elapsed: 5.344 sec
```

You can even extend the upgrade test to make sure it works on other OSGi frameworks, as you did with the original Apache Felix Configuration Admin Service integration tests. You'll see that the test passes on all three frameworks, which is more proof that this service implementation is truly independent of the underlying OSGi framework.

This was only a small test; but if you look at the management examples from chapters 3 and 10, we hope you can see that you can easily script larger, more complex scenarios in Java (or any other JVM language) by using the standard OSGi lifecycle and deployment APIs. Imagine building up a modular library of management actions (install, start, stop, upgrade, and downgrade) that you can quickly tie together to test a particular task. Such management testing can help squash potential problems well in advance, minimizing real-world downtime.

Earlier in this chapter, we showed you how to test an application all the way up from individual classes to single bundles and combinations of bundles. Just now, we looked at testing different management strategies, such as upgrading and downgrading components, to make sure the application as a whole (and not just this release) continues to behave over its lifetime. At this point, you should be ready to move on to system and acceptance tests. These tests don't need special treatment regarding OSGi, because OSGi is just an implementation detail. As long as the application can be launched, it can be tested.

7.4 Summary

This chapter covered three different approaches to testing OSGi applications:

- Bundling existing non-OSGi tests to run inside OSGi
- Mocking existing OSGi tests to run outside of OSGi
- Using OSGi test tools to automate test deployment

In an ideal world, you'd use a combination of these three approaches to test all your code, both inside and outside one or more OSGi containers. In the real world, projects have deadlines and developers need their sleep, so we suggest using tools such as Pax Exam to automate as much of the test-bundling and -deployment work as possible. These tests should grow along with your application, giving you confidence that you do indeed have a robust, modular application. But what should you do if one of your tests fails inside OSGi? What tools and techniques can you apply to find the solution? Help is available in chapter 8.

8 Debugging applications

This chapter covers

- Debugging bundles using jdb
- Debugging bundles using Eclipse
- Understanding and solving class-loading issues
- Tracking down memory leaks and dangling service references

You just learned how to test individual bundles and application deployments in OSGi, but what should you do when an integration test unexpectedly fails with a class-loading exception or a load test runs out of memory? If you were working on a classic Java application, you'd break out the debugger, start adding or enabling instrumentation, and capture various diagnostic dumps. Well, an OSGi application is still a Java application, so you can continue to use many of your well-honed debugging techniques. The key area to watch out for is usually related to class loading, but that's not the only pitfall.

OSGi applications can have multiple versions of the same class running at the same time, requiring greater awareness of versioning; missing imports can lead to groups of classes that are incompatible with other groups; and dangling services can lead to unexpected memory leaks when updating bundles. In this chapter, we'll show you examples of how to debug all these problems and suggest best practices based on our collective experience of working with real-world OSGi applications in the field.

Let's kick off with something simple. Say you have an application composed of many working bundles and one misbehaving bundle: how do you find the bad bundle and debug it?

8.1 Debugging bundles

Applications continue to grow over time—more features get built on top of existing functionality, and each code change can introduce errors, expose latent bugs, or break original assumptions. In a properly modularized OSGi application, this should only lead to a few misbehaving bundles rather than a completely broken application. If you can identify these bundles, you can decide whether to remove or replace them, potentially fixing the application without having to restart it. But first, you need to find out which bundles are broken!

Take the paint example you've worked on in previous chapters. Imagine that you get a request to allow users to pick the colors of shapes. Your first step might be to add a `setColor()` method to the `SimpleShape` interface:

```
/**
 * Change the color used to shade the shape.
 *
 * @param color The color used to shade the shape.
 **/
public void setColor(Color color);
```

You probably think adding a method to an API is a minor, backward-compatible change, but in this case the interface is implemented by various client bundles that you may not have control over. In order to compile against the new `SimpleShape` API, they need to implement this method; so from their perspective, this is a major change. You should therefore increment the API version in the main paint example build.xml file to reflect this. The last version you used was 5.0, so the new version is

```
<property name="version" value="6.0"/>
```

You now need to implement the `setColor()` method in each of the three shape bundles. Here's the updated implementation for the triangle shape bundle.

Listing 8.1 Implementing the `setColor()` method for the triangle shape

```
public class Triangle implements SimpleShape {

  Color m_color = Color.GREEN;                                  <-- Remembers assigned color

  public void draw(Graphics2D g2, Point p) {
    int x = p.x - 25;
    int y = p.y - 25;
    GradientPaint gradient =
        new GradientPaint(x, y, m_color, x + 50, y, Color.WHITE);   <-- Applies color to gradient
    g2.setPaint(gradient);
    int[] xcoords = { x + 25, x, x + 50 };
    int[] ycoords = { y, y + 50, y + 50 };
```

```
    GeneralPath polygon =
        new GeneralPath(GeneralPath.WIND_EVEN_ODD, xcoords.length);
    polygon.moveTo(x + 25, y);
    for (int i = 0; i < xcoords.length; i++) {
      polygon.lineTo(xcoords[i], ycoords[i]);
    }
    polygon.closePath();
    g2.fill(polygon);
    BasicStroke wideStroke = new BasicStroke(2.0f);
    g2.setColor(Color.black);
    g2.setStroke(wideStroke);
    g2.draw(polygon);
  }

  public void setColor(Color color) {
    m_color = color;                                   <-- Updates assigned color
  }
}
```

The paint frame bundle contains another implementation of the `SimpleShape` API: `org.foo.paint.DefaultShape`. This class lazily delegates to the real shape via the OSGi service registry, so it also needs to implement the new `setColor()` method. The correct implementation follows the same approach used in `DefaultShape.draw()`: check that you have access to the real shape from the registry and, if you don't, request it. You'll use a broken implementation instead and assume you already have access to the shape instance:

```
public void setColor(Color color) {
  m_shape.setColor(color);
}
```

This sort of mistake could be made by a new team member who doesn't know about the lazy delegation approach and assumes that `m_shape` has been initialized elsewhere. If the application happened to call `draw()` early on, this bug could go unnoticed for a long time, because `m_shape` would always be valid by the time the code reached `setColor()`. But one day, someone may reasonably change the application so it calls `setColor()` first, as follows from the `ShapeComponent` class, and the bug will bite. (This example may seem a little contrived, but it's surprisingly hard to write bad code when you really want to!)

```
protected void paintComponent(Graphics g) {
  super.paintComponent(g);
  Graphics2D g2 = (Graphics2D) g;
  g2.setRenderingHint(RenderingHints.KEY_ANTIALIASING,
                      RenderingHints.VALUE_ANTIALIAS_ON);
  SimpleShape shape = m_frame.getShape(m_shapeName);
  shape.setColor(getForeground());
  shape.draw(g2, new Point(getWidth() / 2, getHeight() / 2));
}
```

You now have a broken OSGi application, which will throw an exception whenever you try to paint shapes. Let's see if you can debug it using the JDK provided debugger, jdb (http://java.sun.com/javase/6/docs/technotes/tools/solaris/jdb.html).

8.1.1 Debugging in action

The Java Debugger (also known as jdb) is a simple debugging tool that primarily exists as an example application for the Java Platform Debugger Architecture (JPDA, http://java.sun.com/javase/technologies/core/toolsapis/jpda/index.jsp) rather than a product in its own right. This means it lacks some of the polish and user-friendly features found in most other debuggers. But jdb is still a useful tool, especially when you're debugging on production servers that have limited installation environments.

DEBUGGING WITH JDB

You first need to build the broken example. When that's done, you can start jdb:

```
$ cd chapter08/debugging-bundles

$ ant dist

$ jdb -classpath launcher.jar launcher.Main bundles

Initializing jdb ...
>
```

Jdb starts up, but it won't launch your application until you type `run`:

```
> run
run launcher.Main bundles
Set uncaught java.lang.Throwable
Set deferred uncaught java.lang.Throwable
>
VM Started:
>
```

You should see the updated paint window appear, as shown in figure 8.1. All you had to do is use the `jdb` command instead of `java` and specify the class path and main class (the `jdb` command doesn't support the `-jar` option). You didn't have to tell jdb anything about your bundles or the OSGi framework; from jdb's perspective, this is just another Java application.

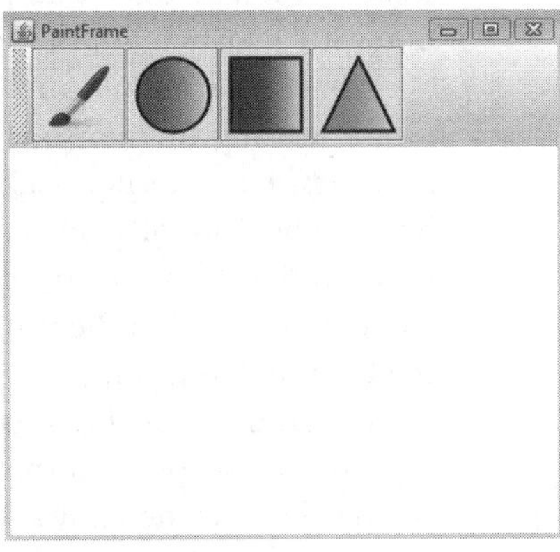

Figure 8.1 Updated paint example running under jdb

> **Felix bundle cache**
>
> If you happen to see several I/O exceptions mentioning the felix-cache, check that you haven't got any leftover debugged Java processes running. When you forcibly quit jdb using Ctrl-C, it can sometimes leave the debugged process running in the background, which in this case will stop new sessions from using the local felix-cache directory.

If you try to draw a shape in the paint window, jdb reports an uncaught exception in the AWT event thread:

```
Exception occurred: java.lang.NullPointerException (uncaught)
    "thread=AWT-EventQueue-0", java.awt.EventDispatchThread.run(),
        line=156 bci=152

AWT-EventQueue-0[1] where

  [1] java.awt.EventDispatchThread.run (EventDispatchThread.java:156)
```

This exception has percolated all the way up to the top of the AWT event thread, and jdb doesn't give you an easy way to see where it was originally thrown. You can ask it to stop the application when this sort of exception occurs again, like so:

```
AWT-EventQueue-0[1] catch java.lang.NullPointerException

Set all java.lang.NullPointerException

AWT-EventQueue-0[1] resume

All threads resumed.
```

Keep resuming the program until you see a long exception stack trace appear on the jdb console. This isn't a new exception: it's the AWT thread printing out the original uncaught exception. The top of the exception stack confirms that it was caused by your faulty code inside `DefaultShape`, which you know is contained inside the paint frame bundle. Notice that jdb doesn't give you a way to correlate the exception location with a particular JAR file.

What if you didn't know which bundle contained this package? You could try to locate it using the console, but most framework consoles only let you see exported packages. For internal packages, you would have to come up with a list of candidate bundles by manually checking the content of each bundle and comparing the exception location with the appropriate source. As you'll see in a moment, tracking a problem to a specific bundle is much easier when you use an OSGi-aware debugger, such as the Eclipse debugger.

Returning to the broken example, try to paint another shape. Jdb now detects and reports the exception at the point at which it's thrown inside `setColor()`. But because you haven't attached any source files, it doesn't show you the surrounding Java code:

```
Exception occurred: java.lang.NullPointerException
    (to be caught at: javax.swing.JComponent.paint(), line=1,043 bci=351)
        "thread=AWT-EventQueue-0", org.foo.paint.DefaultShape.setColor(),
            line=126 bci=5

AWT-EventQueue-0[1] list

Source file not found: DefaultShape.java
```

No problem—you need to attach your local source directory:

```
AWT-EventQueue-0[1] use org.foo.paint/src

AWT-EventQueue-0[1] list

122           g2.drawImage(m_icon.getImage(), 0, 0, null);
123         }
124
125         public void setColor(Color color) {
126 =>        m_shape.setColor(color);
127         }
128     }
```

When you print the current value of m_shape, you can finally see why it failed:

```
AWT-EventQueue-0[1] print m_shape
 m_shape = null
```

If you're an experienced Java programmer this should be familiar; no special OSGi knowledge is required. But take another look at the command where you attached your source directory:

```
use org.foo.paint/src
```

This command has no knowledge of bundles or class versions; it merely provides a list of candidate source files for jdb to compare to debugged classes. Jdb allows only one version of a given source file to be used at any one time, which makes life difficult when you're debugging an OSGi application containing multiple bundle versions. You have to know which particular collection of source directories to enable for each debug session.

DEBUGGING WITH ECLIPSE

Thankfully, this is merely a limitation of jdb. If you use an IDE such as Eclipse, which knows that multiple versions of a class can coexist in the same JVM, you don't have to worry about which source relates to which bundle version. The IDE manages that association for you as you debug your application.

To see this in action, generate Eclipse project files for the two paint examples from chapters 4 and 8:

```
$ cd ../../chapter04/paint-example
$ ant clean pde
$ cd ../../chapter08/debugging-bundles
$ ant clean pde
```

Now import these two directories into Eclipse as existing projects. You should end up with 10 new projects: half marked version 4, the rest version 6. To debug these bundles in Equinox, the OSGi framework used by Eclipse, click the drop-down arrow next to the bug icon (circled at the top of figure 8.2), and select Debug Configurations.

Doing so opens the Debug Configurations dialog box. Follow these instructions to configure a minimal Eclipse target platform for debugging the paint example:

1. Double-click OSGi Framework.
2. Change the name from New_configuration to ch8_debugging_example.
3. Deselect Include Optional Dependencies as well as Add New Workspace Bundles.
4. Select Validate Bundles Automatically.
5. Deselect the top-level Target Platform.
6. Click Add Required Bundles.
7. Click Apply.

When you're happy with your selection, click the Debug button to launch the debugger. Two different paint frames appear, as shown in figure 8.3. This is because you have two versions of the code running simultaneously in the same JVM.

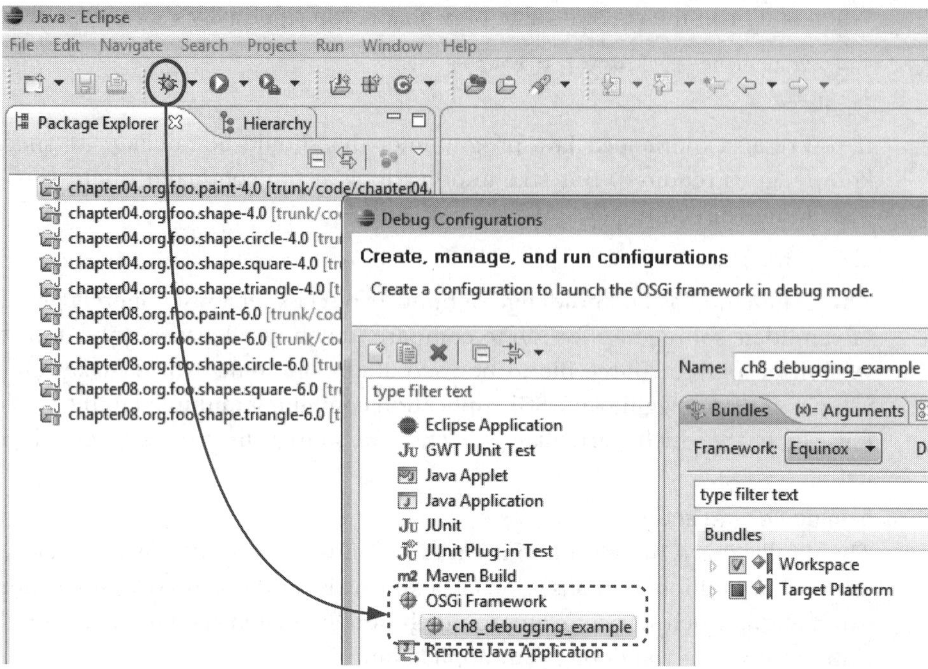

Figure 8.2 Configuring the Eclipse Debugger

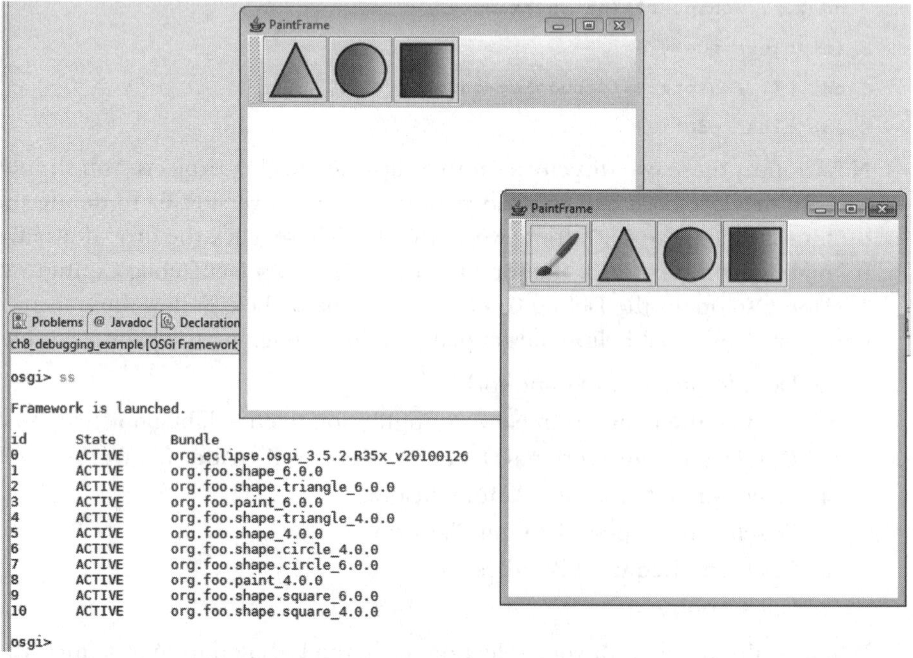

Figure 8.3 Debugging the paint example in Eclipse

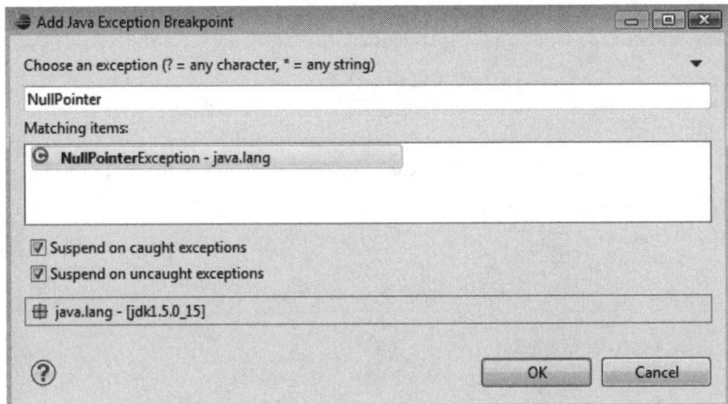

Figure 8.4 Watching for `NullPointer-Exceptions`

Before you start to paint, let's add a breakpoint so the debugger will stop when someone tries to use a null object reference. Choose Run > Add Java Exception Breakpoint to open the dialog box shown in figure 8.4. Select `java.lang.NullPointerException` and click OK.

You now have the two paint examples running in the Eclipse debugger. If you try to paint with the original version, which has three shapes in its toolbar, everything works as expected. But if you try to paint with the new version—the one with the paintbrush in its toolbar—the debugger stops (see figure 8.5).

Look closely at the title bar. The debugger has correctly identified that the affected source code is from chapter08 even though there are multiple versions of this class loaded in the Java runtime. Again, the problem is caused by a null shape object. Using the Eclipse IDE, you can trace the exception back to the specific bundle project. You can also click different frames in the stack trace to see what other bundles (if any) were

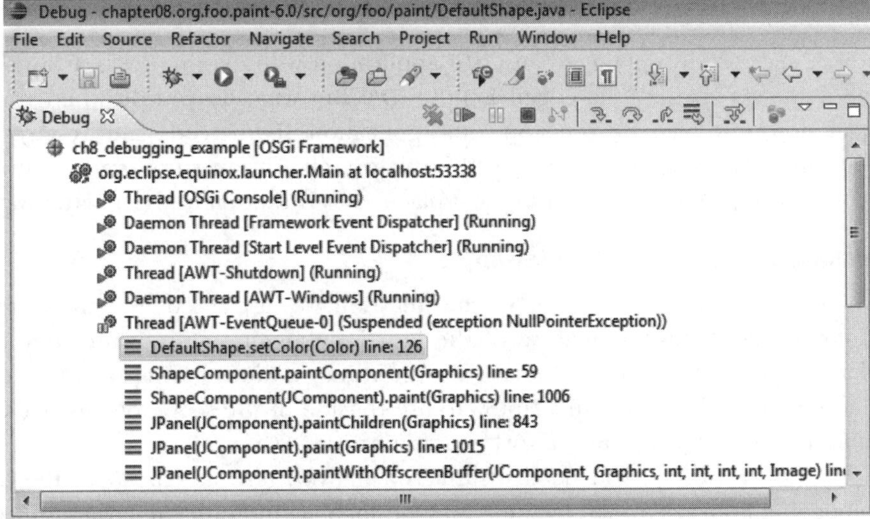

Figure 8.5 Exception caused by a bad `setColor()` method

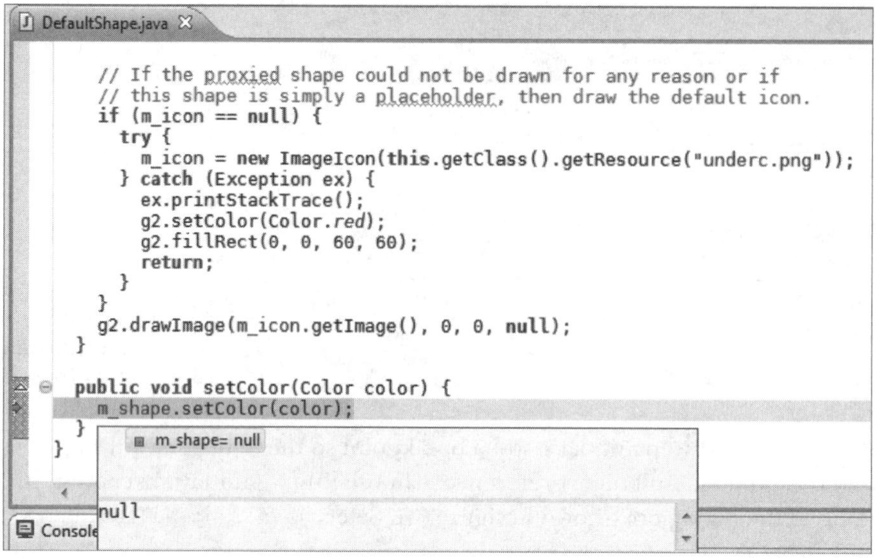

```
// If the proxied shape could not be drawn for any reason or if
// this shape is simply a placeholder, then draw the default icon.
if (m_icon == null) {
  try {
    m_icon = new ImageIcon(this.getClass().getResource("underc.png"));
  } catch (Exception ex) {
    ex.printStackTrace();
    g2.setColor(Color.red);
    g2.fillRect(0, 0, 60, 60);
    return;
  }
}
g2.drawImage(m_icon.getImage(), 0, 0, null);
}

public void setColor(Color color) {
  m_shape.setColor(color);
}
}
```

Figure 8.5 ***(continued)*** **Exception caused by a bad `setColor()` method**

involved. Compare this to jdb, where it was difficult to tell which bundles were involved in a given stack trace without a good understanding of the source distribution.

> **Embedding source inside OSGi bundles**
>
> OSGi defines a standard place for embedding documentation inside bundles: OSGI-OPT. Bundles containing source code under OSGI-OPT/src can be debugged in Eclipse even when you don't have a project associated with them in your workspace.

You've successfully debugged an OSGi application with existing tools, from the basic jdb debugger to the full-fledged Eclipse IDE. But what do you do when you finally track down the bug? Do you stop your application, fix the code, and restart? What if your application takes a long time to initialize, or if it takes hours to get it into the state that triggered the bug in the first place? Surely there must be a better way!

8.1.2 *Making things right with HotSwap*

Thankfully, there is an answer to the question we just asked. You may know it as HotSwap. HotSwap is a feature of the Java 5 debugging architecture that lets you change the definition of a class at execution time without having to restart the JVM. The technical details behind HotSwap are outside of the scope of this book; what's more interesting is whether it works correctly with OSGi.

To use HotSwap, you need to attach a native agent at startup to the low-level debugging hooks provided by the JVM. One such agent is attached whenever you run an application under jdb. Although jdb provides a basic redefine command to swap in newly compiled classes, it won't work for the previous example. Jdb refuses to redefine classes that have multiple versions loaded, because it can't determine which version should be redefined. But what about Eclipse? Can it help you update the right version of `DefaultShape`?

HOTSWAP WITH ECLIPSE

In the previous section, you successfully used the Eclipse debugger to manage multiple versions of source code while debugging. Will Eclipse come to the rescue again and let you fix the broken `DefaultShape` implementation while leaving earlier working versions intact? If you still have the Eclipse debugger instance running, you can skip to the next paragraph. Otherwise, you need to relaunch the example by clicking the drop-down arrow next to the bug icon (circled in figure 8.2) and selecting ch8_debugging_example. Trigger the exception again by attempting to paint a shape.

You should have the paint example suspended in the debugger at the point of failure, as you saw in figure 8.5. Unlike jdb, which has to be told which classes to redefine, the Eclipse debugger automatically attempts to redefine any class whose source changes in the IDE (provided you have automatic builds enabled). This means all you need to do to squish this bug is change the `setColor()` method in the open DefaultShape.java window so that `m_shape` is initialized before you use it, and save the file. For a quick solution, you can copy and paste the relevant code from the `draw()` method, as follows.

Listing 8.2 Fixing the `setColor()` method

```
public void setColor(Color color) {
  if (m_context != null) {
    try {
      if(m_shape == null) {
        m_shape = (SimpleShape) m_context.getService(m_ref);
      }
      m_shape.setColor(color);
    } catch (Exception ex) {}
  }
}
```

Copying code this way is fine for a quick debugging session, but it's better to extract the initialization code into a common method for use by both the `draw()` and `setColor()` methods. Reducing code duplication makes testing and debugging a lot easier. For now, you'll keep things simple: paste the code from listing 8.2 over the broken `setColor()` implementation. When you're ready, click Save to squish the bug!

What happened? Most, if not all, of you got an error message like the one in figure 8.6, saying the JVM couldn't add a method to an existing class. This happened because Eclipse tried to update *both* versions of the `DefaultShape` class. Although it was able to redefine the broken `setColor()` method in the version from this chapter, there is no such method in the `DefaultShape` class from chapter 4. Instead, the debugger attempted to add the `setColor()` method to the old class, but adding methods isn't supported by the current Sun implementation of HotSwap. Even

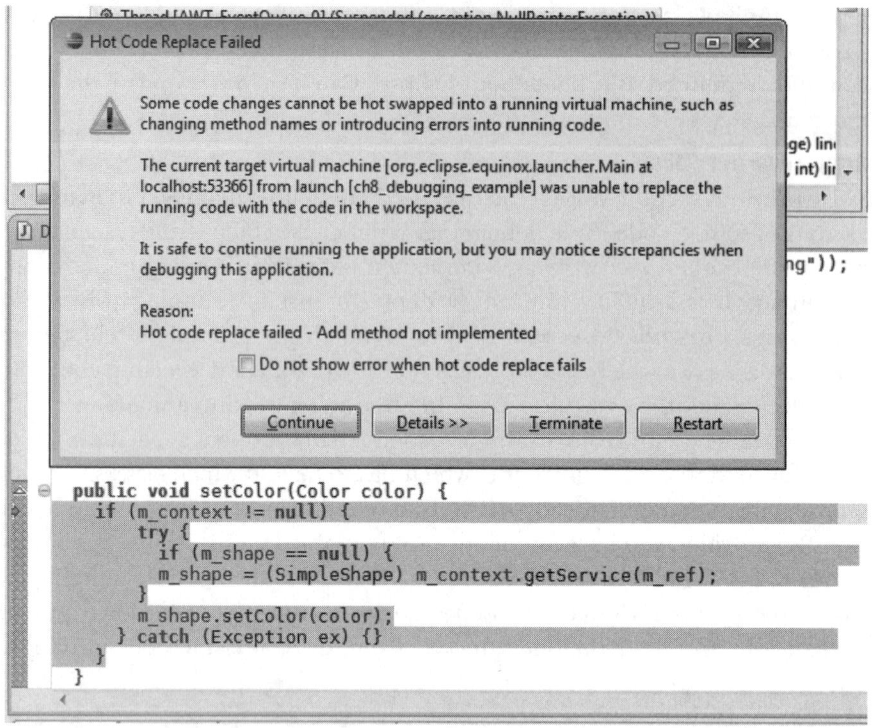

Figure 8.6 HotSwap failure updating `DefaultShape`

worse, if you decide to ignore this error message and continue, you still get the same exception as before when painting shapes.

Alternative implementations of HotSwap do support adding methods. You can find one such implementation in the IBM JDK (www.ibm.com/developerworks/java/jdk/). If you debug the same example using IBM Java 6 as the target runtime (remembering, of course, to first revert the `setColor()` method back to the broken version), you can successfully fix the problem without restarting the process. Figure 8.7 confirms that even after using HotSwap to squish the bug, both the old and new paint examples continue to work on the IBM JDK.

Although you eventually managed to use HotSwap to fix the problem in your bundle, this isn't exactly what you want, because *all* versions of `DefaultShape` were updated. By chance, this didn't affect the old paint example because you were adding a completely new method. It has no effect on the old application and sits there unused. But what if you wanted to change a method that was tightly coupled to existing code? You could end up fixing one version only to find out you'd broken all the others by unintentionally upgrading them with the new logic. This may not be a big deal during development, because you'll probably be focusing on one version at a time; but can you do better when debugging OSGi applications in the field?

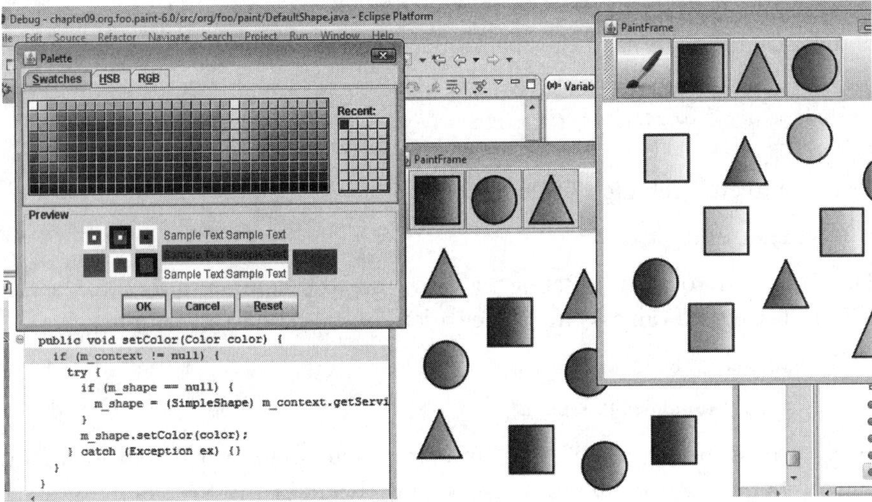

Figure 8.7 Successful HotSwap with the IBM JVM

HOTSWAP WITH JREBEL

Yes, you can do better. A JVM agent called JRebel (formerly known as JavaRebel; www.zeroturnaround.com/jrebel/) behaves in a way similar to HotSwap but has much better support for custom class-loading solutions like OSGi. For those who don't know, a JVM *agent* is a small native library that attaches to the process on startup and is granted low-level access to the Java runtime. Whenever you recompile a class, JRebel automatically updates the appropriate version loaded in the JVM without affecting any other versions of the class. This makes it easy to develop, debug, and compare different releases of an application at the same time.

What are the downsides? The main downside is reduced performance due to the extra tracking involved. JRebel also needs to know how custom class loaders map their classes and resources to local files. It currently supports the Equinox OSGi implementation, but there's no guarantee it will work with other OSGi frameworks. Finally, you need to add an option to the JVM command line to use it, which is problematic in production environments that lock down the JVM's configuration. Some places won't let you use JVM agents at all because of the potential security issues involved. Agents have access to the entire process and can redefine almost any class in your application. Adding an agent to your JVM is like giving root access to a user in Linux. For these reasons, JRebel is usually best suited to development environments.

But what if you're working somewhere that forbids the use of debuggers or JVM agents? Is there any other way you can update the broken bundle without restarting the whole process?

HOTSWAP THE OSGI WAY

Update is the key word here. Back in section 3.7, we discussed the update and refresh parts of the OSGi lifecycle. Well, you can use them here to deploy your fix without having to restart the JVM. To see this in action, you first need to revert the `setColor()` method of the local `DefaultShape` class back once again to the broken implementation:

```
public void setColor(Color color) {
  m_shape.setColor(color);
}
```

Next, completely rebuild the example:

```
$ ant clean dist
```

This time, you won't use a debugger. Also, add your command shell to the current set of bundles, so you can ask the framework to update the fixed bundle later:

```
$ ant add_shell_bundles
$ java -jar launcher.jar bundles
```

First, confirm that you have the broken implementation installed by attempting to paint a shape (you should see an exception). Then, in another operating system shell, fix the `setColor()` method of the `DefaultShape` class using the code from listing 8.2, and rebuild the paint frame bundle in a new window:

```
$ cd chapter08/debugging-bundles/org.foo.paint
$ ant
```

You can now try updating your fixed bundle. Go back to the OSGi console, and type the following:

```
-> update 6
```

Here, 6 is the ID of the paint frame bundle, as reported by the `bundles` command. When you issue the `update` command, the framework updates the bundle content by reloading the bundle JAR file from its original install location. It also stops and restarts the paint frame bundle, so you should see the paint frame window disappear and reappear. The paint example is now using the fixed code, which means you can paint multicolored shapes as shown in figure 8.8. Notice that you didn't need to follow the update with a refresh. This is because the paint frame bundle doesn't export any packages, so you know there are no other bundles hanging onto old revisions of the `DefaultShape` code.

Unlike JRebel, the OSGi update process doesn't depend on a special JVM agent. It also doesn't have any significant effect on performance. These reasons together mean you can use the OSGi update process in a production environment. The downside is that you have to update and restart the entire bundle, potentially destroying the current state, rather than redefine a single class. If you wanted to keep any previously drawn shapes, you would need to persist them somehow when stopping and restore them when restarting.

You've just seen how you can debug and fix problems in OSGi applications using everyday development tools such as jdb and Eclipse. You looked at more advanced techniques, such as HotSwap and JRebel, and finally used the tried-and-tested OSGi update process to fix a broken bundle. We hope these examples made you feel more comfortable about

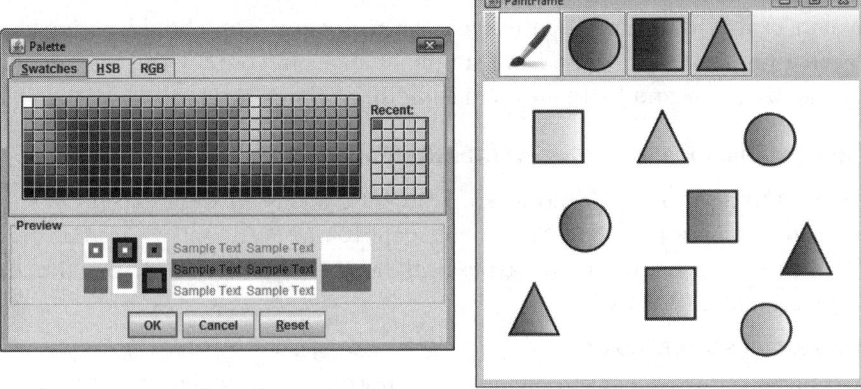

Figure 8.8 Painting with the fixed example

debugging your own OSGi applications. In the next section, we'll take a closer look at a set of problems you'll eventually encounter when using OSGi: class-loading issues.

8.2 Solving class-loading issues

OSGi encourages and enforces modularity, which, by its nature, can lead to class-loading issues. Maybe you forgot to import a package or left something out when building a bundle. Perhaps you have a private copy of a class you're supposed to be sharing or forgot to make sure two tightly coupled packages are provided by the same bundle. These are all situations that break modularity and can lead to various class-loading exceptions. The right tools can help you avoid getting into these situations in the first place, but it's still worthwhile knowing what can happen and what the resulting problem signatures look like. The following sections take you through a number of common class-loading problems, what to look out for, what might be the cause, and how to solve them.

All the exceptions discussed in this section come from the same example application: a simple hub-and-spoke message system that uses the OSGi extender pattern (see section 3.4) to load spoke implementations at execution time. The basic architecture is shown in figure 8.9. The only thing that changes throughout this example is the

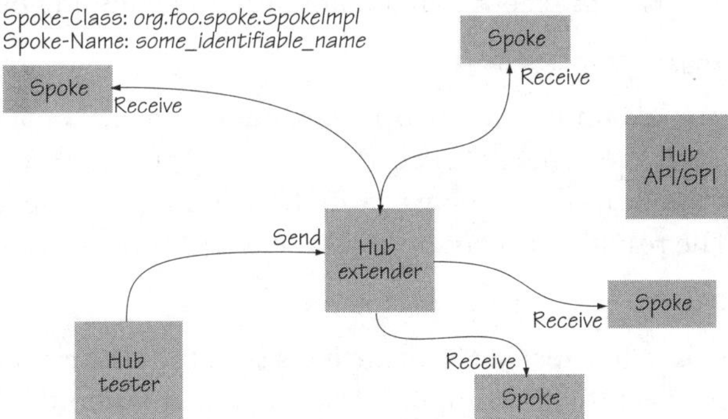

Figure 8.9 Simple hub-and-spoke message system

content of the spoke implementation bundle; the API, hub extender, and test bundles remain exactly the same. By the end of this section, you should understand which class-loading issues can arise from simple changes in content and metadata and how you can diagnose and fix them when something goes wrong.

8.2.1 ClassNotFoundException vs. NoClassDefFoundError

The first thing you should do when debugging a class-loading exception is look and see if the exception is `ClassNotFoundException` or `NoClassDefFoundError`. A subtle difference between these two types will help you understand why the exception occurred and how to fix it.

CLASSNOTFOUNDEXCEPTION

A `ClassNotFoundException` means the reporting class loader wasn't able to find or load the initial named class, either by itself or by delegating to other class loaders. This could occur in a Java application for three main reasons:

- There's a typo in the name passed to the class loader (common).
- The class loader (and its peers) have no knowledge of the named class.
- The named class is available, but it isn't visible to the calling code.

The third case, visibility, is where things get interesting. You know all about `public`, `protected`, and `private` access; but how many of you know what *package private* means? *Package-private* classes are those without any access modifier before their `class` keyword. Their visibility rules are unique: in addition to only being visible to classes from the same package, they're also only visible to classes from the same *class loader*. Most Java programs have a single application class loader, so this last rule hardly ever comes up. OSGi applications contain multiple class loaders, but as long as each package is loaded by only one class loader, it's effectively the same as before. The real problem arises with split packages (see section 5.3), which span several class loaders. Package-private classes from a split package in one bundle aren't visible to fellow classes in other bundles. This can lead to `ClassNotFoundExceptions` or `IllegalAccessExceptions` that wouldn't happen with a single application class loader.

Figure 8.10 shows three different package-private scenarios: one classic and two involving split packages. Each scenario has subtly different class visibility.

To see a common `ClassNotFoundException` situation, run the following example:

```
$ ./chapter08/classloading/PICK_EXAMPLE 1
```

This builds and deploys a spoke bundle with incorrect extender metadata concerning its implementation class: it lists the name as `MySpokeImpl` instead of `SpokeImpl`. This is an easy mistake to make in applications configured with XML or property files because of the lack of type safety. The resulting exception gives the name of the missing class:

```
java.lang.ClassNotFoundException: org.foo.spoke.MySpokeImpl
```

You should use this information to check if the name is correct, the class is visible, and the package containing the class is either imported or contained inside the bundle.

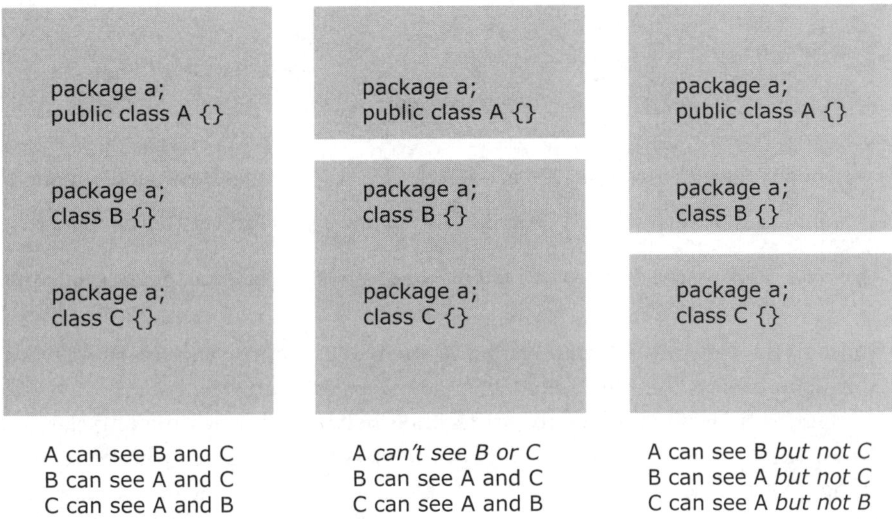

Figure 8.10 Split packages and package-private visibility

Most `ClassNotFoundExceptions` are easily solved by checking bundle manifests and configuration files. The hardest problems involve third-party custom class loaders; you inevitably need access to the class loader's source code to determine why it couldn't see a particular class, as well as have the patience to unravel the exception stack.

That's `ClassNotFoundException`, but how is `NoClassDefFoundError` any different?

NOCLASSDEFFOUNDERROR

First, this is an error rather than an exception, which means applications are discouraged from catching it. Second, it means the initial class that started the current load cycle *was* found, but the class loader wasn't able to finish loading it because a class it depends on was missing. This can happen when a class is compiled against a dependent API, but the resulting bundle neither contains nor imports that package.

Continuing with the exceptional example, type the following:

```
$ ./chapter08/classloading/PICK_EXAMPLE 2
```

This time, the extender metadata in the spoke bundle is correct, but the bundle doesn't import the `org.foo.hub.spi` package containing the `Spoke` interface. The runtime begins to load the spoke implementation but can't find the named interface when defining the class:

```
java.lang.NoClassDefFoundError: org/foo/hub/spi/Spoke
...
Caused by: java.lang.ClassNotFoundException: org.foo.hub.spi.Spoke
```

Debugging a `NoClassDefFoundError` involves tracing back through the dependencies of the class being loaded to find the missing link (or links). Although the cause in this example is clear, developers often get side-tracked by assuming the initial class is at fault. The real culprit may be hidden down at the bottom of the stack as the original

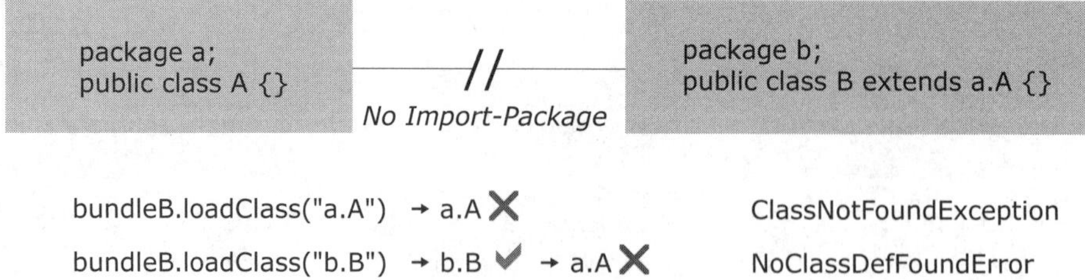

Figure 8.11 Differences between `ClassNotFoundException` and `NoClassDefFoundError`

cause of the exception. When you know the real cause, you can use the same problem-solving approach used in `ClassNotFoundException` to fix the issue.

Figure 8.11 summarizes the difference between the two missing-class exception types; together, they make up many of the class-loading issues you'll encounter when using OSGi. Just remember: `ClassNotFoundException` means a class is missing, whereas `NoClassDefFoundError` means one of its dependencies is missing.

Unfortunately, these two exceptions don't have a monopoly on confusing OSGi developers. A classic puzzle for people new to class loading goes something like this: you're given an object that says its type is `org.foo.Item`, but when you try to cast it to `org.foo.Item` you get a `ClassCastException`! What's going on?

8.2.2 Casting problems

How many of you would expect a `ClassCastException` from the following code?

```
ServiceTracker itemTracker =
    new ServiceTracker(bundleContext, "org.foo.Item", null);

itemTracker.open(true);

Item item = (Item) itemTracker.getService();
```

At first glance, it looks correct: you configure a service tracker to track services of type `org.foo.Item` and cast the discovered service, if any, to the same type. But notice how you open the tracker. Instead of calling the no-argument `open()` method as usual, you pass in a Boolean: `true`. This tells the service tracker to track *all* services whose type name matches the `org.foo.Item` string, not just the ones that are class-loader compatible with your bundle (we discussed a similar situation back in section 4.5.1). If another bundle provides an `Item` service and happens to get the `org.foo` package from a different class space than you did, you'll see a `ClassCastException` at the last line.

How can this be? Recall from chapter 2 that class loaders form part of a type's identity at execution time, so the exact same class byte code loaded by two different class loaders is considered to be two distinct types. This makes all the difference, because OSGi uses a class loader per bundle to support class-space isolation in the same Java runtime. It also means you can get `ClassCastExceptions` when casting between types that look identical on paper.

To see this in practice, run the third example:

```
$ ./chapter08/classloading/PICK_EXAMPLE 3
```

You should see a `ClassCastException` involving the `Spoke` class. This is because your spoke bundle contains its own private copy of `org.foo.hub.spi`, instead of importing it from the hub bundle. The spoke and hub end up using different class loaders for the same API class, which makes the spoke implementation incompatible with the hub:

```
java.lang.ClassCastException: org.foo.spoke.SpokeImpl
  cannot be cast to org.foo.hub.spi.Spoke
```

The fastest way to investigate these impossible `ClassCastExceptions` is to compare the class loaders for the expected and actual types. OSGi frameworks sometimes label their class loaders with the bundle identifier, so calling `getClassLoader().toString()` on both sides can tell you which bundles are involved. You can also use the framework console to find out who's exporting the affected package and who imports it from them. Use this to build a map of the different class spaces. The specific commands to use depend on the framework; at the time of writing this book, the OSGi Alliance is still standardizing a command shell. On Felix, the `inspect package` command is the one to use. On Equinox you would use the `packages` or `bundle` commands. Once you understand the different class spaces, you can adjust the bundle metadata to make things consistent to avoid the `ClassCastException`. One approach might be to add `uses` constraints, which we first introduced at the end of chapter 2.

8.2.3 Using uses constraints

Think back to chapter 2, specifically the discussion about consistent class spaces in section 2.7.2. Bundles must have a consistent class space to avoid running into class-related problems, such as visibility or casting issues. When you have two tightly coupled packages, it's sometimes necessary to add `uses` constraints to make sure these packages come from the same class space. Perhaps you don't think you need all these `uses` constraints cluttering up your manifest—after all, what's the worst that can happen if you remove them?

Let's find out by running the fourth example in the class-loading series:

```
$ ./chapter08/classloading/PICK_EXAMPLE 4
```

Yet again you get a class-loading exception, except this time it happens inside the spoke implementation. The Java runtime notices that you attempted to load two different versions of the `Message` class in the same class loader—in other words, your class space is inconsistent:

```
java.lang.LinkageError: loader constraint violation: loader (instance of
  org/apache/felix/framework/searchpolicy/ModuleImpl$ModuleClassLoader)
    previously initiated loading for a different type with name
      "org/foo/hub/Message"
```

How did this happen? Your new spoke bundle has an open version range for the hub API, which means it can import any version after 1.0. It also provides a new 2.0 version of the `org.foo.hub` package that includes a modified `Message` interface. You may wonder what this package is doing in your spoke bundle—maybe you're experimenting with a new design, or perhaps it was included by mistake. How it got there isn't important. What *is* important is that you have a 2.0 version of `org.foo.hub` floating around without a corresponding 2.0 version of the `Spoke` Service Provider Interface (SPI). Let's see how this affects the package wiring.

The hub extender and test bundles still have the original, restricted version range:

```
Import-Package:
 org.foo.hub;version="[1.0,2.0)",
 org.foo.hub.api;version="[1.0,2.0)",
 org.foo.hub.spi;version="[1.0,2.0)"
```

They get `Spoke` and `Message` from the original API bundle, but your spoke bundle has

```
Import-Package:
 org.foo.hub;version="1.0",
 org.foo.hub.spi;version="1.0"
```

This means it gets the original `Spoke` interface from the API bundle and the updated `Message` from itself. (Remember, the framework always tries to pick the newest version it can.) Thus the `Spoke` interface and your implementation see different versions of the `Message` interface, which causes the `LinkageError` in the JVM. Figure 8.12 shows the mismatched wiring.

You must tell the framework that the various hub packages are related, so it can stop this mismatch from happening. This is where the missing `uses` constraints come in. Edit the chapter08/classloading/org.foo.hub/build.properties file and remove this line from the bnd instructions:

```
-nouses: ${no.uses}
```

Removing this re-enables bnd support for `uses` constraints. If you run the example again,

```
$ ./chapter08/classloading/PICK_EXAMPLE 4
```

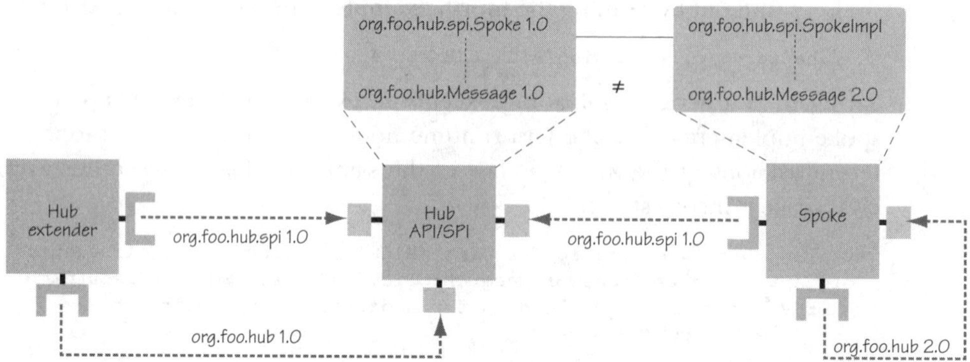

Figure 8.12 Mismatched wiring due to missing `uses` constraints

you no longer see any exceptions or linkage errors:

```
SPOKE org.foo.spoke.no_uses_constraints RECEIVED Testing Testing 1, 2, 3...
```

You just saw how `uses` constraints can help you avoid inconsistent class spaces and odd linkage errors, but what happens if they can't be satisfied? You can find out by tweaking the version range for `org.foo.hub` in the spoke bundle. By using a range of `[2.0, 3.0)`, you leave only one matching exporter of `org.foo.hub`: the spoke bundle itself. But this breaks the `uses` constraints on the SPI package exported from the main API bundle, because it has a range of `[1.0, 2.0)` for `org.foo.hub`. These two ranges are incompatible: there's no way you can find a solution that satisfies both. The fifth example demonstrates the result:

```
$ ./chapter08/classloading/PICK_EXAMPLE 5

Error starting framework: org.osgi.framework.BundleException:
  Unable to resolve due to constraint violation.
```

Unfortunately, the framework exception doesn't tell you which constraint failed or why. Determining why a solution wasn't found without help from the framework can be time consuming, because the search space of potential solutions can be large. Fortunately, Equinox has a `diag` command to explain which constraints were left unsatisfied. With Felix, you can add more details to the original exception by enabling debug logging.

For example, if you change the last line in the `PICK_EXAMPLE` script to

```
java "-Dfelix.log.level=4" -jar launcher.jar bundles
```

this enables Felix debug logging, which prints the following message before the exception is thrown:

```
$ ./chapter08/classloading/PICK_EXAMPLE 5

DEBUG: Constraint violation for 1.0 detected;
  module can see org.foo.hub from [1.0] and org.foo.hub from [2.0]
```

The message tells you the unsatisfied constraint is related to the `org.foo.hub` package. It also gives you the identifiers of the bundles involved. This is another reason why it's a good idea to use `uses` constraints. Without them, you'd have to debug confusing class-loading problems with no support from the framework. By using `uses` constraints, you can avoid linkage errors to begin with and help the framework explain why certain sets of bundles aren't compatible. But it can only do this if the constraints are valid and consistent, which is why we recommend you always use a tool to compute them, such as bnd.

So far, we've concentrated on what happens when your bundle metadata is wrong; but even a perfect manifest doesn't always guarantee success. Certain coding practices common to legacy code can cause problems in OSGi because they assume a flat, static class path. One practice worth avoiding is the use of `Class.forName()` to dynamically load code.

8.2.4 Staying clear of Class.forName()

Suppose you're writing a module that needs to look up a class at execution time based on some incoming argument or configuration value. Skimming through the Java platform API, you spot a method called `Class.forName()`. Give it a class name, and it returns the loaded class. Perfect, right? Its ongoing popularity suggests many Java programmers agree; but before you sprinkle it throughout your code, you should know it has a flaw: it doesn't work well in modular applications. It assumes the caller's class loader can see the named class, which you know isn't always true when you enforce modularity.

How does this affect you as an OSGi developer? Any class you attempt to load using `Class.forName()` must either be contained, imported, or boot-delegated by the bundle making the call. When you're loading from a selection of known classes, this isn't a big deal; but if you're providing a general utility (such as an aspect-weaving service), there's no way to know which classes you may need to load. And even if you happen to know, you may decide to keep things flexible for the future. If you remember our discussion on discovering imports from section 6.1.3, you may think this sounds like a job for dynamic imports:

```
DynamicImport-Package: *
```

But dynamic imports only work when the wanted packages are exported. In addition, your bundle can get wired to many different packages in numerous client bundles. If any one of these bundles is refreshed, your bundle will also end up refreshed, which in turn may affect the other bundles. Finally, you can import only one version of a package at any one time. If you want to work with non-exported classes or handle multiple versions of the same code concurrently, you need to find another way to access them.

Whenever you work with OSGi class loading, always remember that well-defined rules govern visibility. It's not some arbitrary decision about who sees what. Every loaded class must be visible to at least one class loader. Your bundle may not be able to see the client class, but the client bundle certainly can. If you can somehow get hold of the client class loader, you can use it to load the class instead of using your own class loader. This job is much easier if the method arguments already include a type or instance of a type that you know belongs to the client. Let's see how easy it can be with the help of the sixth spoke implementation.

Listing 8.3 Audited spoke implementation

```
public class SpokeImpl implements Spoke {

  String address;

  public SpokeImpl(String address) {
    this.address = address;
  }

  public boolean receive(Message message) {
    if (address.matches(message.getAddress())) {

      Class msgClazz = message.getClass();
      String auditorName = msgClazz.getPackage().getName() + ".Auditor";
```

Assumes same package

```
        try {
          Class auditClazz = Class.forName(auditorName);         <-- Don't use ClassforName()!

          Method method = auditClazz.getDeclaredMethod(
              "audit", Spoke.class, Message.class);

          method.invoke(null, this, message);                    <-- Calls auditor method

          return true;

        } catch (Throwable e) {
          e.printStackTrace();
          return false;
        }
      }
      return false;
    }
}
```

This spoke assumes each `Message` implementation has an accompanying `Auditor` class in the same package and uses reflection to access it and log receipt of the message. The reason behind this design isn't important; you can imagine that the team wants to support both audited and non-audited messages without breaking the simple message API. What's important is that by using `Class.forName()`, the spoke bundle assumes it can see the `Auditor` class. But you don't export your implementation packages, so when you run the example, we hope you aren't too surprised to see an exception:

```
$ ./chapter08/classloading/PICK_EXAMPLE 6

java.lang.ClassNotFoundException: org.foo.hub.test.Auditor
```

You know the `Auditor` sits alongside the `Message` implementation in the same package, so they share the same class loader (you don't have any split packages). You need to access the `Message` implementation class loader and ask it to load the class like so:

```
Class auditClazz = msgClazz.getClassLoader().loadClass(auditorName);
```

Remove the `Class.forName()` line from the spoke implementation in listing 8.3, and replace it with the previous line. You can now run the example without any problem:

```
$ ./chapter08/classloading/PICK_EXAMPLE 6

Fri Sep 18 00:13:52 SGT 2009 - org.foo.spoke.SpokeImpl@186d4c1
  RECEIVED Testing Testing 1, 2, 3...
```

`Class.forName()` considered harmful!

You may wonder why we don't use the longer form of `Class.forName()`—the method that accepts a user-given class loader instead of using the caller's class loader. We don't use it because there's a subtle but important difference between these statements:

```
Class<?> a = initiatingClassLoader.loadClass(name);
Class<?> b = Class.forName(name, true, initiatingClassLoader);
```

> ***(continued)***
>
> First, consider `loadClass()`. The initiating class loader is used to initiate the load request. It may delegate through several class loaders before finding one that has already loaded the class or can load it. The class loader that defines the class (by converting its byte code into an actual class) is called the *defining class loader*. The result of the load request is cached in the defining class loader in case anyone else wants this class.
>
> Now consider `forName()`. Although it behaves like `loadClass()` when looking for new classes, it caches the result in both the defining and initiating class loaders. It also consults the initiating loader cache before delegating any load request. With `loadClass()`, the resulting class can depend on your context, perhaps according to which module you're currently running in. But with `forName()`, you get the same result regardless of context. Because this extra caching may lead to unexpected results in a dynamic environment such as OSGi, we strongly recommend you use `loadClass()` instead of `forName()`.

In the last example, you found the client class loader by examining one of the arguments passed into your method and used that to look up the client's `Auditor` class. What if none of the method arguments relate to the client bundle? Perhaps you can use a feature specifically introduced for application frameworks in Java 2: the Thread Context Class Loader.

8.2.5 *Following the Thread Context Class Loader*

The Thread Context Class Loader (TCCL) is, as you may expect, a thread-specific class loader. Each thread can have its own TCCL; and, by default, a thread inherits the TCCL of its parent. You can access the TCCL with a single line of Java code:

```
ClassLoader tccl = Thread.currentThread().getContextClassLoader();
```

The TCCL is useful when you're writing code that needs dynamic access to classes or resources but must also run inside a number of different containers such as OSGi. Instead of adding a class-loader parameter to each method call, you can instead use the previous code to access the current TCCL. All the container needs to do is update the TCCL for each thread as it enters and leaves the container. When done properly, this approach also supports nesting of containers, as shown in figure 8.13.

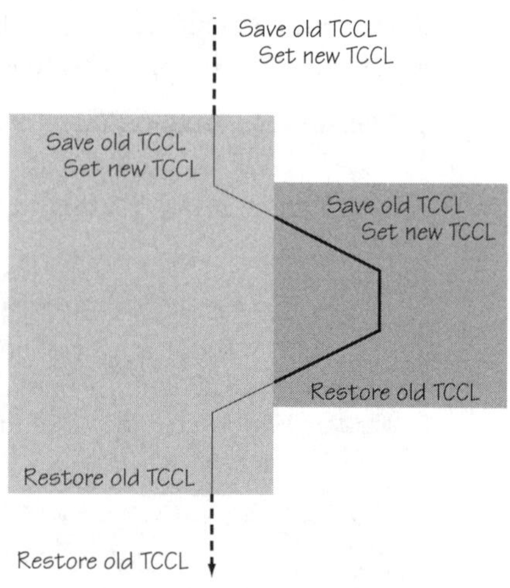

Figure 8.13 Using TCCL with nested containers

You should use a `try-catch-finally` block to guarantee that the correct TCCL is restored even if an exception or error occurs somewhere inside the container code:

```
ClassLoader oldTCCL = Thread.currentThread().getContextClassLoader();
try {
  Thread.currentThread().setContextClassLoader(newTCCL);
  ...
} catch (Throwable e) {
  ...
} finally {
  Thread.currentThread().setContextClassLoader(oldTCCL);
}
```

Let's see how the TCCL can help you solve a class-loading issue without affecting the API. Run this example:

```
$ ./chapter08/classloading/PICK_EXAMPLE 7
```

You should see an exception when the spoke attempts to load the `Auditor` class:

```
java.lang.ClassNotFoundException: org.foo.hub.test.Auditor
```

If you look at this spoke implementation, you'll see that it uses the TCCL, as shown here.

Listing 8.4 Audited spoke implementation with TCCL

```
public class SpokeImpl implements Spoke {

  String address;

  public SpokeImpl(String address) {
    this.address = address;
  }

  public boolean receive(Message message) {
    if (address.matches(message.getAddress())) {

      Class msgClazz = message.getClass();
      String auditorName = msgClazz.getPackage().getName() + ".Auditor";

      try {
        Class auditClazz = Thread.currentThread()
            .getContextClassLoader().loadClass(auditorName);     <-- Uses current TCCL

        Method method = auditClazz.getDeclaredMethod(
            "audit", Spoke.class, Message.class);

        method.invoke(null, this, message);

        return true;

      } catch (Throwable e) {
        e.printStackTrace();
        return false;
      }
    }
    return false;
  }
}
```

As long as the TCCL is assigned properly by the container or the caller, this should work. The OSGi standard doesn't define what the default TCCL should be: it's left up to the framework implementers. This example uses Apache Felix, which leaves the default TCCL unchanged; in other words, it'll be set to the application class loader. Unfortunately, the application class loader has no visibility of the `Auditor` class contained within the test bundle, which explains why you see a `ClassNotFoundException`.

To avoid this exception, you need to update the TCCL in the test bundle before sending the message. To be consistent, you should also record the original TCCL and reset it after the call completes. This last step is important if you want to nest or share containers inside the same process, as you saw in figure 8.13. Look at the test activator contained under `org.foo.hub.test`; following are the changes needed to set and reset the TCCL.

Listing 8.5 Setting and resetting the TCCL

```
public Object addingService(ServiceReference reference) {
  ClassLoader oldTCCL = Thread.currentThread().getContextClassLoader();

  try {
    Thread.currentThread().setContextClassLoader(
        getClass().getClassLoader());

    Hub hub = (Hub) ctx.getService(reference);
    hub.send(new TextMessage(".*", "Testing Testing 1, 2, 3..."));

  } catch (Throwable e) {
    e.printStackTrace();
  } finally {
    Thread.currentThread().setContextClassLoader(oldTCCL);
  }
  return null;
}
```

This listing saves the old TCCL, sets the new TCCL, and then restores the old TCCL. With these three changes, you can rerun the test without any class-loading problems:

```
$ ./chapter08/classloading/PICK_EXAMPLE 7

Fri Sep 19 00:13:52 SGT 2009 - org.foo.spoke.SpokeImpl@186d4c1
  RECEIVED Testing Testing 1, 2, 3...
```

That wraps up our discussion of class-loading problems. You used the same example code to see a wide range of different exceptions you may encounter when developing OSGi applications. We hope this will provide you with a foundation for any future class-loading investigations. If you can relate a particular exception with one of the examples here, the associated solution will also help fix your problem.

Unfortunately, class loading isn't the only problem you'll encounter when working with OSGi, but the next topic we'll look at is indirectly related to class loading. OSGi enforces modularity with custom class loaders. An OSGi application contains several class loaders, each one holding on to a set of resources. Unused class loaders are freed as bundles are uninstalled and the framework is refreshed, but occasionally a rogue reference keeps a class loader and its associated resources alive. This can turn into a memory leak.

8.3 Tracking down memory leaks

Memory leaks occur in OSGi applications as in any other Java application. All you need is something like a rogue thread or static field hanging on to one end of a spaghetti ball of references to stop the garbage collector from reclaiming the objects. In a desktop Java application, you may not notice any memory leaks because you don't leave the application running for a long time. As soon as you restart the JVM, your old application with its ever-growing heap of objects is gone, and you get a brand-new empty heap to fill.

Server-side OSGi applications, on the other hand, can have longer lifetimes; an uptime of many months isn't unreasonable. One of the strengths of OSGi is that you're able to install, update, and uninstall bundles without having to restart the JVM. Although this is great for maximizing uptime, it means you have to be careful not to introduce memory leaks in your bundles. You can't always rely on the process being occasionally restarted. Furthermore, updating a bundle introduces a new class loader to hold the updated classes. If there's anything holding on to objects or classes from the old class loader, it won't be reclaimed, and your process will use more and more class loaders each time the bundle is updated or reinstalled.

> **Introducing the PermGen heap**
>
> Class-loader leaks can be more problematic than simple object leaks because some Java runtimes, like Sun's HotSpot JVM, place classes in a separate heap space called the Permanent Generation, or PermGen for short. This class heap is much smaller than the main object heap, and its capacity is controlled by a different GC setting: `-XX:MaxPermSize`. If every bundle update adds hundreds of new class revisions without unloading anything, you'll probably exhaust the PermGen before you run out of object heap space.

Any leak is a cause for concern, but depending on your requirements, not all leaks warrant investigation. You may not even notice certain leaks if they add only a few bytes to the heap every now and then. What's the best way to find leaks in an OSGi application?

8.3.1 Analyzing OSGi heap dumps

As with debugging, you can continue to use your existing heap analysis skills to examine OSGi applications. Sure, there are more class loaders than in a normal Java application; but standard Java EE containers also contain multiple class loaders, and that doesn't stop developers from finding memory leaks inside web applications.

Let's see what an OSGi application heap dump looks like. The leaky application is under chapter08/memory-leaks in the online examples. It consists of a single bundle that creates and accesses a `ThreadLocal` variable every time the bundle starts and fails to remove it when the bundle stops. Here's the bundle activator.

Listing 8.6 Leaky bundle activator

```
public class Activator implements BundleActivator {
  static class Data {
    StringBuffer data = new StringBuffer(8 * 1024 * 1024)
  }

  static final ThreadLocal leak = new ThreadLocal() {
    protected Object initialValue() {
      return new Data();
    };
  };

  public void start(BundleContext ctx) {
    leak.get();
  }

  public void stop(BundleContext ctx) {}
}
```

Each leaked `ThreadLocal` takes up a noticeable 8 MB. Following recommended practice, the `ThreadLocal` is a static member of the class. This is safe because the JVM guarantees to supply a distinct instance of the data object for each thread accessing the `ThreadLocal`. But how does forgetting to remove the `ThreadLocal` cause a memory leak? If you read the `ThreadLocal` Javadoc, you may expect the JVM to clear up stale references (http://java.sun.com/javase/6/docs/api/java/lang/ThreadLocal.html):

> *Each thread holds an implicit reference to its copy of a thread-local variable as long as the thread is alive and the ThreadLocal instance is accessible; after a thread goes away, all of its copies of thread-local instances are subject to garbage collection (unless other references to these copies exist).*

If the bundle has been updated and the framework refreshed, surely the stale data object is no longer accessible and should be removed, right? Unfortunately, the Java 5 `ThreadLocal` implementation has a subtle behavior that causes it to hang on to values longer than is strictly necessary.

> **`ThreadLocal` behavior in Java 5**
>
> The Java 5 `ThreadLocal` implementation only clears stale thread-local map entries if `set()` or `remove()` is called on *another* `ThreadLocal` for the *same thread*. In the worst case, even this isn't guaranteed to purge all stale thread-local map entries.

As you'll soon see, missing the `remove()` call in `stop()` means that the data object is kept alive indefinitely because you don't use any other `ThreadLocals` in the example. This in turn keeps your class loader alive. Let's see this leak in action:

```
$ cd chapter08/memory-leaks

$ ant dist

$ java -verbose:gc -jar launcher.jar bundles
```

```
[GC 4416K->318K(15872K), 0.0066670 secs]
[GC 926K->327K(15872K), 0.0040134 secs]
[Full GC 327K->327K(15872K), 0.2674688 secs]
Bundle: org.foo.shell.tty started with bundle id 3
->
```

Try updating the leaky bundle:

```
-> update 1
```

Here, 1 is the ID of the leaky bundle, as reported by the `bundles` command. You should see the heap expand each time you call `update`:

```
[GC 17857K->16753K(32324K), 0.0376856 secs]
[Full GC 16753K->16750K(32324K), 0.0329633 secs]
```

If you continue to update the bundle, you'll eventually get an `OutOfMemoryError`:

```
org.osgi.framework.BundleException:
  Activator start error in bundle org.foo.leaky [1].
...
Caused by: java.lang.OutOfMemoryError: Java heap space
...
Unable to execute: update 1
```

Let's try to analyze this memory leak. Restart the framework with heap dumps enabled:

```
$ java -XX:+HeapDumpOnOutOfMemoryError -jar launcher.jar bundles
```

Repeatedly update the leaky bundle until the `OutOfMemoryError` occurs:

```
java.lang.OutOfMemoryError: Java heap space
Dumping heap to java_pid1916.hprof ...
Heap dump file created [238744986 bytes in 16.578 secs]
```

You should now have a heap-dump file in your current working directory. Plenty of open-source tools work with heap dumps; in this case, you'll use the Eclipse Memory Analyzer (MAT, http://eclipse.org/mat/). This tool provides a graphical view of the heap and several useful reports to quickly identify potential leaks. Let's see how it copes with an OSGi application. Figure 8.14 shows the leak suspect report for the captured heap dump.

Notice how it correctly identifies the `ThreadLocal` as the root of the leak. But can it tell you what application code was responsible? To find out, click the Details link at the bottom. Doing so opens a detailed page about the `ThreadLocal`, including the various thread stacks that created the instances (see figure 8.15). It clearly shows the bundle activator `start()` method is the one responsible for creating all these instances. With your knowledge of the OSGi lifecycle, you can infer that the problem is in the activator `stop()` method.

To solve this leak, all you need to do is go back to the bundle activator and add a call to `remove()` the `ThreadLocal` in the `stop()` method. This forces the underlying data object to be cleared and means the bundle's class loader can be collected on each update/refresh. You should now be able to continually update the bundle without incurring an `OutOfMemoryError`.

Leak Suspects

System Overview

▾ Leaks

▾ Overview

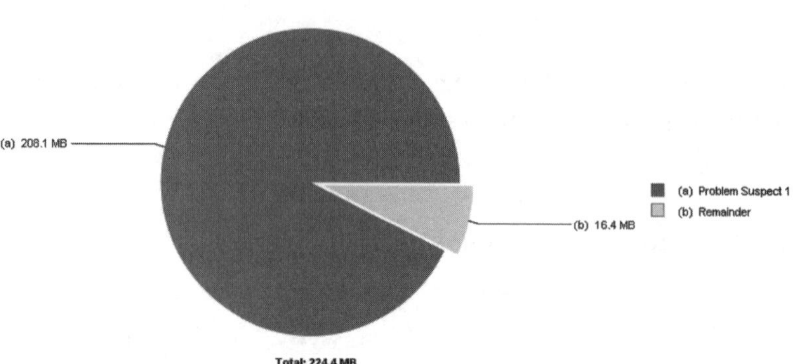

▾ Problem Suspect 1

The thread **java.lang.Thread @ 0x2a69a398 Thread-1** keeps local variables with total size **218,156,632 (92.70%)** bytes.

The memory is accumulated in one instance of **"java.lang.ThreadLocal$ThreadLocalMap$Entry[]"** loaded by **"<system class loader>"**.

The stacktrace of this Thread is available. See stacktrace.

Keywords
java.lang.ThreadLocal$ThreadLocalMap$Entry[]

Details »

Figure 8.14 Leak suspects reported by the Eclipse Memory Analyzer

▾ **Thread Stack**

```
Thread-1
  at java.lang.AbstractStringBuilder.<init>(I)V (Unknown Source)
  at java.lang.StringBuffer.<init>(I)V (Unknown Source)
  at org.foo.leaky.Activator$Data.<init>()V (Activator.java:53)
  at org.foo.leaky.Activator$1.initialValue()Ljava/lang/Object; (Activator.java:71)
  at java.lang.ThreadLocal.setInitialValue()Ljava/lang/Object; (Unknown Source)
  at java.lang.ThreadLocal.get()Ljava/lang/Object; (Unknown Source)
  at org.foo.leaky.Activator.start(Lorg/osgi/framework/BundleContext;)V (Activator.java:76)
  at org.apache.felix.framework.util.SecureAction.startActivator(Lorg/osgi/framework/BundleActivator;Lorg/osgi/framework/
  at org.apache.felix.framework.Felix.activateBundle(Lorg/apache/felix/framework/BundleImpl;Z)V (Felix.java:1700)
  at org.apache.felix.framework.Felix.startBundle(Lorg/apache/felix/framework/BundleImpl;I)V (Felix.java:1622)
  at org.apache.felix.framework.Felix.updateBundle(Lorg/apache/felix/framework/BundleImpl;Ljava/io/InputStream;)V (Felix.
  at org.apache.felix.framework.BundleImpl.update(Ljava/io/InputStream;)V (BundleImpl.java:933)
  at org.apache.felix.framework.BundleImpl.update()V (BundleImpl.java:920)
  at org.foo.shell.commands.UpdateCommand.exec(Ljava/lang/String;Ljava/io/PrintStream;Ljava/io/PrintStream;)V (UpdateComm
  at org.foo.shell.commands.ExecuteCommand.exec(Ljava/lang/String;Ljava/io/PrintStream;Ljava/io/PrintStream;)V (ExecuteCc
  at org.foo.shell.commands.HistoryDecorator.exec(Ljava/lang/String;Ljava/io/PrintStream;Ljava/io/PrintStream;)V (History
  at org.foo.shell.Shell.run()V (Shell.java:39)
  at java.lang.Thread.run()V (Unknown Source)
```

Table Of Contents **Created by** Eclipse Memory Analyzer

Figure 8.15 Leaking thread stack identified by the Eclipse Memory Analyzer

This example shows that analyzing heap dumps from OSGi applications is similar to analyzing dumps from everyday Java applications. You've also seen that misbehaving code can cause memory leaks in OSGi as with any other container. But are any leaks specific to OSGi?

8.4 Dangling services

In addition to the everyday leaks Java developers have to be careful of, the OSGi framework introduces a new form of memory leak to trap the unwary: dangling services. But what exactly do we mean by *dangling*?

In section 4.3.1, we discussed why it's a bad idea to access a service instance once and store it in a field: you don't know when this service is unregistered by the providing bundle. Your bundle continues to keep a strong reference to the original service instance and its entire graph of references long after the providing bundle has been updated or uninstalled (see figure 8.16). You're also keeping alive the class loaders of any classes used by this instance. As with many memory leaks, you can end up with a significant amount of space being kept alive by a single field. Clearing this field frees everything and allows your application to continue running.

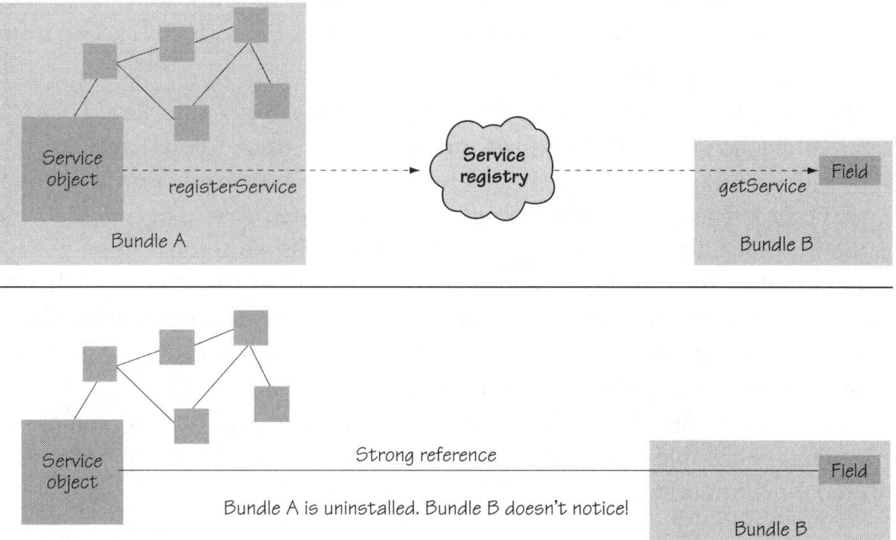

Figure 8.16 Classic dangling service

How do you find this one field in the metaphorical haystack that is your application?

8.4.1 Finding a dangling service

In an ideal world, your application won't resemble a haystack! Often, you'll have some idea where the leak may be, because of the bundles involved. For example, if bundle A leaks when it's updated, and you know that it's used only by bundles X and Y, you can concentrate your search on those three bundles. This is another benefit of modularity: by enforcing module boundaries and interacting indirectly via the service registry, you reduce the contact points between modules. You no longer have to read through or instrument the entire code base for potential references, because different concerns are kept separate from one another. But regardless of how much code you have to look through, you can use a couple of techniques to narrow the search, ranging from high-level queries to low-level monitoring.

QUERYING THE FRAMEWORK

You can perform high-level monitoring by using facilities built into the OSGi framework to track service use. The `Bundle` API has a method called `getServicesInUse()` to tell you which services the OSGi framework believes a given bundle is actively using at any given time. Remember from chapter 4 that this is done by tracking calls to `getService()` and `ungetService()`. Unfortunately, many developers and even some service-based frameworks don't call `ungetService()` when they're done with a service, which can lead you to think there is a leak where there isn't one. This approach also doesn't detect when a direct reference to the service escapes from the bundle into some long-lived field. You can also use the `getUsingBundles()` method from the `ServiceReference` API to perform a reverse check and find out which bundles are using a given service, but this too doesn't account for incorrectly cached instances.

MONITORING WITH JVMTI

Low-level monitoring is possible using the JVM Tools Interface (JVMTI, http://java.sun.com/javase/6/docs/platform/jvmti/jvmti.html). JVMTI is a native API that provides several ways to interrogate, intercept, and introspect aspects of the JVM such as the Java heap, locks, and threads. There are open source agents that can analyze the heap to find leak candidates. It should be possible to take these generic agents and develop them further to add knowledge about OSGi resources, so they can watch for references to OSGi service instances on the Java heap and determine which bundle is responsible for holding on to them. A recent example of this is the OSGi inspector agent (http://wiki.github.com/mirkojahn/OSGi-Inspector/).

Just as you saw when debugging, it's one thing to find out why something is happening; being able to do something about it (and, in this case, protect against it) is even more important.

8.4.2 Protecting against dangling services

The simplest way to protect against dangling services is to let a component framework such as Declarative Services manage services for you. Component frameworks are discussed in detail in chapters 11 and 12; for now, you can think of them as watchful parents that protect their children from the harsh realities of the world. But even component frameworks may not be able to help against rogue clients that stubbornly refuse to relinquish references to your service. You somehow need to give these bundles a reference that you can clear yourself, without requiring their cooperation.

One way to do this is by using a delegating service proxy. A *delegating service proxy* is a thin wrapper that implements the same set of interfaces as the original service. It contains a single reference to the real service implementation that can be set and cleared by methods only visible to your registering bundle. By registering this delegating proxy with the service registry instead of the real service implementation, you stay in control. Because client bundles are unaware of the internal indirection, they can't accidentally keep a reference to the underlying service. As figure 8.17 shows, you can decide to sever the link at any time.

Notice that there's still a small leak, because the rogue client maintains a strong reference to the service proxy. But this should be much smaller than the graph of objects and classes referenced by the actual service implementation; otherwise, you don't gain much by using a proxy.

You can see an example of a service proxy in the code examples:

```
$ cd chapter08/dangling-services

$ ant dist

$ java -jar launcher.jar bundles
<3> thread="main", bundle=2 : logging ON
->
```

The log client is taken from the `broken_lookup_field` service example from chapter 4. It caches the log service instance in a field and repeatedly calls it every few seconds:

```
<3> thread="LogService Tester", bundle=2 : ping
```

Try stopping the log service by going to the OSGi console and typing

```
-> stop 1
<3> thread="Thread-1", bundle=2 : logging OFF
```

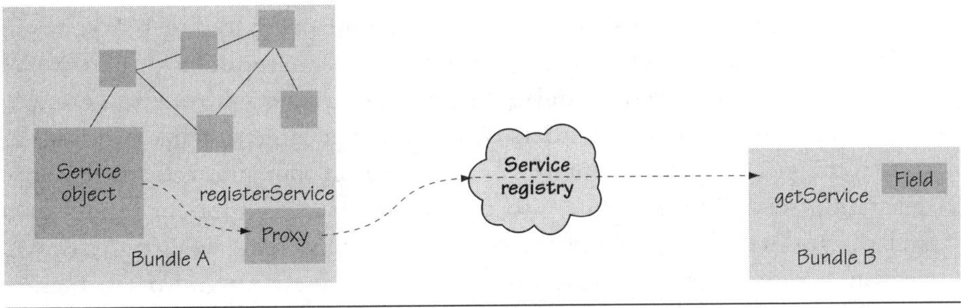

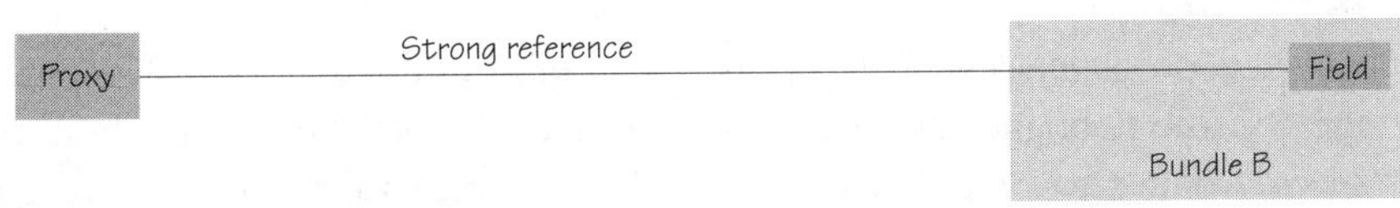

Figure 8.17 Delegating service proxy

where 1 is the ID of the log service bundle, as reported by the bundles command. You should see an exception when the log client next calls the service:

```
Exception in thread "LogService Tester"
  java.lang.IllegalStateException: LogService has been deactivated
```

Your log service proxy has detected that the underlying logger is no longer available and has thrown an IllegalStateException back to the client. In an ideal world, this would make the client take action and clean up after itself. If it doesn't, the only leak is the service proxy. But what does the service proxy look like? The following listing shows the sample implementation.

Listing 8.7 Delegating service proxy

```
Proxy.newProxyInstance(
  LogService.class.getClassLoader(),
  new Class[] { LogService.class },
  new InvocationHandler() {
    @Override
    public Object invoke(Object proxy, Method method, Object[] args)
      throws Throwable {
      LogService cachedService = (LogService) loggerMap.get(bundle);
      if (cachedService != null) {
        return method.invoke(cachedService, args);
      }
      throw new IllegalStateException("LogService has been deactivated");
    }
  });
```

You use JDK reflection to create the proxy, because this approach is less error-prone than creating a new implementation by hand and delegating each method individually. The proxy is defined in the same space as the LogService class and provides the same API. Active logger instances are tracked with an internal shared map. You use reflection to delegate method calls to active loggers and throw exceptions for inactive loggers.

You could manually create delegating service proxies up front, but doing so would only make sense for small numbers of services. For large systems, you want a generic service that accepts a set of interfaces at execution time and returns the appropriate delegating service proxy. Note also that some OSGi component frameworks, which we'll discuss in chapters 11 and 12, will automatically create delegating service proxies for you. There's some overhead involved in both memory and performance, so you may only want to consider using a delegating service proxy only when you don't trust client bundles to do the right thing or your service uses so many resources that even a single leak could be dangerous.

8.5 Summary

We started this chapter with a practical guide to debugging OSGi applications using the console debugger (jdb) and an advanced IDE (Eclipse). We then moved on to specific issues you may encounter while working with OSGi, including seven class-loading problems:

- `ClassNotFoundException`
- `NoClassDefFoundError`
- `ClassCastException`
- Missing `uses` constraints
- Mismatched `uses` constraints
- `Class.forName` issues
- TCCL loading issues

This was followed by a couple of related resource discussions:

- Memory/resource leaks
- Dangling OSGi services

The next couple of chapters should be a welcome break from all this low-level debugging and testing. Look out for fresh, high-level concepts as we discuss managing OSGi bundles and applications!

9 Managing bundles

This chapter covers

- Versioning packages and bundles in a meaningful way
- Configuring bundles using the Configuration Admin Service
- Describing bundle configuration data using the Metatype Service
- Saving bundle settings using the Preferences Service
- Deferring bundle startup using lazy activation

We've covered a lot of ground so far. You know how to use modularity to improve the cohesiveness of your application code; how to use lifecycles to bring dynamic installations and updates to application environments; and how to use services to decouple your modules via interface-based programming techniques. You've also learned approaches and techniques for creating, testing, and debugging bundles. In this chapter and the next, we'll move our focus away from coding bundles to issues of managing bundles and OSGi-based applications.

With the OSGi Service Platform, your deployed set of bundles becomes your application's configuration. As such, the task of managing bundles is one of the most important skills you'll need to fully master OSGi. In this chapter, we'll explore different aspects of bundle management, including the following:

- Evolving a bundle using versioning policies
- Managing a bundle's configuration data
- Configuring a bundle's activation policy

With these skills, you'll be better equipped to deploy and manage bundles in various application configurations. Let's start by looking at versioning.

9.1 Versioning packages and bundles

From what you've learned so far, you know that versioning is a core part of any OSGi application. Both bundles and their exported packages have versions. When the framework resolves bundle dependencies, it takes these versions into account. In this section, we'll discuss the recommended policy for versioning these artifacts and discuss advantages and disadvantages of different versioning strategies. To get things started, let's provide some motivation for OSGi's approach to versioning.

9.1.1 Meaningful versioning

In traditional Java programming, versioning is an afterthought. OSGi, on the other hand, treats versioning as a first-class citizen, which makes it easier to handle versioning in a meaningful way. This emphasis on versioning means that a proper versioning strategy is important for maintaining application consistency.

You must be thinking, "Hey! I already version my JAR files!" Tools like Maven and Ivy let you specify versions for JAR files and declare dependencies on those versions. These tools work with module-level dependencies, which we talked about in chapters 2 and 5. You know that module-level dependencies are brittle when it comes to expressing fine-grained dependencies between units of code.

Likewise, applying versions only at the module level has some drawbacks. Such a model is too simple and forces all packages in a JAR file to be versioned in lockstep with the other packages. Let's look at some of these issues in more detail.

MODULE VERSIONING IS OPAQUE

Consider a case where you bundle related packages together and assign a version number to the resulting JAR file. Later, you may need to alter some code in one of the contained packages; such a change may be the result of a bug fix or a change to the API contract. This new JAR file needs a new version number associated with it.

With a single version number for all the packages, it's left to upstream users of the JAR file to decide whether the change warrants their making the update. Because the only information they have is the module-level version-number change, it's often a stab in the dark as to whether the updated functionality is required for their application. Upstream users don't typically use all the functionality provided by a JAR file and depend on only a subset of it. Depending on which subset they use, it's possible that nothing of importance has changed for them.

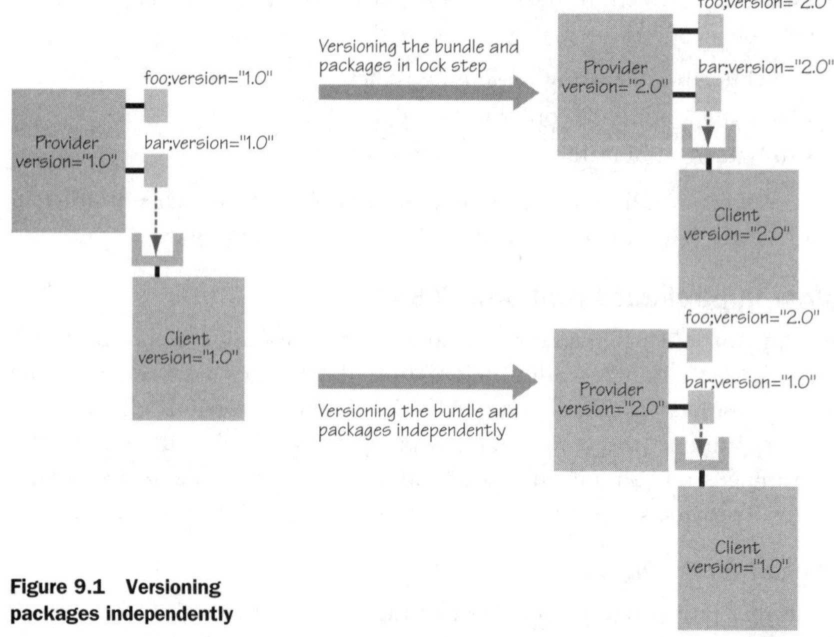

Figure 9.1 Versioning packages independently

A counterargument is that if the bundle is highly cohesive, it makes no sense to update a single package without its siblings. Although this is true, it's not uncommon for JAR files to be less than optimally cohesive. OSGi already caters to this situation with `uses` constraints, which we introduced in chapter 2. These constraints ensure that the cohesiveness of packages is maintained by capturing internal package dependencies. This means upstream users aren't forced to depend on anything more than the API-level contract of the exported packages.

Luckily, in OSGi, you can version your packages either independently or in lock-step with the bundle, as shown in figure 9.1. The OSGi approach of package-level versioning and dependencies leads to less churn in the development lifecycle. Less churn implies less risk, because existing modules are better understood than updated modules, which may introduce unexpected behavior into a complex system. This concept is extremely powerful and removes a lot of the pain from assembling applications out of independent JAR files, because you can make better-informed decisions about when and what to update.

MULTIPLE VERSIONS IN THE SAME JVM

Package-level versioning is also helpful when it comes to running different versions side by side. Java doesn't explicitly support this by default, but OSGi does. In many cases, this seemingly unimportant feature frees you from worrying about backward compatibility or changes to artifacts outside your control. Your bundles can continue to use the versions of packages with which they're compatible, because your entire application no longer has to agree on a single version to place on the class path.

There's a price to pay for this flexibility. Versioning must be done as a core task throughout the development process, not as an afterthought. Versioning packages and maintaining a versioning policy is a lot of work. One easy way to reduce the amount of work is to have less to version. In OSGi, you have the option to not expose the implementation packages of a bundle (assuming that no other bundle needs them). As a consequence, the simplest option you have is to not export packages to avoid the need to version them. When you need to export packages, then you need to version them. Let's look more closely at how you can implement a versioning policy for packages in OSGi.

9.1.2 Package versioning

Let's consider a package named `org.foo` with a version of `1.0.0.r4711` provided by a bundle called `foo` that is itself at version `1.0.0`. Its manifest looks like this:

```
Bundle-ManifestVersion: 2
Bundle-SymbolicName: foo
Bundle-Version: 1.0.0
Export-Package: org.foo;version:="1.0.0.r4711"
```

As we mentioned previously, the OSGi specification doesn't define a versioning policy, which means you can use any scheme that makes sense to you. But the OSGi specification does recommend the following policy behind version-number component changes:

- *Major number change*—Signifies an incompatible update
- *Minor number change*—Signifies a backward-compatible update
- *Micro number change*—Signifies an internal update (such as a bug fix or performance improvement)
- *Qualifier change*—Signifies a trivial internal change (such as line-number refactoring)

This is a common version compatibility policy. Why? Versions are important for the consumer to specify what's needed, and this policy makes it possible to easily express a floor and a ceiling version in between which all versions are acceptable. As you saw in chapter 2, a version range is expressed as a pair of version numbers inside braces or parentheses. This follows mathematical interval notation, where a square brace signifies an inclusive value and a parenthesis signifies an exclusive value. As an example, consider a typical definition of a package import:

```
Import-Package: org.foo;version:="[1.0,2.0)"
```

The `org.foo` package is imported from version `1.0.0` up to, but excluding, `2.0.0`. This makes sense if the recommended version policy is being used, because it includes all backward-compatible versions and excludes all non-backward-compatible versions, which a change in the major number would signify. Being able to specify such ranges is useful because the import can be satisfied by a wider range of exports. This scheme works only if producers and consumers operate with a shared understanding of the kind of compatibility being expressed by a given version number.

DOWNSIDES AND PITFALLS

The recommended OSGi versioning policy sounds good, and it's been used successfully by many projects. But new users should still take care due to a subtlety regarding the use of Java interfaces, which is related to whether an interface is being used or implemented.

The difference seems trivial, but it becomes important in the context of versioning. Consider the following `1.0.0` version of the `Foo` interface:

```
public interface Foo {
  Bar getBar();
}
```

What happens if you change this simple interface? For example, suppose you add a method:

```
public interface Foo {
  Bar getBar();
  void setBar();
}
```

The question to ponder is whether this change should cause a major or minor version-number increase. It depends on whether the interface is intended to be implemented or used by the consumer. In the former case, the addition of the method is a binary-incompatible change to the interface and should cause the major version number to increase to 2.0.0. In the latter case, increasing the minor version number to 1.1.0 is sufficient because method addition is a backward-compatible update to the interface. Figure 9.2 shows the situation.

If you're in control of all the bundles, you can define a policy to ensure that method addition always causes a change in the major version number, which allows all consumers of a package to use a `[1.0,2.0)` version range. In reality, you're unlikely to be in control of all the bundles. Furthermore, such a drastic policy would limit the reusability of your bundles, because consumers only using the interfaces would have no way to express that they're fine with an added method.

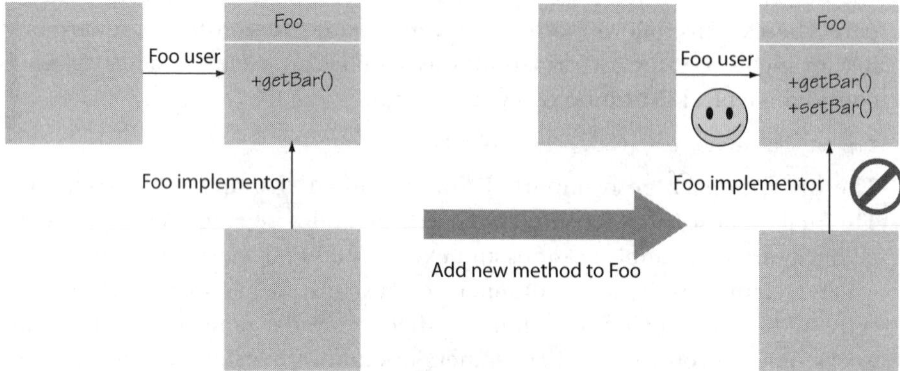

Figure 9.2 Impact on versioning between using and implementing the interface

A refined approach

The best strategy devised so far is to shift the burden to the consumer. This is pretty straightforward and requires implementers to specify a version range of `[1.0,1.1)`, while users can specify the broader version range of `[1.0,2.0)` as shown in the following figure.

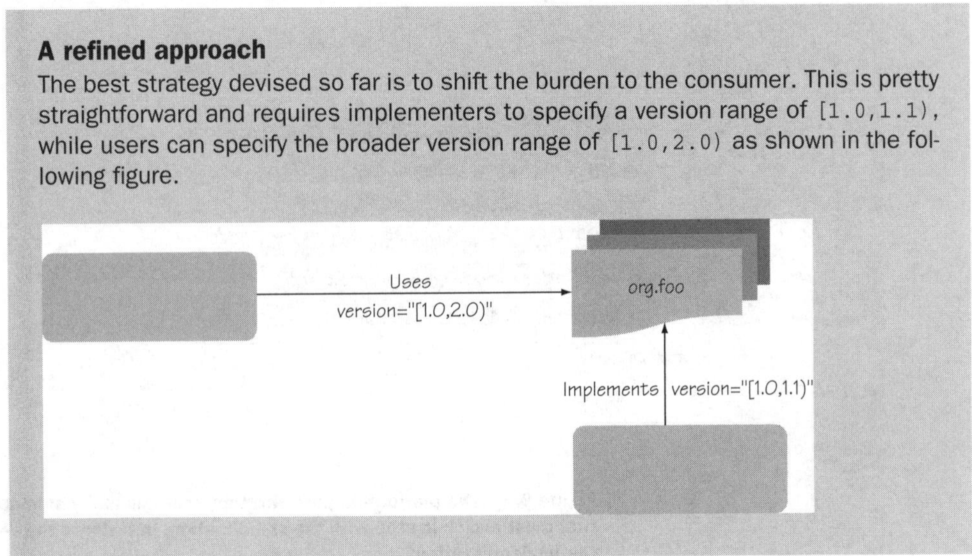

Another important requirement for versioning is consistency. You don't want to define your versioning policy on a bundle-by-bundle basis. So, whether you follow the recommended approach or not, you should at least try to use the same policy globally.

This gives you a fairly good understanding of versioning policy for packages, but what about versioning bundles? We'll explore bundle-versioning policies next.

9.1.3 Bundle versioning

Bundles and packages are related through containment: bundles contain packages. Because both bundles and packages have version numbers, what is the relationship between them? You need to adopt a versioning policy to define this relationship. Let's look at that in more detail.

In the simple case, a bundle may contain several related implementation packages, all with the same version number. Here it's advisable to make the bundle version mirror the version of the implementation packages. When you're dealing with a bundle containing packages of different versions, the most consistent versioning policy is to increment the bundle version based on the highest change of a package inside it. For example, if any package has a major number increase, the major number of the bundle should increase as well; the same is true if the highest change was to a minor or micro portion of the version. With this policy, it's possible to judge the impact of an updated bundle based on its version number. Unfortunately, this may not always make sense, especially if the versions of the individual packages represent a well-known product version.

For example, let's assume you want to create a bundle for the core API of the OSGi framework. In this case, you have several independently versioned packages, but the

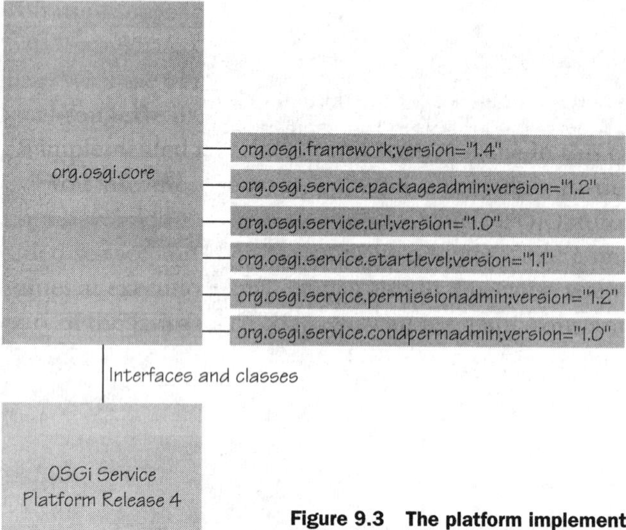

Figure 9.3 The platform implementation contains many subpackages that must evolve in step with the specification, but what's the version of the implementation?

collection of packages in this bundle has a version number based on the OSGi specification. Figure 9.3 graphically depicts this situation.

Now, the question is, what version should you assign to the `org.osgi.core` bundle? There's no single answer. You could increase the major number on every major release of the OSGi specification, but this would indicate a binary-incompatible change in at least one of the provided packages, which clearly isn't the case (as indicated by the individual package versions). Another approach is to keep the version number at 1, indicating that no binary-incompatible change has happened. You would then need to use the minor number to match the release number of the specification. Because the OSGi specification has also had minor number releases (such as 4.1), you would then need to use the micro number for the minor number of the specification.

Unfortunately, this wouldn't be exactly what you want either, because there have been updates in the minor numbers of the contained packages. To make matters worse, if you ever needed to update the bundle for a different reason (like a packaging mistake), then you'd need to use the qualifier to express that the bundle had changed. In the specific case of the core OSGi specification, the OSGi Alliance makes API JAR files available based on the version of the specification (4.1.0, 4.2.0, and so on).

Although there's no single policy you can prescribe for versioning bundles, at a minimum you should try to reflect incompatible changes at the package level in your bundle version number. The management task to take away from this section is that versioning is important and shouldn't be left as an afterthought. If done correctly, the OSGi concept of versioning is extremely powerful and removes a lot of the pain from assembling applications. To get it right, you need to define a versioning policy and enforce it on all your bundles and exported packages.

With versioning covered, let's look into another important management task: configuring your bundles.

9.2 Configuring bundles

To make your bundles more reusable, it's a good idea to introduce configuration properties to control their behavior. Recall from chapter 3, when we introduced the shell example, that you used configuration properties to alter its behavior, such as the port on which it listened for client connections. Configuring bundles is an important aspect of using them, so it would be beneficial if there was a standard way of managing this. At a minimum, it would be nice to have the following:

- A common way to set the configuration information for a given bundle
- A common format for specifying the type of configuration data a given bundle expects
- A common mechanism for bundles to safely store bundle- and user-related configuration information

Fortunately, the OSGi Alliance defines the following three compendium specifications to help you address these issues:

- *Configuration Admin Service*—Manages key/value pair configuration properties for bundles
- *Metatype Service*—Allows bundles to describes their configuration properties
- *Preferences Service*—Provides a place to store bundle- and user-related information

Even with these specifications to help you, adding bundle configurations to the mix creates more issues for you to worry about. Configuration data becomes yet another artifact to manage. For example, you have to make sure to consider this data when you change the bundles in your systems, because configuration data generally isn't compatible across bundles or even bundle versions. The data is subject to deployment and provisioning just like bundles.

In the remainder of this section, we'll introduce you to these configuration-related services and show you how you can manage configurations. We'll start with the Configuration Admin Service.

9.2.1 Configuration Admin Service

The Configuration Admin Service is an important piece of the deployment of the OSGi Service Platform. It allows you to set the configuration information of deployed bundles. You use this service to set a bundle's configuration data, and it ensures that the bundle receives the data when it becomes active.

What happens is pretty simple. Consider the scenario in figure 9.4, where a bundle needs an integer `port` number and a Boolean `secure` property. In this case, you provide these values to the Configuration Admin Service, and it provides these values to the bundle when it's activated. Using this approach, bundles have a simple, standard way of obtaining configuration data.

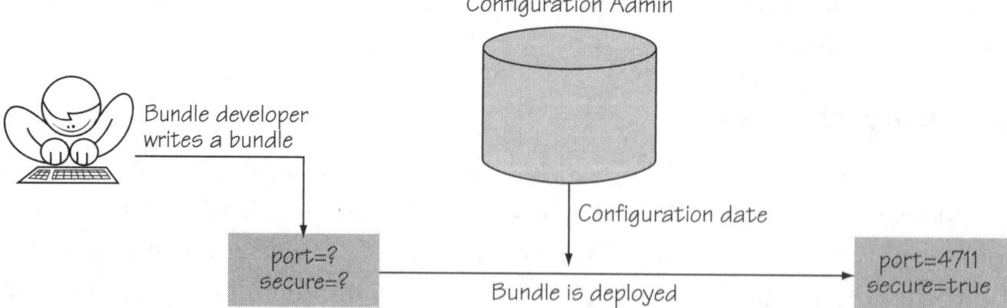

Figure 9.4 An administrator configures a bundle in the framework by interacting with the Configuration Admin Service. This approach decouples the administrator from having to know the internal workings of the bundle using the configuration data.

How does this work? The Configuration Admin Service maintains a database of `Configuration` objects, each of which has an associated set of name-value pair properties. The Configuration Admin Service follows the whiteboard pattern and monitors the service registry for two different managed services: `ManagedService` and `ManagedServiceFactory`. If you have a bundle that needs configuration data, it must register one of these two services defined in the Configuration Admin specification. The difference between these two is that a `ManagedService` accepts one configuration to configure a single service, whereas a `ManagedServiceFactory` accepts any number of configurations and configures a different service instance for each configuration; figure 9.5 illustrates this difference.

When you're registering one of these managed services, you need to attach a `service.pid` (service persistent identity) service property to it. Each managed `Configuration` object also has a `service.pid` associated with it, which the Configuration Admin Service uses as a key to match configuration data to the bundle needing it.

You may have noticed you're dealing with two conceptually different layers when using the Configuration Admin Service. On one layer, you have a published `ManagedService` or `ManagedServiceFactory` service. On the other layer, you have a bundle and the services it provides that you want to configure. The Configuration Admin Service

What is a PID?

In a nutshell, you can associate a persistent identity, or PID, with each registered service by specifying it in the service property dictionary when you register its managed service. If you specify a `service.pid` property, it must be unique for each service. Its purpose is to uniquely and persistently identify a given service, which allows the Configuration Admin Service to use it as a primary key for bundles needing configuration data. This means the Configuration Admin Service requires the use of a PID with `ManagedService` and `ManagedServiceFactory` service registrations. As a convention, PIDs starting with a bundle identifier and a dot are reserved for the bundle associated with that identifier. For example, the PID `42.4711` belongs to the bundle associated with bundle identifier 42. You're free to use other schemes for your PIDs; just make sure they're unique and persistent across bundle activations.

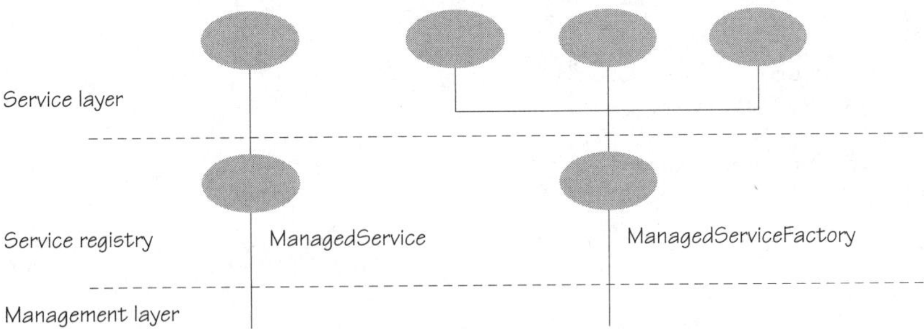

Figure 9.5 Difference between a ManagedService and ManagedServiceFactory

connects these two layers together when it delivers the configuration data. Of course, the reverse is also possible, and the Configuration Admin Service may tell a managed service that its configuration has gone away, which means it needs to stop performing its functionality because it no longer has a valid configuration. This approach gives you a flexible system, where you can configure and control any kind of service or any number of service instances in a common way. Let's look into the details of implementing a managed service next.

IMPLEMENTING A MANAGED SERVICE

Now that you understand the underlying basics of how the Configuration Admin Service works by associating configuration data to managed services, let's explore an example. The actual interface you need to implement looks like the following:

```
public interface ManagedService {
  public void updated(Dictionary properties) throws ConfigurationException;
}
```

The following listing shows an example `ManagedService` implementation.

Listing 9.1 Example of a managed service

```
public class ManagedServiceExample implements ManagedService {
  private EchoServer m_server = null;

  public synchronized void updated(Dictionary properties)
    throws ConfigurationException {
    if (m_server != null) {
      m_server.stop();
      m_server = null;
    }
    if (properties != null) {
      String portString = (String) properties.get("port");
      if (portString == null) {
        throw new ConfigurationException(null, "Property missing");
      }
      int port;
      try {
        port = Integer.parseInt(portString);
      } catch (NumberFormatException ex) {
        throw new ConfigurationException(null, "Not a valid port number");
```

```
        }
        try {
          m_server = new EchoServer(port);
          m_server.start();
        } catch (IOException e) {
          e.printStackTrace();
        }
      }
    }
  ...
}
```

The ManagedService interface has a single updated() method. The argument to this method is a Dictionary containing the configuration properties.

> **Configuration properties**
>
> A configuration dictionary contains a set of properties in a Dictionary object. The name or key of a property must always be a String object and isn't case sensitive during lookup, but preserves the original case. The values should be of type String, Integer, Long, Float, Double, Byte, Short, Character, Boolean, or the primitive counterparts. Furthermore, they can be arrays or collections of them. For arrays and collections, they must only contain values of the same type.

In this example, a simple echo server listens on a port and sends back whatever it receives. Because it's good practice, you make the port configurable. When you receive a new configuration, you first stop the existing server, if there is one. Then, you check whether you received a null configuration, which indicates that the previous configuration was deleted and there is no new one. If this is the case, there's nothing else to do. Otherwise, you get the port number from the dictionary and verify its existence. If it exists, you parse it and create and start a new server for the given port.

A ManagedService is associated with one configuration object. A bundle can register any number of ManagedService services, but each must be identified with its own PID. You should use a ManagedService when configuration is needed for a single entity in the bundle or where the service represents an external entity like a device. Then, for each detected device, a ManagedService is published with a PID related to the identity of the device, such as the address or serial number.

What about cases where you want to configure more than a single entity using the same PID, such as creating multiple instances of the same service with different configurations? You use a ManagedServiceFactory, which we'll explore next.

IMPLEMENTING A MANAGED SERVICE FACTORY

You should use a ManagedServiceFactory when a bundle doesn't have an internal or external entity associated with the configuration information, but can handle more than one configuration at the same time. Remember, with a ManagedService, there's only one configuration: the configuration for the specific PID. With a ManagedServiceFactory, the same factory can have any number of configurations. Using this approach, you can instantiate a service for each configuration associated with your managed service factory, for example. This way, by creating a new configuration for the managed service factory, you create new service instances. A slightly different use case is related to services representing entities that can't be identified directly, such as devices on a USB port that can't provide information about their type. Using a `ManagedServiceFactory`, you can define configuration information for each available device attached to the USB port.

How does this work with respect to the PIDs? The trick in this case is that you register the `ManagedServiceFactory` with a `factory.pid` service property. This way, the Configuration Admin Service can differentiate between a managed service factory and a managed service. For the managed service factory, it assigns a new and unique PID to each created configuration for the factory. The interface to implement looks like this:

```
public interface ManagedServiceFactory{
  public String getName();
  public void updated(String pid, Dictionary properties)
    throws ConfigurationException;
  public void deleted(String pid);
}
```

The following example uses a `ManagedServiceFactory` to configure echo services that read from their configured port and send back whatever they receive along with their name.

Listing 9.2 `ManagedServiceFactory` example

```
public class ManagedServiceFactoryExample implements
  ManagedServiceFactory {
  private final Map<String, EchoServer> m_servers =
    new HashMap<String, EchoServer>();

  public synchronized void deleted(String pid) {
    EchoServer server = m_servers.remove(pid);
    if (server != null) {
      server.stop();
    }
  }

  public String getName() {
    return getClass().getName();
  }

  public synchronized void updated(String pid, Dictionary properties)
    throws ConfigurationException {
    EchoServer server = m_servers.remove(pid);          ❶ Accepts PID
    if (server != null) {
      server.stop();
    }
    if (properties != null) {
      String portString = (String) properties.get("port");
      if (portString == null) {
```

```
        throw new ConfigurationException(null, "Property missing");
      }
      int port;
      try {
        port = Integer.parseInt(portString);
      } catch (NumberFormatException ex) {
        throw new ConfigurationException(null,"Not a valid port number");
      }
      try {
        server = new EchoServer(port);
        server.start();
        m_servers.put(pid, server);          // ❷ Adds server instance to server list
      } catch (IOException e) {
        e.printStackTrace();
      }
    }
  }
  ...
}
```

This example isn't significantly different from the last one. You now implement the `ManagedServiceFactory` interface. Because you're going to manage a number of servers, you introduce a map to hold them. The factory interface defines two new methods, `deleted()` and `getName()`. The latter is a descriptive name for the factory, and the former notifies your factory that a previously updated configuration has gone away, which results in you stopping the corresponding server. Notice that the `updated()` method has a different signature from the `ManagedService` interface ❶. It now accepts a PID, which is necessary because your managed service factory needs to know the PID for the supplied configuration; it correlates the PID with a specific echo server. For each one, you need a PID and a configuration. The rest is similar to what you did for a single server in the `ManagedService` example. The only exception is that now you must add the resulting server instance to your list of servers ❷.

This covers the basics of what you need to do to make your bundles configurable. Now we need to look into how you configure bundles by creating configurations.

CREATING CONFIGURATIONS

It's one thing to make your bundles configurable, but you need some way to specify and set the property values you want to use to configure them. You need to learn how to create and manage configurations; you use the Configuration Admin Service for this. It provides methods to maintain configuration data by means of `Configuration` objects associated with specific configuration targets that can be created, listed, modified, and deleted. The `ConfigurationAdmin` service interface is defined as follows:

```
public interface ConfigurationAdmin{
  public Configuration createFactoryConfiguration(String factoryPid)
    throws IOException;
  public Configuration createFactoryConfiguration(String factoryPid,
    String location) throws IOException;
  public Configuration getConfiguration(String pid, String location)
    throws IOException;
```

```
  public Configuration getConfiguration(String pid) throws IOException;
  public Configuration[] listConfigurations(String filter) throws
    IOException, InvalidSyntaxException;
}
```

Configuration objects are represented by the following interface:

```
public interface Configuration{
  public String getPid();
  public Dictionary getProperties();
  public void update(Dictionary properties) throws IOException;
  public void delete() throws IOException;
  public String getFactoryPid();
  public void update() throws IOException;
  public void setBundleLocation(String location);
  public String getBundleLocation();
}
```

To illustrate how these all fit together, you continue to improve the shell example in the following listing by creating a new command to manage configurations.

Listing 9.3 ConfigurationAdmin service shell command

```
public class ConfigAdminCommand extends BasicCommand {
  public void exec(String args, PrintStream out, PrintStream err)
    throws Exception {
    args=args.trim();
    if (args.startsWith("list")) {
      listConfigurations(args.substring("list".length()).trim(),
        out);
    } else if (args.startsWith("add-cfg")) {
      addConfiguration(args.substring("add-cfg".length()).trim());
    } else if (args.startsWith("remove-cfg")) {
      removeConfiguration(args.substring(
        "remove-cfg".length()).trim());
    } else if (args.startsWith("add-factory-cfg")) {
      addFactoryConfiguration(args.substring("add-factory-
      cfg".length()).trim());
    } else if (args.startsWith("remove-factory-cfg")) {
      removeFactoryConfiguration(args.substring(
        "remove-factory-cfg".length()).trim());
    }
  }
```

In this example, you create a cm command that accepts five different subcommands: list, add-cfg, remove-cfg, add-factory-cfg, and remove-factory-cfg. The code is largely responsible for delegating to private methods to perform the functionality of the subcommands.

The following code shows how cm list lists available configurations.

Listing 9.4 Implementing the cm list subcommand

```
private void listConfigurations(String filter, PrintStream out)
  throws IOException, InvalidSyntaxException {
  Configuration[] configurations = admin().listConfigurations(
```

```
      ((filter.length() == 0) ? null : filter));
    if (configurations != null) {
      for (Configuration configuration : configurations) {
        Dictionary properties = configuration.getProperties();
        for (Enumeration e = properties.keys(); e.hasMoreElements();) {
          Object key = e.nextElement();
          out.println(key + "=" + properties.get(key));
        }
        out.println();
      }
    }
    ...
}
```

You get the `ConfigurationAdmin` service and use its `listConfigurations()` method to get the `Configuration` objects. You can optionally specify an LDAP filter to limit which configurations are returned; specifying no filter results in all configurations. In either case, an array of `Configuration` objects is returned, which are the holders of the actual configuration properties. Then you print the configuration properties, using the `getProperties()` method of the `Configuration` object to retrieve them.

You can use the `add-cfg` subcommand to create new `Configuration` objects. The subcommand accepts the PID of the `ManagedService` and the configuration properties as a whitespace-delimited list of name-value pairs, where the name and value are separated by an equals sign. The implementation is as follows:

```
private void addConfiguration(String args) {
  String pid = args.substring(0, args.indexOf(" ")).trim();
  Configuration conf = admin.getConfiguration(pid, null);
  createConfiguration(args.substring(pid.length()).trim(), pid, conf);
}
```

To create a `Configuration` object, you call `getConfiguration()` on `ConfigurationAdmin`. This method creates the `Configuration` object on the first call and returns the same object on subsequent calls. You initialize the new configuration with a call to the private method `createConfiguration()`, which is defined next.

Listing 9.5 Private method to initialize `Configuration` objects

```
private void createConfiguration(
  String args, String pid, Configuration conf) throws IOException {
  conf.setBundleLocation(null);
  Dictionary dict = conf.getProperties();
  if (dict == null) {
    dict = new Properties();
  }
  StringTokenizer tok = new StringTokenizer(args, " ");
  while (tok.hasMoreTokens()) {
    String[] entry = tok.nextToken().split("=");
    dict.put(entry[0], entry[1]);
  }
  conf.update(dict);
}
```

This sets the `Configuration` object's bundle location to `null`, which means it isn't currently associated with any bundle. You finish initializing the new configuration by getting any existing properties, parsing the specified properties and merging them with existing properties, and finally updating the configuration. Because you handle existing properties, you can use the `add-cfg` subcommand to create and modify configurations.

Configuration and location binding

When you create a `Configuration` object using either `getConfiguration()` or `createFactoryConfiguration()`, it becomes bound to the location of the calling bundle. You can obtain this location via the calling bundle's `getLocation()` method. Location binding is a security feature to ensure that only management bundles can modify configuration data, and other bundles can only modify their own configuration data.

If the bundle location of a configuration for a given PID is set to `null` (as in listing 9.5), the Configuration Admin Service binds the first bundle registering a managed service with the given PID to this configuration. After the bundle location is set, then configurations for the given PID are only delivered to the bundle with that location. When this dynamically bound bundle is subsequently uninstalled, the location is set to `null` again automatically so it can be bound again later.

You can use the `remove-cfg` subcommand to remove `Configuration` objects. The implementation of this subcommand is much simpler:

```
private void removeConfiguration(String pid) {
  Configuration conf = admin.getConfiguration(pid);
  conf.delete();
}
```

The subcommand accepts a PID that you use to get the `Configuration` object from the `ConfigurationAdmin` service. When you have the `Configuration` object, you call `delete()` on it.

The `add-factory-cfg` subcommand creates a `Configuration` object for a managed service factory. It's implemented as follows:

```
private void addFactoryConfiguration(String args) {
  String pid = args.substring(0, args.indexOf(" ")).trim();
  Configuration conf = admin.createFactoryConfiguration(pid, null);
  createConfiguration(args.substring(pid.length()).trim(), pid, conf);
}
```

It accepts the PID of the managed service factory and the configuration properties as a whitespace-delimited list of name-value pairs. It's similar to the `add-cfg` subcommand, except that you use `ConfigurationAdmin.createFactoryConfiguration()` to create a new `Configuration` object for the factory. This always creates a new `Configuration` object for the factory service (unlike `getConfiguration()`, which creates one only the first time for a given PID).

The remove-factory-cfg subcommand allows you to remove a factory configuration. It's implemented as follows:

```
private void removeFactoryConfiguration(String pid) {
  Configuration[] configurations = admin.listConfigurations(
    "(service.pid=" + pid + ")");
  configurations[0].delete();
}
```

The subcommand accepts a PID that you use to find the associated configuration using listConfigurations() with a filter. When you have it, you call delete() on it as before.

To experiment with this new command, go into the chapter09/combined-example/ directory of the companion code. Type ant to build the example and java -jar launcher.jar bundles to execute it. To interact with the shell, use telnet localhost 7070. This example uses the Apache Felix Configuration Admin implementation (http://felix.apache.org/site/apache-felix-configuration-admin-service.html). Here's a session using the cm command:

```
-> cm add-cfg org.foo.managed.service port=6251
-> cm add-factory-cfg org.foo.managed.factory port=6252
-> cm list
service.pid=org.foo.managed.service
port=6251

service.pid=org.foo.managed.factory.89706c08-3902-4f4d-87f5-7da5a504cb94
port=6252
service.factoryPid=org.foo.managed.factory

-> cm remove-cfg org.foo.managed.service
-> cm remove-factory-cfg
[CA]org.foo.managed.factory.89706c08-3902-4f4d-87f5-7da5a504cb94
-> cm list
->
```

This session creates configurations for your managed service and managed service factory. As you should be aware now, the result of these two commands is subtly different. The first directly configures the service associated with the PID, whereas the latter causes a service to be created from the managed service factory. For the combined example, if you go to another operating system shell after performing the first two steps, you can telnet into your configured echo servers using the specified port numbers. Finally, you remove the configurations.

That finishes our quick tour of the Configuration Admin Service. You should now be able to use Configuration Admin to create externally configurable bundles, instantiate services using configurations, and manage configurations. But wait, how do you know what kind of data your configurable bundles accept? All we've said so far is that managed services are configured with simple name-value pairs. Sometimes that may suffice, but often you may want to tell other bundles or entities, such as a user, about the structure of your bundle's configuration data. The Metatype Service, which we'll introduce next, allows you to define your own metatypes and associate them with your bundles and services.

9.2.2 Metatype Service

Assume for a moment that you're deploying a new bundle for the first time into a framework that has your Configuration Admin shell command available. If this new bundle provides some services that are configurable, you can use your shell command to configure it, right? Unfortunately, because this bundle is new to you, you have no idea which properties it accepts, nor which ones are required for it to operate. In this kind of scenario, it would certainly be helpful if the bundle could convey to you what a valid configuration look likes.

The OSGi standard Metatype Service makes this possible. It aggregates *metatypes* (descriptions of types) contributed by bundles and allows others to look up these definitions. Using this service allows you to introspect what a managed service accepts as a valid configuration and also validate configurations against these schema, which are subject to the same update and versioning mechanisms as the bundles that provide them.

As you can see in figure 9.6, there are two ways to provide metatype information about your managed services:

- A bundle can contain XML resources in its OSGI-INF/metatype directory, which are picked-up by the Metatype Service using the extender pattern.
- A managed service can implement a second interface called `MetaTypeProvider`.

If for some reason a bundle does both, only the XML resources are considered, and the `MetaTypeProvider` service is ignored.

From a client perspective, the Metatype Service defines a dynamic typing system for properties. This allows you, for example, to construct reasonable user interfaces dynamically. The service itself provides unified access to the metatype information provided by deployed bundles. A client can request `MetaTypeInformation` associated with a given bundle, which in turn provides a list of `ObjectClassDefinition` objects for this bundle. An object class contains descriptive information and a set of name-value pairs. Here's what this looks like for the example echo server:

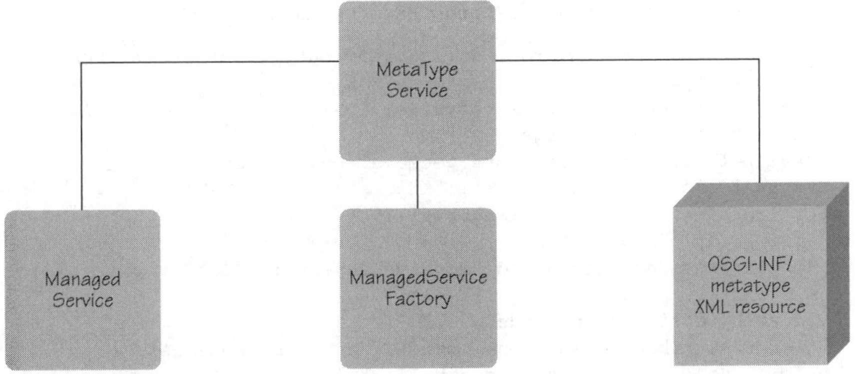

Figure 9.6 Metatype Service overview

```
<?xml version="1.0" encoding="UTF-8"?>
<MetaData xmlns="http://www.osgi.org/xmlns/metatype/v1.0.0">
  <OCD name="EchoServer" id="4.7.1.1" description="Echo Server Config">
    <AD name="port" id="4.7.1.1.1" type="Integer"
     description="The port the Echo Server listens on"/>
  </OCD>
 <Designate pid="org.foo.managed.service">
  <Object ocdref="4.7.1.1"/>
 </Designate>
</MetaData>
```

Don't let this somewhat obtuse XML fool you. It's simple. You first define an `ObjectClassDefinition` (OCD) called `EchoServer`, with a unique identifier of `4.7.1.1` (if you have a matching LDAP/X.500 object class OSGi object identifier (OID), you can use that one; otherwise, use any other reasonably unique name that follows the same grammar as the LDAP/X.500 OID and a human-readable description). You specify an attribute definition (AD) to describe the configuration properties the echo server needs. In this case, there's only one: `port`. Notice the `Designate` element: this is where you make the link between the type (the OCD) and the instance (the PID). In this example, the `EchoServer` description applies to the configurations of managed services with the PID `org.foo.managed.service`.

USING METATYPE INFORMATION

To use metatype information, you use the Metatype Service to look up metatype definitions. The Metatype Service is represented by the following interface:

```
public interface MetaTypeService {
    public MetaTypeInformation getMetaTypeInformation(Bundle bundle);
}
```

Using the discovered metatype information, you can generate user interfaces or validate configurations, for example. To demonstrate how to use the Metatype Service, let's add a `type` command to the shell to display metatype information, as follows.

Listing 9.6 Metatype Service shell command example

```
public class MetaDataCommand extends BasicCommand {

  public void exec(String args, PrintStream out, PrintStream err)
    throws Exception {
    MetaTypeService mts = getMetaTypeService();
    Bundle b = getBundle(args);
    MetaTypeInformation mti = mts.getMetaTypeInformation(b);
    String[] pids = mti.getPids();
    for (int i = 0; i < pids.length; i++) {
      out.println(pids[i]);
      ObjectClassDefinition ocd = mti.getObjectClassDefinition(
        pids[i], null);
      AttributeDefinition[] ads = ocd
        .getAttributeDefinitions(ObjectClassDefinition.ALL);
      for (int j = 0; j < ads.length; j++) {
        out.println("\tOCD=" + ocd.getName());
```

```
            out.println("\t\tAD=" + ads[j].getName() + " - " +
              ads[j].getDescription());
          }
        }
      }
    
      private MetaTypeService getMetaTypeService() {...}
    }
```

The command is simple: you ask the `MetaTypeService` if a specified bundle has `MetaTypeInformation` objects associated with it. The `type` command accepts a bundle identifier as an argument. You get the `MetaTypeService` and retrieve the `Bundle` object associated with the specified bundle identifier. You invoke the `getMetaTypeInformation()` method to retrieve the associated metatype information. If there is metatype information, you get the PIDs; and for each PID, you get the object class definition. Likewise, for each object class definition, you get the `AttributeDefinitions` and print their names and descriptions. You can now use this command to get a list of all known PIDs and their respective properties for any given bundle identifier.

To run this example, go back into the chapter09/combined-example/ directory of the companion code. If you haven't already done so, type `ant` to build the example and `java -jar launcher.jar bundles` to execute it. To interact with the shell, use `telnet localhost 7070`. This example uses the Apache Felix Metatype implementation (http://felix.apache.org/site/apache-felix-metatype-service.html). Here's a session using the `type` command:

```
-> bundles
...
[   2] [    ACTIVE] managed.service
                    Location: file:bundles/managed.service-2.0.jar
                    Symbolic Name: org.foo.managed.service
...
-> type 2
org.foo.managed.service
    OCD=EchoServer
       AD=port - The port the Echo Server listens on
->
```

All you need to do is execute the `type` command with the bundle identifier of a bundle providing metadata, and you get a description of what kind of properties any associated PIDs can understand. This makes it a little easier to properly configure arbitrary services.

Where are we now? You've learned how to configure bundles and provide metatype information about configuration properties. This combination allows you to create externally and generically configurable applications. What more do you need? Not all configuration information is intended to be externally managed; for example, most preference settings in an application fall in this category. Where should a bundle store such configuration information? The OSGi Preferences Service can help you here; let's look at how it works next.

9.2.3 Preferences Service

In many cases, applications need to store preferences and settings persistently. Of course, this chapter is about managing bundles, and, technically, dealing with preference settings isn't really a management activity. Still, we include it here because it's related to configuration data in general, and this gives us an opportunity to present another standard OSGi Compendium service.

The OSGi Preferences Service gives bundles a mechanism to persistently store data. You may recall from chapter 3 that a bundle already has a private file system area, which it can access via `BundleContext.getDataFile()`. You could use this mechanism to store preference settings, but the Preferences Service has several advantages:

- It defines a standard way to handle such data.
- It supports a hierarchical system and per-user settings.
- It doesn't require a file system.
- It can abstract access to the underlying operating system's settings mechanism, if one exists.

The Preferences Service provides simple, lightweight access to stored data. It doesn't define a general database service but is optimized to deliver stored information when needed. It will, for example, return defaults instead of throwing exceptions when the back-end store isn't available.

The Preferences Service data model is a multirooted hierarchy of nodes: a *system root* node exists for system settings, and you can create any number of named *user root* nodes for user settings. Each one of these root nodes is the root of a tree of `Preferences` objects. A `Preferences` object has a name, a single parent node (except for a root node, which has no parent), and zero or more child nodes. It's possible to navigate a tree either by walking from one node to its parent or children or by addressing nodes directly via a relative or absolute path. This is possible using the node names separated with the / character, much like file system paths. Figure 9.7 shows a conceptual picture of such trees.

Each `Preferences` object has a set of key/value pairs, called *properties*. The *key* is a case-sensitive string that lives in a separate namespace from that of the child nodes, which means a node can have a property with the same key as one of its children. The

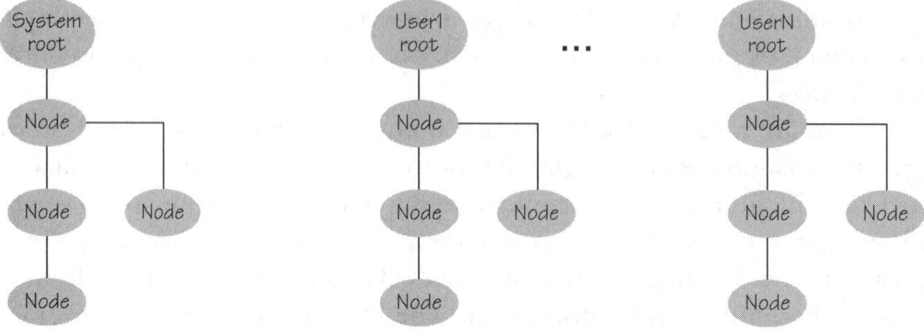

Figure 9.7 System and user-preferences trees

value must always be able to be stored and retrieved as a string. Therefore, it must be possible to encode/decode all values into/from strings. A number of methods are available to store and retrieve values as primitive types.

Preferences are per bundle

The preferences saved by one bundle are completely distinct from the preferences saved by another bundle. The Preferences Service doesn't provide a mechanism for one bundle to access another bundle's preferences storage. If this is needed, you must obtain a reference to the source bundle's preferences in another way, such as directly passing a reference to the other bundle.

Using the Preferences Service is straightforward. It's represented by the following simple interface:

```
public interface PreferencesService {
  Preferences getSystemPreferences();
  Preferences getUserPreferences(String name);
  String[] getUsers();
}
```

The `getSystemPreferences()` method provides access to the system preferences root, whereas the `getUserPreferences()` method provides access to a given user's preferences root. You can use the `getUsers()` method to enumerate all usernames that have stored preferences.

When you have a node, you can navigate the preference tree using the `childrenNames()`, `parent()`, and `node()` methods on the returned `Preferences` node. For setting values, the `Preferences` interface offers some simple methods to store key/value pairs:

```
public void put(String key, String value);
public void putInt(String key, int value);
public void putLong(String key, long value);
public void putBoolean(String key, boolean value);
public void putFloat(String key, float value);
public void putDouble(String key, double value);
public void putByteArray(String key, byte[] value);
```

For each of these methods, a corresponding getter method exists. Getter methods always accept two arguments: the first to specify the key of the property to retrieve, and the second to specify a default value in case the property doesn't exist (or in case of errors). For instance:

```
public float getFloat(String key, float def);
```

Assuming you want to store the last time your bundle was started, you can do this using the system preferences:

```
Preferences startPreferences =
  service.getSystemPreferences().node("start");
startPreferences.putLong("time", new Date().getTime());
```

This stores the current time as a `long` in the system preferences `start` node. As you can see, this is pretty simple stuff, but it's convenient to have a standard service definition rather than having to invent it yourself.

> **Isn't this just Java Preferences?**
>
> Generally speaking, the Preferences Service is similar to `java.util.prefs.Preferences`, introduced in Java 1.4. One of the reasons the OSGi Preferences service exists is because the Java Preferences API isn't available before Java 1.4 and OSGi still supports Java 1.3. At the same time, the OSGi Preferences Service saves preferences for each bundle independently of other bundles, whereas Java Preferences saves preferences of one user of the system independently of other users. So the two, although similar, aren't identical.

This concludes our discussion of bundle configuration. We've covered a lot of ground. The combination of the Configuration Admin, Metatype, and Preferences Services provides for flexible approaches when it comes to configuring your bundles, which can save you a lot of management effort.

So far in this chapter, we've talked about how to manage versions and spent a fair amount of time showing how to manage bundle configuration data. Now we'll switch to our final topic: managing when a given bundle is activated after it's started.

9.3 Starting bundles lazily

From chapter 3, you know that starting a bundle involves invoking the `Bundle.start()` method on its corresponding `Bundle` object. If the bundle has a `BundleActivator`, and it's resolvable, the framework creates an instance of the bundle's activator and invokes `start()` on it, allowing the bundle to initialize itself. The act of starting a bundle and of it being activated are two independent concepts, although typically they occur together. Sometimes you may want to start a bundle but not necessarily activate it until some later time. Why? There are two main reasons:

- Your bundle's exported packages aren't able to function properly without a `BundleContext` (for example, perhaps they require a service from the registry).
- Your bundle's initialization is costly, and you want to defer it until it's needed.

The OSGi specification allows bundles to declare a lazy activation policy, which indicates to management agents that something like one of the previous two issues applies to it. Of course, you can use alternative approaches to deal with these situations. For the first issue, you can program the bundle classes to always throw exceptions until activated. For the second, you can minimize initialization in the bundle activator and use threads to do work in the background. Sometimes these alternative approaches are feasible, but sometimes throwing exceptions isn't so clean, nor is it possible to completely reduce all startup overhead, especially if you're starting lots of bundles. In these cases, you can use the lazy activation policy.

9.3.1 Understanding activation policies

Although the OSGi specification defines activation policies in an open-ended way, there's currently only one activation policy: *lazy*. The main gist of the lazy activation policy is this:

1. A bundle declares itself to be lazy.
2. A management agent installs a lazy bundle and starts it lazily. The framework marks the bundle as started but doesn't yet activate it.
3. The lazy bundle's activation is deferred until a class is loaded from it.
4. After a class is loaded from the lazy bundle, the framework completes its activation as normal.

This is fairly straightforward, but some small details lurk inside. Let's revisit the bundle lifecycle diagram in figure 9.8 to get a better understanding of the impact.

The bold arrows in figure 9.8 depict additional transitions in the bundle lifecycle state diagram. When a bundle is started lazily, it transitions to the `STARTING` state, which is denoted by the framework by firing a `BundleEvent` of type `LAZY_ACTIVATION`, instead of the normal `STARTING` event. The bundle stays in this state until it's stopped or a class is loaded from it. Stopping a lazy bundle in the `STARTING` state returns it to the `RESOLVED` state and results in `STOPPING` and `STOPPED` bundle events. When a class is loaded from a lazy bundle in the `STARTING` state, this acts as a trigger for the framework to automatically activate the bundle, which completes the normal process of creating the bundle activator and calling its `start()` method, resulting in the normal `STARTING` and `STARTED` bundle events.

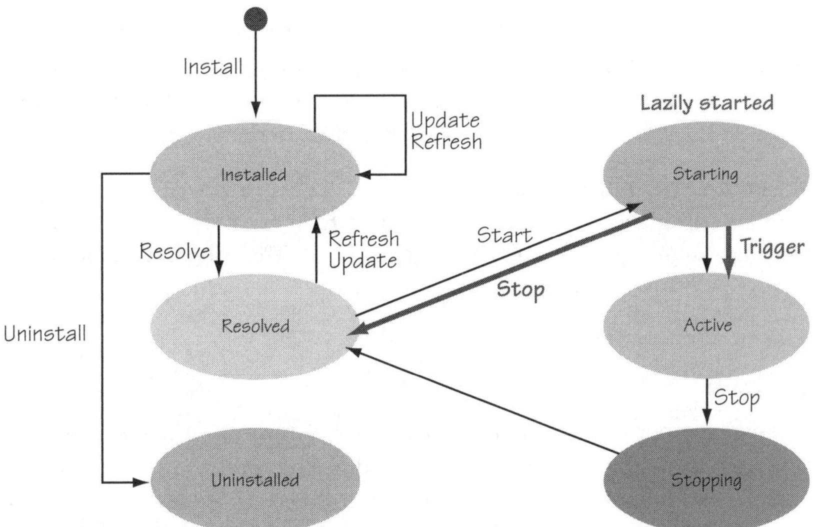

Figure 9.8 The lazy activation policy causes a bundle to defer activation and linger in the `STARTING` state until a class is loaded from it, at which point the framework completes its activation.

Because loading a class from one lazy bundle may require other classes to be loaded from other lazy bundles, the framework may end up activating chains of lazy bundles. The framework doesn't activate the lazy bundles as it loads classes from them, because this can lead to arcane class-loading errors. Instead, the framework delays the activation of each lazy bundle it discovers in a class-loading chain until it finishes loading the instigating class. At that point, the framework activates the detected lazy bundles in reverse order. For example, assume `ClassA` is loaded from bundle A, which requires `ClassB` from bundle B, which in turn requires `ClassC` from bundle C. If all of the bundles are lazy and in the `STARTING` state, the framework will activate bundle C, bundle B, and then bundle A before returning `ClassA` to the requester.

> **Attention!**
> Be aware that loading resources from a bundle doesn't trigger lazy activation, only classes. Also, the specification doesn't unambiguously define how the framework should treat the class-loading trigger, so the precise behavior may vary. In particular, some frameworks may scope the trigger to the lifetime of the bundle's class loader (it needs to be re-triggered only if the bundle is refreshed), whereas others may scope the trigger to the bundle's `ACTIVE` lifecycle state (it needs to be re-triggered after the bundle is stopped and restarted).

Now that you know how the lazy activation policy works, let's look into the details of using it.

9.3.2 Using activation policies

The process of using activation policies involves both the bundle wishing to be lazily activated and the management agent deciding whether to start a bundle lazily. For the first, when you create a bundle that can be lazily activated, you use the `Bundle-ActivationPolicy` header in its manifest metadata to declare the activation policy.

> **BUNDLE-ACTIVATIONPOLICY** Specifies the activation policy of a bundle where the only defined policy is lazy activation, which is specified with the value `lazy`. The default behavior is eager activation, although there is no explicit way to specify this value.

To use this in the bundle manifest, you do this:

```
Bundle-ActivationPolicy: lazy
```

Only bundles containing this manifest header can have their activation deferred. It's not possible to lazily activate an arbitrary bundle. The reasoning behind this goes back to one of the main use cases motivating deferred activation: a bundle that requires a `BundleContext` for its exported packages to function properly. In this use case, only the bundle itself knows if this is the case; thus, only the bundle itself can declare the policy.

This may sound a little odd, because deferring activation sounds like a good thing to do all the time. Why pay the cost of activating a bundle before it's needed? You could start all bundles lazily and they would only activate when another bundle used them, right? There's a fly in the ointment with this approach. Suppose your bundle provides a service. If your bundle isn't activated, it won't ever get a chance to publish its service in its bundle activator. Thus, no other bundles will be able to use it, and it will never be activated lazily. So, even if it were possible to apply an activation policy to a bundle externally, it wouldn't always end up working the way you intended.

One final detail for bundles declaring an activation policy: the specification offers fine-grained control over which precise packages trigger lazy activation. The specification defines `include` and `exclude` directives, which declare a comma-separated list of included and excluded packages, respectively. For example:

```
Bundle-ActivationPolicy: lazy; include:="com.acme.service"
```

A bundle with this metadata will only be lazily activated if a class is loaded from its `com.acme.service` package.

Assuming you have bundles with the declared lazy activation policy, the management agent has the final say as to whether their activation is deferred. In chapter 3, you learned about using `Bundle.start()` to start and eagerly activate a bundle. If you call `Bundle.start()` with no arguments on a bundle with lazy activation policy, it will be activated eagerly, as normal. To start the bundle with lazy activation, you must call `Bundle.start()` with the `Bundle.START_ACTIVATION_POLICY` flag. When you use this flag, you're saying that you want to start the bundle using its declared activation policy. A bundle with no activation policy will be started eagerly as usual, whereas one with the lazy policy will have its activation deferred as described in the previous section.

There's no requirement to start bundles declared as "lazy" lazily. Eagerly starting a bundle is always acceptable; it means you're willing to pay for the startup cost immediately. In most cases, eager activation is more than sufficient, so you won't need to worry about activation policies. But in those situations where it's required, it can make your life simpler.

That's it! We've covered a variety of bundle management topics. Let's review what you've learned in this chapter.

9.4 Summary

In this chapter, we discussed how to manage bundles, including a range of issues:

- You must carefully consider the versioning of both packages and bundles when working with OSGi.
- The OSGi specification recommends, but doesn't prescribe, versioning policies. It's up to you to define and adhere to such as policy.
- Managing bundles also involves managing bundle configuration data.

- The Configuration Admin Service provides a way to externalize and standardize management of bundle configuration data, and the Metatype Service provides a standard way to describe a bundle's configuration data.
- Related to configuration data, the Preferences Service provides a standard mechanism for bundles to manage system- and user-preference settings.
- The lazy activation policy defers bundle activation until a class is loaded from the lazily started bundle, allowing management agents to defer the cost of bundle startup.

These topics have given you a fairly good foundation for managing your bundles. Next, let's look at how to build and manage OSGi-based applications. This is the topic of the next chapter.

10 Managing applications

This chapter covers

- Discovering and deploying bundles using the OSGi Bundle Repository
- Deploying applications using Deployment Admin
- Controlling bundle activation order using start levels

In the last chapter, we focused on issues relating to the management of individual bundles, such as how to version them, manage their configuration data, and control their activation policies. Now, we'll move beyond managing individual bundles to issues related to managing OSGi-based applications composed of many bundles. As we've mentioned previously, in OSGi-based applications the deployed set of bundles is your application's configuration. This is a powerful aspect of the OSGi approach, so understanding this point and knowing how to manage sets of bundles is important to be able to fully take advantage of OSGi technology.

In this chapter, we'll explore a couple of different aspects of application management:

- Deploying applications using the OSGi Bundle Repository or Deployment-Admin
- Controlling bundle activation order using the StartLevel service

With these tools, you'll be better equipped to build, deploy, and configure sophisticated OSGi-based applications. Let's start by looking at bundle deployment.

10.1 Deploying bundles

When you've created some configurable bundles and versioned them according to a meaningful policy, you need to install them into an OSGi framework. In chapter 3, we looked at the various details of the lifecycle layer API, which allows you to install, start, update, and uninstall bundles from a running framework. Given the nature of modularity, it's likely your applications will grow over time to include too many bundles for you to manage their deployment in an ad hoc fashion. Manually installing and updating tens, hundreds, or even thousands of bundles becomes impractical. What can you do? This is when it becomes important to think about how you (or your users) are going to discover and deploy bundles.

10.1.1 Introducing management agents

The solution, in OSGi lingo, is to create a specific type of bundle called a *management agent*. Although we've shown how to programmatically manipulate the lifecycle of a bundle, it's typically not a good idea for a bundle to change its own state or the state of other bundles. Such a bundle is difficult to reuse in other compositions, because it's tightly bound to the other bundles it expects to control. The solution employed by most management agents is to externalize the information about which bundles to install or start. For example, management information can refer to bundles using URIs and aggregate useful groups of bundles using some sort of composition language/mechanism. A management agent can generically process such information, leaving it nicely decoupled from the bundles it's managing.

A simple example of a management agent is the shell from chapter 3. Granted, it's perhaps too simplistic because it only accepts and executes commands; but if such capabilities are sufficient for your application, it's fine. A management agent can be much more powerful, however. Even for your shell, you could easily extend it to handle command scripts for executing commands in batches. You could then create a couple of scripts, one for each configuration you need. Switching between application configurations would then be trivial.

More sophisticated management agents are possible. Your shell assumes human interaction to either directly or indirectly make the correct decisions and issue commands to manage the bundles. You could devise a system with rules to automate some of this by reacting to certain conditions autonomously. Consider a home-automation system that's able to detect a new device, automatically discover a driver for it in a remote repository, and subsequently install the driver along with its dependencies. Or you may have an application that automatically adapts itself to the language of the current user by installing the necessary locale bundles.

In essence, a management agent manages a running framework. OSGi supports you in developing such an agent by providing you with the means to monitor and manipulate a running framework. One of the more critical aspects of managing the framework is determining which bundles should be deployed to it. Various strategies are possible to manage complex sets of interdependent bundles. The two most prominent at the moment are the OSGi Bundle Repository (OBR) and Deployment Admin.

OBR and Deployment Admin address bundle deployment from different angles, but both can help when it comes to developing a management agent. The difference in focus between the two can be summarized as follows:

- OBR focuses on remote discovery and deployment of individual bundles and their dependencies.
- Deployment Admin focuses on the deployment of sets of bundles and associated resources.

In the following sections, we'll explore these two technologies in more detail and show you how to use them to provision or deploy your applications and bundles.

Alternative technologies

A number of other technologies attempt to address deployment and provisioning for OSGi, including Apache Ace, Paremus Nimble, and Equinox p2:

- Ace is a software distribution framework based on Deployment Admin. It focuses on centrally managing target systems, and distributing software components, configuration data, and other artifacts to them. The target systems are usually OSGi-based, but they don't have to be.
- Nimble is based on open source work from the Newton project and focuses on building an extensible resolver architecture that can deal with other types of dependencies outside of the OSGi modularity layer, such as service-level dependencies. For example, if a bundle containing servlets is deployed and activated, a servlet container should be deployed and activated alongside it.
- p2 is a subproject of the Eclipse Equinox framework. p2 focuses on extending the types of deployable artifacts to encompass things outside of an OSGi environment, including Unix RPM packages or Windows services, for example.

We won't discuss the details of any of these in the remainder of this book. If you're interested in them, they're just a Google search away.

10.1.2 OSGi Bundle Repository

The OSGi Bundle Repository (OBR) is officially not an OSGi standard specification; rather, it's a proposal for a specification, internally referred to as RFC 112 in the OSGi Alliance. Because OBR is only an RFC, its details may change in the future, but it's still a useful tool as it is.

OBR started life as the Oscar Bundle Repository, which was associated with the Oscar OSGi framework (which ultimately became the Apache Felix framework). OBR is intended to address two aspects of bundle deployment:

- *Discovery*—Provide a simple mechanism to discover which bundles are available for deployment
- *Dependency deployment*—Provide a simple mechanism to deploy a bundle and its transitive set of dependencies

To achieve the first goal, OBR defines a simple bundle repository with an API for accessing it and a common XML interchange format for describing deployable resources. An OBR repository can refer to other OBR repositories, defining a federation of repositories. But it's not necessary to define federations, so it's possible to create independent repositories specifically for your own purposes and applications. One of the main goals of OBR was simplicity, so it's easy for anyone to provide a bundle repository. One of the benefits of using an XML-based repository format is that no server-side process is needed (although server-side processes are possible). Figure 10.1 shows the federated structure of an OBR repository.

The key concept of an OBR repository is a generic description of a resource and its dependencies. A *resource* is an abstract entity used to represent any type of artifact such as a bundle, a certificate, or a configuration file. The resource description allows an agent to discover applicable artifacts, typically bundles, and deploy them along with their transitive dependencies. Each resource description has

- Zero or more requirements on other resources or the environment
- Zero or more capabilities used to satisfy other resources' requirements

Resource requirements are satisfied by capabilities provided by other resources or the environment. OBR maps bundle metadata from `Import-Package` and `Require-Bundle` headers onto resource requirements and from `Export-Package` and `Bundle-SymbolicName` headers onto resource capabilities. Figure 10.2 shows the relationship among the repository entities.

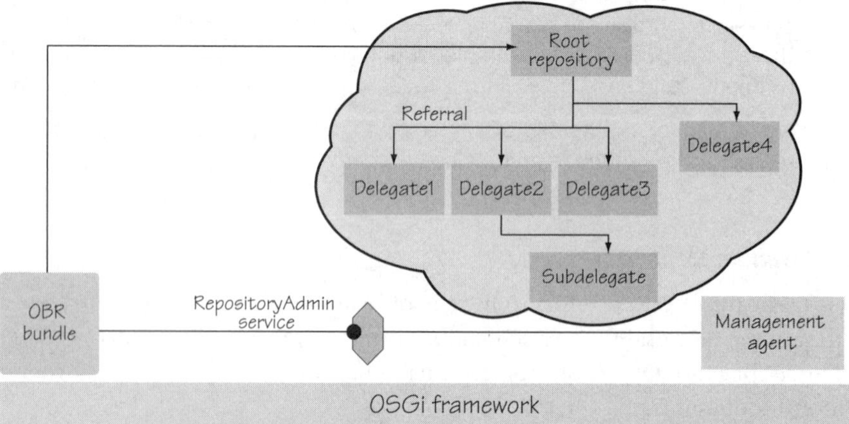

Figure 10.1 The OBR proposed specification provides a federated index that allows a management agent to resolve and install large numbers of bundles from a number of remote locations. The OBR index files are aggregated by a `RepositoryAdmin` service that resolves bundle dependencies on behalf of a management agent.

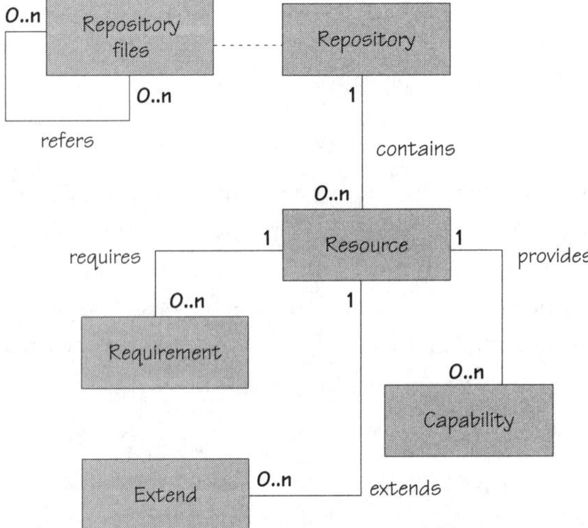

Figure 10.2 Relationships among the OBR repository entities

Using this information, an OBR implementation is able to resolve a consistent set of bundles for deployment given an initial set of bundles to be deployed. OBR's dependency-resolution algorithm is basically the same as the framework's dependency-resolution algorithm.

> **OBR vs. framework resolution**
>
> Although the dependency-resolution algorithms for OBR and the framework are similar, they aren't identical. OBR starts from a given set of bundles and pulls in resources from its available repositories in an attempt to satisfy any dependencies. The framework's resolution algorithm will never pull in additional resources; it only considers installed bundles.
>
> Another gotcha is the fact that the current OBR RFC doesn't currently mandate `uses` constraints when resolving dependencies. This can lead to unexpected failures at execution time if a `uses` constraint prevents bundles from resolving. OBR is an active area of work within the OSGi Alliance, so future revisions of the RFC may address this issue.

With this overview of OBR, let's look at how you can create a repository for it.

CREATING OBR REPOSITORIES

To illustrate how to create an OBR repository, let's use the bundles from the service-based paint program example. The repository is just an XML file containing the metadata of the bundles. We'll go through the entries in the XML file and explain the schema along the way. Assume you have the bundles from the example in a directory called paint-bundles. The directory contains the paint frame bundle, the API bundle, and the three shape bundles:

```
paint-bundles/
  frame-4.0.jar
  circle-4.0.jar
  triangle-4.0.jar
  shape-4.0.jar
  square-4.0.jar
```

You could create the repository XML file by hand, but you can use several different tools to create one instead. This example uses BIndex (http://www.osgi.org/Repository/BIndex), which is provided by the OSGi Alliance. For Maven users, there's also Maven support, which we'll discuss in appendix A. To create a repository using BIndex, run the following from above the bundles directory (this example assumes you're in the chapter10/combined-example/ directory of the companion code):

```
java -jar bindex.jar -r repository.xml -n Paint paint-bundles/*.jar
```

This creates a repository.xml file that contains the metadata of the bundles from the example. The main XML element is a `repository` tag defining the repository:

```
<repository lastmodified='20090215101706.874' name='Paint'>
...
</repository>
```

The `lastmodified` attribute is used as a timestamp by the OBR service to determine whether something has changed. The most interesting element is the `<resource>` tag: it describes a bundle you want to make available. The created repository XML file contains one resource block per bundle. The shape API bundle converted into OBR is as follows.

Listing 10.1 Shape API bundle converted into OBR repository XML syntax

```
<resource id='org.foo.shape/4.0.0' presentationname='shape'
 symbolicname='org.foo.shape' uri='paint-bundles/shape-4.0.jar'
 version='4.0.0'>
  <size>
5742
  </size>
  <license>
    http://www.apache.org/licenses/LICENSE-2.0
  </license>
  <documentation>
http://code.google.com/p/osgi-in-action/
  </documentation>
  <capability name='bundle'>
    <p n='manifestversion' v='2'/>
    <p n='presentationname' v='shape'/>
    <p n='symbolicname' v='org.foo.shape'/>
    <p n='version' t='version' v='4.0.0'/>
  </capability>
  <capability name='package'>
    <p n='package' v='org.foo.shape'/>
    <p n='version' t='version' v='4.0.0'/>
  </capability>
```

❶ Capability element representing bundle

❷ Capability element representing package

```
  <require extend='false' filter='(&amp;(package=org.foo.shape)
(version&gt;=4.0.0)(version&lt;5.0.0))' multiple='false' name='package'
 optional='false'>
    Import package org.foo.shape ;version=[4.0.0,5.0.0)
  </require>
</resource>
```

Requirement element ❸

The capability elements ❶ and ❷ represent what the bundle provides. In this case,❶ represents the bundle itself, because the bundle can be required (for example, `Require-Bundle`), whereas ❷ represents the package exported by the bundle. Bundle dependencies are represented as requirement elements, such as the one for an imported package ❸. Both capabilities and requirements have a name, which is actually a namespace; it's how capabilities are matched to requirements. For example, capabilities representing exported packages and requirements representing imported packages both have the `package` namespace.

In general, a *capability* is a set of properties specified using a `<p>` element with the following attributes:

- `n`—The name of the property
- `v`—The value of the property
- `t`—The type of the property, which is one of the following:
  - `string`—A string value, which is the default
  - `version`—An OSGi version
  - `uri`—A URI
  - `long`—A long value
  - `double`—A double value
  - `set`—A comma-separated list of values

Looking more closely at the bundle capability ❶, you see it's a fairly straightforward mapping from the bundle identification metadata:

```
Bundle-ManifestVersion: 2
Bundle-Name: Simple Paint API
Bundle-SymbolicName: org.foo.shape
Bundle-Version: 4.0
```

Likewise, the package capability ❷ is also a simple mapping from the bundle's `Export-Package` header:

```
Export-Package: org.foo.shape;version="4.0"
```

A *requirement* is an LDAP query over the properties of a capability. So, to match a requirement to a capability, first the namespace must match. If that matches, the requirements LDAP query must match the properties supplied by the capabilities. Even with the LDAP query, the package requirement ❸ is a fairly easy mapping from the `Import-Package` header:

```
Import-Package: org.foo.shape;version="[4.0,5.0)"
```

One reason the filter ❸ looks somewhat more complicated than necessary is that version ranges aren't directly supported by the filter syntax and must be expressed as the lower and upper bound.

If your bundle had a `Require-Bundle`, `Fragment-Host`, or `Bundle-Execution-Environment` header, it would be mapped to requirements. Even though the mappings are straightforward, it's still nice to have a tool like BIndex doing this for you. You can even integrate BIndex into in your build cycle so your repository is updated whenever your bundles change.

The repository XML is all well and good, but you're probably wondering how you can use repositories in your management agent. You don't need to know anything about the XML format to use OBR. All you need to do is grab the service implemented by OBR and use it. Let's take a closer look at this.

BROWSING OBR REPOSITORIES

The best way to familiarize you with how to use repositories is to give an example and explain what it does along the way. Let's use the shell example again and extend it with a new command to add/remove/list repositories and browse the bundles inside them. The programmatic entry point to the OBR specification is the `RepositoryAdmin` service, which is represented by the following interface:

```
public interface RepositoryAdmin {
  Resource[] discoverResources(String filterExpr);
  Resolver resolver();
  Repository addRepository(URL repository) throws Exception;
  boolean removeRepository(URL repository);
  Repository[] listRepositories();
  Resource getResource(String respositoryId);
}
```

This `RepositoryAdmin` service provides centralized access to the federated repository. An OBR implementation implements this interface as well as the other types referenced by it. Figure 10.3 shows the relationships among the involved entities.

The code in the following listing shows the code for the new `obr-repo` command. It uses `RepositoryAdmin` to add, remove, and list repositories as well as to discover resources.

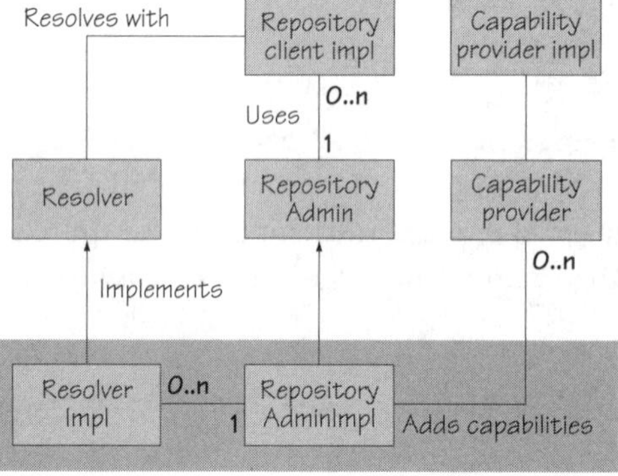

Figure 10.3 UML diagram of the `RepositoryAdmin` service. An external repository client uses the `RepositoryAdmin` and `Resolver` interfaces to download and install bundles and their transitive dependencies.

Listing 10.2 OBR repository shell command example

```
public class RepositoryCommand extends BasicCommand {
  public void exec(String args, PrintStream out, PrintStream err)
    throws Exception {
    args = args.trim();
    RepositoryAdmin admin = getRepositoryAdmin();
    if (admin != null) {
      if ("list-urls".equalsIgnoreCase(args)) {
        for (Repository repo : admin.listRepositories()) {
          out.println(repo.getName() + " (" + repo.getURL() + ")");
        }
      } else if (args != null) {
        if (args.startsWith("add-url")) {
          admin.addRepository(
            new URL(args.substring("add-url".length())));
        } else if (args.startsWith("remove-url")) {
          admin.removeRepository(
            new URL(args.substring("remove-url".length())));
        } else if (args.startsWith("list")) {
          String query = (args.equals("list"))
            ? "(symbolicname=*)"
            : args.substring("list".length()).trim();
          for (Resource res : admin.discoverResources(query)) {
            out.println(res.getPresentationName() + " ("
            + res.getSymbolicName() + ") " + res.getVersion());
          }
        }
      } else {
        out.println(
          "Unknown command - use {list-urls|add-url|remove-url|list}");
      }
    } else {
      out.println("No RepositoryAdmin service found...");
    }
  }

  private RepositoryAdmin getRepositoryAdmin() {
    ...
  }
}
```

❶ Lists repositories
❷ Adds repository
❸ Removes repository
❹ Discovers resources

The obr-repo command has the following subcommands: list-url, add-url, remove-url, and list. A RepositoryAdmin provides access to a number of repositories referenced by URLs. You implement the list-url subcommand ❶ to list these repositories by retrieving the RepositoryAdmin service and calling its listRepositories() method, which gives you access to the associated Repository objects. In this case, you loop through the repositories and print their names and URLs.

You can add or remove repository URLs with the add-url and remove-url subcommands, respectively. As you can see at ❷ and ❸, there's a one-to-one mapping to the addRepository() and removeRepository() methods of the RepositoryAdmin service. Finally, the list subcommand expects an LDAP query which it passes to discoverRepositories() to discover resources ❹. If no query is specified, all resources are listed. You loop through the discovered resources and print their presentation name, symbolic name, and version.

You can now use this command to configure repositories and discover bundles. After you've discovered a bundle you want to use, you need to deploy it. You'll implement a separate command for that next.

DEPLOYING BUNDLES WITH OBR

Discovering bundles is one half of the OBR story; the other half is deploying them and their dependencies into the framework. The `RepositoryAdmin.getResolver()` method gives you access to a `Resolver` object to select, resolve, and deploy resources. A `Resolver` has these methods:

```
public interface Resolver {
  void add(Resource resource);
  Requirement[] getUnsatisfiedRequirements();
  Resource[] getOptionalResources();
  Requirement[] getReason(Resource resource);
  Resource[] getResources(Requirement requirement);
  Resource[] getRequiredResources();
  Resource[] getAddedResources();
  boolean resolve();
  void deploy(boolean start);
}
```

The process for deploying resources is fairly simple. Follow these steps:

1. Add desired resources using `Resolver.add()`.
2. Resolve the desired resources' dependencies with `Resolver:resolve()`.
3. If the desired resources resolve successfully, deploy them with `Resolver.deploy()`.

The following listing implements an `obr-resolver` shell command to resolve and deploy resources.

Listing 10.3 OBR resolver shell command example

```
public class ResolverCommand extends BasicCommand {
  public void exec(String args, PrintStream out, PrintStream err)
    throws Exception {
    RepositoryAdmin admin = getRepositoryAdmin();
    Resolver resolver = admin.resolver();
    Resource[] resources = admin.discoverResources(args);
    if ((resources != null) && (resources.length > 0)) {
      resolver.add(resources[0]);                         ❶ Resolves
      if (resolver.resolve()) {                              resource
        for (Resource res : resolver.getRequiredResources()) {
          out.println("Deploying dependency: " +
            res.getPresentationName() +
            " (" + res.getSymbolicName() + ") " + res.getVersion());
        }
        resolver.deploy(true);                     ❷ Deploys bundle
      } else {
```

```
            out.println("Can not resolve " + resources[0].getId() +
              " reason: ");
            for (Requirement req : resolver.getUnsatisfiedRequirements()) {
              out.println("missing " + req.getName()
                + " " + req.getFilter());
            }
          }
        } else {
          out.println("No such resource");
        }
      }

      private RepositoryAdmin getRepositoryAdmin() {
        ...
      }
    }
```

You first get the Resolver from the RepositoryAdmin service. Then you use the RepositoryAdmin.discoverResources() method with a LDAP filter argument to discover a resource to deploy. If you find any resources, you add the first one to the Resolver and call resolve() to resolve its dependencies from the available repositories ❶. If the resource is successfully resolved, you print out all of the dependencies of the resource you're deploying. Then you use Resolver.deploy() to install and start the discovered bundle and its dependencies ❷. If the resource couldn't be resolved, you print out the missing requirements.

To run this example, go to the chapter10/combined-example/ directory of the companion code. Type ant to build the example and java -jar launcher.jar bundles to execute it. To interact with the shell, use telnet localhost 7070. This example uses the Apache Felix OBR implementation (http://felix.apache.org/site/apache-felix-osgi-bundle-repository.html). The following session uses the obr-repo and obr-resolver commands:

```
-> obr-repo add-url file:repository.xml
-> obr-repo list-urls
Paint (file:repository.xml)
-> obr-repo list
circle (org.foo.shape.circle) 4.0.0
frame (org.foo.paint) 4.0.0
shape (org.foo.shape) 4.0.0
square (org.foo.shape.square) 4.0.0
triangle (org.foo.shape.triangle) 4.0.0
-> obr-resolver (symbolicname=org.foo.paint)
Deploying dependency: shape (org.foo.shape) 4.0.0
-> obr-resolver (symbolicname=org.foo.shape.circle)
```

In this session, you first use the add-url subcommand to add your repository containing the paint program bundles. You verify the configured repository using the list-url subcommand. Using the list subcommand, you browse the bundles contained in the repository. Then, you use the obr-resolver command with an LDAP filter to select and deploy the paint-frame bundle, which also installs its dependencies. Finally, you install the circle bundle.

That's about all you need to know to start using OBR to discover and deploy your bundles. Often, this is enough to manage the growing complexity of your applications. But sometimes you'll be faced with a slightly different scenario that doesn't fit as well with what OBR provides. Perhaps you want to package your application in a single deployment unit composed of several bundles. What can you do in this case? Another OSGi Compendium specification targets such needs. Let's look at that next.

10.1.3 Deployment Admin

With OBR, you tend to think about deploying specific bundles and letting OBR automatically calculate and deploy any dependent bundles. With Deployment Admin, your thinking changes to deploying entire applications or subsystems as a single unit. The Deployment Admin specification standardizes some of the responsibilities of a management agent; specifically, it addresses lifecycle management of interlinked resources on an OSGi Service Platform.

Deployment Admin defines a way to package a number of resources in a deployment package. A *deployment package* is a JAR file with a format similar to a bundle. You can install deployment packages using the `DeploymentAdmin` service. The `DeploymentAdmin` service can process bundle resources itself, but other types of resources in the deployment package are handled by passing them to a `ResourceProcessor` service for that specific type of resource. The chosen `ResourceProcessor` service appropriately processes the given resource type. The uninstallation and update of a deployment package works similarly: bundles are processed by the `DeploymentAdmin` service, and other types of resources are handed off to `ResourceProcessors`. All `ResourceProcessor` services are notified about any resources that are uninstalled or updated. If all resources have been processed, the changes are committed. If an operation fails, all changes are rolled back.

NOTE Although we're talking in terms of commits and rollbacks, a Deployment Admin implementation isn't guaranteed to support all features of transactions. Most implementations tend to provide only a best effort rollback.

This sounds fairly promising for managing applications. To get a better idea of how it works, we'll present some of the details of deployment packages next. After that, we'll give an example of how you can use the Deployment Admin to install and manage deployment packages.

CREATING DEPLOYMENT PACKAGES

As an example, let's think about how to provision your paint program. The paint program has the following artifacts:

```
paint-4.0.jar
shape-4.0.jar
circle-4.0.jar
square-4.0.jar
triangle-4.0.jar
```

To be able to show all of what deployment packages have to offer, let's assume you want to provide a core version of the program containing the drawing frame and the shape API bundles. This way, you're able to deploy the actual shape implementations separately via an extension pack. The extension pack contains the square, circle, and triangle bundles. Let's go with this approach and explore the different ways you can use deployment packages to make it work.

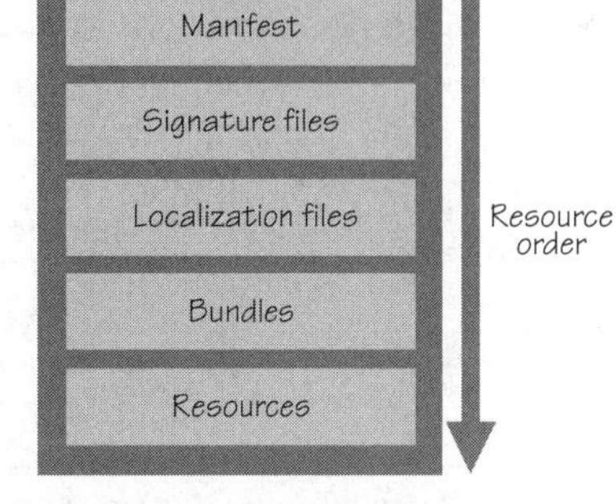

Figure 10.4 Structure of a deployment package JAR file

The general structure of a deployment package is shown in figure 10.4. This ordering is carefully designed to allow deployment packages to be streamed in such a way that the contents can be processed without needing to download the entire JAR file.

The deployment package design has a few other desirable characteristics. First, the deployment package puts metadata in its manifest, similar to bundles, which allows you to turn it into a named and versioned set of resources. Second, by taking advantage of the fact that JAR files can be signed, you can use signed JAR files to make your deployment packages tamperproof.

For this example, you can do either of the following (see figure 10.5):

- Create a deployment package for the core bundles and one package for all shape bundles.
- Create a deployment package for the core bundles and individual deployment packages for each shape bundle.

The difference is obviously that in the first case, you'll deploy either all shapes or none; and in the second case, you can extend the core bundle piecemeal. The important point to understand, though, is that you can't use both approaches at the same time: you must choose one.

In terms of the example, you need to make a decision. In this case, you'll go with the first approach and create a single deployment bundle for all shapes. But because deployment packages can be updated, you can gain some flexibility by starting with only one shape in the deployment package and then adding another one in an updated version and

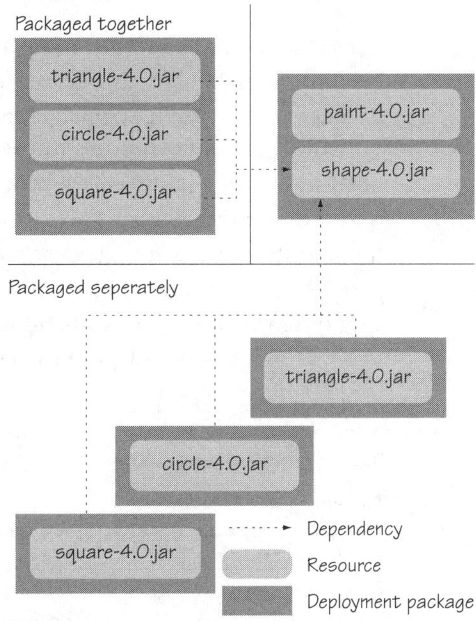

Figure 10.5 Paint program packaging alternatives

> **Deployment packages are greedy**
>
> These two different packaging strategies can't be used simultaneously. The specification only allows resources to belong to a single resource package. Using both approaches at the same time or changing your approach after the fact would move ownership of the bundle resources to another deployment package and thus violate the specification.
>
> A deployment package is defined as a set of resources that must be managed as a unit. The resources in a deployment package are assumed to be tightly coupled, such as a bundle and its configuration data. As a consequence, a resource can belong to only one deployment package; otherwise, for example, you could run into situations where you had two different, conflicting configurations for the same bundle.

another for the third or other combinations. When you create an update that adds or removes resources from a previous version, you don't even have to package the resources inside the update; instead, you can use *fix packages.*

> **FIX PACKAGE** A deployment package that minimizes download time by excluding resources that aren't required to upgrade or downgrade a deployment package. It can only be installed if a previous version of that deployment package is already installed. A fix package contains only the changed and new resources. A fix package (called the *source*) therefore must specify the range of versions that the existing deployment package (called the *target*) must have installed. You'll see this shortly when we walk through the example.

Let's assume that you want to be able to add new shapes to the application when they become available. In this scenario, it makes sense to start with a core deployment package and create fix packages, adding new shapes as they become available.

Now that you've figured out your packaging approach, how do you proceed? You need to create a manifest for the target that contains the paint frame and shape API bundles; you'll use this to provision the paint program core. Then you need to create the manifest of the fix package that you'll use to add the three shape bundles to the core. When you have your manifests, you need to create two JAR files with the corresponding manifests and your bundles, you can optionally sign them, and you're good to go. Here's the manifest of the core deployment package:

```
Manifest-Version: 1.0
DeploymentPackage-SymbolicName: org.foo.paint
DeploymentPackage-Version: 1.0.0

Name: paint-4.0.jar
Bundle-SymbolicName: org.foo.paint
Bundle-Version: 4.0.0

Name: shape-4.0.jar
Bundle-SymbolicName: org.foo.shape
Bundle-Version: 4.0.0
```

You first specify the deployment package's symbolic name and version. Next, you specify the list of resources contained in the JAR file. You specify the name of a resource, its symbolic name, and its version; you must do this for each resource. For this example, you only have bundle resources. To finish, you need to use the `jar` tool to create the JAR file with the appropriate content, and you're finished with your first deployment package.

> **Signing deployment packages**
>
> In this example, you don't sign your deployment package, nor is it required for you to do so. If you want to create a signed deployment package, you use the `jarsigner` tool from the standard Java SDK. The signing process is no different than signing a normal JAR file; it results in the signatures being placed in the deployment package JAR file in the META-INF directory and after the MANIFEST.MF file. Additionally, each entry section in the manifest contains a digest entry.

Now you need to create the manifest for your fix package containing the shape bundles. This manifest is as follows:

```
Manifest-Version: 1.0
DeploymentPackage-Symbolicname: org.foo.paint
DeploymentPackage-Version: 2.0
DeploymentPackage-FixPack: [1,2)

Name: paint-4.0.jar
Bundle-SymbolicName: org.foo.paint
Bundle-Version: 4.0.0
DeploymentPackage-Missing: true

Name: shape-4.0.jar
Bundle-SymbolicName: org.foo.shape
Bundle-Version: 4.0.0
DeploymentPackage-Missing: true

Name: triangle-4.0.jar
Bundle-SymbolicName: org.foo.shape.triangle
Bundle-Version: 4.0.0

Name: circle-4.0.jar
Bundle-SymbolicName: org.foo.shape.circle
Bundle-Version: 4.0.0

Name: square-4.0.jar
Bundle-SymbolicName: org.foo.shape.square
Bundle-Version: 4.0.0
```

Because the fix package is an update to your core package, the symbolic name stays the same, but the version is upgraded to `2.0.0`. The `DeploymentPackage-FixPack` header indicates that this is a fix package; you use version-range syntax to indicate that the fix package can be applied to any previously installed version of the deployment package from `1.0.0` inclusive to `2.0.0` exclusive. This version-numbering scheme expresses the assumption that only major version-number changes indicate added bundles. You don't need to package the bundles already present in the core package, but you still need to mention them in the manifest. You use the `DeploymentPackage-Missing` header to do this. Then you specify the shape bundles in the same fashion as before. To use the deployment packages, you need to make each available via a URL.

> **NOTE** If you make deployment packages available via a protocol that supports MIME types, the standard MIME type for deployment packages is `application/vnd.osgi.dp`.

Next, you can use the provided `DeploymentAdmin` service in your management agent to install, update, and uninstall deployment packages.

MANAGING DEPLOYMENT PACKAGES

To demonstrate how a management agent can use Deployment Admin, you'll again return to the shell and create a new dpa shell command to list, install, and uninstall deployment packages. This command will use the `DeploymentAdmin` service, which is represented by the following interface:

```
public interface DeploymentAdmin {
  DeploymentPackage installDeploymentPackage(InputStream in)
    throws DeploymentException;
  DeploymentPackage[] listDeploymentPackages();
  DeploymentPackage getDeploymentPackage(String symbName);
  DeploymentPackage getDeploymentPackage(Bundle bundle);
  boolean cancel();
}
```

The following listing shows the implementation of the command.

Listing 10.4 Deployment Admin shell command example

```
public class DeploymentPackageCommand extends BasicCommand {

  public void exec(String args, PrintStream out, PrintStream err)
    throws Exception {
    DeploymentAdmin admin = getDeploymentAdmin();

    if (admin == null) {
      out.println("No DeploymentAdmin service found.");
      return;
    }
    if (args != null) {
      if (args.trim().equalsIgnoreCase("list")) {
        for (DeploymentPackage dp : admin.listDeploymentPackages()) {
          out.println(dp.getName() + " " + dp.getVersion());
        }
      } else if (args.trim().startsWith("uninstall ")) {
        DeploymentPackage dp = admin.getDeploymentPackage(
          args.trim().substring("uninstall ".length()));
        if (dp != null) {
          dp.uninstall();
        } else {
          out.println("No such package");
        }
```

1. Gets installed deployment packages
2. Uninstalls deployment package

```
    } else if (args.trim().startsWith("install ")) {
      DeploymentPackage dp = admin.installDeploymentPackage(new URL(
        args.trim().substring("install ".length())).openStream());
      out.println(dp.getName() + " " + dp.getVersion());
    }
  } else {
    out.println("Use {list|install <url>|uninstall <name>}");
  }
}

private DeploymentAdmin getDeploymentAdmin() {
  ...
}
}
```

Installs deployment package ❸

Like the previous example commands, you more or less map the command onto the `DeploymentAdmin` service interface. You get installed deployment packages using the `listDeploymentPackages()` service method and print their names and versions ❶. Then, you uninstall an existing deployment package associated with a specified symbolic name using `DeploymentPackage.uninstall()` ❷. Finally, you install a deployment package from the specified URL using the `installDeploymentPackage()` service method ❸. The approach is fairly similar to managing bundles.

To run this example, go to the chapter10/combined-example/ directory of the companion code. Type `ant` to build the example and `java -jar launcher.jar bundles` to execute it. To interact with the shell, use `telnet localhost 7070`. This example uses the Apache Felix Deployment Admin implementation (http://felix.apache.org/site/apache-felix-deployment-admin.html). Here's the command in action:

```
-> dpa install file:org.foo.paint-1.0.dp
org.foo.paint 1.0.0
-> dpa install file:org.foo.paint-2.0.dp
org.foo.paint 2.0.0
-> dpa list
org.foo.paint 2.0.0
-> dpa uninstall org.foo.paint
```

This session installs the core paint program deployment package. You then update it to include the fix package for the shapes. You list the installed deployment packages and then uninstall the deployment package. (Note that the Apache Felix implementation of Deployment Admin doesn't currently implement the uninstall functionality.) This highlights the difference between the OBR and Deployment Admin approaches, because you can manage your bundles as a single unit of deployment rather than individual bundles.

Before concluding our discussion on Deployment Admin, we'll discuss resource processors. Resource processors are an important part of the Deployment Admin specification, because they extend OSGi deployment beyond bundles.

RESOURCE PROCESSORS

Deployment Admin can process bundle resources in deployment packages by itself; but when it comes to other types of resources, it needs to enlist the help of `ResourceProcessor` services. A `ResourceProcessor` is a service used to appropriately process arbitrary resource types; it implements the following interface:

```
public interface ResourceProcessor {
  void begin(DeploymentSession session);
  void process(String name, InputStream stream)
    throws ResourceProcessorException;
  void dropped(String resource) throws ResourceProcessorException;
  void dropAllResources() throws ResourceProcessorException;
  void prepare() throws ResourceProcessorException;
  void commit();
  void rollback();
  void cancel();
}
```

Deployment Admin connects resource types to resource processors using the `Resource-Processor` header in the resource entry of the deployment-package manifest. You use this header to specify the service PID of the needed resource processor. These kinds of services are provided by *customizer* bundles delivered as part of the deployment package.

You indicate a customizer bundle by using the `DeploymentPackage-Customizer` header in the resource entry for a bundle in the deployment package. This allows Deployment Admin to start customizers first, so they can provide the necessary `ResourceProcessor` services to handle the deployment package content. Resource processors may result in new file system artifacts but can perform other tasks like database initialization or data conversion, for example. Each nonbundle resource should have a processor associated with it. With the necessary resource processor specified, Deployment Admin is able to process all resource package content.

Before processing of the deployment package starts, Deployment Admin creates a session in which all actions needed to process the package will take place. A session isn't visible to clients of the `DeploymentAdmin` service; it's used to join the required resource processors to the processing of the deployment package. If an exception is raised during a session by any of the resource processors or the session is canceled, Deployment Admin rolls back the changes. As we mentioned before, this may only be a best-effort rollback, but it's normally sufficient to leave the framework in a consistent state. If no exceptions are raised during a session, Deployment Admin commits the changes. During a commit, `Deployment-Admin` tells all joined `ResourceProcessor` services to prepare and subsequently commit their changes. Figure 10.6 shows the transactional aspects of the session.

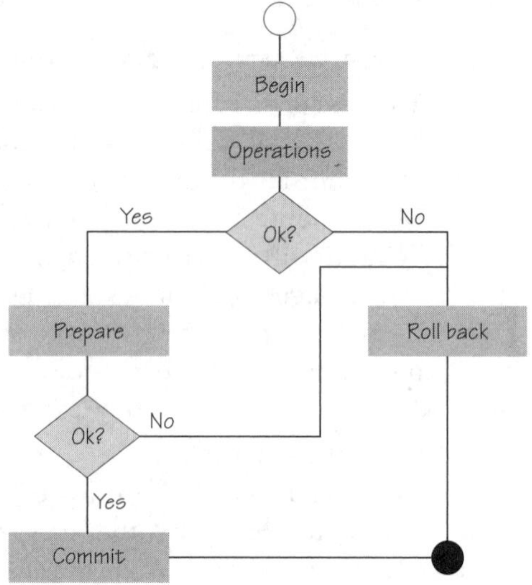

Figure 10.6 Transactional aspects of a session

As you can see, this essentially provides a two-phase commit implementation. It allows `ResourceProcessors` to cleanly handle rollbacks. But rolling back a bundle update, as well as reinstalling a stale bundle, requires an implementation-specific back door into the OSGi framework, because the framework specification isn't transactional over multiple lifecycle operations. This is why the Deployment Admin specification doesn't mandate full transactional behavior.

In this section, we've looked at two different ways of deploying bundles. Which approach to choose depends on your needs. OBR is geared toward discovery and installation of bundles together with the transitive closure of their dependencies. Deployment Admin provisions sets of bundles and their required resources as complete units. These provide solutions to many of the deployment and discovery tasks you'll need for a management agent. Of course, if necessary, you can always use the core OSGi API to create something for your specific needs.

Now that you know how to deploy bundles to the OSGi framework, we need to look at one final management-related task. After deploying a set of bundles, sometimes you need to control their relative activation order. We'll discuss this management activity next.

10.2 Ordering bundle activation

In certain scenarios, you may need to control the relative order in which deployed bundles are activated and/or deactivated. There are some good reasons to control such ordering, but there are many more bad ones. Best practice dictates that you should create your bundles to be independent of activation and deactivation ordering. OSGi allows bundles to listen for lifecycle events from other bundles because it eliminates the need to order dependencies and allows bundles to be aware of changes and react to them. Ordering constraints are another form of coupling among bundles, which severely limits their ability to be reused and arbitrarily composed. A bundle shouldn't require that functionality from another bundle be available for it to be started itself; instead, it should wait for the functionality to become available and then continue with its own functionality.

Having said that, there are a few valid reasons why you may want to ensure that a given bundle is activated before another. For example, you may want to implement a splash screen to display the progress of your application's startup. If your splash screen is developed as a bundle, you need a way to ensure that it's activated first. After all, what good would a splash screen showing the startup progress be if it came up last? You can generalize this kind of functionality as a high-priority feature, which in general requires ordering because it needs preferred treatment. In addition to high-priority features, ordering may be needed in two other scenarios:

- When a bundle violates the best practices mentioned earlier and relies on implicit activation ordering during startup. In reality, you should consider fixing or replacing such a bundle; but if you can't, then you must ensure that the bundles it depends on are started first. Again, this is extremely bad practice, and you should feel a generous amount of shame until the bundle is fixed.
- When bundles can be grouped into sets with certain desirable properties. For example, you may define a set of bundles comprising a safe mode, where you deactivate all but a small set of trusted bundles and provide limited core functionality for safety or security reasons. Other examples include diagnostic or power save modes.

How can you influence and control relative activation and deactivation ordering among bundles? By using the standard Start Level Service provided by the OSGi framework.

10.2.1 Introducing the Start Level Service

The Start Level Service allows a management agent to control the relative activation/deactivation order among bundles as well as when transitions should occur. The idea is simple, and you may already be familiar with it from other contexts, such as in UNIX environments where system services are started or stopped based on the system's current run level.

In OSGi, the framework has an active start level associated with it, which is a non-negative integer indicating the start level in which it's executing. The framework starts with an active start level of zero and, by default, transitions to an active start level of one when it's fully running. Each bundle also has an integer start level associated with it, which indicates the required start level of the bundle. Only bundles with a start level less than or equal to the framework's active start level are allowed to be in the `ACTIVE` state. The Start Level Service is represented by the following interface:

```
public interface StartLevel {
  int getStartLevel();
  void setStartLevel(int startlevel);
  int getBundleStartLevel(Bundle bundle);
  void setBundleStartLevel(Bundle bundle, int startlevel);
  int getInitialBundleStartLevel();
  void setInitialBundleStartLevel(int startlevel);
  boolean isBundlePersistentlyStarted(Bundle bundle);
  boolean isBundleActivationPolicyUsed(Bundle bundle);
}
```

This service interface supports the following operations:

- *Modifying the active start level of the framework*—You can change the framework's active start level with `setStartLevel()`. Doing so results in all active bundles with a higher start level being stopped, and bundles with a lower or equal start level that are persistently marked as started being activated.
- *Assigning a specific start level to a bundle*—You can change an individual bundle's start level with `setBundleStartLevel()`. The framework activates the bundle if it's persistently marked as started and the new start level is less than or equal to the active start level or stops the bundle if the new start level is greater than the active start level.
- *Setting the initial start level for newly installed bundles*—All bundles are installed with a default start level of 1. With `setInitialBundleStartLevel()`, you can change this default value to any desired initial start level. This only impacts subsequently installed bundles.
- *Querying relevant values*—You can query the framework's active start level, the start level of a bundle, and the initial bundle start level. Additionally, you can query whether a given bundle is persistently marked as started.

What does all this mean in simple terms? The framework's active start level and a bundle's start level control whether a bundle can be started. This means that if you explicitly start a bundle (invoke `Bundle.start()` on it), it won't activate unless the bundle's start level is less than or equal to the framework's active start level. In such a case, the only effect of invoking `Bundle.start()` is that the bundle is persistently marked as started. If the framework's active start level is eventually changed to a greater or equal value, the bundle will be automatically activated by the framework.

As you can imagine, changing the active start level of the framework can have a dramatic impact on the framework, because a lot of bundles may be started or stopped as a result. When you use the Start Level Service to change the framework's active start level, all active bundles with start levels greater than the target start level are stopped, whereas all bundles persistently marked as started with start levels less than or equal to the target start level are started. When you invoke `StartLevel.setStartLevel()`, the actual process occurs on a background thread, so the method returns immediately. The background thread effectively increments or decrements the current active start level one step at a time, depending on whether the new active start level is greater than or less than the current active start level, respectively. At each step, the background thread starts or stops the bundles at that level until the new target level is reached.

10.2.2 Using the Start Level Service

To illustrate how you use the Start Level Service, you'll add `startlevel` and `bundlelevel` commands to the shell. These two commands, implemented in the following listing, perform the four functions mentioned earlier.

Listing 10.5 Start Level Service shell commands example

```
package org.foo.shell;

import java.io.PrintStream;
import org.osgi.service.startlevel.StartLevel;

public class StartLevelCommand extends BasicCommand {

  public void exec(String args, PrintStream out, PrintStream err)
    throws Exception {
    if (args == null) {
      out.println(getStartLevelService().getStartLevel());    ❶ Prints framework's active start level
    } else {
      getStartLevelService().setStartLevel(
        Integer.parseInt(args.trim()));
    }
  }
...
}
...

public class BundleLevelCommand extends BasicCommand {

  public void exec(String args, PrintStream out, PrintStream err)
```

```
    throws Exception {
    StringTokenizer tok = new StringTokenizer(args);
    if (tok.countTokens() == 1) {
      out.println("Bundle " + args + " has level " +
        getStartLevelService().getBundleStartLevel(
          getBundle(tok.nextToken())));
    } else {
      String first = tok.nextToken();
      if ("-i".equals(first)) {
        getStartLevelService().setInitialBundleStartLevel(
          Integer.parseInt(tok.nextToken()));
      } else {
        getStartLevelService().setBundleStartLevel(
          getBundle(tok.nextToken()), Integer.parseInt(first));
      }
    }
  }
...
}
```

❷ Outputs bundle's start level

Executing the `startlevel` command without an argument prints the framework's active start level ❶. You implement this with the `StartLevel.getStartLevel()` method. If the `startlevel` command is passed an argument, the new active start level is parsed from the argument, and you call the `StartLevel.setStartLevel()` method, which causes the framework to move to the specified active start level.

Next, the `bundlelevel` command allows you to set and get the start level of an individual bundle. When the command is given only one argument, you use the argument as the bundle identifier and retrieve and output the associated bundle's start level with `StartLevel.getBundleStartLevel()` ❷. You add a `-i` switch to the command to set the initial bundle start level using the `StartLevel.setInitialBundleStartLevel()` method. Finally, you add the ability to change an individual bundle's start level by using the `StartLevel.setBundleStartLevel()` method.

When the framework's active start level is changed, the background thread doing the work fires a `FrameworkEvent.STARTLEVEL_CHANGED` event to indicate that it's finished doing the work. Here's a simple session demonstrating what you can do with these commands.

Listing 10.6 Using the `startlevel` and `bundlelevel` commands

```
-> bundles
  ID       State        Name
[   0] [   ACTIVE] System Bundle
                   Location: System Bundle
                   Symbolic-Name: system.bundle
[   1] [   ACTIVE] Simple Shell
                   Location: file:org.foo.shell-1.0.jar
                   Symbolic-Name: org.foo.shell
-> startlevel
1
-> bundlelevel -i 2
```

```
-> install file:foo.jar
Bundle: 3
-> start 3
-> bundles
   ID       State        Name
[   0] [   ACTIVE] System Bundle
                   Location: System Bundle
                   Symbolic-Name: system.bundle
[   1] [   ACTIVE] Simple Shell
                   Location: file:org.foo.shell-1.0.jar
                   Symbolic-Name: org.foo.shell
[   3] [INSTALLED] Foo Bundle
                   Location: file:foo.jar
                   Symbolic-Name: org.foo.foo
-> startlevel 2
-> bundles
   ID       State        Name
[   0] [   ACTIVE] System Bundle
                   Location: System Bundle
                   Symbolic-Name: system.bundle
[   1] [   ACTIVE] Simple Shell
                   Location: file:org.foo.shell-1.0.jar
                   Symbolic-Name: org.foo.shell
[   3] [   ACTIVE] Foo Bundle
                   Location: foo.jar
                   Symbolic-Name: org.foo.foo
-> bundlelevel 3 3
-> bundles
   ID       State        Name
[   0] [   ACTIVE] System Bundle
                   Location: System Bundle
                   Symbolic-Name: system.bundle
[   1] [   ACTIVE] Simple Shell
                   Location: file:org.foo.shell-1.0.jar
                   Symbolic-Name: org.foo.shell
[   3] [ RESOLVED] Foo Bundle
                   Location: file:foo.jar
                   Symbolic-Name: org.foo.foo
```

In this example session, you first use the `startlevel` command to display the framework's current active start level, which is 1 by default. You use the `bundlelevel` command with the `-i` switch to set the initial bundle start level of installed bundles to 2. Subsequently, when you install and start the `foo` bundle, you can see from the following `bundles` command output that it's not started yet. This is expected, because the bundle's start level is 2, but the framework's active start level of 1 is less than that. You raise the framework's active start level to 2, which ultimately causes the `foo` bundle to be started. Using the `bundlelevel` command to set the `foo` bundle's start level to 3 stops the bundle again.

That's all there is to the Start Level Service. You'll not likely need this service often, because bundle activation ordering isn't good practice, but it can come in handy in certain situations. We've finished covering application management; let's summarize what we've discussed.

10.3 Summary

In this chapter, we discussed how to manage your OSGi-based applications. We covered the following issues:

- One of the key management tasks is deploying bundles to the OSGi framework. You can use multiple techniques to do so, including rolling your own approach or using technologies like OBR and Deployment Admin.
- OBR focuses on discovering and deploying bundles and the transitive closure of their dependencies, whereas Deployment Admin focuses on defining and deploying sets of bundles and needed resources.
- You can use the Start Level Service to control the relative activation order of your deployed bundles, which may be needed in a few situations like creating splash screens and different execution modes.

These topics have given you a fairly good foundation for managing your bundles. Now that you know how to build and manage your OSGi applications, we'll move into more advanced topics, such as service-oriented component models.

Part 3

Advanced topics

In the first part of the book we looked into the core OSGi framework specification and explained its most important features and capabilities. In the second part of the book, we turned to the pragmatic issues of developing OSGi-based applications. In this third and final part of the book, we'll explore a variety of advanced topics. To help you simplify OSGi development, we'll introduce OSGi-based component frameworks. These component frameworks should be interesting for all OSGi developers. We'll also look into launching and embedding the OSGi framework, enabling security in OSGi-based applications, and developing web and distributed applications in OSGi. After completing this final part of the book, you should have a good idea of all the possibilities that OSGi technology provides.

11 Component models and frameworks

This chapter covers

- Understanding component-oriented concepts and terminology
- Explaining how OSGi relates to component orientation
- Exploring the OSGi Declarative Services component framework

So far in this book, we've shown you how to develop applications using the core OSGi framework layers: module, lifecycle, and service. In chapter 2, we mentioned the similarities between module- and component-oriented programming. In chapter 4, we mentioned how the OSGi service model can work alongside component models. There's obviously some degree of synergy between OSGi and component technologies. This has led a variety of existing component technologies to integrate with OSGi as well as a variety of new component frameworks being built on top of it.

Component-oriented approaches have become incredibly popular in Java development over the past decade, and a vast number of approaches are available, including Enterprise JavaBeans (EJB), Spring Beans, Google Guice, Service Component Architecture (SCA), and Fractal, to name just a few. The variety and variation among component-oriented approaches is staggering, but one thing is typically common: they ignore or only pay lip service to modularity issues related to deployment and execution-time verification and enforcement. This means OSGi technology provides a perfect foundation for integrating existing component approaches or defining new ones.

In this chapter and the next, we'll introduce you to component orientation in general and as it relates to OSGi technology. This chapter will cover introductory aspects and present the first OSGi standard component framework, called *Declarative Services*, which is lightweight and fairly representative of how component frameworks are integrated with OSGi. In the next chapter, we'll introduce a couple more advanced component frameworks. We'll reuse the example paint program to illustrate how these component frameworks simplify OSGi-based development. Let's start with background information and motivation.

11.1 Understanding component orientation

Although component-oriented programming has been around for a while, there's no single definition for most of the concepts it embodies (which is similar to module orientation). Therefore, you shouldn't take the discussion in this section as the bible for all component-oriented approaches. The main questions we intend to address for the scope of this chapter and the next are, what are components, and why do we want them? We'll answer these questions in the following two subsections, respectively.

11.1.1 What are components?

A key aspect of all component technologies is that they describe functional building blocks that are typically more coarse-grained than what we normally associate with objects (although object orientation isn't required for component orientation). These building blocks are typically business logic; they provide functionality via interfaces. Conversely, components may consume functionality provided by other components via their interfaces. Components for a given approach are usually programmed according to a particular pattern defined by a *component model*. A *component framework* is used to execute components.

> **Component model vs. component framework**
>
> A component model describes what a component looks like, how it interacts with other components, and what capabilities it has (such as lifecycle or configuration management). A component framework implements the runtime needed to support a component model and execute the components. The relationship between the two isn't strictly one-to-one. For example, the Common Object Model (COM) defines a component model that's implemented by different component frameworks for different platforms. Likewise, it's also possible for a component framework to support multiple component models, such as the JBoss Microcontainer.

(continued)
Component frameworks aren't constrained by the component model they support and may provide additional capabilities. This is common when vendors try to differentiate implementations of standard component models; think about how Java EE application servers try to differentiate themselves. The reality is that no clear line separates a component model from a component framework. The important differentiation to take away is that a component model describes what it means to be a component, and the framework provides the runtime to execute components adhering to a component model.

Generally speaking, components have some explicit way of declaring their provided interfaces. This can be done through certain patterns, such as implementing an interface or extending a base class, or it can be done more explicitly at execution time by publishing provided interfaces, such as using an interface repository. Likewise, components may have some explicit way of declaring their dependencies on the provided interfaces of other components, such as with declarative metadata, or they may be responsible for managing their own dependencies at execution time, such as querying an interface repository. Often, components are packaged as independent deployment units, such as JAR files or DLLs, but this isn't strictly necessary.

Modules vs. components

Doesn't it sound like modules and components have a lot in common? They both provide stuff to each other and consume stuff from each other. They're also packaged as independent deployment units. Couldn't these two be considered one and the same or at least be combined? Yes, they could, but components and modules serve different purposes and are somewhat orthogonal (they're not completely orthogonal, because components are made from code that can ultimately be packaged into modules).

Modules deal with code packaging and the dependencies among code. Components deal with implementing higher-level functionality and the dependencies among components. Components need their code dependencies managed, but they technically don't need a module system to do it (often it's us programmers doing it via the class path).

A good summary is that you can think of modules as dealing with static code and compile-time dependencies, whereas components deal with instances and execution-time dependencies.

The general approach for creating an application from components is to compose it. This means you grab the components implementing the functionality you need and *compose* them (match required interfaces to provided interfaces) to form an application. Component compositions can be *declarative,* such as using some sort of composition language to describe the components and bindings among them; or *implicit,* where the composition is the deployed set of components. For the application to execute, the application's constituent components must somehow be loaded into the component framework and instantiated. Figure 11.1 shows a trivial component composition.

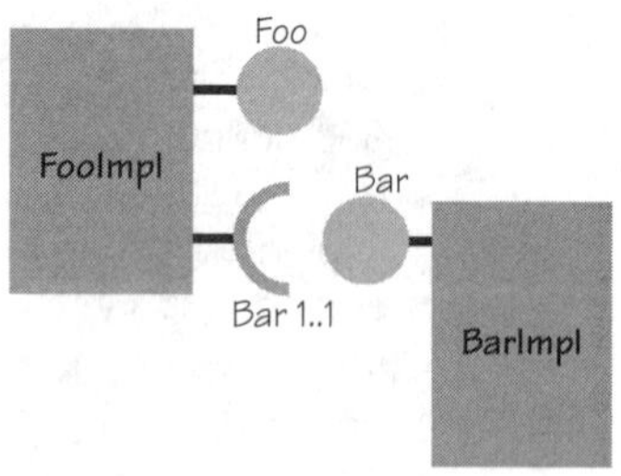

Figure 11.1 Trivial component composition of two components: `FooImpl` and `BarImpl`

This description of component orientation is by no means complete. Depending on the component model, components may have a variety of capabilities, such as explicit lifecycle control. Some component models and frameworks differentiate between component types and instances (for example, there can be multiple component instances from a given type), whereas others treat them as being the same (only one instance per component). You'll see some of these differences rear their heads in our later discussions of specific OSGi-based component frameworks. For now, it's sufficient if your general understanding of component orientation is as a programming approach promoting coarse-grained, composable application building blocks. Now let's look at why we want it.

11.1.2 Why do we want components?

The long-held promise of component orientation is that we'll be able to create applications easily and quickly by snapping them together from readily available, reusable components. The actual merits of this rosy view of component orientation are debatable, but there are benefits to be gained by adhering to a component model. First and foremost, it promotes separation of concerns and encapsulation with its interface-based approach. This enhances the reusability of your code because it limits dependencies on implementation details.

Another worthwhile aspect of an interface-based approach is substitutability of providers. Because component interaction occurs through well-defined interfaces, the semantics of these interfaces must themselves be well defined. As such, it's possible to create different implementations and easily substitute one provider with another. You may have noticed that these benefits are pretty much the same as we described for OSGi services. This is part of the reason why such a strong synergy exists between OSGi and component technologies; more on this shortly.

Because component models typically make the provided and required interfaces of components explicit (or at least explicitly focus on them), you end up with more reusable software that's amenable to composition. And because component models typically require a specific pattern or approach for development, your code ends up more uniform and easier to understand. This uniformity also leads to another potential benefit: external management.

This last point isn't necessarily obvious; but by creating components following a specific model, external entities can understand more about your code and potentially take some tasks off your hands. For example, transactions and persistence are handled automatically for components in EJB. Another example is distribution, where some component frameworks automatically make components remotely accessible. And as you'll see in this chapter, execution-time dependency management is also possible.

This all sounds useful, but are there any downsides to using components? Yes, there are always issues to be considered in any architectural decision. Table 11.1 details some general issues you should consider when choosing whether to use components.

Table 11.1 Potential issues associated with component orientation

Problem	Description	Analysis
Bloat	Some component frameworks are relatively heavy, so they may not be appropriate for small applications.	How complex are your application dependencies? Is the extra functionality provided by a component framework required?
Diagnosis	Debugging service-dependency problems requires a new set of tools to figure out what's going on when your services aren't published as expected.	Debugging dependency problems is often simplified by having generic tools that can be applied to common component models.
Side-file syndrome	Build- or execution-time problems caused by component configuration files becoming stale with respect to Java source code can be frustrating to debug.	IDE tooling can definitely help by providing refactoring support and early analysis. A number of projects are building in support of component models, and they will only increase over time.

Overall, we feel the positives far outweigh the potential negatives. Given this general motivation for component orientation, let's move on to discussing how all this relates specifically to OSGi.

11.2 OSGi and components

For those reading between the lines in the last section, it may not come as a complete surprise, but there's a reason why the synergy between OSGi and component technologies is so strong. The core OSGi specification defines a component model and the framework for executing the corresponding components. Yes, that's right: OSGi developers are component developers. The type of component model defined by OSGi is a special kind, called a *service-oriented component model*. Let's take a minute to look at the specification in this new light.

11.2.1 OSGi's service-oriented component model

The high-level description of the OSGi component model can be understood by equating bundles with components and services with component interfaces. We'll put a little more meat on this description by breaking down how the OSGi core specification maps to the component-oriented concepts of the last section.

COMPONENTS AND THEIR INTERACTION

For a bundle to be a component, it implements a bundle activator. The activator also allows for lifecycle management. Another capability includes external configuration management using `BundleContext.getProperty()`, although the exact details are left to the framework implementation.

The bundle JAR file is the independent unit of deployment for a component. In OSGi, the logical bundle (the component) is equated with the physical bundle JAR file (the module). Technically, this means there can be only one component per module and, further, only one component instance. Later, you'll see that most OSGi-based component frameworks break this one-to-one physical-to-logical mapping, but this mapping isn't the important part of the OSGi component model. OSGi's killer feature is in the richness of its dynamic module layer. Some component models and frameworks deal with modularity (the code level), but few if any provide such rich features.

At the module level, as you've learned, bundles have a way of explicitly describing the code they provide and require. At the component level, the core OSGi specification doesn't define a way for bundles to explicitly declare the services they provide and require. Instead, these issues are left to be handled manually by the bundle at execution time.

COMPONENT FRAMEWORK

The distinction between component model and framework is definitely blurred in the OSGi specification, because it goes to great lengths to ensure that the component framework has standardized behavior. This ultimately makes aspects of what might ordinarily be thought of as belonging to the component framework part of the component model.

The OSGi-based component frameworks described here and in the following chapter can be seen as extensions to the OSGi component model and framework. This is sometimes confusing because the distinction of what is part of the model, the framework, or components themselves isn't always obvious. For example, the OSGi Configuration Admin Service defines how bundles can be configured. But it isn't part of the OSGi component model, nor the OSGi component framework; it's an agreement among the Configuration Admin component and its client components.

But this is how it should be. Keep the model and framework simple and small. Try to do everything else in the layers above. The framework should be the execution environment for components and little else.

COMPONENT COMPOSITION

Just as there isn't an explicit way for bundles to declare their provided and required services, the core OSGi specification doesn't define an explicit way to compose an application. In OSGi, the composition of a component-based application is the set of deployed bundles. The interesting part is how the composition is constructed (matching provided services to required services), which is done at execution time via the service registry. This service-oriented interaction pattern among components is what makes the OSGi approach a service-oriented component model.

Using execution-time service binding means dependencies are resolved late. Further, the use of an interfaced-based interaction via services enables substitutability of providers. Combining late binding and provider substitutability results in a flexible

> **Service-oriented component models**
>
> Service-oriented component models rely on execution-time binding of provided services to required services using the service-oriented interaction pattern (publish-find-bind). Often, execution-time dynamism is also associated with service-oriented component models, but this isn't technically a requirement to receive some of the benefits. For example, COM follows a similar approach of execution-time binding to required components, but it doesn't assume that these components will also come and go during application execution. Still, following this approach allows you to treat the deployed set of components as the application configuration, which leads to flexibility in your application composition.

component model where compositions are malleable, because they don't specify explicit component implementations, nor precise bindings among them. In the OSGi model, this also opens up the possibility of advanced scenarios based on execution-time dynamism.

The OSGi approach is flexible, but it's also a little low-level. For example, although OSGi uses an API-based approach, many modern component models use or are moving toward an API-less approach, such as using Plain Old Java Objects (POJOs) as components. This has led to the creation of several OSGi-based component frameworks and/or extensions to the core OSGi approach. In the next section, we'll provide an overview of what these additional component frameworks are trying to achieve.

11.2.2 Improving upon OSGi's component model

The main weakness of the OSGi component model is its reliance on components manually managing their own service-level dependencies, even though module-level dependencies are automatically managed. Some of the earliest work on improving the OSGi component model was done to address this complexity, such as by Beanome (www.humbertocervantes.net/papers/ISADS2002.pdf) and Service Binder (www.humbertocervantes.net/papers/ESEC2003.pdf). All of the component frameworks we'll discuss in this chapter and the next also address this issue. Because the approaches have a lot of similarities, we'll try to describe some of the issues in a general way here.

GENERAL APPROACH

OSGi-based component frameworks adopt the bundle JAR file as the deployment unit for components. In general, they break the "one component per JAR file" approach of the standard OSGi component framework and allow any number of components to be contained in it. They all define additional, component-related metadata, which is packaged in the bundle to describe the components contained in the bundle JAR file. They then employ the extender pattern to listen for bundles containing components to come and go so they can start managing the contained components, as shown in figure 11.2. A component's description defines which services it provides and which it requires; we'll go into a little more depth on this topic shortly.

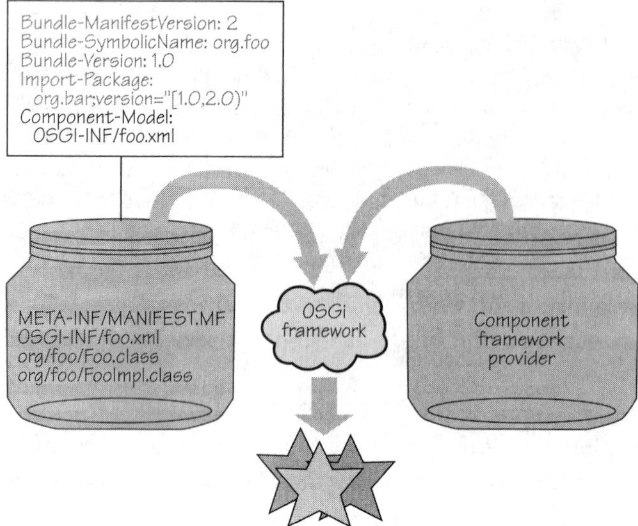

Figure 11.2 Component frameworks in OSGi are generally implemented as other bundles using the extender pattern. They remove boilerplate code from user bundles (often using metadata files—OSGI-INF/foo.xml in this case), allowing the deployer to build complex business services out of modular building blocks.

The lifecycles of components contained in a bundle are subservient to their containing bundle, meaning that components can only be active if their containing bundle is active. Beyond that, the lifecycle of an individual component is based on its own dependencies and constraints. Component frameworks typically define valid and invalid component lifecycle states based on whether a component's dependencies are satisfied. Because the lifecycle of the contained components is managed by the component framework, component bundles typically don't have bundle activators. A component framework listens for bundle lifecycle state changes in the component bundles to trigger management. As a result, component frameworks introduce some other sort of callback mechanism (a *lifecycle hook*) for components wishing for such notification; you can think of this as a component activator. Luckily, such lifecycle hooks are usually unnecessary, because services and service dependencies are managed automatically, which was the main purpose for having a bundle activator in the first place.

AUTOMATING SERVICE MANAGEMENT

The most immediate benefit of having the component framework manage service dependencies is the simplification it brings. It removes redundant boilerplate code for handling each service dependency, and it also eliminates some of the complex, error-prone aspects.

Consider a trivial example where a component `FooImpl` depends on service `Bar` and should only publish its service when `Bar` is available. This is the scenario shown in figure 11.1; the following listing shows the code necessary to achieve it using a `ServiceTracker` (refer to chapter 4 for a reminder of how `ServiceTracker` works).

Listing 11.1 `ServiceTracker` handling one-to-one dependency on a service

```
class BarTracker extends ServiceTracker {
  private final FooImpl foo;
  private final BundleContext ctx;
```

```
  private LinkedList<Bar> found = new LinkedList<Bar>();
  private ServiceRegistration reg;

  BarTracker(FooImpl foo, BundleContext ctx) {
    super(ctx, Bar.class.getName(), null);
    this.foo = foo;
    this.ctx = ctx;
  }

  @Override
  public Object addingService(ServiceReference reference) {
    Bar bar = (Bar) super.addingService(reference);
    found.add(bar);                                          // 1 Stores backups
    if (foo.getBar() == null) {                              // 2 First Bar service found?
      foo.setBar(bar);
      reg = ctx.registerService(Foo.class.getName(), foo, null);
    }
    return bar;
  }

  @Override
  public void removedService(ServiceReference reference, Object service) {
    found.remove(service);
    if (foo.getBar() == service) {                           // 3 Bar service removed?
      if (found.isEmpty()) {
        reg.unregister();
        foo.setBar(null);
        reg = null;
      }
      else {
        foo.setBar(found.getFirst());                        // 4 Replaces removed service with backup
      }
    }
    super.removedService(reference, service);
  }
}
```

BarTracker tracks Bar services. If one is discovered, it checks whether this is the first Bar service it has found ❷. If so, it calls the FooImpl.setBar() method prior to registering the Foo service of FooImpl. If more than one Bar service is found, backups are stored ❶. If BarTracker detects that the Bar service being used has been removed ❸, it replaces that service with one of the backups ❹. If no backup is available, it unregisters the Foo service and calls the FooImpl.setBar() method with null.

You may be looking at this code and thinking that it looks complicated. We agree that it's reasonably so, particularly if you also consider that it covers only a single, one-to-one service dependency. Things get more complex (and redundant) as you get more dependencies. OSGi-based component frameworks allow you to describe these types of issues; then the frameworks worry about it for us. Typically, the component frameworks let you describe the following:

- *Provided services*—Services implemented by the component
- *Required services*—Services needed by the component in order to provide its services

If the component's required services are satisfied, the component framework can instantiate the component and publish its provided services into the service registry. The descriptions of provided services are normally straightforward (just mentioning the interfaces under which to publish the component), but the descriptions of required services can be rich. A service's dependency description may include the following:

- *Service type*—Actual type of required service
- *Optionality*—Whether the dependency is mandatory or the component can function without it
- *Cardinality*—Whether the dependency is for a single service instance (one-to-one) or for an aggregate number of service instances (one-to-many)
- *Lifecycle impact*—Whether execution-time changes are visible to the component (dynamic) or invalidate the entire component instance (static)

Most of these characteristics are reasonably self-explanatory. The last one, lifecycle impact, is a little trickier. Because dynamism adds complexity, some component frameworks allow components to control how much service dynamism a component sees. If a component wants to treat a given dependency as having a static lifecycle, it won't see new services arriving after instantiation and will be completely invalidated if a service being used goes away. On the other hand, dependencies having a dynamic lifecycle can potentially see (and handle) service dynamism at execution time without being invalidated. For example, you may want to create a component with an optional, dynamic dependency on a log service. If the log service isn't there, your component can function without it; but if one arrives, your component can start using it as soon as it's available.

Don't worry if these service dependency characteristics are a little fuzzy at this point; they'll become clearer as we look into the various component frameworks in more detail.

SIMPLIFYING OTHER MANAGEMENT AREAS

Another area where component frameworks can help in removal of boilerplate code is in the management of component configuration. In chapter 9, you saw how you can use the Configuration Admin Service to configure OSGi services using a simple portable model. Still, the developer must provide some boilerplate code to interact with this service. Most component frameworks provide ways to simplify component configuration and interaction with the Configuration Admin Service.

Finally, a number of component frameworks allow for custom extension points to allow third-party providers to provide advanced capabilities such as audit management, persistent state, and transaction management using declarative hooks (either in user code or via side files). These sorts of capabilities turn component frameworks into rich programming environments, allowing you to strip away the layers and focus your code on the core of your business process without sacrificing portability.

Having introduced component models and how they relate to modularity in general and OSGi specifically, let's now turn our attention to a practical demonstration of using component models and frameworks in OSGi.

11.2.3 Painting with components

In this chapter and the next, we'll look at three different OSGi-based component frameworks: Declarative Services, Blueprint Container, and iPOJO. You'll re-create the example paint program using each of these component frameworks. For each, you'll have the components shown in figure 11.3, where each component is packaged in its own bundle (although this isn't strictly necessary).

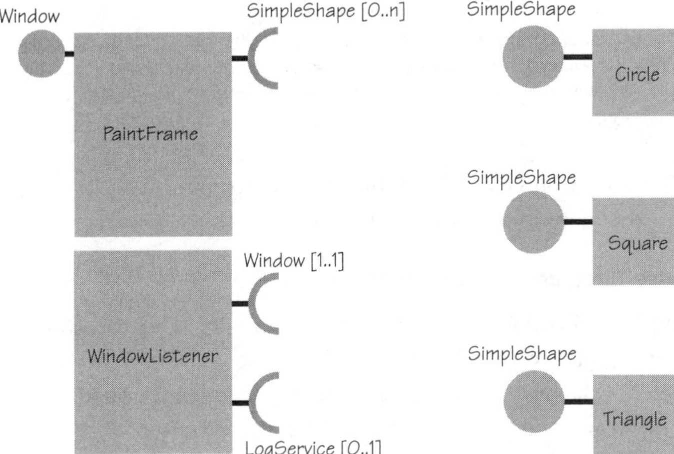

Figure 11.3 Components used in the modified paint application

The `PaintFrame` component provides a `Window` service and has an aggregate dependency on `SimpleShape` services. The shape components each export a single `SimpleShape` service, with no service dependencies. The `WindowListener` component has a mandatory, one-to-one dependency on a `Window` service; it shuts down the framework when the window it's bound to closes. The `WindowListener` also has an optional, one-to-one dependency on a `LogService` to log a message when the window is closed.

All versions of the paint program function like the original, but how they achieve this varies quite a bit. Let's take this high-level of view of OSGi-based component frameworks and make it concrete by turning our attention to the first component framework on the list: Declarative Services.

11.3 Declarative Services

The Declarative Services specification was defined by the OSGi Alliance as part of the R4 compendium specification. It defines a lightweight approach for managing service dependencies. The focus of the Declarative Services specification is to address three main areas of concern, outlined in table 11.2.

The Declarative Services specification addresses these issues by managing service publication and dependencies for components. Managing service publication on behalf of components allows Declarative Services to defer service creation and improve both startup performance and the memory footprint; and managing service

Table 11.2 The Declarative Services' raison d'être

Area of concern	Discussion
Startup time	Because many bundles have bundle activators, the initialization time of each bundle adds to the initialization time of the entire application.
Memory footprint	Registering services often implies the creation of many classes and objects up front to support the services. These classes and objects needlessly consume memory and resources even if these services are never used.
Complexity	A large amount of boilerplate code is required to handle complex service-dependency scenarios. Management of this code in small scenarios is at a minimum a chore, but in large environments this boilerplate code represents a real risk in terms of software maintenance.

dependencies reduces complexity. We'll look into precisely how Declarative Services does these things in the remainder of this chapter.

11.3.1 Building Declarative Services components

Let's start by example. Consider the circle bundle converted to use Declarative Services (the square and triangle bundles follow the same pattern). If you inspect the contents of the new circle bundle in the chapter11/paint-example-ds/ directory of the companion code, you'll see that it has the following contents:

```
META-INF/MANIFEST.MF
OSGI-INF/
OSGI-INF/circle.xml
org/
org/foo/
org/foo/shape/
org/foo/shape/circle/
org/foo/shape/circle/Circle.class
org/foo/shape/circle/circle.png
```

If you remember the previous version, the first thing you'll notice is that it no longer contains a `BundleActivator` implementation. Interesting. If the bundle doesn't have an activator, how does it provide and use services? The clue you need is located in the bundle's manifest file, which has the following new entry:

```
Service-Component: OSGI-INF/circle.xml
```

This header is defined by the Declarative Services specification. It serves two purposes: its existence tells the Declarative Services framework that this bundle contains components and the referenced XML file contains metadata describing the contained components. When a bundle is installed into the OSGi framework, the Declarative Services framework follows the extender pattern and probes for this manifest entry. If it exists, the Declarative Services framework takes over management of the contained components according to the information in the referenced file.

In Declarative Services, the convention is to place component description files in the bundle's OSGI-INF/ directory following an OSGI-INF/<component-name>.xml naming convention, but the files can go anywhere within the bundle. It's possible to include multiple component files in a single bundle using a comma-delimited set, a * wildcard pattern, or a mixture of the two.

Fragmented components

It's also possible to place component descriptions into bundle fragments (which we covered in chapter 5). In this scenario, only the host bundle's `Service-Component` manifest header is read, although the XML files may reside in the bundle fragments. A possible use case for doing this is if you want to support several different component configuration options where you choose at deployment time which is instantiated. We don't classify this as a recommended use case, because fragments bring in all sorts of complex lifecycle issues and break a number of best practices with respect to modular boundaries, but we cover it here for the sake of completeness.

This explains the lack of a bundle activator for your component bundle, but how exactly does your `SimpleShape` service get published? Next, we'll look more closely at the component description file to see how components declare their provided services.

11.3.2 Providing services with Declarative Services

The following code snippet shows the declaration used to tell the Declarative Services framework to publish your `Circle` class as a service in the OSGi service registry under the `SimpleShape` interface:

```
<?xml version="1.0" encoding="UTF-8"?>
<scr:component xmlns:scr="http://www.osgi.org/xmlns/scr/v1.1.0">
  <property name="simple.shape.name" value="Circle" />
  <property name="simple.shape.icon" value="circle.png" />
  <scr:implementation class="org.foo.shape.circle.Circle" />
  <scr:service>
     <scr:provide interface="org.foo.shape.SimpleShape"/>
  </scr:service>
</scr:component>
```

In this metadata, you define two properties for your component. Properties may be used to configure a component (which we'll look at shortly), but they also act as service properties and are automatically attached to services published by a component. In this case, these properties are used by your paint frame to identify the shape. You define the component's implementation class, which must be reachable on the bundle class path where this component description is located. Finally, you declare that the component provides the `SimpleShape` service. Let's now look at the `Circle` class.

Listing 11.2 `Circle` class used in the Declarative Services paint example

```
public class Circle implements SimpleShape {
  public void draw(Graphics2D g2, Point p) {
    int x = p.x - 25;
    int y = p.y - 25;
```

```
    GradientPaint gradient =
      new GradientPaint(x, y, Color.RED, x + 50, y, Color.WHITE);
    g2.setPaint(gradient);
    g2.fill(new Ellipse2D.Double(x, y, 50, 50));
    BasicStroke wideStroke = new BasicStroke(2.0f);
    g2.setColor(Color.black);
    g2.setStroke(wideStroke);
    g2.draw(new Ellipse2D.Double(x, y, 50, 50));
  }
}
```

This `Circle` class is exactly the same as the prior version. All you do is drop the associated bundle activator and add the component description instead. Before moving on to consuming services, let's discuss component properties a little further.

COMPONENT PROPERTIES

For the circle component, you use the component properties to specify service properties. This follows a pattern of property propagation similar to what you saw in chapter 9 for Configuration Admin, where configuration properties are attached to the service. In the paint example, you statically declare the properties in a component XML file using the `<property>` element. This is the last place a Declarative Services framework looks for component properties. Component properties may come from

1. Properties passed to the `ComponentFactory.newInstance()` method (we'll cover component factories in section 11.3.4)
2. Properties retrieved from the Configuration Admin service using the component name as the PID
3. Properties defined in the component description file

The priority of these properties is as listed, with the first having the highest priority. This means properties coming from a higher-priority source override the same property coming from a lower-priority source. This precedence behavior allows a developer to assign default component properties, but another user or system administrator can change the configuration at execution time to suit their specific needs.

> **Declarative Services have simple attribute types**
>
> One limitation arises from using Declarative Services as opposed to the core OSGi framework API: Declarative Services components can only use service properties with simple Java types (`String` [default], `Long`, `Double`, `Float`, `Integer`, `Byte`, `Character`, `Boolean`, and `Short`). In the previous version of the paint program, you added the shape icon object directly as a service property using the following code:
>
> ```
> dict.put(SimpleShape.ICON_PROPERTY,
>   new ImageIcon(this.getClass().getResource("circle.png")));
> ```
>
> In the vast majority of situations, this limitation isn't a big deal, but it's something to consider. We'll return to this topic briefly in the next section and in the following chapter when we discuss the Blueprint and iPOJO component frameworks.

Providing services is straightforward: a component declares which internal class implements which provided service interface, and the Declarative Services framework publishes the service at execution time after the bundle containing the component descriptions is activated. What happens if the component has dependencies on other services?

11.3.3 *Consuming services with Declarative Services*

To see how Declarative Services components can use services, let's turn our attention to the paint program's paint frame. Again, you modify the bundle to contain a component description in OSGI-INF/paint.xml, as shown next.

Listing 11.3 Declarative Services' description of `PaintFrame` component

```
<?xml version="1.0" encoding="UTF-8"?>
<scr:component xmlns:scr="http://www.osgi.org/xmlns/scr/v1.1.0"
  name="paint"
  immediate="true">

  <scr:implementation class="org.foo.paint.PaintFrame" />

  <scr:reference
    interface="org.foo.shape.SimpleShape"
    cardinality="0..n"
    policy="dynamic"
    bind="addShape"
    unbind="removeShape"/>

  <scr:service>
     <scr:provide interface="java.awt.Window"/>
  </scr:service>

  <scr:property name="name" value="main"/>
</scr:component>
```

❶ Defines reference to service

There's quite a bit of information in this component description. Looking at some of the aspects that are similar to the circle component, you see the component declaration, but this time you assign `paint` as its name. You specify the component implementation class, which you indicate as providing a `java.awt.Window` service with a service property, called `name`. You introduce a new element ❶, defining a "reference" (a dependency) to a service implementing the `SimpleShape` interface.

If you're familiar with other dependency-injection frameworks, such as Spring, this should be starting to feel familiar. You specify the method `PaintFrame.addShape()` to use for injecting discovered `SimpleShape` services. Also, because you're in an OSGi environment where services can come and go, you specify the method `PaintFrame.removeShape()` to use when a shape service goes away. There are other service-dependency characteristics, but before we go into the details of those, let's talk more about binding methods.

BINDING METHOD SIGNATURES

The Declarative Services specification defines the following method signatures for binding methods:

- void <method-name>(ServiceReference);
- void <method-name>(<parameter-type>);
- void <method-name>(<parameter-type>, Map);

The first form injects the service's associated ServiceReference into the component instead of the service object itself. This allows the component to find out which services are available in the framework without retrieving them. This method is typically used in conjunction with the ComponentContext, which we'll discuss a little later, to implement extremely lightweight solutions where service objects are created only when absolutely necessary.

The second form should look familiar to most programmers who have used some form of dependency-injection framework. Using this binding method, the Declarative Services implementation retrieves the actual service object from the OSGi service registry and injects it into the component. The component developer may choose to store a reference to the service object; but you must take care to dereference the service when the corresponding unbind method is called, to prevent memory leakage.

The third form behaves much like the second, except that the associated service properties are also injected into the component. Because you need the service properties to retrieve the shape name and icon for the paint frame component, this is the form you'll use. The PaintFrame.addShape() method is as follows:

```
void addShape(SimpleShape shape, Map attrs) {
  final DefaultShape delegate = new DefaultShape(shape);
  final String name = (String) attrs.get(SimpleShape.NAME_PROPERTY);
  final Icon icon = new ImageIcon(shape.getClass().getResource(
    (String) attrs.get(SimpleShape.ICON_PROPERTY)));

  m_shapes.put(name, delegate);
  ...
}
```

The Declarative Services framework calls this addShape() method when any SimpleShape service is published in the OSGi service registry, passing in the service and the associated map of service properties. You read the name property of the shape and load its ImageIcon representation. As we mentioned earlier, the Declarative Services specification is only able to handle simple property types, so in this version of the paint frame component you have to explicitly load the resource via the shape object's class loader. Finally, you store a reference to the shape service object in an internal map for use later.

Conversely, when a shape service is removed from the service registry, the Declarative Services framework invokes the PaintFrame.removeShape() method:

```
void removeShape(SimpleShape shape, Map attrs) {
  final String name = (String) attrs.get(SimpleShape.NAME_PROPERTY);

  DefaultShape delegate = (DefaultShape) m_shapes.remove(name);

  ...
}
```

You use the binding method form that supplies the service attributes as a map. You use the `name` property from the map to figure out which component has been removed and remove your reference to the service object from the internal map.

Binding method accessibility

You may have noticed that the binding methods you've defined have package-private visibility. The Declarative Services specification states the following with regard to method visibility:

- `public`—Access permitted
- `protected`—Access permitted
- package private—Access permitted if the method is declared in an implementation class or any superclass within the same package
- `private`—Access permitted if the method is declared in an implementation class

As a matter of best practice, you should generally protect binding methods, because doing so prevents external code from injecting services out of band of the main service-registry lifecycle (assuming the Java security manager is enabled—we'll look at security in chapter 14).

Now, let's return our attention to how components describe their service dependencies. So far, we've discussed that the component service dependency description includes a service interface and binding methods. Other, more sophisticated dependency characteristics are available.

SOPHISTICATED SERVICE DEPENDENCY CHARACTERISTICS

Many service dependencies fall into the category of being a hard dependency on a single service object. But what if your component is different? Recall the following snippet from listing 11.3:

```
<scr:reference
  interface="org.foo.shape.SimpleShape"
  cardinality="0..n"
  policy="dynamic"
  bind="addShape"
  unbind="removeShape"/>
```

We haven't discussed the cardinality and policy dependency characteristics yet, but they help you address more sophisticated service dependency situations. The notion of *cardinality* plays two roles in the Declarative Services specification:

- *Optionality*—Cardinality values starting with 0 are treated as optional, whereas values starting with 1 are treated as mandatory.
- *Aggregation*—Cardinality values ending with 1 are treated as a dependency on a single service object of the specified type, whereas values ending in n are treated as a dependency on all available service objects of the specified type.

The possible cardinality values defined by the Declarative Services specification are `0..1` (optional, singular dependency), `1..1` (mandatory, singular dependency), `0..n` (optional, aggregate dependency), and `1..n` (mandatory, aggregate dependency). From the snippet, you can see that the paint frame has an optional, aggregate dependency on shape services; this means it wants to be bound to all available shape services, but doesn't need any to function. Cardinality is fairly straightforward, but the dependency policy is a little trickier to understand.

A component service dependency can be declared with either of two policy values: dynamic or static. What does this mean? A dynamic policy means that the component is notified whenever the service comes or goes, whereas with a static policy, the service is injected once and not changed until the component is deactivated. In essence, if you use a dynamic policy, your component needs to cope with the possible issues (such as threading and synchronization) resulting from service dynamism. If you use a static policy, you don't need to worry about issues related to service dynamism, but your component sees only one view of the services published in the OSGi registry while it's active.

This dependency policy also relates to component lifecycle management. For example, the paint frame component specifies a dynamic policy. Therefore, if a shape it's using goes away, it sees the change immediately and dynamically adapts accordingly. You've seen this in earlier examples, where you dynamically added and removed shapes. If this dependency were specified as static, then if a shape service being used by the paint frame departed, the paint frame component instance would need to be thrown away, because a static policy means the component isn't programmed such that it can handle service dynamism. We'll continue this discussion about component lifecycle in the next subsection.

Another characteristic of service dependencies is a target filter. To illustrate, let's look at the `WindowListener` component of the modified paint program; its Declarative Services component description is as follows.

Listing 11.4 Metadata for `WindowListener` with optional `LogService` dependency

```
<?xml version="1.0" encoding="UTF-8"?>
<scr:component xmlns:scr="http://www.osgi.org/xmlns/scr/v1.1.0"
  name="windowlistener">
  <scr:implementation class="org.foo.windowlistener.WindowListener" />

  <scr:reference
    name="window"
    interface="java.awt.Window"
    policy="static"
    cardinality="1..1"
    target="(name=main)"
    bind="bindWindow"
    unbind="unbindWindow"/>
  <scr:reference
    name="logService"
    interface="org.osgi.service.log.LogService"
    policy="dynamic"
```

❶ Window service dependency

❷ Specifies filter

```
    cardinality="0..1"
    bind="bindLog"
    unbind="unbindLog"/>
</scr:component>
```

The `WindowListener` component has a static, singular, and mandatory dependency on a `Window` service ❶. You specify a target LDAP filter to locate the specific `Window` service of interest ❷; recall that the filter references the property you associated with the `PaintFrame` component's `Window` service in its component description in listing 11.3. Additionally, the `WindowListener` component has a dynamic, singular, and optional dependency on a log service.

Target reference properties

You saw earlier that component properties can be used to define the service properties associated with a component's provided service. Component properties can also be used to configure service-dependency target filters at execution time. To do this, the property name must be equal to the name associated with the service reference appended with `.target`. In this case, you could override the window target using a property of this form:

```
<property name="window.target" value="(name=other)" />
```

This binds the window listener to windows attributed with the `name=other` identifier. Doing this directly in the static component description is of relatively low value. But if you remember the discussion on component properties, these values can also be set at execution time via the Configuration Admin Service or using component factories, which opens up a set of interesting use cases.

Filtering services based on attributes is relatively easy and, at first glance, dealing with optional services appears equally easy. But there are some subtle mechanics of which you need to be aware when using the dynamic dependency policy. Here are the relevant lines from the `WindowListener` component.

Listing 11.5 `WindowListener` with optional `LogService` dependency

```
public class WindowListener extends WindowAdapter {
...
  private AtomicReference<LogService> logRef =
    new AtomicReference<LogService>();

  protected void bindLog(LogService log) {
    logRef.compareAndSet(null, log);
  }

  protected void unbindLog(LogService log) {
    logRef.compareAndSet(log, null);
  }
...
  private void log(int level, String msg) {
    LogService log = logRef.get();
```

```
      if (log != null) {
        log.log(level,msg);
      }
    }
}
```

Here, you use a `java.util.concurrent.AtomicReference` object to hold the `LogService`, which you set in the binding methods. You use an `AtomicReference` to protect yourself from threading issues related to the service being bound or unbound while your component is using it. You also need to be aware of the fact that the `LogService` may in fact not be bound because it's optional, so you check whether the service is bound and log a message if so. The use of a wrapper method to achieve this is one possible mechanism; for a more advanced solution, you could use null objects to protect other areas of code from this execution-time issue.

So far, you've seen how to describe components that publish and consume services, but we've only indirectly discussed component lifecycle management. Next, we'll provide more details about the lifecycle of Declarative Services components.

11.3.4 Declarative Services component lifecycle

Having described your components, the next issue to consider is their lifecycle. When are components created? When are they destroyed? Are there any callbacks at these stages? How can you access the `BundleContext` if there is no `BundleActivator`? We'll deal with each of these questions in this section.

COMPONENT LIFECYCLE STAGES

In chapter 3, we introduced the bundle lifecycle: in essence, bundles are installed, then resolved, and then activated. Declarative Services defines a similar lifecycle for components, where they're enabled, then satisfied, and then activated. The Declarative Services specification defines the following stages to a component lifecycle:

- *Enabled*—A simple Boolean flag controls whether the component is eligible for management.
- *Satisfied*—The component is enabled, its mandatory dependencies are satisfied, any provided services are published in the service registry, but the component itself isn't yet instantiated.
- *Activated*—The component is enabled, its mandatory dependencies are satisfied, any provided services are published in the service registry, and the component instance has been created as a result of a request to use its service.
- *Modified*—The configuration associated with the component has changed, and the component instance should be notified.
- *Deactivated*—Either the component has been disabled or its mandatory dependencies are no longer satisfied, so its provided services are no longer available and its component instance, if created, is dereferenced for garbage collection.

You can enable/disable a component declaratively using the `enabled` attribute of the `<component>` XML element and programmatically using the `ComponentContext` interface, which you'll see shortly. A simple use case for this is to reduce startup time by disabling all but a small number of components and then enabling additional components later as needed. Similarly, neither the enabled nor satisfied stages result in instantiating the component class in an effort to avoid unnecessary work.

When a component is enabled, it may become satisfied. A component can become satisfied only if all of its mandatory dependencies are satisfied. After it's satisfied, it may become activated if its provided service is requested. Activation results in the component being instantiated. Each component description ultimately is reified as a single component instance that will be managed by the Declarative Services framework; by default, a one-to-one mapping exists between a component description and a component instance.

The component lifecycle is coupled to the lifecycle of its containing bundle. Only components in activated bundles are eligible for lifecycle management. If a bundle is stopped, the Declarative Services framework automatically deactivates all activated components contained in it.

Let's dive into some code to see what this means in practice for the paint application. First, let's look at the `PaintFrame` class.

Listing 11.6 Lifecycle-related code from Declarative Services `PaintFrame` class

```
public PaintFrame() {
  super("PaintFrame");
...
}
...
void activate(Map properties) {
  Integer w = (Integer) properties.get(".width");
  Integer h = (Integer) properties.get(".height");

  int width = w == null ? 400 : w;
  int height = h == null ? 400 : h;

  setSize(width, height);

  SwingUtils.invokeAndWait(new Runnable() {
    public void run() {
      setVisible(true);
    }
  });
}

void deactivate() {
  SwingUtils.invokeLater(new Runnable() {
    public void run() {
      setVisible(false);
      dispose();
    }
  });
}
...
}
```

You define a default, no-argument constructor for the component class; Declarative Services component classes must define such a constructor. You define an `activate()` callback method to be invoked by the Declarative Services framework when the component is activated, along with a corresponding `deactivate()` callback method to be called when the component is deactivated.

> **Declarative Services callback methods**
>
> The names of callback methods (`activate()` and `deactivate()`) are defaults. If you wish to use a different pattern or are migrating legacy code, you can define the names of these callback methods via attributes on the `<component>` XML element. For example, the following code snippet redefines the activation and deactivation methods to be `start()` and `stop()`, respectively:
>
> ```
> <component name="org.foo.example"
>            activate="start"
>            deactivate="stop">
> ```
>
> The activation and deactivation methods are optional, so if your component has no need to track its activation state, you can leave them out. Also, if you use the default `activate()` and `deactivate()` method names, there's no need to define these in the component declaration because the Declarative Services framework will discover them automatically.
>
> Although it isn't shown in the example, there's also a callback method for the modified component lifecycle stage. Unlike the activation and deactivation methods, this lifecycle callback has no default method name, so you must define the method name in the `<component>` element, as follows:
>
> ```
> <component name="org.foo.example" modified="modified">
> ```
>
> This indicates that the component is interested in being notified about configuration updates and specifies the name of the callback method.

You may be wondering about the `Map` passed into the `activate()` method, which you use to configure the size of the component. The Declarative Services lifecycle callback methods accept a number of different argument types to give the component additional information, which we'll describe next.

LIFECYCLE CALLBACK METHOD SIGNATURES

The lifecycle callback methods follow the same method-accessibility rules laid out earlier for binding methods. They may also accept zero or more of the following argument types (ordering isn't important):

- `ComponentContext`—Receives the component context for the component configuration
- `BundleContext`—Receives the bundle context of the component's bundle
- `Map`—Receives an unmodifiable map containing the component's properties

- `int` or `Integer`—Receives the reason why the component is being deactivated, where the value is one of the following reasons:
  - 0—Unspecified.
  - 1—The component was disabled.
  - 2—A reference became unsatisfied.
  - 3—A configuration was changed.
  - 4—A configuration was deleted.
  - 5—The component was disposed.
  - 6—The bundle was stopped.

Of these arguments, you know little yet about `ComponentContext`. What is its purpose?

USING THE COMPONENTCONTEXT

The Declarative Services framework creates a unique `ComponentContext` object for each component it activates. This object plays a role for components similar to the role the `BundleContext` object plays for bundles—it provides access to execution environment facilities. The `ComponentContext` interface is as follows:

```
public interface ComponentContext {
  public Dictionary getProperties();
  public Object locateService(String name);
  public Object locateService(String name, ServiceReference reference);
  public Object[] locateServices(String name);
  public BundleContext getBundleContext();
  public Bundle getUsingBundle();
  public ComponentInstance getComponentInstance();
  public void enableComponent(String name);
  public void disableComponent(String name);
  public ServiceReference getServiceReference();
}
```

The `getProperties()` method allows a component to access its configuration properties. The methods for locating services provide an alternative approach to service injection for using services; this alternative strategy is discussed in the "Lookup strategy" sidebar. The `getBundleContext()` method provides access to the containing bundle's `BundleContext` object. The `getUsingBundle()` method is related to component factories, which we'll discuss later.

The `getComponentInstance()`, `enableComponent()`, and `disableComponent()` methods provide a component with a way to programmatically control the component lifecycle; we'll discuss them further in the next section. Finally, the `getServiceReference()` method allows a component to access the `ServiceReference` of this component if it provides a service.

In the general case, whether or not a component is satisfied is dictated by whether or not its service dependencies are satisfied. But this isn't the only type of dependency considered by Declarative Services; another situation is where a component is dependent on its configuration properties.

Lookup strategy

So far in this section, we've shown you how to inject services into components using binding methods. This pattern is known as the *Hollywood principle*: "Don't call us, we'll call you." In some circumstances, it's useful to apply the Reverse Hollywood principle, "Do call us, we won't call you."

The Declarative Services specification supports both approaches; it refers to the injection approach as the *event strategy* and the alternative as the *lookup strategy*. The event strategy provides instant notification about service changes, whereas the lookup strategy is able to defer service creation until the last minute.

The family of `locateService()` methods on the `ComponentContext` facilitate the lookup strategy. These methods each take a `String` argument that specifies the name of the associated service reference in the component description XML file to retrieve. For example, you could change the paint frame description to be the following:

```
<scr:reference
  interface="org.foo.shape.SimpleShape"
  cardinality="0..n"
  policy="dynamic"
  name="shape"/>
```

In this case, you don't have bind or unbind methods. To access any bound services, you need to use the `ComponentContext`, like this:

```
void findShapes(ComponentContext ctx) {
  Object[] services = ctx.locateServices("shape");
  for (Object s : services) {
    SimpleShape shape = (SimpleShape) s;
  }
}
```

It's possible to mix and match these approaches. You can use the event strategy for some service references and the lookup strategy for others. You can even use a hybrid approach, using the event strategy with a binding method accepting a `ServiceReference` combined with the `locateService(String, ServiceReference)` method of the `ComponentContext`. This option provides a highly responsive but lightweight approach to service binding.

CONFIGURATION POLICY

We've mentioned that it's possible to configure a Declarative Services component by specifying an entry in the Configuration Admin Service with PID corresponding to the name of the component. These configuration properties override any specified in the XML description and provide a way to tweak the behavior of a component at execution time. It's also possible to define a policy for how dependencies on configuration properties should be handled.

Declarative Services defines the following configuration policies: `optional`, `require`, and `ignore`. The default configuration policy is `optional`, indicating that Configuration Admin will be used if available. If `require` is specified, the component won't be satisfied until there's a configuration for it in Configuration Admin. The `require` policy is useful in cases where no sensible default value can be given for a configuration property (such as a database URL). The `ignore` policy indicates that only the declared component properties should be considered.

You specify configuration policies like this:

```
<component name="org.foo.example" configuration-policy="require">
```

In this example, the component requires a corresponding configuration to be present in Configuration Admin, or else it can't be satisfied.

> **Configuration Admin Service factories**
>
> In chapter 9, you saw that it's possible to use the Configuration Admin Service with one of two types of managed services, either a `ManagedService` or a `ManagedServiceFactory`. The first takes a single configuration and uses it to configure a service provided by a bundle; the second allows multiple configurations to be created—each corresponding to a new service.
>
> This pattern can be applied to Declarative Services components. If the component name matches a registered PID for a nonfactory configuration, the Declarative Services framework creates a single instance of the component. But if the component name matches a registered factory PID, a new component instance is created for each configuration associated with the factory PID. This provides a lightweight way of constructing several different component instances from a common component definition.

Components can be satisfied by the availability of their service dependencies and configuration, but the Declarative Services framework still won't activate (instantiate) a component until another bundle requests its provided service. What about a component that doesn't provide a service? How will it ever be activated?

IMMEDIATE VS. DELAYED COMPONENTS

Many components, such as the shape components in the paint example, exist solely to provide a function to other parts of an application. If no other deployed bundles consume the services these bundles provide, there's no need to expend resources activating the associated components. Components that provide services are delayed by default in Declarative Services. Sometimes this delayed behavior is problematic. If you look again at the component declaration of the paint frame, you see that it specifies the `immediate="true"` attribute:

```
<scr:component xmlns:scr="http://www.osgi.org/xmlns/scr/v1.1.0"
  name="paint"
  immediate="true">
```

This turns off the delayed behavior and forces the Declarative Services implementation to construct the paint frame as soon as it's satisfied. Because the paint frame component provides a service, it would be delayed by default. You need it to be `immediate` because you need it to create the window for the paint program. For components that don't provide a service, it's an error to set `immediate` to `false` because they would never be instantiated; instead, they're implicitly defined as immediate components.

COMPONENT FACTORIES

The final tool in the Declarative Services toolbox is component factories. These provide a programmatic mechanism to instantiate new instances of components. In many ways, this is similar to the factory PID mechanism of creating components mentioned earlier; but instead of going via the `ConfigurationAdmin` interface, the Declarative Services specification provides a mechanism to declare a component as explicitly providing a factory API, which is then manipulated by a secondary service to construct actual instances of the components.

To see how this works, let's consider a slight variation of the original paint example where a shape component factory is registered to provide shape components on demand. You create a component factory by declaring the component using the `factory=<factory.identifier>` attribute on the top-level component declaration:

```
<scr:component xmlns:scr=http://www.osgi.org/xmlns/scr/v1.1.0
 factory="shape.factory" name="shape">
```

This results in the Declarative Services framework publishing a `ComponentFactory` service into the service registry. Component factory services can be used like any normal services; for example, client code wishing to be injected with this component factory can do the following:

```
<reference
  name="shape"
  interface="org.osgi.service.component.ComponentFactory"
  target="(component.factory=shape.factory)"
  cardinality="1..1"
  policy="static"
  bind="addShapeFactory"
  unbind="removeShapeFactory"/>
```

Here the target attribute of the reference element is set to the name of the factory attribute of the declared component. To create a new shape instance, you use the following code.

Listing 11.7 Using a component factory

```
import org.osgi.service.component.ComponentFactory;

public class ShapeManager {
  private AtomicReference<ComponentFactory> factoryRef =
    new AtomicReference<ComponentFactory>();

  void addShapeFactory(ComponentFactory factory) {
    factoryRef.set(factory);
  }

  void removeShapeFactory(ComponentFactory factory) {
    factoryRef.set(null);
```

❶ Registers component factory

```
    }

    public void createShape(String name) {
      ComponentFactory factory = factoryRef.get();
      if ( factory == null )
        throw new IllegalStateException("No factory registered");

      Hashtable config = new Hashtable();
      config.set("name", name);
      factory.newInstance(config);                    <-- 2 Builds shape instance
    }
  }
```

The component factory is registered with the `ShapeManager` component using callback methods ❶. You use the `factory.newInstance()` method to instruct the Declarative Services runtime to build another instance of a shape with the specified name ❷, which will then be registered in the OSGi registry as before.

> **Component factories vs. Configuration Admin Service factories**
>
> The component factory provides an alternative mechanism to the Configuration Admin managed service factory approach mentioned earlier. Which approach you take is largely a matter of preference. Note that the component factory approach and the managed service factory approach are mutually exclusive: it's not possible to create a component factory that is instantiated by a factory PID.

This concludes our introduction to component models in OSGi and review of the Declarative Services specification. If you want a closer look at the Declarative Services version of the paint program, go to the chapter11/paint-example-ds/ directory of the companion code. Type `ant` to build the example and `java -jar launcher.jar bundles` to run it. The example uses the Apache Felix Service Component Runtime (SCR; http://felix.apache.org/site/apache-felix-service-component-runtime.html) implementation of Declarative Services.

11.4 Summary

In this chapter, we reviewed the general principles and motivation of component-oriented programming and looked at how components and modules intersect and interact in an OSGi context. The topics we discussed included the following:

- Components are application building blocks that adhere to a component model.
- Components further support separation of concerns by separating interface from implementation.
- Components support external management of concerns, allowing you to offload mundane and potentially error-prone tasks to component frameworks.
- The OSGi framework is a component framework, where bundles are equivalent to components that interact via services.

- Additional, more advanced component frameworks can be layered on top of the OSGi framework to further enhance the core component model.
- Declarative Services is an OSGi standard component framework that manages service publication, service dependencies, and configuration dependencies on behalf of components.

Component orientation in general and Declarative Services in particular are worthwhile approaches when you're working with OSGi. In the next chapter, we'll push even further by looking at two more advanced component frameworks, in case Declarative Services doesn't address all your needs.

12 Advanced component frameworks

This chapter covers

- Exploring the OSGi Blueprint component framework
- Exploring the Apache Felix iPOJO component framework
- Using Declarative Services, Blueprint, and iPOJO in a single application

In the last chapter, we introduced you to component-oriented programming and how it relates to OSGi. We also introduced a lightweight component framework defined by the OSGi Alliance, called Declarative Services, which you used to re-create your paint program. Declarative Services is just one possible component framework for OSGi. In this chapter, we'll introduce you to two more: Blueprint and iPOJO. These component frameworks provide more advanced capabilities than Declarative Services.

The numerous component frameworks for OSGi may at first seem daunting, but the good news is that you aren't necessarily constrained to a single decision for all time. Choose whichever one seems best to you now. We'll show at the end of this chapter that it's possible to have different component frameworks collaborate in a single application.

Let's get started with the Blueprint component framework.

12.1 Blueprint Container

One of the popular component frameworks in Java today is Spring Beans. The Blueprint Container specification (Blueprint for short) from the OSGi R4.2 Enterprise specification is based heavily on the Spring/OSGi integration work done in Spring Dynamic Modules. One benefit of standardizing this work is that it has resulted in several implementations of this specification from other vendors, including the Apache Aries and Eclipse Gemini projects.

One to rule them all?

It may seem confusing that the OSGi Alliance has defined two "standard" component frameworks: Declarative Services and Blueprint. There's a method to this apparent madness. Both specifications are interoperable at execution time (see section 12.3) via services, so either can be used to implement a given service interface without impacting clients. Additionally, each specification caters to different use cases:

- Declarative Services focuses on building lightweight components with quick startup times.
- Blueprint focuses on building highly configurable enterprise-oriented applications.

As usual, one size doesn't fit all. We see this throughout computing: often there are numerous ways to accomplish similar, but not quite identical, tasks. From the OSGi Alliance's perspective, it makes sense to have different communities standardizing their approaches around OSGi technology, rather than trying to dictate a single approach for everyone.

Let's look into the Blueprint architecture, after which we'll discuss how you can build the paint program using Blueprint.

12.1.1 Blueprint architecture

Blueprint defines a component in terms of a number of elements, each of which has an underlying manager in the Blueprint component container. Each Blueprint component definition can contain zero or more of the managers listed in table 12.1.

Table 12.1 Blueprint component container managers

Manager	Description
Bean	Provides components with the same basic semantics as Spring beans: ■ Construction via reflective construction or static factory methods ■ Support for singletons or prototype instances ■ Injection of properties or constructor arguments ■ Lifecycle callbacks for activation and deactivation
Reference	Gets a single service from the OSGi service registry for the component based on the service interface and an optional filter over the service properties

Table 12.1 Blueprint component container managers *(continued)*

Manager	Description
Reference list	Gets one or more services from the OSGi service registry for the component based on the service interface and an optional filter over the service properties
Service	Allows components to provide OSGi services
Environment	Provides components access to the OSGi framework and the Blueprint container, including the bundle context of the component

Let's now look at a concrete example of Blueprint in action.

12.1.2 *Providing services with Blueprint*

In this section, we'll explore how to use the Blueprint specification to build the example paint program. As with Declarative Services from the previous chapter, we'll start by looking at the converted circle bundle. Again, this bundle no longer contains a bundle activator class, but it does contain the circle.xml file shown in the following listing.

Listing 12.1 Blueprint component definition for the circle component

```
<?xml version="1.0" encoding="UTF-8"?>
<blueprint xmlns="http://www.osgi.org/xmlns/blueprint/v1.0.0">
  <bean id="circle" class="org.foo.shape.circle.Circle" />

  <service id="shape" interface="org.foo.shape.SimpleShape" ref="circle">
    <service-properties>
      <entry key="simple.shape.name" value="Circle"/>
      <entry key="simple.shape.icon">
        <bean class="org.foo.shape.circle.IconFactory"
              factory-method="createIcon"/>
      </entry>
    </service-properties>
  </service>
</blueprint>
```

Notice that Blueprint uses a different XML syntax than Declarative Services. If you're familiar with Spring, some of this XML should look a little familiar. For example, Blueprint uses the `<bean>` element to describe components, which you use here to define the circle component. You also use it again to specify a value for a service property. Spring users should also be familiar with the `<entry>` element, which is used by Spring and Blueprint to define the entries of map objects. You use `<entry>` in this case to define the service properties for your service interface. Some less familiar aspects are as follows:

- The top-level `<blueprint>` element (with a new namespace) as compared to the classic `<beans>` element from Spring
- The `<service>` element, which you use to publish the bean associated with the `ref` identifier `circle` into the OSGi service registry with the declared set of nested service properties

Let's dig a little deeper into the details of precisely how you provide services using Blueprint.

BLUEPRINT SERVICE ATTRIBUTES

At a glance, there appear to be only syntactic differences between the Declarative Services version of this component and the Blueprint one. There's one big functional difference: the ability to define complex attribute objects. Blueprint introduces a factory bean concept, which you use in the example to create an `ImageIcon` service property. The code required to implement the factory bean is

```
public class IconFactory {
  public static ImageIcon createIcon() {
    return new ImageIcon(IconFactory.class.getResource("circle.png"));
  }
}
```

This factory bean allows you to provide a class to perform the nontrivial actions required to create an `ImageIcon` from the XML model. The factory-bean pattern also lets Blueprint create objects with nontrivial constructors and use them in the component as services, parameters, or service properties.

SERVICE INTERFACES

To provide the circle's `SimpleShape` service, you directly specify the interface name as an attribute of the `<service>` element. Blueprint supports a couple of other options for supplying the service interface: the `<interfaces>` element and the `auto-export` attribute. To demonstrate, consider the following trivial XML bean definition:

```
<bean id="fooImpl"  class="FooImpl"/>
```

This corresponds to a class definition like this:

```
public class FooImpl implements Foo { ... }
```

Given this bean and class definition, you can describe the component's provided `Foo` service in any of the following equivalent ways:

- ```
  <service id="foo" ref="fooImpl">
       <interfaces>
         <value>com.acme.Foo</value>
       </interface>
     </service>
  ```
- `&lt;service id="foo" interface="com.acme.Foo" ref="fooImpl"/&gt;`
- `&lt;service id="foo" auto-export="interfaces" ref="fooImpl"/&gt;`

The first is the longhand form of a service definition, which allows a Blueprint component to export more than one interface for a given bean. The second is the shorthand form for explicitly exporting a single service interface. The last is an automatic form, where the service manager reflectively calculates the interfaces under which the bean should be registered. For this last form, you must specify one of the following `auto-export` attribute values:
  ```

- `disabled`—No autodetection of service-interface names is undertaken; the interface names must be explicitly declared. This is the default mode.
- `interfaces`—The service object is registered using all of its implemented public Java interface types, including any interfaces implemented by super classes.
- `class-hierarchy`—The service object is registered using its actual type and any public supertypes up to the `Object` class (not included).
- `all-classes`—The service object is registered using its actual type, all public supertypes up to the `Object` class (not included), as well as all public interfaces implemented by the service object and any of its super classes.

A limitation for providing services

Blueprint requires using Java interfaces for services, whereas basic OSGi and Declarative Services allow (but don't recommend) you to use a Java class as a service. You may wonder why Blueprint requires services to be interfaces. Blueprint injects services into components using dynamic proxies (`java.lang.reflect.Proxy`), which require interfaces. We'll discuss Blueprint's use of proxies more later.

After you've described your component and the services it provides in your XML description, you need some way to tell the Blueprint implementation about it. As with Declarative Services, Blueprint introduces a new manifest header to reference the component description file. If you examine the circle bundle's manifest, you see it has the following entry:

```
Bundle-Blueprint: OSGI-INF/circle.xml
```

Following the same approach as Declarative Services, Blueprint employs the extender pattern and probes bundles to determine if they contain this manifest header. If so, the Blueprint implementation manages the contained components; if not, the bundle is ignored.

Fragmented components

The `Bundle-Blueprint` header can take one of a number of forms:

- *Absolute path*—The path to a resource on the bundle class path. For example: `Bundle-Blueprint: OSGI-INF/circle.xml`.
- *Directory*—The path to a directory on the bundle class path. Here, the path must end in a slash (/). For example: `Bundle-Blueprint: OSGI-INF/`.
- *Pattern*—The last component of the path specifies a filename with an optional wildcard. The part before is the path of the directory in the bundle class path. For example: `Bundle-Blueprint: OSGI-INF/*.xml`.

One interesting point to note is that a single logical component can be defined over many Blueprint XML files. This idea is borrowed from Spring Beans, where it's useful if you need to switch the behavior of a component in different environments—say, for local testing versus enterprise deployment.

> ***(continued)***
> Recall from chapter 5 that we discussed bundle fragments. With fragments, it's possible to define different component configurations by installing different fragments into the OSGi framework, where the host bundle is the base component bundle. In real-world scenarios, you can use this approach to specify entirely new object graphs or service relationships. This is potentially powerful but also very low level because it relies on intimate knowledge of the components being extended in this fashion. Thus you should use this feature with care.

We've covered the basics of providing services with Blueprint; next, let's look at how you consume them.

12.1.3 Consuming services with Blueprint

Blueprint tries to simplify dealing with the dynamic nature of OSGi services by using a proxy approach, instead of binding components directly to an OSGi service. The injected proxy is backed by actual service objects from the service registry, as shown in figure 12.1.

Service proxies are injected into Blueprint components using either the reference or reference-list manager. Let's look into both.

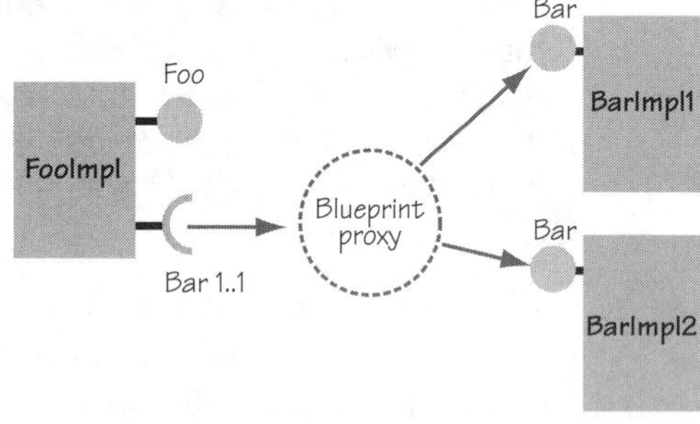

Figure 12.1 Blueprint injects a proxy object, which masks changes in the OSGi service registry. If the underlying service provider goes away and returns, the client code is insulated from this dynamism.

BLUEPRINT REFERENCES A, B, C'S

The easiest way to demonstrate service reference behavior is with a simple example of injecting a service `A` into a client `B`. The following code defines the service interface:

```
public interface A {
  void doit();
}
```

And here's the simple client:

```
public class B {
  private A a;
  public void setService(A a) { this.a = a }
  public void someAction() { a.doit(); }
}
```

In this example, you have a class `B` that depends on a service `A`, which will be injected via a `setService()` method. In Blueprint, you can express this dependency as

```
<reference id="a" interface="A"/>
<bean id="b" class="B">
  <property name="service" ref="a"/>
</bean>
```

Given this declaration, the Blueprint container knows it must inject an instance of A from the service registry into the component by calling the setService() method. It's also possible for Blueprint to inject the service proxy via a constructor. The following class C has a dependency on service A, which is injected via a constructor argument:

```
public class C {
  private A a;
  public C(A a) { this.a = a }
  public void someAction() { a.doit(); }
}
```

In this case, the Blueprint service-dependency description looks like this:

```
<reference id="a" interface="A"/>
<bean id="c" class="C">
  <argument ref="a"/>
</bean>
```

What if your client code doesn't depend on a single service instance, but instead wants to aggregate several service instances? The following example shows a class D that aggregates many A services from the OSGi service registry:

```
public class D {
  private List<A> list;
  public void setServices(List<A> list) { this.list = list }
  public void someAction() {
    for (A a : list) {
      a.doit();
    }
  }
}
```

In this case, class D is injected with a proxied list that aggregates the OSGi services. Changes in the OSGi service registry are reflected in the list. New services are appended to the end of the list, and old services are removed. The XML to describe this sort of dependency in Blueprint is as follows:

```
<reference-list id="a" interface="A"/>
<bean id="d" class="D">
  <property name="services" ref="a"/>
</bean>
```

This is similar to the previous dependency on a single service. The difference is that you replace the XML <reference/> element with the <reference-list/> element.

Proxies and service dynamism

Blueprint uses proxies to mask OSGi service dynamism so you don't have to worry about the concurrency issues in your code. This approach can't solve all issues related to dynamism. For example, in this static view of services, what happens if the underlying service goes away and no replacements are available? In this case, the service proxy blocks the calling thread, waiting for a replacement service, and will eventually throw an org.osgi.framework.ServiceUnavailableException after a certain timeout period if no replacement service arrives.

> ***(continued)***
> This also applies to the reference-list approach of aggregating services. The Blueprint specification ensures that the `hasNext()` and `getNext()` operations are safe with respect to changes in the OSGi service registry. But if a service is removed and `hasNext()` has already been called, a dummy object is returned that throws `ServiceUnavailableException`s when any methods are called, instead of throwing a `ConcurrentModificationException` during the iteration. These types of issues aren't specific to Blueprint, but to how Blueprint handles OSGi's service dynamism.

This covers the basics of service injection. Now let's look at how Blueprint lets components have a dynamic view of services using reference listeners.

REFERENCE LISTENERS

Reference listeners allow a component to receive services via bind and unbind callbacks. Consider the following example:

```
public class E {
  private volatile A a;
  public void addService(A a) { this.a = a }
  public void removeService(A a) { this.a = null }
  public void someAction() {
    A a = this.a;
    if ( a != null ) a.doit();
  }
}
```

In this example, class `E` receives callbacks via the `addService()` and `removeService()` methods when an `A` service is registered or unregistered in the OSGi service registry, respectively. The body of the `someAction()` method must guard against the fact that the service may be `null`. You express this sort of dependency in Blueprint XML as follows:

```
<bean id="e" class="E"/>
<reference id="a" interface="A">
  <reference-listener
    bind-method="addService"
    unbind-method="removeService"
    ref="e"/>
</reference>
```

A reference-listener callback can have any of the following signatures, which have the same semantics as their Declarative Services equivalents (from the last chapter):

- `public void <method-name>(ServiceReference)`
- `public void <method-name>(<parameter-type>)`
- `public void <method-name>(<parameter-type>, Map)`

One issue to keep in mind: the Blueprint specification mandates that binding methods have `public` method access. Although the risk is probably minor in most scenarios, it does open Blueprint components exposed as services to the possibility that external code using reflection can inject dependencies even if a security manager is enabled. Concerned users can work around this using a nonservice helper delegate that manages the reference list—although this is a lot of work compared to marking the methods as nonpublic.

Let's use your newfound Blueprint knowledge and continue to convert the paint program to use it.

PAINTING WITH BLUEPRINT

Your paint frame component has a dependency on `SimpleShape` services, and it provides a `Window` service. The following listing provides its definition in the Blueprint XML syntax.

Listing 12.2 Blueprint definition of the `PaintFrame` component

```
<?xml version="1.0" encoding="UTF-8"?>
<blueprint xmlns="http://www.osgi.org/xmlns/blueprint/v1.0.0">
  <bean id="paintFrame" class="org.foo.paint.PaintFrame"
        init-method="activate"
        destroy-method="deactivate"/>

  <reference-list id="shape"
                  interface="org.foo.shape.SimpleShape"
                  availability="optional">          ❶ Listens for SimpleShape services
    <reference-listener
      bind-method="addShape"
      unbind-method="removeShape"
      ref="paintFrame"/>                            ❷ Injects services
  </reference-list>

  <service id="window"
           interface="org.foo.windowlistener.api.Window"
           ref="paintFrame"/>
</blueprint>
```

You begin by defining the paint frame component and specifying lifecycle methods to be invoked by the Blueprint container after its properties have been injected; we'll leave the details of these for the next section. You use the `<reference-list>` element at ❶ to ask the Blueprint container to listen for all `SimpleShape` services it finds in the OSGi service registry.

Notice that you use the `availability` attribute on the `<reference-list>` element. As with Declarative Services, Blueprint includes the notion of mandatory and optional service dependencies, where mandatory dependencies impact the component lifecycle and optional ones don't. We'll discuss this more when we cover the Blueprint component lifecycle. Possible values for the `availability` attribute are `optional` and `mandatory`; the default is `mandatory`.

Nested in this `<reference-list>` element is a `<reference-listener>` element ❷. This tells the Blueprint container to inject the services into the `addShape()` and `removeShape()` methods of the paint frame component. You choose this approach because your paint frame needs to react dynamically to the arrival and departure of shape services.

Finally, you use the `<service>` element to publish the paint frame bean as a service in the OSGi service registry. Recall that you can't register classes as services in Blueprint; you must use an interface. As a result, you must define a new interface class to provide the `java.awt.Window` methods you need to use in the window-listener component. You define this new interface as

```
public interface Window {
  void addWindowListener(WindowListener listener);
  void removeWindowListener(WindowListener listener);
}
```

The `addShape()` and `removeShape()` methods for the paint frame component look basically the same as the Declarative Services example, but with one minor difference. Here's the `addShape()` method:

```
public void addShape(SimpleShape shape, Map attrs) {
  final DefaultShape delegate = new DefaultShape(shape);
  final String name = (String) attrs.get(SimpleShape.NAME_PROPERTY);
  final Icon icon = (Icon) attrs.get(SimpleShape.ICON_PROPERTY);
  m_shapes.put(name, delegate);

  SwingUtils.invokeAndWait(new Runnable() {
    public void run() {
      //...
    }
  });
}
```

You're given the `Icon` object directly versus having to look it up from the shape's class loader, as is required for Declarative Services.

You've now seen how to define a component, how to publish services, and how to consume services. The next area of the Blueprint specification we'll explore is the component lifecycle.

12.1.4 Blueprint component lifecycle

Similar to Declarative Services, Blueprint is responsible for managing the lifecycles of its components. Blueprint also supports lifecycle callbacks, eager/lazy component activation, and access to the execution-time container environment. Additionally, Blueprint introduces some new concepts, such as service damping and grace periods. We'll look into each of these topics in more detail, starting with general Blueprint component lifecycle management.

COMPONENT LIFECYCLE MANAGEMENT

Similar to Declarative Services, a Blueprint component's lifecycle is controlled overall by its containing bundle's lifecycle. For individual beans, their lifecycle is tied to the state of their service dependencies. All mandatory service dependencies must be satisfied for a bean to become enabled. When a bean is enabled, any service managers associated with it can register their associated service interfaces in the OSGi service registry.

Reference listener != service dependency

One important point to note is that for a Blueprint container to treat a bean as dependent on a service reference, the bean must be bound to the service via an injection mechanism—either a property or a constructor argument. A reference-listener callback *is not* treated as an injection mechanism. So, even though a bean receives a callback when the service appears and disappears, it won't necessarily stop providing its services unless it has the property or argument injection relationship as well.

For Declarative Services, you learned that if a mandatory service dependency is broken, the component instance immediately becomes invalid. Blueprint handles this differently via the concepts of damping and grace periods.

SERVICE DAMPING

As we previously mentioned, Blueprint injects proxies into components instead of the actual service objects. These proxies are the mechanism Blueprint uses to provide service-dynamism damping; said a different way, it uses this approach to hide service dynamism from the component.

When a mandatory service is removed from the service registry, the Blueprint container first stops providing any services offered by the impacted component. Additionally, any attempts by the component to use the proxy associated with the missing service block the calling thread. Blueprint proxies block for a configurable amount of time (five minutes by default). If the timeout expires and no new service is found to replace the missing service, the proxy throws a `ServiceUnavailableException`. Client code should therefore be coded defensively to gracefully deal with execution-time exceptions, but this is true in general and not just in Blueprint.

The benefit of this approach is it eliminates service unpublish/publish waves rippling throughout the framework during bundle updates. But if you're unaware, it can lead to unexpected lockups in your application, which is particularly interesting in GUI scenarios.

To configure the timeout behavior, you specify the `timeout` attribute on a service reference. This value specifies the number of milliseconds to wait until the service reappears. The timeout value must be equal to or greater than zero, where a timeout of zero signifies an indefinite wait. In the window-listener component, you can see this in action:

```
<reference id="window" interface="org.foo.windowlistener.api.Window"
 timeout="1">
```

Damping isn't the only mechanism Blueprint employs to hide service dynamism; another one is grace periods.

GRACE PERIODS

Normally, a Blueprint component container doesn't enable its component until the component's mandatory service dependencies are satisfied. The *grace period* is a period of time the component container waits during component startup for mandatory service dependencies. The grace period ends in success if all mandatory dependencies can be satisfied or in failure if its timeout is exceeded. If the grace period was a success, the component is enabled and its services are registered. If the grace period was a failure, the container is destroyed and the component isn't created. You can see how this affects the Blueprint component lifecycle in figure 12.2.

You can configure the grace period timeout value using directives on the `Bundle-SymbolicName` manifest header in the Blueprint component bundle. For example:

```
Bundle-SymbolicName: com.acme.foo; blueprint.graceperiod:=true;
 blueprint.timeout:=10000
```

Here, you set the grace period timeout to be 10 seconds. It's also possible to completely disable the grace period by using `blueprint.graceperiod:=false`. In this case, the Blueprint container won't wait for any mandatory service references to be

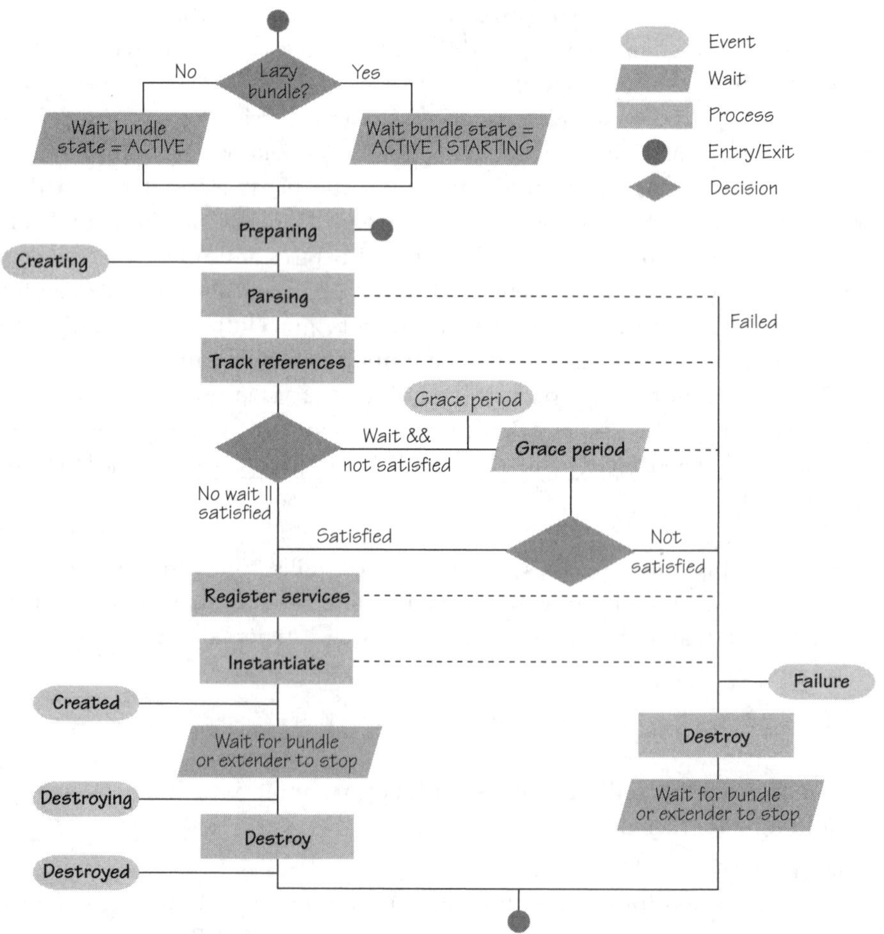

Figure 12.2 The Blueprint component lifecycle

satisfied and will create any Blueprint components contained in the bundle. This results in components being injected with service proxies, which may or may not have backing services available. For those components without backing services for mandatory dependencies, the Blueprint container won't publish their provided services. This is similar to the case where required services depart at execution time, which means that if any threads try to use them, those threads are blocked.

ACTIVATION CALLBACKS

In listing 12.2, you saw that the Blueprint XML declaration allows you to define callback methods that are invoked by the Blueprint container to initialize and destroy beans when they're enabled and disabled, respectively. In the paint frame component, you use these callbacks to control when the component is visible, as shown next.

Listing 12.3 Callback methods used in the `PaintFrame` application

```
public void activate()
{
  SwingUtils.invokeAndWait(new Runnable() {
    public void run() {
      setVisible(true);
    }
  });
}

public void deactivate()
{
  SwingUtils.invokeLater(new Runnable() {
    public void run() {
      setVisible(false);
      dispose();
    }
  });
}
```

You still have an issue regarding precisely when your component—in this case, the paint frame—is created. We'll deal with that next.

LAZY VS. EAGER INITIALIZATION

As with Declarative Services, Blueprint components are lazy by default, which means components aren't created in advance to delay class loading until a published service is requested by another bundle. If you need your component to be created eagerly, you can request this behavior from the container. You declare Blueprint managers as eager or lazy using the `activation` attribute on the associated XML element with a Boolean argument. For example:

```
<bean id="foo" class="Foo" activation="eager" />
<reference id="bar" interface="Bar" activation="lazy" />
<service id="baz" interface="Baz" activation="lazy" />
```

The laziness of a component is also impacted by how it provides its services. If the `auto-export` attribute from section 12.1.2 is used, the Blueprint container must activate the underlying component to perform class loading to calculate the service interfaces.

The final lifecycle-related issue we'll discuss is how Blueprint components gain access to the underlying OSGi execution environment.

ENVIRONMENT MANAGER

As you've seen so far, the Blueprint specification uses managers to control various aspects (such as services, references, and beans) of a component. Each manager defines and controls the specific lifecycle characteristics of its associated aspect. The same pattern is applied to entities outside of the component; these are called *environment managers.* In this case, environment managers are effectively property-value macros. They come in four types:

- `blueprintContainer`—Provides access to the Blueprint container object and allows various forms of component introspection
- `blueprintBundle`—Provides access to the Blueprint bundle's `Bundle` object
- `blueprintBundleContext`—Provides access to the Blueprint bundle's `BundleContext` object
- `blueprintConverter`—Provides access to an object implementing the `Converter` interface, which we'll discuss shortly

Let's look at how you use the `blueprintBundleContext` manager in the paint application to access the `BundleContext`. The `WindowListener` needs the bundle context so it can retrieve the system bundle to shut down the OSGi framework when the paint frame is closed. In the following snippet's `WindowListener` component XML description, you use the environment manager to inject the bundle context into the `WindowListener` class as a property:

```
<bean id="listener" class="org.foo.windowlistener.WindowListener">
  <property name="bundleContext" ref="blueprintBundleContext" />
</bean>
```

This follows the same pattern as the reference-injection mechanism of accessing service references. The implementation code in the `WindowListener` class looks like this:

```
private BundleContext m_context;
...
public void setBundleContext(BundleContext context) {
  m_context = context;
}
```

The bundle context ends up being injected using an ordinary setter method.

With this, we'll conclude the discussion of the Blueprint version of the paint program. To see it in action, go to the chapter12/paint-example-bp/ directory of the book's companion code. Type `ant` to build the example and `java -jar launcher.jar bundles/` to run it. This example uses the Apache Aries (http://incubator.apache.org/aries/) implementation of the Blueprint specification.

In the final section on Blueprint, we'll look at some other advanced features it provides.

12.1.5 Advanced Blueprint features

The features of Blueprint we've described so far are largely comparable to those of Declarative Services. But because Blueprint is an evolution of Spring Dynamic Modules, a lot of experience from that work was carried over into creating the Blueprint specification. This heritage has resulted in some advanced concepts, such as manager values, scopes, type converters, and metadata, which we'll discuss in this section.

MANAGER VALUES

If you've developed Spring applications in the past, you likely know it's possible to define complex object graphs using the Spring XML model. This gives software architects a number of options when composing applications, because the overall program structure doesn't need to be hardcoded in Java. This is particularly useful for scenarios such as desktop testing versus enterprise deployment; with just a few tweaks of XML, you can wire together a raft of new functions without recompiling code.

Blueprint has inherited this ability and supports several constructs in the XML declaration:

- `<value>`—An object that can be directly constructed from its text string contents.
- `<ref>`—A reference to a top-level manager in the same Blueprint container.
- `<idref>`—The ID of another manager that is checked by the Blueprint container. This is the preferred mechanism to pass in a manager ID compared to an unchecked string value, which would show up later at execution time.
- `<map>`—A `java.util.Map` containing a sequence of associations between a key and an object.
- `<props>`—A `java.util.Properties` containing string keys and values.
- `<list>`—A `java.util.List` containing other values.
- `<set>`—A `java.util.Set` containing other unique values.
- `<array>`—A primitive array containing other values.

It's also possible to use the various Blueprint managers we've been discussing inline in these constructs. Every Blueprint manager has a particular value it provides, similar to macro expansion. You've already seen this in action in the way reference managers give access to underlying service references, where the value of a service-reference manager is either a service object or a `ServiceReference` to a service object. For completeness, table 12.2 lists the value objects associated with each Blueprint manager.

Table 12.2 Blueprint manager value objects

Manager	Value
<bean>	The instantiated object created by this bean.
<service>	A proxy object wrapping the service registration created as a result of registering the service in the OSGi service registry. (A proxy is returned because the `unregister()` method isn't supported and throws an exception.)

Table 12.2 Blueprint manager value objects *(continued)*

Manager	Value
<reference>	A proxy object to the service registered in the OSGi service registry.
<reference-list>	A `java.util.List` containing proxies to the registered services or `ServiceReferences`.

This capability makes it possible to define reasonably sophisticated constructions in the component XML descriptions. Consider a contrived example in the following XML snippet:

```
<bean class="com.acme.FooImpl">
  <property name="services">
    <map>
      <entry key="bar">
        <service interface="com.acme.Bar">
          <bean class="com.acme.BarImpl"/>
        </service>
      </entry>
    </map>
  </property>
</bean>
```

In this example, you construct a `Foo` object into which you inject its `services` property with a `Map`. For the map, you set the `bar` key to the `ServiceRegistration` object for a service `Bar`. The `Bar` service is provided by an inlined bean, constructed from the `BarImpl` class. The `FooImpl` class looks something like this:

```
public class FooImpl {
  public void setServices(Map<String, ServiceRegistration> services) {
    for (Map.Entry<String, ServiceRegistration> e : services.getEntrySet())
    {
      String key = e.getKey();
      ServiceRegistration val = e.getValue();
      System.out.println("Registered service " + key + "=" + val);
    }
  }
}
```

Here, the `FooImpl` class is injected with a property whose value is wholly constructed from the Blueprint XML model. This is definitely a contrived example, but it shows the flexibility of the Blueprint model.

SCOPES

As with manager values, Blueprint has inherited the concept of scope from Spring Dynamic Modules. A scope can be applied to bean and service managers; it defines the lifetime over which the specified manager is applicable. Blueprint defines two scopes—*singleton* and *prototype*—but they imply subtly different behavior depending on whether they're applied to a bean or a service manager, as shown in table 12.3.

Table 12.3 How Blueprint scopes apply to different managers

	Singleton	Prototype
Bean	One instance of the bean object is constructed when the bean is activated. This pattern is usually applied to stateless services and core components. This is the default scope for bean managers.	A new instance of the bean object is constructed each time it's requested from the Blueprint container using the `getComponentInstance()` method. All inlined beans (which you saw in the last subsection) are automatically prototype scope.
Service	A single service object is shared by all clients of the service.	A new service object is returned to each bundle, which provides a similar result if your bean implements an OSGi `ServiceFactory`.

TYPE CONVERTERS

The Blueprint specification defines a rich inversion of control (IoC) framework for wiring objects together at execution time. Often, you need to convert between types in order to perform an injection. The most obvious example is converting from `String` values in XML to `integer`, `boolean`, or other basic Java types. The Blueprint specification defines a default set of type converters that can convert a `String` value to a target typed value.

The Blueprint specification also allows you to extend the default set of type converters. Type converters are defined in the `<type-converters>` XML element, which is a child element of the top-level `<blueprint>` element. In the `<type-converters>` element, you can use `<bean>` or `<reference>` elements, which let you define local converters for one particular Blueprint definition or shared converters in the OSGi service registry. Consider the following XML snippet:

```
<type-converters>
  <bean class="AtomicConverter">
    <argument ref="blueprintConverter"/>
  </bean>
</type-converters>
```

Here, you define a type converter using the class `AtomicConverter` that takes a reference to the top-level Blueprint converter as an argument in its constructor. A type converter doesn't need to implement any specific interface, although it must implement two methods:

- `canConvert(Object, ReifiedType)`
- `convert(Object, ReifiedType)`

The code for the atomic conversion class is shown in the following listing.

Listing 12.4 Converter class to coerce an `Object` to an `AtomicReference`

```
public class AtomicConverter {
  Converter bpc;
  public AtomicConverter(Converter bpc) { this.bpc=bpc; }

  public boolean canConvert(Object s, ReifiedType T) {
```

```
    return T.getRawClass() == AtomicReference.class
      && bpc.canConvert(s, T.getActualTypeArgument(0));
  }
  public Object convert(Object s, ReifiedType T)
    throws Exception {
    Object obj = bpc.convert(s, T.getActualTypeArgument(0));
    return new AtomicReference<Object>(obj);
  }
}
```

The `canConvert()` method checks whether it can convert the supplied object to the given reified type. The `convert()` method is called by the Blueprint container if the `canConvert()` method returns `true`. The top-level Blueprint converter is injected into the constructor of the `AtomicConverter` class to allow it to convert generic arguments. For example, `AtomicConverter` can use the top-level converter to convert a source object to an `Integer` and then create an `AtomicReference` to this converted object.

> **WARNING** Type converters shouldn't require type conversion in their initialization because the state of the converter isn't well defined at this time. The Blueprint built-in type converter delegates to registered converters, so a call to the converter during construction may fail because a needed type converter may not have been registered yet.

Having defined this converter, any injection targeting an `AtomicReference<T>` value is automatically converted into an `AtomicReference` of the appropriate type using the example converter. To illustrate, consider the following code:

```
public class Foo<T extends Integer> {
  public Foo(AtomicReference<T> v) {}
}
```

Here's the corresponding XML snippet:

```
<bean id="foo" class="Foo"> <argument value="6"/></bean>
```

This pattern of conversion is useful if you have to adapt third-party code that you can't change, but you nonetheless want to have a common model at execution time.

Next, we'll discuss metadata, which is the last advanced Blueprint feature before we move on to the iPOJO component framework.

METADATA

Metadata is a programmatic representation of the XML description of the Blueprint component. In Spring, the main use case for accessing metadata is to dynamically modify the model (add new elements, modify elements, and so on) at execution time. This forms a flexible component pipeline much like aspect weaving in Java code, but at the component level. But in the current Blueprint specification, this model is largely for informational purposes. Still, it's useful because it can be used to build diagnostic tools to analyze the structure of Blueprint components, for example.

The Blueprint specification defines many classes to model the Blueprint components. We won't list every method and its meaning here, but figure 12.3 provides a view of the Blueprint metadata interface hierarchy.

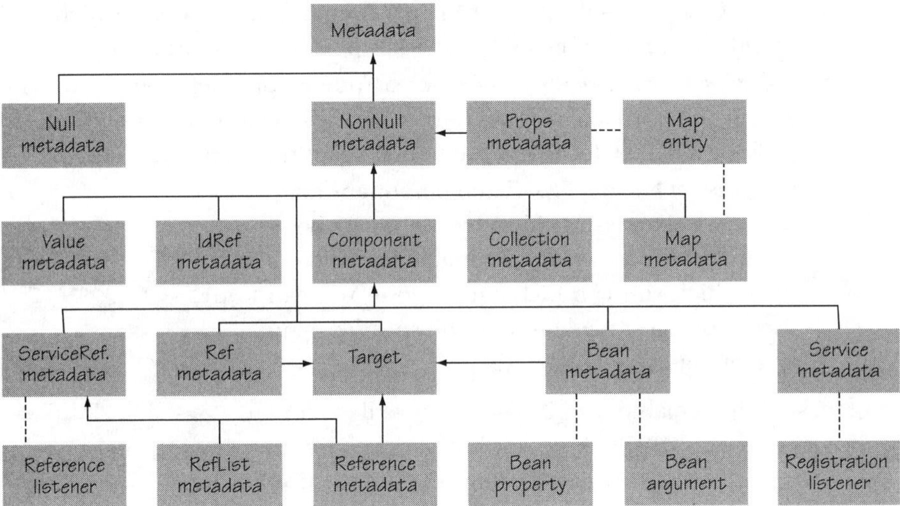

Figure 12.3 The Blueprint metadata interface hierarchy

To access the metadata model, the Blueprint specification provides the `BlueprintContainer` interface, which serves a purpose similar to the `ComponentContext` in Declarative Services. It has the following signature:

```
public interface BlueprintContainer {
  void Set getComponentIds();
  Object getComponentInstance(String id);
  ComponentMetadata getComponentMetadata(String id)
  Collection getMetadata(Class type);
}
```

This concludes our look at the OSGi Blueprint Container specification. We'll now turn our attention to the last component framework on our list: iPOJO, from the Apache Felix project.

12.2 Apache Felix iPOJO

Outside of the OSGi Alliance, a number of different component models have been built for or ported to the OSGi environment:

- Google Guice peaberry (http://code.google.com/p/peaberry/)
- ScalaModules (http://wiki.github.com/weiglewilczek/scalamodules/)
- Apache Felix iPOJO (http://felix.apache.org/site/apache-felix-ipojo.html)

In this section, we'll focus on iPOJO due to its novel features and because we (the authors) are all involved in the Apache Felix project. One of the main goals of iPOJO is to simplify creating dynamic, service-oriented applications in OSGi. The biggest difference between iPOJO and Declarative Services or Blueprint is its approach, which includes the following:

- *Byte-code weaving*—iPOJO instruments component byte code, which enables it to provide features not possible (or easily possible) with other approaches.
- *Metadata format agnosticism*—Whereas other approaches force you into using the single approach they support to describe your components (XML, annotations, or API), iPOJO allows you to use any of these approaches.
- *High level of extensibility*—The component management features provided by the iPOJO component container are implemented by handlers from which you can pick and choose. You can also create custom handlers for specific management tasks; see figure 12.4.

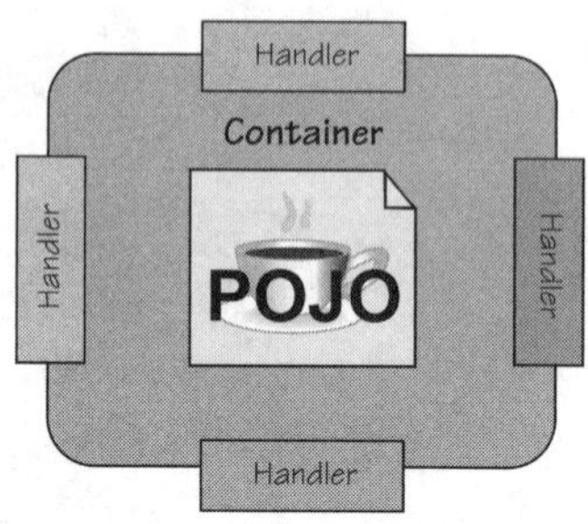

Figure 12.4 iPOJO components are an aggregation of handlers attached to the component container at execution time.

In most of the remainder of this chapter, we'll explore the features of iPOJO, but we won't cover everything. For starters, we'll focus on using the annotation approach for describing components, because you've already seen enough XML and API. But keep in mind that everything you do with annotations you can do with the XML- and API-based description approaches—it depends on your preference.

12.2.1 Building iPOJO components

iPOJO uses byte-code manipulation to instrument component class files. This instrumentation inserts hooks into the component class file so it can be externally managed. Although iPOJO also supports execution-time byte-code instrumentation, the simplest way to get it done is with a build-time step to process your components. To achieve this, iPOJO integrates with Ant, Maven, and Eclipse. As an example, here's the Ant task for the circle bundle:

```
<taskdef name="ipojo"
         classname="org.apache.felix.ipojo.task.iPojoTask"
         classpath="${lib}/felix/org.apache.felix.ipojo.ant-1.6.0.jar" />
<ipojo input="${dist}/${ant.project.name}-${version}.jar"
       metadata = "OSGI-INF/circle.xml"/>
```

Upon completion of this build step, iPOJO has instrumented the byte code of any components contained in the referenced bundle. The details of how iPOJO instruments the component byte code aren't as important; but for the curious, iPOJO instruments all components in a single, generic way to enable intercepting member field and method accesses. All functionality provided by the iPOJO component framework (providing services, requiring services, and so on) is provided by handlers using these interception hooks. The hooks themselves don't change the component behavior; the modified component classes behave the same as before and can still be use without iPOJO, although they now have some code dependencies on it.

What about that XML file?

We said you'd use annotations, but the previous Ant task references a circle.xml file. What's the deal?

iPOJO tries to maintain a fairly strict separation of concepts between component types and component instances. In Declarative Services and Blueprint, a component description is typically a component instance description, meaning it results in a component instance. In iPOJO, component descriptions describe a component type; instances must be explicitly instantiated. As you'll soon see, the circle.xml file doesn't describe the component: you use it to create an instance.

In addition to instrumenting the component byte code, the iPOJO build step also converts the component description to a canonical form. This approach offers three benefits:

- If you use XML to describe your components, an XML parser is needed only during build time and not at execution time.
- If you use annotations to describe your components, they're needed only at build time, and the resulting JAR file can still be used on an older JVM.
- Parsing the resulting descriptions at execution time is more efficient, because it's in a simplified and less verbose form.

As with the other component frameworks, you want to achieve three main tasks with iPOJO: publishing services, consuming services, and configuring components. Let's look into each of these.

12.2.2 Providing services with iPOJO

As we mentioned, iPOJO supports a variety of approaches for describing components. For this chapter, you'll use annotations. As before, let's start with the circle component; the iPOJO version of its source code is shown in the following listing. One of the benefits of using annotations is that the metadata is closely associated with the source code it's describing.

Listing 12.5 iPOJO declaration of circle component type using annotations

```
@Component(immediate=true)
@Provides
public class Circle implements SimpleShape {

  @ServiceProperty(name=SimpleShape.NAME_PROPERTY)
  private String m_name = "Circle";

  @ServiceProperty(name=SimpleShape.ICON_PROPERTY)
  private ImageIcon m_icon =
    new ImageIcon(this.getClass().getResource("circle.png"));

  public void draw(Graphics2D g2, Point p) {
    ...
  }
}
```

You use @Component to declare the Circle class as an iPOJO component; see the sidebar "Immediate components and service properties" for why you use the immediate flag. With the @Provide annotation, you indicate that your component provides a service. You leave iPOJO the task of determining the type of the service, which defaults to all implemented interfaces (only SimpleShape in this case).

You use the @ServiceProperty annotation to declare the m_name and m_icon member fields as service properties, which iPOJO automatically attaches to your provided service and even dynamically updates if the component code changes the field values at execution time. Notice also that because you're using annotations, which are part of the Java source code, you can use static constant fields for the attribute names, unlike in Declarative Services or Blueprint; this greatly reduces the risks of metadata rot due to changing attribute names.

Immediate components and service properties

Just as with Declarative Services and Blueprint, iPOJO delays class loading and component instance creation for as long as possible. Sometimes this delay is inconvenient, and you want the component created immediately. When using @ServiceProperty, iPOJO uses the member field value as a service-property value. But if component creation is deferred (which is the default behavior), iPOJO can't get the field value because the field doesn't yet exist.

As a result, iPOJO first registers the service with no service properties. When the service is requested by another component, then the component is instantiated, which causes the field to be initialized and added to the service. To rectify this situation, @ServiceProperty supports a value attribute to set the default value of the service property; but this works only for simple types, not for complex types like this example's icon. To deal with complex types, you need to use the immediate attribute of @Component to tell iPOJO to instantiate the component immediately.

In listing 12.5, you use the default behavior of @Provides to tell iPOJO to register all of the component's implemented interfaces as service interfaces, including inherited interfaces. You can also explicitly specify interfaces or classes to provide, as shown in the following snippet:

```
@Component
@Provides(specifications=java.awt.Window.class)
public class PaintFrame extends JFrame
  implements MouseListener, MouseMotionListener {
```

As with Declarative Services and Blueprint, the circle bundle no longer needs to have a bundle activator because iPOJO manages service publication. As mentioned previously, you have to modify the component's build process to include the iPOJO Ant task, but that's all there is to it. iPOJO takes care of everything at execution time.

Now, let's look into consuming services.

12.2.3 Consuming services with iPOJO

iPOJO defines two mechanisms for injecting services into a component: method injection and field injection. In most cases, the two can be used interchangeably or mixed and matched. In either case, a component service dependency description can include (among others)

- *Service specification*—The actual service type of interest
- *Optionality*—Whether it's mandatory (default) or optional
- *Aggregation*—Whether it's for a single service or many
- *Filter*—An LDAP filter over service properties for additional constraints
- *Binding policy*—How dynamism is handled with respect to the component's lifecycle (we'll discuss this more when we look at the iPOJO component lifecycle)
- *Proxy injection*—Whether injected services are proxied

Given the similarities between method and field injection, the approach you choose often comes down to preference. Still, there are some things you can do only with one or the other. For example, if you want to be notified whenever a desired service becomes available, you need to use method injection to get a callback, which makes it possible to react immediately to dynamic changes. Yet it's possible to use field injection and method injection at the same time to get the best of both worlds.

> **To proxy or not to proxy**
>
> By default, iPOJO injects proxies instead of the actual service object. This creates a managed reference to the service that can be passed around internally in the component. iPOJO uses byte-code generation instead of Java's dynamic proxy mechanism, which improves performance and avoids the limitation of working only with interfaces. For platforms like Android where dynamic byte-code generation isn't supported, iPOJO reverts to Java's dynamic proxies.
>
> Note that iPOJO proxies aren't like Blueprint proxies, in that they don't do any sort of blocking of the calling thread if no backing service is available. Instead, by default, they hide the fact that the service is missing by using the null-object pattern, which we'll discuss shortly. If you'd rather not use proxies, you can disable them on a dependency-by-dependency basis or completely.

We'll first explore method injection, because it's similar to the mechanisms you saw in Declarative Services and Blueprint.

METHOD INJECTION

iPOJO defines `@Bind` and `@Unbind` method-level annotations to declare the binding methods for a specific service dependency, where `@Bind` is associated with the method used to inject a service and `@Unbind` is associated with the method used to remove a previously injected service. These annotations can be applied to methods with any of the following signatures:

- void <method-name>()—A parameterless binding method useful as a simple notification mechanism.
- void <method-name>(ServiceReference ref)—The component receives the service reference associated with the service.
- void <method-name>(<S> svc)—The component receives the service object.
- void <method-name>(<S> svc, ServiceReference ref)—The component receives the service object and its associated service reference.
- void <method-name>(<S> svc, Map props)—The component receives the service object and its associated service properties as a java.util.Map.
- void <method-name>(<S> svc, Dictionary props)—The component receives the service object and its associated service properties as a java.util.Dictionary.

In the first two cases, you need to specify the type of the service dependency using the specification parameter in the annotation; in all the other cases, iPOJO infers the service type from the method signature. Let's look at some examples. The binding methods for the window-listener component are as follows:

```
@Bind(filter="(name=main)")
protected void bindWindow(Window window) {
  m_log.log(LogService.LOG_INFO, "Bind window");
  window.addWindowListener(this);
}

@Unbind
protected void unbindWindow(Window window) {
  m_log.log(LogService.LOG_INFO, "Unbind window");
  window.removeWindowListener(this);
}
```

You annotate the bind and unbind methods right in the Java code. From the method signatures, iPOJO infers that the type of service dependency is java.awt.Window. The particular window service in which your window listener is interested has a name service property with the value main, to differentiate it from other window services that may be in the service registry. To make sure your window listener tracks the correct window, you use the filter attribute of the binding annotation to specify an LDAP filter matching the name service property. This particular dependency is on a single service instance, which is the default in iPOJO.

How do you declare an aggregate dependency? You can see an example in the iPOJO version of the PaintFrame shown in the following listing.

Listing 12.6 Bind and unbind methods for the iPOJO PaintFrame

```
@Bind(aggregate=true)
public void bindShape(SimpleShape shape, Map attrs) {
  final DefaultShape delegate = new DefaultShape(shape);
  final String name = (String) attrs.get(SimpleShape.NAME_PROPERTY);
  final Icon icon = (Icon) attrs.get(SimpleShape.ICON_PROPERTY);

  m_shapes.put(name, delegate);
```

```
    SwingUtils.invokeAndWait(new Runnable() {
      public void run() {
        ...
      }
    });
  }

  @Unbind
  public void unbindShape(SimpleShape shape, Map attrs) {
    final String name = (String) attrs.get(SimpleShape.NAME_PROPERTY);

    DefaultShape delegate = null;

    synchronized (m_shapes) {
      delegate = (DefaultShape) m_shapes.remove(name);
    }
  }
```

Here you declare the paint frame's binding methods. Because the paint frame depends on all available shape services, you use the `aggregate` annotation attribute to inform the iPOJO framework. At execution time, iPOJO injects all discovered shape services into the component. The service properties of injected services are also needed to get the service name and icon, so you use the binding method signature that includes the service properties.

Bind/unbind method pairs

Conceptually, a bind method is paired with an unbind method. You aren't technically required to have both, but if you do, iPOJO treats them as a logical pair. What does this mean exactly? In the previous examples, when you use an attribute (for example, `filter` or `aggregate`) on `@Bind`, you don't repeat it on `@Unbind`. This is because iPOJO creates a union of attributes out of paired bind/unbind methods, so it isn't necessary to repeat the attributes. If you do repeat attributes, they must have the same value, or iPOJO complains.

iPOJO automatically infers bind and unbind pairs based on method names. If the method name starts with `bind` or `unbind`, the remaining part of the method name is used as an identifier to match pairs. For example, iPOJO determines that `bindFoo()` and `unbindFoo()` are a matched pair with an identifier of `Foo`. Sometimes it isn't possible to name your methods following the bind/unbind naming convention: for example, if you're dealing with legacy or third-party components. In these cases, you can use the `id` annotation attribute to explicitly specify the pair's identifier. For identifiers, you should repeat the `id` attribute in both the `@Bind` and `@Unbind` annotations so iPOJO can correctly pair them.

All the component frameworks we've covered provide mechanisms to simplify the task of accessing OSGi services; but accessing services is only one part of the challenge. Another issue is dealing with the dynamic nature of services. If services can come and go at any point, you must code a service consumer defensively. Doing so involves one or more of the following patterns:

- Using synchronization logic such as synchronized blocks, AtomicReference, or CopyOnWriteArraySet
- Using timeouts if the service removal is only temporary (during a software upgrade)
- Declaring dependencies as mandatory such that a component is shut down if its dependencies become unsatisfied during execution time

iPOJO offers another option through the use of the @Requires annotation, which we'll look at next.

FIELD INJECTION

iPOJO defines the @Requires field-level annotation to associate a service dependency with a component class-member field, rather than a pair of binding methods. As we mentioned previously, iPOJO performs byte-code instrumentation on components to enable field-access interception. For the @Requires annotation, the iPOJO framework intercepts field access at execution time to provide components access to their required services. At a very high level, this acts as if you've sprinkled your code with a liberal number of AtomicRefererences. This ensures that the component always sees a consistent view of the services as they appear in the OSGi service registry at a given moment, without all the tedious boilerplate synchronization code in the source files.

The @Requires annotation also works with collections or arrays to aggregate multiple services from the OSGi service registry. In addition, it can create default objects or null objects if an optional service isn't available, which greatly simplifies your source code because you don't need to perform null checks throughout.

Let's look at how you can use these features in the paint program. The WindowListener component has an optional dependency on the OSGi Log Service. In Declarative Services and in Blueprint, you use an AtomicReference to ensure that you have a consistent view of the service in your component. In iPOJO, you declare the log service dependency on a field, like so:

```
@Requires(optional=true)
private LogService m_log;
```

To access the log service, you use the field like this:

```
@Override
public void windowClosed(WindowEvent evt) {
  try {
    m_log.log(LogService.LOG_INFO, "Window closed");
    m_context.getBundle(0).stop();
  } catch (BundleException e) {
  } catch (IllegalStateException e) {
  }
}
```

In Declarative Services and Blueprint, you have to use the AtomicReference to hold the log service and then check for null before using it. In iPOJO, you can use the log service, because optional dependencies automatically receive a null object if no real service is available. A null object implements the target service interface but doesn't do anything meaningful.

Null objects and default implementations

Unless you explicitly tell it not to do so, iPOJO injects a null object in place of missing optional service dependencies. These null objects are created using a trivial mock object pattern where any method that returns `void` takes no action, and methods that return values return the default `false`, `0`, or `null`, depending on which is appropriate.

If you're using service proxies (which is the default), this means the service proxies are injected with null objects if a backing service isn't available. If you aren't using proxies, then your component is injected with a null object directly. This approach saves you from having to check for `null` in your component code. If you don't desire this behavior, you can disable null object creation like this:

```
@Requires(nullable=false)
private Foo foo;
```

If you disable null objects and you're using proxies, your component code must be prepared to catch runtime exceptions when accessing a proxy object if the backing service is missing (similar to the unavailable service exceptions in Blueprint and indicative of OSGi service dynamism in general). If you aren't using proxies, you'll need to check for `null` service values in your component code. When using proxies, it's recommended to keep the default behavior of null object creation, because the whole point of proxies is to try to insulate the component from dynamism, but the choice is yours.

In the case where you're using null objects without proxies, it's possible for your component to determine whether it has a null object using `instanceof`, because all null objects implement the `Nullable` interface.

As a final comment, because a null object is just a default service implementation that doesn't do anything, iPOJO provides one more wrinkle. You can supply your own default service implementation instead of the normal null object:

```
@Requires(default-implementation=org.foo.DefaultFoo)
private Foo foo;
```

When you do this, iPOJO constructs an instance of the `DefaultFoo` class and injects it into the proxy or component whenever a real `Foo` service is unavailable.

The `@Requires` annotation goes even further with respect to service dynamism. The iPOJO runtime ensures that a given field access always returns the same service instance from the moment in time a given calling thread enters a component method and uses a service until it ultimately exits the original entry method. This means that even if the calling thread somehow calls out to another component and reenters the original component, it always sees the same service instances until it exits the original component once and for all. Essentially, iPOJO associates a shadow copy of a component's field after a thread accesses it and while the thread executes inside the component. Suppose you have a method that does something like this:

```
@Requires
private Foo m_foo;

public void statelessAccess() {
  m_foo.doA()
  m_foo.doB()
  m_foo.doC()
}
```

Accesses to `m_foo` always return the same service instance at the time of the first access to `m_foo`. This allows iPOJO to simplify the task of dealing with stateful services in the dynamic service environment provided by OSGi. This is cool, but it doesn't mean you don't have to worry about anything! Due to dynamism, accessing a service is similar to using remote services, which means they can throw exceptions for unknown reasons. For example, if `Foo` represents some device that becomes physically disconnected, its service methods are likely to throw exceptions when you access them. In short, you still need to code defensively, just as in distributed computing.

You now know how to describe your components' provided and required services. Like the other component frameworks you've seen, your components' lifecycles are controlled and managed according to these component characteristics. We'll look more deeply at the iPOJO component lifecycle next.

12.2.4 iPOJO component lifecycle

As with the other component frameworks, iPOJO component instances are either valid or invalid depending on whether their mandatory service dependencies are satisfied. When a component is valid, iPOJO can publish its provided services in the OSGi service registry. When a component is invalid, iPOJO must remove its provided services from the service registry and release the associated component instance if one was created. At execution time, the iPOJO runtime watches for bundles containing components to be installed into the running OSGi framework. After these bundles are activated, iPOJO takes over their management.

Overall, the component lifecycle is fairly straightforward. iPOJO provides a number of additional ways to impact or hook into a component lifecycle, such as service-dependency binding policy, temporal service dependencies, lifecycle callback methods, component lifecycle participation, and bundle context access. We'll look into each of these.

SERVICE-DEPENDENCY BINDING POLICY

In addition to treating all service dependencies as either mandatory or optional, iPOJO treats them as either static or dynamic; this is called a *binding policy*. This concept is also present in Declarative Services and has the same meaning here. The best way to understand the difference between a static and dynamic service dependency is to consider a specific service dependency, such as an aggregate dependency on the `SimpleShape` service.

For a component with a dynamic, aggregate dependency, iPOJO adds services to and removes them from the component at execution time as the associated services appear and disappear in the service registry without invalidating the component instance (in other words, the component instance lifetime spans service dynamism). For a component with a static, aggregate dependency, iPOJO injects the component with a snapshot of the available services when the component instance was created. iPOJO doesn't inject later-arriving services; and if a service being used departs, iPOJO invalidates the component instance and throws it away (the component instance lifetime doesn't span service dynamism).

The main benefit of using static service dependencies is that your component code is simpler because it never has to worry about dealing with dynamism; but, by default, iPOJO assumes service dependencies are dynamic. You can explicitly choose which binding policy iPOJO uses for a given service dependency. The possible values are as follows:

- `static`—Dependencies are treated as static.
- `dynamic`—Dependencies are dynamic, but not with respect to service priority (default).
- `dynamic-priority`—Dependencies are dynamic and automatically change if a higher-priority service appears, and/or aggregate dependencies are re-sorted.

The `dynamic-priority` policy uses the OSGi service ranking algorithm to determine service priority, but iPOJO also allows you to specify custom sorting algorithms based on `java.util.Comparators`. You declare the binding policy with the policy annotation attribute on either `@Requires` or `@Bind`:

```
@Requires(policy=static)
private LogService m_log;
```

The binding policy should be determined on a case-by-case basis for each of your component's service dependencies. This gives you pretty rich control over your component's service dependencies, but sometimes this still isn't sufficient—for dependencies that are potentially very short-lived, for example. For this, iPOJO supports temporal service dependencies.

TEMPORAL SERVICE DEPENDENCIES

Service dependencies are generally *mandatory* (they must be satisfied to instantiate the component) or *optional* (they aren't needed to instantiate the component). But some types of service dependencies don't fit neatly into these two categories. For example, perhaps your component needs a specific service during startup but then never needs it again. Such a dependency can't be declared optional, because you need it at startup. At the same time, if you declare it mandatory, and it goes away later, your component instance will be invalidated even though it didn't need the service anymore.

In this scenario, the component only has a dependency on the service at a particular point in time. For this reason, iPOJO supports temporal service dependencies, which don't impact the overall component lifecycle like optional dependencies, but must be present when used by the component. How does iPOJO ensure this? It blocks the calling thread if a matching service isn't available.

Declaring a temporal dependency is similar to a normal service dependency. Consider a temporal dependency for a log service:

```
@Requires
private LogService m_log;
```

Although the name is the same, this isn't the same `@Requires` annotation. The original annotation is `org.apache.felix.ipojo.annotations.Requires`; this annotation is `org.apache.felix.ipojo.handler.temporal.Requires`. By using it, whenever a thread accesses `m_log`, it either gets a log service or blocks until one is available. You can use the `timeout` annotation attribute to specify a timeout value, which when expired results in a service exception. If you'd rather not receive an exception, you can use the `onTimeout` annotation attribute to indicate that you'd rather receive a `null` value, a null object, or a default implementation.

> **Damping, anyone?**
>
> The behavior of iPOJO's temporal dependencies is similar to the damping concept used by Blueprint. Technically, if you used temporal dependencies liberally, you'd end up with a similar effect of having all your dependencies damped. Although this is possible, it isn't the intended use case for temporal dependencies, and we advise against it. Generally speaking, most service dependencies are either mandatory or optional. Temporal dependencies are for specific situations as described. The use of damped dependencies may result in systems that exhibit odd behavior when faced with service dynamism.

LIFECYCLE CALLBACK METHODS

iPOJO defines two method-level annotations for declaring lifecycle callback methods in components: `@Validate` and `@Invalidate`. The `@Validate` annotation is applied to component methods to be called when all mandatory service dependencies are satisfied. For example, the paint frame component uses this mechanism to make its frame visible:

```
@Validate
protected void activate() {
  SwingUtils.invokeAndWait(new Runnable() {
    public void run() {
      setVisible(true);
    }
  });
}
```

The `@Invalidate` annotation is applied to component methods to be called when any of the mandatory service references become unsatisfied and iPOJO is going to release the component instance. The paint frame component likewise uses this mechanism to close and dispose of its frame:

```
@Invalidate
protected void deactivate() {
  SwingUtils.invokeLater(new Runnable() {
    public void run() {
      setVisible(false);
      dispose();
    }
  });
}
```

> **WARNING** Be careful about using services in the `@Invalidate` callback, because service departure is the likely cause of the invalidation. This means not all service references are necessarily usable.

Callback methods such as these are nice if you want your components hooked into their own lifecycle. But what if you want them to actively participate in it?

COMPONENT LIFECYCLE PARTICIPATION

In addition to lifecycle-callback methods, iPOJO components can directly participate in their own instance and service-lifecycle management using the `@Controller` and `@ServiceController` annotations, respectively. Both of these annotations can be associated with a `boolean` member field in the component. For example:

```
public class MyComponent implements MyService {
  @Controller
  private boolean isValid = true;
  ...
}
```

This tells the iPOJO runtime to monitor this field to control the lifecycle of the component. If the component sets `isValid` to `false`, iPOJO invalidates the component instance and throws it away. You can use this approach to model exceptional conditions, such as an invalid configuration with no reasonable defaults.

`@ServiceController` is a little more dynamic and allows the component to control when its provided services are published:

```
public class MyComponent implements MyService {
  @ServiceController
  private boolean isProvided = true;
  ...
}
```

In this case, if the component sets `isProvided` to `false`, the iPOJO runtime removes the instance's service from the service registry. If `isProvided` is set to `true` again, iPOJO publishes the service into the service registry again. You can specify the precise service interface using the `specification` annotation attribute, if the component provides more than one service. By default, `@ServiceController` applies to all provided services.

BUNDLE CONTEXT ACCESS

As with the other component frameworks, you can access the underlying OSGi `BundleContext` object associated with the bundle containing the components. In iPOJO, you do so by declaring the component class with a constructor that accepts `BundleContext` as a parameter. Here's an example from the window listener:

```
@Component(immediate=true)
public class WindowListener extends WindowAdapter {
  private BundleContext m_context;

  public WindowListener(BundleContext context) {
    m_context = context;
    m_log.log(LogService.LOG_INFO, "Created " + this);
  }
```

iPOJO automatically injects the `BundleContext` into your component when it's instantiated. So how do you instantiate your components in iPOJO? You'll find out next.

12.2.5 Instantiating components with iPOJO

At this point, you've seen how to define an iPOJO component using Java annotations, and we've looked into component lifecycle issues; but, surprisingly, nothing you've learned so far creates any component instances. Unlike Declarative Services and Blueprint, where component definitions are typically treated as configured component instances, iPOJO always treats a component definition as a type definition. The distinction is the same as between a class (type) and an object (instance).

An iPOJO component description defines a template for creating component instances; but creating an instance requires an extra step, much like using `new` in Java to create an object. How do you accomplish this in iPOJO? There are four possibilities:

- Static XML when the component is instrumented
- Static `@Instantiate` annotation in the Java source code
- Programmatically using an iPOJO component factory service
- Programmatically using the `ConfigurationAdmin` service

We'll look into each of these options in this section.

XML INSTANCE CREATION

Recall earlier that when we discussed setting up the build process for an iPOJO component, you saw the following Ant task referencing a circle.xml file:

```
<ipojo input="${dist}/${ant.project.name}-${version}.jar"
       metadata = "OSGI-INF/circle.xml"/>
```

Now you can see what this file contains:

```
<?xml version="1.0" encoding="UTF-8"?>
<ipojo>
  <instance component="org.foo.shape.circle.Circle"/>
</ipojo>
```

This instructs iPOJO to create an instance of the circle component. Although the circle.xml file is contained in the same bundle as the circle component, this needn't be the case. The beauty of iPOJO's strict separation between component type and instance is that you can package all your component types into bundles, deploy which types you need, and then separately deploy a bundle containing an application configuration describing which instances of which components to create and how to configure them. For example, consider the following simple component:

```
@Component(name="hello")
@Provides
public class HelloImpl implements Hello {
  @Property
  private String name;
  public void sayHello() {
    System.out.println("Hello my name is " + name);
  }
}
```

This component prints a message telling you its name, where its name is injected into the member field `name`. You indicate this by using the iPOJO `@Property` annotation. Here's how to create and configure four different instances of the component:

```
<instance component="hello">
   <property name="name" value="David"/>
</instance>
<instance component="hello">
   <property name="name" value="Karl"/>
</instance>
<instance component="hello">
   <property name="name" value="Richard"/>
</instance>
<instance component="hello">
   <property name="name" value="Stuart"/>
</instance>
```

You declare four different component instances and uniquely configure each. When the bundle containing this component configuration is activated, the iPOJO runtime finds the component type associated with the name `hello` and instantiates it four times, injecting the appropriate configuration into the corresponding instance. In addition to simple name-value properties, iPOJO also supports lists, maps, arrays, sets, and dictionaries as configuration properties.

This is the recommended approach for creating component instances. And remember, the XML is only parsed at build time—no XML parsing goes on at execution time. Regardless, some people wish to avoid XML, which brings us to the next approach.

@INSTANTIATE INSTANCE CREATION

iPOJO also supports the `@Instantiate` annotation. It provides a way to create a component instance without XML and is largely equivalent to declaring a static singleton in Java code. You use it like this:

```
@Instantiate
@Component
@Provides
public class FooImpl implements Foo {
   public void doFoo() {
```

```
      // Do something...
    }
}
```

The `@Instantiate` annotation results in iPOJO creating a component instance at execution time when the containing bundle is activated and the component becomes valid. The main downside of this approach is that it hinders component reusability, because it presupposes that the number and configuration of your component instances are the same for every scenario in which they're used. This isn't typically the case.

Although the XML and annotation approaches likely satisfy the majority of use cases for most people, they don't cover all possibilities. For example, what if you need to dynamically create component instances? iPOJO provides two different ways to accomplish this.

FACTORY SERVICE INSTANCE CREATION

We've told you that iPOJO maintains a strict separation between type and instance, but we didn't tell you how iPOJO does this. For each described component type, iPOJO registers an `org.apache.felix.ipojo.Factory` service in the OSGi service registry at execution time. The `Factory` interface is fairly straightforward and largely defines methods for creating configured component instances.

Internally, iPOJO uses these factory services to create the component instances you declare using XML or `@Instantiate`. To differentiate one component factory service from another, iPOJO registers them with unique `factory.name` service properties, which is the name of the component class by default but can be any name you choose. How does this allow you to dynamically create component instances? Because these are just OSGi services, you can look them up in the service registry and use them like any normal service. The following listing shows an example.

Listing 12.7 Creating components using the component factory service

```
@Component(immediate=true)
public class Creator {
  @Requires(filter="(factory.name=hello)")            ① Dependent on component
  private Factory helloFactory;                          factory service

  private Map<String, ComponentInstance> instances =
    new HashMap<String, ComponentInstance>();

  public void create(String name) {
    Hashtable props = new Hashtable();
    props.put("name", name);
    ComponentInstance instance =                         ② Creates
      helloFactory.createComponentInstance(props);         instance
    instances.put(name, instance);
  }

  public void rename(String oldName, String newName) {
    ComponentInstance instance = instances.remove(oldName);
    if (instance != null) {
      Hashtable props = new Hashtable();
      props.put("name", newName);
```

```
      instance.reconfigure(props);                  Configures previously
      instances.put(newName, instance);           ❸ created instances
    }
  }

  public void dispose(String name) {
    ComponentInstance instance = instances.remove(name);
    if (instance != null) {
      instance.dispose();
      System.out.println(name + " says: Eeek!");
    }
  }
}
```

In this example, you define a component with a dependency ❶ on a component factory service for the previous trivial `Hello` component implementation. You specify the desired factory using the `filter` attribute of `@Requires`; in this case, you previously named the component type `hello`. Like any normal service dependency, the `Creator` component becomes valid only if a matching factory service is available.

In the `create()` method, you prepare a new `Hello` instance configuration by setting the `name` property to the passed-in value and then use the factory to create the instance ❷. In the `rename()` method ❸, you use the `ComponentInstance` object returned from the factory service to configure previously created instances. When you're finished with the instance you dispose of it in `dispose()`.

This approach is well-suited to pooling, allowing you to programmatically create and release component instances. If you swapped your `Hello` implementation for a database connection pool or a thread pool, for example, instances could be programmatically created as other components in the framework noticed degradation in application performance. Although this mechanism lets you dynamically create instances at execution time, it ties components to the iPOJO API. But this effect can be minimized: iPOJO provides another approach to eliminate this coupling.

CONFIGURATION ADMIN INSTANCE CREATION

The final option for creating component instances uses the `ManagedServiceFactory` interface from the OSGi Configuration Admin specification. This approach is fairly similar to the iPOJO factory service, except that it uses the standard OSGi interface rather than an iPOJO-specific one. To illustrate, the next listing shows the previous `Creator` component refactored to use the `ConfigurationAdmin` service instead.

Listing 12.8 Creating components using Configuration Admin

```
@Component(immediate=true)
public class Creator {                                           Creates ❶
  @Requires                                          Configuration object
  private ConfigurationAdmin ca;

  public void create(String name) throws IOException {
    Configuration config = ca.createFactoryConfiguration("hello");
    Hashtable props = new Hashtable();
    props.put("name", name);
```

```
    config.update(props);
  }

  public void rename(String oldName, String newName)
    throws IOException, InvalidSyntaxException {
    String filter = "(&(service.factoryPid=hello)(name=" + oldName + "))";
    Configuration[] configs = ca.listConfigurations(filter);      <-- Finds Configuration object ❷
    if (configs != null) {
      Hashtable props = new Hashtable();
      props.put("name", newName);
      configs[0].update(props);
    }
  }

  public void dispose(String name)
    throws IOException, InvalidSyntaxException {
    String filter = "(&(service.factoryPid=hello)(name=" + name + "))";
    Configuration[] configs = ca.listConfigurations(filter);
    if (configs != null) {
      configs[0].delete();          <-- Disposes of Configuration object ❸
    }
  }
}
```

This version of the `Creator` component requires the Configuration Admin Service. You use it in `create()` to create a `Configuration` object for the factory associated with your component ❶; iPOJO automatically registers a Configuration Admin `ManagedServiceFactory` for component factories and uses the factory name as its PID (see chapter 9 for a refresher on Configuration Admin). You then set the configuration property with the passed-in name and update the configuration. This results in Configuration Admin creating an instance from the `ManagedServiceFactory`, which is backed by the iPOJO `Factory` service.

To update the component, in `rename()` you find the `Configuration` object associated with the passed-in name ❷. If it's found, you update its `name` property with the specified value. Finally, in `dispose()` you again find the `Configuration` object associated with the passed-in name and delete it ❸, which disposes of the instance. Although this approach is somewhat less direct than using iPOJO factory services, the component now only depends on standard OSGi APIs.

We haven't touched on all of iPOJO's features (such as composite service description, which goes beyond what we can cover in this section), but we've discussed most of what you'll need to get started. To see the iPOJO version of the paint program in action, go to the chapter12/paint-example-ip/ directory of the book's companion code. Type `ant` to build the example and `java -jar launcher.jar bundles/` to run it.

12.3 Mix and match

In this and the preceding chapter, we've shown you three OSGi-based component frameworks. You may be wondering which to choose. Unfortunately, there's no one-size-fits-all answer. You have to pick based on your requirements, but table 12.4 provides a summary of some of the features of each to make this task a little easier.

Table 12.4 Summary of component framework features

Feature	Declarative Services	Blueprint	iPOJO
Dependency injection			
Callback injection	Yes	Yes (but methods must be public)	Yes
Constructor injection	No	Yes	No
Field injection	No	No	Yes
Setter injection	Yes	Yes	Yes
Proxy injection	No	Yes	Yes
List injection	No	Yes	Yes
Nullable injection	No	No	Yes
Lifecycle			
Callbacks (activate/deactivate)	Yes	Yes	Yes
Factory pattern	Yes	Yes	Yes
Lazy initialization	Yes	Yes	Yes
Damping	No	Yes	Yes
Field synchronization	No	No	Yes
Component lifecycle control	Yes	Partial	Yes
Service lifecycle control	No	No	Yes
Configuration			
Property configuration	No	Yes	Yes
Field configuration	No	No	Yes
Configuration Admin	Yes	No	Yes
Services			
Custom attribute type	No	Yes	Yes
Lazy initialization	Yes	Yes	Yes
Composite services	No	No	Yes
Description approach			
XML	Yes	Yes	Yes
Java annotations	No	No	Yes
API	No	No	Yes
Nonfunctional			
Multiple providers	Yes	Yes	No

Before closing out this chapter, we'll let you in on a little secret about OSGi component frameworks: you don't have to choose just one. They can all work together via the OSGi service layer. To a large degree, you can use any combination of these component frameworks in your application. To show this in action, let's convert the paint application to use the following components:

- Paint frame from Declarative Services
- Shape API from standard OSGi
- Circle from Declarative Services
- Square from Blueprint
- Triangle from iPOJO
- Window listener from iPOJO

To achieve this goal, you need to make a handful of minor changes to your components so they'll play well together. We hear you asking, "Wait! Why do we need to change the components? I thought you said they can work together." Technically, they can; but there are some issues due to disparate feature sets. You need to smooth over one or two discontinuities among the various component models; table 12.5 summarizes these issues.

Table 12.5 Component model discontinuities

ID	Difference	Discussion
1	Declarative Services' simple service properties	In Declarative Service components, you use simple string service properties with class loading to load icons. This approach causes issues with Blueprint due to issue 2.
2	Blueprint's use of proxy objects	Because Blueprint injects proxies into the callback methods, you can't use the service object to load a resource (i.e., `service.getClass().getResource()` would search the proxy's class loader, not the service object's).
3	Blueprint's requirement of only interfaces as services	For Blueprint, you needed to create an interface to represent the `java.awt.Window` API. All components need to agree on the interfaces they'll expose.

Practically, you need to make the following changes:

- In the `SimpleShape` interface, add an `Icon getIcon()` method and remove the `ICON_PROPERTY` constant that's no longer used. Doing so bridges the gap between Declarative Services capabilities and Blueprint capabilities with respect to service attributes.
- As a consequence, each `SimpleShape` implementation now loads its own `ImageIcon`. Also, the `DefaultShape` class delegates the `getIcon()` call to the `SimpleShape` implementation where possible and handles the loading of the under-construction icon when the service is no longer available.
- The `PaintFrame` class uses the `getIcon()` method on `SimpleShape` to load the icon versus handling this itself.

To run this combined paint program, go to the chapter12/paint-example-mixed directory of the book's companion code. Type `ant` to build the example and `java -jar launcher.jar bundles` to execute it. All the components from the different frameworks integrate nicely into a single application.

12.4 Summary

Component frameworks can simplify the task of creating OSGi-based applications and add useful capabilities, including lazy initialization, complex service-dependency management, and configuration externalization. Often, you'll end up having to do a lot of this work yourself, so using a component framework can free you from the drudgery.

The following list summarizes the component frameworks we've investigated in the past two chapters:

- Declarative Services is an OSGi specification and is the simplest framework, offering management of service dependencies and component configuration.
- Blueprint is also an OSGi specification and provides features similar to Declarative Services, but with a richer configuration model. It's familiar to developers who come from a Spring background.
- iPOJO is an open source solution that uses byte-code instrumentation of components to offer a well-rounded and sophisticated framework for building dynamic, service-based applications.
- With any of these component frameworks, you can build rich, dynamic, OSGi-based applications, with the added bonus that they can all integrate and collaborate via the OSGi service registry.

Now we'll switch focus from dealing with the internal structure of your applications to external concerns. Until now, we've assumed that applications are a set of bundles running inside an OSGi framework, but sometimes they're more complicated. For example, you may need to be in control of how your application is launched, or you may not be able to package an entire application as bundles. What do you do then? In the next chapter, we'll look at how to launch and/or embed an OSGi framework.

13 Launching and embedding an OSGi framework

This chapter covers

- Introducing the OSGi framework launching and embedding API
- Explaining the generic bundle launcher used throughout the book
- Embedding the OSGi framework into an existing application

We've spent a lot of time talking about creating, deploying, and managing bundles and services. Interestingly, you can't do anything with these unless you have a running OSGi framework. For such an important and necessary topic, we've spent very little time discussing how precisely to achieve it. Not only is it necessary, but by learning to launch the framework, you'll have the ability to create custom launchers tailored to your application's needs. It even opens up new use cases, where you can use an instance of an OSGi framework inside an existing application or even embedded inside a bundle. Interesting stuff.

In this chapter, you'll learn everything you need to know about launching the OSGi framework. To help you reach this goal, we'll dissect the generic bundle launcher you've been using to run the book's examples. You'll also refactor the paint program to see how to embed a framework instance inside an existing application. Let's get going.

13.1 Standard launching and embedding

As we mentioned back in chapter 3, you face a dilemma when you want to use a bundle you've created. You need a `BundleContext` object to install your bundle into the framework, but the framework only gives a `BundleContext` object to an installed and started bundle. So you're in a chicken-and-egg situation where you need an installed and started bundle to install and start your bundle. You need some way to bootstrap the process.

Traditionally, OSGi framework implementations from Apache Felix, Equinox, and Knopflerfish devised implementation-specific means for dealing with this situation. This typically involved some combination of auto-deploy configuration properties for each framework implementations' custom launchers and/or shells with textual or graphical interfaces. These mechanisms worked reasonably well but weren't portable across framework implementations.

With the release of the OSGi R4.2 specification, the OSGi Alliance defined a standard framework launching and embedding API. Although this isn't a major advance in and of itself, it does help you create applications that are truly portable across framework implementations. You may wonder if this is really necessary or all that common. There are two main reasons why you may want to create your own framework instance:

1. Your application has custom startup requirements that aren't met by your framework's default launcher.
2. For legacy reasons, you can't convert your entire application into a set of bundles that run inside an OSGi framework.

Previously, if either of these applied to your project, you had to couple your project to a specific framework implementation by using its custom API to launch it. Now, R4.2-compliant frameworks share a common API for creating, configuring, and starting the framework. Let's dive into its details.

13.1.1 Framework API overview

As we previously mentioned, at execution time the OSGi framework is internally represented as a special bundle, called the *system bundle*, with bundle identifier zero. This means active bundles are able to interact with the framework using the standard `Bundle` interface, which we reiterate in the following listing.

Listing 13.1 Standard `Bundle` interface

```
public interface Bundle {
  String getSymbolicName();
  Version getVersion();
```

Content-access methods

```
  Dictionary getHeaders();
  Dictionary getHeaders(String locale);
  URL getEntry(String path);
  Enumeration getEntryPaths(String path);
  Enumeration findEntries(String path, String pattern, boolean recurse);
  URL getResource(String name);
  Enumeration getResources(String name) throws IOException;
  Class loadClass(String name) throws ClassNotFoundException;
  Map getSignerCertificates(int signersType);
  void start() throws BundleException;
  void start(int options) throws BundleException;
  void stop() throws BundleException;
  void stop(int options) throws BundleException;
  void update() throws BundleException;
  void update(InputStream input) throws BundleException;
  void uninstall() throws BundleException;
  int getState();
  BundleContext getBundleContext();
  long getBundleId();
  String getLocation();
  long getLastModified();
  ServiceReference[] getRegisteredServices();
  ServiceReference[] getServicesInUse();
  boolean hasPermission(Object permission);
}
```

Content-access methods

Lifecycle-control methods

Execution-time state- and context-access methods

Although this provides an internal framework API for other bundles, it doesn't help externally when you want to create and start framework instances. When the R4.2 specification looked to address this situation, the logical place to start was with the `Bundle` interface. This was a good starting point, but it wasn't completely sufficient. To address the missing pieces, the R4.2 specification defines a new `Bundle` subtype, called `Framework`, which is captured in the following snippet:

```
public interface Framework extends Bundle {
  void init() throws BundleException;
  FrameworkEvent waitForStop(long timeout) throws InterruptedException;
}
```

All R4.2-compliant framework implementations implement the `Framework` interface. Because it extends `Bundle`, this means framework implementations now look like a bundle externally as well as internally via the system bundle.

> **NOTE** Although this new API represents the framework instance internally and externally as a `Bundle` object, the specification doesn't require the internal system bundle object to be the same object as the external `Framework` object. Whether this is or isn't the case depends on the framework implementation.

As you can see, the `Framework` interface is a simple extension, so you don't have too much new API to learn. In the following subsections, we'll fully explore how to use this API to configure, create, and control framework implementations in a standard way.

13.1.2 Creating a framework instance

It's great to have a standard interface for framework implementations, but you can't instantiate an interface; you need a way to get a concrete implementation class. It isn't possible for the OSGi specification to define a standard class name, so it adopts the standard Java approach of specifying service-provider implementations in JAR files: META-INF/services.

In this case, META-INF/services refers to a directory entry in a JAR file. Just as a JAR's META-INF/MANIFEST.MF file contains metadata about the JAR file, so does its META-INF/services directory. More specifically, it contains metadata about the service providers contained in a JAR file. Here the term *service* isn't referring to an OSGi service, but to well-known interfaces and/or abstract classes in general. All in all, the concept is similar to the OSGi service concept.

The META-INF/services directory in a JAR file contains service-provider configuration files, which refer to a concrete implementation class for a given service. Concrete service implementations are connected to their abstract service type via the name of the file entry in the directory, which is named after the fully qualified service it implements. For example, a service implementation for the `java.text.spi.DateFormatProvider` service would be named

```
META-INF/services/java.text.spi.DateFormatProvider
```

The content of this file is the name of the concrete service-implementation class:

```
org.foo.CustomDateFormatProvider
```

Figure 13.1 depicts this hypothetical example. At execution time, when a service provider is required, the code needing it queries the service-provider configuration file

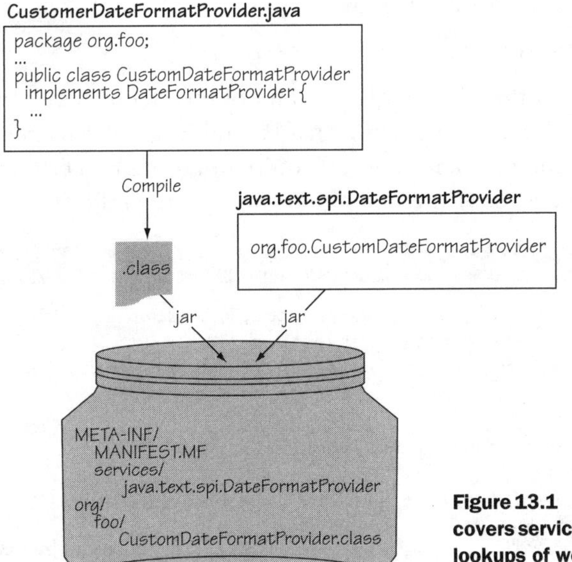

Figure 13.1 The Java META-INF/services approach discovers service providers at execution time by performing lookups of well-known named resource files to acquire concrete service-implementation class names.

like any normal resource using the well-known service name as the name of the resource file. When a concrete type is obtained from the content of the file, the code needing the service can load and instantiate the associated class.

The OSGi specification uses this mechanism to provide a standard way to get the concrete framework implementation class. But rather than directly retrieve a framework implementation class, OSGi defines a framework factory service as follows:

```
public interface FrameworkFactory {
  Framework newFramework(Map config);
}
```

This interface provides a simple way to create new framework instances and pass a configuration map into them. As a concrete example, the Apache Felix framework implementation has the following entry in its JAR file declaring its service implementation:

```
META-INF/services/org.osgi.framework.launch.FrameworkFactory
```

The content of this JAR file entry is the name of the concrete class implementing the factory service:

```
org.apache.felix.framework.FrameworkFactory
```

Of course, these details are only for illustrative purposes, because you only need to know how to get a framework factory service instance. The standard way to do this in Java 6 is to use `java.util.ServiceLoader`. You obtain a `ServiceLoader` instance for a framework factory like this:

```
ServiceLoader<FrameworkFactory> factoryLoader =
    ServiceLoader.load(FrameworkFactory.class);
```

Using the `ServiceLoader` instance referenced by `factoryLoader`, you can iterate over all available OSGi framework factory services like this:

```
Iterator<FrameworkFactory> it = factoryLoader.iterator();
```

In most cases, you only care if there's a single provider of the factory service; you can invoke `it.next()` to get the first available factory and use `FrameworkFactory.newInstance()` to create a framework instance. If you're not using Java 6, you can also use the `ClassLoader.getResource()` method as illustrated in the following listing.

Listing 13.2 Retrieving a `FrameworkFactory` service manually

```
private static FrameworkFactory getFrameworkFactory() throws Exception {
  URL url = Main.class.getClassLoader().getResource(
    "META-INF/services/org.osgi.framework.launch.FrameworkFactory");    <-- 1 Looks up framework factory provider
  if (url != null) {
    BufferedReader br =
      new BufferedReader(new InputStreamReader(url.openStream()));
    try {
      for (String s = br.readLine(); s != null; s = br.readLine()) {
        s = s.trim();
        if ((s.length() > 0) && (s.charAt(0) != '#')) {
```

```
            return (FrameworkFactory) Class.forName(s).newInstance();   <-- Instantiates provider class (2)
          }
        }
      } finally {
        if (br != null) br.close();
      }
    }
    throw new Exception("Could not find framework factory.");
  }
```

The `getFrameworkFactory()` method in listing 13.2 isn't as robust as it could be, but it's sufficient to get the job done. It queries for the standard service-provider configuration file ❶. If it finds one, it reads the content of the file. Within the loop, it searches for the first line not starting with # (the comment character) and assumes that the line contains the name of the concrete class it should instantiate at ❷. The method throws an exception if an error occurs during this process or if a factory provider couldn't be found.

This method is fairly simple and will work for all R4.2-compliant frameworks; you'll use it for the generic launcher in section 13.2. Next, we'll look into how you use the factory service to configure a framework instance.

13.1.3 Configuring a framework

When you have a framework factory service, you can create an instance of `Framework`. Typically, you don't use a default framework instance; instead, you often want to configure it in some way, such as setting the directory where the framework should store cached bundles. This is why `FrameworkFactory.newInstance()` takes a `Map`, so you can pass in configuration properties for the created framework instance.

> **No configuration required**
>
> You don't have to pass in configuration properties when creating a framework; `null` is an acceptable configuration. The OSGi specification says framework implementations must use reasonable defaults, but it doesn't explicitly define all of them. This means some defaults are implementation-specific. For example, by default the Apache Felix framework caches installed bundles in a felix-cache/ directory in the current directory, whereas the Equinox framework uses configuration/org.eclipse.osgi/bundles/ in the directory where the Equinox JAR file is located. Be aware that you won't necessarily get the same behavior unless you explicitly configure it.

Prior OSGi specifications defined a few standard configuration properties; but until the framework factory API, there was no standard way to set them. As part of the R4.2 specification process, several new standard configuration properties were also introduced. Table 13.1 shows some of the standard configuration properties.

The properties listed in table 13.1 can be put into a `Map` and passed into the `FrameworkFactory.newInstance()` method to configure the resulting framework instance;

Table 13.1 Some standard OSGi framework configuration properties

Property name	Spec	Meaning
`org.osgi.framework.storage`	R4.2	A file system path to a directory, which will be created if it doesn't exist. If this property isn't set, a reasonable default is used.
`org.osgi.framework.storage.clean`	R4.2	Specifies if and when the storage area for the framework should be cleaned. If no value is specified, the framework storage area isn't cleaned. Currently, the only possible value is `onFirstInit`, which causes the framework instance to clean the storage area the first time it's used.
`org.osgi.framework.system.packages`	R4	Using standard `Export-Package` syntax, specifies a list of class path packages to be exported from the system bundle. If not set, the framework must provide a reasonable default for the current VM.
`org.osgi.framework.system.packages.extra`	R4.2	Specifies a list of class path packages to be exported from the system bundle in addition to those from the previous system-packages property.
`org.osgi.framework.startlevel.beginning`	R4.2	Specifies the beginning start level of the framework.
`org.osgi.framework.bootdelegation`	R4	Specifies a comma-delimited list of packages with potential wildcards to make available to bundles from the class path without `Import-Package` declarations (for example, `com.sun.*`). By default, all `java.*` packages are boot delegated. We recommend avoiding this property.
`org.osgi.framework.bundle.parent`	R4.2	Specifies which class loader is used for boot delegation. Possible values are `boot` for the boot class loader, `app` for the application class loader, `ext` for the extension class loader, and `framework` for the framework's class loader. The default is `boot`.

Table 13.1 Some standard OSGi framework configuration properties *(continued)*

Property name	Spec	Meaning
`org.osgi.framework.library.extensions`	R4.2	Specifies a comma-separated list of additional library file extensions that must be used when searching for native code.
`org.osgi.framework.command.execpermission`	R4.2	Specifies an optional OS-specific command to set file permissions on a bundle's native code.

property names are case insensitive. We won't go into the precise details of all the standard configuration properties, so consult the R4.2 specification if you want details not covered here. With this knowledge, you know how to configure and instantiate a framework instance; let's look at how to start it.

13.1.4 Starting a framework instance

When you have a `Framework` instance from `FrameworkFactory`, starting it is easy: invoke the `start()` method inherited from the `Bundle` interface. The `start()` method implicitly initializes the framework by invoking the `Framework.init()` method, unless you explicitly initialize it beforehand. If the `init()` method wasn't invoked prior to calling `start()`, then it's invoked by `start()`.

You can relate these methods to the framework lifecycle transitions, similar to the normal bundle lifecycle:

- `init()` transitions the framework instance to the `Bundle.STARTING` state.
- `start()` transitions the framework instance to the `Bundle.ACTIVE` state.

The `init()` method gets the framework ready but doesn't start executing any bundle code yet. It performs the following steps:

1. Framework event handling is enabled.
2. The security manager is installed if it's enabled.
3. The framework start level is set to 0.
4. All cached bundles are reloaded, and their state is set to `Bundle.INSTALLED`.
5. A `BundleContext` object is created for the framework.
6. All framework-provided services are made available (Package Admin, Start Level, and so on).
7. The framework enters the `Bundle.STARTING` state.

The `start()` method starts the framework instance and performs the following additional steps:

1. If the framework isn't in the `Bundle.STARTING` state, the `init()` method is invoked.
2. The framework sets its beginning start level to the configured value, which causes all reloaded bundles to be started in accordance with their activation policy and start level.
3. The framework's state is set to `Bundle.ACTIVE`.
4. A framework event of type `FrameworkEvent.STARTED` is fired.

You may wonder why the `init()` method is necessary and why all the steps aren't performed in the `start()` method. In some cases, you may want to interact with the framework instance before restarting cached bundles, but some interactions can only happen via the framework's `BundleContext` object. Because bundles (including the framework) don't have a `BundleContext` object until they've been started, `init()` is necessary to transition the framework to the `Bundle.STARTING` state so you can acquire its context with `Bundle.getBundleContext()`.

To summarize, in the normal case, call `start()`. But if you want to perform some actions before all the cached bundles restart, call `init()` first to do what you need to do followed by a call to `start()`. When the framework is active, subsequent calls to `init()` and `start()` have no effect.

Next, we'll look at how you shut down a running framework.

13.1.5 Stopping a framework instance

As you may guess, stopping an active framework involves invoking the `stop()` method inherited from the `Bundle` interface. This method asynchronously stops the framework on another thread, so the method returns immediately to the caller. If you want to know when the framework has finished shutting down, call `Framework.waitForStop()` after calling `stop()`, which blocks the calling thread until shutdown is complete.

The following steps are performed when you stop a framework:

1. The framework's state is set to `Bundle.STOPPING`.
2. All installed bundles are stopped without changing each bundle's persistent activation state and according to start levels.
3. The framework's start level is set to 0.
4. Framework event handling is disabled.
5. The framework's state is set to `Bundle.RESOLVED`.
6. All resources held by the framework are released.
7. All threads waiting on `Framework.waitForStop()` are awakened.

NOTE Calling `waitForStop()` doesn't start the framework shutdown process, it waits for it to occur. If you want to stop the framework, you must call `stop()` on it first.

The `waitForStop()` method takes a timeout value in milliseconds and returns a `FrameworkEvent` object whose type indicates why the framework stopped:

- `FrameworkEvent.STOPPED`—The framework was stopped.
- `FrameworkEvent.STOPPED_UPDATE`—The framework was updated.
- `FrameworkEvent.ERROR`—An error forced the framework to shut down, or an error occurred during shutdown.
- `FrameworkEvent.WAIT_TIMEDOUT`—The timeout value expired before the framework stopped.

When the framework has successfully stopped, it can be safely discarded or reused. To start the framework again, call `start()` or `init()/start()`. The normal startup process will commence, except the bundle cache won't be deleted again if the storage-cleaning policy is `onFirstInit`, because that applies only the first time the framework is initialized. Otherwise, you can stop and restart the framework as much as you like.

That's all there is to creating and launching frameworks with the standard framework launching and embedding API from the R4.2 specification. Let's explore your newfound knowledge by examining the generic bundle launcher.

Launching vs. embedding

Why is this called the framework launching and embedding API? The term *launching* is largely self explanatory, but the term *embedding* is less clear. What is the difference between the two? The conceptual difference is that *launching* refers to creating and starting a framework instance in isolation, whereas *embedding* refers to creating and starting a framework instance within (embedded in) another application. Technically, there's very little difference between the two, because creating, configuring, and starting a framework instance with the API is the same in either case.

The main technical differences are in your objectives. When you launch a framework, all functionality is typically provided by installed bundles, and there's no concern about the outside world. But when you embed a framework, you often have functionality on the outside that you want to expose somehow on the inside or vice versa. Embedding a framework instance has some additional constraints and complications that we'll discuss later in this chapter.

13.2 Launching the framework

The general steps for launching a framework are straightforward:

1. Set the desired configuration properties.
2. Create a framework instance using the configuration properties.
3. Start the framework instance.
4. Install some bundles.

These are the same basic steps the generic bundle launcher uses, as we'll introduce in the following subsections by breaking the example into short code snippets. The complete source code for the generic launcher is in the launcher/ directory of the book's companion code.

13.2.1 Determining which bundles to install

As you've seen throughout the book, the generic bundle launcher installs and starts all bundles contained in a directory specified as a command line argument. The launcher is composed of a single class, called `Main`, which is declared in the following code snippet.

Listing 13.3 Main class declaration for generic bundle launcher

```
public class Main {
  private static Framework fwk;

  public static void main(String[] args) throws Exception {
    if (args.length < 1 || !new File(args[0]).isDirectory()) {
      System.out.println("Usage: <bundle-directory>");
    } else {
      File[] files = new File(args[0]).listFiles();
      Arrays.sort(files);
      List jars = new ArrayList();
      for (int i = 0; i < files.length; i++)
        if (files[i].getName().toLowerCase().endsWith(".jar"))
          jars.add(files[i]);
      ...
```

The static member variable holds the framework instance you're going to create. You verify that a directory was specified as a command line argument. If a directory was specified, you get the files contained in it and save all files ending with .jar into a list to be processed later.

13.2.2 Shutting down cleanly

You can't always guarantee that the launcher process will exit normally, so it's a good idea to try to ensure your framework instance cleanly shuts down. Depending on the framework implementation, you can end up with a corrupted bundle cache if you don't shut down cleanly. The following listing adds a shutdown hook to the JVM process to cleanly shut down your framework instance.

Listing 13.4 Using a shutdown hook to cleanly stop the framework

```
...
if (jars.isEmpty()) {
  System.out.println("No bundles to install.");
} else {
  Runtime.getRuntime().addShutdownHook(new Thread() {
    public void run() {
      try {
```

```
        if (fwk != null) {                      ◁ Checks if
          fwk.stop();                           ❶ framework exists
          fwk.waitForStop(0);
        }
      } catch (Exception ex) {
        System.err.println("Error stopping framework: " + ex);
      }
    }
  });
  ...
```

The JVM shutdown hook mechanism requires a Thread object to perform necessary actions during process exit; you supply a thread to cleanly stop the framework. When the shutdown thread executes, you verify that a framework instance was created ❶ and, if so, you stop it. Because shutting down the framework happens asynchronously, the call to fwk.stop() returns immediately. You call fwk.waitForStop() to make the thread wait for the framework to completely stop. It's necessary to have your thread wait; otherwise, there's a race condition between the JVM process exiting and your framework stopping.

Using a shutdown hook isn't strictly necessary. The process is in an awkward state during shutdown, and not all JVM services are guaranteed to be available. There's also the potential for deadlock and hanging the process. In short, it's a good idea to try to cleanly shut down the framework, but be aware of the potential pitfalls and do as little work as possible in the shutdown hook.

13.2.3 Configuring, creating, and starting the framework

In section 13.2.1, you determined which bundles you want to install; all you need now is a framework instance. The following snippet shows how you create it:

```
...
Bundle mainBundle = null;
try {
  List bundleList = new ArrayList();
  Map m = new HashMap();
  m.putAll(System.getProperties());
  m.put(Constants.FRAMEWORK_STORAGE_CLEAN, "onFirstInit");
  fwk = getFrameworkFactory().newFramework(m);
  fwk.start();
  ...
```

You begin by creating a variable to hold a reference to your *main* bundle, which is a bundle with a Main-Class entry in its manifest file; we'll come back to this concept in a couple of sections. After that, you create a list to hold the bundles you successfully install.

In the setup for the framework instance, you create a configuration map for it. For the generic launcher, you copy the system properties in the configuration map as a convenience and only set one configuration, which cleans the bundle cache on first initialization. In most cases, you likely won't want to do this; but for the purposes of the book examples, this makes sense to be sure you always start with a clean framework instance. Next, you get the framework factory service and use it to create a framework instance using the configuration map. To get the framework factory service, you use the `getFrameworkFactory()` method introduced in listing 13.2. Finally, you start the framework.

13.2.4 Installing the bundles

Now you have a configured and started framework instance. Because you configured the framework to clean its bundle cache on first initialization, you know your framework has no bundles installed in it. You need to remedy that. The following snippet shows how to install the bundles contained in the directory specified on the command line:

```
...
BundleContext ctxt = fwk.getBundleContext();
for (int i = 0; i < jars.size(); i++) {
  Bundle b = ctxt.installBundle(
    ((File) jars.get(i)).toURI().toString());
  bundleList.add(b);
  if (b.getHeaders().get("Main-Class") != null) {
    mainBundle = b;
  }
}
...
```

You first get the `BundleContext` object associated with the system bundle; this is possible because the `Framework` object extends `Bundle` and represents the system bundle. You loop through the JAR files discovered in the specified directory and install them using the system bundle context; any exceptions cause the launcher to fail. After you install a bundle, you add it to the list of installed bundles and probe to see if its manifest contains a `Main-Class` header, which you'll use later. If there's more than one bundle with a `Main-Class` header, you use the last one you discover.

13.2.5 Starting the bundles

You've installed all of the bundles, but they aren't doing anything yet. You need to start them. You can accomplish this in a simple loop over all installed bundles, invoking `start()` on each one:

```
...
for (int i = 0; i < bundleList.size(); i++) {
  if (!isFragment((Bundle) bundleList.get(i))) {     ❶ Starts nonfragment bundles
    ((Bundle) bundleList.get(i)).start();
  }
}
...
```

You may wonder why you don't start each installed bundle right after installing it. It's better to install and start bundles in two passes: one pass for installing and one pass for starting. This approach helps alleviate ordering issues when it comes to dependency resolution. If you install a bundle and start it immediately, it may fail to resolve because it may depend on some bundle that's not yet installed. By installing all the bundles first, you stand a better chance of successfully resolving the bundles when you activate them.

Notice also that you don't call `start()` on all bundles ❶; instead, you only call `start()` on bundles that aren't fragment bundles. Fragments can't be started and will throw an exception if you try to start them, which is why you avoid doing so. How do you know a bundle is a fragment? This simple approach works:

```
private static boolean isFragment(Bundle bundle) {
  return bundle.getHeaders().get(Constants.FRAGMENT_HOST) != null;
}
```

You check to see if the bundle's manifest headers contain the `Fragment-Host` header. If so, it must be a fragment, and you don't want to start it.

13.2.6 Starting the main bundle

You've installed and started all the bundles contained in the specified directory. In most cases, this would be good enough. But for the examples in this book, you need one more step. In chapter 2, we showed how you can use the module layer all by itself to modularize the paint program. In that example, none of the bundles contained a `BundleActivator`, because activators are part of the lifecycle layer. In such an scenario, you need a way to start your application: you can use the standard Java `Main-Class` JAR file manifest header as a way to define a main bundle from which you can load the main class and execute its `static void main()` method.

> **NOTE** The notion of a main bundle with a main class isn't an OSGi convention or a standard. We defined this approach for this book to show that it's possible to use the OSGi modularity layer to modularize OSGi-unaware applications. You could also consider introducing a custom manifest header for this purpose to avoid confusion with the standard `Main-Class` header.

The next listing shows how to load the main class and invoke its `main()` method.

Listing 13.5 Invoking the main class from the main bundle

```
...
if (mainBundle != null) {
  final String className =
    (String) mainBundle.getHeaders().get("Main-Class");
  if (mainClassName != null) {
    final Class mainClass = mainBundle.loadClass(className);
    try {
      Method method = mainClass.getMethod(
        "main", new Class[] { String[].class });
      String[] mainArgs = new String[args.length-1];
      System.arraycopy(args, 1, mainArgs, 0, mainArgs.length);
      method.invoke(null, new Object[] { mainArgs });     ❶ Invokes static main method
    } catch (Exception ex) {
      System.err.println("Error invoking main method: "
```

```
            + ex + " cause = " + ex.getCause());
        }
      } else {
        System.err.println("Main class not found: " + mainClassName);
      }
    }
    ...
```

If you have a main bundle, you need to invoke its main class's `main()` method; you won't necessarily have a main bundle if the bundles have activators. First, you get the name of the class from the `Main-Class` manifest header. Using this name, you load the class from the main bundle. Then, you use reflection to get the `Method` object associated with the main class's `main()` method. You make an array to contain any additional command line arguments passed into the launcher after the specified directory. Finally, you use reflection to invoke the `main()` method ❶, passing in any command line arguments.

13.2.7 Waiting for shutdown

At this point, your launcher should have your bundled application up and running. What's left to do? Not much; just sit around and wait for it to finish, like this:

```
          ...
          fwk.waitForStop(0);
          System.exit(0);
        } catch (Exception ex) {
          System.err.println("Error starting framework: " + ex);
          ex.printStackTrace();
          System.exit(0);
        }
      }
    }
}
```

You first call `Framework.waitForStop()`, which doesn't stop the framework—it waits for it to stop somehow. Why do you do this? Why not let the calling thread run off the end of your main method, similar to what you do with Swing applications? Unlike Swing applications, which result in a non-daemon thread starting for Swing event delivery, you don't have any guarantee that the OSGi framework will create any non-daemon threads. (If you aren't familiar with the concept of daemon threads, it's a fancy way of saying *background threads.*) For the Java VM, if only daemon threads are present, the VM process terminates. You need to explicitly wait for the framework to stop, because you know the main thread is non-daemon and will keep the VM process alive.

For similar issues, you call `System.exit()` to end the VM process. If you didn't call `exit()` here, and a bundle started a non-daemon thread that wasn't properly stopped, then the VM process wouldn't exit after stopping the framework. This is similar to Swing applications, which require an explicit call to `exit()` because the Swing event thread is non-daemon.

That's all there is to it. You've successfully created a completely generic launcher that will work with any OSGi R4.2 framework implementation. To use this launcher with an arbitrary framework implementation, put it on the class path with the launcher, and you're good to go. But what about situations where you can't convert your entire application into bundles? In that case, you may want to embed a framework instance inside your application. We'll look into that next.

13.3 Embedding the framework

In some situations, it isn't possible to convert your entire application into bundles, where everything runs inside the OSGi framework. This can happen in legacy situations where conversion into bundles is prohibitively expensive, or in situations where there's resistance or uncertainty about converting the entire application. Even in these sorts of situations, you can use OSGi technology for specific needs. For example, it's not uncommon for Java-based applications to provide a plugin mechanism for extensibility purposes. If your application has a plugin mechanism or you're thinking about adding one, an embedded OSGi framework can do the trick (in chapter 6, you saw how to convert jEdit's plugin mechanism to use OSGi).

You may be thinking, "Wouldn't I be better off creating my own simple plugin mechanism in this case?" Typically, the answer is, no. The dynamic class-loading aspects of plugin mechanisms are difficult to get right. Over time, you'll likely need to add more advanced features, such as support for library sharing, side-by-side versions, or native libraries, at which point you'll start to enter complicated territory and have to reinvent the wheel. By using OSGi, all this is taken care of for you, so you can concentrate on implementing your application's core functionality. If you're concerned about the size of OSGi frameworks, remember that they're intended to run on embedded devices, and most implementations aren't too hefty. In addition, you get the benefit of having a known standard, which makes it easier for your plugin developers and provides the opportunity to reuse existing bundles.

Embedding an OSGi framework instance into an application may sound pretty exotic; but thanks to the standard framework launching and embedding API, it's largely the same as launching the framework. You do need to understand some differences and a few issues; in the remainder of this section, we'll discuss these issues as well as present an example of embedding a framework instance into an application.

13.3.1 Inside vs. outside

The main issue around embedding a framework instance into an application is the distinction between being on the *inside* of the framework versus being on the *outside* of the framework. The bundles deployed into the embedded framework live in a nice insulated world and know nothing about the outside. Conversely, the application lives in the external rough-and-tumble world. Figure 13.2 illustrates the situation.

It's possible to traverse the isolation boundary provided by the framework, but the inside/outside distinction places some constraints on how the application can interact with installed bundles and vice versa.

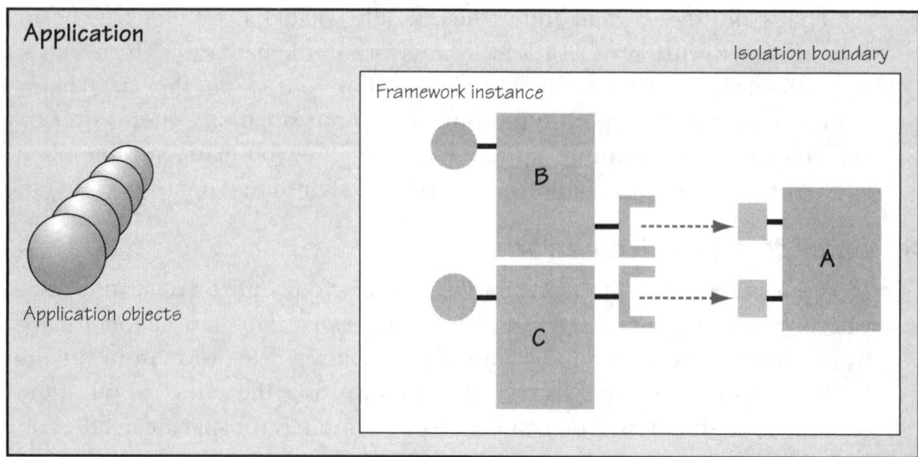

Figure 13.2 The embedded framework instance forms an isolation boundary between the bundles on the inside and the application objects on the outside.

> **Avoid being on the outside**
>
> The best approach for dealing with the inside/outside divide is to eliminate it by converting your entire application to bundles. If you're on the fence about this issue, you can start with an embedding approach and later convert the rest of your application to bundles. But if you have a choice up front, start with all bundles.

If you decide to embed a framework instance, what are some of the things you'll likely want to do with it? You'll probably want to

- Interact with and manage the embedded framework instance
- Provide services to bundles and use services from bundles

Let's look at what you need to do in each of these cases.

INTERACTING WITH THE EMBEDDED FRAMEWORK

You already know how to interact with an embedded framework instance: through the standard launching and embedding API. When you create an instance of an R4.2-compatible framework implementation, you get an object that implements the `Framework` interface. As you saw previously, this interface gives you access to all the API necessary to control and inspect the framework instance. The framework instance represents the system bundle and provides you a passage from the outside to the inside of the framework, as depicted in figure 13.3.

From the system bundle, you can start and stop the framework as well as deploy, manage, and interact with bundles. If you're using an embedded framework instance as a plugin mechanism in your application, you use this API to deploy plugin bundles by loading them from a directory or providing a GUI for user access, for example. It's also through this API that you can provide services to bundles and use services from bundles.

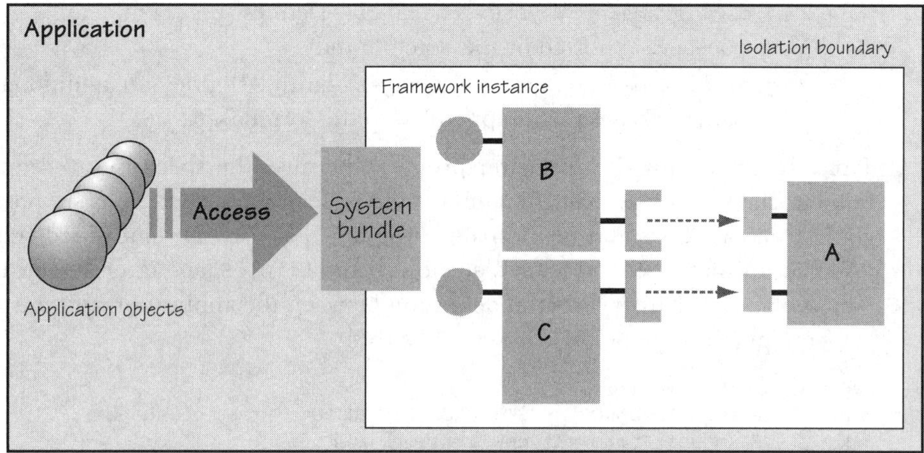

Figure 13.3 A framework instance represents the system bundle and provides the means to manage the framework instance as well as interact with deployed bundles.

PROVIDING SERVICES AND USING BUNDLE SERVICES

Luckily, there's no new API to learn when it comes to providing application services to embedded bundles or using services from them. You learned about providing and using services in chapter 4, and that knowledge applies here. The only real difference is that you use the system bundle to do everything, because the application has no bundle associated with it.

Because you need a `BundleContext` to register or find services, you use the `BundleContext` associated with the system bundle. You can get access to it by calling `getBundleContext()` on the framework instance. From there, registering and using services is pretty much the same as if the application were a bundle. Simple, right? As you may expect, there is one main constraint.

> **NOTE** An application embedding a framework instance can only interact with contained bundles using objects whose class definition is the same for both the application and bundles.

By default, the application on the outside and the bundles on the inside only share core JVM packages, so it would be possible for the application and bundles to interact using objects from classes defined in core JVM packages. For example, you can provide or use `java.lang.Runnable` services, because you know the application and the bundles use a common class definition for `Runnable`. This works out fairly well if everything you need is in a core JVM package, but this isn't typically the case.

Luckily, there's a rudimentary way to share packages from the application to the contained bundles via framework configuration. The launching and embedding API defines two previously mentioned configuration properties for this purpose:

- `org.osgi.framework.system.packages`—Defines the complete set of class path packages exported by the system bundle
- `org.osgi.framework.system.packages.extra`—Defines an additional set of class path packages that is appended to the former set

Typically, you'll only use the latter property, because the specification requires the framework to set a reasonable default for the former. For an example, suppose you're going to create a version of the paint program that used an embedded framework instance. In that case, you likely want to put the `SimpleShape` interface on the class path so you can share a common definition between the application and the bundles. You configure the framework instance like this:

```
Map m = new HashMap();
m.put(Constants.FRAMEWORK_SYSTEMPACKAGES_EXTRA, "org.foo.shape");
fwk = getFrameworkFactory().newFramework(m);
fwk.start();
```

The syntax to use when specifying the property is exactly the same as for the `Export-Package` manifest header, which means you can specify additional packages by separating them with commas; you can also include version information and attributes.

Necessary, but not sufficient

It's necessary to specify this configuration property to share class path packages with bundles, but it isn't sufficient to only do this. You must also ensure that the specified packages are available on the class path when you start your application. You do so the standard way (by specifying them on the JVM class path).

The need to perform this configuration is an extra step for the application, but from the bundle's perspective it's business as usual. Bundles need to specify the package on their `Import-Package` manifest header, as normal, and the framework gives them access to the package following normal OSGi rules.

What about the situation where you don't have a common class available from the class path? Because the application can't import packages from bundles, there isn't much you can do here. The main option is to resort to reflection, which is possible because OSGi service lookup can be performed by the class name. Of course, you should use `BundleContext.getAllServiceReferences()` instead of `BundleContext.getServiceReferences()`, because the framework will potentially filter results if it determines that you don't have access to the published service type. This gives you access to the `ServiceReference` that you can use to get access to the service object so you can invoke methods on it using reflection.

If you have different definitions of the service class on the outside and inside, you can try to get fancy and use dynamic proxies to bridge the two types in a generic way. But this is beyond the scope of this chapter and can easily be avoided by converting your entire application to bundles.

13.3.2 Who's in control?

If you're going to pursue the embedded framework route, you may run into a few other issues related to who's expecting to be in control. Generally speaking, the OSGi framework assumes it's in control of the JVM on which it's running. If you're embedding a framework, you probably don't want it to be in control or at least want it to share control with the application in which you're embedding it. It's not uncommon to run into issues related to JVM singleton mechanisms, such as URL and content handler factories or security.

Singleton mechanisms like these are only intended to be set once at execution time. OSGi framework implementations need to be responsible for initializing these mechanisms to properly implement specification functionality. When a framework is embedded in another application, often the application assumes it's in control of these singletons. The OSGi specification doesn't specifically address these aspects of framework embedding, so how implementations deal with it is undefined. Some frameworks, like Apache Felix, go to lengths to try to do the right thing, but the right thing often depends on the specific use case. If you run into issues in these areas, you'll have to consult the documentation or support forums for your specific framework implementation.

Another area where issues arise is in the use of the Thread Context Class Loader (TCCL). If you're not familiar with this concept, each thread in Java has a class loader associated with it, which is its *context class loader*. The TCCL provides a backdoor mechanism to subvert Java's normal, strict hierarchical class loading. Application servers and various frameworks use this mechanism to deal with class-loading dependencies that can't be shoehorned into hierarchical class loading. Unfortunately, this crude attempt at dealing with class-loading dependencies doesn't mesh well with OSGi modularity.

Thread Context Class Loader travails

The TCCL can be both a blessing and a curse. Used correctly, it can enable access to classes in places where it wouldn't otherwise be possible; but it can have unexpected side effects in cases where modularity is enforced. Embedding an OSGi framework is a typical example of where things may go wrong. This can happen if the outside application or container sets the context class loader. In this case, it's leaking classes into the class space of bundles being accessed from the outside. Typical examples of situations in which problems can occur include the following:

- Libraries that prefer the TCCL over their own class loader
- Libraries that rely on the TCCL mechanism and don't attempt to get the correct class loader
- An outside container that expects a certain TCCL on a callback

One prime example for the first case is logging. Consider a situation where you're embedding an OSGi framework inside a container using log4j for logging. The container will obviously have log4j on its class path. Now, if the container happens to set the TCCL to its own class loader and then calls into the framework, a bundle using log4j may end up with unexpected problems because classes from the container can be found that shouldn't, or vice versa.

(continued)

To get around this, bundles can set the TCCL to their own class loader before touching log4j, but this is a fragile solution and can confuse the container.

Dealing with the TCCL is tricky. Because the OSGi specifications don't address this issue, you can't be sure it's handled the same way by different frameworks. For example, Apache Felix doesn't do anything in regard to the TCCL, whereas other frameworks try to automagically set it to the "correct" bundle class loader.

One piece of useful advice to keep in mind is that the TCCL is inherited by threads. So if you set the TCCL of a given thread, and it in turn creates a new thread, it'll inherit the same TCCL. Of course, this can be a good or a bad thing, depending on your situation. The important part is to think about what the TCCL will be for any threads created by the framework and/or bundles; it will be implicitly inherited if you don't explicitly set it.

13.3.3 Embedded framework example

For a simple illustration of framework embedding, you'll convert the service-based paint program from chapter 4 into a standalone application with an embedded framework instance. Because the service-based paint program is completely composed of bundles, you need to transform it into a Java application. The new standalone paint program uses an embedded framework instance as a plugin mechanism by which it can deploy custom shape implementations. Figure 13.4 shows the before and after states.

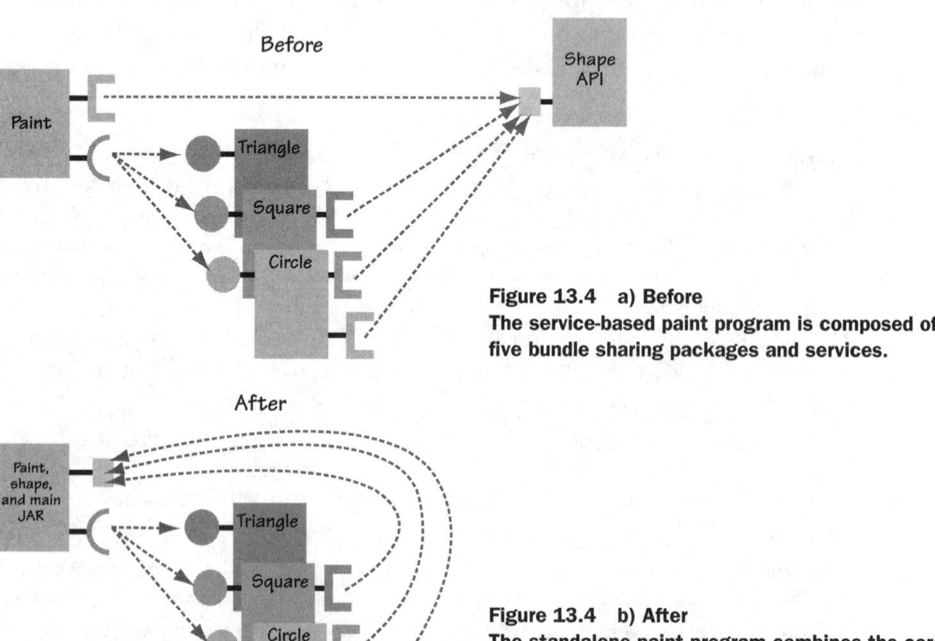

Figure 13.4 a) Before
The service-based paint program is composed of five bundle sharing packages and services.

Figure 13.4 b) After
The standalone paint program combines the core paint program, shape API, and launcher into a single JAR file that provides and shares the API with the bundles and uses their services.

For the standalone paint program, you don't need to change the shape bundles. What does need to be changed? The original service-based paint program didn't need a launcher, because the bundle activator in the paint bundle served this purpose. For the standalone paint program, you need a launcher that creates the paint frame and the framework instances and wires everything together. Additionally, because the paint program needs a common class definition to interact with bundles implementing shapes, you must move the shape API into the standalone application so the application and bundles can use the same `SimpleShape` service-interface definition. Note that figure 13.4 depicts the application as a quasi bundle with an exported package and service dependencies. This is just for illustrative purposes: the application is a normal JAR file. The structure of the modified paint program source code is as follows:

```
org/foo/paint/
  DefaultShape.java
  Main.java
  PaintFrame.java
  ShapeTracker.java
  ShapeComponent.java
  underc.png
org/foo/shape
  SimpleShape.java
```

What's the design of the standalone paint program? Recall the original design of the paint program: the main paint frame was designed in such a way as to be injected with shape implementations. This approach had the benefit of allowing you to limit dependencies on OSGi API and to concentrate your OSGi-aware code in the shape tracker. In keeping with these design principles, you'll do most of the work in the launcher `Main` class, which creates the embedded framework instance, deploys the shape bundles, creates the paint frame, and binds the paint frame to the embedded shape services.

Perhaps at this point you're thinking that this sounds similar to the generic framework launcher you created in the previous section. You're correct. Using the framework in an embedded way isn't all that different, other than the issues we outlined previously. As a result, the launcher code for the standalone paint program will bear a striking resemblance to the generic launcher. The different aspects it illustrates are as follows:

- Sharing code from the class path to bundles
- Using services on the outside
- Providing services to the inside

This last aspect doesn't have an analogue in the original service-based paint program, but we include it to demonstrate that it's possible to provide services from the outside. As before, we'll break the launcher into small snippets and describe each one. Let's get started.

PERFORMING THE MAIN TASKS

Because the paint program is no longer a bundle, you replace its bundle activator with a `Main` class. The primary tasks this class performs are easy to discern from the `main()` method.

Listing 13.6 Standalone paint program main() method

```
public class Main {
  private static Framework fwk;
  private static PaintFrame frame = null;
  private static ShapeTracker shapeTracker = null;

  public static void main(String[] args) throws Exception {
    addShutdownHook();
    fwk = createFramework();
    publishTrapezoidService();
    createPaintFrame();
  }
  ...
```

The performed functionality is a combination of the generic launcher and the old bundle activator: adding a shutdown hook, creating a framework instance, and creating a paint frame. The only new task is publishing an external trapezoid shape service, which you'll see is pretty much the same as publishing a normal service.

Let's continue to look into the details. Because adding a shutdown hook is basically identical to what you did for the generic launcher, we'll skip that step and go directly to creating the framework instance.

CONFIGURING AND CREATING THE FRAMEWORK

The `createFramework()` method follows fairly closely to the launcher, so we'll go over the details quickly. The method starts, like the launcher, with discovering which bundles it should install into the framework instance:

```
...
private static Framework createFramework() throws Exception {
  File[] files = new File("bundles").listFiles();
  Arrays.sort(files);
  List jars = new ArrayList();
  for (int i = 0; i < files.length; i++)
    if (files[i].getName().toLowerCase().endsWith(".jar"))
      jars.add(files[i]);
...
```

Here you get the contents of the bundles directory in the current directory and add all contained JAR files to a list. This is rather simplistic, but it's sufficient for this example. Now you can create the framework instance and deploy the discovered bundles. The following listing shows these steps.

Listing 13.7 Creating the framework instance and deploying discovered bundles

```
  ...
  try {
    List bundleList = new ArrayList();
    Map m = new HashMap();
    m.putAll(System.getProperties());
    m.put(Constants.FRAMEWORK_STORAGE_CLEAN,
      Constants.FRAMEWORK_STORAGE_CLEAN_ONFIRSTINIT);
    m.put(Constants.FRAMEWORK_SYSTEMPACKAGES_EXTRA,
      "org.foo.shape; version=\"4.0.0\"");
```

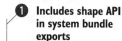

1 Includes shape API in system bundle exports

```
    fwk = getFrameworkFactory().newFramework(m);
    fwk.start();
    BundleContext ctxt = fwk.getBundleContext();
    for (int i = 0; i < jars.size(); i++) {
      Bundle b = ctxt.installBundle(
        ((File) jars.get(i)).toURI().toString());
      bundleList.add(b);
    }
    for (int i = 0; i < bundleList.size(); i++) {
      ((Bundle) bundleList.get(i)).start();
    }
  } catch (Exception ex) {
    System.err.println("Error starting framework: " + ex);
    ex.printStackTrace();
    System.exit(0);
  }

  return fwk;
}
...
```

❷ Starts all installed bundles

As with the generic launcher, you configure the framework to clean its bundle cache on first initialization. For performance reasons, you probably wouldn't want to do this if you were using the framework as a plugin mechanism, because it's slower to repopulate the cache every time. You do it in this case to make sure you're starting from a clean slate. An important difference from the launcher, which we alluded to previously, is at ❶. Here you configure the framework to export the `org.foo.shape` package from the class path via the system bundle. This allows bundles to import the package from the application, thus ensuring that they're both using the same interface definition for shape implementations. You also need to ensure that this package is on the class path; but because you're going to package it in the application JAR file, it should definitely be available.

Next, you create the framework with the defined configuration and start it. You get the system bundle's bundle context, which you use to install the discovered bundles. Finally, you start all installed bundles ❷. Any errors cause the JVM to exit.

Now let's look at how you publish an external service into the framework instance.

PUBLISHING AN EXTERNAL SERVICE

The `publishTrapezoidService()` method is simple, as the following code snippet illustrates:

```
...
private static void publishTrapezoidService() {
  Hashtable dict = new Hashtable();
  dict.put(SimpleShape.NAME_PROPERTY, "Trapezoid");
  dict.put(SimpleShape.ICON_PROPERTY,
    new ImageIcon(Trapezoid.class.getResource("trapezoid.png")));
  fwk.getBundleContext().registerService(
    SimpleShape.class.getName(), new Trapezoid(), dict);
}
...
```

This code is basically the same as what you saw back in chapter 4 for publishing services. The only difference is that you use the system bundle's bundle context to register the service, because the application doesn't have its own bundle context. Of course, what makes this possible is the fact that you're using the same `org.foo.shape` package on the inside and the outside, which means your trapezoid shape works just like the shapes provided by any of the shape bundles.

Now you're ready to bind everything together to complete the functioning paint program.

CREATING THE PAINT FRAME

The `createPaintFrame()` method performs nearly the same functionality as the bundle activator for the original paint bundle from chapter 4. The details are shown in the following listing.

Listing 13.8 Creating the paint frame and binding it to the framework instance

```
...
private static void createPaintFrame() throws Exception {
  SwingUtilities.invokeAndWait(new Runnable() {
    public void run() {
      frame = new PaintFrame();
      frame.setDefaultCloseOperation(JFrame.DO_NOTHING_ON_CLOSE);
      frame.addWindowListener(new WindowAdapter() {
        public void windowClosing(WindowEvent evt) {
          try {
            fwk.stop();
            fwk.waitForStop(0);
          } catch (Exception ex) {
            System.err.println("Issue stopping framework: " + ex);
          }
          System.exit(0);
        }
      });
      frame.setVisible(true);

      shapeTracker = new ShapeTracker(fwk.getBundleContext(), frame);
      shapeTracker.open();
    }
  });
}
```

❶ Creates and starts shape tracker

You create the paint frame itself and then add a window listener to cleanly stop the embedded framework instance and exit the JVM process when the frame is closed. Then you display the paint frame; but at this point it isn't hooked into the embedded framework instance. You get the system bundle's bundle context and use it to create a shape tracker for the paint frame ❶; this is what binds everything together. Due to the original design, you don't need to spread OSGi API usage throughout the application.

To run the standalone paint program, go into the chapter13/paint-example/ directory. Type `ant` to build the program and `java -jar paint.jar` to run it. Figure 13.5 shows the result.

As you can see, the bundle-provided shape services and the application-provided shape service integrate nicely in the paint frame. You didn't need to do anything to make this happen, other than ensure that the application and the bundles used the same service interface. Cool.

That's all there is to the OSGi R4.2 standard launching and embedding API. Don't be afraid to use it.

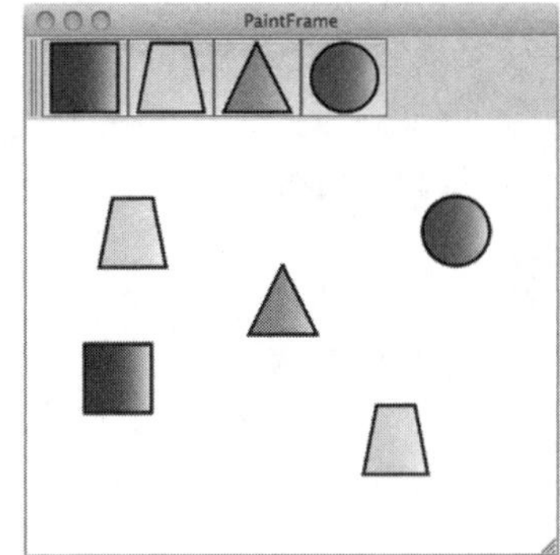

Figure 13.5
The standalone paint program

13.4 Summary

The OSGi specification doesn't define a standard launcher with a standard way to configure and launch a framework. Consequently, most OSGi framework implementations provide their own approach. The standard launching and embedding API introduced in OSGi R4.2 is the next best thing to a standard launcher, because it allows you to create a single launcher that works across framework implementations. In this chapter, you learned the following:

- The OSGi R4.2 specification introduced the `Framework` interface to represent a framework instance.
- The `Framework` interface extends the existing `Bundle` interface, which extends your existing knowledge of managing bundles to framework instances.
- The `Framework` instance represents the system bundle, which provides access to the system bundle's bundle context for performing normal bundle tasks (such as installing bundles and registering services).
- The META-INF/services approach finds a `FrameworkFactory` provider, which enables framework creation without knowing a concrete framework implementation class name.
- The OSGi specification defines numerous framework configuration properties to further improve framework implementation independence; you can pass these into `FrameworkFactory.newInstance()` when creating a framework instance.
- Although using completely bundled applications is the preferred approach, the launching and embedding API also simplifies embedding framework instances into existing applications.
- When you embed a framework instance into an application, the main constraint involves dealing with the difference between being on the outside versus the inside. If direct interaction with bundles is required, you often need to share common class definitions from the class path.
- Other than some additional constraints, embedding a framework instance is nearly identical to launching a framework instance.

With this knowledge under your belt, you can use it to create your own framework launchers for specific purposes and do so in a framework implementation-neutral way. In the next chapter, we'll look into configuring framework instances to deal with security.

14 Securing your applications

This chapter covers

- Providing an overview of the Java security architecture
- Using OSGi Conditional Permission Admin to manage permissions
- Signing bundles and granting permissions based on bundle signers
- Creating custom permission conditions for advanced use cases

OSGi allows you to create loosely coupled, extensible applications. In such applications, bundles can come and go at any time, and it's easy to allow third parties to extend your application in a well-defined way. But as with most things in life, there's a downside to this flexibility: you open yourself (or your users) to security vulnerabilities because third-party bundles can't be completely trusted.

Luckily, the Java platform has built-in support for secure sandboxes, and the OSGi framework is designed to take advantage of them. Unfortunately, secure sandboxes and their restrictions are difficult to get right and often hard to manage. This is especially true in an environment as dynamic as the OSGi framework. To help with this situation, OSGi defines an extensive and powerful security model to ease security management.

In this chapter, we'll familiarize you with the Java security model and how OSGi uses it to securely deploy and manage applications. You'll learn how to create secure applications and well-behaved bundles for security-enabled OSGi frameworks. Before we start with that, let's look at some general issues you'll need to consider when trying to secure your applications.

14.1 To secure or not to secure

Modern applications and software solutions increasingly center around loosely coupled, extensible architectures. Component and service orientation are applied to almost all areas of application development including distributed systems, ubiquitous computing, embedded systems, and client-side applications. One of the main drawbacks of loosely coupled, extensible applications is the potential security issues around executing untrusted code. There are two common reasons for running untrusted software:

- *Permission management is often extremely complicated.* Often, users are left to make security policy decisions, and they're typically unable to assess the impact of granting a given permission. Further, because the user is typically using an application to perform some task, security is largely viewed as an obstacle because it doesn't contribute to the task at hand.
- *It's inherently tricky to establish meaningful identity of third-party software providers.* It's often necessary to differentiate between providers or types of providers to properly grant or deny permissions. Often the origin of the software artifact (where it came from) is used for this purpose, but techniques like digital signatures are also needed to ensure that the software hasn't been tampered with. Digital signatures introduce the complicated process of creating and maintaining certificates and trust between certificates, which can be onerous for both users and developers.

This raises perhaps the biggest issue with securing code: it adds another burden to development. Even if you don't plan to run with security enabled, your code has to be aware of security if you want it to be possible for other people to use the code when security is enabled. Then, to make matters worse, if you decide to enable security, the fine-grained security checks impose an execution-time performance penalty.

Despite these issues, security isn't something that can or should be ignored, because plenty of people are willing to take advantage of software vulnerabilities. What do you need to do? Providing meaningful security management involves three key aspects:

- Establishing identity
- Establishing policies to manage permissions
- Performing permission checks and privilege management

As we mentioned previously, identity can be established by the location or origin of the software artifact or by cryptographic measures using digital certificates. Especially for the latter approach, the software provider generally needs to make the code available in such a way that you can establish the needed credentials. When you have identity established, you need to define the permissions that code should have. For OSGi, this is the responsibility of whoever is managing the framework, which can be a gateway operator, a server administrator, or even an end user. As a consequence, permission management should be kept as simple as possible. Last but not least, security must be built into the code itself. You have to think about internal security checks to prevent external code from performing undesired operations and also how to limit privileges so external code can perform potentially sensitive operations in a safe way.

Assuming you're able to develop your code with all the security checks in the right place, define a reasonably policy to manage permissions, and sign it using a trusted certificate for establishing identity, is all the work worth it?

Clearly, it depends on your specific situation. In some cases, it's not within the scope of your application. Either the performance impact is too great or the development costs are too high. Often, these issues serve as the determining factor for creating security-enabled applications. This is compounded by the fact that if code isn't *designed* to be usable in security-enabled environments, it's unlikely to happen by accident. This results in a catch-22 type of situation, where the difficulty associated with creating secure code results in security being ignored, which makes it next to impossible to use such code with security enabled, thus further raising the barriers for deciding to develop with security in mind in the first place.

All hope isn't lost. In the remainder of this chapter, we'll show you that taking advantage of the security capabilities of the OSGi framework needn't be too difficult. In the next section, we'll start by taking a high-level view of Java and OSGi security.

14.2 Security: just do it

So you want to secure your OSGi-based application. Great—but where do you start? Let's begin at the beginning and look at the Java security architecture and its permission model, on which the OSGi security model is based.

14.2.1 Java and OSGi security

It's important to understand the Java security architecture; but to keep this chapter tightly scoped, we'll introduce only the parts needed to understand the remainder of the chapter. Welcome to Java security boot camp!

The Java security architecture is fundamentally about the assignment of `java.security.Permission` subclass objects to code. Specific permissions allow access to specific, sensitive operations, such as file system or network socket access. How do you grant `Permission` objects to code? The Java security architecture is based on the two fundamental concepts of domain- and role-based security:

- Domain-based security revolves around granting code permissions based on its origins (also referred to as its *code base*).
- Role-based security revolves around authenticating users or processes and granting them permissions based on who they are.

The OSGi framework security model relies on Java's domain-based approach; the role-based approach is possible, but only as a layer on top. In standard Java, role-based security is provided by the Java Authentication and Authorization Service (JAAS) framework, but OSGi also provides its own API in the form of the User Admin Service. We won't deal with role-based security in this chapter; for more information on the User Admin Service, refer to the OSGi compendium specification. Now, let's delve a little deeper into domain-based security.

PERMISSIONS

The Java permission model is fairly simple. The `Permission` class is a base class from which more specific permissions can be derived via subclassing. You grant `Permission` objects to code to give it the ability to perform sensitive operations. Additionally, the `Permission` class has a method called `implies()` that accepts another `Permission`. This method checks to see if the supplied permission is implied by the target permission (similar to being a subset). Thus, `Permission` objects are used to both grant and check permissions.

PROTECTION DOMAINS

You grant permissions to code, but how are they associated with it? For domain-based security, Java uses a special concept called a *protection domain*, which is represented by the `java.security.ProtectionDomain` class, to encapsulate the security characteristics of a domain. Permissions are granted to protection domains, and all classes belong to a single protection domain. Sound complicated? Actually, in OSGi it's pretty simple, because a domain is mapped one-to-one with a bundle; you can think of it as a bundle protection domain. All classes originating from a given bundle are members of the same bundle protection domain.

BUNDLE PROTECTION DOMAIN Maintains a set of permissions granted to a given bundle. All classes loaded from a bundle are associated with the bundle's protection domain, thus granting them the permissions granted to the bundle.

To understand how protection domains enable permission checking, consider code that performs a sensitive operation, such as creating a file. The code in the JRE for file access performs security checks internally to make sure the invoking code has permission to perform the operation. Internally, the code associated with performing file system operations triggers a specific permission check by using the security-checking methods of `SecurityManager` or `AccessController`. When triggered, the JVM collects the `ProtectionDomains` of all classes on the call stack leading to the invocation of the sensitive operation. It checks that each protection domain on the call stack has at least one permission implying (granting) the specific permission being checked by the method. Figure 14.1 shows how this looks in practice.

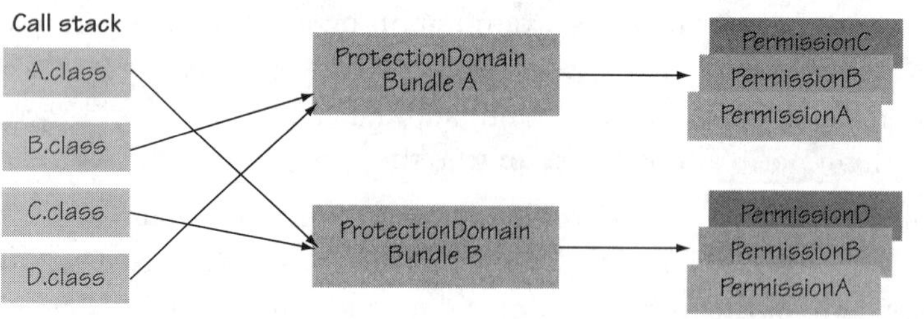

Figure 14.1 The JVM checks permissions by collecting all protection domains associated with classes on the call stack and seeing if each involved protection domain has the specified permission granted to it.

In this case, assume that class `D` performs a sensitive operation that triggers an internal permission check using the `AccessController.checkPermission(Permission p)` method. This checks whether at the point of the permission check, all protection domains on the call stack have permission `p`. Looking at figure 14.1, the JVM performs a stack walk from the class performing the security check and determines that classes `A`, `B`, `C`, and `D` are involved. Subsequently, it determines that classes `A` and `C` originate from the protection domain of Bundle B, and classes `B` and `D` originate from the protection domain of Bundle A. With this information, the JVM checks whether all protection domains have some permission implying the checked permission. If not, then a security exception is thrown.

This provides a good foundation for understanding the Java security architecture, but there's one final piece to the puzzle: privileged calls.

PRIVILEGED CALLS

You now know that checking a specific permission triggers a complete stack walk to collect all involved protection domains and verify that they all imply that permission. This is useful, but it's too restrictive by itself. For example, assume you have a service with a method for appending a message to a log file. Because disk operations trigger file system–related permission checks, all code on the call stack must have permission to write to the file. This may be fine if only trusted code is involved; but in an extensible and collaborative environment like OSGi, you generally want to allow arbitrary bundles to share code and services, so it's likely that some code on the call stack won't be trusted.

In such cases, if a permission check always walks up the entire call stack, you either have to disallow all nontrusted code or grant code-sensitive permissions to untrusted code. Neither choice is palatable, which is why Java supports privileged calls. A *privileged call* is a mechanism to short-circuit the stack walk when performing a permission check. In practice, this allows trusted code to perform sensitive operations on behalf of code with insufficient permissions.

You achieve this by using the `AccessController.doPrivileged()` method, which takes a `PrivilegedAction` instance (it has a `run()` method similar to a `Runnable`). When the `doPrivileged()` method is invoked, it invokes the `run()` method of the passed-in `PrivilegedAction`. Any subsequent permission checks triggered by the `PrivilegedAction` stop walking the call stack at the last privileged call. Thus, only the protection domains from the privileged action onward are considered by subsequent permission checks.

Returning to the example of a service for appending a message to a log file, you trust the bundle containing the service implementation, but you don't want to give direct file system access to anyone else. To do this, your service must encapsulate its file system operations inside a `PrivilegedAction` and use `doPrivileged()` like this:

```
public void append(String msg) {
  SecurityManager sm = System.getSecurityManager();
  if (sm != null) {
    AccessController.doPrivileged(new PrivilegedAction() {
      public Object run() {
        doFileAppend();
      }
    });
  }
  else {
    doFileAppend();
  }
}
```

Any triggered permission checks stop walking the call stack at the `run()` method, which means nontrusted code further up the stack won't have its protection domain checked for the triggered permissions. Pushing this example further, you may decide to limit which code can call the `append()` method. To so this, you can create your own `Permission` subclass, which you can grant to code. For the append method, if you create an `AppendPermission`, it can check the permission before performing the privileged call:

```
public void append(String msg) {
  SecurityManager sm = System.getSecurityManager();
  if (sm != null) {
    sm.checkPermission(new AppendPermission());
    AccessController.doPrivileged(new PrivilegedAction() {
      public Object run() { doFileAppend(); }});
  } else {
    doFileAppend();
  }
}
```

Here your service asks the `SecurityManager` to check whether the code on the call stack has been granted the custom `AppendPermission`. If so, it can continue to perform the file-append operation; otherwise, a security exception is thrown.

> **WARNING** You may have noticed that you check whether the security manager is `null` before performing security checks. You do it this way because you want to perform security checks only if security is enabled, to avoid performance penalties when it's not enabled.

That pretty much sums up the important pieces of the Java security architecture. These mechanisms provide for flexible, fine-grained security management. A potential downside is that managing all these permissions can be complex. Luckily, the OSGi specification lessens some of this complexity by defining services to help you perform permission management. We'll look at these services shortly; first, let's examine OSGi-specific permissions defined by the OSGi specification.

14.3 OSGi-specific permissions

Certain methods in the OSGi framework API perform sensitive operations or provide access to sensitive information. To control which code can access these sensitive methods, the OSGi specification defines a few custom permissions, as you learned about in the last section. You can group these permissions by the layers of the OSGi framework, as shown in table 14.1.

Table 14.1 Permissions defined by the OSGi specification

Layer	Permission(s)
Module	`PackagePermission`—Controls which packages a bundle is allowed to import and/or export
	`BundlePermission`—Controls which bundles a bundle is allowed to require
Lifecycle	`AdminPermission`—Controls which bundles are allowed to perform sensitive lifecycle operations
Services	`ServicePermission`—Controls which services a bundle is allowed to publish and/or use

We'll introduce these OSGi permissions in the following subsections, and you'll subsequently use them when we discuss permission management.

> **Names and actions**
>
> Standard Java permissions typically have constructors that accept two parameters: a `name` string and an `actions` string. The meaning of these parameters is determined by the specific permission. For example, `java.io.FilePermission` expects a file path for `name` and a comma-delimited value that may include `READ`, `WRITE`, `EXECUTE`, or `DELETE` for actions. The combination of `name` and `actions` allows you to express everything the permission allows you to control. All of the OSGi-specific permissions follow this pattern, as you'll see.

14.3.1 PackagePermission

`PackagePermission` is a module-layer permission giving you the ability to limit which packages a bundle can import or export. For example, we discussed how methods can use `AccessController.doPrivileged()` to allow code with insufficient privileges to perform sensitive operations. You may not want any arbitrary code using the packages containing these privileged operations. In that case, you can use `PackagePermission` to limit which bundles can import the packages containing the associated classes. Likewise, you can use `PackagePermission` to control which bundles can export a given package, because you may only want trusted bundles providing some packages.

To grant a specific PackagePermission, you need to supply the name and actions parameters for its constructor; these parameters are described in table 14.2.

Table 14.2 PackagePermission constructor parameters

Parameter	Description
String name	Name of the package or packages to which this permission applies
String actions	Comma-delimited list of the actions granted by the permission (export, import, or exportonly)

For convenience, you can use * or a trailing .* as a wildcard to target several packages with a single permission. For the actions, import gives a bundle permission to import the named packages, export gives a bundle permission to export and import the package, and exportonly does as its name implies. You may wonder why export also gives permission to import the named packages. It's to support bundles' ability to import packages they export (that is, substitutable exports), as described in section 5.1.1.

To get an idea of how PackagePermission works, let's take a conceptual look at how the framework uses it. Assume you have a bundle with the following imports and exports:

```
Import-Package: org.foo, org.bar
Export-Package: org.bar
```

When the framework resolves this bundle, it checks to see whether the bundle has the following permissions granted to it:

- PackagePermission.IMPORT permission for the org.foo package
- PackagePermission.IMPORT permission for the org.bar package
- PackagePermission.EXPORT permission for the org.bar package

For these checks to succeed, you'd have to grant the necessary permissions, such as

```
new PackagePermission("org.foo", PackagePermission.IMPORT);
new PackagePermission("org.bar", PackagePermission.EXPORT);
```

Notice that you don't need to grant the bundle permission to import org.bar, because it's implied by the export action.

That's the basics for PackagePermission; let's move on to the next OSGi permission.

14.3.2 BundlePermission

Similar to PackagePermission, BundlePermission is a module-layer permission for controlling bundle and fragment dependencies. To grant a BundlePermission, you need to construct it with the parameters shown in table 14.3.

As with PackagePermission, you can use * or a trailing .* as a wildcard to target several packages with a single permission. To control bundle dependencies, the provide action gives a bundle permission to be required by bundles matching the supplied

Table 14.3 `BundlePermission` constructor parameters

Parameter	Description
`String symbolicName`	Symbolic name of the bundle to which this permission applies
`String actions`	Comma-delimited list of the actions granted by the permission (`provide`, `require`, `host`, or `fragment`)

symbolic name, whereas `require` gives it permission to require matching bundles. Fragment dependencies are controlled by the `host` and `fragment` actions, which give a bundle the ability to be a host bundle for matching fragments or be a fragment for matching hosts, respectively. Another similarity to `PackagePermission` is that the `provide` action implies the `require` action.

Using `BundlePermission` isn't sufficiently different from using `PackagePermission`, so we won't look into it any further. Instead, we'll move on to the next OSGi permission.

14.3.3 AdminPermission

`AdminPermission` is a lifecycle-layer permission to control access to sensitive framework operations and information. The operations and information protected by `AdminPermission` are diverse, which makes it somewhat complex but fairly powerful. Table 14.4 shows the parameters needed to create such a permission.

Table 14.4 `AdminPermission` constructor parameters

Parameter	Description
`String filter`	LDAP filter to specify matching bundles
`String actions`	Comma-delimited list of the actions granted by the permission (`class`, `execute`, `extensionLifecycle`, `lifecycle`, `listener`, `metadata`, `resolve`, `resource`, `startlevel`, or `context`)

When you grant `AdminPermission` to a bundle, that bundle is allowed to perform the specified actions on the bundles matching the filter. The filter uses the same LDAP filter syntax used by the OSGi service registry, but only the following attributes are defined for matching:

- `signer`—Identity information about the bundle provider
- `location`—Bundle location
- `id`—Bundle identifier
- `name`—Bundle symbolic name

We'll give some filter examples shortly. First we'll briefly describe what the granted actions allow on the matching bundles:

- `class`—Load a class
- `execute`—Start, stop, and set the start level

- `extensionLifecycle`—Manage extension bundles
- `lifecycle`—Install, update, and uninstall
- `listener`—Add/remove a synchronous bundle listener
- `metadata`—Retrieve bundle headers and location
- `resolve`—Resolve and refresh
- `resource`—Get resources
- `startlevel`—Set the start level, and initial the start level
- `context`—Get the bundle context

The special action `*` represents all actions. As you can see, `AdminPermission` gives you fine-grained control over which bundles can do what on which bundles. For example, assume a bundle wants to install another bundle using code like this:

```
context.installBundle("file:bundle.jar").start();
```

This triggers the framework to check whether all code on the call stack has the following:

- `AdminPermission.LIFECYCLE` permission for the installed bundle
- `AdminPermission.EXECUTE` permission for the installed bundle

This is relatively straightforward, although granting the permission can be a little confusing. The thing to remember about `AdminPermission` is that you use it to grant a bundle the right to perform specific operations on other bundles. The `filter` constructor parameter is how you specify the bundles that can be controlled. For a more complicated example, you can grant an `AdminPermission` like this:

```
new AdminPermission("(&(signer=CN=core,O=baz,C=de)(name=org.foo.*)
  (location=file://*)(id>=10))", AdminPermission.LIFECYCLE + "," +
  AdminPermission.EXECUTE);
```

The bundle granted this permission can perform the operations associated with `AdminPermission.LIFECYCLE` and `AdminPermission.EXECUTE` on bundles with a signer matching `CN=core,O=baz,C=de` (more on signing later), a symbolic name starting with `org.foo`, a location starting with `file://`, and a bundle identifier greater than 10. Granted, this is completely contrived, but it illustrates the possibilities.

You've now seen the module- and lifecycle-layer permissions, which means you have one framework layer to go—services.

14.3.4 ServicePermission

`ServicePermission` is a service-layer permission for controlling which services a bundle can provide or use. As with the other permissions, the actual permission granted is controlled by its constructor parameters, as shown in table 14.5.

You can use `*` or a trailing `.*` as a wildcard to target several service interfaces or classes with a single permission. The `get` action grants the ability to use the specified services, whereas the `register` action grants the ability to provide the specified services. For the `get` action, you can also use an LDAP filter for `name`, which matches

Table 14.5 `ServicePermission` constructor parameters

Parameter	Description
`String name`	Service interface or class name(s)
`String actions`	Comma-delimited list of the actions granted by the permission (`get` or `register`)

against the associated service properties in addition to the same set of bundle properties described for `BundlePermission` (`signer`, `location`, `id`, and `name`).

To get a better understanding of how this permission is used, consider the following snippet of code a bundle can use to find a service and to register a service:

```
context.getServiceReference("org.foo.Service");
context.registerService("org.bar.Service", new Service(), null);
```

Here you find an `org.foo.Service` service and register an `org.bar.Service` service. This triggers the framework to check whether all code on the call stack has the following:

- `ServicePermission.GET` for the `org.foo.Service` interface
- `ServicePermission.REGISTER` for the `org.bar.Service` interface

These permission checks are straightforward. For the associated bundle to perform these tasks, you can grant it these permissions:

```
new ServicePermission("org.foo.*", ServicePermission.GET);
new ServicePermission("org.bar.Service", ServicePermission.REGISTER);
```

In the first permission, you use a wildcard to allow it to access all services in the `org.foo` package. In the second permission, you specifically allow it to register `org.bar.Service` services.

That completes the OSGi-specific permissions you can grant to bundles. Before we move on to discussing permission management, let's briefly discuss file permissions, because they behave slightly differently in an OSGi environment.

14.3.5 Relative file permissions

Although `java.io.FilePermission` isn't defined by the OSGi specification, it's still impacted by how the framework interprets it. In a standard Java environment, a file permission created with a relative path is interpreted as being relative to the directory from which the Java process was started (the current working directory). This isn't the case in an OSGi environment. Instead, it's treated as relative to the root of the private data area of the associated bundle.

Typically, this doesn't have much of an effect, especially because the framework automatically grants bundles permission to read, write, and delete files in their own private area. The main thing this enables is the ability to grant a bundle additional permissions for files in its private data area, such as the execute permission.

Enough of describing permissions. Next, we'll discuss how you manage them with the Conditional Permission Admin Service.

14.4 Managing permissions with Conditional Permission Admin

Until now, we've talked mostly about the details of permissions (what they look like and what they mean) and otherwise glossed over how you grant permissions to bundles. Individual permissions in and of themselves aren't that useful. The useful part is being able to grant and manage permissions for groups of bundles in accordance with your desired security policies. To help you achieve this goal, the OSGi specification defines the Conditional Permission Admin Service.

Whereas standard Java offers a file-based policy approach for permission management, OSGi only defines an API-based approach, because it fits better with the inherently dynamic nature of the OSGi environment. The Conditional Permission Admin Service is the one place to go to define and maintain your security policy. Further, it introduces a new way of performing permission management by defining the concept of *conditional* permission management, which is how it got its name. Let's explore this concept first.

14.4.1 Conditional permissions

If you're at all familiar with standard Java permission management, you know that the basic approach is to grant permissions to code using a policy file. A standard Java policy file may look something like this:

```
grant signedBy "sysadmin" {
  permission java.security.AllPermission;
};
grant codeBase "file:/app/main.jar" {
  permission java.security.AllPermission;
};
grant {
  permission java.io.FilePermission "/tmp/*", "read,write";
};
```

In this policy file, you granted all permissions to classes signed by `sysadmin` and from file:/app/main.jar. All other classes are only granted read/write access to the /tmp/ directory. Although this example assigns only a single permission for each case, you can assign any number of permissions in a single group. When the security manager walks up the call stack to check permissions at execution time, the permissions for a given class are determined by effectively using either its signer or code base as a key to look up the associated protection domain to see which permissions have been granted to it. If the protection domain has the permission, the call can proceed; if not, the call fails.

This approach works, but it's somewhat simplistic. In particular, it allows you to grant permissions only based on one of two conditions:

- Who cryptographically signed the class
- The originating location of the class (that is, the code base)

The Conditional Permission Admin Service improves on this by introducing an abstract condition concept, which allows you to grant permissions based on arbitrary conditions. A condition acts as a Boolean guard that determines whether a permission group is applicable; a permission group can be guarded by zero or more conditions. Because permissions are granted to bundles in OSGi, conditions are evaluated against the bundles on the call stack to determine which permissions have been granted to a bundle. If multiple conditions are associated with a permission group, all conditions must be satisfied for the permissions to apply (a logical AND).

If it isn't already clear, this is pretty powerful. Not only does it allow you to introduce your own arbitrary conditions for granting permissions, but these conditions can also be much more dynamic and fine-grained. For example, you can create a condition to only grant permissions based on license status via remote server communication or even the time of day. We'll get into creating custom conditions later; for now, we'll continue to explore what's provided by the Conditional Permission Admin Service.

What about performance?

If you know anything about Java security, you probably know it can have a significant impact on execution-time performance. Evaluating all conditions for all bundles on the call stack on every permission check can get expensive. Luckily, the Conditional Permission Admin Service provides a way to mitigate this cost in a lot of cases by differentiating between mutable and immutable conditions. This means the Boolean results for immutable conditions only need to be calculated once per bundle protection domain. You'll see an example of an immutable condition shortly.

14.4.2 Introducing the Conditional Permission Admin Service

Let's look at the API behind the Conditional Permission Admin Service, which is the `ConditionalPermissionAdmin` service interface shown in the following listing.

Listing 14.1 The `ConditionalPermissionAdmin` interface

```
public interface ConditionalPermissionAdmin {

  ConditionalPermissionInfo addConditionalPermissionInfo(
    ConditionInfo[] conds, PermissionInfo[] perms);

  AccessControlContext getAccessControlContext(String[] signers);

  ConditionalPermissionInfo getConditionalPermissionInfo(String name);

  Enumeration getConditionalPermissionInfos();

  ConditionalPermissionInfo setConditionalPermissionInfo(
    String name, ConditionInfo[] conds, PermissionInfo[] perms);

  public ConditionalPermissionUpdate newConditionalPermissionUpdate();

  public ConditionalPermissionInfo newConditionalPermissionInfo(
    String name, ConditionInfo[] conditions, PermissionInfo[] permissions,
    String access);

  public ConditionalPermissionInfo newConditionalPermissionInfo(
    String encodedConditionalPermissionInfo);
}
```

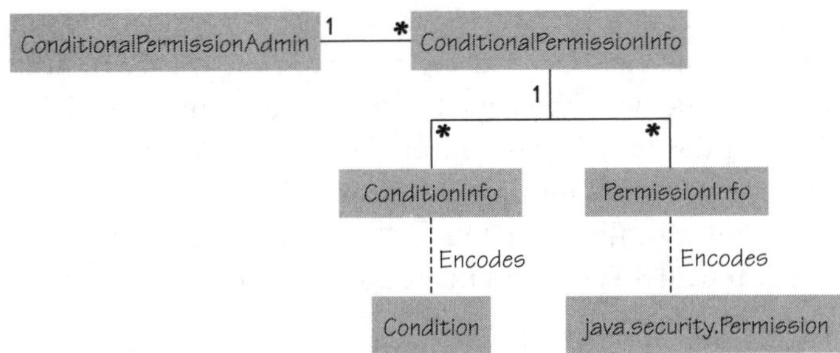

Figure 14.2 Conditional Permission Admin Service overview

With this service, you can grant permissions to bundles. To achieve this, you use the service to maintain a persistent set of `ConditionalPermissionInfo` objects, which as a whole embody your current security policy. A `ConditionalPermissionInfo` object is a tuple containing a set of `ConditionInfo` objects and a set of `PermissionInfo` objects. Figure 14.2 depicts these relationships.

The set of `ConditionInfo` objects encodes the conditions that must be true for the permissions to apply, and the set of `PermissionInfo` objects encodes the permissions to be granted. You may wonder why you need `ConditionInfo` and `PermissionInfo` objects to encode the conditions and permissions, respectively, rather than directly creating instances of conditions and permissions. This is because the bundle assigning permissions may not have access to the associated classes, because you're in a modular environment. Both of these info objects encode a target class name and its constructor arguments.

More specifically, a `ConditionInfo` encodes two arguments: the class name of the condition and an array of `String` objects for any constructor arguments for the condition class. The `PermissionInfo` object, on the other hand, encodes three arguments: the class name of the permission and the standard `name` and `actions` arguments of the permission class constructor. As a simple example, you can construct a `PermissionInfo` object like this:

```
new PermissionInfo(
  AdminPermission.class.getName(), "(id>10)", AdminPermission.EXECUTE);
```

This encodes the `AdminPermission` with the `name` of `(id>10)` and `actions` of `execute`, which grants the right to start and stop bundles with a bundle identifier greater than 10. To see a `ConditionInfo` example, you'll need a concrete condition to play with, so we'll introduce one next. After that, we can get down to brass tacks and show you the steps involved in using `ConditionalPermissionAdmin`.

14.4.3 Bundle location condition

We've talked abstractly about conditions, but we haven't yet discussed any concrete condition types. The OSGi specification defines two: `BundleLocationCondition` and `BundleSignerCondition`. Intuitively, you can probably guess that these conditions correspond to the two types of conditions that exist in standard Java policy files. You'll learn about the former right now and the latter when we discuss bundle signing a little later.

You construct a `BundleLocationCondition` with a location string, which it uses to match against bundles on the call stack during a permission check. In other words, this condition matches bundles with the same location string, which for all intents and purposes is equivalent to the bundle's origin or code base. The condition location string may contain `*` as a wildcard to match multiple locations. As we mentioned previously, to use this condition with the `ConditionalPermissionAdmin` service, you need to encode it in a `ConditionInfo`, such as in the following example:

```
new ConditionInfo(BundleLocationCondition.class.getName(),
  new String[] { "*://foo.org/*" });
```

Here you encode the name of the `BundleLocationCondition` class and its constructor arguments. This particular example matches all bundles coming from the `foo.org` domain using any protocol. Since the OSGi R4.2 specification, `BundleLocationCondition` also accepts a second parameter; you can use `!` to negate the evaluated result. For example:

```
new ConditionInfo(BundleLocationCondition.class.getName(),
  new String[] { "file:bundle/foo.jar", "!" });
```

This results in a `BundleLocationCondition` that matches all bundles except a bundle with the location file:bundle/foo.jar. With this concrete condition under your belt, you can now see what's involved in using the `ConditionalPermissionAdmin` service in practice.

14.4.4 Using ConditionalPermissionAdmin

The steps for using `ConditionalPermissionAdmin` are straightforward:

1. Get the service from the OSGi service registry.
2. Give your bundle `AllPermission`.
3. Set permissions for other bundles to implement a security policy.

Nothing too surprising here, but these steps do assume you're starting from a clean slate. When an OSGi framework is started for the first time with security enabled, all bundles have `AllPermission`. This essentially means that the first bundle to get the `ConditionalPermissionAdmin` service and set a security policy is in control, because any permissions it sets are persistently recorded. If your bundle isn't the first, it may not be able to get the service or may get a security exception when it tries to change the security policy, because `AllPermission` is required to change permissions. For now, let's assume your bundle is first or at a minimum has `AllPermission`.

When you've retrieved the service, you want to use the `ConditionalPermissionAdmin.newConditionalPermissionUpdate()` method to create a session for modifying permissions. The `ConditionalPermissionUpdate` object has a `getConditionalPermissionInfos()` method for retrieving a mutable list of `ConditionalPermissionInfo` objects that make up the current security policy. To make changes to the policy, modify the returned list and then call `ConditionalPermissionUpdate.commit()` to write your changes. For example, the following code snippet shows how a bundle can give itself `AllPermission` (steps 1 and 2 from earlier).

Listing 14.2 Using the `ConditionalPermissionUpdate` to set permissions

```
ConditionalPermissionAdmin cpa = getConditionalPermissionAdmin();
ConditionalPermissionUpdate u = cpa.newConditionalPermissionUpdate();
List infos = u.getConditionalPermissionInfos();
infos.clear();
infos.add(
  cpa.newConditionalPermissionInfo(
    "management agent all permission",
    new ConditionInfo[] {
      new ConditionInfo(
        BundleLocationCondition.class.getName(),
        new String[] { context.getBundle().getLocation() })
      },
    new PermissionInfo[] {
      new PermissionInfo(
        AllPermission.class.getName(), "", "")
      }
    },
    ConditionalPermissionInfo.ALLOW));
u.commit();
```

Going step by step through the code, you begin by using a utility method to retrieve the `ConditionalPermissionAdmin` service, and then you use the service to get a `ConditionalPermissionUpdate` object. From the update object, you get a list of `ConditionalPermissionInfo` objects representing the current security policy (which is an empty list initially). Although it may not technically be necessary, you clear the list to make sure there aren't any other random permissions in your security policy. Then you add a new `ConditionalPermissionInfo` object, which you construct using the `newConditionalPermissionInfo()` method of the `ConditionalPermissionAdmin` service. This method takes four arguments: the name associated with the `ConditionalPermissionInfo`, an array of `ConditionalInfo` objects, an array of `PermissionInfo` objects, and an access-decision flag.

What does this particular permission entry do? The name you set is a unique key to identify the entry and has no inherent meaning; if you specify `null` for the name, a unique name will be generated for you. The single `ConditionInfo` and `PermissionInfo` objects in their respective arrays match your bundle and grant it `AllPermission`. We'll expand on the last argument, the access-decision flag, in the next section.

The last step after adding the `ConditionalPermissionInfo` object is to commit it, which you do using the update object. Assuming this completes successfully, you've successfully modified the security policy. To set permissions for other bundles, you follow a similar set of steps: get an update object, add or remove any desired permissions, and then call `commit()`. Pretty simple. Just make sure you don't delete the entry giving your own bundle `AllPermission`!

Now let's look into what the access-decision flag means.

Are you stuck in the past?

The approach we just outlined for using the `ConditionalPermissionAdmin` service is simplified by the introduction of the `ConditionalPermissionUpdate` API in the OSGi R4.2 specification. If you're using a framework that implements an older R4 specification, the steps are conceptually the same, but the details are different. For example, after getting the `ConditionalPermissionAdmin` service, you need to directly add `AllPermission` for your bundle:

```
ConditionPermissionInfo myCPI = cpa.addConditionalPermissionInfo(
  new ConditionInfo[] {
    new ConditionInfo(
      BundleLocationCondition.class.getName(),
      new String[]{context.getBundle().getLocation()}) },
  new PermissionInfo[] {
    new PermissionInfo(
      AllPermission.class.getName(), "", "") });
```

You assign permissions to other bundles in a similar fashion. To remove unexpected or unwanted permission entries, you need to loop through any existing `ConditionalPermissionInfo` objects and delete them, like this:

```
Enumeration e = cpa.getConditionalPermissionInfos();
while (e.hasMoreElements()) {
  ConditionalPermissionInfo info =
    (ConditionPermissionInfo) e.nextElement();
  if (!info.equals(myCPI)) {
    info.delete();
  }
}
```

Notice that in this example, you take care not to delete your own `ConditionalPermissionInfo`; otherwise, you'd lose the ability to set permissions. This highlights the most important difference between this older (and deprecated) approach and the newer update approach: changes happen immediately and don't require any sort of commit operation.

ALLOW- VS. DENY-ACCESS DECISIONS

Until this point, we've talked about granting permissions to allow code to perform some operation. This is the standard way to think about permissions in Java. The OSGi R4.2 specification introduced a new wrinkle: deny-access decisions. Instead of only using permissions to say what code is allowed to do, you can also use them to say what code isn't allowed to do. You saw the standard case in listing 14.2, where you added a condition with an access decision of `ConditionalPermissionInfo.ALLOW`; this corresponds to the normal case of saying what is allowed. But now you can use `ConditionalPermissionInfo.DENY` to say what isn't allowed.

Being able to allow/deny permissions makes it possible to use a white list/black list approach for handling security. Deny-access decisions can significantly simplify some security policies because they let you easily handle an exception to a general rule. Consider a case where you want to allow a bundle to import all packages except those with names starting with org.foo.secure. How can you implement such a policy with only allow-access decisions? You'd have to exhaustively grant permissions to import every package except the ones you want to exclude. This wouldn't even be possible in an open-ended system. This is where a deny-access decision becomes valuable.

Assume you add a ConditionalPermissionInfo with a deny-access decision. During a permission check, if the associated conditions match and the permission being checked is implied by the associated permissions, the bundle on the stack will be denied permission to perform the operation. To complete the hypothetical example, you can grant a bundle the following permission:

```
infos.add(admin.newConditionalPermissionInfo(
  "deny-secure-packages",
  new ConditionInfo[] { new ConditionInfo(
    BundleLocationCondition.class.getName(),
    new String[] { "file:foo.jar" }) },
  new PermissionInfo[] { new PermissionInfo(
    PackagePermission.class.getName(),
    "org.foo.secure.*", PackagePermission.IMPORT)
  }, ConditionalPermissionInfo.DENY));
```

This prevents it from importing packages starting with org.foo.secure. Of course, to give it permission to import everything else, you also have to grant it the following permission:

```
infos.add(admin.newConditionalPermissionInfo(
  "allow-non-secure-packages",
  new ConditionInfo[] { new ConditionInfo(
    BundleLocationCondition.class.getName(),
    new String[] { "file:foo.jar" }) },
  new PermissionInfo[] { new PermissionInfo(
    PackagePermission.class.getName(),
    "*", PackagePermission.IMPORT)
  }, ConditionalPermissionInfo.ALLOW));
```

This allows it to import everything else. This also raises another important point when mixing allow and deny decisions into a single security policy: ordering. With allow- and deny-access decisions, the order of ConditionalPermissionInfo objects in the policy table managed by the ConditionalPermissionAdmin service becomes important. When a permission check is triggered, the entries in the policy table are traversed in ascending index order until the first one is found where the conditions are satisfied and the required permission is present. If the associated access policy is DENY, the check fails. If it's ALLOW, the checking continues with the next bundle protection domain on the stack. Thus, in the example, to implement the policy correctly the denied permission must be added before the allowed permission.

That covers the basics of using the ConditionalPermissionAdmin service. To provide a slightly more familiar approach to defining a security policy for seasoned Java developers, you'll now use this API to create a policy-file reader. A lot of what you need for doing this is provided by the OSGi specification already, so it's pretty easy to accomplish.

14.4.5 Implementing a policy-file reader

The main purpose behind implementing a policy-file reader is to give you a convenient way to populate the ConditionalPermissionAdmin service with ConditionalPermissionInfo objects composing your desired security policy. To achieve this, you need a way to encode/decode ConditionalPermissionInfo objects to/from human-readable text. As luck would have it, the Conditional Permission Admin Service specification standardizes such an encoding.

To encode an object, you use the ConditionalPermissionInfo.getEncoded() method, which returns a String representing the associated object. To decode an object, you use the ConditionalPermissionAdmin.newConditionalPermission(String) method, which returns the corresponding decoded ConditionalPermissionInfo object. It can't get much simpler than that. The encoded format is

```
access { conditions permissions } name
```

Here, access is the access decision (either ALLOW or DENY), conditions is zero or more encoded conditions, permissions is one or more encoded permissions, and name is the name associated with the ConditionalPermissionInfo object. Drilling down, the encoded format of a ConditionInfo is

```
[type "arg0" "arg1" ...]
```

where type is the fully qualified class name of the condition and the remaining are the quoted arguments for its constructor. In a similar fashion, the encoded format of a PermissionInfo is

```
(type "name" "actions")
```

As with conditions, type is the fully qualified class name of the permission, and the remaining are the quoted name and actions for its constructor. A more concrete example looks like this (we've added line breaks for readability):

```
ALLOW {
  [org.osgi.service.condpermadmin.BundleLocationCondition "file:foo.jar"]
  (org.osgi.framework.PackagePermission "*" "IMPORT")
} "allow-all-packages"
```

With this standard encoding format, you can implement a simple policy-file reader bundle that populates the ConditionalPermissionAdmin service by reading encoded ConditionalPermissionInfo objects from a file upon activation. All you'll need to do to set and/or change your security policy is to edit your policy file and then start this bundle. More precisely, its start() method looks like the following listing.

Listing 14.3 Policy-file reader bundle activator start() method

```
public void start(BundleContext context) {
  File policyFile = getPolicyFile(context);
  List<String> encodedInfos = readPolicyFile(policyFile);
  encodedInfos.add(0, "ALLOW {"
    + "[org.osgi.service.condpermadmin.BundleLocationCondition \""
```

```
    + context.getBundle().getLocation() + "\"]"
    + "(java.security.AllPermission \"*\" \"*\")"
    + "} \"Management Agent Policy\"");
  ConditionalPermissionAdmin cpa =
    getConditionalPermissionAdmin(context);
  ConditionalPermissionUpdate u = cpa.newConditionalPermissionUpdate();
  List infos = u.getConditionalPermissionInfos();
  infos.clear();
  for (String encodedInfo : encodedInfos) {
    infos.add(cpa.newConditionalPermissionInfo(encodedInfo));
  }
  if (!u.commit()) {
    throw new ConcurrentModificationException(
      "Permissions changed during update");
  }
}
```

This method combines most of your knowledge about the `ConditionalPermissionAdmin` service. You get the policy file, which defaults to a file called `security.policy` but can be configured. Next, you read in the encodings of the `ConditionalPermissionInfo` objects contained in the policy file and add an encoding for an `AllPermission` at the beginning of the list for the policy-file reader bundle. The previous step is necessary to make sure the policy-reader bundle has sufficient permission to make future changes to the security policy.

After this, you get the `ConditionalPermissionAdmin` service, create a new `ConditionalPermissionUpdate`, and use it to get the current list of `ConditionalPermissionInfo` objects. You clear the existing policy to make sure you're starting with a clean slate, and then loop through the encoded permissions to decode them and add them to your list of objects. The only thing left to do is commit the update. Because the update may fail if the permissions were changed concurrently, you throw an exception in this case.

To see the full details of this bundle, go to the chapter14/combined-example/org.foo.policy/ directory of the book's companion code. This bundle is generic and can be used in any security-enabled framework to put a policy file into effect. You'll see it in action a little later when we show a complete example with digitally signed bundles and a custom condition. We'll introduce bundle signing next.

14.5 Digitally signed bundles

Defining a security policy by assigning permissions to bundles is a workable approach, but being able to step up a level can simplify things. For example, you may trust a particular provider, so it's nice to be able to assign permissions based on the provider rather than individual bundles. Doing so simplifies defining a security policy, because it raises the level of abstraction. Digitally signed bundles can help you achieve this; specifically, they help you do two things:

- Authenticate the provider of a bundle
- Ensure that bundle content hasn't been modified

The former provides the ultimate goal, but without the latter, the former would be meaningless. You'll learn about both as we discuss digital signing and certificates. We'll show you how to create certificates and use them to digitally sign your bundles. Then we'll introduce `BundleSignerCondition`, which gives you the ability to grant permissions based on the identity established via certificates. First, let's get some terminology out of the way.

14.5.1 Learning the terminology

The domain of digital cryptography is complex and sophisticated. Providing a complete and detailed description is beyond the scope of the book, so we'll focus on describing just enough to have it make sense. With that in mind, table 14.6 introduces some relevant terms we'll use throughout the remainder of the chapter.

Table 14.6 Digital cryptography terminology

Term	Definition
Digital signing	A mathematical approach for verifying the authenticity of digital data. Specifically, used to verify the identity of the provider and that the data hasn't been modified.
Signature	A unique value calculated when data is digitally signed.
Public key cryptography	A form of digital signing using two mathematically related keys: a public key and a private key. The private key is a guarded secret used to sign data. The public key is shared with others in the form of a certificate, which they can use to verify that a signature was generated with the private key. This allows you to infer the identity of the provider and determine whether someone has tampered with the data.
Certificate	A form of metadata about a public key, binding it to the identity of the private key holder. This binding is achieved by having a well-known (trusted) third party sign the public key/identity pair.
Distinguished name	The identification portion of a certificate; specifically, as defined by the X.509 ITU-IT standard. Identifies the holder of the private key.
Certificate chain	A certificate has a reference to the certificate of its third-party signer, which includes a reference to the certificate of its signer, and so on, until the root. This is a certificate chain. The root of the certificate chain is a self-signed certificate.

A general understanding of these terms should be sufficient. You don't need a complete understanding of digital cryptography to use the technology effectively. We'll start looking at the basics.

14.5.2 Creating certificates and signing bundles

You'll be using digital signing based on public key cryptography, which involves a public key and a private key. The public key is shared with the world in the form of a certificate. The private key is kept secret and used to sign data by performing a computation over it. The resulting value can be verified by performing another calculation over the data using the public key. This verifies that the signer has access to the private key and that the data hasn't been modified.

In OSGi, the signer of a bundle is associated with it. With this association, you can grant permissions to a bundle based on its signers. For example, you can assign permissions to all bundles from a particular company, if the company signs its bundles. You can also grant permissions to perform operations on bundles signed by specific principles. These approaches provide a simple yet powerful way to control who can do what inside your application.

Effectively, bundle signing creates a powerful delegation model. An administrator can grant a restricted set of permissions to a signer, after which the signer can create bundles that use those permissions or some subset, without any intervention or communication with the administrator for each particular bundle. To understand how this all fits together, consider the following scenario.

Assume you have a system that features a set of core bundles (which we'll call the *core domain*) and an arbitrary number of third-party plugin bundles (which we'll call the *third-party domain*). This means you expect fully trusted bundles and not completely trusted bundles to exist in your system, but you want to provide a level of isolation between them. Your goal is to create a simple security policy that lets you manage core and third-party bundle domains without knowing the precise bundles in each set. We'll delve into the details of doing this next.

CERTIFICATES AND KEYSTORES

To implement the desired security policy for this scenario, you need to create two root certificates for the core and third-party domains. These root certificates will be used by the framework to establish a chain of trust for the two domains. With these two certificates, you can then sign certificates of core and third-party providers with the appropriate certificate. When they use their individual certificates to sign bundles they've created, the framework can use the root certificates to establish a chain of trust and determine to which domain a bundle belongs.

The details of all this are based on Java 2 JAR file signing, which means the same tools you use to sign JAR files can be used for OSGi. To create the needed certificates and their associated public and private keys, you'll use the `keytool` command provided by the JDK. It can create and manage certificates and keys inside a *keystore*, which is an encrypted file defined by Java for this purpose. For this scenario, you use `keytool` to create two certificates and their associated public/private keys for the core and third-party domains like this:

```
keytool -genkey -keystore keys.ks -alias core -storepass foobar  \
  -keypass barbaz -dname "CN=core,O=baz,C=de"
keytool -genkey -keystore keys.ks -alias third-party \
  -storepass foobar -keypass barbaz -dname "CN=third-party,O=baz,C=de"
```

This creates a keystore called `keys.ks` containing two new key pairs and a certificate for each pair with aliases of `core` and `third-party`. The keystore is protected by the password `foobar`, and the keys themselves have the password `barbaz`. The `-dname` switch allows you to specify the distinguished name you use to identify yourself, which in this case is the `baz` organization in Germany (`de`).

> **DISTINGUISHED NAME** A standard X.509 structured name, officially identifying a node in a hierarchical namespace. For our purposes, it's sufficient to recognize a distinguished name (DN) as a set of comma-delimited attributes, such as in the example: `CN=core,O=baz,C=de`. These attributes specify the common name, organization, and country, respectively. The hierarchical aspect of this namespace is that it goes from the least significant (but most specific) attribute to the most significant. The root of the tree for these attributes is the country, which is then divided into organization, and further divided into common names within an organization. Order is significant. Two DNs with the same attributes but different order are different DNs.

The next thing to do is sign your key pair certificates with themselves. It may sound a little strange, but this is how you make them root certificates. It's a common thing to do, as you can see by the fact that the `keytool` command has support for it:

```
keytool -selfcert -keystore keys.ks -alias core -storepass foobar \
  -keypass barbaz -dname "CN=core,O=baz,C=de"
keytool -selfcert -keystore keys.ks -alias third-party \
  -storepass foobar -keypass barbaz -dname "CN=third-party,O=baz,C=de"
```

The only difference from the previous command is that you use `-selfcert` instead of `-genkey`.

Now you have key pairs that you can use to sign other certificates or bundles to make them part of your trusted certificate chain. To allow other people to verify your signatures, you need to extract the certificates from the `keys.ks` keystore and import them into a new keystore called `certificates.ks`. Why? Because the `keys.ks` keystore contains your private keys; you need another keystore that contains only your public keys to share with the outside world. Currently, your certificates are saved as key entries (a public/private key pair and its certificate) in the keystore. You need to export them and re-import them as certificate-only entries, which you do like this:

```
keytool -export -v -keystore keys.ks -alias core \
  -file core.cert -storepass foobar -keypass barbaz
keytool -export -v -keystore keys.ks -alias third-party \
  -file third-party.cert -storepass foobar -keypass barbaz
keytool -import -v -keystore certificates.ks -alias core-cert \
  -file core.cert -storepass foobar -keypass barbaz
keytool -import -v -keystore certificates.ks -alias third-party-cert \
  -file third-party.cert -storepass foobar -keypass barbaz
```

You can verify the contents of your keystores like this:

```
> keytool -list -keystore certificates.ks -storepass foobar

third-party-cert, 08.01.2010, trustedCertEntry,
fingerprint (MD5): 15:9B:EE:BE:E7:52:64:D4:9C:C1:CB:5D:69:66:BB:29
core-cert, 08.01.2010, trustedCertEntry,
fingerprint (MD5): CE:37:F8:71:C9:37:12:D0:F1:C8:2B:F9:85:BE:EA:61

> keytool -list -keystore keys.ks -storepass foobar

core, 08.01.2010, PrivateKeyEntry,
fingerprint (MD5): CE:37:F8:71:C9:37:12:D0:F1:C8:2B:F9:85:BE:EA:61
third-party, 08.01.2010, PrivateKeyEntry,
fingerprint (MD5): 15:9B:EE:BE:E7:52:64:D4:9C:C1:CB:5D:69:66:BB:29
```

You have everything in place now, which means we can look into signing bundles to make them members of one of your domains.

SIGNING BUNDLES

A bundle JAR file can be signed by multiple signers; the signing follows normal Java JAR signing rules. The only additional constraint for a bundle is that all entries inside the bundle must be included in the signature, but entries below the META-INF/ directory aren't included. Normal Java JAR file signing allows for partially signed JAR files, but OSGi doesn't. It's lucky that signing all entries except those below META-INF/ is the default in JAR signing, so you can use the `jarsigner` tool included in the JDK. The following will sign a bundle with your core private key:

```
jarsigner -keystore file:keys.ks \
  -storepass foobar -keypass barbaz core-bundle.jar core
```

Signing another bundle with your third-party private key looks very similar. You specify the appropriate alias:

```
jarsigner -keystore file:keys.ks \
  -storepass foobar -keypass barbaz third-party-bundle.jar third-party
```

For verification, you need the keystore containing the certificates. You can use the `jarsigner` tool for verification as well:

```
jarsigner -verify -keystore file:certificates.ks core-bundle.jar
jarsigner -verify -keystore file:certificates.ks third-party-bundle.jar
```

This command should output `jar verified` if you've correctly signed the bundles. Assuming you have, you now have one bundle in the core domain and one in the third-party domain. This makes it easy for you to grant permissions to either, based on the signer of a bundle, as you'll see next.

14.5.3 BundleSignerCondition

To assign permissions to bundles based on who signed them, you need a condition. The OSGi specification defines the `BundleSignerCondition` for certificate matching, which is specifically based on DN matching. DN matching can seem somewhat complicated, but it needn't be. We'll discuss the details of it shortly; first, let's look at how you construct a `BundleSignerCondition`.

The `BundleSignerCondition` is initialized with a DN matching expression as its first argument and an optional second argument of `!`. If you specify the exclamation mark, it negates the result of the DN matching expression. Consider the following snippet of an encoded `ConditionalPermissionInfo` object containing a `BundleSignerCondition`:

```
ACCEPT {
[org.osgi.service.condpermadmin.BundleSignerCondition "CN=core,O=baz,C=de"]
...
}
```

This matches a bundle on the call stack if it's signed by the core certificate of the example, which means any permissions associated with this entry will be granted to the bundle. On the other hand, the following won't match a bundle if it was signed by the core certificate:

```
ACCEPT {
[org.osgi.service.condpermadmin.BundleSignerCondition
  "CN=core,O=baz,C=de" "!"]
...
}
```

The DN matching expression in these two examples illustrates how simple DN matching can be. It can also be sophisticated, because it supports various flavors of wildcard matching. We'll describe that next.

DISTINGUISHED NAME MATCHING DETAILS

You saw that a DN is composed of multiple attributes, like country, organization, and common name. When performing DN matching, you're matching against these attributes using a comma-delimited list, such as what you saw earlier with `CN=core, O=baz,C=de` to match the core certificate. Additionally, because certificates can be signed by other certificates, you can match against the other certificates in the chain: you delimit different certificates with a semicolon.

To match certificates in a chain, use DN matching expressions against the DN associated with each certificate you're trying to match. For example, consider the following DN matching expression:

```
CN=extensions,O=bar,C=fr;CN=core,O=baz,C=de
```

This matches a bundle that was signed by the `bar` organization from France using its extensions certificate, which was signed by your core certificate. You need to understand two important points about chain matching:

- Matching occurs naturally against the most specific certificate. Certificates further up the chain that aren't mentioned are ignored.
- Order is important, because reversing it indicates the opposite signing relationship.

When you match certificate chains, you're specifying an interest from the most specific certificate of the chain onward.

Both attribute matching and certificate chain matching support wildcards, but the rules for comparison are more complicated than string-based wildcard matching. The different cases are described in table 14.7.

Table 14.7 Certificate DN wildcard matching

Case	Description

Specific attribute wildcards	If a wildcard is used as part of the right-hand argument of an attribute, such as
	`CN=*,O=baz,C=de`
	this matches either of the two certificates (core and third-party). You can also use a wildcard for more than one attribute:
	`CN=*,O=baz,C=*`
	This matches any certificate from the `baz` organization from any country.

Table 14.7 Certificate DN wildcard matching *(continued)*

Case	Description

Arbitrary attribute wildcards	If a wildcard is used standalone, such as
	`*,O=baz,C=de`
	this matches any attributes coming before `O` and `C`, regardless of their name or value. For the example, it's another way to match both of your certificates. This kind of wildcard can also be combined with the previous:
	`*,O=baz,C=*`
	This also matches all certificates from the `baz` organization from any country.

Certificate chain wildcards	The attribute wildcard can be used in a certificate chain and behaves as described earlier, but when used standalone it matches at most one certificate. For example:
	`*;CN=core,O=baz,C=de`
	This matches either a bundle signed by another certificate that was signed by your core certificate or a bundle signed directly by your core certificate. The hyphen wildcard matches zero or more certificates:
	`-;CN=core,O=baz,C=de`
	This matches any bundle signed by your core certificate anywhere in the certificate chain.

The rules for certificate matching are also relevant to `AdminPermission`, discussed in section 14.3.3. If you recall, `AdminPermission` accepts an LDAP filter over a limited number of attributes to describe target bundles. The value for the `signer` attribute of the LDAP filter is a DN matching expression.

ESTABLISHING TRUST

In addition to DN matching, a `BundleSignerCondition` will only match if all the certificates in the chain are trusted or are signed by a trusted certificate. Certificates are *trusted* when they're known by the OSGi framework. How do they become known? Prior to OSGi R4.2 specification, this was implementation-specific; but now the standard way is to specify keystores containing trusted certificates using the `org.osgi.framework.trust.repositories` framework configuration property. For example:

```
org.osgi.framework.trust.repositories=\
  /var/trust/keystore.jks:~/.cert/certs.jks
```

The value is a list of file paths, where the paths are separated by the system-specific `File.pathSeparator`. Each file path must point to a JKS keystore, which can't have a password. The framework uses the keystores as trust repositories to authenticate certificates of trusted signers. The stores must be used only as read-only trust repositories to access public keys.

You should now understand how to use certificates to sign your bundles and grant permissions based on the bundle signer. With that out of the way, let's look at how you can use local permissions to know which permissions a bundle needs.

14.6 Local permissions

Bundle signing provides a powerful yet fairly simple mechanism for creating desired security policies. But it doesn't help address one nagging issue: how do you know which permissions to grant a bundle? Even if you've verified a bundle's signature and know that the bundle comes from a trusted provider, you still need to answer this question. Even if you fully trust a provider, it's better to limit a bundle's permissions to a precise set of required permissions to further prevent intended or unintended security breaches.

The standard Java security architecture doesn't help you here; instead, you must rely on prior knowledge about the code's requirements or trial and error. OSGi specifically addresses this issue with a concept called *local permissions*. Local permissions are defined by a resource contained in the bundle, which describes the maximum set of permissions required by the bundle. This set of permission is enforced by the OSGi framework. A bundle can be granted fewer permissions than its local permissions, but it never gets more permissions.

At first blush, it may seem a little odd to have a bundle define its own permissions, but the purpose is more for the deployer to audit and analyze a bundle. Bundles aren't guaranteed to receive the permissions they request and therefore should be programmed to degrade gracefully when they receive less. As a deployer, though, local permissions simplify your life because you can easily determine what permissions are required and which you're willing to give. For example, if the local permissions request the use of network sockets, it's clear that the bundle has the potential to access the wider internet. If you decide this is acceptable, you can trust this audit because it's enforced by the framework at execution time.

What do local permissions look like in practice? The bundle-permission resource is a file in the bundle's OSGI-INF/ directory called permissions.perm. It contains a listing of all of the bundle's required permissions. As a simple example, let's assume you provide a bundle that only wants to export a single package, org.foo. This bundle's OSGi-INF/permissions.perm file is as follows:

```
# Tuesday, Dec 28 2009
# Foo Bundle
( org.osgi.framework.PackagePermission "org.foo" "IMPORT,EXPORT" )
```

Lines that start with a # are comments. All other non-empty lines describe required permissions as encoded `PermissionInfo` objects. This is simple but effective when it comes to auditing the security impact of a given bundle.

You've now learned about some powerful tools for defining a security policy; but in the infamous words of many infomercials, "Wait! There's still more!" In the next section, we'll cover the most advanced tool available: the ability to create custom conditions for your security policy. We'll explore *why* you may want to do this and show you *how* to do it by implementing two custom conditions.

14.7 Advanced permission management

At this point, you've seen the two standard conditions defined by the OSGi specification: `BundleLocationCondition` and `BundleSignerCondition`. Although these are often sufficient to implement reasonable security policies, in some cases you may want or need more. To address these situations, you can create custom conditions. This extensibility gives you a lot of power. In this section, we'll show you how to harness this power by creating two custom conditions: a date-based condition and a user-input condition.

14.7.1 Custom conditions overview

As you may imagine, providing custom conditions is a security-sensitive process. You certainly don't want a malicious bundle to shadow an actual condition with a faulty one. For this reason, providing conditions isn't possible via normal bundles. Custom conditions are valid only if they're made available from the framework's class path (that is, they're provided by the system bundle). Otherwise, implementing a custom condition is pretty easy.

When you use `ConditionInfo` to construct a new condition instance, the framework loads the specified condition class from the class path and tries to call a static method on it that looks like this:

```
public static Condition getCondition(Bundle bundle, ConditionInfo info)
```

This is a factory method, although it need not return a new instance for each call. If such a method isn't available, the framework falls back to trying to find a constructor to invoke with the following signature:

```
public X(Bundle bundle, ConditionInfo info)
```

Assuming it finds one or the other, it uses the condition as part of the permission check. The custom condition must implement the `Condition` interface, which is defined as follows:

```
public interface Condition{
  public static Condition TRUE;
  public static Condition FALSE;
  public boolean isPostponed();
  public boolean isSatisfied();
  public boolean isMutable();
  public boolean isSatisfied(Condition[] conditions, Dictionary context);
}
```

The static `TRUE` and `FALSE` objects are used for conditions that are always true or false, respectively. This may seem odd, but think about `BundleLocationCondition`. Its `getCondition()` method can determine immediately whether the supplied bundle's location matches; it only needs to return `TRUE` for matches and `FALSE` for nonmatches, because these values will never change. Other than that, the interface is reasonably simple, but the best way to explain the remaining methods is by way of some examples.

14.7.2 Date-based condition

Assume you want to restrict certain permission sets to be available before a given point in time, but not after. Imagine that you want to associate permissions with a period of validity, where the ability to perform certain operations expires after some time. The following listing shows a condition you can use to make this possible.

Listing 14.4 `BeforeDateCondition` example

```
class BeforeDateCondition implements Condition {
  private final long m_date;
  public static Condition getCondition(Bundle bundle, ConditionInfo info){
    return new BeforeDateCondition(Bundle bundle, info);
  )
  private BeforeDateCondition(Bundle bundle, ConditionInfo info){
    m_date = Long.parseLong(info.getArgs()[0]);          ◁─┐ Condition
  }                                                        ❶ constructor
  public boolean isMutable(){
    return m_date > System.currentTimeMillis();
  }
  public boolean isPostponed(){
    return false;
  }
  public boolean isSatisfied(){
    return System.currentTimeMillis() < m_date;
  }
  public boolean isSatisfied(Condition[] conditions, Dictionary context){
    return false;
  }
}
```

As you can see, this implementation is pretty simple. When the framework evaluates this condition, it uses the static `getCondition()` method to create an instance for the target bundle. The condition's constructor ❶ converts its argument to a `long`, which sets the date. The framework then checks whether the condition is postponed by calling the `isPostponed()` method. This tells the framework whether the condition should be evaluated immediately or deferred; this condition is immediate, but you'll see an opposite example later. Because this condition isn't postponed, the framework invokes the `isSatisfied()` method immediately to test the condition. This method checks whether the current time in milliseconds is still lower than the ending date supplied in the constructor argument. Note that the second `isSatisfied()` method is only used for postponed conditions and is ignored here.

The `isMutable()` method is purely used by the framework to optimize condition evaluation. If a condition is immutable, the framework only needs to call its `isSatisfied()` method one time and can cache the result. For mutable conditions, the framework needs to evaluate the condition on every check. For this particular condition, you have an interesting case because it's mutable until the ending date is reached, after which it becomes immutable.

You can now use this custom condition to define your security policy like the standard conditions. For example, in the policy file you can do something like this:

```
ACCEPT {
  [ org.foo.BeforeDateCondition "1282684888" ]
  ( java.security.AllPermission "*" "*" )
} "DATE CONDITION"
```

As we mentioned previously, you need to put this condition on the class path of the framework to use it. You can achieve this by adding it directly to your application class path or by using a special kind of bundle called an *extension bundle*. Because it's more dynamic, you'll use an extension bundle.

Extension bundles

Extension bundles can deliver optional parts of the framework implementation or provide functionality that must reside on the boot class path. For example, a framework vendor can supply optional services like Conditional Permission Admin and Start Level as framework-extension bundles instead of building them into the framework for more modular framework deployments.

An extension bundle is treated as a fragment of the system bundle. The system bundle has a standard bundle symbolic name, `system.bundle`, but it also has an implementation-specific alias. For example, the following example uses the `Fragment-Host` header to specify an extension bundle for the Felix framework implementation:

```
Fragment-Host: org.apache.felix.framework; extension:=framework
```

Because extension bundles are special, there are certain restrictions on what you can do with them. For example, extension bundles can't specify any of the following headers: `Import-Package`, `Require-Bundle`, `Bundle-NativeCode`, `DynamicImport-Package`, and `Bundle-Activator`. Typically, they're used to add stuff to the class path and possibly to export additional packages from the system bundle.

To package this custom condition inside an extension bundle, you create a bundle with the following manifest:

```
Manifest-Version: 1.0
Bundle-ManifestVersion: 2
Bundle-SymbolicName: org.foo.beforedatecondition
Bundle-Name: Before Date Condition Extension Bundle
Bundle-Version: 1.0.0
Fragment-Host: system.bundle; extension:=framework
Export-Package: org.foo
```

Now you need to install this bundle into your framework, after which you can use the condition in your security policy. That was fairly easy, so let's move on to a more sophisticated example.

14.7.3 User-input condition

Often, the only means to determine whether some code is allowed to perform an operation is to ask the user. We see this regularly when running Java applications from a web browser or on a mobile phone. As you may guess, you can implement such a custom condition, but the scenario is trickier. In particular, permission checks tend to be fine-grained, and in this case executing the condition is costly (and potentially annoying to the user). Luckily, the Conditional Permission Admin Service specification defines mechanisms to deal with such situations.

POSTPONED CONDITIONS

Certain conditions can be costly to evaluate, such as asking the user for permission. In such situations, you should evaluate the conditions as *postponed conditions*. Doing so causes the framework to delay their verification until the end of the permission check.

A condition informs the framework that it's postponed by returning `true` from the `Condition.isPostponed()` method. A condition must always return the same value for the `isPostponed()` method, so that the Conditional Permission Admin Service can cache the value. If the method returns `false`, the no-argument version of the `isSatisfied()` method checks the permission, which is intended to be used for quick evaluations. On the other hand, if the method returns `true`, the version of `isSatisfied()` that takes arguments is used; it's intended for more costly evaluations.

For example, a condition can verify whether a mobile phone is roaming. This information is readily available in memory, and therefore this condition need not be postponed. Alternatively, a condition obtaining authorization over the network should be postponed to avoid the delay caused by network latency if not necessary.

Looking more closely at the parameters of the `isSatisfied()` method used to evaluate postponed conditions, you see that it takes an array of `Condition` objects and a `Dictionary`. The array always contains a single element: a reference to the receiving condition. This behavior was introduced in the R4.2 specification, because prior specification versions could verify multiple conditions at the same time. As a result, this change makes the array relatively worthless. The method was reused to avoid creating a breaking change for existing custom conditions. The `Dictionary` parameter is a context object for the condition implementation, which it can use to maintain state between invocations. The same `Dictionary` object is passed into all postponed conditions of the same type during a single permission check.

> **Impact on creating security policies**
>
> From the point of view of the security-policy creator, it doesn't matter whether a condition is postponed. The impact is in how the framework processes the conditions and/or how the condition implementation optimizes evaluation. The important result is that the framework evaluates postponed conditions only when no immediate condition entry implies the required permission, which allows the framework to avoid costly condition evaluation if possible. When you're creating a security policy, you can ignore this aspect of conditions.

You now understand the theory behind postponed conditions. Let's implement an example that asks the user to authorize permissions.

ASKING THE USER

You'll implement the ask-the-user condition by splitting it into two parts:

- An `AskTheUser` class that presents the user with a Swing dialog box asking to authorize permission requests
- `AskTheUserCondition`, which is a postponed condition that uses the `AskTheUser` class to evaluate its condition

This is a good example for postponed conditions, because you don't want to bother the user with questions if the check fails for other reasons and user interaction is slow. The following listing shows the `AskTheUser` implementation.

Listing 14.5 `AskTheUser` dialog box implementation

```
public class AskTheUser implements Runnable {
  private final String m_question;
  private volatile boolean m_result;

  public AskTheUser(String question) {          ❶ Question to ask
    m_question = question;
  }
  public void run() {
    m_result = (JOptionPane.YES_OPTION ==
      JOptionPane.showConfirmDialog(null, m_question, "Security",
        JOptionPane.YES_NO_OPTION));
  }
  public boolean ask() throws Exception {          ❷ Asks question
    SwingUtilities.invokeAndWait(this);
    return m_result;
  }
}
```

The constructor accepts the question to ask ❶, which you display in the `ask()` method ❷. In the `ask()` method, you use a `JOptionPane` confirmation dialog box to query the user. You return `true` or `false` depending on whether the user confirms or rejects the request, respectively. The next listing shows how you implement the condition itself.

Listing 14.6 `AskTheUserCondition` implementation

```
public class AskUserCondition implements Condition {
  private final Bundle m_bundle;
  private final String m_question;
  private final boolean m_not;
  private boolean m_result = false;
  private boolean m_alreadyAsked = false;

  private AskUserCondition(Bundle bundle, ConditionInfo info){
    m_bundle = bundle;
    m_question = info.getArgs()[0].replace(
      "$symbolic-name", bundle.getSymbolicName());
    m_not = (info.getArgs().length == 2 && "!".equals(info.getArgs()[1]));
  }
```

```
  public static Condition getCondition(Bundle b, ConditionInfo i) {
    return new AskUserCondition(bundle, i);
  }
  public boolean isMutable() {
    return false;
  }
  public boolean isPostponed() {
    return true;
  }
  public boolean isSatisfied() {
    return false;
  }
  public synchronized boolean isSatisfied(Condition[], Dictionary) {
    ...
  }
}
```

Delegates to constructor ❶

❷ Stubbed out

You provide a static factory method ❶ which delegates to the private constructor. The constructor is initialized with the question you need to ask the user, which comes from the first argument of a corresponding `ConditionInfo` object. In the constructor, you automatically replace any occurrence of `${symbolic-name}` in the question with the symbolic name of the bundle making the permission request. Additionally, if there's a second argument in the `ConditionInfo` of `!`, you use it as an indication to negate the eventual result.

The condition is immutable and postponed. Because the condition is postponed, you can stub out the other `isSatisfied()` method ❷.

Now let's look at how to implement the postponed `isSatisfied()` method, which is shown in the following listing.

Listing 14.7 `AskTheUserCondition isSatisfied()` method implementation

```
public synchronized boolean isSatisfied(Condition[] cs, Dictionary) {
  if (alreadyAsked) {
    return m_result;
  }
  Boolean result = ((Boolean) AccessController.doPrivileged(
    new PrivilegedAction() {
      public Object run() {
        AskTheUser question = new AskTheUser(m_question);
        try {
          return question.ask() ? Boolean.TRUE : Boolean.FALSE;
        } catch (Exception e) {
          return Boolean.FALSE;
        }
      }
    }));
  }
  m_alreadyAsked = true;
  if (m_not) {
     return (m_result = !result.booleanValue());
  } else {
    return (m_result = result.booleanValue());
  }
}
```

❶ Calls ask() method

❷ Creates AskTheUser

❸ Marks question as already asked

Here you check whether you've already asked the user by looking at the m_alreadyAsked flag, which is only necessary to avoid a race condition if multiple threads are trying to set the initial value; after that, the framework will cache the result because the condition is immutable. If the user hasn't already been asked, you create a new AskTheUser object with your question ❷ and call its ask() method. When you get the result, you set the alreadyAsked flag to true ❸ to make sure that the user is asked only one time for the given bundle. Finally, you return the result or invert the result if "!" was specified in the ConditionInfo.

A slightly complicated part of this example is that you need to perform the call to the ask() method using AccessController.doPrivileged() ❶. This is because the use of Swing will result in a lot of additional permission checks, so you must limit the protection domains involved to the protection domain of the condition itself. Because the condition must be on the class path, it'll have the protection domain of the framework, which needs to have AllPermission. If, for whatever reason, you get an exception, you return false.

This completes the AskTheUserCondition implementation. If you package it as an extension bundle or add it to the framework class path, you can use it to let the user make security decisions by including it in your policy file like this:

```
ACCEPT {
  [ org.foo.AskTheUserCondition "Do you want to allow $symbolic-name to
  provide a shape?" ]
  ( org.osgi.framework.ServicePermission "org.foo.shape.SimpleShape"
  "register")
}
```

We've covered a lot of ground in this chapter, so you should be commended for making it this far. To wrap up the discussion on security, we'll look at an example that pulls everything together.

14.8 Bringing it all back home

What's left is to show you how to start a framework with security enabled. You need to make sure a security manager is installed in the system and tell the framework where it can find the trusted root certificates. You can either set a custom security manager or have the framework install its own security manager. Typically, you need to set the following two framework-configuration properties:

- org.osgi.framework.security—Tells the framework to set the security manager
- org.osgi.framework.trust.repositories—As mentioned earlier, specifies the repositories of trusted certificates

The org.osgi.framework.security property value can be either an empty string or osgi. In either case, the framework sets the JVM security manager to an implementation-specific one when started. If the property isn't specified, the framework doesn't set the security manager; security will still work if a security manager is already set, but not all features of OSGi security may work. In particular, if the existing security manager uses AccessController, postponed conditions won't work.

Even though some aspects of enabling security are standardized, not all aspects are. As a result, enabling security is handled a little differently by different framework implementations. We'll use the Apache Felix framework to show a concrete example. The Felix framework is special because it provides its Conditional Permission Admin Service implementation as an extension bundle. This means that in addition to setting the previous properties, you also need to deploy the security provider bundle. Luckily, this is easy to do with the bundle launcher; add it to the directory containing the bundles you want to launch.

This gets you a framework with security enabled and an initial security policy. If you want to allow for bundles signed by trusted certificates, you can use the `org.osgi.framework.trust.repositories` property to point to the keystore containing the certificates you trust, but typically a keystore requires the use of a password. Because keystores used with this configuration property can't have passwords, you need to resort to an implementation-specific means to give you what you want. For the Felix framework, you do the following:

```
java -Dorg.osgi.framework.security=osgi \
    -Dfelix.keystore=file:certificates.ks \
    -Dfelix.keystore.pass=foobar \
    -Dfelix.keystore.type=jks \
    -jar launcher.jar bundles
```

In this case, the initial security policy file contains the following:

```
grant { permission java.security.AllPermission; };
```

This sets up your framework with a keystore and the password necessary to access it.

To illustrate what you can do with all of this, let's add to the paint program a security policy that uses the security features you've learned about. The security policy will allow core providers to provide shapes automatically; all others will require explicit approval from the user. Other than provide shape services, bundles are allowed to do anything. Start by creating a policy file with an entry to grant `AllPermission` to bundles signed by the core certificate:

```
ALLOW {
  [ org.osgi.service.condpermadmin.BundleSignerCondition
    "CN=core,O=baz,C=de" ]
   ( java.security.AllPermission "*" "*" )
} "Signed by core"
```

Next, create an entry to grant all other bundles permission to register a shape service based on the condition that the user approves it. For this, use your custom condition like this:

```
ALLOW {
  [ org.foo.condition.ask.AskUserCondition
    "Do you want to allow ${symbolic-name} to provide a shape?" ]
  ( org.osgi.framework.ServicePermission
    "org.foo.shape.SimpleShape" "register" )
} "Ask the user"
```

If a bundle that isn't signed by your core certificate tries to register a shape service, the user is asked to grant or deny that request. Pretty simple, right? This entry only deals with asking the user to approve shape services from non-core bundles; you still need to create an entry to grant these bundles the ability to do everything else. In that case, you need to grant them `AllPermission` except for registering shape services. You can use a `DENY` access decision, like this:

```
DENY {
  ( org.osgi.framework.ServicePermission
    "org.foo.shape.SimpleShape" "register" )
} "Deny register"
ALLOW {
  ( java.security.AllPermission "*" "*" )
} "All other"
```

All these entries combined form your defined security policy. You may wonder whether the policy is correct. If you follow the rule ordering in the policy file, it looks like it will always prompt the user if a bundle isn't signed by the core. But this isn't the case, because `AskUserCondition` is a postponed condition. That means it's evaluated only if no other rule with an immediate condition implies the permission. Your security policy is evaluated like this:

1. If a bundle is signed by the core certificate, it immediately matches the first rule, which allows it to do anything.
2. If a non-core signed bundle performs any secure operation other than registering a shape service, the first rule doesn't apply, the second rule is postponed, the third rule doesn't apply, and ultimately the fourth rule is matched that allows the bundle to do anything.
3. If a non-core signed bundle tries to register a shape service, the first rule doesn't apply, the second rule is postponed, the third rule applies because the permission is implied, and this rule fails due to the `DENY` access decision. This causes the framework to evaluate the postponed second rule because it logically came before the failed entry, which prompts the user and grants the permission based on the user's reply.

As you can see, you only ask the user at the end if all other rules don't provide the needed permission. The `DENY` access decision of the third rule provides a way to short-circuit the rule evaluation. To see this security policy in action, go into the chapter14/combined-example/ directory of the book's companion code; type `ant` to build it and the following to run it:

```
java -Dorg.osgi.framework.security=osgi -Djava.security.policy=all.policy \
  -Dfelix.keystore=file:certificates.ks -Dfelix.keystore.pass=foobar  \
  -Dfelix.keystore.type=jks -jar launcher.jar bundles
```

This starts your shell in a security-enabled framework running your security policy. You first need to install the bundles of the paint program:

```
-> install file:paint-example/shape-4.0.jar
Bundle: 8
-> install file:paint-example/paint-4.0.jar
Bundle: 9
-> start 9
```

These bundles were signed by the core certificate and have `AllPermission`, so you should see an empty paint program (one with no shapes) after starting the paint bundle. Next, install and start the unsigned circle bundle:

```
-> install file:paint-example/circle-4.0.jar
Bundle: 10
-> start 10
```

Doing this causes the user to be prompted to grant the permission, as shown in figure 14.3. If you grant the bundle permission, you get a circle shape in the paint program, as shown in figure 14.4.

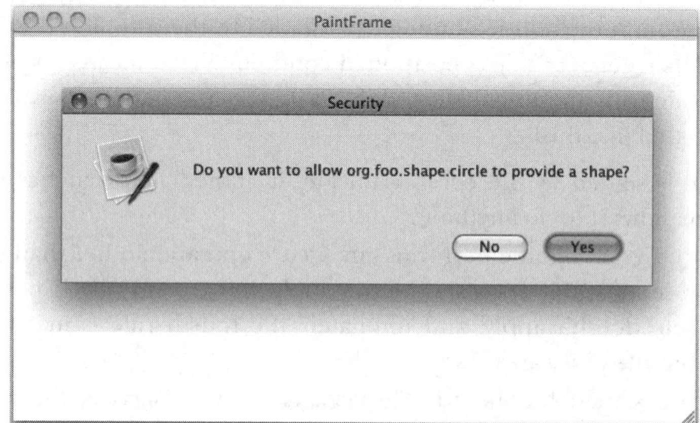

Figure 14.3 Secured paint program prompting the user to grant the unsigned circle bundle permission to provide a shape service

Figure 14.4 Secured paint program after the user has granted permission to the unsigned circle bundle

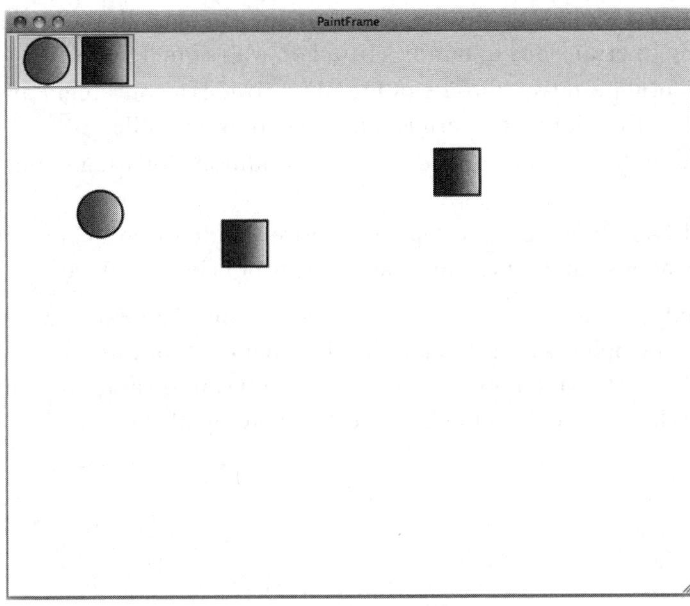

Figure 14.5 Secured paint program with an unsigned circle bundle and a signed square bundle

Finally, to show that core-signed bundles can provide shapes without prompting the user, install and start the square bundle:

```
-> install file:paint-example/square-4.0.jar
Bundle: 11
-> start 11
```

You should now have a paint program with circle and square shapes, as shown in figure 14.5.

Congratulations! If you've made it this far, you know just about everything there is to know about securing your OSGi-based applications. Just do it!

14.9 Summary

In this chapter, we introduced you to the Java security model and showed how OSGi uses it to provide the infrastructure to deploy and manage applications that must run in secure environments. You've learned the following:

- It's important to have security in mind when you're writing bundles, because otherwise they probably won't be good citizens in a security-enabled environment.
- Java security provides the foundation of the OSGi security model.
- OSGi provides the necessary permissions to express security policies for bundles with respect to the three key layers of the OSGi framework: module, lifecycle, and services.
- The Conditional Permission Admin Service introduces a new way of managing security by means of conditions that must be satisfied in order for certain permissions to be applicable.

- You can make your life a lot simpler by signing your bundles with certificates and assigning permissions to bundles based on who signed them.
- Specifying local permission inside of bundles provides a convenient and simple way to audit and enforce the permissions needed by a bundle.
- It's easy to implement and provide custom conditions for use in your security policies.
- Postponed conditions let you defer expensive condition evaluation until the end, which allows you to fine-tune your security policies for efficiency.

With this knowledge under your belt, you can secure your framework according to your specific security policies and develop bundles that can work in security-enabled frameworks. In the next chapter, we'll look into how you can use and provide web services in OSGi as well as how to build web applications on top of OSGi.

15 Web applications and web services

> **This chapter covers**
>
> - Using the OSGi HTTP Service specification to serve content and servlets
> - Using the OSGi Web Applications specification to deploy WAR files
> - Using the OSGi Remote Services specification to provide and consume web services

This is it: the last chapter. We hope that throughout the course of this book, we've been able to convince you that OSGi technology is fairly easy to use and extremely powerful. This final chapter touches on an area that we haven't covered yet but that is hugely important to many modern developers: web applications and web services. We'll show you how to build and deploy web applications using OSGi, and the benefits this technique can bring to traditional web-development frameworks. You'll reuse a lot of knowledge from earlier in the book to build a dynamic, distributed OSGi application.

Web-related technologies are ubiquitous. Almost all organizations and many individuals have some form of web presence, whether via social networking sites, static HTML pages, simple one-tier web applications, medium-sized n-tiered architectures, or massive global behemoths. Developers of these types of systems are familiar with a number of key technologies, including web services for back-end communication between business tiers and web applications for user interaction via a browser.

If you're reasonably familiar with Java, you know that a plethora of tools and technologies are available to help you build such applications. In fact, there are so many that it's impossible for us to cover all the possibilities in a single chapter. Instead, we'll pick a few of the more popular Java toolkits and show you how OSGi can improve on their design and usage. From here, you should be able to extend the general principles we cover to integrate OSGi with other toolkits of your choice.

To illustrate our points, we'll look at a number of simple examples before explaining how you can extend an existing stock-watcher web application from the Google Web Toolkit (GWT) tutorial to use OSGi. For the purposes of brevity, we'll focus on the aspects of these technologies that directly relate to OSGi and skip over (or even ignore) some of the more complex aspects of web development and distributed computing in general. Our goal is to show you how OSGi can work in a web context, not how to build and manage all aspects of web applications or services. Let's get started.

15.1 Creating web applications

We'll start our foray into web technologies by looking at web applications, before moving on to web services. Unless you've been living on the moon for the last decade, you must've had some exposure to web applications, whether as a user or as a developer. Web applications are a class of applications that present their user interface in a standard web browser such as Internet Explorer, Firefox, or Safari. They range from consumer shopping carts to online banking, from travel booking to social networking, from games to employment to government—the list is pretty much endless.

In this section, we'll look at using OSGi with the following web-application technologies:

- Static content
- Java Servlets
- JavaServer Pages (JSP)
- Google Web Toolkit (GWT)

Figure 15.1 provides a simple diagram of the components you'll build in this chapter. What benefits can OSGi bring to web-application development to cause you to break from the status quo? The major benefits are related to OSGi's different layers:

- The module layer provides an improved physical and logical structure, so web applications are easier to maintain and deploy.
- The lifecycle layer enables managing web-application installation and activation, to control what is available and when.
- The services layer supports a more loosely coupled application development approach, making it easy to swap in different implementations or even move those pieces to other machines to improve performance without changing a single line of client code.

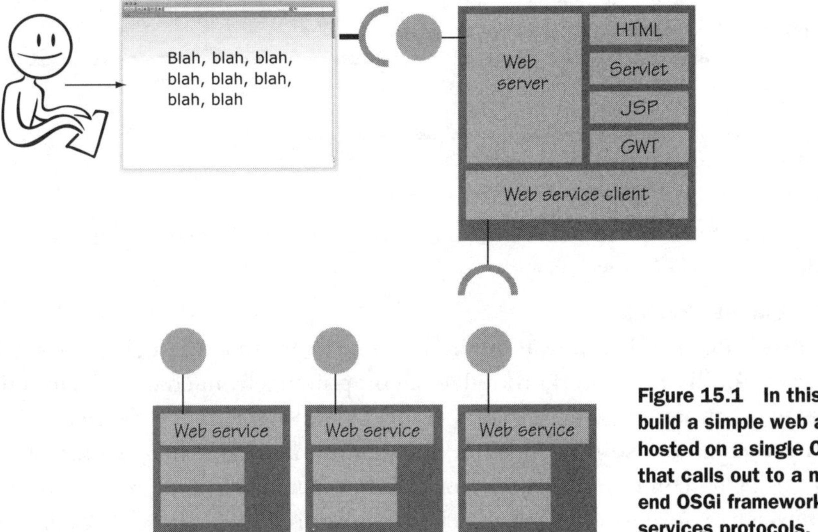

Figure 15.1 In this chapter you'll build a simple web application hosted on a single OSGi framework that calls out to a number of back-end OSGi frameworks using web-services protocols.

There are two main routes into the OSGi framework for web applications: the OSGi HTTP Service specification and the Web Applications specification. The HTTP Service specification is an OSGi Compendium specification. It enables programmatic registration of servlets and static resources. The Web Applications specification is one of the R4.2 Enterprise specifications and defines a web application bundle (WAB). A WAB is a special web archive (WAR) file that supplies OSGi metadata and relies on the OSGi framework's lifecycle layer to control when its resources are made available. We'll look at HTTP Service first.

15.1.1 Using the HTTP Service specification

If you're starting a web application from scratch, the simplest way of providing it in OSGi is to use the HTTP Service, which is represented by the `org.osgi.service.http.HttpService` interface. You find the HTTP Service like any other OSGi service, by looking in the service registry using the `BundleContext`:

```
String name = HttpService.class.getName();
ServiceReference ref = ctx.getServiceReference(name);
if (ref != null) {
  HttpService svc = (HttpService) ctx.getService(ref);
  if (svc != null) {
    // do something
  }
}
```

Having found the HTTP Service, what can you do with it? The `HttpService` interface provides methods to register and unregister static resources (for example, images or HTML pages) and Java servlets. The `HttpService` interface is defined as follows:

```
public interface HttpService {
  HttpContext createDefaultHttpContext();
  void registerResources(String alias, String name, HttpContext context);
  void registerServlet(
    String alias, Servlet servlet,
    Dictionary initparams, HttpContext context);
  void unregister(String alias)
}
```

Let's look at how you use this interface; you'll start with registering static resources and then move on to servlets.

REGISTERING RESOURCES

Let's dive into a web application by creating a bundle to register a set of static resources. You'll reuse your knowledge of components from chapter 12 to build a simple iPOJO component that registers resources with the HTTP Service. Listing 15.1 shows the complete source code for this component. You may wonder why you're using an iPOJO component instead of a simple `BundleActivator`. The reason is the complex startup-ordering issues associated with using multiple services, because your component uses the HTTP Service and the Log Service. You could do this without a component framework, but using one makes life simpler.

Listing 15.1 `ResourceBinder` component class

```
@Component
public class ResourceBinder {
  @Requires(optional=true)
  private LogService s_log;

  @Requires(id="http")
  private HttpService s_http;

  @Bind(id="http")
  protected void addHttpService(HttpService service) {
    register(service);
  }

  @Unbind(id="http")
  protected void removeHttpService(HttpService service) {
    unregister(service);
  }

  @Validate
  protected void start() {                                  <-┐
    register(s_http);                                         │
  }                                                           │ ❶ Responds to
                                                              │   lifecycle events
  @Invalidate                                                 │
  protected void stop() {                                   <-┘
    unregister(s_http);
  }                                                              ❷ Registers content
                                                                   from /html
  private void register(HttpService service) {            <-┘
    try {
      service.registerResources("/", "/html", null);
```

```
      service.registerResources("/images", "/images", null);
    } catch (NamespaceException e) {
      s_log.log(
        LogService.LOG_WARNING, "Failed to register static content", e);
    }
  }

  private void unregister(HttpService service) {
    service.unregister("/");
    service.unregister("/images");
  }
}
```

❸ **Unregisters content** (annotation on `unregister(HttpService service)`)

The iPOJO runtime automatically injects the Log Service into the `s_log` field and uses the `addHttpService()` and `removeHttpService()` methods to bind and unbind (respectively) the HTTP Service. The `ResourceBinder` component responds to lifecycle events ❶. The real work, for this example, is done when you register content from the /html directory within your bundle to the root context of the HTTP Service ❷. In other words, the file /html/index.html from within your bundle is served as /index.html from the HTTP Service. You unregister it when the service is removed or the component is deactivated ❸. What does the end result look like? Figure 15.2 shows the service- and bundle-level dependencies of the `ResourceBinder` component.

To see this example running, go into the chapter15/httpservice/ directory of the book's companion code. Type `ant` to build the example and `java -Dorg.osgi.service.http.port=8080 -jar launcher.jar bundles` to execute it. In addition to using iPOJO, this example uses the Apache Felix HTTP Service (http://felix.apache.org/site/apache-felix-http-service.html) and Apache Felix Log Service (http://felix.apache.org/site/apache-felix-log.html) implementations.

After launching the example, navigate to http://localhost:8080/index.html; you should see the web page shown in figure 15.3.

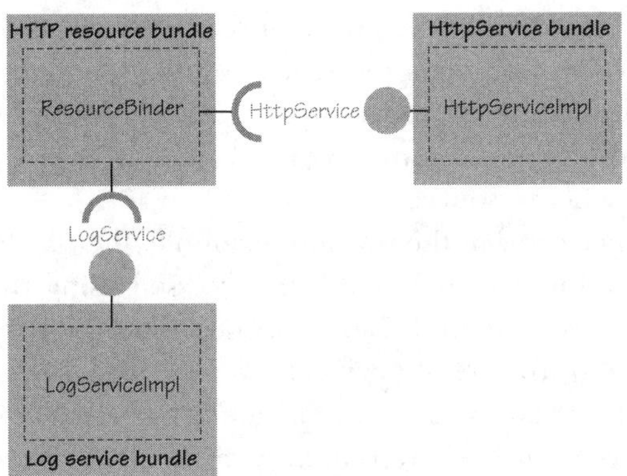

Figure 15.2 The `ResourceBinder` has a mandatory dependency on the HTTP Service for providing content and an optional dependency on the Log Service for logging errors.

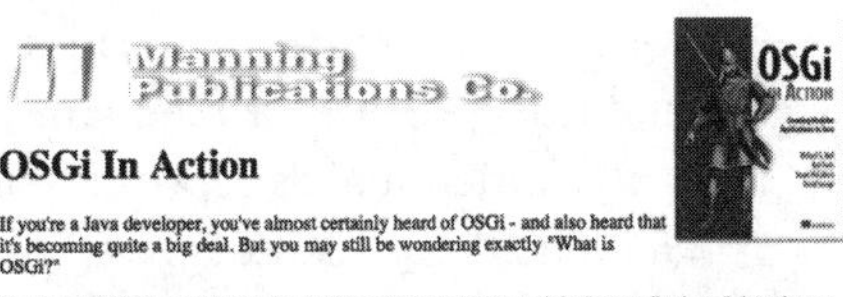

Figure 15.3 Static content served from the OSGi HTTP Service

> **Configuring the HTTP Service**
>
> The HTTP Service is registered by an implementation bundle. The client has no control over the port or URL on which the service is running. That's the job of the administrator of the OSGi framework. The HTTP Service specification defines framework properties to configure the service ports:
>
> - `org.osgi.service.http.port`—Specifies the port used for servlets and resources accessible via HTTP. The default value is 80.
> - `org.osgi.service.http.port.secure`—Specifies the port used for servlets and resources accessible via HTTPS. The default value is 443.
>
> You can set framework properties using the launching API covered in chapter 13. In this case, the launcher passes system properties through to the framework properties. It's also generally possible to configure the HTTP Service implementation using the Configuration Admin Service, but that is implementation-dependent.

SETTING THE HTTPCONTEXT

You may have noticed the `HttpContext` parameter in the `HttpService.registerResources()` method. In the previous example, you passed in `null`, but what does this parameter do? `HttpContext` provides a way to inject the HTTP Service with resource-lookup and -access policies. Let's first look at the API, followed by an example, to show what this allows you to do. The `HttpContext` interface is defined as follows:

```
public interface HttpContext {
  boolean handleSecurity(HttpServletRequest req, HttpServletResponse res)
    throws IOException;
  URL getResource(String name);
  String getMimeType(String path);
}
```

The `handleSecurity()` method provides a callback to allow the HTTP Service to verify whether a request should be allowed for a given resource. The `getResource()` method provides a mechanism to define how a particular resource is mapped to a URL, which makes it possible to host contents from any scheme accessible from URLs. Finally, the `getMimeType()` provides a mechanism to control the MIME type headers returned with the stream of a particular resource.

If you use `null` for the `HttpContext`, as in the previous example, the HTTP Service uses a default context implementation, which can also be accessed using the `HttpService.createDefaultHttpContext()` method. Table 15.1 describes the behavior of the default `HttpContext` as defined by the OSGi specification.

To demonstrate how to use the `HttpContext`, let's create a `ResourceTracker` to track bundles and automatically register their resources with the HTTP Service. To accomplish this, you'll use the `org.osgi.util.tracker.BundleTracker` introduced in the OSGi R4.2 Compendium specification. Listing 15.2 shows the body of the `addBundle()` method of the `BundleTracker` subclass.

Table 15.1 Default behavior of `HttpContext` implementations

Method	Behavior
handleSecurity()	Implementation-specific authentication, although all known open source implementations return `true`
getResource()	Maps requested resources to the content of the registering bundle
getMimeType()	Always returns `null`

OSGi R4.2 bundle tracker

The `BundleTracker` class provided by the OSGi R4.2 Compendium simplifies the task of tracking bundles much as `ServiceTracker` simplifies tracking services. As with `ServiceTracker`, which we introduced in chapter 4, `BundleTracker` supports a filter pattern based on bundle states and a customizer object to fine-tune which bundles are tracked and/or to create a customized object to track with the bundle.

Compared to the simple `BundleTracker` you created in chapter 3, the OSGi `BundleTracker` performs the same task, but does so in a more sophisticated way. In particular, it handles concurrency issues better and allows you to track bundles based on desired states, instead of just the `ACTIVE` state as the simple implementation did.

Listing 15.2 Tracking HTTP resources in `ResourceTracker`

```
@Override
public Object addingBundle(Bundle bundle, BundleEvent event) {
  ArrayList<String> aliases = new ArrayList<String>();

  String[] resources = findResources(bundle);        ❶ Checks whether bundle specifies resources

  if (resources != null) {
    HttpContext ctx = new ProxyHttpContext(bundle);

    for (String p : resources) {
      String[] split = p.split("\\s*=\\s*");
      String alias = split[0];
      String file = split.length == 1 ? split[0] : split[1];
      try {
        http.registerResources(alias, file, ctx);
        aliases.add(alias);
      } catch (NamespaceException e) {
        e.printStackTrace();
      }
    }
  }

  return aliases.isEmpty()
    ? null : aliases.toArray(new String[aliases.size()]);
}
```

In this example, you define an HTTP-Resources manifest header that bundles can use to specify resources they wish to register with the HTTP Service. You check whether a bundle specifies any resources in the HTTP-Resources header ❶. The format of this header is a comma-delimited list of directories that may optionally be aliased (you'll see this working in a second). If any resources are found, you create a ProxyHttpContext (shown in the following listing) and register the resources with the HttpService.

Listing 15.3 ProxyHttpContext for reading resources from a bundle

```
public class ProxyHttpContext implements HttpContext {

  private final Bundle bundle;

  public ProxyHttpContext(Bundle bundle) {
    this.bundle = bundle;
  }

  public URL getResource(String name) {
    return bundle.getResource(name);          <- ❶ Passes getResource() to tracked bundle
  }
...
}
```

If you used the default HttpContext, the HTTP Service would try to find the requested resources in your ResourceTracker bundle, which clearly isn't correct. ProxyHttpContext attempts to find the resources in the bundle you're tracking. You create a unique ProxyHttpContext for each tracked bundle. The key line of code in this class passes the getResource() call through to the tracked bundle ❶.

To demonstrate how to use the resource tracker, the org.foo.http.resource bundle in the chapter15/httpservice/ directory of the companion code contains the following header:

```
HTTP-Resources: /resource=html,/resource/images=images
```

If you deploy this bundle into an OSGi framework along with an HTTP Service and your ResourceTracker, then its resources are registered; you can browse them at http://localhost:8080/resource/index.html. This is just one trivial usage of the HttpContext object. Other possible scenarios might include the following:

- Managing authenticated access to web content
- Mapping local file system resources into the HTTP Service

Now that you're familiar with registering static resources with the HTTP Service, let's look at how it allows you to use servlets in an OSGi environment.

REGISTERING SERVLETS

Java servlets are the building block on which a vast number of web applications have been built. Some of the key advantages of the servlet specification are the relative simplicity of the API and the huge number of tools and frameworks available to help you develop web applications with it. Similar to static content, the HTTP Service provides a mechanism to dynamically register servlets using the following `HttpService` method:

```
void registerServlet(String alias, Servlet servlet,
  Dictionary initparams, HttpContext context);
```

In the example using static content with the HTTP Service, we showed how you can use the `registerResources()` method to dynamically register content. Can you do the same for servlets? Yes, you can. But because the `registerServlet()` method expects an instance of a servlet, instead of using the `BundleTracker`, you'll find servlets in the OSGi service registry and automatically register them with the HTTP Service.

The following listing shows a snippet from an iPOJO component that maps servlets registered in the service registry with a `Web-ContextPath` service property to any available `HttpServices`.

Listing 15.4 Binding servlets in the OSGi service registry using iPOJO

```
@Component(immediate=true)
public class ServletManager {

  @Requires(optional=true)
  private LogService log;

  private LinkedList<HttpService> services = new LinkedList<HttpService>();
  private Map<String, Servlet> servlets = new HashMap<String, Servlet>();

  @Bind(aggregate=true)
  void bindHttp(HttpService http) {
    Map<String, Servlet> snapshot;

    synchronized (servlets) {
      snapshot = new HashMap<String, Servlet>(servlets);
      services.add(http);
    }

    for (Map.Entry<String, Servlet> entry : snapshot.entrySet()) {
      String ctx = entry.getKey();
      Servlet s = entry.getValue();
      try {
        http.registerServlet(ctx, s, null, null);      ❶ Registers servlets
      } catch (ServletException e) {
        log.log(LogService.LOG_WARNING, "Failed to registerServlet", e);
      } catch (NamespaceException e) {
        log.log(LogService.LOG_WARNING, "Failed to registerServlet", e);
      }
    }
  }
```

In this example, you declare an optional service dependency on the `LogService` to allow you to inform the outside world of any exceptions. You synchronize on the current servlets to create a snapshot of them and to add the `HttpService` to the set of known services. Then you iterate over the current servlets and register them with the recently discovered `HttpService` ❶. Because this is a dynamic environment, you also need to consider the case where servlets come before or after an `HttpService`. Hence you need similar logic in the `bindServlet()` method, shown in the next code snippet.

Listing 15.5 Binding servlets in the OSGi service registry using iPOJO (continued)

```
@Bind(aggregate=true)
void bindServlet(Servlet servlet, Map attrs) {
  String ctx = (String) attrs.get("Web-ContextPath");       ❶ Reads web context path
  if (ctx != null) {
    LinkedList<HttpService> snapshot;

    synchronized (servlets) {          ❷ Stores servlet and snapshots available HTTP Services
      servlets.put(ctx, servlet);
      snapshot = new LinkedList<HttpService>(services);
    }

    for (HttpService s : snapshot) {        ❸ Registers servlet with available HTTP Services
      try {
        s.registerServlet(ctx, servlet, null, null);
      } catch (ServletException e) {
        log.log(LogService.LOG_WARNING, "Failed to registerServlet", e);
      } catch (NamespaceException e) {
        log.log(LogService.LOG_WARNING, "Failed to registerServlet", e);
      }
    }
  }
}
```

In this method, you read the `Web-ContextPath` from the service headers ❶. If this isn't `null`, you then snapshot the `HttpServices` and store the servlet using the same object lock as in listing 15.4—ensuring that you don't miss any services ❷. Finally, you iterate over the available `HttpServices` and register the new servlet ❸.

The final piece of the puzzle is the actual registration of a servlet. Here you create the trivial `HelloServlet` shown in the following listing, which prints a message in the web browser.

Listing 15.6 Binding servlets in the OSGi service registry using iPOJO (continued)

```
@Component(immediate = true)
@Provides(specifications = Servlet.class)
public class HelloServlet extends HttpServlet {
  @ServiceProperty(name = "Web-ContextPath")
  String ctx = "/hello";

  @Override
  protected void doGet(HttpServletRequest req, HttpServletResponse resp)
      throws IOException {
    ...
  }
}
```

You register this component using the `Servlet` interface and add the `Web-ContextPath` service property with iPOJO annotations.

To see this example in action, go into the chapter15/httpservice/ directory of the book's companion code; type `ant` to build it and `java -Dorg.osgi.service.http.port=8080 -jar launcher.jar bundles/` to launch it. Then browse to http://localhost:8080/hello with a web browser.

> **The relationship between the servlet and HTTP contexts**
>
> The HTTP Service specification specifies that only servlets registered with the same `HttpContext` object are part of the same `ServletContext`. The HTTP Service implementation creates a `ServletContext` for each unique `HttpContext` object that is registered. If `null` is passed in, the HTTP Service calls `createDefaultHttpContext()`, which puts the registered servlet in a separate `ServletContext`.

PAX WEB SUPPORT

Before leaving this section on the HTTP Service, we should also point out the support provided by the Pax Web project (http://wiki.ops4j.org/display/paxweb/Pax+Web). This project defines a `WebContainer` service interface that extends the standard OSGi `HttpService` interface. This new interface provides a number of extra methods to register other servlet-related services, including JSP, servlet filters, and servlet event listeners.

We won't cover Pax Web in depth, but we'll show you how to run a shopping cart example from another Manning publication, *Web Development with Java Server Pages, Second Edition* (Fields, Kolb, and Bayern, 2001), in an OSGi context. The following listing shows a Declarative Services component for registering JSPs when the `WebContainer` service is published in the OSGi service registry.

Listing 15.7 Binder to register JPS pages in the Pax Web `WebContainer`

```
public class Binder {
  private volatile HttpContext http;

  protected void bindWebContainer(WebContainer c) {
    http = c.createDefaultHttpContext();
    c.registerJsps(new String[] { "*.jsp" }, http);
  }

  protected void unbindWebContainer(WebContainer c) {
    c.unregisterJsps(http);
    http = null;
  }
}
```

This component registers all JSPs in the bundle under a shared `HttpContext` and unregisters the JSPs. The next listing shows the Declarative Services component description.

Listing 15.8 Declarative Services component definition for JSP binder

```
<?xml version="1.0" encoding="UTF-8"?>
<component name="sample.component" immediate="true">
  <implementation class="org.foo.webapp.jspapp.Binder" />
```

```
  <reference name="webcontainer"
        interface="org.ops4j.pax.web.service.WebContainer"
        cardinality="1..1"
        policy="static"
        bind="bindWebContainer"
        unbind="unbindWebContainer"
    />
</component>
```

You specify the component implementation class and declare the component as `immediate`, so an instance is created as soon as the component's dependencies are satisfied. Then you specify a one-to-one dependency on a `WebContainer` service, which you want injected into your component using the specified binding methods. We'll leave it as an exercise for you, but you can trivially extend this to use the `BundleTracker` approach from listing 15.2 to track JSP bundles centrally, rather than duplicating binding logic in different bundles.

To see this example running, go into the chapter15/pax-web/ directory of the book's companion code. Type `ant` to build the example and `java -jar launcher.jar bundles` to execute it. To see the shopping-cart application in action, go to http://localhost:8080/jsps/catalog.jsp. When you do, you should see a simple shopping cart page. Add a couple of items to the cart to verify that it works, as shown in figure 15.4.

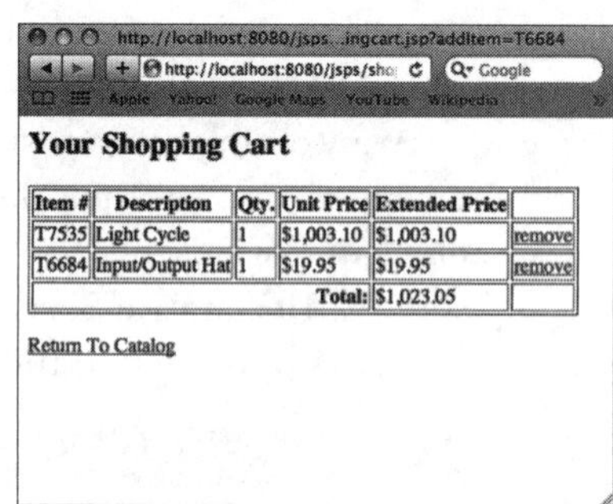

Figure 15.4 JSP shopping cart application running in an OSGi environment

We've shown you how to deploy a range of web-application technologies from static resources to servlets to JSPs using the HTTP Service or its extensions. This may leave you wondering, "What about my WAR files?" Good question. In the next section, we'll look at the standard way to deal with WAR files in OSGi.

15.1.2 Using the Web Applications specification

Since the Servlet 2.2 specification came out in August 1999, we've been packaging and deploying servlets, JSPs, and other web technologies in WAR files. WAR files provide a standard way to map a range of web technologies to a servlet-container context. Despite the widespread use of WAR files, until recently there was no standard way to use WAR files in an OSGi framework. Due to the increasing use of OSGi technology in the enterprise domain, member companies in the OSGi Alliance are now producing enterprise-related specifications.

The OSGi R4.2 Enterprise specification is the result of this effort. The Enterprise specification defines another set of compendium specifications specifically targeting enterprise technologies. One of these specifications is the Web Applications specification, which provides a standard way for servlet and JSP application components to execute within an OSGi framework by defining a web application bundle (WAB).

WAB is pretty much a standard WAR file that has been converted into a bundle. More specifically, it's a WAR file that adheres to the Servlet 2.5 and JSP 2.1 specifications and additionally declares its dependencies using the standard OSGi metadata. To demonstrate the process of creating a WAB, you'll take the stock-watcher application from the GWT tutorial and convert it to run in an OSGi context. You can use bnd to convert the WAR file generated by the GWT build into a bundle using the following Ant target:

```
<target name="osgi">
  <path id="bnd.class.path">
    <fileset dir="${root.dir}/lib" includes="osgi.*.jar"/>
    <fileset dir="build" includes="*.war"/>
  </path>
  <mkdir dir="../bundles" />
  <pathconvert pathsep=":" property="bnd.cp" refid="bnd.class.path"/>
  <bnd files="build.properties" classpath="${bnd.cp}" exceptions="true"/>
</target>
```

Bnd takes its configuration properties from the build.properties file in the same directory, which contains the following:

```
Bundle-SymbolicName: com.google.gwt.sample.stockwatcher
Bundle-ClassPath: WEB-INF/lib/gwt-servlet.jar,WEB-INF/classes
Include-Resource: war
Import-Package: \
  com.google.gwt.benchmarks;resolution:=optional,\
  junit.framework;resolution:=optional,\
  *
Web-ContextPath:  /stockwatcher/stockPrices
```

Most of these headers look similar to those introduced in chapter 2; if you aren't familiar with bnd syntax, refer to appendix A. Briefly, you first specify the bundle symbolic name for your WAB. Next, you set up the bundle class path to include the gwt-servlet.jar file, which is embedded in the WAR file, and the WEB-INF/classes directory, which contains the classes of your application. You embed the various resources used by this application, including JavaScript files and images. Then you specify two optional package imports that are only used in testing scenarios.

The only new header here is `Web-ContextPath`. It's used to identify the bundle as a WAB. The header is used by the *web container extender* bundle. This bundle is defined in the Web Application specification; it uses the extender pattern, which we discussed in chapter 3, to track bundles with the `Web-ContextPath` header and register the servlet resources specified in these WABs as a web application, similar to the previous examples in this chapter. The value of this header specifies the context root that the web container uses to register the web application. All web-accessible resources in the bundle are served up relative to this path.

Before we delve any further into the inner workings of WAB files, let's launch the GWT application to show it in action. Go into the chapter15/gwtapp/ directory of the book's companion code. Type `ant` to build the example and `java -jar launcher.jar bundles` to execute it. Browse to http://localhost:8080/stockwatcher/stockPrices/, which should look something like figure 15.5.

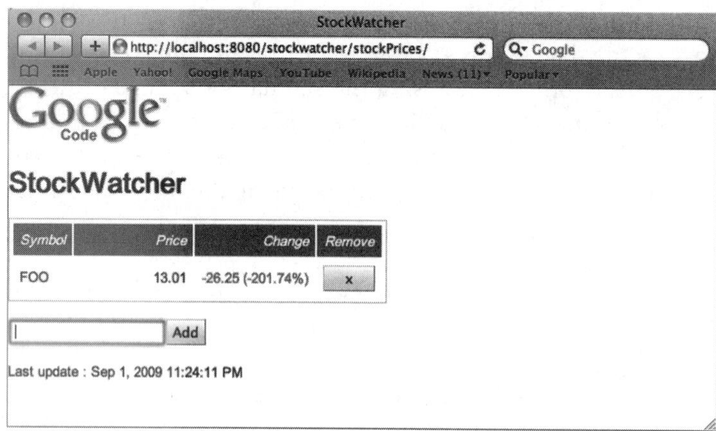

Figure 15.5 The Google stock-watcher application running in an OSGi context

The Web Applications specification allows you to take advantage of OSGi's module layer to share classes installed elsewhere in the OSGi framework, ensure that you have the correct dependencies installed, and enforce defined module boundaries. You can also use the lifecycle layer to allow dynamic installation, update, and removal of your web application.

Modularity improves memory consumption

In this trivial example, sharing classes offers relatively little value, because the stock watcher has few external dependencies. But consider the benefits of being able to share classes in a large web application environment. In standard WAR development, each application must embed its own set of dependencies in its WAR file under the WEB-INF/lib directory. For utility classes, such as collections libraries, XML parsers, and logging frameworks, this can mean a lot of duplicate classes get loaded into the VM for each WAR file installed in your application server. These classes can eat up memory. In an OSGi environment, you can move dependencies into separate bundles that are then shared among installed applications, reducing the overall memory footprint.

You've got modularity. You've got lifecycle. What about services? Yep, the example uses services too! The following listing shows how.

Listing 15.9 Accessing the `BundleContext` from within a servlet

```
public class StockPriceServiceImpl extends RemoteServiceServlet
  implements StockPriceService {

  private BundleContext ctx;

  @Override
  public void init() throws ServletException {
    ctx = (BundleContext) getServletContext()
      .getAttribute("osgi-bundlecontext");
```

```
  }

  @Override
  public void destroy() {
    ctx = null;
  }
}
```

Here you extend `com.google.gwt.user.server.rpc.RemoteServiceServlet` with your own implementation class. Although the details of GWT aren't important for this example, note that you override the `init()` and `destroy()` methods of `javax.servlet.GenericServlet`. You grab a reference to the `BundleContext` from an attribute on the `javax.servlet.ServletContext`. Having cached a reference to the `BundleContext`, you can use it to discover other services in the framework.

EXTENDING THE GWT SAMPLE WEB APPLICATION FOR OSGI

To demonstrate how you can use services in a WAB context, you can make a minor change to the sample GWT application to discover a trivial `StockProvider` service from the OSGi registry using the following interface:

```
public interface StockProvider {
  Map<String, Double> getStocks(String[] symbols);
}
```

This service returns a `Map` of stock prices for the given symbols. In the `StockPriceServiceImpl.getPrices()` method, you look up a `StockProvider` service and use it to get stock prices as shown in the next listing.

Listing 15.10 Reading stock prices from the `StockProvider` service

```
public StockPrice[] getPrices(String[] symbols)
  throws DelistedException, ServiceUnavailableException {
  StockPrice[] prices = null;

  StockProvider provider = (StockProvider) tracker.getService();
  if (provider != null) {
    prices = readPrices(provider, symbols);
  } else {
    throw new ServiceUnavailableException();
  }

  return prices;
}
```

You see whether a `StockProvider` service is registered using a `ServiceTracker`. If one is available, you use it to read prices for the specified symbols or throw a checked exception to indicate that an error message should be displayed to the user.

You've now taken an existing servlet application and deployed it to an OSGi environment using the WAB format. You've also extended this application to discover services from the OSGi registry. As it stands, this is a trivial example; but you'll see in the next section how to extend the example further by using the service abstraction to allow your application to be divided into a multiprocess application. First, we'll briefly cover one remaining area of interest: how to support standard WAR files in OSGi.

> **OSGi and JNDI**
>
> Retrieving the OSGi bundle context from the `ServletContext` is the most direct way to interact with the OSGi environment. Many existing servlets use JNDI to discover Java EE services—wouldn't it be great if a bridge existed between these two worlds? Such a bridge does exist in the R4.2 Enterprise specification, so rest assured that you can use this mechanism to access services. The technical details of how this interaction works are beyond the scope of this book; refer to the specification for more information (www.osgi.org/Download/Release4V42).

15.1.3 Standard WARs: the Web URL Handler

As a convenience for users who wish to migrate web applications to OSGi but don't wish to undertake the effort of converting a WAR file to a WAB, the Web Applications specification provides a utility mechanism to convert a WAR file to a WAB at execution time: the Web URL Handler. It uses the OSGi URL Handlers Service to turn WARs into WABs.

> **URL Handlers Service specification**
>
> The OSGi URL Handlers Service specification provides a service-based approach for bundles to offer custom stream and content handlers associated with URLs. The normal approach for dealing with stream and content handlers in Java is to set a `URLStreamHandlerFactory` and/or a `ContentHandlerFactory` on `URL` and `URLConnection`, respectively. Unfortunately, these are singletons, so they can't be shared and they aren't dynamic. The URL Handlers specification addresses both of these issues.
>
> The URL Handlers Service works by setting the `URLStreamHandlerFactory` and `ContentHandlerFactory` objects once; it then uses the whiteboard pattern to discover services offered by bundles implementing custom stream and content handlers. When the URL Handlers service receives a request for a specific protocol or content type, it delegates the request to the appropriate underlying service to perform the processing.

To use the Web URL Handler, all you need to do is prefix any existing URL pointing to a WAR file with the `webbundle` protocol when installing the WAR file into the framework. For example, you could use your shell's install command like this:

```
install webbundle:http://www.acme.com/acme.war?Bundle-SymoblicName=
     com.example&Web-ContextPath=acme
```

The Web URL Handler converts the referenced WAR file into a WAB on the fly prior to the OSGi framework installing. The Web URL Handler makes a best-effort attempt to convert a WAR to a WAB, but in certain circumstances you may have to give it extra hints to help the process go smoothly. In this example above, you specify a `Bundle-SymbolicName` as a parameter in the query portion of the URL. The Web URL Handler also supports a number of other parameters that affect the outcome of the conversion; these parameters are listed in table 15.2.

Table 15.2 Parameters supported by the Web URL Handler

Parameter	Description
`Bundle-SymbolicName`	Desired symbolic name for the resulting WAB.
`Bundle-Version`	Version of the resulting WAB. The value of this parameter must follow OSGi versioning syntax.
`Bundle-ManifestVersion`	Desired bundle manifest version. Currently, the only valid value for this parameter is `2`.
`Import-Package`	List of packages on which the WAR file depends.
`Web-ContextPath`	Context path from which the servlet container should serve content from the resulting WAB. If the input JAR is already a WAB, this parameter is optional but may be used to override the context path. Otherwise, it must be specified.

In the first half of this chapter, we've looked at a range of web-application technologies and shown how they can be integrated with OSGi. We've highlighted a number of themes:

- Using the HTTP Service to provide static and dynamic content
- The benefits modularity brings at execution time due to improved memory consumption from the use of shared classes
- Flexible collaboration between functional units due to the use of service patterns
- Converting WAR-style applications to WABs using OSGi R4.2 Enterprise features

In the second half of this chapter, we'll turn our attention to making OSGi services available across process boundaries—that is, how to build distributed OSGi applications.

15.2 Providing and consuming web services

Until this point in the book, all your applications have resided in a single JVM process; but this is rarely the case for web-based applications. The entire ethos of internet-based development is predicated on distributed processes communicating over network protocols. You saw how to do this at a low level in chapter 3, where you built a simple telnet implementation. But this is the early twenty-first century, and the zeitgeist for distributed computing today is web services. In this section, we'll investigate OSGi-based technologies for communicating between JVM processes using web-service protocols.

Obviously, we'll only be able to scratch the surface of distributed computing, because the topic is too large and complex to cover in a single section of a chapter. Instead of going into a lot of detail about specific web-service protocols or technologies, we'll introduce you to some of the key features of the Remote Services specification, which is another specification in the OSGi R4.2 Enterprise specification.

The Remote Services specification and its sibling specifications, Remote Services Admin and SCA Configuration Type, provide a comprehensive model for building distributed computer systems in OSGi. Their key purpose is to provide a common model

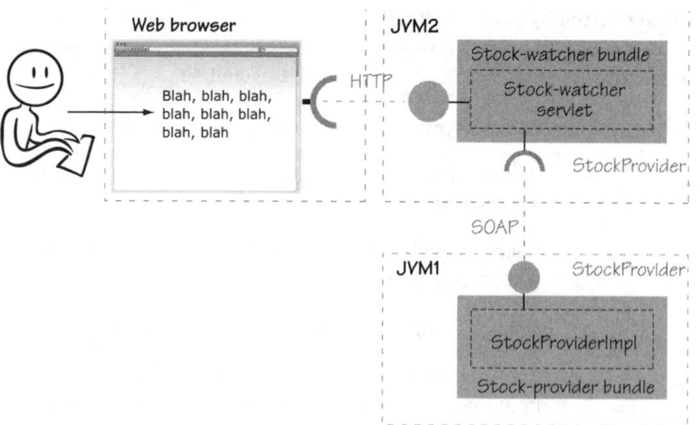

Figure 15.6 The Google stock-watcher application running in an OSGi context

to import remote services (provided over any protocol, such as SOAP, RMI, or JMS) into the OSGi service registry and symmetrically export services from the OSGi service registry so they can be accessed by other processes external to the JVM.

To see how this works in practice, let's look at the stock-watcher application you built in the last section. It has a three-tier architecture, consisting of a web browser connected to a back-end servlet engine that talks to an in-process `StockProvider` service. A logical step in this section of the book is to split the `StockProvider` service into a separate JVM process and communicate with it using an over-the-wire protocol, such as SOAP. The new architecture is shown in figure 15.6. Let's look into how you can realize this design using the Remote Services specification.

15.2.1 Providing a web service

The first step in making a distributed OSGi application is to create the remote implementation of the `StockProvider` service. To do this, create the `BundleActivator` shown in the following listing.

Listing 15.11 Reading stock prices from the `StockProvider` service

```
public class Activator implements BundleActivator {

  public void start(BundleContext ctx) throws Exception {
    Dictionary props = new Hashtable();

    props.put("service.exported.interfaces", "*");
    props.put("service.exported.intents", "SOAP");
    props.put("service.exported.configs", "org.apache.cxf.ws");
    props.put("org.apache.cxf.ws.address",
      "http://localhost:9090/stockprovider");

    ctx.registerService(StockProvider.class.getName(),
      new StockProviderImpl(), props);
  }

  public void stop(BundleContext ctx) throws Exception {
  }
}
```

As you can see, this is a fairly typical `BundleActivator`. You're basically registering a service with a set of properties. You may be asking yourself, "Where is the remote communication?" That's the cool thing about the Remote Services specification: it shields you from those messy details. The specification defines a set of service properties you can attach to your services to indicate that they should be made available remotely. The actual remote communication is handled by another bundle or set of bundles; these types of bundles are classified as *distribution provider* bundles.

The key service property in listing 15.11 is `service.exported.interfaces`, which tells any distribution providers that you intend for your service to be made available remotely. The value `*` indicates that all interfaces specified when registering the service should be exported remotely. You can also change this to a `String` array to specify a specific set of interfaces.

> **NOTE** This opt-in approach is reasonable, because not all services make sense in a remote context. For example, consider the whiteboard pattern for servlets that we provided earlier, in section 15.1.1. It makes little sense to register a Java5 servlet interface remotely, because it's entirely an in-memory API.

The rest of the attributes specify either intents or configuration for the distribution provider, which it uses to decide how to publish the remote service. We'll look at intents and configuration in more detail a little later; for now, you can probably intuitively guess that you're requesting that your service be exposed using a SOAP interface from the specified URL.

To create a remote service, you need to select a distribution provider. For this example, we've chosen to use the Apache CXF Distributed OSGi implementation (http://cxf.apache.org/distributed-osgi.html), which is a Remote Services distribution provider built on top of Apache CXF. To run your remote service, go into the chapter15/webservice/ directory of the book's companion code. Type `ant` to build the example and `java -jar launcher.jar bundles/` to run it. You can test your intuition by visiting http://localhost:9090/stockprovider?wsdl in a web browser. You should see something like the following (truncated):

```
<wsdl:definitions name="StockProvider"
 targetNamespace="http://stockprovider.foo.org/">
  <wsdl:types>
    <xsd:schema attributeFormDefault="qualified"
     elementFormDefault="qualified"
     targetNamespace="http://stockprovider.foo.org/">
      <xsd:complexType name="string2doubleMap">
        <xsd:sequence>
          <xsd:element maxOccurs="unbounded" minOccurs="0" name="entry">
```

That's all there is to it! By deploying the `StockProvider` bundle into an OSGi framework along with a distribution provider, you're able to make it available remotely. Pretty neat. Before we move on to the client side of the example, let's look a little more at intents and configuration.

UNDERSTANDING INTENTS AND CONFIGURATION

To understand intents and configuration it's useful to consider the actual mechanics of how OSGi distribution providers publish a service remotely. This process follows the classic whiteboard pattern, where the distribution provider waits around listening for services to be registered with the `service.exported.interfaces` service property. This is the cue for it to make the corresponding service available remotely.

Given no other information, a distribution provider can pick any number of ways to make the service available remotely. It can use various protocols (SOAP, REST, RMI, and so on). It can use a range of different security or authentication mechanisms (such as SSL, DSA, Blowfish, LDAP, or Kerberos). There are even many different transport technologies (HTTP, JMS, Unicast, Multicast, and P2P). This dilemma is shown in figure 15.7.

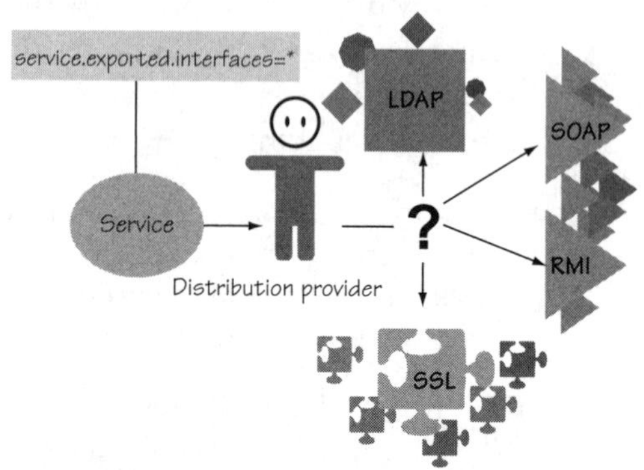

Figure 15.7 When making remote services available, the number of options is bewildering: protocols, transports, authentication schemes, and encryption algorithms all play their part.

There's no single best choice for any of these options. When you're building distributed applications, as with most applications, one size doesn't fit all. Different techniques are appropriate in different scenarios. Having said that, it doesn't make sense for business-level services to specify the minute details of how they should be made available remotely. Coming back full circle to the theme from chapter 2, this is another area where separation of concerns is applicable.

Intents and configurations provide a layer of indirection between the service provider and the distribution provider. They allow the service provider to specify just enough information to ensure that the service behaves as expected, yet still allow the distribution provider to optimize communications for the environment in which they're deployed. Now that you understand what intents and configuration are in the abstract, let's look at them in concrete terms.

INTENTS

Intents are a pattern borrowed from the Service Component Architecture (SCA) specification. An *intent* is a string value with agreed-on distribution-level semantics. To make this concept less abstract, let's look at an example of an intent you might attach to a registered service:

```
props.put("service.exported.intents",
  new String[] { "propagatesTransaction", "authentication" });
```

In this case, you're communicating two different intents to the distribution provider. The first, `propagatesTransaction`, says the service should be made available in such a way that transactional boundaries are transmitted to the service. The second, `authentication`, says the client application should be authenticated prior to using the service.

The precise details of how these intents are accomplished is left up to the distribution provider.

> **Qualified intents**
>
> Intent values are hierarchical. This is expressed by delimiting the intent value with the . character. For example, `authentication.transport` indicates that the service should use transport-level authentication. The practical upshot is that a service specifying `authentication` as an intent may be implemented by a provider that provides `authentication.transport`. But a service specifying `authentication.transport` may not be implemented by a provider only providing `authentication`.

Because the meaning of the intents is well-known, a distribution provider can make its best attempt at how to achieve them in its underlying implementation. This aids in decoupling distributed applications, because you can specify the qualities of the desired remote communication without tying yourself to a particular distribution technology. If you move your application to a different environment, a different distribution provider may make equally valid but potentially different choices. The SCA specification defines many intent values, but the precise details are beyond the scope of this book—for more information on SCA, visit the OSOA consortium website (www.osoa.org).

A service provider specifies intents, and the distribution provider realizes them. Is this the end of the story? Not exactly. The distribution provider must honor the requirements of the service provider, but it's free to add any behaviors it feels are appropriate. These may include default communication protocols, authentication schemes, and buffering strategies, as shown in figure 15.8.

In summary, intents provide a distribution provider with some flexibility when it comes to deciding how to distribute a service. Sometimes, though, you know exactly how you want your service to be made available remotely. In these situations, you need a mechanism to give specific instructions to the distribution provider. This leads us to Remote Services configuration properties.

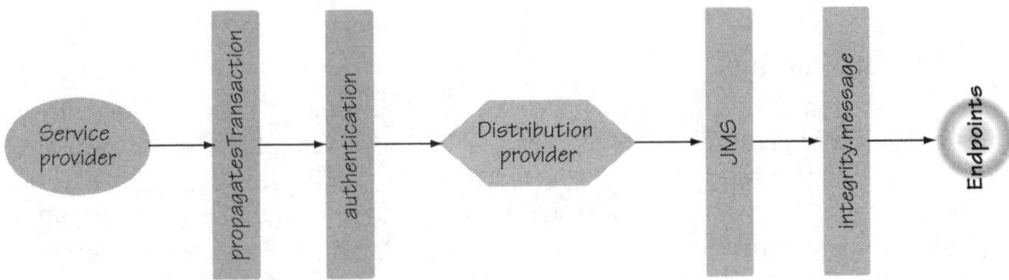

Figure 15.8 Service providers and distribution providers can each define intents that are applied to a service endpoint.

CONFIGURATION

Configuration properties provide a mechanism for the service provider to communicate explicit settings to the distribution provider. Given the range of possible configuration schemes, the Remote Services specification defines a mechanism for how the configuration is encoded. In the earlier example, you added the following property to the service:

```
props.put("service.exported.configs","org.apache.cxf.ws");
```

This specifies that the configuration properties follow the CXF web-services configuration scheme or configuration type. Note that this doesn't mean that only CXF can be used to distribute the service; it means the semantics of the configuration properties are defined by CXF. The Remote Services specification suggests a naming convention for configuration properties, which is the configuration type followed by `.` and a key. In the example, you specified a single configuration property:

```
props.put(
  "org.apache.cxf.ws.address","http://localhost:9090/stockprovider");
```

Here, the configuration type is `org.apache.cxf.ws` and the key is `address`. It's possible to use a number of different configuration types, in which case you may see something like this:

```
props.put("service.exported.configs", new String[]{"foo","bar"});
props.put("foo.key1","value1");
props.put("foo.key2","value2");
props.put("bar.key1","value3");
props.put("bar.key2","value4");
```

The idea behind using configuration properties from multiple configuration types is to make your service's configuration more broadly applicable. Clearly, the Apache CXF distribution provider understands the `org.apache.cxf.ws` configuration type. Some other distribution providers may understand it too, but not all of them will. By using additional configuration types, you make your service's configuration understandable to a wider range of distribution providers.

This concludes our overview of intents and configurations. They provide an extensible and flexible mechanism for service providers to specify to distribution providers

> **SCA configuration**
>
> For interoperability purposes, the OSGi R4.2 Enterprise specification introduces a standard configuration type based on the SCA XML format. This configuration format uses the configuration type `org.osgi.sca` and defines a single configuration attribute `org.osgi.sca.bindings` which points to a named service definition. This forms a recommended approach for different distribution providers to share configuration data in a vendor-neutral format. A full description of this functionality is outside the scope of this book, but you can refer to the OSGi Enterprise specification for more information (www.osgi.org/Download/Release4V42).

how services should behave in a distributed environment. In general, intents and configuration should be kept to a minimum to allow distribution-provider flexibility. Let's now turn our attention to the other side of the equation: client-side distributed services.

15.2.2 Consuming a web service

Returning to the stock-watcher example, what do you need to do it to make it use the remote `StockProvider` service? Currently, it looks for the `StockProvider` service in the OSGi service registry; what needs to change? With respect to your application, nothing at all.

Because your client bundle runs in a separate JVM, all you need to do is install a distribution provider into the client-side OSGi framework and configure it to discover the distributed `StockProvider` service. The distribution provider will automatically create a proxy of the remote service and inject it into the local service registry, which the stock-watcher application will discover and use as normal. This scenario is shown in figure 15.9.

If you're familiar with technologies such as Zeroconf, SSDP, UDDI, and Jini, you're acquainted with the concept of *discovery*. Even if you aren't familiar with these technologies, it should be relatively intuitive that discovery is a pattern used in distributed computing to allow a service provider to announce the presence of a service and for a consumer to find it. Often, this is achieved using a central registry or peer-to-peer mechanism, such as multicast TCP or multicast DNS. With such approaches, services are discovered as needed by client applications. The Remote Services specification provides an extensible pattern for implementing service discovery, which we'll cover in more depth in the next section. For now, we'll look at what you need to do to configure your distribution provider to discover the remote `StockProvider` service.

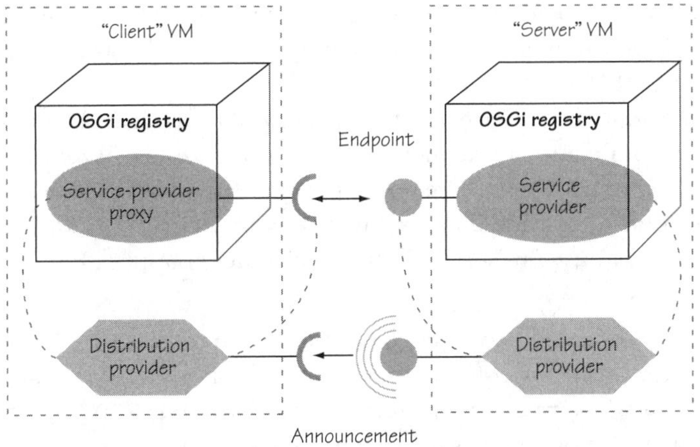

Figure 15.9 The distribution provider bundle creates a remote endpoint for the service provider. It may also announce the location and type of this endpoint for other distribution provider bundles to find. The client-side distribution provider discovers remote endpoints and creates proxies to these services, which it injects into the local OSGi service registry.

CONFIGURING THE DISTRIBUTION PROVIDER FOR DISCOVERY

The Remote Services specification doesn't explicitly define how discovery is implemented, only how it should behave. The Apache CXF Distributed OSGi implementation provides discovery based on the Apache Hadoop Zookeeper project (http://hadoop.apache.org/zookeeper/), but its usage is beyond the scope of this book. Luckily, Apache CXF Distributed OSGi also provides a static version of discovery based on the Remote Services Admin Endpoint description from the R4.2 Enterprise specification. With this approach, the discovery process is directed by XML files contained in bundles installed in the framework. The following listing shows the XML that describes the `StockProvider` service, which is nearly identical to the configuration for publishing the service.

Listing 15.12 XML discovery file for the `StockProvider` service for Apache CXF

```
<service-descriptions xmlns="http://www.osgi.org/xmlns/sd/v1.0.0">
  <service-description>
    <provide interface="org.foo.stockprovider.StockProvider" />     ❶ Defines provided service interface
    <property name="service.exported.interfaces">*</property>
    <property name="service.exported.configs">                      ❷ Specifies configuration information
      org.apache.cxf.ws
    </property>
    <property name="org.apache.cxf.ws.address">
      http://localhost:9090/stockprovider
    </property>
  </service-description>
</service-descriptions>
```

For this example, package this file in OSGI-INF/remote-service/remote-services.xml of a new bundle called stockprovider-client-1.0.jar. You define the interface that the discovered service will provide ❶. Then you provide the configuration entries needed by the distribution provider to bind to the remote service into the OSGi service registry ❷. In this example, this new bundle is purely for configuring the discovery process, so it only contains this XML file.

That's all there is to it. The service is automatically published into the OSGi service registry; you can look it up and invoke methods on it, which results in remote method invocations being sent using SOAP to the server proxy created in the remote JVM.

You now know how to provide and consume remote services. Let's wrap up this example by seeing how to use this service in the stock-watcher application.

USING YOUR WEB SERVICE

It's time to see the updated stock-watcher application in action. Go into the chapter15/webservice/ directory of the book's companion code. Type `ant` to build the example and `java -Dorg.osgi.service.http.port=8081 -jar launcher.jar bundles/` to execute it. Doing so starts the remote `StockProvider` service.

Now you need to start the stock-watcher application. In a separate command shell, go into the chapter15/webservice-client/ directory of the companion code. Type `ant` to build the application and `java -jar launcher.jar bundles/` to start it. Browse to http://localhost:8080/stockwatcher/stockPrices/, and enter the stock name foo. You should see results appear in the browser and in the output of the first console, as follows:

```
Retrieved {FOO=4.736842484258008}
Retrieved {FOO=48.88924250369791}
Retrieved {FOO=22.847587831790904}
```

This output shows that the method invocation of the local StockProvider service is being sent across the wire from the stock-watcher JVM using SOAP to the stock-provider JVM. Very cool!

Dealing with failure

One thing that should be obvious to experienced developers of distributed software is that remote services are unreliable. In RMI, for example, this unreliability is dealt with by using java.rmi.RemoteException, which is a checked exception to inform the client when things go wrong during attempts to communicate with a remote service. In OSGi, the equivalent exception is osgi.framework.ServiceException, but in this case it's an unchecked exception. Regardless, you should expect these types of exceptions to occur when dealing with a remote service.

As you can see, it's fairly straightforward to configure a distribution provider to import a remote service for use locally. In the example, the client isn't particularly picky about which StockProvider service it uses: it takes whichever one is available in the service registry. The Remote Services specification allows the consumer to be more selective; we'll conclude this section by looking into how it does so.

MATCHMAKING SERVICES

Earlier, we covered how the service provider uses intents and configuration to have control over how its service is exposed remotely. In a symmetric fashion, clients often need to use services with specific characteristics. For example, a medical insurance web application may require encrypted communications to ensure patient confidentiality, or a financial trading application may require a certain protocol to communicate between services for performance or regulatory reasons. Using the OSGi service registry's query mechanism, clients can select services using filters over the intents and configurations specified on published services.

Let's consider the simplest case of differentiating between local and remote services. In this case, the Remote Services specification requires distribution providers to automatically add a service.imported service property to imported remote services. If you explicitly want to bind to only a remote service, you can use a filter like the following:

```
ServiceReference ref =
  context.getServiceReferences(
    MyService.class.getName(),"(service.imported=*)")
```

Alternatively, if you explicitly want to bind to only a local service, you use a filter like the following:

```
ServiceReference ref =
  context.getServiceReferences(
    MyService.class.getName(),"(!(service.imported=*))")
```

Now, let's consider the more complex case of matching remote-service qualities. You saw earlier that a service provider can specify various intents (`propagatesTransaction`, `authentication`, and so on) when publishing its service. We also mentioned that a distribution provider can augment this set. The Remote Services specification requires distribution providers to automatically add a `service.intents` service property to imported remote services, which contains the union of the service provider and distribution provider intents. Therefore, if you want a service that propagates transactions and uses encryption, you can use a filter like the following:

```
ServiceReference ref =
  context.getServiceReferences(
    MyService.class.getName(),
    "(&(service.intents=propagatesTransaction)
      (service.intents=confidentiality))")
```

Matching qualified intents and configurations

One slightly thorny area surrounds the matching of qualified intents where, for example, the client requires `service.intents=confidentiality`, but a service provides `service.intents=confidentiality.message`. These two intents should match because the client doesn't care how the confidentiality is achieved, but a pure LDAP filter match would fail. To work around such issues, the Remote Services specification requires distribution providers to expand all implied qualified intents on services so LDAP queries function intuitively. For example, `service.intents=confidentiality.message` becomes `service.intents="confidentiality,confidentiality.message"`.

We've looked at how the Remote Services distribution provider makes it easy to publish and consume remote services within an OSGi-based environment. What if you're coming at this from the other side? What if you're a distributed software developer and want to import/export services from/to the OSGi service registry using your own distribution technology of choice? In that case, you'll need to implement your own distribution provider. We'll briefly look into doing this next.

15.2.3 Distributing services

In this section, we'll lead you through a short example showing how you can implement a trivial distribution-provider framework. The goal isn't to create something particularly useful, but to show the underlying mechanics at play.

For the purposes of this example, you'll create a simple `RemoteRegistry` interface to abstract away the details of dealing with remote services. You'll first see how you can export local OSGi services into your remote registry; then you'll see how to import remote services into the local OSGi service registry. Figure 15.10 provides a view of the classes involved in this example.

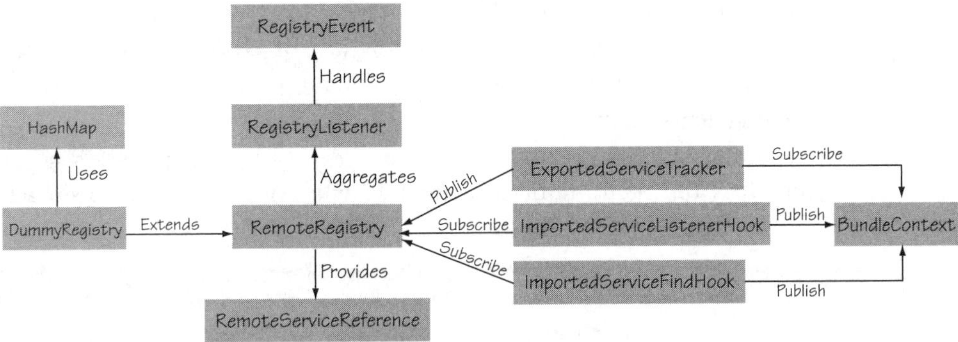

Figure 15.10 Simple registry scheme that abstracts mechanism of service discovery

> **Remote Services Admin**
> If you're interested in building this sort of technology, we advise you to look at the Remote Services Admin chapter of the OSGi R4.2 Enterprise specification. It provides a more complete model for building pluggable discovery and transport schemes, but it goes beyond the scope of this book.

During this example, we'll focus on the following classes:

- `ExportedServiceTracker`
- `ImportedServiceListenerHook`
- `ImportedServiceFindHook`

But before we get there, let's look briefly at the other classes in this diagram. The `RemoteRegistry` interface provides a simple lookup and listener scheme similar to those of the OSGi service registry. The `RegistryListener` interface receives notifications of `RegistryEvents`, which contain details of added or removed `RemoteServiceReferences`.

For the purposes of providing a concrete implementation of this API, you'll implement a `DummyRegistry` that performs no remote communication at all; instead, it tracks the available remote services using a `java.util.HashMap`.

> **Hash map?**
> You may think we're cheating a little by using a `HashMap` in this example—and we are. But this `HashMap`-based approach demonstrates all the key functionality of implementing a Remote Services distribution provider, which involves dealing with an externally managed service registry. By necessity, we must ignore the complex issues in the area of distributed computing, such as network-discovery protocols, remote procedure calls, and object marshaling. These are all important topics, but they're beyond the scope of this book. We leave you as architects or developers with the task of choosing your favorite distributed technologies if you wish to implement a real remote registry.

Having described the general registry architecture, let's look more closely at the ExportedServiceTracker, which handles the task of exporting local services with the service.exported.interfaces service property into the remote registry.

EXPORTEDSERVICETRACKER

The ExportedServiceTracker class extends the ServiceTracker class you met in chapter 4. As the name implies, it tracks any services that have been marked for export. Here's how you do this.

Listing 15.13 Constructing an exported service tracker

```
public ExportedServiceTracker(BundleContext ctx, Registry registry,
  String[] intents, String[] configs) {
  super(ctx, createFilter(ctx), null);
  this.ctx = ctx;
  this.registry = registry;
  this.intents = intents == null ? new String[0] : intents;
  this.configs = configs == null ? new String[0] : configs;
}

private static Filter createFilter(BundleContext ctx) {
  try {
    return ctx.createFilter("(service.exported.interfaces=*)");
  } catch (InvalidSyntaxException e) {
    throw new IllegalStateException(e);
  }
}
```

You call the ServiceTracker constructor, passing in an LDAP filter that you create to match all services with a service.exported.interfaces attribute of any value; the * is interpreted by the LDAP syntax to be a wildcard that matches any value. Then you store the intents and configurations supported by your remote registry. You'll see a little later how these are derived; for now, let's look at the overridden addingService() method in the next listing.

Listing 15.14 Dealing with new exported services

```
@Override
public Object addingService(ServiceReference ref) {
  Object svc = super.addingService(ref);

  if (isValidService(ref)) {
    String[] ifaces = findExportedInterfaces(ref);
    for (String iface : ifaces) {
      registry.registerService(ref, iface, svc);
    }
  }

  return svc;
}
```

This method is called by the ServiceTracker super-class whenever a service published in the OSGi service registry matches the filter specified in listing 15.13. In this method, you first get a reference to the matching service by calling the addingService()

method of the `ServiceTracker` super class. You check whether the service's intents match the supported intents and configurations passed into the constructor. If so, you determine the set of interfaces by which the service should be exported. Finally, the service is exported to your remote registry.

> **NOTE** This example exports the service multiple times for each desired interface. In a real-world scenario, it might be more appropriate to register the service once with multiple interfaces. The approach used in this book is for conceptual simplicity only.

The next listing shows how to check whether a matching service is supported by the registry. The process compares the matching intents and configurations with the ones supplied to your `ExportedServiceTracker`'s constructor.

Listing 15.15 Checking if a service matches supported intents and configurations

```
private boolean isValidService(ServiceReference ref) {
  List<String> list = readIntents(ref);
  list.removeAll(Arrays.asList(intents));
  if (list.isEmpty()) {
    list = readConfigs(ref);
    list.removeAll(Arrays.asList(configs));
    return list.isEmpty();
  }
  else {
    return false;
  }
}
```

This code reads the intent and configuration values from the matching service's service properties. You then use `String.equals()` via `List.removeAll()` to verify that the service doesn't export any intents and configurations your remote registry doesn't support, respectively.

> **NOTE** The `isValidService()` method is a naïve implementation for checking whether a given service matches your remote registry's supplied intents and configurations. It's naïve because it doesn't take into account the qualified naming convention mentioned in section 15.2.1. A proper implementation needs to do this, but the logic to achieve it is too long to list here and doesn't add much to the discussion. We'll neatly skip over it and leave it as an exercise for you.

You now need to find out the interfaces that matching services wish to export remotely. The following listing shows how to find these interfaces. The method `findExportedInterfaces()` returns a `String[]` containing the interface names or `null` if the service isn't exported.

Listing 15.16 Checking the exported interfaces of a service

```
private String[] findExportedInterfaces(ServiceReference ref) {
  Object ifaces = ref.getProperty("service.exported.interfaces");
  if (ifaces == null) {
```

```
      return null;
    }
    else {
      String[] strs = PropertyUtil.toStringArray(ifaces);
      if (strs.length == 1 && "*".equals(strs[0])) {
        ifaces = ref.getProperty(Constants.OBJECTCLASS);
        strs = PropertyUtil.toStringArray(ifaces);
      }
      return strs;
    }
  }
```

You first look for the appropriate service property indicating whether the service is to be exported. If it is, you use a utility class to return the interfaces. Then you check to see whether the name of the exported interface is `*`. If it is, you get the interfaces from the standard OSGi `objectClass` service property, which lists all the registered service interfaces of the service object.

You also need to override the `ServiceTracker` methods for handling when matching services are modified or removed, but we'll skip describing these in detail because they're fairly similar to adding services. If you're curious, you can look at the companion code in chapter15/webservice-impl/org.foo.dosgi.

Let's turn our attention away from exporting local services to a remote registry and toward importing remote services into the local OSGi service registry. To facilitate this, the OSGi R4.2 core specification introduced a way to hook into the OSGi service registry using two new service interfaces:

- `org.osgi.framework.hooks.service.FindHook`
- `org.osgi.framework.hooks.service.ListenerHook`

To save ourselves from repeating boilerplate code in the following examples, you define a `RegistryWatcher` helper class to handle the lookup of services from the

Framework service registry hooks

The OSGi R4.2 core specification allows third-party code to inject various hooks into the framework service registry. These hooks let you monitor or even mask service lookup, service discovery, and service registrations. The new interfaces:

- `FindHook` detects when services are requested from the framework.
- `ListenerHook` detects when service listeners are registered.
- `EventHook` detects service registrations, modifications, or removals, and enables the masking of these events.

Services implementing these interfaces are registered in the OSGi service registry, just like any other service, but they're picked up by the framework implementation. These interfaces can provide some extremely powerful patterns, but you should be highly wary because they have the capacity to create complex situations that are difficult to debug. That being said, they're the only practical way to build distributed service models on top of the OSGi service registry, so here we are.

remote registry and injection into the OSGi service registry. To give context for the example, the following listing shows the implementation of the `addWatch()` method of `RegistryWatcher`.

Listing 15.17 `RegistryWatcher` helper `addWatch()` method

```
public void addWatch(String clazz, String filter) {
   Watch watch = new Watch(clazz, filter);
   synchronized (watches) {
     Integer count = watches.get(watch);
     if (count == null) {
       log.info("Adding watch " + clazz + " -> " + filter);
       Collection<RegistryServiceReference> services = registry
           .findServices(clazz, filter);
       for (RegistryServiceReference ref : services) {
         if (!regs.containsKey(ref)) {
           log.debug("Registering " + ref);
           Future<ServiceRegistration> future = exec
               .submit(new Registration(ref));
           regs.put(ref, future);
         }
         else {
           log.debug("Already registered " + ref);
         }
       }
     } else {
       watches.put( watch, count + 1 );
     }
   }
 }
```

You begin by checking whether this a new `Watch`—a unique class and filter request. If it is, you find the existing services that match your watch criteria from the `RemoteRegistry`. For each service, you check whether you've already imported it for a different watch. If this is in fact a new service, you create a new `Registration` callable object. Here, the `Registration` callable object is submitted to a background thread executor to avoid deadlock scenarios that can occur if you execute external code while holding the object lock on the `m_watches` object. Finally, you store the future `ServiceRegistration` for tidying up later, should the `Watch` be removed.

The next listing shows the code for the `Registration` inner class.

Listing 15.18 `Registration` callable

```
public class RegistryWatcher {
...
  class Registration implements Callable<ServiceRegistration> {
    private final RemoteServiceReference ref;

    public Registration(RemoteServiceReference ref) {
      this.ref = ref;
    }

    public ServiceRegistration call() throws Exception {
```

```
      Hashtable props = new Hashtable(ref.getProperties());
      return ctx.registerService(
        ref.getInterface(), ref.getService() ,props);
    }
  }
...
}
```

This class passes through the service properties of the remote service and registers the service object in the OSGi service registry.

The final area to look at is what happens if a new remote service is discovered by the watcher.

Listing 15.19 `RegistryListener` event handling

```
private void handleAdd(RemoteServiceReference ref) {
  synchronized (m_watches) {
    if (!m_regs.containsKey(ref)) {
      for (Watch w : m_watches.keySet()) {
        if (w.matches(ref)) {
          Future<ServiceRegistration> future = exec
              .submit(new Registration(ref));
          m_regs.put(ref, future);
          break;
        }
      }
    }
  }
}
```

This method is called as a result of a `RegistryListener` event indicating that a new remote-service reference has been added to your `RemoteRegistry`. You check whether this is a new service reference and whether any existing watch has been created for this service. If so, you create another background registration and store the future OSGi service registration.

In summary, using your helper class and the service-hook interfaces, you can find out when a remote service is needed and inject it into the local OSGi service registry on demand. Let's see how this works in practice.

IMPORTEDSERVICELISTENERHOOK

`ImportedServiceListenerHook` tracks service-listener registrations and adds a watch in the remote registry for the associated services. You keep track of which types of services other bundles are interested in so you know which types of remote services you should import. The following listing shows how to process service-listener registrations.

Listing 15.20 `ListenerHook` that tracks registered service listeners

```
public void added(Collection listeners) {
  for (final ListenerInfo info : (Collection<ListenerInfo>) listeners) {
    if (!info.isRemoved()) {
      LDAPExpr expr = LDAPParser.parseExpression(info.getFilter());
      expr.visit(new ExprVisitor() {
```

```
            public void visitExpr(LDAPExpr expr) {
              if (expr instanceof SimpleTerm) {
                SimpleTerm term = (SimpleTerm) expr;
                if (term.getName().equals(Constants.OBJECTCLASS)) {
                  watcher.addWatch(term.getRval(), info.getFilter());
                }
              }
            }
          });
        }
      }
    }
```

You first check whether the listener is removed. This may seem a little odd, given that it happens in the `added()` method, but it protects your listener against race conditions due to asynchronous event delivery. You then inspect the body of the LDAP expression by using a utility class to walk your way through the filter expression to find references to the `objectClass` service property, indicating the service interfaces of interest. Finally, you add a watch in your remote registry for the discovered service interfaces specified.

Now, when another bundle registers a service listener, your listener hook will find any matching remote services in the remote registry and add them to the local OSGi service registry. This lets you handle asynchronous service lookup; but how do you handle direct service queries? We'll look at this next.

IMPORTEDSERVICEFINDHOOK

When a bundle invokes `BundleContext.getServiceReference()`, you'd like to be able to intercept it and inject a remote service into the OSGi service registry. You can achieve this using a find hook:

```
public class ImportedServiceFindHook implements FindHook {
...
  public void find(BundleContext ctx, java.lang.String name,
      java.lang.String filter, boolean allServices, Collection references)
  {
    watcher.findServices(name, filter);
  }
}
```

This implementation is trivial because it asks the registry watcher to find any matching services in the remote registry, which then adds the services to the local OSGi service registry.

PUTTING IT ALL TOGETHER

We'll skip over the implementation of the `DummyRegistry`, because it's indeed trivial (the curious can look in the companion code). You can complete the example by creating a test bundle that exports a `Foo` service using the `service.exported.interfaces=*` service property as follows:

```
Hashtable props = new Hashtable();
props.put("service.exported.interfaces","*");
context.registerService(Foo.class.getName(), new FooImpl(), props);
```

In a second bundle, add a ServiceTracker that finds the "remote" service in listing 15.21. Because all of this example is happening in the same OSGi framework (it isn't distributed), you explicitly look for the service.imported service property to ensure that you find the "remote" version of your service versus the local service, both of which are published in the local framework's service registry.

Listing 15.21 Tracking the "remote" service

```
Filter filter = context.createFilter(
  "(&(" + Constants.OBJECTCLASS + "=" + Foo.class.getName()
  + ")(service.imported=*))");
ServiceTracker tracker = new ServiceTracker(context, filter, null) {
  @Override
  public Object addingService(ServiceReference reference) {
    System.out.println("Found " + reference + " !!!!!!!");
    return super.addingService(reference);
  }

  @Override
   public void removedService(ServiceReference reference, Object service) {
    System.out.println("Lost " + reference + " !!!!!!!");
    super.removedService(reference, service);
  }
};
tracker.open();
```

To see this in action, go into the chapter15/webservice-impl/ directory of the companion code. Type ant to build the example and java -jar launcher.jar bundles to run it. You should see the following output:

```
Found [org.foo.dosgi.test.Foo] !!!!!!!
```

Although this Remote Services distribution provider is simplistic, it demonstrates the general outline and underlying mechanics for getting remote services to work seamlessly with existing OSGi applications.

15.3 Summary

In this chapter, we've shown you how to build web applications and web services that take advantage of the OSGi framework. We built on the advanced features of the OSGi framework and demonstrated the extensibility of the OSGi framework, including the following topics:

- Using the HTTP Service to provide static resources and simple servlet-based applications in an OSGi framework
- Using the Pax Web extensions to the HTTP Service to deploy JSP applications in an OSGi framework
- Converting a more complex WAR-style application based on the stock-watcher application for the Google Web Toolkit into a web application bundle

- Exporting a local OSGi service into a remote JVM using a Remote Services distribution provider, which, thanks to the flexibility of service-based programming, required no changes to the client application
- Examining at a high level the mechanics of implementing an OSGi Remote Services distribution provider

Let's quickly review what we've covered during the course of this book. We started by introducing you to the core concepts of OSGi development provided by its module, service, and lifecycle layers. In the middle of the book, we moved on to practical considerations of developing OSGi, including migrating, testing, debugging, and managing OSGi-based applications. Finally, in this last part of the book, we covered a number of advanced topics including component development, launching and embedded use cases, how to manage security, and building web applications.

We've covered a lot of ground, and you deserve congratulations for making it all the way through. We think you'll agree that OSGi is both flexible and powerful—and now you have the skills and knowledge required to build your own dynamic modular applications using OSGi. Thanks for reading.

appendix A: Building bundles

Throughout this book, you've been building OSGi bundles with the bnd tool, using Ant to manage the builds. If you're a fan of Maven, you may be feeling a bit left out at this point, but don't worry. You can build bundles with Maven using the same bnd instructions, thanks to the maven-bundle-plugin. To build a bundle, all you really need is the ability to customize the JAR manifest; you don't need to change to an OSGi-specific build system. On the other hand, the more a build system understands about *what* it's building, the more it can assist you—so which build systems work particularly well with OSGi?

We start by revisiting bnd and Ant, but this time explaining the various bnd instructions used in the book along with some advanced ones with which you may not be familiar. After that, we'll show you how to migrate a Maven project to use bnd and introduce some features specific to the maven-bundle-plugin. Finally, we'll round things off with a brief overview of more OSGi-specific build systems, including Eclipse Plug-in Development Environment (PDE) and Maven Tycho. But first, let's return to where we left off: building bundles with Ant.

A.1 Building with Ant

Apache Ant (http://ant.apache.org) is a build system for Java that uses XML to describe a tree of targets, where each target describes a sequence of tasks. Ant is extended by writing new tasks in Java, such as the bnd tool's `bnd` task that can generate one or more bundles from a given class path. But what exactly is bnd?

A.1.1 Introducing the bnd tool

The bnd tool (www.aqute.biz/Code/Bnd) was written by Peter Kriens to take the pain out of developing bundles. Usually, when you create a JAR, you take a directory and archive its contents. This is fine for plain JARs, but it isn't always ideal for OSGi bundles—there's no easy way to tell if the OSGi manifest matches the contents or to quickly slice a large project class path into a consistent set of bundles.

Bnd is different because it takes a pull approach to assembling bundles: it doesn't just archive everything it's given. Developers write instructions using OSGi-style headers, which can either be written as properties in the build or stored in separate property files. The bnd tool uses these instructions to pick the classes and resources that should go into each bundle. Because the tool knows each class and resource pulled into a bundle, it can make sure they form a consistent set and generate a valid OSGi manifest that represents the contents. It can also glean information from other bundles on the class path, such as version information, and use that to automatically version imports.

Bnd instructions can be categorized into four types:

- OSGi-style headers, which start with a capital letter
- Low-level directives, which start with a dash
- Variables, which start with a lowercase letter
- Built-in macros, which start with `$`

Let's begin by looking at what headers are available.

A.1.2 Headers

Bnd headers follow the same pattern of comma-separated clauses defined in the OSGi specification, so you don't have to learn yet another syntax to write instructions. The bnd tool accepts standard OSGi headers such as `Export-Package` and `Import-Package`, as well as its own headers like `Private-Package` and `Include-Resource` that let you define additional bundle contents that are neither imported nor exported. To make life easier, you can use wildcard patterns and negation in package headers; you don't have to be explicit and list every single package in detail. Bnd expands wildcards and normalizes versions, so the final bundle always has valid OSGi headers.

The following are some of the bnd headers you've used so far in this book.

EXPORT-PACKAGE

This header is a comma-separated list of packages that should be contained and exported from this bundle. By default, this is `*`, which pulls the complete class path into the bundle. This is fine when you're creating a mega bundle, but you'll usually want to limit the packages pulled into the bundle and give them an explicit version:

```
Export-Package: org.foo;version=1.0
```

If you want to export all packages except any internal or implementation packages, you can use a negated pattern. But remember that the negated pattern must appear before the normal pattern, because the bnd tool processes patterns from left to right:

```
Export-Package: !*.internal.*,!*.impl.*,org.foo;version=1.0
```

As discussed in chapter 5, it's often a good idea to import your own exported API packages. Older versions of bnd automatically added imports for all exports, whereas the latest versions try to make better guesses about which exported packages should be imported. If you don't want to import an exported package, you can add an attribute to each clause as follows:

```
Export-Package: org.foo;version=1.0;-noimport:=true
```

IMPORT-PACKAGE

This is a comma-separated list of packages that should be imported into this bundle. By default, this is also `*`, which the bnd tool expands into any packages that are referenced from but not contained inside the bundle. Ideally, you should use this header to tweak the results of the generated list, rather than explicitly list the packages you want imported. The most important thing to remember is to leave the `*` at the end of the header; otherwise, you limit the ability of bnd to manage the set of imported packages for you:

```
Import-Package: !org.foo.test,org.foo.runtime,*
```

PRIVATE-PACKAGE

This is a comma-separated list of packages that should be included in this bundle but not exported. This isn't a standard OSGi header, so it won't have any effect at execution time; it's only used when assembling the bundle. If a package matches both `Export-Package` and `Private-Package`, it will be exported.

INCLUDE-RESOURCE

This is a comma-separated list of resource paths to include in this bundle. This isn't a standard OSGi header, so it won't have any effect at execution time; it's only used when assembling the bundle. The simplest form of this header doesn't accept any regular expressions and strips away directories when including resources. The following example includes two resources, both at the root of the bundle:

```
Include-Resource: src/foo/plugin.xml, plugin.properties
```

To place resources in a subdirectory, you must use the assignment form. All you need to do is put whatever location you want (followed by `=`) before the resource:

```
Include-Resource: META-INF/model=src/model
```

If you want to preprocess resources and replace any property placeholders (`$...`) with values at build time, put curly braces around the resource clause:

```
Include-Resource: {META-INF/model=src/model}
```

Embedding a JAR inside your bundle is as simple as naming it. You don't need to know its exact location because bnd automatically scans the project class path for it. This feature is useful when you're using bnd with repository-based build systems like Maven, where a dependency JAR can come from anywhere:

```
Include-Resource: foo.jar
```

If you want to unpack the full JAR instead of embedding it, put an `@` at the front:

```
Include-Resource: @foo.jar
```

And if you only want certain parts, you can select them using Ant-style path expressions:

```
Include-Resource: @foo.jar!/**/*.xml
```

SERVICE-COMPONENT

Normally, this header points to an XML resource describing Declarative Service components. The bnd tool goes a step further and also accepts inline short descriptions of components, automatically generating valid XML at build time. You can even use bnd annotations to mark up component classes and setter methods; list the component class names in the header, and bnd will do the rest. The official bnd site has a complete description of the `Service-Component` header as well as detailed examples.

A.1.3 Directives

If headers describe the *what* of bundles, then directives describe the *how*. They let you fine-tune the packaging process so you get exactly the bundle you want. Some of the more popular directives are as follows:

- `-classpath`—Comma-separated list of additional class path entries.
- `-donotcopy`—Regular expression of filenames that shouldn't be copied into the bundle. The default excludes CVS and .svn directories.
- `-exportcontents`—Same syntax as `Export-Package`, but doesn't pull anything into the bundle. Useful in multimodule projects when you want to provide some general export instructions, but you don't want to affect the bundle contents.
- `-failok`—Still creates a bundle, even if errors are found in the instructions or content.
- `-include`—Comma-separated list of properties files containing additional bnd instructions. Properties from included files override existing properties unless the name is prefixed with ~. A missing filename causes a build error unless the name is prefixed with -.
- `-manifest`—Uses the given manifest file for the bundle instead of generating one.
- `-nouses`—Disables generation of `uses` constraints. This can be useful if you expect to deploy the bundle on Equinox or Eclipse, as the additional constraints can slow down the bundle-resolution process on certain frameworks.
- `-output`—Writes the generated bundle to the given file location.
- `-plugin`—List of plugin class names that augment or extend the bundling process. Bnd includes optional plugins that can process Spring XML or generate bundles on demand in the style of Make.
- `-removeheaders`—Comma-separated list of headers to remove from the final manifest. Useful if you don't want bnd-specific headers like `Include-Resource` ending up in your final bundle.
- `-sources`—Automatically adds the source for any classes pulled into the bundle under OSGI-OPT/src. The source code must either exist in a directory or JAR on the class path, or be listed under the `-sourcepath` directive. OSGi-aware IDEs like Eclipse automatically look for embedded sources and use them when debugging, so adding them can help developers.
- `-versionpolicy`—Defines the policy to use when selecting import ranges. The default policy is to only include the major and minor segments of the version, with no upper limit. To give a concrete example: if you were building a bundle against SLF4J 1.5.8 with the default version policy, any generated import for the `org.slf4j` package would use an open-ended range of `org.slf4j;version="1.5"`.

We'll cover version policies in more detail in section A.1.5 and suggest some common policies.

A.1.4 Variables and macros

Instructions beginning with a lowercase letter are taken as variables (also known as *properties*), which can be used with macros to control or parameterize the bundle contents. Bnd accepts curly, square, round, and angled brackets around macros; this can be useful if your build system attaches its own meaning to a specific bracket type, such as Maven and `${}`. For consistency, we'll stick to using round brackets throughout this appendix, because they won't conflict with Maven property interpolation.

The simplest macro is the property placeholder consisting of just a variable name:

```
$(variable)
```

Bnd defines other macros of varying complexity that can parse, search, and filter bundle contents—essentially providing its own mini-language to control the build process. All bnd macros start with a keyword, followed by one or more parameters separated by semicolons:

```
$(keyword;param1;param2)
```

Let's look at some of the more useful macros:

- `$(classes;query)`—Searches the content of the bundle for classes that match the given query. You can use this to select all public classes that implement a certain interface:

  ```
  $(classes;PUBLIC;IMPLEMENTS;org.foo.Extension)
  ```

  Or those that use certain annotations somewhere in the class:

  ```
  $(classes;ANNOTATION;*.Inject)
  ```

  This macro is useful for scanning component details at build time and recording the results in the manifest, so you can avoid having to repeatedly scan the bundle class path at execution time. You can find the full query syntax on the bnd site.
- `$(env;name)`—Evaluates to the value of the named environment variable.
- `$(filter;list;regex)`—Takes a comma-separated list and keeps only the entries that match the regular expression.
- `$(filterout;list;regex)`—Takes a comma-separated list and removes any entries that match the regular expression.
- `$(findname;regex;replacement)`—Searches the project class path for resources whose names match the regular expression. You can provide an optional replacement string for the resource name, which can also contain the usual back references to groups in the matched pattern. The following example macro evaluates to the names of all class resources, but with *.java* replacing *.class*:

  ```
  $(findname;(.*)\.class;$1.java)
  ```

- `$(findpath;regex;replacement)`—Similar to `findname`, but matches against the complete path rather than just the name.

- `$(if;condition;true;false)`—Evaluates to the `true` section when the condition string is empty; otherwise, evaluates to the `false` section. This macro is a bit counterintuitive: a condition string of `false` is treated as true, because it's non-empty.
- `$(join;list;list;...)`—Concatenates a series of comma-separated lists into one list.
- `$(now)`—Evaluates to the current date and time.
- `$(replace;list;regex;replacement)`—Replaces any entries in the list that match the regular expression with the replacement string. As with `findname`, the replacement string can contain references to matched segments.
- `$(sort;list)`—Sorts the given comma-separated list according to lexicographical order.
- `$(toclassname;list)`—Replaces entries (such as org/foo/Test.class) with their class name equivalent (such as org.foo.Test).
- `$(toclasspath;list;extension)`—Replaces class names (such as org.foo.Test) with their path equivalent (such as org/foo/Test.extension).
- `$(version;mask;version)`—Takes a version string and alters it according to the given mask. The mask contains one to four characters, each representing a segment of the version: major, minor, micro, and qualifier. An = character means *leave the segment unchanged*, whereas + or - means *increment or decrement the segment value*. Using fewer than four characters truncates the version. As you'll see in the next section, you can use this macro to automatically create ranges for any given version.

A.1.5 Choosing a version policy

As we mentioned at the end of section A.1.3, the default policy for generated import versions is to keep the major and minor segments but drop the rest. Using the resolution rules from chapter 2, this means the bundle won't resolve against previous incompatible releases, but it will continue to resolve against any future release.

If the default version policy isn't for you, you can define your own with the help of the version macro from the last section, with `$(@)` representing the detected import version. To explicitly define the default policy, you write

```
-versionpolicy: $(version;==;$(@))
```

The default policy gives you maximum flexibility in the future while stopping the bundle from accidentally resolving against older, incompatible releases. To strengthen the lower bound further and only accept versions strictly older than the ones you built and tested against, use the entire version and don't drop any segments:

```
-versionpolicy: $(@)
```

What if you want to guard against future breaking changes and exclude future versions that aren't binary compatible? You can do this by adding an upper bound to the range:

```
-versionpolicy: [$(version;==;$(@)),$(version;+;$(@)))
```

An import version of 1.5.8 using this policy maps to a version range of `[1.5,2)`. If you find all these similar brackets confusing, remember that bnd lets you mix bracket types, so you can always rewrite this last policy more clearly:

```
-versionpolicy: [$<version;==;$(@)>,$<version;+;$(@)>)
```

A.1.6 Mending split packages

As you saw back in chapter 6, when you're modularizing legacy applications, you may encounter the thorny issue of split packages, where two different JARs contain the same package but with different contents. Bnd warns you when it detects split packages, but it still creates the bundle. These warnings can be irritating if you already know about (and don't mind) the split package. Indeed, you may be creating this bundle in order to merge the different parts together. To remove these warnings, add the following package attribute to any known split packages:

```
Private-Package: org.foo.bean;-split-package:=merge-first
```

This tells bnd to silently merge the contents of the `org.foo.bean` package together but not overwrite existing entries if there's any overlap. You can also choose not to perform any merging by using the `;-split-package:first` attributes.

You now know the various headers, directives, and macros available to us when building bundles with bnd in Ant, but what if you're using another system, such as Maven? Do you have to learn yet another syntax, or is there a way to reuse your existing knowledge of bnd?

A.2 Building with Maven

You saw in chapter 6 how easy it is to take an existing Ant-based project and migrate it to OSGi with bnd. But what if you use Maven? Maven (http://maven.apache.org) is another popular build tool from Apache that also uses XML to describe builds, but this time the description is declarative rather than procedural. Instead of listing the steps required to build a JAR (also known as an *artifact*), you list the packaging as `jar` in the project XML.

Maven favors convention over configuration; follow the Maven way, and you can keep your XML relatively lean and uncomplicated. The problem is when you need to do something special outside of the normal Maven build process. You can end up with pages of XML detailing each step of your customized build.

How well does OSGi fit with Maven? Will you need pages of configuration to assemble your bundle?

A.2.1 Introducing the maven-bundle-plugin

The Maven build process is extended by adding plugins to projects. Maven plugins contain one or more Maven plain old Java objects (mojos), each of which represents a specific goal, such as assembling a JAR from classes and resources. A well-written plugin complements the Maven process and requires minimal setup by following the convention-over-configuration mantra.

One such plugin is the maven-bundle-plugin (http://felix.apache.org/site/apache-felix-maven-bundle-plugin-bnd.html) from the Apache Felix project. It adds a new packaging type called `bundle` that tells Maven how to package, install, and deploy OSGi bundles. Add this plugin to your project XML (or parent project) and change the packaging to `bundle`, and it should create a bundle instead of a plain old JAR. Let's try this out!

First, you need a simple Maven project. You can create one with the archetype plugin:

```
$ mvn archetype:generate -DinteractiveMode=false \
    -DgroupId=examples -DartifactId=mybundle -Dpackage=examples.osgi
```

This creates a new Java project in the mybundle directory with example source and tests. To build this project, type the following:

```
$ cd mybundle
$ mvn clean install
```

You should see Maven compile, test, package, and install a JAR called mybundle.jar. If you look at the manifest inside the final JAR, it only contains a few entries about who built it:

```
$ jar xvf target/mybundle-1.0-SNAPSHOT.jar META-INF/MANIFEST.MF
$ cat META-INF/MANIFEST.MF
Manifest-Version: 1.0
Archiver-Version: Plexus Archiver
Created-By: Apache Maven
Built-By: me
Build-Jdk: 1.6.0_22
```

Let's change this into an OSGi build. Open the project file (pom.xml), and add the additional lines shown here:

```
<project>
  ...
  <build>
    <plugins>
      <plugin>
        <groupId>org.apache.felix</groupId>
        <artifactId>maven-bundle-plugin</artifactId>
        <version>2.1.0</version>
        <extensions>true</extensions>
      </plugin>
    </plugins>
  </build>
  ...
</project>
```

Setting `extensions` to `true` tells Maven that this plugin contains a new packaging type, in this case `bundle` packaging. To use this to build your project, you need to change the packaging listed in the project's pom.xml from

```
<packaging>jar</packaging>
```

to

```
<packaging>bundle</packaging>
```

You can now ask Maven to rebuild your project:

```
$ mvn clean install
```

If you compare the console output to the previous build, you should see that it uses the maven-bundle-plugin to package the project. The JAR manifest now contains the appropriate OSGi headers:

```
Manifest-Version: 1.0
Export-Package: examples.osgi
Bundle-Version: 1.0.0.SNAPSHOT
Build-Jdk: 1.6.0_22
Built-By: me
Tool: Bnd-0.0.357
Bnd-LastModified: 1289004026415
Bundle-Name: mybundle
Bundle-ManifestVersion: 2
Created-By: Apache Maven Bundle Plugin
Import-Package: examples.osgi
Bundle-SymbolicName: examples.mybundle
```

Notice how you didn't need to add anything else to the project—the maven-bundle-plugin uses existing information (project metadata, resources, and source code) to generate reasonable defaults for the OSGi manifest. But what are these defaults, and how can you customize the bundle?

A.2.2 Going undercover

You may have noticed a couple of bnd headers in the last manifest. This is because the maven-bundle-plugin leans on the bnd tool to do the heavy work of assembling the bundle and generating the manifest. In other words, the main task of the maven-bundle-plugin is to translate Maven metadata into bnd instructions, so developers don't have to repeat themselves over and over again. The default translations are listed in table A.1.

Table A.1 maven-bundle-plugin defaults

OSGi header	Maven metadata
`Bundle-Name`	`${project.name}`
`Bundle-SymbolicName`	`${project.groupId}.${project.artifactId}` with duplicate segments removed
`Bundle-Version`	`${project.version}` normalized to the OSGi format
`Bundle-Description`	`${project.description}`
`Bundle-License`	`${project.licenses}`
`Bundle-DocURL`	`${project.organization.url}`

Table A.1 maven-bundle-plugin defaults *(continued)*

OSGi header	Maven metadata
`Bundle-Vendor`	`${project.organization.name}`
`Export-Package`	All Java packages in the current project (except *.internal.* and *.impl.*)
`Private-Package`	All Java packages in the current project
`Include-Resource`	All project resources in the current project (with property substitution)

Although these defaults are usually enough for most Maven projects, you'll occasionally want to tweak or add additional instructions to fine-tune the bundling process. Because the maven-bundle-plugin uses bnd, you can use the exact same instructions covered in the first part of this appendix. Let's look at a real-world example. The following listing contains a customized maven-bundle-plugin configuration taken from the Google Guice project.

Listing A.1 Google-Guice maven-bundle-plugin configuration

```
<groupId>org.apache.felix</groupId>
<artifactId>maven-bundle-plugin</artifactId>
<version>2.1.0</version>
<configuration>
  <instructions>
    <module>com.google.inject</module>
    <_include>-${project.basedir}/build.properties</_include>
    <Bundle-Copyright>Copyright (C) 2006 Google Inc.</Bundle-Copyright>
    <Bundle-DocURL>http://code.google.com/p/google-guice/</Bundle-DocURL>
    <Bundle-Name>${project.artifactId}</Bundle-Name>
    <Bundle-SymbolicName>$(module)</Bundle-SymbolicName>
    <Bundle-RequiredExecutionEnvironment>
      J2SE-1.5,JavaSE-1.6
    </Bundle-RequiredExecutionEnvironment>
    <Import-Package>!com.google.inject.*,*</Import-Package>
    <_exportcontents>
      !*.internal.*,$(module).*;version=${guice.api.version}
    </_exportcontents>
    <_versionpolicy>
      [$(version;==;$(@)),$(version;+;$(@)))
    </_versionpolicy>
    <_nouses>true</_nouses>
    <_removeheaders>
      Embed-Dependency,Embed-Transitive,
      Built-By,Tool,Created-By,Build-Jdk,
      Originally-Created-By,Archiver-Version,
      Include-Resource,Private-Package,
      Ignore-Package,Bnd-LastModified
    </_removeheaders>
  </instructions>
</configuration>
```

Most of this customization is tweaking the Maven-produced manifest to match the one generated by the existing Ant build. You can avoid this by extracting the common bnd instructions to a shared file and using the `-include` directive to pull it into both Ant and Maven builds. Using a separate file for bnd instructions also avoids two formatting issues that can plague Maven bundle developers:

- XML tags can't start with -, so bnd directives listed in XML instead start with _.
- Maven attempts to process any text containing `${...}`, so use `$(...)` for bnd macros.

Other issues to watch out for when you start bundling Maven projects include the following:

- The complete project class path is passed to bnd; so `Export-Package: *` will embed the *entire* class path, dependencies and all—which may or may not be what you want.
- Bnd uses a pull approach. It doesn't zip up target/classes; so, if any classes are missing or you see any unexpected additional classes, check your bnd instructions.

If you want to know more about how the maven-bundle-plugin translates your project details into bnd instructions, you can use `mvn -X install` to enable debug logging. But watch out: this output includes debug from all plugins used in the build, so you probably want to save it somewhere so you can search for bundle details at your leisure.

You now know how to take an existing Maven project and turn it into a bundle using the maven-bundle-plugin. Just as you did with Ant, you can use bnd instructions to tweak the manifest and select the bundle content. Is that all the maven-bundle-plugin does?

A.2.3 Embedding dependencies

In addition to translating project details into bnd instructions, the maven-bundle-plugin adds a few headers of its own that let you embed Maven dependencies without having to write lengthy `Include-Resource` headers. It also keeps the `Bundle-ClassPath` header in sync, so any embedded JARs are automatically available on the bundle's class path.

You won't be surprised to learn that the main header is called `Embed-Dependency`. It accepts a comma-separated list of patterns that are matched against the project's Maven dependency tree. Matching dependencies can either be embedded or selectively unpacked inside the bundle. The full syntax of the `Embed-Dependency` header is as follows:

```
dependencies ::= clause ( ',' clause ) *

clause ::= MATCH ( ';' attr '=' MATCH | ';inline=' inline )

attr ::= 'groupId' | 'artifactId' | 'version' | 'scope' | 'type' |
         'classifier' | 'optional'

inline ::= 'true' | 'false' | PATH ( '|' PATH ) *

MATCH ::= <globbed regular expression>

PATH ::= <Ant-style path expression>
```

Pretty complicated, no? You may have noticed a resemblance between this syntax and the bnd tool syntax for selecting packages. Perhaps a few examples will make things clearer; the following listing is taken from the Apache Felix documentation for the maven-bundle-plugin.

Listing A.2 Embed-Dependency examples

```
<!-- embed all compile and runtime scope dependencies -->
<Embed-Dependency>*;scope=compile|runtime</Embed-Dependency>

<!-- embed any dependencies with artifactId junit and scope runtime -->
<Embed-Dependency>junit;scope=runtime</Embed-Dependency>

<!-- inline all non-pom dependencies, except those with scope runtime -->
<Embed-Dependency>*;scope=!runtime;type=!pom;inline=true</Embed-Dependency>

<!-- embed all compile and runtime scope dependencies,
     except those with artifactIds in the given list -->
<Embed-Dependency>
  *;scope=compile|runtime;inline=false;
    artifactId=!cli|lang|runtime|tidy|jsch
</Embed-Dependency>

<!-- inline contents of selected folders from all dependencies -->
<Embed-Dependency>*;inline=images/**|icons/**</Embed-Dependency>
```

In addition to `Embed-Dependency`, the maven-bundle-plugin adds headers to do the following:

- Select where to embed dependencies in the bundle (`Embed-Directory`)
- Remove the `groupId` from the embedded name (`Embed-StripGroup`)
- Remove the version from the embedded name (`Embed-StripVersion`)
- Consider transitive dependencies as well as direct ones (`Embed-Transitive`)

Now, you may be thinking that `Embed-Dependency` coupled with `Embed-Transitive` is a quick way to create a mega bundle containing everything you need for your application (see section 6.2.1). Often this is true, but occasionally you end up pulling in a vast list of optional dependencies that aren't needed at execution time. Forget about downloading the internet—you can end up embedding it!

You should also be careful when mixing the `Export-Package` header (which pulls in classes and resources) with `Embed-Dependency`. You can easily end up with duplicated content: one pulled in, the other embedded. Instead, try to use the `-exportcontents` directive when you want to export packages contained in embedded dependencies.

A.2.4 Deploying artifacts to OBR

In addition to embedding, the maven-bundle-plugin has built-in support for the OSGi Bundle Repository (OBR; see section 10.1.2). Whenever you use Maven to build and install a project of packaging type `bundle`, the maven-bundle-plugin automatically updates an OBR index file (called repository.xml) at the top of your local Maven repository. You can use this file to select and deploy your project bundles onto OSGi frameworks:

```
-> obr-repo add-url file:/Users/foo/.m2/repository/repository.xml
-> obr-repo list
-> obr-resolver deploy ...
```

You can even use it to remove stale bundle entries from your local OBR:

```
$ mvn bundle:clean
```

But how about non-local OBRs, like the one listing official Apache Felix bundle releases at http://felix.apache.org/obr/releases.xml? You can configure the maven-bundle-plugin to automatically update a remote OBR whenever it deploys a bundle to a remote Maven repository, but this isn't enabled by default. For more details about enabling and configuring remote OBR updates, see the plugin documentation on the Apache Felix website.

A.2.5 Bundling non-JAR projects

What if you don't want to change your project packaging type to `bundle`? Can you still get Maven to generate OSGi metadata for you? You'll be pleased to hear that the answer is, yes—the maven-bundle-plugin provides a `manifest` goal that you can use to generate the OSGi manifest during other types of builds. To allow the use of this goal with other packaging types, you first need to tell the maven-bundle-plugin to process them, like so:

```
<groupId>org.apache.felix</groupId>
<artifactId>maven-bundle-plugin</artifactId>
<configuration>
  <supportedProjectTypes>war,ear,jar,zip</supportedProjectTypes>
</configuration>
```

Next, add an plugin execution to generate the manifest as part of the build lifecycle:

```
<executions>
  <execution>
    <phase>prepare-package</phase>
    <goals>
      <goal>manifest</goal>
    </goals>
  </execution>
</executions>
```

Finally, you need to get Maven to include the generated manifest in the final artifact. Exactly how this happens depends on the packaging you're using, but most archives support some way to use an existing manifest file.

You've now built bundles using Ant and Maven. What about other build tools and IDEs?

A.3 For your consideration

Bnd and the maven-bundle-plugin aren't the only option when developing OSGi bundles. As you saw back in chapter 7, Eclipse includes support for developing bundles courtesy of its Plug-in Development Environment (PDE). NetBeans and IDEA also provide add-ons for OSGi, and there are additional Ant tasks and Maven plugins specifically designed for developers targeting Eclipse or Spring. Whatever your workflow, you should be able to find something that works for you.

Let's take a quick look at the alternatives currently available, starting with Eclipse PDE.

A.3.1 Eclipse PDE

The PDE (www.eclipse.org/pde) adds a new perspective for developing Eclipse plug-ins, but it can also be used to build plain OSGi bundles. Unlike bnd, which generates a manifest based on a small recipe of instructions, Eclipse PDE provides dialog boxes and wizards for working directly with the manifest. What you see is what will appear in the bundle. Although this often leads to simpler manifests, it also means you have more responsibility for keeping the manifest up to date. PDE helps by integrating closely with the Java development tools, but you do need to invest significant effort to do headless builds.

A.3.2 Apache Felix Sigil

Sigil (http://felix.apache.org/site/apache-felix-sigil.html) is a tool that applies the OSGi modularity concepts to the build environment. It extends build-time resolution technologies such as Maven and Ivy to resolve project dependencies primarily using the same `Import-Package` semantics encouraged by OSGi best practices. This leads to a greater degree of decoupling and has been shown in real-world scenarios to reduce extraneous dependencies by up to a factor of 10 compared to module-level dependencies. The Sigil project structure encourages delegation to avoid duplicated configuration and supports a flexible repository management framework. Sigil integrates with Eclipse and Ant/Ivy.

A.3.3 Eclipse bndtools

Bndtools (http://njbartlett.name/bndtools.html) is an alternative to Eclipse PDE based on the bnd tool. It provides dialog boxes and wizards for managing bnd instructions in Eclipse as well as menu options to run, test, and debug OSGi applications. Developers already used to bnd should have no problem picking up bndtools; others will find its forms, syntax highlighting, and auto-completion a useful introduction to building bundles from recipes.

A.3.4 IDEA Osmorc

Osmorc (http://www.osmorc.org) is a plugin for IntelliJ IDEA that lets you choose whether to use an existing manifest for your bundle or have the IDE generate it. Osmorc can generate a manifest based on either a simple form or a set of bnd instructions. You can also use it to run and debug OSGi applications on all the major frameworks.

A.3.5 NetBeans Netisgo

Netisgo (http://netbeans.org/features/java/osgi.html) is a plugin for NetBeans that forms a bridge between the NetBeans module system and OSGi. It allows native modules and OSGi bundles to interoperate by mapping their metadata at runtime. NetBeans also provides templates for simple Ant- or Maven-based OSGi builds.

A.3.6 Maven Tycho

Tycho (http://tycho.sonatype.org) is a collection of plugins specifically developed for building Eclipse plugins, applications, and update sites in Maven. Its primary goal is to make the command line build match the Eclipse IDE build by replacing the standard Maven dependency resolution by a P2-based resolver. Developers can choose between an Eclipse style manifest-first approach or a maven-bundle-plugin style pom-first approach. Management of target platforms is also much easier with Tycho: add your required dependencies, and it will compute and download the appropriate target platform for you.

A.3.7 Spring Bundlor

Bundlor (http://www.springsource.org/bundlor) is an alternative to bnd that works with Ant, Maven, and Eclipse. Like bnd, it generates the bundle manifest from a recipe and uses instructions based on OSGi headers, but it uses a different syntax to control the results. Bundlor also scans non-Java dependencies like Spring or Blueprint configuration files to find references that don't appear in Java code but still need to be imported into the bundle.

appendix B: OSGi standard services

This appendix lists the Core, Compendium, and Enterprise services defined in release 4.2 of the OSGi specification. All services are optional: some are available from framework vendors, others are available from third-party vendors. Most service implementations work with any OSGi R4 framework.

B.1 Core OSGi services

Table B.1 lists the services defined in the OSGi Core specification. All of them are optional singleton services provided by the framework, except for the Service Hooks which may have zero or more instances registered by other bundles.

Table B.1 Core OSGi services

Name	Description	Package	Version
Package Admin	Provides the ability to control and reflect over bundle- and package-level wiring	`org.osgi.service.packageadmin`	1.2
Start Level	Controls the relative order of bundle startup by assigning start levels to bundles	`org.osgi.service.startlevel`	1.1
Conditional Permission Admin	Enables permission assignment to bundles based on arbitrary conditions	`org.osgi.service.condpermadmin`	1.1
Permission Admin	Enables permission assignment to bundles based on bundle location	`org.osgi.service.permissionadmin`	1.2
URL Handlers	Multiplexes URL and content-handler factories to allow bundles to provide custom handlers	`org.osgi.service.url`	1.0
Service Hooks	Allows bundles to monitor and limit service registry events and access	`org.osgi.framework.hooks.service`	1.0

B.2 Compendium OSGi services

Table B.2 lists the services defined in the OSGi Compendium specification. These services are provided by optional bundles installed on the base OSGi framework. There can be zero or more versions of a service registered at the same time.

Table B.2 Compendium OSGi services

Name	Description	Package	Version
Log	Provides a lightweight logging facility for bundles	`org.osgi.service.log`	1.3
HTTP	Defines a simple HTTP server supporting dynamic servlet and resource registration	`org.osgi.service.http`	1.2
Device Access	Manages the linking of devices and device drivers	`org.osgi.service.device`	1.1
Configuration Admin	Manages bundle configuration data storage and injection	`org.osgi.service.cm`	1.3
Metatype	Provides a schema or type description mechanism	`org.osgi.service.metatype`	1.1
Preferences	Provides storage and access to preferences and settings data	`org.osgi.service.prefs`	1.1
User Admin	Manages user identities and associated attributes	`org.osgi.service.useradmin`	1.1
Wire Admin	Defines and connects data producers to consumers	`org.osgi.service.wireadmin`	1.0
IO Connector	Adaptation of the J2ME `javax.microedition.io` communication infrastructure	`org.osgi.service.io`	1.0
Initial Provisioning	Defines a packaging format and delivery approach to deploy an initial set of bundles	`org.osgi.service.provisioning`	1.2
UPnP	Provides infrastructure to publish and discover UPnP services	`org.osgi.service.upnp`	1.1
Declarative Services	Defines a lightweight service-oriented component model	`org.osgi.service.component`	1.1
Event Admin	Provides publish-and-subscribe and topic-based event notification	`org.osgi.service.event`	1.2
Deployment Admin	Defines a packaging format and delivery approach for deploying bundle-based applications	`org.osgi.service.deploymentadmin`	1.1

Table B.2 Compendium OSGi services *(continued)*

Name	Description	Package	Version
Application Admin	Defines an abstract application manager concept for managing arbitrary application types	`org.osgi.service.application`	1.1
DMT Admin	Defines an API for managing a device using concepts from the OMA DM specifications	`info.dmtree`	1.0
Monitor Admin	Defines how bundles can publish status variables and how administrative bundles can discover, read, and set status variables	`org.osgi.service.monitor`	1.0
Foreign Application Access	Enables foreign applications to participate in the OSGi service-oriented architecture	`org.osgi.application`	1.0
Blueprint Container	Defines a service-oriented component model closely aligned with Spring	`org.osgi.service.blueprint`	1.0
XML Parser	Addresses how the classes defined in JAXP can be used in OSGi	`org.osgi.util.xml`	1.0

B.3 Enterprise OSGi services

Table B.3 lists the services defined in the OSGi Enterprise specification and specifically relating to using OSGi in an enterprise environment. These services are provided by optional bundles installed on the base OSGi framework. There can be zero or more versions of a service registered at the same time.

Table B.3 Enterprise OSGi services

Name	Description	Package	Version
Remote Service Admin	Addresses how remote services can be provided inside an OSGi framework and discovered in a network	`org.osgi.service.remoteserviceadmin`	1.0
JTA	Provides the JTA specification as a service-based model	`javax.transaction`	1.1
JMX	Exposes an OSGi framework via JMX	`org.osgi.jmx`	1.0
JDBC	Enables OSGi-aware JDBC drivers	`org.osgi.service.jdbc`	1.0
JNDI	Defines how JNDI can be utilized from within an OSGi framework	`org.osgi.service.jndi`	1.0
JPA	Specifies how persistence units and JPA providers work in an OSGi framework	`org.osgi.service.jpa`	1.0

index

Symbols

A

B

C

D

E

J

K

L

M

P

RELATED MANNING TITLES

Tuscany SCA in Action

by Simon Laws, Mark Combellack, Raymond Feng, Haleh Mahbod, Simon Nash

ISBN: 978-1-933988-89-4
472 pages, $59.99
February 2011

Spring in Action, Third Edition

by Craig Walls

ISBN: 978-1-935182-35-1
700 pages, $49.99
May 2011

Spring Dynamic Modules in Action

by Arnaud Cogoluègnes, Thierry Templier, and Andy Piper

ISBN: 978-1-935182-30-6
548 pages, $59.99
September 2010

Spring Batch in Action

by Arnaud Cogoluègnes, Thierry Templier, Gary Gregory, and Olivier Bazoud

ISBN: 978-1-935182-95-5
350 pages, $69.99
July 2011

For ordering information go to www.manning.com

YOU MAY ALSO BE INTERESTED IN

Event Processing in Action
by Opher Etzion and Peter Niblett

ISBN: 978-1-935182-21-4
384 pages, $49.99
August 2010

Mule in Action
by David Dossot and John D'Emic

ISBN: 978-1-933988-96-2
432 pages, $44.99
July 2009

Camel in Action
by Claus Ibsen and Jonathan Anstey

ISBN: 978-1-935182-36-8
552 pages, $49.99
December 2010

Java Persistence with Hibernate
Second Edition of Hibernate in Action
by Christian Bauer and Gavin King

ISBN: 978-1-932394-88-7
880 pages, $59.99
November 2006

For ordering information go to www.manning.com